RICHARD FINDLATER

Lilian Baylis

THE LADY OF THE OLD VIC

ALLEN LANE

Copyright © 1975 Richard Findlater
First published in 1975
Allen Lane
Penguin Books Ltd
17 Grosvenor Gardens, London SW1 W OBD
ISBN 0 7139 0902 1
Printed in Great Britain by
Ebenezer Baylis and Son Ltd
The Trinity Press, Worcester, and London
Designed by Gerald Cinamon

To the friends of Lilian Baylis
and the heirs of her national theatres

Contents

List of Plates   9

Foreword   11

1   Prelude   17

2   Emma   23

3   The Purified Hall   43

4   Enter Lilian   65

5   Acting Manager   87

6   Lilian's War   113

7   The Building Years   145

8   The Way to the Wells   175

9   Private Worlds   211

10   The Triple Crown   245

11   Enigma Variations   281

Notes   301

Bibliography   307

Index   311

List of Plates

Frontispiece: Lilian Baylis in her forties

1. The Old Vic (*c.* 1914)
2. Emma Cons
3. Lilian at sixteen
4. Robert Atkins
5. Sir Philip Ben Greet
6. Charles Corri, sketched by Harry Powell Lloyd
7. Evelyn Williams
8. Father Andrew
9. Reginald Rowe
10. Clarkie
11. Lilian in the 1920s, with the Vic queue
12. Cutting a *Twelfth Night* cake on stage
13. John Gielgud
14. Sybil Thorndike
15. Ninette de Valois
16. Lawrance Collingwood
17. Lilian picnicking with Louie Davey
18. At the seaside with Harriet Webster
19. Miss Baylis, making music
20. Miss Baylis, Companion of Honour and Hon. MA (Oxon)
21. At a Vic first night
22. At Elsinore in 1937

Foreword

When I agreed to attempt the biography of Lilian Baylis nearly twenty years ago, at the instigation of a Governor of the Old Vic, Patricia Strauss, I was blithely blind to the Andes in my path. No terrain, it seemed to me, could be as difficult to explore as the lost world of Regency pantomime – I had recently written the first biography of Grimaldi since 1838, the year after his death. I had started it for the simple and (as I thought) sufficient reason that I wanted to know more about what he actually *did*, what it was that made so many people think he was a Kean of the harlequinade, and what he was really like behind the grinning mask of Joey the Clown. A similar impulse prompted me to accept Mrs Strauss's invitation to write about Lilian Baylis. I had never met her, but during my schooldays I had seen her in her box from the Old Vic gallery (where my theatrical education began); and since then I had come to marvel at her achievements, of which the books I had read and the anecdotes I had heard provided no satisfying explanation. The Baylis myth, like the Grimaldi legend, led me on; and there was at least one seductive, though, as it turned out, somewhat misleading, difference. She had died precisely a century after Grimaldi (with whom she shared a devotion to Sadler's Wells) and many of the people who worked for her were still irrefutably alive. The evidence must be there, I assumed, for the taking. So, armed with a tape-recorder lent by the generous Pat Strauss and with an unteachable faith in the accessibility of the past, I began to put out groping and very tentative feelers towards that buried life into which – I had the temerity and the hubris to believe – I might intrude to plumb its mysteries.

It rapidly became clear to me, however, that I should have to follow in detail the history of the Old Vic from at least 1880, when it was taken over by Lilian's aunt, Emma Cons; and the fact that

Miss Baylis was a century closer to me than Grimaldi did not make nearly as much difference as I had supposed. Many essential documents had disappeared, and there was a dearth of autobiographical material. Most of Miss Baylis's letters were brisk, businesslike and impersonal. The diaries extant record little more than appointments, telephone numbers and sums (theatrical and domestic); and although towards the end of her life she began to dictate some autobiographical notes to her private secretary, Annette Prevost, she did not get very far or go very deep. Miss Prevost, who has given me the most generous, valuable and illuminating help that any biographer could wish for, was herself going to write the life of Miss Baylis, but had to give up the project because of her husband's illness. I had underestimated, moreover, the difficulties of writing about a *manager* – and a manager who did not direct, or design, or present much new work, or mix with other managers. For most of her singers, dancers and actors most of the time, she was, in her later years, a background matriarch, 'a power and a joke', as Dame Peggy Ashcroft says, half frightening, half funny, omnipotent but remote. They had little to do with her, and knew next to nothing about her after their salary was fixed, apart from the snowballing anecdotes. What many people 'remember' is not first-hand experience but what they have heard and read; and (as in Miss Baylis's case) the legend tends to cover up the facts deeper and deeper every year.

What is more, Miss Baylis did a good deal to bury her own tracks in her lifetime, by accident and/or design. Her memory was eccentric, like so many other things about her: she 'misremembered' names, dates, events. More dismayingly, from a biographer's point of view, she told different anecdotes about the same episodes that were not only confused but contradictory. Even in the same stories about her, passed on by old friends and colleagues, there are sometimes antithetical interpretations. To take a tiny example, Lilian, even in the minds of some who knew a part of the truth, used to say, 'We'll have no betting in my theatre. Only on the certs.' To Clarkie (Mrs Clark, her box-office manager at the Vic) this was another of Miss Baylis's endearingly innocent Malapropisms: what she meant was not 'certs' but 'classics'. To Bruce Worsley (her front-of-house manager and trustee) it was a sign of the Baylis shrewdness and hatred of waste. I find little difficulty in choosing between these two readings; but other anecdotes yield far more puzzling glosses.

Again, I discovered that Lilian's private life was, for years, largely inseparable from her work. She had little time for anything but the Vic. The theatre was her autobiography in action. Outside it her main interests were God and his intermediary, Father Andrew, her confessor for over twenty years; and neither was available for consultation.

As the magnitude of the task and the meagreness of all but the spiritual rewards became painfully evident, I regretfully decided that to write a biography of Lilian Baylis was a luxury that I (and my family) could not afford. I felt guilty about this abdication of responsibility, especially when the obituary columns reminded me, from time to time, of what was being lost to theatrical and biographical research. Three years ago, prompted by the imminence of the centenary of Miss Baylis's birth, and released from acute economic pressures, I returned to the excavations. The work was interrupted, once again, by outside diversions – notably by the loss of notes on interviews and library research, when my car was stolen. But I finished it – as far as any biography of this kind can be finished – a week after her centenary celebrations ended, an irony that the Lady (as she was known from the 1920s) might have relished. She might also, I feel, have enjoyed my distracting and largely unavailing quest for more information about her astonishing Aunt Emmie and the Cons family; the sudden discovery, when I was nearing the end of this book, of a cache of her father's notebooks; and the even more surprising emergence, *after* I had finished, of a Cons family tree and of Lilian's nephew from South Africa, Dr Robert Dunning, who had long been out of touch with the Vic and visited it by chance during the celebrations, knowing nothing of what was going on in honour of his aunt.

All this is by way of explanation for the genesis of the book, its shape, its sources, its omissions and variations on the legend. Much of it is based upon conversations with and letters to the author. Main quotations from books are identified in end-notes to each chapter, when this is feasible, although much of the narrative is beyond annotation, as printed, manuscript and oral sources are, necessarily, compounded. I have drawn heavily, inevitably and (I think) properly upon several books about Miss Baylis and the Old Vic published shortly after her death. Dozens of people (dead and alive) have contributed their memories and opinions to the mosaic. For the total effect, and the overall interpretation, I am of course solely responsible.

The structure of the book is, like its subject, somewhat unconventional. I have devoted two chapters to Emma Cons and the pre-Baylis Vic. Although Lilian rarely appears in them, I believe it is impossible to understand her without some knowledge of her aunt. And in one chapter I have concentrated on her private life: it comes late in the book because the evidence for it relates largely to her last decade. There is little documentation about Lilian's first twenty years at the Vic, and scarcely any about her life outside it, until near her death. At the same time, although Lilian's biography is entwined with the theatre's history, I have had to omit even a mention of many names that fill the long roll of honour during her forty years at the Old Vic and seven years at Sadler's Wells. The full and proper record of artists and productions in drama, opera and ballet during the Baylis regime must be reserved for the complete (and overdue) history of her theatres. I can do no more than touch on a few of the talents.

My thanks are due to all those who have talked and written to me over the years and have generously allowed me to tap their knowledge and experience. They include the late Frances Briggs, Sir Lewis Casson, Mrs Firminger, Canon Hutchinson, Andrew Leigh, Ernest Milton, Nora Nicholson, Winifred Oughton, Miss Poggi, J. Baxter Somerville, Madge Whiteman, Harcourt Williams; John Allen, Dennis Arundell, Dame Peggy Ashcroft, Sumner Austin, Jane Bacon, Eileen Beldon, Henry Cass, Edith Coates, Lawrance Collingwood, Joan Cross, Dame Ninette de Valois, Leslie French, Sir John Gielgud, Marius Goring, Natalie Kent (Agnes Carter), John Laurie, Harry Powell Lloyd, Oliver Messel, Marie Ney, Lord Olivier, Anthony Quayle, Margaret Rankin, Sir Michael Redgrave, Iris Roberts, Dame Flora Robson, Athene Seyler, Robert Speaight, Dame Sybil Thorndike, W. J. Townsend, Molly Veness, Bruce Worsley; W. Baxter (Whitefriars Glass), Professor Quentin Bell, Captain Evelyn Broadwood, David Carrington, Dr Robert Dunning, Mrs Fuller, Miss D. N. Gomm (Islington and Shoreditch Housing Association), Rev. Harry Johnson (St Peter's, Paddington), Dr John Hopkins, W. Kirby (Highgate Cemetery), Cecil Leslie, Raymond Mander and Joe Mitchenson, John McKee (who has constructed a Cons family tree), Miss E. D. Mercer (GLC Archives), Professor Allardyce Nicoll, Dr C. C. G. Rawll (All Saints, Margaret Street), Denis Richards (historian of Morley College), S. V. Rugg, Molly Sole (Clerk to the Governors of the Old Vic), Sylva Stuart Watson, Rev. J. Whitelam (St Agnes, Kennington), Miss M. Y. Williams (Lambeth Archives), Bryan Wood (City Parochial Foundation); those who wrote to me from South Africa, especially Ernest Hunt,

J. M. Kennedy, Mrs V. Randall and Mrs Pearl Stam; and from Australia, especially Frank Haycox, Mrs A. V. Maher, Reginald Monkhouse, Mrs Annetta Morris and Mrs Lilias Oliver (Lilian Baylis's niece); the staff of the Enthoven Collection, and the libraries of the Vic–Wells Association, the Greater London Record Office, the Royal Academy of Music, the Royal College of Art, the Housing Centre Trust, the Shakespeare Centre at Stratford-upon-Avon, the Public Record Office, the BBC Sound Archives, Morley College; and the Bodmin, Stockport, Marylebone, Holborn, St Pancras and Buckingham Palace Road libraries.

I am especially grateful to Patricia Strauss for starting me off, and to the Governors of the Old Vic; to Mrs Clark ('Clarkie') and Mrs Chamberlain ('Prevost'), without whom the book would never have been written; to David Astor, for allowing me the time and opportunity to complete it; to John Trewin and Peter Roberts for their advice on the draft, which was also read by Clarkie, Prevost and (in part) Sumner Austin; and to Prevost, Peter Roberts and Dame Sybil Thorndike for reading the proofs.

For permission to quote, at length, from copyright sources my thanks are due to Annette Prevost Chamberlain, the Governors of the Royal Victoria Hall, the Greater London Council, the trustees of Robert Atkins, the Raymond Mander and Joe Mitchenson Collection (for extracts from Lilian Baylis's letters to Ivy Smithson), Peter Roberts (for extracts from the Centenary Festival Memorial Programme), Victor Gollancz Ltd (extracts from *The Same Only Different* by Margaret Webster), Hamish Hamilton (*A Life in the Theatre* by Tyrone Guthrie), the Bodley Head (*Vic–Wells*, edited by Harcourt Williams), Macdonald & Co (*A Theatre for Everybody* by Edward J. Dent, and *Old Vic Saga* by Harcourt Williams), Chapman & Hall (*Lilian Baylis* by Sybil and Russell Thorndike), David Higham Associates (*Come Dance With Me* by Ninette de Valois), Constable (*Octavia Hill* by E. Moberly Bell), the Society of Authors, on behalf of the Bernard Shaw estate, Anthony Gishford (Joan Cross's contribution to *Tribute to Benjamin Britten*), A. R. Mowbray & Co (*The Life and Letters of Father Andrew* edited by Kathleen E. Burn), Heinemann (*Early Stages*, by John Gielgud), Dr C. C. G. Rawll (the magazine of All Saints' Church, Margaret Street), and to Sheridan Morley and Hutchinsons, publishers of *Theatre 1974*, to which I contributed an essay on which I have drawn for the Foreword.

For their help in illustrating this book I am grateful to Annette

Prevost Chamberlain, Kathleen Clark, Mary Clarke, Peter Roberts, Raymond Mander and Joe Mitchenson, A. R. Mowbray & Co, Molly Sole, Jane Edgeworth, Lawrance Collingwood, Harry Powell Lloyd and the Victoria and Albert Museum.

Prelude

The passage of time will turn Miss Baylis into a myth.
There will be an apocrypha about her, most of it sentimental,
some of it funny, and a little of it true.

St John Ervine (1938)

Do I contradict myself?
Very well then I contradict myself.

Walt Whitman

In the last year of the First World War Eileen Beldon, an actress of seventeen who had just made her stage debut in *Aladdin* at the Theatre Royal, Drury Lane, went for an audition to the Royal Victoria Hall in the Waterloo Road, the only place in London then offering a grounding to both actors and audiences in the plays of Shakespeare. Miss Beldon had not visited the Hall or the surrounding district before, although it was only a few minutes walk from the Strand, over Waterloo Bridge. Until recent years it had been virtually out of bounds to most middle-class ladies, except those bent on missionary work (which included singing in operatic recitals at the Hall). The 'Vic' – as it was known to the locals – stood in the centre of a slummy, sleazy, Cockney quarter long notorious for its street-market, prostitutes, pickpockets and specialists in more violent trades. Since 1914, when it began to stage Shakespeare, it had been acclaimed as a temple of the classic drama, but to Miss Beldon it didn't look a bit like one, that day in 1918. Nearly the entire front of the building, where the foyer and box office ought to have been, was occupied by a workmen's café with trestle tables and sawdust on the floor. There was no commissionaire on duty, and no stage-doorkeeper – in fact there was no stage door.

After circling the barrack-like building in bewilderment and some trepidation, pushing through the crowds at the stalls where the costers shouted under the naphtha flares, averting her eyes from a tart standing at her door in a side-street and the drunks outside the glittering gin-palace who made improper suggestions as she hurried past (she was becoming used to *that* in the Drury Lane area), Miss Beldon managed to get into the theatre through what seemed to be the only entrance. As she stumbled into the dark auditorium, feeling rather like Alice misrouted in Wonderland, the contrast with the Theatre Royal struck her even more sharply. 'No jewels, no laughter, no furs, no crystal chandeliers, no gilt and plush.' It smelt strongly of gas, mixed with fish, size, disinfectant, spirit-gum and stale tobacco. There was an atmosphere of 'intense poverty'. There were wooden benches and sawdust on the floor. Miss Beldon felt damp, cold and lost. On the stage she could dimly see a group of figures who all seemed to be in black, talking in whispers. Behind her she could hear the rattle of crockery in the café at the front of the theatre. She was completely ignored, and felt like crying. This was no place for her. But, as she turned to leave, a voice came raspingly out of the darkness, 'Who are *you*? What are you doing here?'

'It only needed Her to complete the nightmare. The Red Queen? The Duchess? It suddenly became so unreal that I didn't mind any more. Large; ugly; red face with one side slightly slipped, untidy hair piled high on top above a battlement of pins and combs; gold-rimmed glasses on a chain. An ample erect figure encased in a dung-brown dress with a boned bodice bedecked with tucks and lace; a wide skirt down to her feet, and button boots. A familiar figure enough. A well-dressed cook? A headmistress? A matron? A chapel deaconess?' She was, in fact, the manager of the theatre, Lilian Baylis, to whom Eileen Beldon hesitantly explained that she had a letter of introduction.

'Well, wipe your nose and speak up,' said Miss Baylis brusquely, with a near-Cockney snap in her voice. 'We don't want any more actors, but you can come as a student if Mr Greet, the producer, wants you. You won't get paid, and you'll have to put down £5 as a guarantee of good behaviour. You'll get it back at the end of the season if you behave yourself. After you've seen Mr Greet come to my office and collect some handbills that you can leave in the trains and buses.' With a sniff and a glare the button-booted apparition vanished; Eileen Beldon clambered on to the stage and met Ben Greet, who had a shock of white hair and 'the bluest, kindest eyes I ever remember'; shouted Mark Antony's oration over the dead Caesar to an apparently empty theatre (but not *quite* empty: she suddenly saw Miss Baylis peering at her through a curtain in a stage box); was approved by the producer, led to the manager's office (where Miss Baylis pressed a stack of green leaflets into her hand, asked her if she believed in God and barked a dismissive goodbye), and remained at the Vic for most of the next two years – for the second of which she was actually *paid*: 12s. 6d. a week.

That was how the manager of the Old Vic looked and talked in 1918 to a newcomer who came to admire her as 'a great woman' (and went on, herself, to make a long and distinguished stage career). Like many first impressions it was a caricature; but to others, throughout most of her life, Lilian Baylis seemed at first encounter no less bizarre, miscast, formidable and even frightening. During the next decade there were changes in her dress and hair-do, but little alteration in her style and manner. People who later became her friends described her as looking and behaving like a 'seaside landlady', 'a charwoman', 'a schoolmarm' and, most frequently, 'a parish visitor' and 'social worker'. And, in a way, she played all these roles. She certainly bore no resemblance to a theatre manager, of any known kind: either the actor-managers and their managing wives (whose heyday was now over) or the new breed of West End showmen, businessmen and speculators. She did not *think* like other managers: she was not in it for the money, she was opposed to long runs, she resented the well-to-do occupying her seats (though she touted for their donations) and she was deeply suspicious of spectacle, showmanship and glamour. Nor, in many ways, did she *behave* like other managers: she seldom ate out in fashionable restaurants (or restaurants of any sort); her life-style was generally simple; she never visited Broadway or the Paris stage; she nearly always said what she thought, and was often brusque to those over whom other managers would ladle balm and butter; she made few intimate friends inside the theatre; her principal adviser for years was the Superior of a religious order; and she put God a long way before Mammon. There was a further difference: Miss Baylis was the salaried servant of a charitable foundation, which paid her a weekly pittance to run the Royal Victoria Hall. The Old Vic was not *her* theatre, although that is how people thought of it then, and think of it still.

Miss Baylis was not quite as large as she at first appeared to Eileen Beldon. Her height was five foot four, and although she was dumpy and bulky, she was surprisingly light on her feet. Her light-blue eyes, shrewd and penetrating behind her thick glasses, could warm into a smile that gave her at times in her younger days a fleeting beauty. But she was – if not 'ugly' – plain, with a slight deformity that turned down one corner of her mouth, of which she was secretly but painfully conscious. She had a compulsive sniff. She was brusque, even bullying in manner. She had a harsh, somewhat clipped voice with an accent that sounded Cockney to many people, though she said it was South African. She lacked charm and social grace. She had no dress-sense. She was completely tactless. She had little formal education, and was not, in the accepted sense, a cultured woman. She never acted, or produced. She took little interest in other theatres: on her occasional visits she tended to fall asleep, and in later years primed her companion to prod her awake with a knitting needle. Although she could play the mandolin, violin and guitar, her musical knowledge did not stretch far beyond the Palm Court classics. Her favourite dance was the Sir Roger de Coverley. If she hadn't been called by the Almighty to the Vic, she might well (as Ninette de Valois believes) have found her vocation in a convent.

Yet this dowdy, uneducated, eccentric, deeply religious spinster turned a dingy temperance music hall in a London slum into 'the home of Shakespeare and opera in English', with virtually no money or resources, in the middle of a world war. She recruited many of the prime talents in the twentieth-century theatre. She achieved the regeneration of Sadler's Wells, and laid the foundations there of a national opera and a national ballet. Her place as one of the outstanding Englishwomen of the century was recognized by her appointment to the Companionship of Honour. She was a unique theatrical phenomenon.

Since her death Miss Baylis has been both overpraised and undervalued. In dozens of funny, and not so funny, anecdotes she has been much mimicked and not a little mocked. The tales of her gaffes, fights and eccentricities have grown into a theatrical legend that has sometimes obscured not only her real and astonishing achievement, but also the private woman behind the public figure. This book is an attempt to redress the balance; but the balance is hard to find because she appeared to be so full of contradictions. Whereas Russell Thorndike said that 'she looked upon the smallest innovation at the Vic with misgiving and mistrust', his sister Sybil in the same book asserted that Lilian 'had no "settling down" in her composition' and believed in change.[1] To the members of her company she was 'a standing joke, but they all swore by her', said one obituarist. She was 'at once a slave and a tyrant', said another. Many people, in trying to sum up Lilian Baylis, have done so in antitheses. She was, said Edward Dent, a 'singular combination of artistic insight and ignorance, personal goodness and hard-headed business capacity'.[2] Sir Hugh Walpole, in a strenuously over-written defensive tribute, declared that 'she was a brute, a tyrant, ignorant, selfish, conceited – what you like – but she was a great, courageous, inspired figure also, and she was an untidy, ugly, affectionate Cockney child as well'.[3] Robert Atkins, who believed he had good reason to dislike her, said that she was 'cute, crafty, common, vulgar and yet at times in speech and outlook unbeliev-ably beautiful'.[4]

That apparent complexity has to be recognized from the start. So does the fact that the life of Lilian Mary Baylis (1874–1937) is inseparable from the life of the Old Vic Theatre (1818– ?). She had little time for anything outside it, until she discovered Sadler's Wells. She gave herself to the Vic and the Wells. Their history reflects hers; and I have attempted to catch some of the reflections in this book. Yet, although theatrical history and reminiscence are among my main sources, and although she is indivisible from her theatres, I have not found it possible to conceive this study of Lilian Baylis as primarily a 'theatrical biography', for success on the stage (judged by conventional criteria) was not her principal aim. She was concerned with good works in the service of God and the people rather than good theatre in the service of art. And we cannot begin to understand her now, a hundred years after her birth, until we have tried to learn more about her family back-ground, and, in particular, about the importance of her favourite aunt, Emma Cons, with whom it all began. So, before we return to Lilian, we have to look first at the history of Emma and the pre-Baylis Old Vic. This history deserves a book in itself; here it occupies two chapters which, I suggest, must be read by anyone who wants to comprehend the personality of Lilian Baylis and her unique contribution to our national theatres.

Emma

If the history of the Old Vic is to be rightly understood,
it must include a sketch of the woman
who turned it from its evil ways
and whose spirit still influences its work.

Lilian Baylis (1926)

Although Emma Cons (1838–1912) is now little more than a name, even to students of British theatrical history, she deserves a well-lit niche in the Victorian halls of fame and achievement for a cluster of creditable reasons which have little to do with the stage. This tiny, gentle, indomitable London spinster was a pioneer in housing reform; in campaigning for urban parks and open spaces; in setting up crèches and clinics for working-class women; in providing cheap food and entertainment outside the pubs and music halls; in extending evening-school education; in working for women's suffrage and their right to serve in local government. 'To such beneficent ends she gave her very self. Large-hearted and clear-sighted, courageous, tenacious of purpose, and of great personal modesty, her selfless appeal drew out the best in others and was a constant inspiration for service to all those with whom she was associated.'[1] Beatrice Webb rated her as 'one of the most saintly as well as one of the most far-sighted of Victorian women philanthropists'.[2] She may be ranked among the most remarkable Englishwomen of the century; a great do-gooder who rejected the seigneurial condescension and sanctimonious severity that made philanthropy seem a dirty word to a later generation; one of a splendid sisterhood of secular nuns who helped to nurse the consciences of the rich and the cancers of the poor; and it is unfortunate that no detailed study of her life and work has been

23

published, and that so little material for it apparently survives outside the sketch written by her niece and god-daughter Lilian Baylis.[3] Her role in this story is important not only because she opened a new chapter in the history of the Old Vic, but because she was deeply loved, admired and, in some degree, imitated by her niece. To understand Lilian Baylis, it is necessary to know something about her Aunt Emma.

Emma Cons was born in London on 4 March 1837 into an Anglo–German family, lower middle class and, in her childhood at least, fairly prosperous, with a pedigree of three generations (if not more) in the music trade. Her great-grandfather Elias Konss was brought up in the Rhineland town of Anrath, near Cologne, where his parents had spent most of their lives and where he was apprenticed as an organ-case maker.[4] After his father's death in 1768 Elias, then twenty-three, emigrated to France and on to London in 1772. Emma (and, after her, Lilian) proudly preserved and often exhibited a testimonial to his character and skill as a craftsman, given to him in Anrath by his master in 1769, and a passport allowing him to travel in France in 1772. Eleven years later he married an English widow, Mrs Sarah Taylor, at St Pancras Parish Church; and it was in this district that Elias took root and changed his name to Cons. (Lilian wrongly described him as her grandfather.) His second son Frederick (1788–1839) was also in the music trade, as a cabinet maker and pianoforte-case maker in St Pancras; and Frederick's eldest son, also called Frederick (1810–70) followed the same career in the same district of London. He was apprenticed to Broadwood's, the leading British firm of piano manufacturers; and in 1833 he married Esther Goodair, the daughter of a Stockport mill-owner. By then he was probably working for his father at 81 John Street, now Whitfield Street (parallel with Tottenham Court Road), a centre of the crafts and trades connected with the expanding piano industry. It was probably in this house (now destroyed) that Emma Cons was born, and it was certainly here that she spent her childhood and adolescence. The family seems to have been proud of their German ancestry (Uncle Elias – who died a pauper in the local workhouse – kept the original spelling). Emma's youngest sister Elizabeth (Lilian's mother) was usually known as Liebe; and as a singer she reverted to the old spelling of her surname – a tactical asset, no doubt, when many British musicians and dancers assumed foreign names to improve their chances of impressing managers, audiences and critics.

By 1847 Emma had two brothers (Frederick and Charles) and four sisters (Ellen, Esther, Eliza and Elizabeth); she was the second daughter. Frederick Cons appears to have been successful at first. There is a tradition in the Broadwood family – whose head, a century later, has been a governor of the Old Vic and Wells for forty years – that Emma's father was principal assistant to Broadwood's. But a few years after the birth of the last Cons girl, Elizabeth, the family fortunes declined. The cause, according to Lilian Baylis, was that Frederick Cons fell ill about 1851 and remained so until his death (in 1870). His sons were, at that time, too young to carry on the business, and the main responsibility seems to have fallen on their mother, whose long struggle to cope with workshop, husband and children may well have helped to shape both Emma's feminism and her celibacy. She resolved at an early age that she must start earning a living or, at least, contribute to the weekly budget.

In the 1850s this was easier said than done. Victorian convention excluded nearly every paid employment, except that of governess, on pain of social ostracism. Women could not seek jobs in trade, industry or the professions. In 1858 the first issue of the *Englishwoman's Journal*, which 'marked the beginning of the organized women's movement in Britain', included this editorial plea: 'it is work we ask, room to work, an open field with a fair day's wages for a fair day's work'. It was hard to get. The Society for Promoting the Employment of Women, established that year, found it desperately difficult to make any dent on the great wall that middle-class male prejudice had erected, and busily maintained, to keep The Sex in its place (according to its class). During the next few decades a number of determined, courageous women broke through in medicine, education and other fields, without openly challenging male political supremacy, as did the later militant generation of suffragettes. Among these pioneering moderates was Emma Cons.

She started work at the age of fourteen, if not earlier, in the Ladies' Co-operative Guild near Fitzroy Square, a few minutes away from the Cons home. This was one of twelve early experiments in self-governing cooperatives promoted in London by the Christian Socialists (the others, all-male, included tailors, printers – and piano-makers); and it sought to provide 'employment for ladies with artistic ability', which had been detected in Emma at an early age. The main employment was the design and decoration of tables and other commodities from 'consolidated glass', made to carry heavy weights by a special process of reinforcement with a kind of cement. The Guild, established in 1851, was managed by Mrs Caroline Hill, whose daughter Octavia became one of Emma's closest friends: indeed, for a time, her only friend (by Octavia's account). She was to have a decisive effect upon Emma's life. They met at an art school round the corner run by the mother of the Victorian painter Henry Halliday.

The Hill and Cons families had some experiences in common: a sick father, a managing mother, genteel poverty and a preponderance of girls. Among the sisters there were close ties: Octavia and Miranda Hill, like Emma and Ellen Cons, shared a house all their adult lives. But there were, it appears, significant differences between the two clans. The Cons girls were somewhat inferior, not only in social status but also perhaps in creative intelligence and energy (Emma apart), and Emma's distinctive gifts were not at first apparent. She was thought to be an unlikely friend for Octavia: blunt, exuberant and tomboyish, 'so much given to romps that Octavia's fellow-workers (including her sisters) were rather startled at the attraction which her new friend had for her'.[5] (According to her niece, Emma 'kept certain tomboyish tastes' till the end of her life. 'I know, for instance, that she always carried a knife and a piece of string in her pocket even when she was wearing evening dress.')[6] She carried independence of Victorian convention in some respects rather far, even for the free spirits of the Co-operative Guild. On her own initiative, for example, she helped Polish refugees who were building an extension to the Guild, mixing the mortar and whitewashing the walls – though manual work of that kind for ladies was unheard of and, indeed, not done. Emma was not as ladylike, as solemn, as introspective or as intellectual as Octavia; yet behind the boisterous high spirits there was a seriousness and strength of will which her friend cherished and fostered. In 1853, two years after Mrs Hill and her daughters arrived at the Guild, Octavia wrote admiringly of Emma in a letter: 'It seems to me that she is capable of a very great deal.' Two years later she went further:

When she came here, she had not a single person in the world to love or be loved by except her own family. Our Miss Cons, however, has got to know friends; and whoever cares to break through her shell will be well rewarded. I feel, in Miss Cons, whose growth I have watched eagerly, an amazing perseverance, a calmness, a power and a glorious humility before which I bow, and which I feel may be destined to carry out great works more nobly.[7]

Octavia and Emma, now sixteen and seventeen years old, thought a good deal about great works. They were already, it seems, touched by the passionate urge to do good – and the firm conviction that one could readily know what 'good' was and how it could be done – that drove a small elite of high-minded Victorian campaigners to attack and reduce, if not destroy, some of the worst social evils inflicted on the underprivileged majority. The two girls were then Christian Socialists. It was probably Octavia who introduced Emma to what she described, at thirteen, as 'one of the greatest happinesses one can have . . . reading a Socialist book'. Their heroes included such leaders of the movement (then only a few years old) as the Rev. F. D. Maurice and the novelists Thomas Hughes and Charles Kingsley, who were all among Mrs Hill's friends. (It should be remembered that Maurice's definition of Socialism was no more revolutionary than 'the assertion of God's order': a Socialist was one who believed that the principle of cooperation was 'stronger and truer' than the principle of competition.) They were influenced, too, by the major artist-sage of the day, John Ruskin, whose work Octavia had discovered as a revelation at thirteen, together with Maurice's sermons. When he visited the Ladies' Guild two years later Ruskin proved to be no disappointment – to Octavia, at least. He actively encouraged his young disciple, inviting her to visit his art collection at Dulwich (Octavia and Emma walked there from St Pancras!), lending her work to copy, giving her advice. Emma did not completely share Octavia's idolatry of Mr Ruskin. She had reservations about his outlook and behaviour. He was an opponent of feminism: by contemporary standards, a male chauvinist. But he played, indirectly, a significant role in her career.

Apart from their discovery of Ruskin, Hughes and Kingsley, Emma and Octavia read Henry Mayhew's revelations about how the poor lived; and they saw some of the squalor and misery for themselves, not only in the streets around them but in the homes of the 'Ragged School' children who worked in another of the Guild's philanthropic ventures, making toy furniture. These were children of the abyss. 'Desperately poor and very rough . . . they came from wretched and degraded homes, some lived in cellars, some were deformed and disfigured by the hardships they had endured. Many of them were older than Octavia, and all were more experienced in wretchedness and vice.'[8] At first there were 'terrible fights'; but with Emma's help Octavia set out to teach the children with a patience and kindness to which they were not accustomed, encouraging them to work with her, entertaining them, improving their food and taking them on outings into the country. The treatment is said to have worked with remarkable speed on many of these brutalized waifs. Dirty, foul-mouthed guttersnipes dropped their savage armour and became trusting, affectionate children – as long as Octavia and Emma were in charge. For both girls their appalling conditions, and their response to fair and loving control, were prime lessons.

Neither of them set out to be social workers. Both intended to be artists. Emma went to the School of Ornamental Art for Females (established in Gower Street in 1857 under government auspices). Octavia spent over ten years under Ruskin's tutelage, trusting in his method – to learn by copying – and pinning her destiny not to philanthropy but to painting. That was one of the things she had in common with Emma. Lilian Baylis may have oversimplified her aunt's personal drives by saying that 'the principle and motive power behind her many activities . . . was her passion for beauty',[9] yet it appears to be true that such a passion played a larger part in her life than in her niece's. She remained, in essence, more of an artist than Lilian ever was, even by association. It was partly an artist's conscience that spurred Emma on to abandon painting (in whatever medium) as a primary occupation; to reject the notion that art was more important than life. Yet she never gave up painting and sketching in her spare time. 'The fact that she was hard at work on some scheme for the better housing of the working classes did not prevent her from having an illustrated manuscript on hand . . . She could not see a bare building without wanting to adorn it, and her diaries of foreign tours contain sketch after sketch, executed with wonderful care and precision of detail.'[10] She frequently painted the doors, lintels and walls of friends' houses, showing a particular penchant for representing the seasons. Her belief in Beauty was one of her main legacies to Lilian.

In 1856 the Ladies' Guild came to a sudden end. Frederick Maurice had offered to take a Bible class for the toymakers; Octavia enthusiastically accepted; but to some of the Guild's backers Maurice was a dangerous radical, who could not be permitted to imperil the children's souls. He had been removed from his Chair at King's College, London because he declared his refusal to believe in Hell and eternal damnation. Mrs Hill indignantly opposed the committee's decision to reject his offer and, when she was defeated, she resigned. Not long after, the Guild collapsed.

Octavia and Emma, with the other 'artistic ladies', looked for work. Both found it, initially, through Ruskin, who commissioned them to restore some illuminated manuscripts in his collection. Octavia became secretary of the College for Working Women, recently opened by Maurice (while continuing to work for Ruskin). Emma took another course – perhaps after a spell in the Gower Street school. Fired by the discovery that engraving watches in Switzerland was a woman's trade, she and some friends set out to learn its mysteries in London, by apprenticing themselves to a friendly craftsman. Having done so in six months, instead of the statutory seven years, they set up in business – as a kind of Ladies' Co-operative – in a room in Clerkenwell, and spread the word. At first they received a sufficiency of orders, with the help of their middle-class connections; but their success aroused predictably fierce resentment among men in the engraving trade, angered by their competitors' class as well as their gender. This resulted in physical violence, when one of the messengers who collected the watch-cases was beaten up. Manufacturers became chary of handing out work to the girls, and Emma had to give up the fight. Among the little hoard of mementoes that Lilian Baylis kept in a safe at the Old Vic, sixty years later, was an example of her aunt's craftsmanship from this period – 'a watch that Emmie carved most exquisitely, representing a peacock with its tail outspread. It was one of the most fascinating contradictions about her – her wonderfully minute handiwork and her big, broad ideas.'[11]

This experience of male bigotry and jealousy strengthened in Emma her already firm conviction that women, as well as men, had a right to carve out careers for themselves. That conviction was reinforced in her next attempt to find work. The manufacturer who had supplied the glass to the Guild, Arthur Powell of the celebrated Whitefriars factory, offered Emma the job of designing and restoring stained-glass windows, a craft stimulated by the mid-Victorian boom in building and restoring churches. She was the first woman in the factory and she paid the price for it: the men did everything they could to make her life a misery. 'They would smudge the colour of her work while it was still wet and overheat the furnaces in order to crack the glass, and it was only the personal intervention of Mr Powell which put an end to this form of persecution.'[12] One can only guess at the emotional tensions in Miss Cons's work, even after that 'intervention'; but 'in the end her quiet endurance won the day'. Not only did she continue to design and restore windows – including some in the

29

chapel of Merton College, Oxford, where she worked for two years – but she opened the way for her sister Ellen and others, and a new workroom for women was established at the factory.

This was a small victory for Emma Cons, and for women's rights; but, within a few years, restoring stained glass – and whatever jobs, if any, succeeded it during the 1860s – may well have seemed to her increasingly irrelevant against the sombre background of savage squalor to which vast numbers of Londoners were condemned, and which became an object of scandal and concern to the more sensitive members of the privileged minority. This was a city of chronic poverty, alcoholism and prostitution, with none of the safety nets of the welfare state. London had no public health service, no public water supply, no civic sanitation, no adequate municipal authority (the London County Council was not established until 1888). Cholera and typhus still broke out in the slums; deficiency diseases were commonplace; starvation was not unknown. Large areas of the metropolis seemed like human jungles; and the new middle-class activists, with social consciences stimulated by Ruskin, Morris, Carlyle and others, plunged into these jungles like missionaries. Later, in the 1880s, some actually lived and worked among the natives in 'settlements', as they were revealingly called (Toynbee Hall, founded by Samuel Barnett, a close friend of Octavia and Emma, was the pioneering example). Others preferred to get away from the savages at night, back to the comforts of middle-class clearings. Some stood in for rich philanthropists whose social work was vicarious – performed, for instance, by buying slum property and hiring managers to improve it while ensuring that the inmates paid their rent.

Among the first of these benevolent slum-landlords was John Ruskin. When his father died in 1864, he was concerned about the best way of using his inheritance. Octavia Hill, who was still copying his pictures and helping him to illustrate his books, proposed to him that he should invest some of the money in better housing for the poor. He responded cautiously. He would buy a tenement, he said, if she would find one, run it and guarantee him a return of five per cent (compared with the usual fifteen per cent or more) – not for the money, of course, but to give an incentive in setting an example.

After stubborn resistance from property-owners and agents who suspected such unwomanly initiative and the tendency to pamper the lower orders, Octavia acquired in 1865 three slum houses in Marylebone. They were a minute's walk – but worlds away – from the house in Nottingham Place where she lived with her mother and three of her sisters, who had established a school there after the Guild closed. (According to Lilian Baylis, Emma went to this school, but she was nineteen when it opened.) The address of Octavia's new hobby was Paradise Place. From her letters, it sounds like hell. When she took them over, the houses were filthy with grime and excrement. The drains were stopped. All the water came from one dirty, leaking butt. There were no lights on the stairways, and no banisters: they had been burned for firewood. The roofs leaked. Nearly all the windows were broken. Some of the overcrowded rooms swarmed with vermin. There was continual brawling among the men, and the women were frequently beaten up. They were, said Octavia, 'a desperate and forlorn set of people, wild, dirty, violent and ignorant as I have ever seen'.[13] Yet she was undaunted. Within a year she arranged to buy another slice of slum housing on the other side of Marylebone, near the Edgware Road, with an equally piquant name: Freshwater Place. Of wildernesses like these, Octavia wrote:

Such awful dens of darkness . . . narrow, filthy, dark places, winding stairs, where light never comes, three, four or five children and their parents living, of course, in one room only: oh, but such rooms! And the children! their eyes all inflamed with continual dirt, their bare feet, their wild cries, their disordered hair, and clothes looking as if dogs had torn them all round, and carried off great jagged pieces.[14]

These people at first attempted to ignore Octavia Hill; they were shut off behind a barrier of sullen resentment – all the stronger when it became clear that their new landlady, while bent on improving the property, also demanded weekly payment of the rent. On this regularity Octavia was, and remained, adamant. Letting the rent slide into arrears would not only ruin her experiment, but would, she believed, leave these unfortunates for ever in the mire. It is astonishing that she was never attacked or molested, although she went alone and at night into areas where the police patrolled only in pairs. But, of course, she needed help, and foremost among the friends to whom she turned was Emma Cons. It was in these Marylebone middens that Emma discovered what her life was for.

Octavia had been warned at the outset, as Emma was so often to be told, that there was no point in attempting to befriend these people or to improve their homes. They had the housing they deserved. As soon as the drains were cleared, they would be stopped again; as soon as the banisters were replaced, they would be burned; as soon as the windows were repaired, they would be broken; whatever promises were made, they would be broken too. The pessimists were right, at first; but Octavia went on replacing the windows and the banisters, while determinedly carrying on other improvements. She encouraged them to save, and helped the men to get work. She set aside a room at the back of her house in a converted stables, as a kind of club for the women. Against fierce local opposition, she cleared a playground for the children. She planted trees and shrubs, and went on planting more when these were destroyed overnight. She also firmly refused to lend money. She set her face against traditional charity, and gave no free meals or coal tickets. She believed in helping people to help themselves, to keep their independence. With the aid of Emma and other 'visitors' she gained the confidence of the majority of the tenants, although a minority were evicted. Within four years these houses, which had been among the worst in the borough, were cleaned, repaired and filled with tenants whose transformation had to be seen to be believed.

Such an achievement demanded more than the condescending kindliness of the old-style Lady Bountiful or the piety of the more ardent church-workers. Emma had to deal with drunks, thugs and bullies, men brutalized by their environment and taking it out on everyone around them; with scabby, underfed, vandalizing children, shouting obscenities, excreting on the stairways and in the courtyards; with their derelict mothers, seeking refuge from the misery of their lives – like their men – in drink and violence; with rape and incest. She was particularly good with the children, better than Octavia, who found it hard to communicate with these little aliens, whose very language seemed to belong to a different world. Emma's high spirits and direct manner helped with parents and children alike. The fact that she was more 'common' than Octavia narrowed the gulf between the natives and the invaders – for that was, inevitably, how these housing reformers were seen from the viewpoint of the slums. She had no fear, and no side. Lilian Baylis remembered her, many years later, 'turning up her skirts and clinging on to the roof of one of her tenants' houses, to show a recalcitrant workman how slates and gutters should be fixed!'[15] For she learned, at Paradise Place and Freshwater Place, to handle builders and plumbers; policemen and lawyers; bankers and accountants. It was essential for these housing managers to be accurate in their book-keeping, as well as the skills of what a later generation called 'man management'. The whole question, said Octavia, depended on 'extreme care about the details of expenditure', in what Ruskin called 'the partial moralization' of two acres of Marylebone. Emma never forgot these early lessons, and she passed them on to Lilian Baylis.

At first, Emma was only a part-time volunteer (it is not clear whether she was still working at Powell's glass factory). In 1869 she could give no more, so Octavia regretfully reported, than one and a half days a week. But from 1870 onwards (after her father died) she devoted most of her time to housing work. One of her main tasks was the redemption of Barrett's Court, a slum off Wigmore Street bought by one of Octavia's aristocratic sponsors. This was a disaster area, as bad as – if not worse than – Paradise Place. According to Lilian, the exuberant Emma succeeded so well in 'transforming the inhabitants . . . into a state resembling civilization' that Octavia began to single out this former 'den of darkness' as a model court.[16] Among Emma's methods, significantly, was the provision of entertainment on Saturday nights. She started a brass band, and a supporters' society which enlisted eighty members. And in 1874 a concert at the court was given by 'Mrs Baylis and friends' – Lilian's mother, in the year of Lilian's birth. By that time Emma led a team of fifteen workers, nearly all women, each with a block in his or her charge. Octavia believed that, after training, her helpers should be given their heads. Emma also worked in other areas: in, for instance, the Walmer Street district of Marylebone, which Octavia had been invited in 1869 to administer for charitable purposes by the Rector, who was impressed by the success of her methods in Paradise Place and Freshwater Place.

She also organized outings to the country for her tenants, most of whom – as Lilian Baylis put it – 'had never seen a buttercup meadow', certainly not in each other's company. The emphasis in these trips was always on the *family* treat; but there was one rule – 'nobody, from first to last, was allowed to enter a public-house'.

In order to reduce temptation, Emmie used to plan out her route very carefully beforehand, trying to pass as few public-houses as possible. As an additional precaution against breaches of the rule, scouts were posted outside the inns that could not be avoided – the duty of the scouts being to shepherd the excursionists out of the area of temptation. Once, when an outing to Epping Forest had been planned and the weather proved unkind, Emmie found an organ-grinder outside Liverpool Street Station and hired him to come along with the party.

The expedient saved the excursion from failure; the trippers danced in a long empty room and enjoyed themselves so much that there were no attempts to slip off for less innocent amusement.[17]

At Barrett's Court, her niece said, Emma's methods began to show a 'fundamental difference' from those of Octavia.

Octavia swept away the most unruly elements among her tenants – which promptly migrated to defile some other quarter; Emmie, on the contrary, insisted doggedly on keeping her unruly tenants, and badgered and cajoled them into keeping themselves, their homes and their morals cleaner.[18]

Too much, however, should not be made of Emma's relative flexibility of approach. She did not, and could not, believe in 'doggedly keeping her unruly tenants' at all costs: the records of other properties show that she did evict intransigent families or, rather, 'send them away', as she preferred to put it. According to Beatrice Webb, she 'revolted against the self-complacent harshness of doctrine' of the Charity Organisation Society. This body was set up in 1869, with support from Octavia, to rationalize the network of charitable institutions, improve their efficiency and replace indiscriminate hand-outs by selective help. Yet, as her niece makes plain, Emma followed Octavia's faith in 'the importance of aiding the poor without almsgiving' (the title of an influential lecture given by Octavia to the COS shortly after its formation). According to Lilian, Emma 'had one firm rule, she never gave actual money. She knew too well the results of indiscriminate charity and the professional pauperism which was one of the greatest evils she had to fight.'[19]

To the Hills Emma appeared 'something of a rough diamond, downright, often tactless. She did not share Octavia's enthusiasm for Ruskin, she thought but little of her artistic efforts, or of her attempts to beautify the courts and their surroundings.'[20] In some ways she was more extrovert, more directly compassionate, than Octavia. In others she was more puritanical and authoritarian, as in her moral absolutism on the question of temperance ('the one subject on which this exceptionally broad-minded woman was intolerant', said her niece). According to one of Octavia's biographers, the friendship between Emma and Octavia had always been 'a somewhat tempestuous affair; it had its roots deep in their common past, they saw each other with that devastating clearness only possible to those who have shared experience at an early age ... Neither could ever doubt the affection of the other, yet it was not easy for them to work closely together.'[21] The split was inevitable – and proper. By the time it happened there were over 3,500 tenants in Octavia's charge, or ultimate responsibility; and she had become, within a decade of those first struggles in Paradise Place, something of a national figure.

Emma was the first woman in the team to achieve the full autonomy at which Octavia aimed, even before they separated. Octavia had already transferred to Emma responsibility for managing the Central London Dwellings Improvement Company, a shaky enterprise launched with the best of intentions in 1861, before Octavia started her operations in Marylebone, but handed over to her management in 1870 to rescue from disaster. Octavia passed its control to Emma in the same year. It owned slum property in the Drury Lane area and in Clare Market (site of the London School of Economics); clusters of tenements in narrow side-streets, inhabited by an overcrowded colony of market-porters, costermongers, prostitutes and 'members of the criminal classes'. It was not only a dirty but a dangerous neighbourhood, where drunken brawling and clan vendettas were common, and mugging was a popular means of supplementing the family income. Yet Emma Cons went unharmed about these squalid warrens, demanding her rents, lecturing the mothers, trying to befriend the children, haranguing the fathers about the evils of the pubs in which they spent so much of their miserably scanty money. Lilian Baylis doubted that Emma ever thought of the 'strong element of personal danger' here and in other districts where she worked; 'it was to her fearlessness, probably, that she owed her immunity from violence'.[22] She kept her close concern for this corner of London until her death. A block of flats in Newton Street, built under her direction, still stands today; and as late as the 1950s she was remembered there by at least one elderly resident, who recalled that 'Miss Cons was always for the costers'.[23] It was in this district that she launched her coffee-tavern movement.

The 'coffee tavern' was designed as a place where a working man (and his family) could get cheap non-alcoholic refreshment, and perhaps entertainment, but where it was impossible to gamble or to drink. (The first one in Shelton Street was originally called 'coffee house and club', but this name was thought to be too divisively redolent of class distinction.) For Emma Cons the main problem of social reform had become to establish an acceptable alternative to the pub: only by attracting men away from the boozer could she and all the other missionaries in the slums hope to secure any lasting improvement in family life at the bottom of the social ladder. Emma did not, of course, invent the idea of such counter-attractions. From the 1830s onwards the expanding temperance movement had been opening teetotal hotels and building societies, and sponsoring teetotal entertainers. Drink-free concerts began in Liverpool and Birmingham in the mid-1840s. The first 'coffee palace' in London was opened in 1873 by Dr Barnardo in Limehouse. But Emma Cons helped to give the movement a special impetus, in the right direction at the right time.

The Shelton Street 'tavern' was so successful that Emma enlisted the aid of two aristocratic philanthropists whom she had met through her work with Octavia – the Duke of Westminster and Lord Mount Temple (friend of Ruskin, nephew of Lord Melbourne and heir of Lord Palmerston) – to form the Coffee Tavern Company. The movement spread through London and outside it: by 1880 there were fifty-five other companies. Clearly, these temperance cafés filled a need. From the pub times of 5 a.m. till midnight you could get a cup of coffee for a penny, a cup of tea or cocoa for a halfpenny, a plate of hot beef for sixpence. Recreation rooms and sometimes beds were provided. The new establishments flourished. Businessmen saw that there was money in catering for the lower classes, and within a few years of Emma's pioneering 'Safe Shop' – as the local costers dubbed it – chains of cheap eating places, such as Lockharts and the Aerated Bread Company, crowded the coffee and cocoa taverns out of existence.

About this time Emma Cons decided to concentrate her energies in Lambeth, south of the Thames. Not far from Waterloo Station, at the junction of Lambeth and Kennington Roads, she discovered that a manor house and garden, which had belonged to a local JP, were up for sale. Enlisting the aid of rich friends, once again, she bought Surrey Lodge, and in 1879 formed the South London Dwellings Company – with Viscount Hampden as chairman and herself as managing director – to develop the property and run other housing projects in the area. 'Model dwellings for working folk' were built to her design on the site, with plenty of open space (by contemporary standards). They took the shape of a quadrangle around the garden, with four-storey tenement flats on two sides, shops on the ground floor, facing the road, and three-storey workmen's 'cottages' on the other sides. There were wash-houses on the roof, so that clothes could be hung out to dry away from the staircase and playground – an idea which she pioneered. Lavatories were built 'well away' from the living-quarters and kept locked (every family had a key). These precautions were necessary, Emma explained after a decade at Surrey Lodge, because 'only those who have had practical experience of this class of property know how rudimentary are the ideas of these people on matters of cleanliness and sanitation, and how reluctant they are to live where there is any supervision and rules as to order, cleanliness, etc. . . . it is a common habit to regard anything with a hole in it as suitable for the conveyance away of rubbish',[24] including not only tins, mussel-shells and cinders but even pieces of carpet – with obvious effects on the sanitation system. Other difficulties are illustrated by the name given locally to Surrey Lodge, thirty years after it was built: 'Bug Island'. (Badly damaged in the Second World War, it was demolished in the 1960s.)

Emma Cons took two of the six-room 'cottages': 5 and 6 Moreton Place, for herself, her sisters Ellen and Eliza and her friends and helpers. This was to be her office, home and headquarters until she died, thirty years later.

Now it is time to outline the state of the Cons family, ten years after the death of Frederick Cons, as far as it may be discerned – which is not very far at all. His death in 1870 is not recorded on the General Register. With the help of Mr Kirby of Highgate Cemetery I discovered it on the gravestone of the Cons family, where he is proudly recorded as 'of 38 Torrington Square'. The Cons girls continued to live there for a year or two; but by 1873 they had moved to Marylebone. The youngest, Elizabeth, married Edward William Baylis, raised a large family and made a home for her mother until old Mrs Cons died in 1882. Esther emigrated to Western Australia, encouraged by the Bishop of Melbourne, whom she had met in London while teaching in his Sunday school. According to Lilian Baylis, Esther established the first school there: this seems to be a family myth, but she did open the first Sunday school in the port of Bunbury, about 120 miles south of Perth. Here she married a pupil in her Bible class, much younger than herself – Robert Forrest, whose father owned a flour mill, and whose brother was the eminent Australian explorer and statesman, Sir John, later Lord, Forrest. Eliza Cons joined Esther in Bunbury at some time during the next decade. By 1880 Emma's brothers, Frederick and Charles, had set up their own piano-making business in East London (with, at first, frequent changes of address); but they are not even mentioned by name in Lilian Baylis's biographical sketch of her aunt, nor are they listed on the Highgate gravestone. It seems likely that there was a family split over life-styles: Frederick's baby daughter died of syphilis in 1869 aged one. There was alcoholism in the family too. Both Esther Forrest and Elizabeth Baylis are said to have had serious drink problems (though there is no evidence of when these developed); and Emma's single-minded hatred of drink may well have been fuelled by other first-hand experiences of its dangers.

Emma, Eliza and Ellen 'clung together for a good many years', as Lilian Baylis put it; or, more accurately, Ellen and Eliza clung to Emma. 'We used to say that Emmie was like the strong husband and Ellen the devoted wife. Whatever time Emmie came home from her work, there was always every comfort awaiting her; and whatever difficulties had arisen in her absence . . . Ellen dealt with, to the best of her power and ability. Emmie, I am certain, could never have accomplished the half of what she did, without Ellen's loving care at home.'[25] Sadly, that is about all one knows of Ellen, although she served for many years as a governor of the Old Vic, and lived to be eighty-one.

The Cons double-cottage in Moreton Place, where Emma and Ellen settled down in the 1880s, looked much the same as the others, except for the brass knocker on the front door; but the inhabitants' level of income, like their habits and conversation, was notably different from their neighbours'. There, for part of the week, lived Caroline Martineau, a member of the rich Liberal Unitarian family, who became one of Emma's closest friends and disciples. She, too, had trained as one of Octavia's helpers, some seven years after Emma; and she, too, showed a selfless devotion to social service, as well as to Emma, whom she served for some years as a kind of honorary secretary. Another close friend, Ethel Everest, also lived for a time in this 'cottage'. Miss Everest, daughter of the soldier-surveyor after whom the mountain was named, was yet another rich, philanthropic spinster who dedicated herself to good works and to Emma. (Both she and Caroline Martineau left fortunes of over £20,000, compared with Emma's £4,000.)

Emma believed in enlisting the help of her friends on the spot. She also believed in living among 'her people', so that they might know 'that at any hour of the day or night they can come to me if in trouble . . . living in a cottage no better than their own'.[26] And, after an early period of suspicion and resentment, they did come, frequently and persistently. Among her more sensational experiences was her trip to a nearby hospital in a 'fever-wagon' with a tenant suffering from black typhus, because none of his friends or relations would risk the journey; and there was the time she sat up all night in his room with a drunken madman, over a foot taller than herself, 'while the police and the parish authorities were disputing whose duty it was to remove him'.[27] But it was in the less perilous, everyday crises of family life that Emma proved to her tenants that she was no ordinary landlady or philanthropist. As a result, whereas she had first found it 'hard to convince them that we could possibly be right in any complaint or rule we made', she could report after nine years that 'it is generally taken for granted that, unless proved to the contrary, if we find fault there must be some cause for it'.[28] She won the trust of most of her tenants by the patent sincerity of her desire to serve, which combined sweetness of temper with firmness of will. A minor illustration is the distinction she observed between her two annual treats for the tenants, at Christmas and in summer. At Christmas everyone was invited, whether their rent was in arrears or not. The summer picnic was only for those whose accounts were clear.

At the same time, Emma showed that philanthropic experiments could be solvent, if properly managed. Even though her model dwellings made an uneconomic use of space, by commercial standards – only half the ground was built on – the shareholders received a steady four per cent each year. They could get a better return elsewhere, but this was their sacrifice to the cause of improving the conditions of the lower orders. Virtue, however, was not required, among the investing orders, to be its own reward: the steadiness of the dividend was all. Emma was obliged to appeal not only to Christian altruism but to the self-interest of the property-owning classes, among whom at this time there was a persistent fear of anarchy and revolution. Where else could she find the money? She may, like other reformers of the day, be charged with the erroneous 'application of moral force to political economy', because she believed that 'the evil to be combated was not poverty but pauperism . . . with its attendant vices, drunkenness, improvidence, mendicancy, bad language, filthy habits, gambling, low amusements, and ignorance,'[29] and that the solution was essentially a moral one, to be achieved by the spread of teetotalism and encouragement to thrift. Yet to fault her work on such grounds seems not only anachronistic but irrelevant.

A deeply interesting sketch of Emma at Surrey Lodge was made by Beatrice Webb in her notebooks, after a visit in 1885 (when Emma was forty-seven and Beatrice Webb twenty-seven).

Not a lady by birth, with the face and manner of a distinguished woman, almost a ruler of men. Absolute absorption in work; strong religious feeling, very little culture or things outside the sphere of her own action. To her people she spoke with that peculiar combination of sympathy and authority which characterises the modern type of governing woman . . . A calm enthusiasm in her face, giving her all to others. 'Why withhold any of your time and strength?' seems to be her spirit. All her energy devoted to the practical side of her work. No desire to solve the general questions of the hour. These governing and guiding women may become important factors if they increase as they have done lately: women who give up their lives to the management of men; their whole energy, body and mind, absorbed in it. They have the dignity of habitual authority; often they have the narrow-mindedness and social gaucherie due to complete absorption, physical and verbal, in one set of feelings and ideas.[30]

For Emma, the 'general questions of the hour' took second place. No matter how hard she worked for the improvement of housing and home life, there was a more important objective. 'So long as gin-palaces and beer-shops are to be found at nearly every street-corner in the poorer-class neighbourhoods, so long will the greatest part of the money saved by cheaper rent be spent there. And unless recreation, of intellectual and artistic merit, be brought within the reach of the mass of the people (many of whom are fully able to appreciate it) and their intelligence and love of beauty, harmony and order for its own sake, are used, they will speedily reduce these new and improved dwellings to the filth and squalor of the old.'[31] By the time she wrote this, in 1889, she had been trying to supply that kind of 'recreation' to Lambeth costermongers for nearly ten years.

Back in 1861, Henry Mayhew had argued, in the first volume of *London Labour and the London Poor*, that if the costermongers were to be lifted out of 'the moral mire in which they are wallowing, the first step must be to provide them with wholesome entertainment'. Already the way had been shown by the movements concerned with the education and leisure of the skilled working class. The Mechanics' Institutes and Lyceums attempted to meet the competition of the pubs and music halls with singing classes, recitals, lectures and concerts. Octavia had recognized the need too; in 1874 she wrote, 'How to make amusement self-supporting and yet pure and good is the problem'. Her sister Miranda helped in 1877 to found the Kyrle Society, with the aim of 'bringing beauty home to the public'. Her friend Samuel Barnett, the founder of Toynbee Hall, contended that 'The religion of amusement has been lost sight of', and believed that 'by music, one may be helped to find God'. In 1874 the performance of oratorios for East Enders began under his auspices, at St Jude's in Whitechapel; from 1877 concerts were given at fortnightly intervals; and in 1879 the People's Concert Society grew out of these experiments. In the same year Working Men's Concerts were launched in Manchester; and in London Emma Cons took a more direct initiative, driven by her hatred of the Demon Drink.

It was in music halls, just as much as in pubs, that the Demon worked his evil way. She argued that 'entertainment, like refreshment, had been in bondage to the brewer and distiller; and entertainment, like refreshment, should be made independent of drink'.[32] And in the cause of liberation she began to lobby her philanthropic friends and patrons. First, Lord Mount Temple chaired a meeting at the Walmer Castle to discuss her plan 'to provide for the working and lower middle classes recreation such as the music hall offers, without the existing attendant moral and social disadvantages'. The best way, she suggested, was to open new-model music halls providing 'purified entertainment, which shall amuse without degrading them, and to which men and women may take their wives and children, without shaming or harming them'. The meeting resolved to form a Coffee Music Hall Company, with this aim in view, and with Emma as honorary secretary. And at another meeting in February 1880, held in no less a place than the Jerusalem Chamber of Westminster Abbey, the site of the opening experiment in 'purified' teetotal entertainment was chosen: the Victoria Theatre in the Waterloo Road.

The Purified Hall

Always Talent, Always Change.
Slogan on a Royal Victoria Hall bill, 1886

The rich think of the poor as people to send missions to,
to amuse, keep out of pubs
and guard from dangerous opinions.
Henrietta Barnett, c. 1880

The Victoria Theatre in 1880 was a massive, dirty, boozy, melo-drama-house, rearing high above the Lambeth slums, a minute's walk from Waterloo Station and some of the worst brothels and thieves' kitchens in late-Victorian London. Like the district around it, the 'Vic' had changed for the worse in the six decades since it was built, when the Waterloo Road still had a semi-rural surround.

It was on Whit Monday 1818 that the Vic opened its doors for the first time, as the Royal Coburg Theatre, barely a year after the formal inauguration of Waterloo Bridge (on the second anniversary of the battle). The bridge was 'the Vic's first cause';[1] for it was meant to serve not so much the local playgoing population (there wasn't yet enough of that) but rather the expected new flow of North Bankers crossing the river to look for fun, of one kind or another, as they had done since Shakespeare's time. The fun available at the Coburg was usually provided with a musical accom-paniment, because it was a 'minor' house with a burletta licence – like the majority of London showplaces it was forbidden to present the drama of the spoken word, the 'legitimate' plays reserved by royal patent for Covent Garden and Drury Lane (and the Hay-market in summer). Again, like all the others, it broke the licens-ing laws by evasion and camouflage in presenting Shakespeare and other dramatists; and it was built in Lambeth because this was outside the jurisdiction of the Lord Chamberlain as a licenser of buildings (though not as the licenser of plays).

The architect of the Coburg, Rudolf Cabanel, had also designed the stage of the Surrey and the Theatre Royal, Drury Lane; and in spite of its size (it could hold as many as Drury Lane today), the auditorium had the intimacy and immediacy of communication made possible by the horseshoe design of three tiers looped above the pit and connecting directly with the stage, at each side of which were two stage boxes. The theatre boasted a Grand Marine Saloon (later converted by Emma Cons into a Coffee Tavern), and a Grand Looking Glass Curtain, which was briefly one of the sights of Regency London. This ornamental folly was made of sixty-three plates of glass set in a huge gilt frame, and was so heavy (five tons) that it endangered the roof from which it was suspended, and was dismembered a few years later. The pieces of glass were used to decorate the auditorium and saloon, where they remained for nearly a hundred years; some persisted in dressing-rooms until the 1950s.

The theatre was named after Prince Leopold of Saxe-Coburg, who was shortly to marry the Prince Regent's only daughter, Charlotte, heir-presumptive to the Crown. By the time it opened she had died in childbirth; and in 1833 the building was renamed after the fourteen-year-old Princess Victoria, who was now next in line of succession to the throne. In her honour the Royal Arms were set up above the stage, surmounted by a crown on a crimson cushion, with four flags – the Royal Standard, the Union Jack, the Stars and Stripes, and one other, never identified – and these remained unchanged, oblivious of the American Civil War, the First World War and all other contingencies, until they were destroyed in 1941. Princess Victoria visited the theatre with her mother in the year of its redubbing, but never returned as Queen. (It was not until Emma Cons took over that an active connection with the royal family was made and maintained.)

Within a few years it became clear that the promoters of the theatre had overestimated the effect of the new bridge on play-going. The Vic catered increasingly for a local working-class audience, as the surrounding district filled up with overcrowded terraces of jerry-built houses, and the Great Wen oozed over Lambeth, unplanned and uncontrolled, into the fields and market gardens of South London. The social changes in the audience were reflected in the price levels. When the Vic opened, these were on the traditional scale, starting at a shilling for the gallery; but by the mid-1830s this had dropped to twopence. (You could still get into the Vic gallery for twopence eighty years later, when the theatre had become 'the home of Shakespeare'.) During the 1820s and 1830s several great theatrical names appeared there, for a night or two: Phelps, Macready, Edmund Kean, Grimaldi, Paganini (his last English concert). But the standards of the programmes declined with those of the neighbourhood, which was already anathematized in 1840 by a critic, F. G. Tomlins, as one of the worst in London. The theatre was described in the 1840s by one journalist as 'the most degraded in London'; another said that its productions were 'fit for an audience of felons'; a third complained that it was particularly odious at Christmas, when it exhibited 'an appalling amount of loathsome vice and depravity' (unspecified). In 1850 Charles Kingsley, in an often-quoted passage from his novel *Alton Locke*, described how, at half-price time at the Vic 'the beggary and rascality of London were pouring in to their low amusement from the neighbouring gin-palaces and thieves' cellars. A herd of ragged boys, vomiting forth slang, filth and blasphemy, pushed past us, compelling us to take good care of our pockets . . . Look there! Look at these licensed pits of darkness, traps of temptation, profligacy and ruin triumphantly yawning night after night, and then tell me that the people who see their children kidnapped into hell are represented by a Government who licenses such things . . .'

Allowing for evangelistic rhetoric, and the abyss between middle-class and working-class life-styles, the New Cut was clearly not a place for ladies and gentlemen in pursuit of sweetness and light. Two years before Emma Cons took control of the Victoria Theatre a leading journalist, George Augustus Sala, described the district – notorious by now as the site of one of London's busiest street-markets and biggest criminal 'rookeries' – as 'simply Low', neither picturesque, nor quaint, nor curious.

The howling of beaten children and kicked dogs, the yells of ballad-singers . . . and reciters of sham murders and elopements; the bawling recitations of professional denunciators of the Queen, the royal family and the Ministry; the monotonous *jodels* of the itinerant hucksters; the fumes of the vilest tobacco, of stale corduroy suits, of oilskin caps, mildewed umbrellas, of decaying vegetables, of escaping gas, of deceased cats, of ancient fish, of dubious mutton pies and of unwashed, sodden, unkempt, reckless humanity; all these make the night hideous and the heart sick. The New Cut is one of the most unpleasant samples of London that you could offer to a foreigner.[2]

The theatre was nearly as squalid in appearance as the 'tumble-down, dreary and dirty' streets around it. According to the author and manager, John Hollingshead, 'the fittings are faded, the walls are smeared with greasy dirt, the pit floor is muddy and half covered with broken bottles'.[3] At midnight when the Vic emptied there were often drunken brawls outside. Few Saturdays passed, said the police, without seven or eight arrests, sometimes as many as forty (inside the theatre too).

The Vic gallery could – and did – hold over a thousand people on a Saturday night; packed tight, in shirt-sleeves, sweating and quarrelling, and (as Hollingshead said) 'always thirsty'. They used to tie their handkerchiefs together to make a rope for hauling up big stone bottles of beer from the pit, and occasionally the hats they had dropped below. They dropped other things, too – orange peel, nuts, bits of food. They made such a noise that hardly a note could be heard when the orchestra began to play; but the din – and the fights – stopped as soon as the curtain rose. The Vic was, indeed, a 'safety-valve', said Sala, which saved the area from being 'a mere Devil's Acre'. The audience was rowdy, boozy and aggressive. They came not only for the shows but for the drink and the whores – pillars of the popular theatre here, as elsewhere in Victorian London; and their taste was for melodramatic nonsense. 'Fearful Fights', 'Sensation Scenes', 'Final Explosions' and a 'good murder' were what they loved, with a sufficiency of villains to curse and shout at. But these were dramas in which, as Sala said:

for all the jargon, silliness and buffoonery, the immutable principles of right and justice are asserted; in which virtue, in the end, is always triumphant, and vice is punished; in which cowardice and falsehood are hissed, and bravery and integrity vehemently applauded; in which, were we to sift away the bad grammar, and the extravagant action, we should find the dictates of the purest and highest morality.

Even a critic like F. G. Tomlins, who had dismissed the Vic audience as 'of the lowest kind', praised 'the attention and justice with which certainly one of the most uneducated audiences must appreciate genuine pathos and even genuine wit and poetry'.[4]

By the 1870s, however, such commodities were in short supply at the Vic. It failed to hold a regular audience, and to survive the competition of the music halls. (It was only briefly a music hall itself.) Within a few minutes' walk of the Vic you could find the Canterbury, the Winchester, the Union, the South London, the Rotunda, the Bower Saloon, Astley's, the Surrey and several 'penny gaffs'. In 1871 the theatre went up for auction, staggered on till 1874, went up for auction again, then closed down in 1880. The Winchester and the Bower Saloon had collapsed shortly before this: the South Bank pits of darkness seemed to be burning out.

Emma Cons started at the Vic with the highest of hopes and the best of intentions. The Council of the Coffee Music Hall Company declared (in her voice, perhaps) that 'to keep men happy helps to keep men good, and that benefits all, whether rich or poor'; and Miss Cons set out to demonstrate in the Waterloo Road that men could be kept happy in public without the help of alcohol – or blue jokes. In spite of the demands of housing management and other good works, she was clearly determined to supervise the operation herself. John Hollingshead, who had originally proposed the Vic, was ready to handle it for the Company; he soon discovered that his association with the un-purified Gaiety Theatre appeared to carry the threat of infection, and that the honorary secretary had no intention of delegating the direction of her teetotal crusade.

There were three main reasons why the dirty, raffish old building in the New Cut was chosen as the starting-point. It was readily available to anyone who would pay the rent. It was in the centre of one of the capital's poorest districts, and surrounded by gin-palaces and beer-houses; it had a reputation for rowdyism and drunkenness; and thirdly, it was not far from Surrey Lodge. It was, indeed, the popularity of the unregenerate Vic among her tenants that spurred Emma on to redeem it. When she collected rents on Monday morning, she was horrified to discover each week a fresh crop of black eyes and blue bruises among the women; it took the men that way, they said, when they came back drunk from the Vic on Saturday nights. In later years Miss Baylis liked to ram the point home to her actors, as to Laurence Olivier: 'If it hadn't been for drunken men beating their wives, dear boy, we'd never have got this place and you wouldn't be doing Hamlet'.

Having leased the theatre for eighteen years at around £1,000 p.a., Emma Cons set about raising the cash for alterations and redecoration, with the help of her supporting cast of wealthy backers. It cost the Council about £3,000 before the Vic re-opened on Boxing Day 1880, as the Royal Victoria Coffee and Music Hall. The word 'theatre', steeped as it was in impure associations, was dropped – for nearly forty years. But the inaugural programme, a variety bill, was unmistakably theatrical, even though it was carefully vetted and 'freed from anything of a debasing character'. No prostitutes were on parade (not, at least, inside the building) and no spirits or beer were on sale. But tea, coffee and sandwiches were available, served on this special occasion by Emma's friends and relations. Watching the audience filing in that evening, perched in the same box from which she was to rule the Hall for over thirty years, was the founder's six-year-old niece, Lilian Baylis.

Emma Cons and the Council did not want to deter, by too much uplift and education, the possible family audience in search of good, clean music-hall fun. So they presented variety 'purged of innuendo in word and action' (as far, that is, as Miss Cons could tell). The clearest indications of her intentions were signalled by the programme, which carried in the first year two improving quotations from Shakespeare – 'For in my youth I never did apply hot and rebellious liquors in my blood' (*As You Like It*) and 'Oh God, that men should put an enemy in their mouths to steal away their brains' (*Othello*).

But Emma soon discovered that she had underestimated the difficulties of drawing customers without the lure of alcohol. Business on Saturday night was good, as it was throughout London, but when takings dropped away there were no bar profits to balance the budget, as in unregenerate establishments. Emma found that she hadn't enough money to hire a good variety bill every night of the week, and so she began to introduce cheaper if more enlightened diversions. She started with ballad concerts 'of a high type', in which 'Artists as well as Amateurs' gave their services free or at cut rates, lobbied assiduously by Miss Cons and her contacts to do their bit for charity. These concerts were on Thursdays. On Fridays Emma staged a temperance meeting, followed – by way of bait – by an hour's lecture with magic lantern or an hour's variety. On Saturday afternoons there was a variety show, meant for children; on Sundays the Hall was let for Divine Service (of approved denominations).

Emma could see for herself one rapid and tangible result of her labours: an improvement in manners. At first the programme carried a warning note: 'The Manager respectfully reminds the audience that for the true enjoyment of this programme in so large a Theatre, *silence* is an absolute necessity. He begs, therefore, that Whistling and unnecessary noise will not be *practised in the Gallery and Pit*.' But before very long the *Illustrated London News* was noting with surprise that at a ballad concert 'the rough working men are as courteous and enthusiastic as the fashionable folk in St James's Hall' (the chief London concert hall of the day). The *Era* described the 'good order and good humour' of 'whole families taking their tea and coffee'. And another observer reported 'galleries filled to overflowing, and a pit crammed with men fresh from their work to hear and to applaud rapturously a cavatina by Raff and a reverie by Vieuxtemps, on the very spot where, a few nights before the old "Vic" closed, I saw a wretched drunken woman dividing a glass of gin at the gallery bar between herself, a little boy of seven years old, and a baby at her breast'. They seemed, as one journalist surmised after visiting the Hall, 'not only willing but eager to exchange the inanities of the music hall for something better, even at the expense of the cheering glass'; and another, inspired by euphoria, declared that 'Music for the million is . . . the most rational and simple plan . . . to refine the humbler classes'.

However satisfactory the social accountancy might appear, the economic balance-sheet was disturbing. The Vic was a big theatre to fill – it held 2,300 (500 more in a Saturday-night squeeze), and the prices were low: over 800 places in the gallery at twopence, over 500 in the pit at threepence and 120 stalls at a shilling. On Wednesdays and Fridays admission to the gallery was only a penny. Box-office revenue fell alarmingly below running costs (which amounted to nearly £6 a night in rent and gas alone). The Cons crusade, it appeared, had been over-optimistic on four counts: the willingness of the local audience to do without a proper drink on an evening out; the support of the 'more respectable class' of working man; the ease of finding a manager qualified to run such an innovatory venture (the first one left within a year); and the brute facts of theatre economics – e.g. that the profits of tea, coffee and soft drinks could not rationally be compared with those of beer and spirits, or 'wet money', as it was known in the trade. As Lilian Baylis said, 'It must not be imagined that the movement to "elevate the masses" met with immediate success; on the contrary, the masses showed plainly enough that they did not much want to be elevated'.[5]

Within eight months of the opening Emma Cons faced a financial crisis, the first of a long series which were to recur throughout the Vic's next sixty years. The Hall closed down, and it nearly stayed closed: there was a deficit of £2,800. That seemed a great deal, even for the deserving poor; and many directors of the

Coffee Music Hall Company wanted to stop the experiment there and then before 'purified' entertainment made any further inroads on their credit. But Emma stood firm. After many years among the philanthropic elite, she was accustomed to tender monetary consciences and vagaries of will. The work was a *moral* success, she contended with serene obstinacy, and it must go on. To admit defeat, so soon, would be a bad example: in effect, a surrender to the force of darkness (like the brewers). Before the Hall opened, she said in a report, neighbouring clergy had attacked the project of opening another music hall on the South Bank, because 'the others did so much harm to their people', and had urged their flocks not to visit the Vic. But now, reported Emma jubilantly, their attitude had completely changed. They 'concur in saying that wonderful work is being done . . . they all say that the streets are quite different since we came, both for drunkenness and immorality. The police say the same, from the Chief Superintendent downwards.' The 'general charges' in the area had decreased on an average from forty to four, and not one of these had been connected directly with the Vic. 'Without exception every policeman and person to whom I have spoken in the neighbourhood joins in the same theme of thankfulness and rejoicing,' wrote Emma; and she ended, with a trumpet-blast of defiant rhetoric, 'If I were rich I should think no money so well spent: as it is, I can only give my life and that I give freely.'

Put like that, it sounded an astonishing success story. Yet the Vic would have collapsed at this point without the money of Emma's rich friends like the Marchioness of Lothian and Caroline Martineau's mother, whose cheque for £1,000 reinforced Emma's decision to hold out. (Emma got this money because, while helping Mrs Martineau at home in Suffolk to send off a batch of charitable circulars, she broke the news to her that they needed only a halfpenny, not a penny stamp.) Lord Mount Temple undertook to guarantee all losses for a further period of nine months; the directors handed over to a committee (which resolved, poignantly, 'never to run into debt'); and the Hall reopened in October 1881, under a new manager, William Poel.

Poel's place in theatrical history is assured, as a reformer of Shakespearian production. His work had a marked influence, thirty years later, at the Old Vic. But he was then only at the beginning of his experiments – his First Quarto *Hamlet* (two hours, with no scenery) had been staged a few months earlier – and he could have no opportunity to develop them at the Vic, for as it had no theatre licence it was legally prohibited from presenting stage plays. Poel remained as manager for two years. On his departure the committee paid warm tribute to his 'zeal and good management . . . He has not only lessened the expenses . . . but has raised the tone of entertainments'; but he had little impact on the Vic's evolution. Far more valuable help was given from about this time onwards by another of the aristocratic philanthropists whom Emma had met in the 1870s through Octavia Hill: Lady Frederick Cavendish. After her husband was murdered in Phoenix Park, Dublin in 1882 Lady Fred, as she became known at the Old Vic, immersed herself in social work. A deeply religious *grande dame*, she was connected to some of the richest and most powerful people in Britain. Her father was Lord Lyttelton, and her brothers included a general, an admiral, a bishop, a viscount and a head-master of Eton. She was the daughter-in-law of the seventh Duke of Devonshire, sister-in-law of the eighth, and aunt of the ninth. Bishop Talbot (one of Lilian Baylis's idols) was her brother-in-law. Gladstone was one of her uncles, among whom were also the Earl of Carlisle and the Duke of Sutherland. One nephew, Alfred Lyttelton, later played a leading role in the campaign for a National Theatre, as did his second wife, Edith, and his son, Lord Chandos. Lady Fred was also related to the Earls of Liverpool and Antrim, Archbishop Temple, the Duchess of Westminster and Lord Hampden (the chairman of Emma's main project, the South London Dwellings Company). More important to the Old Vic than any of this glittering network of grandees, scarcely any of whom appear to have taken the remotest interest in subsidizing or indeed patronizing the theatre, was Lady Fred's friendship with the royal family – she was Maid of Honour to Queen Victoria and, later, to Queen Alexandra – and her readiness to tug on her connections when the Vic seemed to be in need of visible support from the Palace.

It was probably through Lady Fred's influence that in 1881 the first royal visit was secured. It was made by Queen Victoria's niece, Princess Frederica of Hanover, who came *twice* before Christmas. (On her first visit, Lilian Baylis made her public debut at the Vic by presenting the Princess with a bouquet.) A few weeks later there were even more lustrous visitors in the persons of the Prince and Princess of Wales (later Edward VII and Queen Alexandra), who came for a 'special Irish night'. Miss Cons certainly knew how to pull the strings, or how to win the confidence of other people who were good at pulling them.

In the same month one Thursday night was given up to Mozart: in a foretaste of the future, 'the ladies and gentlemen of the Royal Academy of Music' sang the first act of *Così fan tutte*, in costume, to English words. Another night *The Messiah* was received attentively and enthusiastically by the gallery, 'a great number with knotted handkerchiefs round their necks, and nearly all with the humble "clay" in their mouths'. The mechanics, factory workers and costers who made up most of the audience 'rapturously applauded each soloist . . . and would have encored nearly every solo and chorus had they been permitted'; while 'the girls known on the Surrey side as of the Madame Blackfriars type – girls with white aprons, mysteriously propped up hats, and ridiculous fringes on their foreheads – instead of lolling on their sweethearts' shoulders and absorbing spirits and suggestiveness . . . here sat quiet and attentive'. On variety nights, too, there were noticeable changes in the manners of the artists and the expectations of the customers. 'The Music Hall profession recognize that we are in earnest,' Miss Cons reported. 'We have continually less and less trouble in controlling words and gestures, and when the Hall is let for a benefit our rules are strictly observed, without causing any sign of dissatisfaction on the part of the audience.' (One of those dissatisfied was Beatrice Webb. Having been fired by enthusiasm for Emma Cons's personality, she sampled a Saturday night at the Vic in 1885 but found it 'a dreary performance, sinking to the level of the audience, while omitting the dash of coarseness, irreverence and low humour which give the spice and the reality to such entertainments. To my mind the devil is preferable, and in every way more wholesome, than a shapeless mediocrity.')[6]

Hecklers and rowdies still disturbed the teetotal peace; and there was still employment for the burly chucker-out – who reminded one journalist of a Russian moujik, dressed as he was in a red shirt, standing at the ready with his arms folded across his chest. But there was no doubt that times had changed in what was now sometimes described in the programme as 'The People's Hall, The People's Entertainments, The People's Prices'. 'The People's Entertainments' included not only 'acrobats, niggers and performing animals', but also such treats as 'A Grand Shakespeare Night', with 'Songs, Glees and Scenes selected from Shakespeare's Plays'. A visiting Danish actor, Albert Alberg, played Othello – in scenes from Acts 3 and 5 – while a local favourite Charles Sennett appeared as Iago. Poel also approached the bandmaster of the Life Guards, Dan Godfrey, offering him £20 to bring his band to the Vic and play his current hit, the 'Holly Bush' polka: it was, Poel claimed later, 'the first appearance of any military band on a variety stage'. This all went to prove, said Miss Cons proudly, that 'drink, unseemliness and profanity have no necessary connection with entertainment'.

What is more, Emma extended the scope of the Hall in 1882 from entertainment (and temperance propaganda) to education. She appealed to scientists through the columns of *Nature* to address the Vic audience, and the response was so satisfactory – first from the scientists, then from the public – that in the autumn of 1883 she introduced (with the help of a scientists' committee) a weekly Tuesday lecture. Emma made this the special responsibility of Caroline Martineau, who may well have suggested it and whose passionate interest in science had been aroused by listening to Faraday and Tyndall, the leading scientific sages of the day, at the Royal Institution. Within three years of its opening as a music hall, the Vic now occupied most of its time by non-theatrical activities. Among those who disapproved of this trend was William Poel. After leaving the Vic he said that 'it aimed too high', and that the Committee's didactic and educational priorities were misplaced. They were ignoring what the audience wanted.

Certainly, the moral victories of the Hall were still not reflected in the takings, which continued to fall; and it made no difference when the committee voted (against Miss Cons's wishes) to replace both Tuesday lectures and Friday temperance meetings with variety entertainment. As no financial gain was achieved by this move, it was revoked; and both evenings were recaptured for education and propaganda. But by 1884 the Vic was again on the point of collapse. The guarantee fund was nearly exhausted. There was only enough cash in hand for a few weeks' operations. Emma was now effectively acting as manager of the Hall, in addition to her interests outside it. She took no salary. At this juncture, once again, one of her rich friends came to the rescue. Ethel Everest offered £1,000 anonymously towards the purchase of the lease. Her benefaction was not enough; but it was a spur to finding others. Emma decided to approach one of the great philanthropists of that generation, Samuel Morley.

Morley was a millionaire textile manufacturer, a Liberal MP, a Nonconformist who probably gave away more money than any contemporary, though in small packages; a model of the paternalistic boss (he introduced the first big pension scheme in British industry). He was also an enemy of smoking, a fanatical supporter of total abstinence, and for most of his life – he was now, at seventy-four, nearing the end of it – he had nursed a puritanical dread of 'worldly amusements', including the theatre. Such a man would scarcely seem a likely backer for any music hall, however 'purified'. As a practical reformer, however, Morley was impressed by the rapidity of the Vic's impact upon local manners. He joined the committee; he ventured to watch some of the programmes; and he found, to his astonishment, that he actually enjoyed himself at the Hall. He testified at a meeting that 'I don't know that I have ever laughed so much as on these occasions. I believe in good hearty laughter, it tends to health . . . I have seen thousands listening to good music. . . . I am not a theatre-goer, but I did most heartily enjoy the real fun, absolutely divested of anything gross or immoral . . .' Now, in this moment of crisis, Morley responded to Miss Cons's plea by offering £1,000, if she could get the additional £2,000 needed to buy the lease. He made one condition: that he should appoint a working committee in sympathy with his own ideas about how the Vic should be run. As these ideas concerned the growth of both the lectures and the temperance meetings, it was a condition that Emma was happy to accept. With £2,000 in the kitty, the power of Morley's name, and the help of the Martineau family *en bloc* (no fewer than nine contributed to the fund), the lease was acquired. An expanded Council was formed, with Princess Christian as Patroness and the Duke of Westminster as President. The Patrons included Ethel Everest (and her brother), Caroline Martineau (and her sister) and Ellen Cons; and the Vic was renamed 'The Royal Victoria Hall (and Coffee Tavern)'. The parenthesis was rapidly lost – mainly because, according to William Poel, Charles Santley had refused to sing there while 'Coffee' was in the title – he wrote to Emma that 'Art has nothing to do with eating and drinking'.[7] The Coffee Music Hall Company went into liquidation; it had no successors, and no more temperance showplaces were opened.

Although Samuel Morley's role has sometimes been exaggerated – it is not true that he 'gave us the Old Vic' – his intervention at this phase was of obvious value; and it was not only a question of cash. Having taken to Miss Cons, as so many eminent Victorians did, he decided that the cause needed 'moral support and personal service no less than gifts of money' (and holly from his Kent estate for Christmas decorations), and from then on he devoted much of his energy to what he described, in a letter to Emma, as 'our happy partnership'. Characteristically, he wrote to her in 1886:

I have the impression that you have denied yourself the ease and comfort of having a competent manager because of the expense . . . I must ask you to oblige *me* by losing no time in seeking such help as is competent, at whatever cost may be necessary, in order that we may all be relieved from the distress we really feel, that you have had a great deal more on your hands than it has been kind of us to allow. I have really thought whether, if I were to come and engage some rooms at Surrey Lodge, I could do anything that would be helpful. The result of my cogitations has been, that perhaps I should be in the way.[8]

A few months later he died. Nearly a hundred institutions were represented at his funeral, but it was through the Vic, above all, that Samuel Morley's name was preserved, although few Londoners may now know the origins of Morley College.

Buying the lease was not the final answer. Emma had more obstacles to overcome before she could say that the future of the Hall was reasonably assured. In 1888 the Charity Commissioners, responding to an appeal from the City Parochial Foundation, a fund created out of ancient charitable bequests, agreed to give the Vic an annual endowment of £1,000 on condition that the trustees bought the freehold. Emma ascertained that it was for sale – at a price of £17,000, within four months; the time limit was set by the owner, who claimed that a publican was ready to pay much more. The Duke of Westminster called a meeting at Grosvenor House and started the ball rolling with a gift of £1,000, and Lord Brassey gave the same amount. Encouragement was provided by such eminences as Earl Brownlow ('It is a matter of deep importance that pure recreation should be within the reach of all classes') and Cardinal Manning ('Miss Cons and her assistant are carrying happiness, brightness, rays of light and rays of joy into a multitude of homes into which the rays of the sun never shine'). Lord Mount Temple testified to the shameful poverty of the area: 'there are 9,000 people not wealthy enough to keep a servant'. And Miss Cons, harping on the theme of class reconciliation, observed: 'As the Japanese proverb says, there is nothing that unites the highest and lowest so much as community of entertainment'. It seemed as if community of giving was a more rarefied phenomenon; but although public generosity was painfully slow in coming to the rescue, the full amount was collected a few days before the deadline. Now yet another new opportunity opened for the Vic, with the freehold secure and an annual endowment. In 1891 the freehold of 13,000 square feet in the Waterloo Road was vested in the Charity Commissioners; the Royal Victoria Hall Foundation was formally approved at the Court at Windsor; with eleven Representative and seven Cooptative Governors (of the Representatives, six were to be chosen by the City Parochial Foundation; one each by the University of London, the Royal Academy of Music and the Royal College of Music jointly, and the London County Council; and two by the Borough Road Polytechnic Institute).

The Vic was now devoted to 'the benefit and enjoyment of the people for ever'. This was recorded on a white marble tablet in memory of Samuel Morley, 'one who held his wealth in trust for the benefit of others irrespective of class or creed'.

By then Emma Cons had presided over a major development in the Vic's educational activities. In 1884, after one of the Tuesday lectures, two or three young men approached her from the pit and asked her to introduce regular evening classes in scientific subjects. The lectures were fine as far as they went, said the young men, but left so many questions unanswered. Stirred by their initiative, and undoubtedly encouraged by Caroline Martineau, Emma managed to secure official permission – and put Caroline in charge. Within a year the classes attracted some sixty students, who occupied dressing-rooms behind the stage and met in the saloon. The range and popularity of the classes spread, until the governing body decided to separate the Hall's educational from its theatrical activities under the name of the Morley Memorial College – for working men *and* women. It was opened in 1889. Those who had begun their studies in the theatre proudly signed OVS (Old Vic Student) after their names.

Morley College followed in the path of the evening classes run by Mechanics' Institutes, the Lyceums, the Working Men's College established by F. D. Maurice and the more recent Polytechnic in Regent Street, opened in 1882 and rapidly imitated elsewhere. But there were two big differences between Morley College and other educational institutions. First, it admitted women on equal terms; its first executive head was a woman (*and* its second); and at least three members of its council were, by prescription, women (although most of its students were men). Second, it was a college in a theatre, working around, behind and below a stage. It was subsidized, in its early years, by the Hall; its students were admitted to all entertainments (except Saturday-night variety) at half-price; and the honorary secretary of the College and its Council was also the honorary secretary of the Hall (and its manager) – Emma Cons. Miss Cons's closest friends were also on the College Council – Ethel Everest and Caroline Martineau (and her sister

Constance), together with Lady Frederick Cavendish. When the first Principal resigned after two years, Caroline stood in, and was persuaded to remain until her death in 1902 at fifty-nine. Not only was she unpaid, but she continued – with Constance – to make frequent gifts to the College.

The College stayed inside the Hall, incredibly, for many years. Under the stage were the recreation rooms; above it was the library; behind it were class-rooms – occupying the space that had once been given to dressing-rooms, stage machinery, flies, scene-dock and other standard equipment and services. While the ballad-concerts, temperance meetings, military bands and variety performers were on the stage, all around the building, behind fire-proof (though not necessarily sound-proof) walls, hundreds of students were every night at work or at play in their gymnasium, societies or music classes. Sometimes they used the Hall for gymnastic displays, prize-givings and concerts. Their orchestral society rehearsed with the Hall band.

The Hall also included a café – or, rather, a dining and refreshment room (strictly temperance, of course) – to which there was direct, open access from the pit. This occupied the front of the building for over thirty years, adding its sounds and savours to the extraordinary atmosphere of the place. It was run by John Pearce, one of the entrepreneurs to benefit from the example of Miss Cons's coffee taverns. This ex-barrow boy from Hoxton set up a chain of nearly a hundred temperance eating-houses, 'Pearce and Plenty' – deliberately echoing a Victorian political slogan – of which the Vic's is the best remembered.

In retrospect, it seems something of a miracle that theatrical and musical programmes could be given in a building so devoid of elementary stage facilities, run on such low prices and with such divided purposes. What kind of theatre was this? To Emma Cons, of course, it *wasn't* a theatre. It was the Hall – and the College. Whether she provided ballad-concerts, music-hall turns, lectures on electricity or athletic classes, the ends she had in view were far higher than those (as she understood them) of a mere showplace.

In the light of her reforming ambitions, the problems of stage management, accountancy and even aesthetics diminished in significance. The kind of entertainment she could provide was, in any event, restricted by the Hall's music-hall licence, which prohibited the performance of a stage play; and, as a number of music-hall managers discovered, the term 'stage play' could be so narrowly defined by litigious competitors, supported by the licensing authorities, as to penalize the performance of dramatic sketches, pantomimes and even ballets. In 1880, for instance, the lessee of the nearby Canterbury was summonsed for presenting a ballet, *The Peri of Peru*, which was adjudged a 'stage play' because it had a plot. The fine was a nominal forty shillings, but further convictions might have cost the music hall its licence. Such prosecutions were a matter of luck, spite and accident. As we have seen, the Victoria Hall in 1882 was presenting scenes from Shakespeare in costume, without let or hindrance. But pantomime was a more serious matter. In 1886 Miss Cons was charged with presenting a 'stage play' at Christmas, called *King He's a Bore, The Plague of his Dear-man*. It was a kind of delayed revenge. For the case was brought under pressure from J. Arnold Cave, who had managed the Vic for over a decade, off and on, before Emma took over, and who was then running the Elephant and Castle Theatre. What's more, a key witness was the former musical director of the Vic, Bernard Issacson, who had worked there for many years. Mr Issacson said that he had written over forty pantomimes, and what he saw at the Vic was nothing more nor less than a pantomime, even though only Prince Amoroso actually spoke (everybody else is said to have sung). The fact that one actor had a small speaking part was enough to infringe the law. The fine – half a crown (plus agreed expenses) – was even more conspicuously a token penalty than the one imposed on the Canterbury; yet to Emma the warning was clear. She could apply to the Lord Chamberlain for a dramatic licence, but even if this were granted (with the help of her aristocratic allies) it would entail two measures that Emma could not afford: the prohibition of smoking, and structural changes for reasons of safety. In any event, her prime ambition was not theatrical management. Running the Vic was, for her, a 'recreation' from housing chores and other social work, and the performances were not her main concern. So she kept the music-hall licence, and practised traditional evasions for untraditional reasons.

There seems to have been no repetition during her lifetime of the Grand Shakespeare Night and other dramatic events staged by Poel. The words of Shakespeare and other writers were sometimes heard on the Vic stage, but only in 'dramatic readings' and recitals, usually incorporated in a ballad concert. In music, however, Emma took a more adventurous course. From 1889 onwards she presented, once a fortnight, concerts of excerpts from opera, sung in English. These were recitals, rather than performances. Guest singers of varying celebrity stood in front of the curtain and belted out the most celebrated songs from the most popular operas of the day; and every now and then the curtain rose to reveal a *tableau* of some climactic scene. These *tableaux vivants* – remotely akin to the distinctly less reputable and less fully clothed diversions of the non-temperance halls – were enacted by a number of helpful people, more or less in costume, who struck appropriate attitudes and held them, mutely, till the curtain dropped noisily on to the stage again. To move was, in effect, illegal, a proscription comparable in idiocy with the 'freeze' enjoined on strippers in the nude revues of the pre-permissive era.

It was safer for Miss Cons to present this kind of entertainment than to attempt drama, because it did not compete with the programmes of neighbouring managers. It was also more likely to hold the audience, as the popularity of the ballad concerts suggested. ('People who cannot read, and have a narrow conception of things about them, are more open to the influence of music than to anything else', explained Lord Mount Temple.) And, moreover, an interest in opera was reviving, especially opera in English. This was reflected in the national popularity achieved in the 1880s by the Carl Rosa Company (founded in 1869), the growth of other companies like the Moody Manners ensemble (started in 1897), and such abortive attempts to establish a national opera house as d'Oyly Carte's 1891 Royal English Opera House (now the Palace Theatre).

'Real' opera was still generally identified with Italian opera at Covent Garden, performed by visiting foreign virtuosi. (It was not until 1891 that the Royal Opera House dropped 'Italian' from its title.) These programmes of some eight or ten weeks had for generations featured in the annual rituals of upper-class leisure. The opera season was part of the London season. Grand opera was for grand people, one of the more expensive luxuries of the rich. But meanwhile, down in Lambeth, the opera concerts proved so popular that Emma developed their scope, within the regulations; although the programme expressed the hope that 'before long, the law affecting these matters will be revised, and those who are trying to improve the quality of the entertainment offered to the people will then be less hampered by vexatious restrictions ...' She usually offered, in one concert, some twenty excerpts and twenty *tableaux*. In the 1891–2 season – the only one in this period of which a record survives – selections from nine operas were given fifteen performances: they included *Il Trovatore*, Gounod's *Faust*, *La Sonnambula* and *The Daughter of the Regiment*, as well as such native favourites as *Maritana*, *The Bohemian Girl* and *The Lily of Killarney* (known for years as 'The English Ring'). Many of the performers were amateurs; but a few eminent professionals gave their services free or at cut rates. Among the most famous was Antoinette Sterling, an American Quaker 'obsessed by the conviction that her incomparable voice had been specially bestowed on her by God as an instrument for the conversion of sinners'.[9] That conviction suited the Vic, with which the Sterling family retained a link for over fifty years.

Among the less-qualified musicians in the orchestra pit was, briefly, Bernard Shaw, who was employed in 'filling up the gaps in an anything-but-full band on a grand piano, at a performance of detached acts of *Faust* and *Il Trovatore* for the improvement of the masses ... if the masses were not improved it was not my fault'.[10] Shaw also stood in, on 'one or two similar occasions', as a stage manager, with no more success than as a pianist. In sounding the bell in the Miserere in *Il Trovatore*, he recalled years later, 'I was such a failure that the *prima donna* struck at rehearsal and silenced me; but what could I do with a length of gaspipe on a string and an old poker to hit it with?' Later, in 1883, he attacked the Vic anonymously in the *Musical Review*, for using music as 'a handmaid in the cause of religion and sobriety'. If it failed, Shaw observed, it would not be for want of publicity: 'there has been an amount of trumpet-blowing worthy of the inauguration of a great work'. But he protested that because of 'the association of music with total abstinence ... the Victoria Hall, which might be made a centre for the diffusion of art among the humbler ranks of society, only appeals to one section, and that a comparatively small one ... it would be grossly unfair to gauge the tastes of the entire artisan class by the measure of success obtained in this instance.' After two or three visits, Shaw suggested that 'the management underestimates, rather than overestimates, the critical capacity of its audiences . . .' One concert had been attended by about 1,500 people, 'and if the whole of them had been skilled musicians the verdict on each item could not have been more discriminating. The demeanour of all present was equally remarkable, perfect silence being preserved while the music was being performed'.[11]

It was not until the spring of 1894 that a chorus was added to the opera. This was recruited, characteristically, from the choir of the Church of the Sacred Heart in Camberwell. Its debut was made in a work called *Robert Macaire* (by George Fox), founded on a Vic melodrama of sixty years earlier. The experiment was so successful that Emma decided to establish a regular chorus (largely unpaid, and largely from the Sacred Heart) from the autumn of 1894 onwards. The same church also supplied dancers when required.

Meanwhile, the variety continued on Saturdays, under close supervision. In 1888 the *Pall Mall Gazette* reported that 'No coarse or unseemly jest or allusion, no word with an undesirable double entendre, is permitted to be heard on the stage. To this each acrobat, ventriloquist, comedian, nigger vocalist, clown and dancer pledges himself or herself, and only once in the course of eight years has the curtain been made to fall before the performance has ended on account of the infringement of the stage rules.' Miss Cons inserted a 'special notice' in the programme, to encourage moral vigilantes: 'All possible care is exercised to insure perfect propriety in the Entertainment offered at this Hall. The Managers will, however, be greatly obliged to members of the audience who will report to them anything in the slightest degree objectionable.' Lilian Baylis testified that Emma used to watch the acts 'lest they were tempted to fall into vulgarity'. Sometimes she delegated this task to Caroline Martineau, who was often seen 'quietly sitting in judgement on . . . a popular clown, or legislating firmly, but not too severely, on the costume of a danseuse'.[12] Legend had it, after Emma's death, that she was on guard every night in the prompt corner; and that if one of the acts on the bill showed a tinge of blue she applied instant censorship – by letting down the roller-curtain, on one occasion, right on the offender's head. This is a tribute to the lingering force of her moral authority – like the story that she used to make raids on the gallery to break up necking couples (the same tale is told of Lilian Baylis). An inspector from the LCC noted in 1891 one evening when the Hall was 'closely packed' that 'Miss Cons herself went to any part of the house in which the slightest noise was heard and her presence seemed sufficient to restrain them'.

Certainly, Emma took a close and not always comforting interest in the Vic's theatrical affairs. When Constance Willis, as a girl chorister, got the giggles in *Faust* one night, she was called off the stage by Miss Cons, scolded for 'unmannerly behaviour', made to stand in the wings and not allowed back in the chorus that night. Emma's niece recalled her in a warmer light, sitting at the back of the circle and 'giving a smiling greeting to regular patrons'; quelling a gang of rowdies in the gallery, dressed, as ever, in her 'delicate little lace bonnet'; presiding over Christmas tea parties, where everyone received a 'specially chosen' gift and then watched a variety programme; and entertaining Vic staff and College students at the Kent home of Ethel Everest, Chippens Bank near Hever, where she spent nearly every weekend.[13]

The Hall was, however, only one iron in the fire of Emma's life. Apart from helping to run the affairs of Morley College and managing the Surrey Lodge estate and the Drury Lane property, she served on the executive of the Women's Liberal Federation and became vice-president of a women's suffrage group. She helped to raise the money to keep Vauxhall Park as an open space. In 1892, at fifty-four, she became the first woman student at Swanley Horticultural College – in order to open another area of work for her sex; within six years there were thirty-five women students there, in the House of Residence of Women Gardeners. In 1895 she went to Armenia to report on the Turkish pogroms for the *Daily News*. On the journey back she visited Crete, where many Armenians had taken refuge, and helped to set up a silk factory there to give them employment. She took an ardent interest in a home for backward girls in Bodmin, and a Working Girls' House and Day Nursery near Drury Lane. But, as one historian says, 'it was the boys, especially the naughty boys, who were most dear to her heart. Again and again she says in her reports, "although the boys were troublesome they were not really bad".'

Recognition of Emma's work came in 1889, after the creation of the London County Council, for she was chosen as an alderman, while Miss Cobden and Lady Sandhurst were elected as councillors. Lady Sandhurst's election, however, was disputed by her opponent on grounds of sex. He objected that permission for women to vote in local elections did not imply permission to take office, and his objection was upheld. She was unseated; Miss Cobden's election was challenged in turn; and so Emma felt obliged to resign, after no more than a year as alderman. (This restriction was maintained until 1907, when women were enabled to serve as councillors or aldermen.) But she continued to do social work with the new Council, in spite of the sexual prejudices of some councillors. Her feminism was of the kind that put service before self-dramatization, and work before warfare. She was nagged persistently by a sense of the immensity of what had to be achieved, in London alone, for the majority of the people; and of how little time she had left.

Even for Emma Cons, all this was a heavy load, and her 'recreation' added to it. From 1894 she was helped at the Hall by an acting manager, Miss Phillips (she liked to employ women when she could); but by 1897, when Miss Phillips left, Emma was on the verge of a breakdown. It was at this point in the history of the Vic that her niece Lilian Baylis returned from South Africa, at Emma's invitation, for six months convalescence; and at this point in our narrative we must return to the history of Lilian, with the reminder, in Octavia Hill's words, that 'You will never reach the poor except through people who care about them and watch over them.'

Enter Lilian

The only path of escape known in all the Worlds of God
is Performance.

Emerson

I might have been a great violinist,
but in the Colonies I could not get tuition.

Lilian Baylis

Lilian Mary Baylis has sometimes been romanticized as a Cockney
Cinderella who achieved a throne without a prince. Certainly she
owed a great deal more to her godmother-aunt, Emma, than to
her parents (or so she believed); yet although her childhood seems
to have been hard and joyless, she did not have to endure the full
drudgery of working-class slaveys (her family depended on one
of those); she was not victimized by her sisters (indeed, *she* was the
dominant girl – more, the dominant child); and she was not
obliged to observe the more stifling discriminatory conventions of
the submissive society. Moreover, although she has often been
identified as a South Londoner, because of her forty-year management of the Old Vic, she was brought up on the other side of the
Thames, and her family tree was rooted for three generations in
Marylebone and St Pancras. She was born in Marylebone on 9
May 1874 – the first child of Edward William Baylis and Elizabeth
(or Liebe) Cons. They had married the previous June at All Saints,
Margaret Street, the fashionable Anglo-Catholic church off Oxford
Street where Lilian was christened, and to which she often re-
turned in later life. It has been claimed that she was part-Jewish,
and as such she was included in the *Encyclopaedia Judaica* (on the

presumption that 'Konss' was a corruption of the German version of 'Cohen') – one of the more improbable honours conferred on her after death, and one that she would have relished keenly. But Lilian was an unusually devout Christian brought up in a family of traditional churchgoers. If there were synagogues in the Cons background, they had long been obliterated or transmuted, before her great-great-grandfather left Germany.

Lilian's maternal grandfather, as we have seen, was a Fitzrovian piano-key maker, who died four years before she was born. Her paternal grandfather (whom she probably met in childhood) was a jeweller, William Baylis, whose business in Upper Rupert Street traded for some forty years, until 1886. (He is not mentioned in the fragments of autobiography left by his son, and I can trace no evidence of his death in official records.) His wife, Mary Baylis – who featured, many years later, on Lilian's short list of people whom she remembered in her prayers – was (according to her son) 'a clever musical and literary amateur', who sang in several leading choirs. (She appeared in the chorus of the first Handel Festival: a prime point in her favour, for Lilian's father.) More significantly, she was an 'inseparable pal' of two eminent Victorians, the author Charles Reade and the actress Fanny Stirling, in whose biography she occupied a shadowy role as confidante.

In her youth Mrs Stirling was a leading West End comedienne. Peg Woffington in Reade's *Masks and Faces* was one of her star parts (in old age Lilian's father recalled that he had been present with his parents when the author first read this play to Mrs Stirling). In later years she was best known as Mrs Malaprop and Juliet's Nurse (she was nicknamed 'Nursie'). After retiring from the stage in 1870 she still gave occasional recitals and remained a great name in the Victorian theatre. The actor–manager Sir Frank Benson described her as 'the fairy godmother not only of her profession but of all who came into the sphere of her influence'; and Lilian Baylis, who apparently came into that sphere in childhood, treasured her memory (and several mementoes, including a coat, a coverlet and a cheval glass) until her own death, which arrived over forty years after Mrs Stirling's last exit in 1895. She also employed the actress's great-grandson John Allen, in the Old Vic company in the 1930s, and a great-granddaughter worked on the theatre staff. This was, outside the Vic, perhaps Lilian's main theatrical interest; but, characteristically, it was as a family friend and counsellor, rather than as an actress, that Mrs Stirling was enshrined in her small and selective pantheon. Her father was deeply proud of the family connection with these Victorian celebrities, and often talked about them: they were, perhaps, part of his armour against the overpowering Cons sorority. He was also (according to a family tradition apparently unknown to Lilian's friends) proud of his supposed descent from Isaac Newton. Although this may well have been a fantasy (and the story itself – passed on by his daughter Ethel – may not be true) it does explain why Mr Baylis took 'Newton' for his name as a singer and gave it to two of his sons.

When Lilian was born, Edward Baylis was employed as a book-keeper in the Oxford Street shop of Gillows, London's leading furniture business. He had been on their payroll for eight years, after what appears to have been a false start in his teens, when he spent three years working for his articles in engineering. He was articled to the eminent engineer Sir Charles Gregory, with whom Mrs Stirling lived and whom she married shortly before her death. As Newton Baylis he was an enthusiastic amateur singer; and it was at voice-production classes that he met his future wife. Liebe Cons (or Konss, as he spelled it in his autobiographical notebooks) had, he claimed, studied for three days a week at the School of Ornamental Art (where Emma is said to have gone) and three days at the London Academy of Music, until she finally plumped for music as a profession. (Emma may well have helped to support her little sister, as Lilian later indulged and subsidized *hers*.)

Mr Baylis was not well off when he married at the age of twenty-five (Libby, as he called his wife, was twenty-four). His salary was probably no more than some thirty shillings a week. He could not afford to set them up in a house of their own, and he went to live with Libby and her elder sisters, Emma, Ellen and Eliza, and their mother, in Nottingham Street, off Marylebone High Street. The house was just round the corner from the school-home of Octavia Hill and *her* sisters, and had no doubt been chosen by Emma for that reason. Emma – who was ten years older than Libby – wore the trousers in the household, and Libby's husband, one suspects, had to follow her lead. Lilian was brought up in a tradition of matriarchal domination. In her family, the women ruled, whether they married or not.

It was at 19 Nottingham Street that Lilian was born (a block of flats now stands on the site). Before she was two years old, her parents moved to lodgings in Harewood Place, off Cavendish Square – this was about the time that Emma split from Octavia – but by 1878 they were living again with Emma, Ellen and Eliza *and* Grandmother Cons. The new home was on the 'wrong' side of Maida Vale, off Elgin Avenue, at 17 Grittleton Road. It was from this address that Emma launched her appeal for Coffee Music Halls. When she and Ellen moved across the river to Surrey Lodge, about 1880, the growing family of Baylises remained in Grittleton Road for some ten years.

In 1974, a hundred years after Lilian's birth, Grittleton Road was a dirty, dingy street in a 'twilight zone' with a largely coloured population. The vandalized church at the corner, St Peter's, seemed due for demolition, as was much of the area. The Baylis family-home was, like the other houses, divided into rooms for letting (there is no plaque to mark the decade that Lilian lived here, and no trace of them in the records of St Peter's). But when the Baylises were at number 17 it was, though not such a 'good address' as Lilian's Marylebone birthplace, in the middle of a solidly respectable middle-class district, St Peter's Park.

Lilian had nine brothers and sisters. The first seven after her were christened at All Saints', Margaret Street, although to take them there entailed something of an expedition from Grittleton Road. Her father, a devout Anglican, showed a special allegiance to this high church – he had been a choirboy there and belonged to the Men's Guild (although he was never, as his daughter said, its secretary) – and Lilian recalled that it was one of her earliest treats to be taken there occasionally by him. When she was about twelve, arriving for evensong one Saturday, 'the church was crowded and the sidesman on the right aisle gave me his seat. A few minutes later, however, I was unceremoniously hauled out of it and made to stand by the font. I felt very injured about this until I was told that the Prince of Wales, afterwards King Edward VII, was occupying the seat.' Some years later, when Lilian and her family were entertaining the guests at an aristocratic garden party, the Prince 'spoke so kindly to us and praised our music. I longed to say, "I once gave up my seat at All Saints' to you".'[1]

Five of the Baylis children survived infancy: Lilian, Violet (1875), William (1877), Ray (1879) and Ethel (1885). Margery, born in 1880, survived only thirteen days; Hugh, born in 1881, died at thirteen months; Francis, born in 1883, died at six; Arnold, born in 1886, lasted only three months, and so did Herbert, born in 1887. Mrs Baylis was often ill; and although Mr Baylis managed for some years to keep a servant (and shared a governess, for a time, with his neighbours) the eldest girl was inevitably pressed into service as a 'little mother'. That was not an uncommon lower-middle-class phenomenon in an era of large families; but Lilian may have worked harder and longer as a stand-in mother than many of her contemporaries in the same social group. For one thing, Mrs Baylis does not appear to have been a very practical woman. Although she briefly worked before her marriage as one of Octavia Hill's part-time rent-collectors, she was not very good at the job. Nor does she seem to have been domestically capable; and she found it hard to keep servants. A revealing phrase in her obituary in the *Old Vic Magazine*, clearly emanating from Lilian, describes her as 'an artist above all things, who would never cook'. In a carefully understated judgement intended for the autobiography that Lilian never found time to write, she said: 'My mother, temperamental by nature, found the combined effort of bearing children and carrying on her work something of a strain, and in consequence ours was never a tranquil household.' Lilian's aunts tried to make up for it, by taking her for occasional holidays 'when babies were coming'.

Libby Baylis was a singer and a music teacher, before she was a mother. She put art first: a lesson her eldest daughter assimilated. Under the name of Madame Liebe Konss, she was (according to the *Marylebone Mercury*) 'well known in the borough of Marylebone as a professor of singing and the piano'. She was not so well known outside it. Before her marriage she had toured the provinces for nearly a year with an actor-reciter, Clarence Holt, who presented 'A Night with Shakespeare and Dickens' to which Libby supplied the musical illustrations as pianist and singer. After her marriage her travelling radius was necessarily restricted, but she continued to teach, and to sing and play at charity concerts. With her husband she started what he described as 'a small Vocal, Instrumental and Operetta Party, one of our lines being Lunatic Asylums (public and private)'. Lunatic audiences, he said, were 'most attentive and appreciative'. 'Our first real success was a Costume Recital of a portion of the opera of *Martha*, and we had a very fine chorus of about twenty pupils.' They also sang, on their own, at some of the first concerts at the Old Vic, and performed appropriate numbers after a Temperance Demonstration. Payments were small: from Colney Hatch, to which they returned several times, they obtained three guineas. Prisons paid better: Wormwood Scrubs went up to five guineas. In a year they took as much as £240, but as they lost £110 (through a defaulting manager and other fiascos) the net family income from music was £107. Yet somehow they carried on. They were, no doubt, helped by the Hill connection. Miranda's

Kyrle Society for the Diffusion of Beauty resolved to encourage the performance of music in hospitals and workhouses.

During the 1880s Mrs Baylis organized an annual concert at the Seymour Hall, near Portman Square, in which she exhibited the talents of her more promising pupils, and those of her family, for every Baylis child was dedicated to a musical career as soon as he or she could manage to sing a note and dance in time to Mummy's piano. As she continued between births to appear in public and to train pupils at home, and as Mr Baylis frequently accompanied her in concerts (he was a light baritone, who specialized in sea shanties), Lilian was often in charge of the household at number 17. She very rarely talked about this period in later life (except in connection with her aunt) but when she did so she gave the impression that she had been allowed no real childhood – or, at least, she *felt* she had never had one, which comes to much the same thing. She also gave the impression that her mother was a very selfish woman. Although this may be filially unfair to Mrs Baylis – her concerts and music lessons were, after all, an indispensable support to the family budget as well as to her *amour propre* – the fact that she later allowed two of her children, Violet and Ray, to be adopted by her sister Esther in Western Australia indicates not only the pressure of economic problems but the relative weakness of her maternal instinct. Lilian was undermothered (which helps to explain her over-mothering tendencies in later life); and she undoubtedly found emotional compensation, perhaps a partial mother-substitute, in Aunt Emma.

As soon as Lilian could speak she called her aunt 'Emmie' – 'And from that time onwards, she loved me: an old friend wrote that she said it "rested her to have that little bit of purity and innocence come on Sundays, after the hard week's work in the courts".'[2] From the age of seven Lilian helped Emmie to entertain her tenants, at Christmas parties and in summer picnics, and she held the collecting plate when Emmie organized meetings in the drawing-room to raise funds for her causes. 'I suppose that even then, small child as I was, I must have realized the force of her wonderful personality'; and, after her first meeting with royalty at the Old Vic in 1881, 'I knew . . . that Auntie was a personality and kinship with her an advantage'. A few days after that occasion, when the seven-year-old Lilian presented Princess Frederica with a bouquet, she met Canon J. W. Horsley, chairman of the Old Vic Governors, who had looked after her on the royal visit. He did not quite recognize Lilian, and asked her where he had met her before.

I was very shy as I told him, 'Last week, when I gave the Princess the flowers. I'm Auntie's niece.' He was much tickled with my description of myself, and for many years after refused to call me Lilian and always introduced me to strangers by the name of 'Auntie's niece'.[3]

As a result of this domestic background, Lilian's schooling was erratic and incomplete. All we know of it, from her own account, is that she began her education with a governess employed by a local vicar (apparently shared with the children of deserving believers not rich enough to employ their own). Later she went to a convent school – St Augustine's in Kilburn – every other week, by special arrangement with the nuns (with whom she retained a lifelong connection). The week in between was reserved for home chores and little-mothering. By conventional standards, even those of Victorian girls' schools, she was undereducated, and in later life she became very conscious of this. Musically, she fared better. 'My musical training was the only education I really had. My spelling and punctuation have never quite caught up.'[4] (The punctuation in her surviving handwritten letters is anarchic, but the spelling is in fact rather better than the standard skill of a longer-educated generation today.) At an early age she showed signs of what Libby acclaimed as hereditary talent – enough for her to be exhibited at seven as a 'child prodigy', according to her own recollections. She learned the violin from a regimental bandmaster, and was then taken as a pupil – probably at the Royal Academy of Music – by one of the leading violinists, conductors and teachers of the time, John Tiplady Carrodus, whom later she cited frequently and proudly as her childhood mentor. It was to him rather than to her parents, she said, that she owed her love of opera. The preface to his book, *How to Study the Violin*, post-humously published in the year of his death, 1895, claimed that the name of Carrodus had 'become a household word throughout the length and breadth of the land'. Certainly he had vast theatri-cal experience – he led the orchestra at Covent Garden for twenty-five years; he was a soloist at the Proms and Philharmonic con-certs; and long after Lilian left his classes he was summoned to Balmoral to play before the Queen. There is no evidence of how long Lilian was taught by Carrodus – not, perhaps, long enough, for in maturity her taste and skill were undeveloped; but she cherished her early connection with this forgotten Yorkshire eminence (a native of Keighley, his real name was Carruthers) and his tuition suggests that in childhood at least her talent was above the level of ordinary domestic music-making.

Lilian certainly started young. By the age of nine she was appearing in charity concerts, playing piano duets with Mummy. She had to practise for five hours a day: Carrodus was a martinet. At ten she appeared as a solo violinist in such venues as Epping Town Hall and St Paul's, Portman Square. Among her specialities were 'Alice Where Art Thou?' and 'Home Sweet Home'. She superintended the practising of her mother's piano pupils, and took her own pupils in the violin from eleven onwards. She was big, even bulky, for her age, and as conductors on trams and buses would not believe she was under twelve, she used to carry her birth certificate about with her as proof positive, to avoid paying the full fare.

She began to appear frequently in the family troupe run by her parents under such names as the Concert and Operatic Party, and the Operatic Costume Recital Party. They played and sang at town halls and mission halls; in workhouses and prisons; at Free Concerts for the People and Penny Popular Concerts; on seaside piers (at Bognor and Worthing); at Colney Hatch and the People's Palace. Lilian recalled in the 1930s how, on her way to a concert at the latter establishment, she sat next to the driver on top of a 'knifeboard' horse-bus, and 'had to run the gamut of rotten apples and tomatoes cheerfully flung at the then unexpected apparition of a bus among the stalls in the Mile End Road'.[5] Art, for Lilian Baylis, was from her childhood inextricably entangled with good works and social service, a kind of medicine dispensed to the poor and needy; and she was accustomed to the idea that, although it was good for The People to have it administered to them, they might put up a fight before they discovered that they liked the flavour.

By the time she was fifteen she had played before more conventional audiences at the St James's Hall and the Aeolian Hall. The programmes were Palm Court-ish entertainments of a familiar kind: vocal and instrumental snippets of light opera, ballads, showpieces. In a concert at the Seymour Rooms, for instance, Lilian played first violin in the overture to Suppé's *Poet and Peasant* (there were only two other players: brother Willie on second violin, and Mummy on piano); she gave a solo violin performance of two pieces by Papini; she provided a violin accompaniment to her mother's rendering of 'Unto Thy Heart'; and she joined the family in several numbers from Gilbert and Sullivan operas. Lilian also learned the mandolin, the guitar and the castanets; she deputized for her father as manager of the family concert party; she gave music lessons at a Croydon girls' school ('a most persevering and painstaking teacher', said the Lady Principal); and before she was sixteen her parents set her up as a teacher at their home address. Her qualifications were advertised in the musical press: 'Miss Lilian Konss-Bayliss [sic], VIOLINIST, Pupil of J. T. Carrodus and Certificated Society of Arts, London, Visits and receives Pupils for Violin. Lessons Also Given on Guitar, Mandolin and Pianoforte. Singing and Harmony. Terms Moderate. Concerts attended as Solo Violinist, Leader in Orchestra, or with her "Ladies Orchestra" in Costume. Public and Private Concerts and Entertainments provided in Town or Country.' She was then still taking lessons from Carrodus. The idea of the Ladies Orchestra was inspired by her membership of the first group of this kind (or so she claimed) – the Ladies Orchestra of St James's Restaurant. All the players wore a dark blue coat and skirt, with gold buttons and braid and a scarlet satin waistcoat. To this uniform Lilian looked back, in later years, with affectionate nostalgia.

Was this somewhat premature launching of Lilian's career an act of parental piety and confidence in their eldest daughter, or was it, rather, parental desperation? Some months earlier Madame Konss suffered from severe and prolonged illness (we learn from a newspaper announcement), which must have had a disastrous effect on the family finances. After she recovered, the Baylises moved from Grittleton Road to Dorchester Place, Regents Park; and although it was probably a better address, it was not their own property, not a house but a flat. There are signs that Mr Baylis, far from advancing in prosperity, was considering emigration. He attempted to get a job in the civil service in Western Australia, through the influential connections of his sister-in-law Esther Forrest; and although the attempt failed, it was probably at this time that Esther (who was childless) agreed to take Violet and Ray into her family, to lighten the Baylis load in London. Robert Forrest adopted both children, and both spent nearly all their lives in Australia, mostly in Bunbury. Ray went into the family mill, and Violet worked for a time as housekeeper for her Aunt Esther. She showed, like her sister Lilian, a keen interest in music, churchgoing and good works (she also had a rasping voice and thick pebbled glasses), and she is remembered in

Bunbury for her music lessons and for entertaining seamen at the Sailors Rest, a home founded by her aunt, Eliza Cons (who settled in Bunbury until her death in 1924), with whom Violet then lived. Neither of them married. The Forrest family home was, at first, called Grittleton Lodge, apparently in nostalgic recognition of the home in Grittleton Road.

It is not clear what Newton Baylis did in London after he resigned in 1884 from Gillows (where he had worked for eighteen years) apart from acting as manager of the family concert party and singing occasional ballads. He emerges cloudily from the scanty records as a jaunty, shabby-genteel, Micawberish, churchy man, somewhat henpecked by both his wife and eldest daughter, more cultured – in the widest sense – than either of them, but never very effectual as a breadwinner and inclined to look back to the past, to the relative ease and prosperity of his family background.

The Baylis fortunes apparently took a turn for the better in 1890, when they transformed their concert party into 'The Gipsy Revellers' – described in their publicity as 'A company of Three to Sixteen Vocalists and Instrumentalists in 18th century Neapolitan Costume. The Entertainment consists of Songs, Vocal Concerted Music and Dances, Descriptive of Gipsy Costumes, Life and Pastimes, accompanied by Violins, Violoncellos, Mandelins[sic], Guitars, Tambourines and Castinets [sic]. Engagements accepted for Garden Parties, Receptions, Soirees, "At Homes" and Concerts.' The repertoire included the Gipsy Chorus from *The Bohemian Girl*, the opening of *Maritana*, Schumann's 'Gipsy Life' trio and Glover's 'Gipsies' Laughing Song'. What gave point to the advertisements was the proudly proclaimed climax of the Baylises' career to date: an appearance at 'the Marquess of Hartington's Garden Party, June 13, 1890, in the presence of T.R.H. the Prince and Princess of Wales and a Distinguished Company'. They played, as Mr Baylis fondly recalled thirty years later, in 'a charming dell in the Grounds', alternately with the Scots Guards, who were stationed on the steps of the house. The Prince of Wales arrived at the charming dell just as Lilian was singing her solo in the 'Gipsies' Laughing Song', but she 'did not notice the royalty', Mr Baylis complained, although 'our girls whispered to her'. To make up for it, he sang *his* solo, 'I am your King', and 'looked the Prince of Wales full in the face. He laughed heartily at the fun of it.'

This social *coup* was clearly achieved with the help of the indispensable Aunt Emma, since Lord Hartington was the brother-in-law of Lady Frederick Cavendish, Emmie's loyal ally on the board of the Vic. Emmie's hand is also visible in a below-stairs Society engagement that season for the Revellers – the Household Club of Lady Aberdeen, another of Miss Cons's aristocratic patrons, who had inaugurated concerts for her servants; and the published list of their patrons includes other philanthropists whom Emma had met through Octavia Hill, such as Lady Ducie and the Rev. Samuel Barnett, founder of Toynbee Hall, together with Lords Nelson, Halifax and Hardinge. The names of their Royal Highnesses and the Marquess of Hartington had a tonic if temporary effect upon the Baylises' popularity. Their performing radius widened, into Surrey, Kent and Cheshire, to a Cottagers Show and a Unionist fête. The surviving notices, preserved by Lilian till her death, scarcely suggest an overwhelming success. At a concert in Leighton Buzzard, the local journal noted: 'These sons and daughters of Romany depicted a bright and romantic aspect of Gipsy Life, and one would be led to the conclusion that such a life must be rather a happy one.' The tinge of doubt was reflected in the peroration: 'with a little maturity we should predict that the Gipsy Revellers in the near future would become exceedingly popular'. In London the *Pall Mall Budget* was more positive in its commendation (in May 1891): 'Any lady with a bit of green sward and some trees can give her friends a really pleasant afternoon by extending her invitation to the Revellers ... they are just the thing for a little outdoor fête.' This privileged pastoral audience represented a marked improvement on the workhouse paupers, seaside holidaymakers, East End costers and social workers before whom Lilian and her family had been singing, playing and dancing during the past five years.

It was apparently the gimmick of the Gipsy Revellers that now opened a new chapter in Lilian's life. Their name, and the VIP names on their handouts, caught the attention of a South African manager Ben Wheeler, who signed up the family, with reinforcing talent amounting to five ladies and one tenor, and packed them off to Cape Town in the autumn of 1891 as *Wheeler's* Gipsy Revellers. (There is no truth in the story, passed on by Tyrone Guthrie, that the Baylis exodus was financed by Emma and other members of the family, who clubbed together to buy a one-way ticket so that the improvident Newton and Liebe should be kept out of sight and out of mind.) With the departure down under of Violet and Ray, there were five of them – Madame Liebe Konss, Newton Baylis, Lilian, Willie and baby Ethel.

The Revellers, under Mr Wheeler's banner, were warmly received by the local press, although the notices were largely stolen by the local talent – including Mr Wheeler's brother, Frank, Miss Adeline Parkin the Accomplished Lady Cornetist, Miss Edith Probyn the Unrivalled Lady Violinist, and the Six Royal Lady Bellringers (who specialized in 'Men of Harlech'). Mr and Mrs Ben Wheeler, the *Cape Argus* recorded, 'were received with applause, the public recognizing what they have done as entertainers for several years' (though no reviewer explains more precisely what that was). 'It goes without saying that Mr Frank Wheeler's Negro impersonation was a complete success.' Neither Mr nor Mrs Baylis was given more than a perfunctory mention; but Lilian and Willie fared better. Lilian's turns included a skipping-rope dance while playing the banjo, which, said the *Cape Argus*, she 'handled with the greatest dexterity'; a violin duet; and a mandolin trio of Neapolitan airs. Later she appeared wearing a white wig in the Revellers' version of a nigger minstrel show. The company played in a number of leading towns – East London, Burgersdorp, Maritzburg, Grahamstown, Port Elizabeth – and were described *en route* (in, no doubt, a managerial puff) as 'the first thoroughly organized concert party that has ever visited this country. Their performances are unique and of the very highest order, and should do much to raise the musical tone and propagate the musical culture of South Africa generally.' But before they could complete such a mission Ben Wheeler went bankrupt, and the tour ended in Durban. He offered every Reveller the fare back to England, or £40 in cash.

In spite of warnings by 'globetrotting pros', as Mr Baylis described them, the Baylis family decided to take the money and stay. For one thing, they had let their London flat for a year, and they had nowhere else to go; they could not all land back on Emma at Surrey Lodge. Moreover, Mr Baylis, always the optimist, believed that they could do better in Africa. Although their vocal duets and instrumental solos, their Gipsy choruses and sea shanties, might seem to us to be incongruously genteel entertainment for this crude and often violent new society, threatened by racial and political conflict, the audiences to date had shown rather more enthusiasm than any in England (even, perhaps, the lunatics). Back in England, after all, it was hard for Lilian – one among hundreds of musical ladies on view – to attract the spotlight of fame; but the *Krokstad Advertiser and East Griqualand Gazette*, for instance, saluted her talents immediately. 'It is really a difficult matter to state on which instrument, be it Violin, Zither-Banjo or Mandolin, Miss Lilian Baylis most excels, as she is evidently thoroughly at home with each in turn' (on the whole, the reviewer decided, she was *most* at home in 'pianoforte accompaniments'.) And 'l'Enfant Prodigue', her whistling seven-year-old sister – 'Little Ethel . . . who it is easy to see is the spoilt darling of the family' – achieved a social success in Zululand that could scarcely have been matched at Lord Hartington's garden party.

Lilian fell ill in Durban. After she recovered, she and Willie managed to get a job in the local Christmas pantomime of *Beauty and the Beast* – in which Frank Wheeler surfaced again, with his Negro impersonation – doing their banjo and mandolin turns from the Revellers' repertoire. By the time they were ready to set off into the interior with their own touring company – consisting of little more than the family talent, with no Royal Lady Bell-ringers or Accomplished Lady Cornetist – Mr Baylis had only thirty shillings in capital. It was a desperate venture, carried out in considerable discomfort and some danger, for in the next few months they travelled many hundreds of miles throughout the territories that now comprise the Union in post-carts and mail-coaches, in waggons hauled by mules or oxen, among villages which had not long come under the 'protection' of the whites. For Lilian the coming year was not only one of the most arduous but also the most romantic of her life.

The Konss-Baylis family, as they billed themselves, played well away from the conventional theatrical circuit, in hotels, clubs, court-houses, police-stations, and the 'recreation rooms' of the chief mining-camps on the Rand. Often they had to camp for the night on the veld, and as they rehearsed by the fire the Africans from nearby kraals would gather round 'entranced', as Lilian remembered them. They penetrated into Griqualand, which had been 'settled' shortly before their arrival in Africa; and they were the first visiting company to perform in Eshowe, the capital of Zululand, where a theatre was quickly improvised to accommodate them. Improvisation of a different kind was required here from the Baylises, for the proprietor of the hotel and his family had all rushed off to a gold strike on the coast, leaving only a carpenter and a barman to run the place, and Lilian had to take charge of the kitchen. In one town in Natal a policeman tried to stop the show because they had no licence, but he was effectively dissuaded by the local population, who stripped him and ducked

him in the river. In another town Mr Baylis achieved one of his
finest hours: he conducted divine service, in the absence of the
minister, while his wife played the organ. They had to cope with
the heckling of over-friendly drunks (Little Ethel was useful for
quietening these); with dust storms, dysentery, and implacably
hostile insects; with the breakdowns, hold-ups and other disasters inevitable in crossing newly opened country with primitive
transport; with, not least, the grumbling ineffectuality of Mrs
Baylis. It was she, no doubt, who insisted that the touring should
end; but Lilian always looked back to that pioneering period
with especial affection. It was not only the landscapes she loved,
and the lionization that even a plain, shy girl of seventeen could
expect from the sequestered, randy males of a mining camp or
farming outpost. 'When I sang them "Old Folks at Home" I
moved them to tears and as the banjo tinkled out and my small
clear soprano hovered over the tense silence of that great rough
crowd, I felt that I had some kind of power.'[6]

By the end of 1892 the Baylises established a more sedentary
life in Johannesburg. They lived in Doornfontein, now an industrial area but then a well-to-do residential quarter of this rapidly
expanding boom-town. It was less than a decade since the discovery of the great gold-bearing reef of the Rand. Joburg was
only six years old when Lilian and her family arrived there, and
although the pioneers' tents had given way to wood and iron
buildings, social life in some respects was still close to that of a
mining camp. There were already five theatres – the Theatre
Royal, the Globe, the Standard, the Amphitheatre and the Music
Hall; but only one house of two storeys, according to Lilian's
recollection. Public dog-fights, for big stakes, were scarcely less
popular forms of entertainment. The citizens showed a disposition, well known in frontier societies, to take the law into their
own hands: a visitor who made some unchivalrous observations
about the morals of the ladies in the Joburg suburb of Jeppe was
tarred and feathered, to teach him manners. Theatre criticism was
dangerous, too: in 1893 a local editor was horsewhipped by chorus-
girls who objected to the notice of their show published by his
paper. Brawls and muggings were frequent, guns were generally
carried, and drunks were sometimes inclined to fire into the air, in
order to liven up the town. The railway was still 300 miles away.
The first goods train from the Cape arrived in September 1892, to
be greeted ceremonially by the High Commissioner and other
notables; and the Baylises were there to help in the celebrations,

making 'merry music' at a banquet in the Grand National Hotel, 'ensconced in a shrubbery at the corner of the room . . . arrayed in picturesque Italian costume' (the same Neapolitan gear, no doubt, in which they had shone on Bognor Pier and at the Gloucester Unionist fête). It was a year since they had left England; but they had made a new home.

By the following spring Lilian was engaged to a gold prospector, Jack Webster, who had fallen in love with her when he saw her in her Neapolitan costume in *Beauty and the Beast* the previous year. It seems to have happened rather suddenly. Lilian wrote to Jack's sister, Harriet: 'I did not know that Jack had told any of you yet, as things were not really settled between us till just as he was leaving for Mashonaland.' And in another letter she wrote, 'I was only nineteen last week, and my Mother does not approve of girls getting married before they are twenty, so there is plenty of time . . . I know what it is, leaving those you love and coming out to a horrid strange country.' Is there a hint in this lukewarm reaction that Lilian was already regretting the engagement? Probably not: it lasted for three years, and Lilian spoke of Jack Webster in later life as if her emotions had been deeply involved. But in 1896 she told him that she couldn't go through with it, and broke off the engagement – partly, perhaps, because she felt that she couldn't yet desert her parents, but mainly because she couldn't see herself making a success of motherhood as a prospector's wife (and, perhaps, as a way of life with her own mother's example in mind). Some weeks later Jack failed to return from one of his trips into the interior, and was never seen again. Ever afterwards Lilian seemed to feel a keen personal responsibility for his disappearance, in case her rejection of him had made him reckless in taking precautions against hostile Africans, or had in some other way helped to destroy him. Throughout her life she conscientiously kept in touch with Harriet Webster, who in later years came to stay with Lilian in London every summer, when the prices went up in her seaside boarding-house. Lilian often explained, in introducing Harriet, that she was 'nearly my sister-in-law', though she seldom pursued the subject. However serious her affair with Jack may or may not have been, a sense of guilt about him persisted, as part of a romantic fantasy.

So there were still five members of the family, all together, supplying 'Popular, Refined and Varied Entertainment'. This is how they described themselves (in 1894):

Miss LILIAN KONSS-BAYLIS
Soprano, Vocalist, Violinist,
and acknowledged premier lady Mandolinist
and Banjoist of South Africa

WILLIE BAYLIS
Violinist, Violincellist, Mandolinist, and Banjoist

ETHEL BAYLIS (aged 9 years)
The Celebrated Juvenile Whistler, Vocalist,
Mandolinist and Banjoist

Madame KONSS-BAYLIS
Contralto Vocalist, Guitarist, Pianist and Conductor

Mr NEWTON BAYLIS
Bass Vocalist and Manager

Lilian was the star turn, and was therefore privileged to add her
mother's German name as an accepted index of superior musical
skill. The news of poor Mr Baylis's qualifications is conspicuously
brief; but at least Libby and Lilian didn't make him change his
name.

In this advertisement, the Konss-Baylis family announced that
they had no fewer than six changes of programme, 'including old
favourites and newest Mandolin and Banjo Solos, Duets and
Trios, Songs and Concerted Vocal Music, Musical Sketches, &c.'
In addition, they gave lessons – in the violin, cello, mandolin,
banjo, piano, singing and voice production. That was not all.
They organized Subscription Dances and Social Assemblies.
Lilian ran a Banjo Band (composed mainly of bank clerks, she
said); a Banjo and Guitar Childrens' Orchestra; and a Ladies' Band,
in which several instruments were played by wives of the new
gold-millionaires, like Mrs Solly Joel and Mrs Barney Barnato,
whom she taught the mandolin. From the *Johannesburg Standard* in
1894 we catch a glimpse of the Ladies in action in the Standard
Theatre: 'a perfectly dazzling semi-circle of beauty, in the shape of
about fifteen of Johannesburg's fairest, with Mrs Konss-Baylis
and one of her accomplished daughters Lilian in the centre . . .
when the conductress's baton gave the signal all of the dainty
fingers simultaneously attacked miscellaneous instruments and
drew forth a burst of music that was a pleasure to listen to . . .'
The Baylises also gave lessons in ballroom dancing; and they let
rooms out for private dances, wedding parties and 'other Gatherings'. Among Lilian's more notable temporary pupils, or so she
would claim in later years, was Mark Twain: during his visit to

Johannesburg in 1896 she tried, without much success, to teach him the Lancers. Or was it, as she also said, Twain who tried to persuade Baylis?

Lilian was proud of being the second woman to ride a bicycle in the city, in spite of the social opposition to such a gesture of emancipation. (The Boer children used to call her 'Devil on a Wheel' and throw tin cans at her when she cycled past.) And she was proud to claim that she 'mixed with and taught every degree of society'. The Baylises, in fact, were part of the driving force behind the social transformation of life on the Rand, meeting the demand among the new rich and their imitators for genteel accomplishments and easily acquired social graces, as well as entertainment fit for ladies and gentlemen – the demand for instant civilization, burying the mining-town past and compensating for such pleasures of the present as the dog fights, or the conspicuous red-light district. Over fifty years later the Baylises were still remembered by a handful of veterans; but it was because of the dances they ran ('very jolly affairs') and because of Lilian's later fame, rather than because of their artistic talent. 'As musicians they were just mediocre – all right for those old mining-camp days, but they would not pass muster now,' one senior citizen affirmed in the 1950s. 'Knowing some members of the family,' recalled another, 'I was really surprised that Lilian showed such ability later and made a name for herself.'

It was not all plain sailing for the Baylises – and for Lilian, in particular, there were many accidents and some disasters. On one journey across country the travelling was so rough that she was thrown out five or six times. She was injured on another expedition when the ox-waggon in which they were travelling overturned. She nearly died of enteric fever in Durban; her life was saved – without a fee – by a local doctor, father of the poet Roy Campbell. Lilian never forgot Dr Campbell's kindness. Some forty years later, having read Roy Campbell's book *Flaming Terrapin* while revisiting South Africa, she went to the family house in Durban, photographed it shortly before it was demolished, and sent him a copy. Roy Campbell said of this, 'it was the first and greatest compliment that was ever paid to me as a poet'.[7] Moreover, Lilian was nearly drowned while swimming – one of her lifelong enthusiasms. She got into difficulties in strong currents, panicked and as she was losing consciousness, she recalled in later years, she 'felt as if every wave was battering one side of her face'.[8] After she was rescued, she said, she saw in a mirror that her face looked quite crooked, as if she had had a stroke; and although most of her features returned to normal, her mouth remained slightly twisted – and stayed like that for the rest of her life. This cruel blow had a crucial effect upon Lilian's character and career, for she was deeply and painfully conscious of her disfigurement to the end. Yet it seems doubtful that it happened when she was seventeen, or that a narrow escape from drowning was the cause. For one thing, this was not the only explanation which Lilian gave to friends and acquaintances twenty or thirty years later. Her 'stroke', she said at various times, was due to falling off her bicycle in Johannesburg, and to the news that Jack Webster had disappeared in Mashonaland. But her most dramatic anecdote described how a Kaffir murderer, against whom the family had been warned, broke into the Baylis home in Joburg in the middle of the night. Lilian woke to find him in her room and tried to grapple with him, but he was greased all over and her hands slipped off his naked body. He took fright and escaped through the window – though not before, in one version of the incident, Lilian had hearkened to the voice of the Lord, who said: 'Throw the pot at him, Lilian.' It was the shock of this encounter, said Lilian, that twisted her mouth. In fact all these stories seem highly improbable, if not impossible, on medical grounds. Lilian's 'stroke' was probably due to Bell's palsy, which, though it may be caused by infection through water in the ears, could scarcely have taken such instantaneous effect. And, what is more, it happened before she arrived in Africa. In a studio portrait taken by a Baker Street photographer when she was sixteen the crooked mouth seems unmistakably visible. The true story – or, at least, the story that appears nearest to the truth – is one that Lilian told to very few people. When she was six or seven, her aunts took her on a trip to the seaside. Sitting on a breakwater at high tide above a shelving beach she reached backwards for a doll that had fallen into the water, fell in herself and was swept out to sea. Aunt Ellen splashed in after her, fully dressed in long skirts and button boots; and she, too, was in danger of drowning. Both she and Lilian were rescued by a man near by; but on her return home Lilian became ill. She should have been taken to a doctor, but – said Lilian – her mother refused to spend the money; and the illness left her face twisted. For ever after, she bore a grudge against Madame Konss-Baylis. The fact that she was disfigured from early childhood, and felt herself to be set apart from other girls, makes it easier to comprehend the defensive armour of her later personality; the compensations of her special relationship with God; and the ferocious drive of her career. Talking about Richard III to Sybil Thorndike, she said: 'People don't realize how awful it must be to be deformed – even ever so slightly.' That is surely one reason for her dedication for over twenty years to the service of sufferers from leprosy. But why did she invent the stories? Perhaps she was born with the deformity: it seems visible in a photograph of her aged two and a half. Probably the reason is no more significant than her tendency to dramatize and fantasize her life. A stroke off the coast of Africa *sounded* so much more impressive than catching the palsy at Broadstairs. Yet it is conceivable that Lilian *had* to attribute her personal stigmata to Africa, because Africa occupied a special place in her life, for reasons at which one may only guess.

In some ways, her six years there were – or seemed to her in retrospect – the happiest years of her life. She often talked about them to close friends and intimate colleagues, whereas she scarcely ever talked about her earlier years in London. Perhaps that time, in spite of the hard work and hard living, was a compensation for her lost childhood. It was, or so she made it sound, a 'dashing, exciting life'. Little can now be exhumed of those reminiscent anecdotes, except that they were mainly, if vaguely, to do with risqué episodes, and that some were funny, racy and even 'Rabelaisian'. One favourite concerned her exploits in delivering the illegitimate baby of a friend among a crowd of uncomprehending Zulu women in a village where the unmarried mother had taken refuge. Another story described how she was saved from rape, in the nick of time, by the sudden appearance of a man on a white horse; she clung to the mane, and was whisked off at speed. 'We'll get the white horse today,' her staff used to say, with affectionate irreverence. 'She looks in the mood for it.' In a different vein was a story (left among her papers) in which Lilian was suddenly given additional strength to break away from her attacker (a village postmaster) by hearing the voice of a nun who taught her in Kilburn saying, reproachfully, 'Lilian, *Lilian*!' She gave the postmaster 'a friendly wave' and ran back to her parents. Some months later she heard that the nun had died on the day of the 'attack'. Assaults apart, there were flirtations and at least one more proposal, after Jack Webster, although the wooer's name has been long forgotten.

The fact that it is the risqué anecdotes that predominate in her intimates' recollections of what Lilian told them about South Africa is, no doubt, due to their apparent incongruence with the celibate career of a woman in whose life sex seemed to be so deeply

83

sublimated in her work and religion. But it is not beyond conjecture that, for Lilian Baylis, what had seemed 'a horrid strange country' came to be romanticized as a kind of magic pleasure-ground, the place of lost possibilities. She liked to wear things that reminded her of Africa; to keep in touch with African connections; to dream of returning there. When she did revisit the country in 1924, she said:

> An old Zulu servant said when he placed a Kaffir bangle around my wrist: 'Once this has encircled your arm, it will encircle your heart for ever.' Another native saying is: 'Once you drink of the waters of Africa, you long for them all your life.' Certainly in my case I have proved this.

During 1897, her sixth year in South Africa, Lilian Baylis fell seriously ill. In later years she gave several explanations of this illness; that it was due to a bad attack of typhoid; that her accidents in ox-waggon transport, combined with overwork, led to an operation (unspecified); and that her kidneys had to be operated on. There is no necessary contradiction between the second and third of these stories; although it has also been said that her illness was complicated by emotional troubles verging on a breakdown, Lilian made a slow return to health (she was in bed for some two months) until word came from England. When Emma Cons heard the news she cabled to Lilian's parents offering to pay her return fare to London, as the sea voyage and change of scene would be good for her convalescence. With her, Lilian brought Ethel, then twelve, to complete her education; also, no doubt, at Emma's expense.

On her arrival in London at Surrey Lodge Lilian discovered that her beloved Emmie (then sixty) was 'worn out with her work of housing, fighting for open spaces and all that meant better lives for the poor'.[9] And she soon found herself under pressure from Emmie's closest friends, Ethel Everest and Caroline Martineau, as well as Emmie's sister Ellen, to remain in London and take some of the load off her aunt's shoulders by looking after her 'recreation' – the Royal Victoria Hall – as its manager, because 'the much-sought-after "right person" had never yet materialized'.[10] It was a kind of emotional blackmail (perhaps premeditated, though there is no evidence of this); and although Emmie herself did not apparently join in, being a woman of proudly independent spirit, Lilian found it impossible to resist. She agreed, 'after much consideration', to help – if only for a year. But before the year was over, she had agreed to stay for good.

I had intended to return to my parents and take up again my very profitable teaching on the Rand; but when I saw how things stood, I felt it my duty to stay and be of help to Emmie.

It was not an easy decision, she said. To remain in London was 'a great wrench' which involved, so she claimed in later years, a considerable financial sacrifice. In Johannesburg she had earned £50 a month, sometimes as much as £80. In London she was paid a pound a week, with full board at Surrey Lodge, where she made her home with Emmie and Ellen. She did not see her parents for sixteen years; she never saw her brother Willie again (he died in Durban in 1906, twelve months after his marriage); and it was nearly thirty years before she returned to South Africa.

Acting Manager

It is difficult, perhaps,
to those not acquainted by direct contact and personal experience,
with the way in which the poor live,
to realize the vast gulf in pecuniary value between a penny and
twopence.

Annual Report of Old Vic, 1911–12

Theatrical management in this country
is one of the most desperate commercial forms of gambling.
You must disturb a man's reason
before he will even listen to a proposal to run a playhouse.

G. Bernard Shaw, Preface to The Theatrical World of 1894,
by William Archer

By the time Lilian Baylis started work for her aunt at the Royal
Victoria Hall in 1898, as a plain, plump and frumpish spinster of
twenty-three, she had already tasted a good deal of experience far
outside and well beneath the social range of most of her unmarried
middle-class contemporaries. That was part of her value to Aunt
Emmie. So was the fact that she maintained intense emotional
loyalties to the family (especially to Emmie); that as the practical
member of a hard-up clan she had learned the importance of counting pennies; that she was deeply religious, with a simple but absolute faith in the personal reality, indeed proximity, of God, and a
belief in the abiding importance of good works; and that, although
she may have already given up any thought of becoming a wife,
she had developed a vocation for mothering – with a perceptible
tendency to masochism. These were not commonly considered as

87

sufficient qualifications for the management of a theatre; but then there has never been any theatre like the Vic or any manager like Miss Baylis. And, in any event, Emmie loved her.

For her first fourteen years at the Vic – from 1898, when she became acting manager, until 1912, when Emma Cons died – Lilian worked with dedicated loyalty in the shadow of her loving and beloved aunt. Whereas for Emmie the Hall was one of a dozen causes, for Lilian it was her whole life from breakfast to bedtime – excepting her religious needs and duties. She had to organize ballad concerts, opera recitals, temperance meetings, scientific lectures and variety bills; learn to cope with the police, the builders, the Executive Committee, the staff and the neighbouring publicans, who occupied pride of place in Emmie's demonology. No job was too menial for the acting manager. She sold programmes; she helped with the costumes; she even scrubbed the stage – or so the legend says. (Years later Lilian sometimes used to test the fitness of applicants for the Old Vic by suddenly saying, 'And would you scrub the stage, dear?' When they said 'Yes', as seemed advisable, she seemed quite satisfied: they were not required to prove it.) She helped to keep order, among both staff and audience, and to make sure that nobody was drinking or making love on the premises. Charitable chores went with the job, too. On Tuesday afternoons, for example, Lilian had to collect children from the Surrey Lodge tenements and take them to the Vic, where they were taught games like 'London Bridge is Falling Down' by voluntary helpers on the stage. But she had to chase other children away from the theatre, when they used to sneak up the stairs into the gallery, or put out the lights for a laugh, or lob bottles, stones or rubbish through the windows. If Lilian caught them (and she often did) she would buffet them angrily round the head, till the games began to lose their savour. She had to deal with repentant drinkers anxious to be saved (and rewarded) at the next temperance meeting; and also with the unrepentant drinkers who reeled into the theatre from the neighbouring pubs and had to be wheeled out again. When she got home at night Lilian was still in the thick of it, for Emmie would want to hear about the events she had missed at the Hall, discussing plans, programmes and budgets. And then, like as not, Lilian might be caught up in one of those domestic dramas of Emmie's tenants that often exploded late at night. On one occasion Emmie had arranged to send a sick child to the country to recover, but the father violently objected to any such arrangement and arrived at the front gate of her cottage armed with a revolver. According to Lilian, 'Emmie made me take the child out at the back door and rush her to Victoria while she held the man at bay at the front. It was a most exciting, not to say thrilling experience.' There were not a few such thrills (though no other recorded instances of revolvers). 'Non-stop, it was,' said a tenant. But if Emmie could stand it, so could Lilian.

One of Emmie's recurrent struggles was with the London County Council. For twenty years she fought a running battle against persistent complaints by the Council's inspectors about the structure, condition and maintenance of the Hall, especially in fire precautions. She acquiesced to some demands, refused to comply with others, asked for the postponement of measures on the grounds of hardship and philanthropy: the Old Vic was a special case, not to be judged by the rules applied to mere theatres. When she did agree to carry out improvements, she usually contrived to carry on a delaying action for months, until she could dodge no longer. A typical skirmish flared up over the 'slip' dressing-rooms on the stage, made in lath-and-plaster, for quick-change artists. These were, said the Council in 1894, an appalling fire risk and must be destroyed. That was unthinkable, said Miss Cons, because it would restore 'the old custom . . . of both sexes dressing in public at the wings'. Surely the London County Council was not going to promote *that* kind of immorality? Well, no, said the Council; if Miss Cons had the dressing-rooms rebuilt in brick, they could stay. Brick was far too expensive, Miss Cons answered; and anyway, why had the Council sanctioned the lath-and-plaster when she took over the building in the previous decade? The dressing-rooms were no more dangerous now than they were then . . . And so it went on, till they agreed on Emmie's compromise: to rebuild them in corrugated iron.

The LCC architects and fire officers, however, were understandably uneasy and resentful about the tolerance of the Old Vic shown by the Council. They pressed for detailed surveys of the building and strict enforcement of the regulations. And in 1902 Emmie, Lilian and the Governors were confronted by a list of no fewer than seventy-two Council recommendations concerning the safety, sanitation and structure of the Hall. It was a major and expensive programme, even though Emmie refused to accept every item (she agreed to 'portions' of eleven, and objected to seven recommendations). By 1904 fund-raising appeals had to be set in motion again, with another Duke of Westminster presiding over a meeting at Grosvenor House. The amount was only

£200, but a principle was at stake, as Emmie explained in a letter to *The Times*. The Hall was in debt, and 'we have never been in debt before. Our rule has been never to incur an expense till we had the money to pay it.' That was the school in which Lilian Baylis learned the lessons of theatrical management.

After all this LCC harassment (for so Emmie considered it) the last straw was the Council's insistence that she should install a telephone at the Hall to connect with the local fire station. She flatly refused. She did not want a telephone; it was a totally unnecessary expense to pay £4 10s. a year for a useless instrument. If she wanted the fire brigade, she said, she could shout for it. It was just across the road. The Council threatened that the Hall's licence would not be renewed. Emmie still refused. 'Every music hall and theatre in London has got it now,' said the LCC in 1905, 'and you are the only one who has not.' Emmie was not impressed. 'We have done everything that you have asked us to do . . . for years past . . . We have spent over £40,000 on carrying out different requisitions from successive Councils, not wishing to oppose a body whom we are willing to believe are trying to do their duty, and for the sake of peace . . . every requirement for the safety of the public has been complied with, but as to the telephone communication we think that is a ridiculous waste of money, and we do not mean to have it.'

Emmie could get the licence renewed only by agreeing to install the telephone, but she refused to honour that condition. 'I am quite willing to meet them in open fight,' she said a year later to one of her allies on the Council, when the licence was due for renewal again; and she wrote persuasively to over forty Councillors, setting out her case. The matter was finally put to the vote, and 'the great battle' (as the Vic minutes describe it) was won – on an undertaking by Miss Cons that she would ensure 'means of prompt communication' between the Vic and the fire station. For the moment, the telephone was kept at bay, and £4 10s. a year was saved. Auntie's niece had seen what a really determined manager could do – with a little help from her friends.

Within three years of Lilian's arrival her weekly salary was raised from £1 to £3. Notifying her officially of this decision by the Executive Committee, Caroline Martineau wrote: 'I may add that an opinion was expressed that for the loss to be only £200 more than last year, when the takings are £300 less, shows very good management!' And she appended an unofficial postscript: 'My dear, I hope this will raise your spirits somewhat! and convince you that the Hall is *not* going to the dogs.' Four years later Lilian was voted another rise, of £25 p.a.; but she accepted only on condition that, if the Hall's loss increased, she would be allowed to revert to £150 p.a. – 'as work such as this must be undertaken mainly as a labour of love'. That was the spirit that animated her throughout her life at the Vic, the spirit she expected to see in other people. It was 'Auntie's niece' talking.

The emotional climate at the Vic had a family warmth – and family tensions, too. The staff were small and loyal. In 1909 a letter to *Encore* proudly listed their years of service; two (the bill-poster and assistant stage manager) had been there since Emmie took over in 1880, and, with twelve others, they totalled 245 years, an average of seventeen years each. (The letter was signed by W. J. Townsend, better known as 'Townie', who stayed in harness at the Vic until the 1950s and who was still a flourishing source of reminiscence in 1974.) Outside the Hall, the New Cut was still the site of one of London's busiest street markets (ninth busiest out of over 100 markets), and there was a large colony of coster-mongers, many of them Irish. When, with them in mind, the Hall presented *The Lily of Killarney*, especially on St Patrick's Day, Lilian had to station a couple of extra men in the gallery to keep order. Even if serious drinking was forbidden – 'Anyone bringing intoxicating liquor into this building will be at once expelled,' warned a notice posted strategically through the Hall – there was plenty of serious eating. You could bring in fish and chips, or jellied eels, or meat pies; in Pearce and Plenty you could buy a 'baby's head' (the Cockney slang for a boiled meat pudding) with two veg; or you could patronize the old woman at the foot of the gallery stairs who sold pigs' trotters at a halfpenny each, and buy a baked potato, to go with the trotter, from a cookshop across the street. Manners, though much improved, were still unpredictable. The more impatient consumers of fish and chips in the gallery would sometimes amuse themselves by sprinkling their leavings over the people in the pit below, and following these with the greasy paper. Heckling and brawling were not unknown. Although there was less drunkenness in the district, the neighbouring pubs still flourished from 7.30 in the morning till midnight, and not even Emmie or Lilian could prevent customers from taking a skinful before they arrived, or during the interval.

About one Londoner in every four died on public charity; over half lived three or more to a room; and in Lambeth the poverty was still deep rooted and plain to see, along with what the middle class called 'improvidence' – exhibited, for instance, in the weekly ritual exchanges at the pawnbrokers. 'On Fridays and Saturdays', Townie recalls, 'you'd see the kids sitting on the kerb at 11 o'clock at night, eating their fish and chips, while their mothers and fathers were in the pubs. Then on a Monday you'd see them all lined up at the pawnbrokers, hocking clothes and boots to get through the week till Saturday, when they'd get them out again.' It was not to this audience that Emmie and Lilian could look for financial help. The pennies they paid for admission did not go far towards the cost of the weekly programmes, however Lilian scraped and saved and cadged. It wasn't only money she begged for. The annual report dropped heavy and imploring hints to its philanthropic readers about backstage needs: 'Such a thing as an old-fashioned sofa, for example, would be a great acquisition . . . Old evening dresses are very useful . . .'

The Vic was still not widely known, in artistic or even philanthropic circles. That is illustrated by the failure of Charles Booth even to mention the Hall in the final volume of his great London survey, published in 1903. In discussing the need for better amusements, he regretted that the 'tendency to the direction of drama' in music halls had been checked by licence restrictions, and observed that 'in the minor halls, development is never in the direction of music . . . Perhaps music might some day find its way in through operatic sketches, if these were encouraged.'[1] Had he never been lobbied by Emmie, when she met him at the homes of such friends as Canon Barnett? Or did he think the Vic beneath consideration?

In spite of its relative obscurity, the Hall drew people to it, increasingly, from outside the immediate area. But whoever they were, and wherever they came from, they were all part of the divine pattern – as long as they paid for their tickets. Lilian was there to mother them, scold them, throw them out, if necessary, but see that they were supplied with what was good for them – music, uplift, information, temperance propaganda and non-alcoholic refreshments. They were her people: hers and Emmie's.

Lilian and Emmie were not only bound by ties of family affection. They were, in some ways, much alike – not least in the settled celibacy of their private lives (though both enjoyed working with men), and their dependence on and, at the same time, empire over a circle of faithful female friends and disciples. Both exerted over other women a kind of authority which has been described as 'masculine', though men often quailed before both of them, and both were unmistakably feminine, not mannish, in personality. Lilian was no less religious than Emmie: indeed, a good deal more so. Nor was she less interested in good works: she inherited the missionary tradition and practised it vigorously, if more narrowly, in her own eccentric style. Under her management the Royal Victoria Hall stayed firmly on the lines of educational, didactic and temperance work laid down by Emmie. If she had attempted to make any radical changes in her aunt's lifetime (an unlikely disloyalty), one may be sure that she would not have got very far. Lilian was the servant of the Executive Committee, on which Emmie remained a dominant force until her death, keeping a friendly but minatory eye on everything.

There were, however, differences between them in taste and temperament, manners and education. Indeed, Sir Adrian Boult – who remembered Emma as 'a most sensitive and cultured person' – found it 'hard to think of Emma and Lilian as aunt and niece', partly because of 'the striking difference in their manner of speaking'.[2] Yet compared with her aunt, Lilian showed a more persistent enthusiasm for music (especially opera) and she was all the readier to meet the growing demand for it among the Vic's public. This reflected a new appetite in the theatregoing population: in 1908 Stanford wrote that 'the country is at the highest point of enthusiasm for it'. In addition to the Carl Rosa and Moody Manners companies, four or five groups were often on tour in the provinces. At the Vic old favourites like *The Bohemian Girl* and *The Lily of Killarney* remained in the repertoire for years, but Lilian gradually and very cautiously extended the range. *Tannhäuser* was introduced in 1904 and, as Wagner proved immediately popular, *Lohengrin* followed in 1906, subsidized to some extent by the proceeds of films she showed. (And also by at least one member of the company: Euneta Truscott, then a favourite of the Vic audience, presented Lilian with the balcony set. It was still in use ten years later.) These works had still to be staged as 'recitals'. Lilian was, naturally, impatient about the absurdity of the licensing regulations, and the evasions to which they condemned the Vic. We catch a glimpse of her feelings from an actor who visited her one evening in her stage-box, where she conducted much of her business, during a Costume Operatic Recital of *Cavalleria Rusticana*. While they were talking he suddenly noticed the tenor stepping forward to the front of the stage in mid-opera and looking up apprehensively as the curtain descended behind him. 'Breaking the continuity of the act,' Miss Baylis explained angrily. 'What act?' he asked. 'Wildly and surrealistically she replied – one can hear the peculiar snarl of her voice – "Act of Parliament".'[3] Already in 1906 we find her asking the Executive Committee if they would apply for a theatre licence, as she understood that smoking would now be allowed and such a licence would 'overcome many difficulties in arranging the opera recitals'. But she was wrong about the ban on smoking, one of the Governors' main reasons for sticking to the old type of licence (if the audience couldn't have a drink, they must at least be allowed to smoke). The Governors refused to take action, and their manager had to wait for six years before she had her way. According to Tyrone Guthrie, she also pressed for an opera company long before she got it, but the Governors found it 'not merely impractical but exceedingly sinful'. No evidence of this survives; Sir Tyrone probably saw the records relating to Lilian's first decade (which have now disappeared).

The recitals were presented under considerable difficulties. To say that they were 'produced' would be misleading, for there was no production in the contemporary sense of the term. Programme credits for 'production' were given to Alice Barth from 1900 to 1906, and to Sam Harrison from 1907 onwards, but these were both part-time singers whose function was limited to stage management of an elementary kind. (Harrison, a stocky Northerner with a pronounced Lancashire accent, who later worked during the day for a gramophone company, had made his Vic debut in 1899. He was a pillar of the theatre until 1931, with what Joan Cross calls 'a voice of brass' and a reputation for being able to sing practically any male role in the repertoire.) The chorus was largely amateur, and could not rehearse during the day. Lilian could not afford to pay the orchestra rehearsal fees at night. There was, indeed, only one orchestra rehearsal, without the chorus. Frequent emergencies arose over sudden gaps in the cut-price (or voluntary) cast. Many singers wore their own costumes: 'a corselet belt skirt and apron if Italian or German, a bolero jacket if Spanish or Gipsies. When grand attire was needed many and varied were the evening gowns worn.'[4] They learned their parts on their own, sometimes with less than a fortnight to do it in, and they would hear the orchestration for the first time a couple of days before the performance, with one three-hour rehearsal. Instead of being produced, they were 'built up at the show, according to the experience of the artists'. They stood and sang, as best they could. For the principals the repertoire was familiar; the positions were generally the same as those they occupied on other stages; and, in any event, they could not afford to give the Vic many rehearsals. The only way that Lilian could get her singers cheap, as Edward J. Dent said, was 'by demanding as little as possible from them. If they were not required to rehearse, they had all the more time free for other engagements.'[5] Some members of the chorus paid a small fee, on joining, 'towards wear and tear of music. This unselfish work alone must be a factor for good,' said the Chairman of the Governors in 1913.

Apart from the differences in their attitude to music at the Vic, Lilian was more empirical than Emmie, more responsive to changes in public taste. At the beginning of the century, for instance, she took the initiative in exploiting the appeal of the cinematograph, six or seven years before the first effective cinema opened in London. At first in 1901 the Exhibition of Animated Pictures by Mr E. Holmes's Fireproof Matagraph was dangled as an experimental bait, after such operas as *The Daughter of the Regiment*. By 1903 she advertised the Matagraph on the programme as a coming attraction ('Change of Pictures Each Week'). In the 1904–5 season she gave it an evening on its own, every third Monday. Business was so good that in the next season she obtained permission to run films every alternate Monday, then every Monday. During the 1907–8 season they made a profit over £250. Lilian claimed that in the next two years she netted over £2,000; and although there is no evidence to support this figure – vast, in relation to the Vic penny prices, and smacking of Baylis fantasy – there seems little doubt that without the Matagraph the Hall might have closed down. By 1909 the trade began to fall off, partly because several 'Animated Picture Halls' had opened in the neighbourhood, where the Vic had for some time been the sole supplier. Nonetheless, the Matagraph was used not only on Mondays, but also to follow the Tuesday lectures, precede the Costume Operatic Recitals, conclude the Ballad Concerts and brighten up the Saturday night variety.

Looking for new attractions, in 1905 Lilian had started symphony concerts, which seemed at that time to be a consummation of the Hall's progress in twenty-five years from the original ambition of presenting 'musical entertainments of the music-hall type'. The annual report (which Lilian helped to draft) celebrated the innovation with the assurance that, 'Briefly expressed, "pure entertainment, good music and decent surroundings" has been the main object which the management of the Vic has always had in view,' a marked over-simplification of Emmie's recorded aims. Yet it should be noted that when, two years later, the symphony concerts were already losing so much money that Lilian recommended they should be jettisoned, it was Emmie who vetoed such a quick surrender. In the Baylisian words of the Vic's minutes, Miss Cons 'called attention to the fact that our grant was given us to give good music to the people and raise their taste for same'. Once again, she was putting the brake on her niece. But Lilian knew what she wanted. By 1909 she was negotiating with the 1st Life Guards, the Coldstream and the Grenadier Bands, to see if they could supply a military band to replace the symphony orchestra for part of the season: 'It was the general opinion that the uniform would attract with our audience.' As a result the musical mixture in April–May 1910 included, for example, this sequence on Thursdays: the Coldstreams, a Costume Recital of *Fra Diavolo*, a ballad concert, *Carmen*, a return match of the Coldstreams, *Trovatore*, another ballad concert and *Faust*. Yet, while the Costume Recitals increased in popularity, the Coldstreams' uniform didn't 'attract with' enough customers.

In the field of non-martial music, Lilian was helped by an invaluable, expert ally. In 1899 (according to Grove's) or the end of 1901 (according to Reginald Mander) she had the good luck and the good sense (these are especially hard to distinguish, in explaining her choice of people) to engage Charles Corri as musical director. Corri, who remained with Miss Baylis for over thirty years, stemmed from a dynasty of dancers, composers and instrumentalists, established in England by his great-grandfather Domenico, who emigrated from Italy in the 1750s. One of his ancestors sang at the Vic in 1820, and another had produced plays there. In 1839 Mr M. Corri appeared on the Vic bills as 'Composer and Director of Orchestra'. Charles Corri first came to the Vic as a cellist, having played with the Carl Rosa company, and later deputized for Alfred Dove as conductor and musical director. From the beginning of the century Corri was able to attract and to keep better players than might otherwise have been willing to work under the grim conditions at the Hall, because of his unusual sensibility and professionalism. He continued to play the cello, his brother Bill played the viola, and his eldest son Vernon later took the violin and became leader of the orchestra. In organizing the operatic 'recitals', Corri showed a remarkable gift for re-scoring works for his tiny orchestra of fifteen to eighteen players, using, in Professor Dent's words, 'a composer's imagination to think out

96

how Mozart or Wagner would have scored the operas had they been faced with a small band like this'.[6] What it lacked in volume it made up for in 'general accuracy, good tone and intonation'.[7] Although the orchestra was engaged *ad hoc* for every performance, Corri could count on the regular support of a number of good musicians, and they could count on the regular performance of a number of standard works, which required no more than one rehearsal. He talked little, but when he did use his tongue it often scarified a recalcitrant singer. He is remembered as a reticent, hard-drinking Cockney, unflappably conducting at rehearsals in a bowler hat, puffing on a favoured pipe and spitting emphatically (when Lilian was not watching). He was a 'terrific autocrat' who liked laying traps for singers, and his curious conducting style was described by Powell Lloyd as 'cutting off slices', while frequently telling a singer (whose voice he was deliberately drowning), 'Can't 'ear yer, old boy'; or telling a harpist, 'Come on, tickle it, old boy'. According to Joan Cross, 'he knew the works inside out, backwards and forwards, up and down. I adored him.'

Corri's problems included Miss Baylis, with whom he plunged, every now and then, into blazing rows. She was overheard, on one occasion, threatening to 'put him back in the gutter where she found him'.[8] Yet in spite of such tempests – which blew up periodically in many of her working relationships – they remained firm professional allies, linked in a kind of loving hatred. She was far too shrewd to let Corri go; and in spite of many frustrations, he liked the Vic (and her) too much to leave. Astonishingly, against enormous odds, he improved the quality of the singing and the playing in the 1900–20 period. Professor Dent has testified that his orchestra was 'always satisfactory and in a way adequate, adequate, that is, for its environment'. This is less dismissive praise than it may seem, and it means more than just 'good enough for the Vic'. For Corri deserves a share of the credit given to Miss Baylis as architect of the national opera (English, Welsh and Scottish); even though in his old age he failed, not surprisingly, to keep up with the changes in the 'environment' and his standards then seemed no longer 'adequate'.

By the summer of 1914, the opera at the Vic was recognized to have, for all its imperfections, especial virtues. As one critic wrote:

The scenery is crude, the dresses are garish, the limelight is a will o' the wisp, the orchestra has insufficient bass; but the singing is in tune, the dancing fresh and graceful, the chorus hearty, the audience too intent on the play to eat chocolate; for the applause all of them are in the firing line and there are no reserves; and the prices rise from twopence. Here are the essentials at any rate. It is possible that English Opera might be born south of the Thames, not far from the scene of Shakespeare's activities.

Such a prospect seemed remote, for some years, when the survival of the theatre was perennially in danger. In spite of the successful opera performances, presented only once a fortnight, all was far from well at the Royal Victoria Hall. The acting manager herself was often far from well: indeed, in 1910 she had overstrained herself to the point of a 'nervous breakdown', and was granted three months' holiday to recuperate while the Vic was closed during the summer. She went on a world cruise with her friend Louie Davey (probably paid for by Emmie), and visited – among other places – the West Australian home of her aunts Esther and Eliza, her sister Violet and her brother Ray. When she came back into harness that autumn, the manœuvrings of Lady Frederick Cavendish and her influential friends succeeded in inducing the Prince and Princess of Wales to attend the Old Vic. Royal visits were always good for business and prestige – that, at least, was the prevailing wisdom. The couple were welcomed by the Duke and Duchess of Devonshire, the wife of the Archbishop of Canterbury, the Governors and Emma (who gave them a bouquet and a synopsis of the Hall's history). The Prince and Princess were, they said after her death, 'impressed by the personality of Miss Cons, whose whole life seemed to be centred in her excellent work'.[9] For more than an hour before they arrived, the streets were thronged by crowds which 'rendered the approaches almost impassable'. But such publicity did nothing to solve the essential problem. Emmie and Lilian had to face the fact that only the films and the operas were successful: the ballad concerts, symphony concerts, military bands and variety were all losing audiences and money. Emmie and the Governors allowed Lilian to drop the military bands; but the symphony concerts had to be retained, as a matter of principle (Emmie's principle); and, when in 1911 Lilian proposed jettisoning variety and giving up Saturday nights to films instead, she was defeated by Emmie and her colleagues. They clearly thought that Auntie's niece was going too fast, and trying to change too much.

Yet, as Lilian was only too well aware, the Hall's financial situation was desperate – and desperate remedies seemed, in her view, to be called for. By 1911, Emmie announced, they had spent over £5,000 on redecoration and over £10,000 on structural alterations ordered by the LCC. In the past the Council had not always insisted upon normal requirements; but now it was pressing for an extensive and costly programme of alterations. Meanwhile, the capital had almost disappeared, and the takings were falling. In March Lilian could not meet the weekly cheque for current expenses: the chairman of the Governors had to lend the Hall £200 to pay bills and wages. Even the Sunday service attendances were sinking. Lilian suggested to the Executive Committee that if the minister wanted to run 'Sacred Animated Pictures' it would be as well to consent, as 'Secular Pictures were being shown on every side of the Hall, on Sunday evenings'. But Emmie was not having any of *that*, either.

The decline of business was particularly evident on Saturday nights, and that is why Lilian had proposed abandoning variety. Some performers who later became stars – Hetty King, Chirgwin, Gus Elen, Little Tich and Marie Lloyd – had briefly appeared on the Vic stage. Charlie Chaplin, at the beginning of his career, is said to have tried twice for an engagement, but received no reply – Miss Cons never answered a letter which did not contain a stamped addressed envelope. (In the 1890s he lived with his mother and brother in a basement room in Oakley Street, now Baylis Road.) But it was never a recognized show-place or shop-window for top talent. As it maintained a moral censorship, and could offer only two or three weekly dates (later only one), at chicken-feed pay, it could not compete with music halls in the neighbourhood. And it grew progressively more difficult first for Emmie, then for Lilian, to book talent, and to draw an audience big enough to pay for the turns, however far down the scale these might be. Doing a Saturday at the Vic was a last-resort option, to be ditched at once if anything better came along. When sudden gaps in the bill opened up, Lilian would send someone from the Hall in an attempt to recruit replacements from 'Poverty Corner' (otherwise known as 'Misery Junction' or 'The Rialto'), the area between Waterloo Station and the bridge where dramatic and variety agents' offices attracted a small floating population of unemployed artists. The resulting bills were scarcely on a level with the rest of the Hall's activities. 'Oh, those variety programmes, the place filled with the toughest of the neighbourhood, and a chucker-out at each door.'[10] But to Emmie, no doubt, the termination of these programmes would have represented too sharp a break with the past. The vision that had led her to the Vic thirty years earlier was, after all, that of a reformed music hall – even though, by 1912, the building was dubbed 'The People's Opera House', and housed a college.

That year of 1912 was, however, a turning-point in the history of the Vic; for on 24 July, after a short illness, the seventy-four years-old Emma Cons died at Chippens Bank, Ethel Everest's home in Hever. 'On her death-bed', Lilian wrote fourteen years later, 'she talked to me of her various interests and of those she was leaving in charge of them; some would need guidance, in others she had absolute confidence. "What about the Vic, Emmie?" I said at last, and her answer was, "You are there, dear" . . . I felt humbled at her faith in me.'[11]

Although the passing of this great Victorian, who was hard at work until shortly before her death, was scarcely noticed by the press, Ellen Cons and Lilian Baylis received 'hundreds of letters of sympathy'. Her niece wrote: 'I remember very distinctly that I took in, at the same time, Lord Stamfordham's telegram expressing the regret of the King and Queen and a similar message sent by a scavenger in Lambeth.'[12] The royal message – sent, in fact, to Lady Frederick Cavendish – said: 'The King and Queen have heard with regret of the death of Miss Cons, whom they so well remember meeting at the Royal Victoria Hall, and for whose self-sacrificing life their Majesties had a high regard.' Emmie's will asked for her ashes to be scattered in the daffodil wood at Chippens Bank, in a spot which she had agreed with Ethel Everest. Lilian performed the last service to her aunt, watched by Ellen, Miss Everest and some of Emmie's servants in her causes. (Octavia Hill died the same year, and was buried not far away, in Westerham.) Lilian kept Emmie's memory green not only in her own heart but in her conversation, where her aunt played, at strategic moments, a leading role. One picture of Emmie was presented to the LCC – the inscription read: 'Emma Cons: the pioneer in housing and in recreation for the people. Alderman First London County Council.' Another was hung in the foyer of the Vic, and her name was enshrined there. (Later audiences, however, were sometimes hazy about her identity. On at least one occasion she was mistaken for Queen Victoria, whom she vaguely resembled in coiffure. She was also taken to be 'Shakespeare's mother'.)

Lilian had dedicated herself to the Vic partly for Emmie's sake, and her aunt's death intensified that dedication. Yet, in spite of that, the death was also a liberation. Within a few months Lilian had launched the Vic on a new course, for which she had been impatiently waiting. She relished her new freedom, her new status. Although she was still, of course, answerable to the Executive Committee, the Governors maintained no effective opposition to her main plans, now that Miss Cons had gone.

First of all, in December, Lilian obtained a theatre licence from the Lord Chamberlain (with the help of Lady Frederick Cavendish). From now on she could present full-length operas and felt herself free to produce stage plays of any kind. The Lord Chamberlain acted on the advice of the LCC, who recommended him to grant the licence, in spite of the unsuitability of the building as a full-time theatre, on the understanding – as the Clerk of the LCC reminded Lilian in 1916 – that it was 'only for the purpose of legalizing the presentation of certain selections from plays and operas, with occasional full performances'. This was the reason Lilian had given when requesting it in 1912. Neither the Lord Chamberlain nor the LCC had any idea that she was about to turn the Old Vic into a professional play-house and opera-house combined; but then it seems certain that, at this point, Lilian had no idea either of what precisely she should do next. The fact is that something had to be done, quickly – by the spring of 1913 there was only £15 in the bank. Lilian dropped the ballad concerts and symphony concerts and replaced them by opera recitals, including full operas, *every* Thursday. Then, the following year, she extended the opera performances to Saturday night as well, and variety disappeared. 'On the first Saturday night of the opera', she wrote in 1936, 'we were crowded out, and this has been the rule ever since.' The Cons pattern was quickly being reshaped, and more changes were on the way. The new element, which Auntie's niece introduced at the end of 1913, was drama.

How did this start? Lilian Baylis's own story was that the available films had become too vulgar and sensational for the Vic, and, in looking for something to replace them, 'in despair I turned to Shakespeare'. The explanation is not altogether convincing. The reason for abandoning films was probably not only moral but also financial. The chairman of the Governors told the CPF in March 1914 that the Matagraph, too, was losing money. 'We now hope to try the experiment of giving Shakespearian performances, and if these are successful, we may be able to make arrangements of a permanent nature for the continuance of the work,' the chairman said. Miss Baylis did not *turn* to Shakespeare; she knew very little about his plays, and showed no love of the theatre at large. She was pushed towards him – by accident, expediency and the pressures of the times – and she embraced Shakespeare, at first, with some reluctance and apprehension, for opera was her first love and she feared that it might suffer from the introduction of straight plays. But she did it; she huffed and puffed, prodded and pulled the Vic out of the doldrums, into a new and glorious era; and she did it in Emmie's name, while changing Emmie's course.

As long as the Governors of the Vic had preferred not to seek a theatre licence, there was no practical possibility of staging Shakespeare in the Waterloo Road. Emma Cons apparently had no intention of challenging the law by, for instance, allowing the audience to smoke after obtaining a theatre licence; or of risking legal action, while retaining its old form of licence, by extending the evasive technique of opera 'recitals' to the drama. Solo 'dramatic reciters' could, however, appear without breaking the law, as Charles Fry had done in the early years of the Cons régime. Fry, who was already known for his readings in the 1870s, delivered them at the Vic as late as 1895; but in 1898 (at the age of fifty-three) he formed his own Shakespearian company, and thereafter there is no evidence that he returned to the Vic, although his son asserted, many years later, that Lilian Baylis told Fry that his work had given her the idea of staging Shakespeare.[13] This 'veteran elocutionist and actor', as *The Times* described him in 1908, belonged as a director to the Poel school, and was responsible for the first public production of *Troilus and Cressida* since Shakespeare's day, in 1907 (at the Great Queen Street Theatre, later the Kingsway, with Lewis Casson as Troilus). He presented an annual Shakespearian season at the Royal Court, appeared at the Royalty, the Savoy and other theatres, and by 1908 had produced twenty-one of Shakespeare's plays – at speed, without scenery, on a stage usually draped with green velvet and with only one interval. Perhaps he did influence Lilian Baylis's ideas of Shakespeare; the economy of his staging would have been an irresistible argument in his favour. But whatever Fry's role may or may not have been, a new approach to Shakespeare – putting text before spectacle, aiming at Elizabethan speed and simplicity – was certainly in the air at the time Miss Baylis got her new licence from the Lord Chamberlain.

William Poel had approached her in 1906, offering to stage a production – of a Shakespearian play no doubt – but the Executive Committee declined with regret, 'as we are unable to have dramatic performances'. It seems odd that Poel, who had been manager of the Hall, did not know that its licence was unchanged; but although he may have proposed some form of recital, inside the law, we have no evidence beyond the Vic's refusal. In 1909 an actor with the felicitous name of Shakespeare Stewart offered (as reported in the characteristic Baylis prose of the minutes) 'to bring a first-class company and take ten per cent of the takings. It was decided to do nothing in the matter at present.' In 1912 a more specific and practical proposal was made by two actors who had been in Laurence Irving's company, George Owen and W. Bridges-Adams (later celebrated as a producer at Stratford and as a historian of the theatre). Following Poel's (and Fry's) example, they offered to present Shakespeare plays in costume on a draped stage with no scenery, calling the performance 'recitals'. As it meant 'certain financial loss' Bridges-Adams asked the Governors to what extent he would be subsidized. The Governors answered that they wouldn't subsidize him to any extent. They couldn't afford it. They offered him the theatre for six Wednesdays at five guineas a night, if he and his partner could raise the money for the production. As they couldn't, the project collapsed. Yet another application came that year – before the new licence was acquired – from Philip Carr. As secretary to the Shakespeare Memorial National Theatre Committee, he was arranging events to propagate the cause of a National Theatre, including a Shakespearian Pageant at Knole and a Shakespearian Lord Mayor's Show, and he now inquired about 'hiring the Hall for Shakespearian performances'. Nothing came of this. But suddenly, at Christmas, there were plays at the Vic, for the first time since it had gone temperance with Miss Cons; and they were continued in 1913 for some weeks, although they made a loss.

Maddeningly, there is no exact record of what these plays *were*, or who produced them; but it seems certain that they were not by Shakespeare. In Cicely Hamilton's history of the theatre, she says it had 'already adventured into plays' by 1911 – 'plays considered safer than Shakespeare; hearty melodramas with no vice in them like *The Shaughraun*'.[14] The dating is almost certainly wrong; as is her explanation of the Governors' refusal to accept the Bridges-Adams and Owen plan – that they were 'more than doubtful about the drawing powers of classic dramatists' (doubtful they may have been, but that was surely not the reason). But another chronicler, Winifred Isaac, confirms that melodramas were Lilian's first choice after Emma's death: *Poor Joe, The Streets of London, Lady Audley's Secret* and *Oliver Twist*.[15] It seems apt that it should be with such twopence-coloured drama that the Vic returned after thirty years to the presentation of plays. For it was largely on melodrama that the Vic had once fed the local audience whom Emmie had set out to redeem; and perhaps Lilian felt that, by using the freedom of the licence to restore it, she was following the spirit of her aunt's régime, though she might appear to be departing from the letter. She may also have been encouraged by the growing popularity of short sketches and scenes in music-hall bills, whose managers recruited 'straight' actors to fight the competition of the cinema. In 1912 some 300 short pieces were staged in the halls, including the Vic.

The first Shakespearian productions at the Vic in the spring of 1914 were, in fact, approved by the Governors against some opposition from their manager. Her objections were, it seems, not so much to Shakespeare but to his latest sponsor, Rosina Filippi, and to her threatened interference with Lilian's extended opera programme; for Miss Filippi proposed to stage plays for four nights a week. This was reduced to two nights; but there was no improvement in the relations between Miss Filippi and Miss Baylis.

Rosina Filippi, then forty-eight, had retired from the London stage into married life after winning some *réclame* as an actress, had since made a second reputation as a teacher, and was at this time one of the leading campaigners for a 'People's Theatre' – a concept which, like that of the National Theatre to which it was evidently allied, enjoyed a flurry of publicity among liberal theatrical and literary circles in the last years of Edwardian England. What seems to have distinguished Miss Filippi from other advocates of the project, whose often vaguely visionary gleams shared a common inspiration in such German exemplars as the *Volksbühne* (in Berlin the New People's Theatre Society was nearly twenty-five years old) was that she found her model in Italy. In Milan a philanthropic organization, the Società Umanitaria, had converted a drill-hall into a 2,300-seat theatre, and claimed – according to Miss Filippi – that the effect of its repertory had been 'to reduce not only crime, but Socialism, to improve the intelligence of the people, and to serve as a bridge between primary education and the responsible duties of the voter'. Miss Filippi announced that she was pursuing the same objectives, by producing 'only the best plays by the greatest authors, living and dead, and charging only fourpence for every seat in the house'.[16]

The Old Vic was probably not the first theatre she had lobbied, but it was the first to bite. After some discussion on the Executive Committee perhaps the most incontestably pious member, the

Wesleyan Minister Dr Scott Lidgett, argued that to present 'high-class drama' would be carrying out the principle of the Hall's work, and should not be lightly spurned; and although spurning tendencies were clearly perceptible at that meeting, a later one agreed to accept Miss Filippi's plan to stage 'Shakespeare and other similar Drama'. She asked for March, but Miss Baylis vetoed that. The season opened in April, with a company of thirty, and a programme of three plays: *The Merchant of Venice*, *Romeo and Juliet* and *The School for Scandal*. Miss Filippi had intended to include *Candida*, but when the Governors discovered this plan they were astonished and indignant. They had never thought of Mr Shaw's works as being 'similar' to those of Shakespeare. Indeed, they had not realized that 'modern' plays were to be staged at all. As *Candida* was not, in their view, 'desirable' for the Vic audience, they vetoed it – with, no doubt, their manager's full support. There was more trouble when Miss Filippi revealed this act of censorship, as she saw it, to the press.

By mid-April, however, the People's Theatre campaign had gained some momentum. A special meeting was held at Drury Lane, at which leading actor-managers like Sir George Alexander and Sir Herbert Tree spoke eloquently in support of the idea – and of Miss Filippi. Like Charles Fry she had, said Sir George, done 'great work', and was on the verge of doing even greater things. Tree proposed that 'our People's Society should be extended to the larger provincial cities: thus we may obtain what is sorely needed, the Municipal Theatre – finally perhaps the achievement of a National Shakespeare Theatre'. Meanwhile there was the season at the Victoria Hall. Miss Filippi reported that she had sent out a subscription list for £600, and received £300, on which she had 'started a People's Theatre' in the Waterloo Road, 'with art muslin, two changes of scenery and two hired orange trees'. The audiences, said Miss Filippi, were 'magnificent. There seemed to be a Marconi communication between the players and the audience that was never experienced in the West End.' If she could only extend the season for another fortnight, she claimed, it would be a 'great success'. If it lasted only one week more, it would be a 'tolerable' success. She appealed for subscriptions, and raised £40.[17]

It is not clear whether Miss Filippi's company managed to last for four weeks. What *is* clear is that, far from being a great or even a tolerable success, it was a débâcle. One reason was, perhaps, that Miss Filippi and Miss Baylis could not stand each other.

In Dame Sybil Thorndike's words, 'Rosina and Lilian together would have been a wonderful pair, but they were both too *violent* to work together. They got on very well, as long as they were apart. But when it came to doing anything together, they would bawl at each other and have terrible rows. Rosina had *such* a temper, a terrible temper, and so did Lil.' And Lil's temper is unlikely to have been improved by Rosina's claim that she had started 'the People's Theatre' at *her* Vic. Yet another reason, according to Russell Thorndike (who married Rosina's daughter) is that the manager of the company decamped with all the money. But, in any event, the expectations were far too rosily high; however magnificent the 'Marconi communication' with the audience may have been, not enough of them came. After starting with full houses, the company played to no more than a few dozen people. Miss Filippi, in more modest vein, had thought of her season as a 'trial', in order to see if she could attract 'an audience of the people, as already achieved for opera'. But to build up that opera audience had taken years of patient, cautious experiment and economy. Full-length Shakespeare, without music – at least, none to speak of, or to hum – was completely new for the Vic. No manager could expect instant mobilization of a ready-made audience for it among the public for opera, lectures, films and temperance meetings. What's more, Miss Baylis did little to encourage that audience. Russell Thorndike said she had slips inserted in the opera programme, 'telling the patrons that although they might want to come and see the plays, they must clearly understand that they must not spend their opera pennies upon them. If they couldn't afford to pay for the two shows, they must come only to one, and that one . . . must be the opera . . . She would say: "Shakespeare may be all right in his way, but Opera is entirely right in every way for the success of the Vic".'[18]

In spite of Miss Baylis's reservations about Miss Filippi, however, the programme had to be filled. The Governors had spoken firmly in support of Shakespeare and, more materially, Lilian seems to have decided that there were several points in his favour – as long as Rosina Filippi was not making them. He was cheap to stage, if produced in the right way. He provided a good deal of moral uplift. There were, it seems, plenty of actors eager to act in his plays, who could be persuaded to do it 'mainly as a labour of love', as all things should be done at the Vic. Moreover, Lilian had heard the voice of Shakespeare himself. Or was it God? One night, as she lay awake in tears after the Filippi fiasco, she recorded that 'a strong, manly voice came out of the dark-ness'.

'Why have you allowed my beautiful words to be so murdered?' said the strong manly voice.

'I know something about music and I can run operas,' said Lilian into the darkness. 'But I'm not an actress myself and I had to ask a good player to help me.'

'You must run the plays yourself as you do the operas,' said the voice.

'I don't know enough about Shakespeare. I don't feel able to cast plays.' The voice was inexorable. 'You are to choose your company of players and run the plays yourself.'

So, next day, Lilian obeyed the orders of the 'calm, good voice', by pressing into service Shakespeare Stewart, who had applied to do the job five years earlier. Mr Stewart had acted with Poel; he had the more substantial merit, in Lilian's eyes, of being a light baritone who had sung with 'my dear operas'. He knew what was expected at the Vic, and he was on the spot. In May Mr Stewart conjured up three productions – of *Twelfth Night*, *As You Like It* and *Much Ado About Nothing*. They ran for two performances each, on Mondays and Wednesdays, and lost £50. Yet at the end of the month the *Era* reported that 'there is every prospect, we are told, of Shakespeare being presented through-out the autumn and next season'. It was true; and the Governors agreed in July that Shakespearian performances would be staged in the autumn, until Christmas.

That fateful year of 1914 saw the launching of another public appeal for money to keep the Royal Victoria Hall alive, and, in particular, to keep its music going.

With the inevitable loss during the past thirty years of most of the little band of enthusiasts to whom the work owes its inception, this help has become increasingly difficult to obtain, and through the recent death of Miss Emma Cons we are faced with a financial crisis … If only one half of those who attend regularly Opera and Concerts in more fashionable surroundings will send us the sum which only one evening's enjoyment costs them, we shall have the answer we want. It means so little to them, but so much to us and our humble patrons.

The appeal was headed by powerful names – Princess Christian, the Lord Mayor of London and the Chairman of the LCC, to-gether with such musicians as Dame Nellie Melba, Thomas

Beecham, Edward German and Henry Wood. The prose was eloquent:

> In every direction there is a longing to rise out of all that is low and sordid and ugly. An opportunity now presents itself which has never before arisen in the same degree. If we neglect this, other attractions will intervene. Who can tell what it may foreshadow in the future to put the best forms of entertainment within the reach of those who are already seeking 'higher things'. Even now we are able to see the introduction of High-Class Drama in conjunction with our Operas . . .

But the begging-bowl filled very slowly, this time round. Not only were Emma's allies among the philanthropic old guard fading away, but attitudes among the wealthy upper class were changing towards good works and salvation by them. The condition of the poor had – or was, at least, widely thought to have – improved. Both the temperance movement and the threat of class war had lost their urgency. And the cause of the Royal Victoria Hall was decidedly *vieux jeux*, especially now that the *vieille dame* herself, its main begetter and fund-raiser, had left the stage. By August only £800 had been collected; although the CPF had agreed to make a supplementary grant of £500 p.a. (Lilian wanted £1,000.) In their annual report the Governors said that they would 'very seriously have to consider whether they can possibly continue to run the Hall after the present season'.

The outbreak of war, contrary to expectations, saved the Vic. It re-opened not only with opera but with Shakespeare too. After some hesitation, the Governors had resolved to 'carry out the original arrangement and continue to do so as long as possible'. And Lilian Baylis, by now, was in full support. It seems probable indeed that it was her persistence that won the day against the Executive Committee's initial reluctance to take such risks in wartime. But Shakespeare Stewart had no part in the new season: his vagueness 'drove Miss Baylis up the wall'. And Rosina Filippi never returned. Her People's Theatre campaign was obliterated by the onset of war. A People's Theatre did arise in the Waterloo Road, but it was Lilian Baylis who built its foundations. She did more, in her own way, for the establishment of that exemplary theatre of pre-war dreams than any other contemporary manager, although at the time of her first Shakespearian season she was a complete novice in the management of drama and took no part in the campaigns for the National, the People's or any other kind of Theatre.

How did she do it? Partly, she believed, by the personal help of God. He showed His hand that year, for instance, in immediate response to Miss Baylis's complaint to Him – for once, not on her knees – about the neglect of the Vic by the press. The story, which Lilian told over twenty years later in the parish magazine of All Saints, Margaret Street, deserves reprinting here, because it gives one of the rare opportunities of hearing her authentic and eccentric voice.

In the spring of 1914 my mother lost the sight of one eye and was told her only chance of saving the other was to leave South Africa and return at once to England for a special operation. My parents were greatly troubled financially through the difficulties which followed the Boer War, and I had arranged, with much effort, for them to come and live with my aged aunt and myself.

The strain of re-adjusting my household and the constant burden of Vic work made my eyes so troublesome that I had to consult an oculist. His report was so alarming I felt my sight might fail me quickly. My oculist requested me to take his prescriptions at once to his own chemist near the Queen's Hall. It was exactly a quarter to one and the chemist told me the prescriptions would take half an hour to make up. I was ill and weary and turned into All Saints for twenty minutes while I was waiting.

This was the only time I remember entering a church and not kneeling to pray. I sat and groused to the Almighty. I could hardly shoulder the burden of my aged dear ones with my normal health; my work was bristling with difficulties; my wonderful aunt, who had founded the Vic and had always been such a pillar of strength to me, had passed on some months before. I told God that even the *Daily Telegraph*, which had seldom failed to note my musical programmes, had taken no notice of our last Wagner performance. I had no praise or thanks in my heart – just one hateful grumble.

A few minutes before one o'clock the Editor of the *Telegraph* rang through to one of his staff, who was keen on my work, telling him to go at once to the Carlton and interview Melba who had just arrived in England, and could be caught there at lunch. Tetrazzini had captured the attention of the English public shortly before, and my friend of the *Daily Telegraph* thought it would be a popular thing if Nellie Melba's first visit on her arrival was to the People's Opera House. He persuaded her to come to the Vic that night where we were playing *Rigoletto*. She was charming to the audience, the cast and the staff – it was like a royal visit. She promised to help my work, and the next day sent me a big cheque. I had longed for a word or two in the *Daily Telegraph*: the following morning I had several columns on Melba's visit to my work. My friend told me later that he was back at the newspaper's office by one thirty – everything having been arranged while I was in our beloved church in anything, I am afraid, but a humble and contrite frame of mind.

Whoever else – besides Emmie – was standing by her, as she prepared to steer the Vic through the war, Lilian knew that God was there. Indeed, He wasn't only at her side. 'For Miss Baylis, God was on the staff.'

After Lilian went back to England in 1898, taking Ethel with her, the family finances plummeted in South Africa. The immediate cause was war; but the Baylises missed Lilian's musical talent and energizing optimism, as well as Ethel's box-office charm. They continued to teach music in Johannesburg and to give regular concerts with their pupils. But music, it soon became apparent, was not enough. The Konss-Baylis Academy of Music developed a sideline, the Konss-Baylis Music, Stationery and Haberdashery Store ('Newest Novels and Music by Every Mail'). During the British occupation of the Rand, Mrs Baylis's family name was dropped – perhaps, because it may have seemed Boerish – and Lilian's parents presided over the Rand Academy of Music, Dancing, Art and Literature (with French Classes thrown in). But they failed to thrive; they lived (as neighbours recalled) in 'very poor circumstances'; and their children could give them little help. When Ethel returned in 1902, she set up as a teacher of dancing; she married Robert Dunning in 1908, and had two children, Robert and Gladys. Willie gave some help, while he could, but he died in 1906 before the birth of his daughter Lilian. Lilian could not afford to support her parents on her meagre salary, although she sent frequent remittances. By the spring of 1914 Lilian's financial position had improved, eighteen months after Emmie's death. Emmie left her estate of some £4,000 to Ellen and, at her sister's death, to Lilian, enjoining her beloved niece to continue to make her home with Ellen. (Having given so much of her time and money to charities during her lifetime, she wrote, she had none to leave them now.) So Ellen and Lilian moved from 6 Moreton Place a few miles south, to a small double-fronted house in a quiet suburban street: 27 Stockwell Park Road; and here both remained until they died. Ellen in 1920, Lilian in 1937. It was Ellen, it seems, who paid for the house, out of Emmie's legacy; and Ellen probably also paid for the return fares of her sister and brother-in-law from South Africa in 1914.

For all Lilian's family piety, Madame Konss-Baylis and her

consort can scarcely have been welcome guests in that little Victorian house, whose rooms were stuffed with Victorian furniture and bric-a-brac. There was too much tension between mother and daughter for them to stay. Although within a year or two she settled her parents in a home of their own in Kennington, the responsibility of looking after them, as well as Ellen, was a heavy burden for Lilian to shoulder at such a crisis in the affairs of the Vic.

Lilian's War

I knew nothing about Shakespeare
but I went to those who knew nearly everything.
I have always done that – gone to those who know.

Lilian Baylis

If the great William Shakespeare, that inspired genius,
were to return to earth from the Elysian Fields,
I for my part am very sure that he could not fail
to regard her as his minister and high-priestess,
and to load her with praises and thanks;
inasmuch as it is owing to her
that the name of our greatest poet is cherished
in the minds of a wider audience.

*From the (translated) address of the Public Orator at Oxford University
on the presentation of an Honorary Master of Arts degree
to Miss Baylis in 1924*

Although the existence of the Old Vic was little known before
the First World War in the wider spheres of music, theatre and
the arts at large, great things were already expected of it by a few
enthusiasts of an evangelistic, William Morris-y turn of mind. One
such – signing himself, or herself 'Pilgrim' – wrote to a paper
(unidentified) in November 1913:

Are you going to strengthen those who will not rest until the 'Old
Vic', standing straight on its own self-supporting basis, shall be a
centre of the People's life, of all that belongs to the Ideal, the Beautiful,
the True, and by example and achievement may help to bring back to
country town and teeming factory alike the happier days of old, and
make our England 'merrie' once again?

The old building in the Waterloo Road was a somewhat improbable seed-bed for such Utopian designs; and indeed both Lilian Baylis and the Old Vic might well have appeared to be ludicrously ill equipped even for the more specific enterprise of establishing in the capital under one roof 'the home of Shakespeare and opera in English'. For any London theatre to attempt so vastly ambitious a task with no state grant, civic aid or private fortune behind it would have been wildly audacious at any period. For the Royal Victoria Hall to try it, after the outbreak of a world war, seems in retrospect a kind of sublime insanity, a mad courage robbed of magnificence only by the apparent inability of Miss Baylis, blinking irritably upwards through her thick glasses at the Everest above her, to recognize its height.

Here was a building far from the theatregoing centre, in a working-class district with a lingering reputation for roughness, vice and violence that deterred many genteel middle-class families from visiting it. How, in any event, could they know what was happening there? The Vic did not advertise its programmes in the daily press, and Miss Baylis grudged giving tickets to critics. If they wanted to come, they could jolly well *buy* a ticket. 'Why should we give the bounders free seats and then let them earn their wretched livings by saying scurrilous things about us?' was the indignant rhetorical question posed by the manager.[1] Lilian put her faith in what became known as the Green Leaflet, a flimsy hand-out which detailed all performances of opera and drama for half the season at a time, and was the main channel of publicity for nearly twenty years. Everybody on the staff was expected to do his or her duty by keeping a stock of Green Leaflets always available and giving them the widest possible distribution: passing them out to friends and acquaintances, leaving them in trains, shops and buses, spreading the word. It was not only the staff who had to do it: actors and actresses who came for auditions, visiting clergymen, musicians and officials, unsuspecting *grandes dames* – all came away clutching packs of leaflets that Miss Baylis had pushed unceremoniously and irresistibly into their hands.

To the less sheltered explorers of transpontine pleasures the Vic offered few of the usual comforts and services expected by audiences for music and drama in the West End. There was sawdust on the floor, and no spirits or beer in the bars. Most of the seats were wooden benches covered with red oil-cloth, and the Refreshment Rooms at the back of the pit produced persistent cooking smells (you could get a steak for fourpence) and the sound effects of plates and crockery. The noise of the costers outside, too, could be very disconcerting. Lavatories were 'medieval' and scarce. Mice could often be seen on both sides of the stage. Rats were not unknown. The dramatic critic, William Archer, once discovered one gnawing at his boot during a performance.

Backstage it was even worse. There was a men's dressing-room (a 'longish slit') under the stage, but with a biggish cast many actors had to change in the top boxes. Most of the women dressed in the saloon or, on occasion, in the wings, while the stage staff resolutely looked the other way. Those occupying the saloon had to creep behind the audience through the auditorium, two flights down, and through a pass-door. There was no running water for anybody, not even in the two 'star' dressing-rooms. These were the 'slip' cubicles in the wings, over which Emma had clashed with the LCC. Built for quick-change artists in pre-Shakespearian days, they were so small that two actresses could not put on their dresses at the same time. The leading ladies, like the smaller fry, had to share one basin of water for the whole evening. There was one ladies' lavatory, one tap and one gas-ring. All were very close to Miss Baylis's office, which was also used as a dressing-room for the privileged.

There was virtually no wardrobe. Costumes were begged, borrowed and, when it was quite unavoidable, rented from Raynes, the costumiers, whose original shop was up the road. 'Wigs were hired for the night, and very often they did not arrive until a quarter of an hour before the curtain went up, when it was quite impossible to get them changed.'[2] Props and furniture were scarce and tatty. As an early annual report observed, on Lilian's behalf: 'it adds greatly to the cares of a management already over-burdened, to have to request artistes, before going on the stage, to fling themselves as gingerly as possible on to the furniture with which the scene is set, lest the sofa-leg, or chair-back, which has been mended so often, should prove unequal to a sudden strain, and immediately collapse'. To save money, props were often borrowed. Lilian persuaded the local undertaker, Mr Hurry, to lend her the fittings of his chapel for the chapel scene in *Much Ado*; and thereafter he was always ready to oblige with a coffin when required.

The theatre was lit by gas. Sometimes the battens, naked flames in wire cages, went out while they were being dimmed; and a man would come along with a taper to relight them, to be greeted with laughter and cheers as a kind of family joke. As the general illumination was weak, this had tactical advantages: it hid the full seediness of the scenery, and cut down distracting reflections in the bits of the old looking-glass curtain that still decorated the walls.

Scene-changes were still worked on grooves, tram-lines in the stage along which wings and flats were slid sideways on and off. This had been the standard system throughout most of the past two centuries, but had disappeared from every other London theatre by 1914. There were several stock backcloths – the cottage, the palace and the wood scene – which served incongruously enough on all manner of occasions, thudding down on heavy tumblers. If new scenes were needed imperatively, then flats and cloths were repainted; but this had to be done on the stage or at the back of the gallery, for there was no scene-dock or painting-room, and the Vic had no flies. The painting was done by apprentices and amateurs; and so, indeed, was nearly everything else.

The Vic had no rehearsal rooms, and not much time for rehearsal of any kind. Singers and actors competed for the saloon, and the stage itself. They also competed for wigs, boots, costumes and the attention of the manager. The two companies worked in virtually complete isolation from each other for twenty years, except when Miss Baylis forced some of them to fraternize at her annual garden party in her Stockwell home.

Again, the Vic had no proper foyer: nearly all the front was occupied by Pearce and Plenty. It had no real stage door: the company and staff came in through the gallery entrance. Nor did it have a box office of the conventional kind. Advance bookings were at first rare – even in 1917 half a dozen were 'an event, a thrill' – and nearly all the money was taken at the doors. If you wanted a seat during the day, you came to the 'stage door', and walked up into a stage box. Miss Baylis could often be found here, as well as the box-office manager (though not yet dignified by that title). Lilian was inclined to be impatient with intruders in the morning. On more than one occasion she snapped at customers. 'Get out! We're having a rehearsal,' she'd say. 'Come back at the proper time – two o'clock.' And, according to one of her early secretaries, 'They'd go away with their tails between their legs, saying, "Sorry, Miss!"' In the early evening, the box-office manager would move round to the front of the theatre for the main business at the doors; and sometimes a small queue would follow her, giving her a hand with her ledgers and boxes.

One problem was that the space devoted in less eccentric, less philanthropic theatres to essential theatrical services had been given up to Morley College. Most evenings about a thousand students were scattered around under the same roof, invisible though not always inaudible. Moreover, in 1914 two evenings a week were still ruled out for either opera or drama: Tuesdays for lectures and Friday for temperance meetings. So the two companies had only four nights a week in which to share the less than rudimentary services of the Hall, and to build up their audiences. They started, moreover, on a capital of less than £100; and as the Vic's prices were constitutionally pegged (for ideological reasons) at uneconomically low levels, Lilian Baylis had to dun the rich continually for alms, while spending not a penny more on anything or anybody than seemed to her absolutely necessary. It was a charity, and it depended on the charity of everyone that it employed (and that Lilian tolerated).

So much for the theatre. That is as it stayed, virtually unchanged, for a decade. As for its manager, who was forty when the war broke out, apparently she had never read a play by Shakespeare, and it is doubtful if she had seen any of the Works professionally staged. She had no experience of commercial theatre management and no private income. Who could possibly have predicted, in 1914, what this woman was to achieve in the Vic? It may well have seemed that, in the manner of so many worthy theatrical experiments, it would all be over in a few months – like the war itself.

On the credit side, Lilian Baylis was free from the need to pay dividends to backers, or rents to private landlords. She had no preconceived ideas about Shakespeare, his plays or the way that they should be presented. The building, whatever its drawbacks, had the virtues of the traditional horseshoe shape – warm and intimate, making possible a kind of high-voltage connection from stage to audience and back again: a theatre that Ellen Terry, for one, loved to play in (although she only did so for one or two special performances). The Vic was cheap to run; it was easy to reach by public transport; and it had already established an audience for opera – the popularity of which grew quickly in wartime, now that the recitals were replaced by complete works, uninterrupted by the statutory rise and fall of the curtain. But the venture into Shakespearian production was to be maintained only by desperate improvisation and exceptional good luck.

After the collapse of the Filippi project, and Miss Baylis's quick disillusionment with Shakespeare Stewart, people came to the rescue with a felicity of timing that recurred throughout Lilian's career, and that she credited to God's personal interest in the Vic. One such providential arrival was that of Estelle Stead, actress-daughter of the crusading journalist, W. T. Stead, who had died two years earlier on the 'Titanic'. A graduate of Frank Benson's company, and a keen believer in the national need for Shakespeare (and Spiritualism), she approached Miss Baylis in the spring of 1914, soon after her return from an Australian tour, drawn apparently by the limelight in which the Vic had suddenly been caught by the Filippi experiment. The two women established a personal *rapport*; and Miss Stead volunteered her aid in fund-raising, recruiting a Shakespeare company (with a leading role for herself) and a group of experts to advise Miss Baylis. She wrote innumerable letters to influential people, and although she raised only some £50 in cash, she obtained many promises of advice. With her help and money (and the help, she believed, of her dead father), a Shakespeare Committee was formed in June; and Lilian was given assurances of support, in planning the autumn programme, by leading players and actor-managers such as Frank Benson, Matheson Lang, Ben Webster and Mrs Edward Compton.

The outbreak of war in August, of course, upset everybody's plans. The theatre was, like everything else, in confusion: tours were cancelled, playhouses closed. Some actors disappeared into uniform, others were left stranded and out of work. Not surprisingly, the Vic's VIP committee evaporated. Lilian was warned to give up her plans, and the Governors were at first reluctant to carry on. Yet the chaos of the theatrical world was the Vic's opportunity, one of the ways in which the war proved to be Lilian Baylis's ally. For, although it was hard to keep together a company at the salaries she could pay, she could now hope to attract actors who might well have otherwise ignored her new venture, and she had little or no competition in the field of Shakespeare.

Having overcome the initial opposition of the Governors she set Estelle Stead to scrape a company together by hook or by crook – even (against Lilian's scruples) by advertising. On 9 September 1914 the *Era* published this small ad:

Wanted: Experienced Shakespeare Actors for special performance at Royal Victoria Hall, Waterloo-road, certain of being in London till end of October. Apply by letters only to the Manager, Box 7, 194.

Nothing was said about any plans beyond October; perhaps that was as far as Lilian would allow herself to look. But the advertisement did bring in some useful recruits, including a future director, Andrew Leigh. Matheson Lang and his wife, Hutin Britton, helped at auditions; and the Langs directed the three opening productions, *The Taming of the Shrew*, *Hamlet* and *The Merchant of Venice*. (Hutin Britton played Katherine and Portia.) Lang also lent Lilian costumes and props (what she called 'several pieces of beautiful old furniture'). 'To the end of his life,' said Sir Lewis Casson, 'he was trying to get them back.' 'I owe a tremendous lot to the Langs,' Lilian said. 'They really put my foot on the right road to Shakespeare.' The audience got their money's worth; before *The Shrew* actually started the orchestra played the 'National Airs of the Allies'; Mr James Pursaill sang 'The Lord is my Light'; the band played a bit more; and 'Pictures' followed the play. This seems to have been done as a token compliance with the licensing requirements. By breaking up the programme into items, like a music-hall bill, Lilian felt that she could permit smoking. As the war continued, this restriction was tacitly dropped, and within a year Shakespeare was presented straight, with only an orchestral overture to share the programme. (Charles Corri took over the direction of the music for the plays, and continued it for sixteen years.)

Aid from the Langs was an emergency measure. They had to go off on tour, and Lilian urgently needed more help and guidance. It was arranged that, to fill the gap, Andrew Leigh and Estelle Stead would direct *The Merry Wives of Windsor* and *As You Like It* between them; Leigh handled *Twelfth Night* on his own; Mrs Frank Benson agreed to take *She Stoops to Conquer*, Mrs Edward Compton *School for Scandal* and J. Fisher White *Julius Caesar*. But this was all patchwork improvisation: Lilian needed one person to look after the drama. Twenty years later she described how she found him:

When the Langs had to leave London he said to me, 'God alone knows who will help you now'. And I replied, 'He does know, and will guide me'. That night as the curtain fell Sir Philip Ben Greet came to me from the back of the pit. He told me how he had hurriedly left America to try and do war work in England but had had nothing offered him – was there any way in which he could serve me? He started rehearsing *The Tempest* almost immediately and gave me his constant and unselfish support for four years . . .[3]

According to some stories it was Estelle Stead who was responsible for Ben Greet's arrival; she 'seized' on him, in Dame Sybil's words. But whether she or the Almighty was the immediate cause, it was an event of considerable significance. For just as Charles Corri established opera at the Vic, under Lilian's supervision, so Ben Greet established Shakespeare.

When he came to the Vic in 1914, Greet was already fifty-six, with thirty-five years experience of many kinds of stages, but it was his first visit to the New Cut. Although an ardent playgoer from boyhood, he had been forbidden to attend the Vic by an otherwise broad-minded father; and he obeyed the veto (with, no doubt, little temptation to break it) until the night that he approached Miss Baylis. Trained in the old stock companies – he claimed that he had to play nineteen roles in his first week as an actor – he became a touring manager who at one time had twenty-five companies on the road, playing small provincial dates. He worked with William Poel on experiments in near-Elizabethan production, and in presenting *Everyman*; he ran a school of acting in Bedford Street; he was a pioneer of professional open-air theatre, and (in 1886) inaugurated the Open Air Theatre in Regents Park; for two years he had presented Shakespeare to audiences of LCC schoolchildren at the invitation of the Board of Education; and he had toured with a Shakespearian company throughout America.[4]

The spiritual qualifications of B.G. – as he was usually called – were, for Miss Baylis, more impressive. Like her, he was a devoted Anglican – 'very High Church – it was his whole life', says Dame Sybil. He was a pillar of the Actors' Church Union, and of the Church and Stage Guild. B.G. viewed Shakespeare as a moral oracle who helps us all to achieve 'serenity of mind' and 'the way of gentleness and mercy' and whose works must therefore be brought to the widest possible audience. In Dame Sybil's words, Shakespeare was 'the nearest approach to Almighty God that B.G. knew'. (In the nursing home where he died, many years later, he asked the doctor to change his nurse, because the one in attendance didn't know a line of the Bard.) But if he revered Shakespeare, it was not as someone supernatural and remote. As Margaret Webster put it, 'Shakespeare, to him, was bread, breathing and a cup of tea'. He believed in simplicity – and that suited Lilian Baylis's budget very well.

B.G. was tall and sturdy, with a shock of white hair, deep blue eyes, and a cherubic face, which frequently went scarlet with violent rages. He got angry when he couldn't remember his lines, which happened frequently; he would stuff them up his sleeves, or into his hat, or pin them behind a property tree, but he would still drop sections of speeches, and rhubarb his way through the gap. He got angry when he saw (or imagined) that a property had been moved. In the middle of a speech he would say, quite audibly to the audience. '*That* bloody thing should be *there*' – transferring it to the place in which he expected to see it – or, 'I'll bloody *kill* him (meaning the ASM) when I get off. As I was saying . . .' He was a belligerent, explosive man; and it was not long before he was at war with Lilian. They had terrible rows, forgave each other and then did battle royal again. Both were shrewd enough to realize that they couldn't do without each other, at that time. His value to her is plain. He knew about Shakespeare – as much as, if not more than, anybody in the theatre. He knew about actors: he had trained scores of them, and he brought a number to the Vic. He knew about management and production on the cheap, having to survive one disaster after another and come up smiling – or fighting. He knew about opera – enough, at least, to help in productions. He knew about audiences. As he never demanded – indeed, never encouraged – novel readings or original business, and as most of the actors were used to working together, the plays could be staged in rapid succession with little rehearsal – a necessity at the Vic. And he did it all free – for the first year, at least. Later he took 'expenses'.

That is why Lilian Baylis needed Ben Greet. And why did he stay? Partly because it was his 'war work': he was an old-fashioned patriot. Also, perhaps, because he liked power, even when Miss Baylis had the last word. Although he had, in his time, made a lot of money out of the theatre, he usually lost it quite rapidly; he was financially inept, and he liked to be rid of economic detail. He liked to keep a group of his people together. He grew to like the Old Vic. And he loved Shakespeare's plays. Where else in London could he have hoped to stage so many of them, without the financial risks of management?

It was through B.G., soon after he came to the Vic, that the theatre acquired an actress who was to become one of its wartime pillars, Sybil Thorndike. She was then thirty-two, had been on the stage for ten years, but had never been to the Vic and had never heard of Lilian Baylis, although there were tenuous connections – Lilian had been to her father's church, and her husband's sister, Elizabeth Casson, had been trained as a rent-collector for Octavia

Hill. Ben Greet, with whom she had trained, toured and suffered, wrote to her in 1914:

There's a strange woman running a theatre in the Waterloo Road, you'd find her exciting, Syb, because you're as mad as she is. I'm doing some shows for her with Estelle Stead, so come and join us. *Comedy of Errors* week after next – you play Adriana – I've told them you'd be wonderful, though I don't think you'd really be very good . . . still, you'll like Lilian Baylis, she's got ideals, and don't go telling her you've not played the part before because she says she wants the best and she's going to get it.[5]

So that October Sybil Thorndike went, for the first time, to the Old Vic and met Miss Baylis.

I heard a voice – roughened – a bit cockney – warm, calling out, 'Bob come here, you old devil, I won't have all this muck on my stage' . . . Then she spied me, and I was hailed in friendly fashion. Funny, I don't know what she said to me first, as I was a bit taken aback by the coming-on sweep of her, but I remember, 'Well, you won't get much pay, but you like the work, don't you, and if your husband's in the army you'd better be doing decent work, too – good for you *and* the children'. Then, 'Your father's a priest, isn't he? Church and stage – same thing – should be!'[6]

That often-quoted recollection by Dame Sybil, written over twenty years later, gives a vivid glimpse of the essence of Lilian Baylis – including the summary explanation of the low pay (then ten shillings a performance) echoed in scores of later engagements. It was 'decent work', which ought to be done; it was good for you to do it; and you enjoyed doing it anyway – so why expect to be paid for it? Especially if you shared Lilian's belief that it was God's work, as well as war work. With what went on across the river in the West End she had little concern. Although she was glad when her favourites in the company, like Sybil Thorndike, later did well there, it was not *that* kind of stage that she was thinking of when she said, 'Church and stage – same thing – should be!' It was *her* kind of stage that she meant, even though she'd barely started to use it for Shakespeare.

An even more immediate impression of Lilian was given on the spot by Dame Sybil in a letter to her brother, Russell Thorndike, then on wartime service in Egypt:

She's an absolute scream. You remember, Russell, that we always thought Miss Horniman the oddest person we had ever worked for in the theatre, and so she was. But now, Miss Baylis is much odder, she has the oddest criticisms, too, and uses old-fashioned slang – words like 'bounders' and 'mucky' . . . I rather like her attitude. She treats Shakespeare as a person of the theatre. I'm sure Shakespeare is roaring with laughter at her, especially when B.G. gets all Holy-bobey about him! I'll tell you more about her later, because I simply adore her. She runs the place exactly like we've seen people organize parish rooms. She looks like a church worker, and is one.[7]

Lilian was, said Dame Sybil, 'the most original person I've ever met. Simply dying to play her. She'd be a gorgeous part. She's not a bit like a theatrical manager. Much too keen on "the People", and really the whole thing promises to be great fun. I shall love working for her, as she's one of those people who just make you do things.' Dame Sybil became a close friend and life-long champion of Lilian Baylis, in spite of the ruthless way in which Lilian drove her in those wartime years. A few days after Dame Sybil's third child, Ann Casson, was born, Lilian arrived in her bedroom and told her she must start rehearsing in *Hamlet*.

'You must give me a little time,' said Miss Thorndike.

'I can't put it off any more,' Miss Baylis insisted.

'Ann was late coming.'

'That was her fault, not mine.'

Lilian could be tough, even implacable; but, says Dame Sybil, 'I took it from her because it was all for the Old Vic, never for herself'. The theatre came first.

The first season of combined opera and Shakespeare at the Vic ran from October 1914 until the end of April 1915. In quantity, the programme is staggering. Sixteen operas and sixteen plays were staged in less than thirty weeks. Taking the number of works alone, this represents in contemporary terms the repertoire of two separate theatres over some three seasons each, at a cost to the state of many millions. The operas performed were as follows: *Carmen, The Daughter of the Regiment, Lohengrin, Faust, Traviata, Trovatore, Rigoletto, Lucia di Lammermoor, Pagliacci, Cavalleria Rusticana, Martha, Fra Diavolo, The Lily of Killarney, Maritana, The Bohemian Girl* and *Don Giovanni*, which was staged at the Vic for the first time in January. This innovation was made possible by Charles Manners of the Moody-Manners company, who lent his scores to Corri and gave his advice to Lilian (a fellow-luminary of the Actors' Church Union). The plays were: *The Taming of the Shrew, Hamlet, The Merchant of Venice, The Tempest, Merry Wives of*

Windsor, Comedy of Errors, Twelfth Night, A Midsummer Night's Dream, Macbeth, As You Like It, A Winter's Tale, Othello, Julius Caesar and, in addition, three non-Shakespearian offerings: *She Stoops to Conquer, The School for Scandal* and *King René's Daughter*. The only play to get more than ten performances was *The Tempest* (*Othello* was given twice only); and the most successful operas were *Carmen* and *Faust*, with eight performances each. At the end of the season, in April, Lilian and B.G. ambitiously presented 'Shakespeare's Birthday Festival', which they had confidently announced the previous December. This was in response to pressure from the London Shakespeare League, which B.G. had helped to found, and which for some years had lobbied managers to stage a Shakespeare play every year on his putative birthday. Tree had run a 'festival' of six Shakespeare plays at Easter; but then Tree staged only thirteen of the Works in eighteen years.

The Vic 'festival' occupied a week. Three plays – *Hamlet, Taming of the Shrew* and *Macbeth* – were given twice daily on Monday, Wednesday *and* Friday (a significant pointer), and, on the Birthday itself, a Special Matinée included such distinguished visiting artists as Viola Tree, Lilian Braithwaite and Henry Ainley (in a scene from *Twelfth Night*); H. B. Irving (a soliloquy from *Hamlet*); Basil Gill, Lyn Harding, Constance Collier and Eva Le Gallienne (two scenes from *Julius Caesar*); and Lena Ashwell, reciting 'Love Lyrics'. In addition, what was described as 'the "Vic" Shakespeare Co.' acted scenes from *Macbeth* and *The Shrew*; Gervase Elwes sang three of Roger Quilter's songs, accompanied by the composer; the Dolmetsch family gave a recital; Mrs Henry Wordsworth's girls performed the dances from *A Midsummer Night's Dream*. The afternoon opened with lantern-slides showing scenes at Stratford and Vic prints and playbills, and it ended with the company reciting 'The King's Prayer', from *Ralph Roister Doister*, a B.G. favourite which now came into its own as a patriotic set-piece. This Birthday Matinée was repeated the following April and every April after that with a similar starry mixture, becoming one of the *specialités de la maison* which helped to establish the Vic's reputation. Among the most illustrious guest artists on later occasions was Ellen Terry, for whom Lilian nursed a deep admiration and affection.

Another Vic institution was also introduced that April: *Everyman*, the medieval morality play revived by William Poel in 1901 with immediate success, and later toured by Ben Greet through the provinces and in the USA. Following the Poel tradition of distaff casting, Sybil Thorndike played Everyman in 1915. It was staged on Tuesday evenings in Lent and during Holy Week, preceded by a recital of English music from the sixteenth and seventeenth centuries. *Everyman* made a deep and abiding impression on Lilian Baylis. According to Sybil Thorndike it 'always moved' her, and it was 'one of the few plays she watched through from start to finish', an endurance test that she rarely survived in Shakespeare.

I remember her once as I stood in the wings watching Death who was just about to summon me to go on my last journey and me feeling very exalted and prepared – she tweaked my coat and said, 'Doesn't Death look a joke – that Death always makes me laugh' . . .[8]

That reaction reminded Dame Sybil of a pre-war performance of *Everyman* given by the Greet company in Santa Barbara, California, when a group of monks was allowed to attend. To the consternation of the cast they burst into laughter at the moment of Death's entrance; but a priest explained to the company later that the monks' mental attitude was that of medieval Catholics, who knew that death was not to be taken seriously. Just like Lilian; or so Dame Sybil believed.

The threat of death to the Vic, however, was a different matter, and it naturally preoccupied the manager. On the programmes in April she printed the following appeal *twice*, in blue and red type:

The management request the Members of the Audience who really appreciate the work here and believe it worthy of support to mention it to their friends and help to make it known in every possible way. To ensure the success of the Season commencing in September, and to provide a small Resident Company of Actors and Singers we ask for at least 500 lovers of Shakespeare and 500 lovers of Opera to purchase a guinea book of 25 Stall Tickets, available any time from October to May.

That kind of appeal was to become a familiar ingredient of the programme for the next twenty years.

It was not the opera that was in trouble: the audience for that was growing. The war was not to blame: on the contrary, war was good for business – but not, at first, for Shakespeare business. Opera had been entrenched at the Vic for over twenty years. It was to take more than a year to mobilize a comparable public for Shakespearian drama. The first time that *Hamlet* was staged, there was less than £2 in the house. Dame Sybil remembers an evening which began with 'about five people in the pit and three boys and an orange in the gallery', though this had swelled to a score by the end of the evening. On many evenings it scarcely seemed worth while to give a performance at all; but to Miss Baylis it was always worth while. Of course, the show had to go on. It was *her* show – whatever that old devil B.G. might say. As she admitted in an article in the *Shakespeare League Journal* after the first season, 'we have not yet induced many of our opera gallery to come to Shakespeare'. But she trumpeted, 'It is our glory that we play to the gallery, and we have a preference for a full gallery for the purpose . . . We rejoice more over the presence of one rough lad who has never heard of Shakespeare, than over the attendance of half a dozen Shakespeare students.' After all, as she explained, she was 'trying to bring Shakespeare home to the less educated classes', because it was good for them. And even if money was desperately scarce, Lilian drew on other sources of support: 'we should like to place on record our conviction that we could not have carried our work through either last season or this season without the aid of prayer'.

Prayer apart, the opera takings helped to keep the Shakespeare going – a fact of which Lilian frequently reminded Ben Greet, to his fury, in moments of divergence. Although she would not spend money on advertising, the word slowly spread around London. Critics came increasingly, from the second season onwards, and within a year a new public began to filter into the Vic on Shakespeare nights. The Birthday Matinée helped to make the new venture known, and B.G. and Lilian lobbied leading actors to harangue the opera audience into supporting the plays. People slowly discovered that they had to go to the Waterloo Road if they wanted to see Shakespeare's plays – there was nowhere else in London, where serious drama of any kind had virtually disappeared in wartime. Commercial managers believed they gave the public the featherweight relaxation it wanted; and they could scarcely be said to have been proved wrong, as far as the majority was concerned. But a growing minority wanted to see Shakespeare – in search of a deeper escapism, perhaps, than the trivia of the West End, and maybe partly, as Professor Dent suggested, because of 'the subconscious craving for that moral inspiration that perhaps Shakespeare alone of all men could give' at such a time.[9] It was, in fact, just the right time for the Vic to start on Shakespeare, however hard it might be to meet the bills.

What probably ensured Shakespeare's survival at the Vic for a second season more practically than any other single factor – except Lilian Baylis's conviction that it was God's will – was the new audiences of London schoolchildren. One of the last things that Emma Cons said to her niece before she died was, 'The Vic must help poor children'. Until the outbreak of war that help was limited, as in the past, to Christmas parties and summer outings. (Lilian was obliged to drop the afternoon games on the stage for the Surrey Lodge children.) But in 1914 the stage began to offer the young a different kind of diversion. 'It always seems rather miraculous to me', Lilian wrote in 1926, 'that within eighteen months after Emma Cons's death thousands of schoolchildren were listening at the Vic to a Shakespeare matinée.'[10] The miracle was partly achieved by the Rev. Stewart Headlam (1847–1924), a Fabian parson in the Christian Socialist tradition, and, like Emma Cons, a disciple of F. D. Maurice: indeed, his leading disciple in the Church, where he was regarded as a dangerous radical.

Headlam, who founded the Church and Stage Guild in 1879, played a significant role in reducing anti-theatrical prejudice, and both Henry Irving and Ben Greet avowed that the profession owed him a great debt. (Lilian's mother was on the first council of the Guild, and Lilian's father was a chorister at Headlam's wedding.) He was an early advocate of the ballet (long before it became intellectually chic), an enthusiasm for which he was dubbed 'the dancing parson'; and he believed in the Poel approach to Shakespearian staging (for ten years he was president of the London Shakespeare League). As a member of the London School Board from 1889 to 1904 he pioneered the introduction to schools of swimming, pianos, dinners for needy children and, in 1899, 'Shakespeare instruction', helped by his old friend Ben Greet, an original member of the Guild. Under Headlam's sponsorship, Greet's company began in 1902 to give performances to evening-school students, and, later, to schoolchildren. But it was apparently Lilian Baylis who – while Greet was still in the USA in the early summer of 1914 – revived Headlam's idea of Shakespearian Matinees for schools in the theatres. Headlam (now on the LCC Education Board) lent his support. Through his influence the Vic programmes were advertised in the LCC Gazette; and during the war thousands of children every month made their first acquaintance with Shakespeare at the Vic. As many as 4,000 saw *As You Like It* in a week. The actors were less jubilant than Lilian and B.G. about the children: 'how intensely we disliked them – and their fidgets,' said Sybil Thorndike, *and* the buns and sweets they consumed so noisily. But these matinées rapidly spread in popularity and gave a taste for Shakespeare to a new generation of Londoners. (Among them was Malcolm Muggeridge, who came all the way from Croydon, and says in his autobiography that he enjoyed every minute of the performances.)

The Vic not only hit on the right time to embark on the Works, it found the right way to stage them. Audiences were ready for the simplicity and relative speed of Ben Greet's plain productions, after the opulence of the Irving–Tree spectacular style; and the work of Granville-Barker had helped to disseminate the ideas of Poel, Craig and other advocates of Shakespearian reform. Ben Greet was no reformer. He used the traditional bowdlerized and censored versions, and, for all his reverence of Shakespeare, he cut heavily for reasons of length as well as *pudeur* – more, indeed, than he 'quite approved of' (as he explained in a programme note), but Lilian insisted that her people must be out of the theatre by 10.30 at the latest. In any case, B.G. claimed it was impossible to present the complete text in a theatre like the Vic. He tried 'to make the plays act as closely and rapidly as possible . . . with changes of scenery to make them entertaining and interesting to ordinary audiences. The intellectual ones and the youngsters who study the plays can supply with their knowledge the omitted scenes.' Miss Baylis required him to put on a different play every week, on no more than a couple of pounds for production expenses; and to stage them for young, unsophisticated audiences.

The company played not only to schoolchildren at matinées, but went out to the Northern Polytechnic in Holloway Road; to an East End 'settlement', Oxford House; and to a converted swimming bath in Bethnal Green, where the audience was predominantly Jewish – for Sybil Thorndike, looking back in 1938, 'the most vivid and intelligent audience I've ever played to'. Lilian Baylis was enthusiastic, too.

I do like to see the Jews coming, don't you dear? Even if they aren't Christians, it must do them good, but I wish we didn't have to give them *The Merchant of Venice*, the Christians all behave so badly.[11]

Working for such a wide-potential public, and under such handicaps as those imposed by backstage conditions at the Vic, it was just as well that B.G. had 'no time for fancy theories, farfetched analogies, scholarly discussions or gimmickry'. If much of what he did fitted new 'fancy' theories in the air, it was for empirical economic reasons.

He stripped his stages because he couldn't afford to do otherwise . . . He dressed many of his plays Elizabethan because it was simpler and the costumes would fit several different shows. He didn't fuss about design, but took what God or the local authorities provided . . . He played himself, and directed his actors, in a sort of Elizabethan manner of his own, broadly, lustily, often crudely, but at least without affectations. His actors were expected to do one thing and one thing only – to reach their listeners, to make contact and hold it. Sometimes they did it by fair means and sometimes by foul, but they did it; and they did it with and through the lines alone. Nobody was supposed to intervene between the author and the audience . . .[12]

That was just the right approach for Miss Baylis and her people, and so was B.G.'s readiness for chaos and calamity. To quote Margaret Webster again:

He had done the plays so often, in so many extraordinary ways and places, that I don't think he took any of it seriously any more. In the face of some particularly fearful or ludicrous happening, his eyes would twinkle with enjoyment. Anything short of total disaster simply passed him by . . .[13]

According to Robert Atkins, 'his main exhortations were "Get on with it!" and "I want sincerity".' Yet, although he could muster no higher praise than 'Not too bad', there were moments when 'he would grasp your coat and whisper affectionately a word or two that opened a heaven of invention'.[14]

By the 1915–16 season, Shakespeare had gained another night. Those temperance Fridays, so dear to Emma Cons's heart, were surrendered to the drama with some reluctance by Lilian, 'to enable us to get a permanent company'. As a compromise with her family conscience, and as a gesture to Emmie, she proposed to call these Fridays 'Evening School Nights', to demonstrate that it was not mere art but education in which she was engaged; but she was talked out of using such a label. For the moment, Tuesdays were still devoted to 'Illustrated Lectures for Thinking Men and Women, by the leading Scientists, Travellers and Public Men'. Yet very soon Lilian had to sacrifice another of Emmie's principles by rationing these lectures to two a month in order to let the opera company rehearse on stage once a fortnight.

The new policy won praise if not profits. Actor-managers who had told Lilian it was hopeless paid public tribute to her survival. By the spring of 1916, when Lilian (urged by B.G. and Stewart Headlam) mounted a Tercentenary Festival to mark the 300th anniversary of Shakespeare's death, the critic of the *Athenaeum* could say of the Vic that, although it lacked 'the glitter of fine scenery and the attendance of the fashionable', it had 'done more to educate by the enjoyment and understanding of Shakespeare's plays than its more gaudy competitor'. Some weeks later, when Lilian sent a company to Stratford-upon-Avon for the annual festival, to stand in for Frank Benson (at his suggestion), *The Times* observed that 'excellent work for Shakespeare and England' was being done at the Royal Victoria Hall, where ' "Shakespeare for twopence" has for some years been the symbol of a fine achievement'. Discussing the 'Royal Victoria Theatre Company of Shakespearian Players' in advance of their visit, a writer in the *Stratford-upon-Avon Herald* said: 'What was at first an avowed experiment has now ripened into a confirmed success'.

In the event, the company was given a mixed reception at Stratford. A local critic wrote with such asperity about some of the performances that B.G. and others publicly rebuked him, and the row rumbled on for weeks. And there were backstage battles over, for instance, the fact that Lilian asked Sybil Thorndike to play Lady Macbeth, while B.G.'s choice was Nancy Price. The actresses shared the role amicably, but Lilian and B.G. refused to talk to each other. That did not influence the box office. At least one production – *Henry VIII*, with Lilian Braithwaite as guest-star – was a big success; and though praise often went no further than such epithets as 'well-considered' and 'student-like', allowances were made for the fact that twelve productions had to be prepared in two months. 'Handicapped as the company was, the only thing for surprise is that it was able to do so much with such a modicum of pleasure,' said the *Stratford-upon-Avon Herald*, after it was all over. The 1916 invitation was not repeated, but it showed how quickly Lilian's venture had become known and respected.

It was in 1916 that *Hamlet* in its entirety – a theatrical rarity which turned out to be a box-office hit – was first staged at the Vic; and that Handel's *Elijah* was adapted, with the help of Charles Manners. With *Everyman*, this was for some years Lilian's favourite item in the repertoire, and it took a place in her religious calendar – in Lent. In 1916, too, the words 'The Old Vic' first appeared on the bills of 'The People's Opera, Play and Lecture House', as Lilian now called it. 'We are asked on all sides to call the Vic its old title of Theatre, as Hall is harmful to the work,' she wrote in August to the City Parochial Foundation; but the name was only used on the programmes once, as a sub-title, for the Shakespeare

Tercentenary performance that year. It did not appear regularly and officially until the 1918–19 season, and then for the plays only – not for the opera programmes. Yet, oddly enough, the name had been displayed on a sign outside the theatre, under the clock, probably since 1910.

Financially, it was often touch and go in these years. Early in 1916 the LCC, understandably alarmed by the transformation of the Hall into a theatre, demanded extensive structural alterations, in order to improve the ventilation of the stage, construct new means of escape in case of fire from both stage and dressing-rooms, and generally improve the safety of the building. Lilian replied, in the Cons tradition, by warning the LCC that the Vic might have to close in 1917, as it might not be able to raise the money for such reconstruction. After negotiations by post and in person, the Vic was reprieved, for the time being, on condition that the gallery capacity was reduced to 500; that a competent fireman was always on the stage while the public was in the building; and that 'the scenery, properties, dress baskets, etc. be reduced to a minimum', a condition with which Miss Baylis was only too happy to agree.

So far, so good. But after only a few weeks of the 1917–18 season the theatre lost over £600, because of the slump in takings caused by German air raids. 'I was just dotty as to how to carry on,' she wrote in a letter the following year. 'I wanted the weekly cheque for £275 and had only £150 in the bank.' Lilian is said to have considered giving up Shakespeare and bringing back films, in order to save the Vic from disaster. Perhaps she did; and if so, no doubt B.G. did his best to talk her out of such defeatism; but a more material fact was a subsidiary grant of £500 from the City Parochial Foundation which helped to keep the theatre open. 'A wonderful answer to prayer, I call it', said Lilian. She now gave *more* performances of both opera and Shakespeare. They took alternate Saturday matinées, and by 1918 there were frequent Thursday matinées, too.

In spite of Ben Greet's network of connections, casting grew increasingly difficult, because of the accelerated drain of men into uniform. The Vic offered unusual opportunities to get instant Shakespearian experience if you were unfit for service, waiting to go or invalided out. An actor like Henry Kendall, for instance, had only been in the profession for a year when he joined the company in 1915, and he had never played in Shakespeare; but he had attended B.G.'s drama school for a couple of terms, and he was *needed*. So he was engaged as Paris in *Romeo and Juliet*, and played thirty parts in nine months (including Laertes, Florizel and Claudio – usually with no more than five rehearsals) before disappearing into uniform for three years. But, as the slaughter went on, even men who had first been turned down by the army were demanded for service – including two props of the company, Andrew Leigh and Robert Atkins – and, in Russell Thorndike's words, 'There were left only the old crocks or men discharged as crocks from which to choose. No, not to choose – but to beg to receive a bad salary, and to work hard.'

To get into the company in those days was not difficult. Winifred Oughton, for instance, was a drama student who went for an audition; and, a few weeks later, received a postcard from Lilian saying, *tout court*, 'Walk on tonight in *The Merchant of Venice*'. She found her way backstage, where she'd never been before, and waited in the semi-darkness until she saw a young man walking across the stage. When he asked her what she wanted, she showed him her postcard:

He shrugged his shoulders, and said, 'Oh, she *would*. You'd better go to Raynes and find a costume.' So I went to Raynes, which was just down the road, and they said, 'What are you going to be?' 'I don't know,' I said, feeling pretty silly. 'Well,' they said. 'You'd better be in a crowd of Venetians in the trial scene.' I chose something that looked Venetian, and I went back to the Old Vic. There was nobody there to tell me what to do. Quite inadvertently I changed in the leading ladies' dressing-room, but there was only one of them there, and she was awfully polite. Then Miss Baylis came in, and she just said. 'Turn around, let's see'. She said it would do. And I was installed at the Old Vic.

She was paid 25s. a week the first season, plus a bonus of 7s. 6d. at the end, from Miss Baylis's own purse – 'for shoe-leather, dear', £2 the second and £2 15s. the third – by which time she was a leading lady. Miss Oughton played about a hundred parts, over seventy of them men. Inevitably, women *had* to play male roles – young and old. 'It will do them good', said B.G., 'to put on beards and play some of those lovely parts.' When Miss Baylis approached Sybil Thorndike about this extension of her range, she said: 'You won't mind, dear, will you? Because, after all, there should be no sex in acting – you ought to be able to understand men as well as women.' According to Dame Sybil, none of them minded. 'I frankly loved it; I've always been jealous of the men in Shakespeare. For every good woman's part there are ten good men's.'

One actress who did mind was immediately dispatched by B.G.

and Lilian. 'Oh what a pity,' B.G. said to her. 'Your objection bars you from being a real Shakespearian leading lady. You rule out Rosalind, Viola, Julia, Imogen, Portia, Nerissa and Jessica, any of which parts you might have played this season. You never know. What a pity.'

And Miss Baylis clinched it, characteristically. 'We don't want people here who only think of themselves. We want people who want to help the Vic.'[15]

By 1918 male impersonation, on a wide scale, was another convention that the audience was prepared to accept at 'The Home of Shakespeare' (although it was an inversion of Shakespearian practice). In *Henry V*, for instance, the following roles were all played by women: the Dukes of Bedford, Gloucester and Westmoreland, Lord Scroop, Sir Thomas Grey, Sir Thomas Erpingham, the Dauphin, the English Herald, Orleans, Mountjoy, the Constable of France, the French Ambassador – and Chorus. For actresses the licensed sex-reversals of the New Cut offered rare technical opportunities.

About this time Lilian began to be known by the audience, largely as a result of the speeches she made to them. These began during the German air raids. Ben Greet used to carry out the job of breaking the news to the audience as soon as news of a raid was received; but one night he made his announcement as John of Gaunt on the point of death, in 'a rather ghastly make-up' which (said Lilian) 'so alarmed members of the audience that they fainted'. After that she took it upon herself to deliver the warnings. 'It was my first effort at speechmaking.' And although it was some years before she learned to do it well, she seems to have enjoyed the exercise. Henry Kendall recalled her speech as going something like this: 'Now boys and girls, we're not going to let Kaiser Bill interfere with the Vic, and so we shall carry on with this beautiful play, and if you up there on the top shelf would feel any safer you can come down and sit in the stalls – and I won't charge you any extra.'[16] Or, more brusquely, she would bark: 'Will all those who wish to leave please do so at once? *We* are carrying on.' She gave the company no option. Once, when bombs began to drop during an opera rehearsal, everyone on stage stopped and took shelter in the wings, until Miss Baylis appeared in a blazing temper. First, she had been made to stay in the Tube against her will. Now, she discovered that her company had deserted their posts. 'I'm ashamed of you all,' she shouted at them. 'If you have to be killed, at least die at your job.' A guilty witness reported that 'we all went back to work feeling that somehow we had failed'. One evening a raid began when Sybil Thorndike was on her way to play in *Richard II*. As she came out of the Tube at Waterloo she was stopped by a policeman.

'I can't help the raid,' I cried, clinging to his brass buttons. 'The curtain's up at the Old Vic, and I shan't be on for my entrance.'

'Old Vic, is it,' he said. 'Oh, I know Miss Baylis; yes, you're right,' and a lull coming in the bomb sounds, he gave me a push into Waterloo Road with a: 'Now run for your life, and if you're killed, don't blame me – blame Her.'

I got to the pit door – first door I reached – and found Lilian in a fume and fret.

'Why on earth weren't you in before this?'

'A raid,' I said. 'Everything underground at Waterloo – everything impossible.'

'Raid,' she snorted. 'What's a raid when my curtain's up?'[17]

The fact that the Vic played through the raids helped to give it an aura of special patriotism. On the first night of *King John*, in September 1917, the nine-year-old Agnes Carter, playing Prince Arthur, and Ben Greet, as Hubert, 'went through their scenes without turning a hair'; and the lines at the end

> This England never did, nor never shall
> Lie at the proud foot of a conqueror

brought the house down. These lines were put up above the proscenium arch for the rest of the war. A sign of the status so rapidly acquired by the Vic was that it was here – in February, 1918 – that a roll of honour was erected (somewhat prematurely) with the names of those musicians, actors and writers who had died in wartime service. The roll was placed above the stage door and unveiled by the Bishop of Southwark. Lewis Casson read out the 142 names. And every year thereafter a ceremony of remembrance was held on the eve of Armistice Day, after the performance, at which the Last Post was sounded, a hymn was sung, a wreath was laid and, later, a maroon was fired (or rather misfired) by the master-carpenter.

From giving warnings about raids, Lilian progressed to delivering appeals for support. She caught the taste for speechmaking from the stage, and relished the feeling it gave her of direct contact with her people. Week after week she appeared in front of the curtain, pleading for money, begging for more customers, especially on Monday nights. She usually ended with the slogan: 'And look here, you bounders. Monday nights have got to be better.' This is the kind of speech she made at the end of a season, quoted by Russell Thorndike:

I suppose you want to know something of what we are going to do when we re-open. Well, I can't tell you, because I don't know myself, except that unless Monday nights, which continue to be so mucky, get better, we may have to close down, and I don't intend to, so you must all of you pray that they get better. I shall try to get some more good actors cheap, as a lot of the present ones are going. I don't know whether you'll be interested or not to hear that Russell is staying on, as he wants to play Hamlet. He was Matheson Lang's understudy in the part, and played it in South Africa, so he shouldn't be too bad. I know what you're all thinking. That his legs will look funny in black tights. Well, you may laugh, but do you know I rather like Russell's legs. Perhaps I shouldn't have said that as I'm not married.[18]

Miss Baylis ended this speech by 'asking for the prayers of the audience in order that she might be given grace to pull together with Ben Greet for another season'. She knew that the audience would be 'convulsed' by her speeches, said Russell Thorndike, but she didn't care: 'she just told them what she thought, without preparation'. Being laughed at didn't seem to disturb her (though laughing at the Old Vic could bring down thunderbolts). She would talk to them as if they were all her personal friends, and bully them as if they were a class of students who had been misbehaving.

As we have seen, several observers of the Vic audience in the days of Emma Cons – including Bernard Shaw – had been struck by its responsiveness to opera. A critic of *Musical Opinion*, quoted in the annual report of 1911–12, focusing on the gallery, expressed his 'astonishment at finding these people present, as they mostly look like people to whom a serious work of art would not appeal . . . I have never seen a more attentive and appreciative lot of people.' On a Saturday night in the 1920s, according to Sumner Austin, you could feel the excitement in the air before the curtain rose. There was such enthusiasm that sometimes a singer couldn't finish an aria. The audience would finish it for him, then burst into applause. As the Shakespeare habit grew, this attentive and appreciative response extended to the Works; so that dozens of voices from the house could (and did) prompt an actor who dried (as not a few, not infrequently, did) in Shakespeare.

During her brief visit to the Vic Rosina Filippi, as we have also seen, was struck by the warmth of the *rapport* between the auditorium and the stage; and Lilian Baylis fermented and maintained this warmth in an atmosphere of community that distinguished the Vic in the first decade of its Shakespearian seasons. She established fixed points in the calendar when both the company and the audience participated in family rituals, from which, indeed, there was no escape. On the first night of the season Lilian made a speech brusquely introducing new members of the company, exhorting the audience to bring their friends (and come on Mondays), invoking (as the years went by) the hardships of the past – notably, these wartime austerities. There was 'an embarrassment of bouquets'. Returning favourites were greeted with applause, whether they were on the stage or in the audience. At Christmas there were parties in the theatre – for the company, for old people and for poor children in the area, served with toys, buns and lemonade by volunteers. On Twelfth Night, after the performance, the actors made a processional walk right around the auditorium and back to the stage; a special cake was then cut by Lilian, and slices were handed out to the audience, with cups of lemonade. Later, more intimately, there was the Old Vic Circle (started in 1919) and its Reunion – 'an evening of speeches, songs, recitations and sketches, of ices and lemonade; an evening such as only Miss Baylis, waving her magic wand, could command and carry out successfully'. There was the annual performance of *Everyman* in Lent; and the annual performance of a play by the Old Vic students (who, till the late 1920s, at least, gained most of their training by serving as unpaid extras, stand-ins and small-part players). In April there was the annual Birthday Matinée. From the 1920s onwards there was the Magazine, the Association (started in 1923) and the annual Costume Ball. And the consummation was the last night of the season, when Lilian made her 'hands-across-the footlights speech on the rippingness of camaraderie, the wonderfulness of Shakespeare, the never-to-be-forgotten awfulness of acting during air raids and the need of every sixpence you can spare to further the latest project for spreading the gospel of the Immortal Bard'. More specifically, she announced the names of those who were not coming back and some of the new recruits. Many speeches were made. Many presents were given by members of the audience to members of the companies and staff, notably to Miss Baylis: cigarettes, chocolates, books, jewellery, home-knitted socks and sweaters, a laurel wreath, flowers in profusion. 'Trestle tables stretching the whole width of the stage were piled high with little parcels wrapped in tissue paper, with cards saying "To my favourite Guildenstern" or "Shall never forget your Third Witch".[19] Everybody in the team mustered on the stage, and finally they all linked hands and sang 'Auld Lang Syne' and 'God Save the King', in which the audience lustily joined. In addition to encouraging these ritual occasions, Lilian frequently talked to the audience around the pit and in the gallery, for which she retained a particular affection; and she was known to be – and was frequently seen to be – in her box at the side of the stage.

The wartime Shakespeare programmes helped to improve communication between the audience and the stage, and extend the 'family' feeling. They carried simple explanatory notes on each play, usually written by Ben Greet. He often indicated some of the production problems. Of *Richard III* he wrote, 'We have endeavoured to arrange thirteen scenes as simple settings to avoid as many delays as possible, but our appliances are almost 100 years old, and our friends are asked to be forbearing'; and of *The Merchant of Venice*, 'we do ask our audience to imagine that some of our scenes are in Venice, as we do not at present possess more correct stage settings'. And he always tried to stress the relevance of the plays to contemporary experience. Of *Othello*, he wrote, 'This play could be acted in today's khaki . . . Every scene of it is a human sermon – an epic of common life'; and of *Macbeth*, 'How nearly some of the exploits of the present time assimilate with those of this 1,000-years-old history; lessons to all, who will take them in; both in love of country and love of home; and the reverse.'

In the 1917–18 season these brief commentaries developed into 'Victorian Notes', keeping the audience in touch with news about plays and people – but only the Shakespeare audience: the Notes did not appear on the opera programme. Out of these Notes emerged the *Old Vic Magazine* in 1920.

There were competitions for the audience, too. Prizes were offered for the best essay by a child on the plays in general (by Lady Frederick Cavendish); to 'the student who notices the most errors in the text made by the Actors' (by Ben Greet); and for an essay on Shakespeare's Women (by Miss Baylis). Quotations were flashed on the magic-lantern screen, and a prize was given to the first person to identify the author – and presented, perhaps, on stage by Ben Greet in costume. The link between audience and company was strengthened by more direct participation. Volunteers were sometimes invited to join in crowd scenes – as in *Julius*

Caesar – for the fun of it and, sometimes, for a lemonade and a sausage roll, in the local operatic tradition of remuneration. And the audience was encouraged, on special occasions, to laugh at the actors, themselves, and even Shakespeare. For Lilian allowed the company to produce satirical Christmas revues, starting in 1916, which burlesqued the plays and ridiculed the actors and the staff, even the Governors and Miss Baylis, although she refused to follow Ben Greet's 'sportsmanlike' example by appearing in person and making fun of herself. The Thorndikes nearly talked her into it by the argument that she could use the occasion to vent all her grievances to the audience; but she persuaded Dame Sybil to imitate her instead.

'Go on, Sybil,' she urged. 'You can pad yourself out and speak out of the side of your mouth like I do. Do anything you like to get a laugh out of them . . . I'm not nearly as funny as you all are when you imitate me, you bounders.'

And so Sybil, with a Baylisian wrap thrown around her costume of Columbine, delivered this verse:

> I'm Lilian Baylis, Lessee:
> And manage this show to perfection:
> Now listen, you bounders, to me,
> Who've worked up this blooming connection:
> A little less free with your jaw:
> And a little more free with your money:
> Monday nights will be better, I'm sure,
> When you realize Shakespeare is funny.
>
> To roll de roll roll, de rollay,
> The Vic is for ever defying
> These merchants who constantly say
> That the Drama in England is dying.[20]

Harmless, even laudatory fun, this; it is scarcely surprising if Lilian made no attempt to censor it, though she questioned every line of this and other scripts which 'might sound derogatory' about the Vic itself. And, indeed, the in-jokes and friendly send-ups of these house-revues played their part in establishing Miss Baylis's matriarchal role, by the frequent allusions to her power as well as her personality.

As a manager, she impressed the whole theatre with the strength of her will, her capacity for unremitting hard work and her explosive temper. At least one secretary was frequently reduced to tears: Frances Briggs (who, in later life, became secretary of the British Drama League) 'spent many a lunch-time crying in St John's Church'. Lilian would shriek at the offender (whose offence was often not at all clear to anyone but Lilian) from one end of the theatre to the other. She would quickly work herself up into tantrums, and would scream: 'Fools! I've nothing but *fools* around me.' She could be instantly unjust and irrationally offensive.

One offended party was the stage manager, Madge Whiteman. Among her many duties, she had to control the stage lighting and the front-of-house lights, all gas. One evening when *Henry IV* was coming to an end, Miss Whiteman – who was also playing Mistress Quickly – turned up the lights in the usual way, when a messenger from the manager came 'buzzing through' and said, 'Turn up the lights. The theatre's dark.'

'The switch is on as far as it'll go,' said Miss Whiteman.

Miss Baylis then stormed in. 'Turn up the house lights,' she shouted. 'Do you want my audience to break their necks?'

'The lights *are* turned up,' said Miss Whiteman.

'You're a bloody liar,' answered Miss Baylis, in a fury.

'Come and see,' said Miss Whiteman, but the manager slammed the door.

'Damn her!' Miss Whiteman said, with commendable restraint. The door opened again immediately. 'I heard you!' shouted Miss Baylis, and went off again.

On returning home that evening, Miss Whiteman's father told her not to go back to the Vic; he was not going to have his daughter called a bloody liar. So Miss Whiteman wrote to Ben Greet to tell him so. Meanwhile, Mr Whiteman tried to speak to Miss Baylis on the telephone, but she wouldn't take the calls. Greet sent his missing Mistress Quickly a wire: 'Come and see me. Don't do anything rash.' That night it was *The Merry Wives*, in which she was due to appear again as Quickly; and, according to her, 'Greet depended on me to give him every line in the Garter Inn scenes'. She went to the theatre and told Greet that she wouldn't appear that night unless Miss Baylis apologized to her. He said that he couldn't play without her.

Baylis came into the room, and although Greet was a fat man he moved very quickly and he got between her and the door and said, 'Now, Lilian, what's all this. I hear that Madge and you have had a row.'

'Get away from that door,' she said.

'Now, Lilian, the curtain won't go up without Madge. I won't move until you apologize.'

Baylis used filthy language – as she did on many occasions when roused – and Greet said, 'Don't lose your temper, Lilian, you're too fat to get out of the window'.

She went on with a Billingsgate tirade, but in the end she said she was sorry and I went on that night. After the show she called me to her office and said, 'I think we had better part in two weeks time'.

I went home with the Thorndikes, and Lewis said as there was no clause of notice in my contract she couldn't get rid of me, and I couldn't leave her till the end of the season in May.

So I told Lilian Baylis when I saw her later that week that if she didn't give me my salary till the end of the season, I should give her all the kind of publicity she didn't want. Later she called me, and said, 'I have been praying for you, Madge, and I've decided to give you another chance.'

There were many backstage stories of verbal and even physical combat – like the Nose episode, lovingly elaborated in the succeeding years. The Nose belonged to Miss Baylis, and – after niggling provocation over a trivial incident – it was pulled by Ben Greet, *twice*. 'The awful part about it was that I enjoyed pulling her nose,' he confessed to Russell Thorndike the next day. Lilian's version, reported by Thorndike, began generously:

I'm sure B.G. is a good man really. He *is* a good churchman. You've known him so much longer than I have, and I'm sure you agree that he's full of love for God and the Vic. I don't worry about having my nose pulled, which he did twice, but I don't like to think he has any nasty tendencies, and surely wanting to pull someone's nose *is* a nasty tendency, isn't it, dear boy?

According to Russell Thorndike, 'they both forgave each other, but neither of them ever forgot the incident, and constantly referred to it'.[21]

The rows between Lilian and B.G. increased in frequency and intensity. 'At one time she appeared to be driving him mad while he, in turn, was driving her to the point of insanity. The row might begin during a rehearsal; they would retire to the office, the door would be slammed, and from behind it one would hear their high-pitched tones.' 'Away, *woman*,' he would shout at her. '*Woman*, you don't know what you're talking about.' At a matinée of *Macbeth*, Robert Atkins recalled, they began to quarrel in the wings, stumping up and down, shouting so that the front-of-house could hear, knocking against the flats. The audience began to laugh, especially on the line, 'How is't with me, when every noise appals me?' Lady Macbeth (Sybil Thorndike) begged the squabbling pair to keep quiet, to no effect.

By the last year of the World War, it was clear that Lilian's patience was exhausted, and that B.G.'s services to the Vic were at an end. He left in the summer of 1918. (He was succeeded for a year by the scholarly George Foss, and followed for a further year by the partnership of Russell Thorndike and Charles Warburton.) But Lilian never forgot what B.G. had done for the theatre; and the two adversaries remained in touch, and indeed in friendship, for the rest of their lives.

In the theatre world outside the Old Vic her reputation began to grow – not only as a manager, but as an eccentric. Stories accumulated, as the years went by, into a legend. This featured several main characteristics; her stinginess, naïvety and bossiness; her gaffes and crushingly personal verdicts on performers; her frequent recourse to prayer, and invitations to join with her in it. One archetypal Baylis story, still current in the theatre, is of her notorious wartime prayer, 'Dear God, please send me good actors – and cheap,' a perfectly reasonable request in the circumstances, and well attested in substance, though such pleas (like other appeals for the Vic) were likely to take longer to deliver and were not always answered promptly. Another anecdote in similar vein is of her reply to an actor's plea for a small rise. She would have to pray, she said, for an answer; she left the room for a few minutes, and on returning said, 'Sorry, dear, God says no.' And another: the lavatory accommodation at the Vic was so limited that the ladies of the company and staff, including the manager, had on occasion to queue – as inconspicuously as possible. Exasperated by a particularly long wait one day, Lilian burst out, 'This is simply *ridiculous*. And when I meet my dear Lord, I shall tell him so. It's *such* a waste of time for a very busy woman like me. I shall tell him He's really made a very bad arrangement, and He'll have to do better.' Again: on a wartime visit to Portsmouth, when an actress (Florence Saunders) was taken ill, Lilian began to telephone for emergency aid – the Vic could not afford understudies for some years to come. As she stood with the telephone speaker to her mouth she was heard to say into the instrument, 'God, you've got me into this mess. You've got to get me out of it. You *must* help me . . .' And then, as a mystified voice at the end of the line said, 'I *beg* your pardon,' Lilian explained, 'I'm so sorry.

I quite forgot there was someone else on the line.' There is the story of how, a few years later, a young actress stepped into the breach in a similar crisis to take a leading role, and Lilian greeted her at the curtain's fall by saying, 'Well, dear, you've had your chance. And you've missed it.' There is the story of how, when the actor Ernest Milton came to tell her of his marriage to Naomi Royde-Smith, who met him through reviewing his performances at the Vic, Lilian said: 'Very nice, dear. Come to me in your joys and come to me in your sorrows, but not in between because I've no time for chit-chat.' There is the story of how an infuriated member of the team turned on her and said, 'You *cow*,' and how Lilian replied, with dignity, '*Thank* you. The cow is a clean animal.' There is the story of how one day in the office her secretary announced that a member of the audience wanted to see her – 'There's a Miss Kerridge in the circle . . .' – and Lilian barked quickly, 'Well, don't make a fuss. Clean it up and get on with it.'

The details changed, the frills grew more elaborate, but the eccentric figure behind the legend remained immovably central at the Vic. Among its main characters was Lilian's spiritual adviser, Father Andrew (see Chapter 9). As the Superior of a neo-Franciscan order, which he had helped to establish, Father Andrew habitually wore a robe and skull-cap; and from the time that Lilian met him in 1914 until her death his tall monastic figure was frequently seen at the Vic gliding in and out of her office or her box. Nobody knew much about him, except that he exercised a considerable influence over the manager, with whom he was often closeted in prayer; that he had what Robert Atkins described as 'one of the most arresting yet sinister faces I have ever seen'; that he nursed a passion for the theatre, and Lilian had commissioned a nativity play from him which she insisted on staging at Christmas; and that he had introduced her to a leper colony in Essex, which had become her main charitable concern outside the Vic and to which she frequently took reluctant actors and singers, under strict orders to entertain the patients. Among the Father's good causes was a home for unmarried mothers, for whom Lilian showed somewhat less enthusiasm than for the lepers. On one occasion in later years she opened the gallery to a party from this home, for a performance by the drama students. The women began to laugh in the wrong places and shouted remarks at the stage. Lilian went into action, up into the gallery. ' "You shut up, you poor, stupid, rough women. You shut up and behave yourselves or I'll bang your heads together." ' There was silence. Lilian came down again.

' "Poor, dear, fallen women," she said, with tears in her eyes. "It seems a shame they can't enjoy themselves." '[22]

Her courage, as well as her piety, features in some of the stories – like the one told by Tyrone Guthrie about the evening when she climbed in a long skirt up an iron ladder at the side of the stage to correct a drunken fireman during the garden scene of one of her favourite operas, Gounod's *Faust*. Not only Gounod but God was being mocked. 'He was blaspheming, my dear, in the middle of that lovely quiet bit.' Lilian struggled with him on the electricians' platform over the prompt corner and forced him down the ladder in front of her, 'praying to God to give her strength to hold him if he lost his footing on the rungs'.[23]

In spite of all its handicaps, by 1918 the Old Vic commanded the loyalty of an audience that was, and for some years remained, as unusual as its manager, whose eccentricity, idealism and energy helped to give it a special atmosphere. As the *Tatler* observed: 'There is a life and enthusiasm about everyone which is perhaps the most exhilarating thing to be met with in all the world of London's entertainments.' To that world Miss Baylis had given a lesson during the war. She was to continue it during the next two decades.

The growing reputation of the theatre (and the influence of Lady Fred) attracted the attention of royalty. In October 1918 the Queen came to the gala matinée, to celebrate the theatre's centenary; the following week Princess Beatrice and Princess Marie Louise attended a matinée of *Macbeth*, and in the evening Princess Beatrice came to *Carmen*. Princess Marie Louise was then invited to become a member of the Council – which she did. She later became president of the Old Vic Association (and patron of the lepers' home). No wonder that the *Tatler* was saying, 'It seems as if there is a danger now that the old Vic will be "taken up" fashionably'.

Miss Baylis, however, seemed in no danger of surrendering to fashion, or being awed by the Crown. She showed, at first, no enthusiasm for Queen Mary's presence at the gala matinée, as it meant decorating and refurbishing a box. But she was persuaded that what she lost in cash she would gain in prestige. When the day arrived, she bustled round in a purple overall putting the finishing touches to the royal box, which 'stank of size and was so bedizened by Nottingham lace curtains tied with red bows it would be a wonder if Her Majesty could see a thing'. The theatre's senior citizen, Old Bob Robinson, was sent to watch for the Queen's arrival; but this was delayed by a traffic jam, and Lilian decided that the show must start without Her Majesty. The matinée was to be followed at night by an opera, and one of Lilian's slogans was, 'I won't keep my opera patrons waiting'. She was told that it was just not done to commit lese-majesty of this kind, but Lilian took no notice. 'Queen or no queen, we must make a start,' and up went the curtain on the first scene. Halfway through, Old Bob rushed in shouting, ' 'Ere you are, Miss! 'Ere's the Queen!' Lilian rang down the curtain and hurried to the main entrance. 'I'm glad you've turned up at last, dear,' she said breezily to the Queen, 'and I know it's not your fault being late. But we've got a long programme to get through, so let's get on with things.' As the Queen mounted the steps to the royal box, Lilian dashed forward and said, in a piercing whisper, 'Go on, Corri. She's here. The Queen. The Queen.' The orchestra hastily started the National Anthem, and Lilian said to Her Majesty, with benign satisfaction, 'We *always* play your husband's tune here, right through.' In the box itself she had hung up Emma Cons's picture, as a treat. 'We have always had a photograph of the dear King in this box, but I've hung him over there on the prompt side for today,' she explained. 'His picture isn't as big as Emmie's, but then he hasn't done as much for the Old Vic.' Royal visits become intertwined in the Baylis legend – perhaps on this one Lilian had already contrived her solution to the embarrassing problem presented by the fact that the Vic had only one suitable 'Ladies'. She had several members of the staff holding up screens, to prevent the audience from using the lavatory at the interval. And she had a last-minute inspiration for a finishing touch in this department. 'Put the aspidistra in there,' she told her secretary. 'Makes it look more royal, dear.'

. The Old Vic (c. 1914)

. Emma Cons (c. 1900)

3. Lilian at sixteen

4. Robert Atkins (*c.* 1920)   5. Sir Philip Ben Greet (1930)

6. Charles Corri (*c.* 1930), sketched by Harry Powell Lloyd

7. Evelyn Williams (*c.* 1950)

8. Father Andrew (*c.* 1920)

9. Reginald Rowe (*c.* 1935)

10. Clarkie (*c.* 1925)

11 and 12. Lilian in the 1920s, with the Vic queue; and cutting a
Twelfth Night cake on stage (her father is on the extreme right)

13. John Gielgud (1930)

14. Sybil Thorndike (*c*, 1920)

15. Ninette de Valois (*c*. 1930)

16. Lawrance Collingwood (*c*. 1930)

17. Lilian picnicking with Louie Davey (right foreground)

18. At the seaside with Harriet Webster

19. Miss Baylis, making music

20. Miss Baylis, Companion of Honour with Hon. MA (Oxon)

21. At a Vic first night, with veteran critic S. R. Littlewood

22. Dispensing coffee at Elsinore in 1937, with Annette Prevost

The Building Years

When the war is over and conditions are such
that the state can be approached,
surely yours is the first theatre that should receive state aid.

Matheson Lang to Lilian Baylis (1915)

Our intrepid manager had one of the characteristics
of the great artist;
she did her greatest work when her difficulties were greatest.

James Agate (1937)

I do so believe that the moment we feel our cross,
if we call on Him to help us carry it He does indeed carry it,
and we more often feel only joy – the heaviness goes.

Lilian Baylis (1918)

After the disappearance from the West End of such actor-managers as Alexander, Tree and Forbes-Robertson, few London theatres retained a distinctive, visible policy by the 1920s. Even fewer had a distinctive, visible manager. The Old Vic had both. Lilian Baylis was, indeed, not only visible nearly every evening in her box, but often audible as well.

The box was on the right hand of the audience, between the stalls entrance and the stage, and it served as a listening-point, an observation post, a platform, an auxiliary office and a throne-room for over twenty years. Here Lilian sat at every first night, shaking hands with friends, waving and bowing, holding a kind of gruff court – 'part queen, part showman, but mostly the Lady Bountiful at a mighty Social'.[1] She was grave, even dour, but sometimes warmed into a 'tilted smile' (as Ernest Milton described it). She wore Victorian jewels, chains, rings (which tended to multiply in later years), a crucifix, shawls and, often, nondescript furs – described by her staff as 'Miss Baylis's hearthrug' (the skin was believed to have come from South Africa, but – said 'Clarkie' – from 'no known animal'). In her later years, as she became dressier, she was seen there in a sable cape with a bright mauve lining – 'Nice colour, dear, isn't it? It's a bit of *Julius Caesar*. I swapped it with the wardrobe for an Indian shawl' – and under it a black taffeta coat with enamelled buttons that had belonged to her grandmother's friend, Mrs Stirling.[2] Here she watched dress rehearsals, often far into the night; and here she sat for a part of nearly every performance of drama or opera. She did not stay in the box throughout the evening, and she did not watch all the time she was there. She retired into a recess, behind a dusty red curtain, where she would receive friends and visitors, or write letters with the help of a torch. But she was likely to poke out her head from time to time, and to deliver a running commentary not only on the audience during the intervals but also on the performance during the acts. Tyrone Guthrie gave two examples from a later decade in his brilliantly vivid recollections. 'There's Sir Hugh Walpole, dear – Row D on the OP side – quite a nice writer and a dear good honourable man – did I ever tell you how his father – he was a Canon – smacked me on the BTM the year King Edward died – tell you later.' 'Quite a sweet little Carmen and a dear good honourable woman with a drunken brute of a husband – he's had a stroke now, thank God . . . You see that little girl in the chorus – the one with the tambourine? She's going to have a baby, you wouldn't think she was old enough, would you, dear?'[3] Sometimes she would hiss remonstrances at members of the cast ('For God's sake, girl, throw your bosom out'). Sometimes in earlier days the sound of her conversation, or of a typewriter in the box, 'mingled dangerously' with the play. In a wartime *Macbeth* the audience would hear:

Is this a dagger which I – *tap, tap, tap* – before me,
The handle toward my – *tap-tap* –
Come let me clutch –
Well, my dear (the quiet voice of Father Andrew) if I were you – tap-tap-tap–
I have thee not –
I don't give a damn what the Governors say (Lilian talking) . . .

There followed 'heavy shushing from the audience; then the patter of the stage manager as he rushed through the pass-door to beg silence from the occupants of the box'.[4]

The theatre was run from the box and from the office. There were, in fact, two offices – tiny cubicles in the wings which had also been 'slip' dressing-rooms for quick-change artists. One of them, about ten feet by eight, accommodated – from 1917 on, at least – Miss Baylis's secretary, the treasurer, a girl to check the entertainment tax vouchers, and the director of plays, when he had the time and inclination for correspondence. Apart from the acute shortage of space, work was frequently continued against heavy odds. The door had to be kept shut, because the sound of the typewriter could be heard on the stage; and the window had to be shut, too, 'because some merry heart in the Waterloo Road was fairly certain to throw something through'. Immediately outside the cubicle there were, from time to time, the distractions of stage tempests from the wind-howler and the tin bath (for thunder). The secretary's duties, like the hours, were irregular; they included, for instance, feeding the opera chorus with lemonade and biscuits at the interval. Miss Baylis's room was about the same size; and she vacated it on opera nights so that it could be used as a dressing-room for the veteran ladies of the chorus.

The site and size of her office changed, in later reconstructions and rearrangements, but not its essential decor, atmosphere and significance. As Tyrone Guthrie put it, years later, this was the room in which 'she interviewed us, scolded us, bestowed her rare but heart-warming praise, beat down our salaries, won our undying admiration and deep love'.[5] It was crammed with oddly assorted, old-fashioned furniture, dominated by a big oak roll-top desk covered with papers and knick-knacks such as the brass bowl with rusty paper clips and shrivelled rubber bands. There was usually a tray (Lilian rarely went out for a meal) and a bowl of flowers. A big crucifix on the wall was surrounded by pictures of actors and actresses, of Emmie, of course, and of members of the Baylis family; by a postcard of the Victoria Falls, and by other African mementoes. A reproduction of Dürer's 'Praying Hands' was pinned to the desk: Lilian had a thing about hands. Under the sapphire plush cover of a side-table lived, during the latter part of Miss Baylis's reign, the dogs who shared it, with their basket, bones, water, pervasive smell and continual shrill barking. There was a medallion of Shakespeare on the wall, and his head also appeared on the door, as a knocker. And outside was a gas ring on which she fried sausages, kippers or steaks between performances, and which privileged members of the staff were sometimes invited to share. The smell of Lilian's cooking, drifting across the stage and through the auditorium, became an indispensable part of the legend; but however comic, or smelly, or unhygienic, or eccentric it seemed to other people, it was a practical necessity to Lilian, and she fiercely resisted any attack upon the Ring. Its removal was among the changes regularly demanded by the local Fire Inspector, who was no less regularly repulsed by Miss Baylis. 'It was here in my aunt's time and here it stays,' she would bark at him. 'You tell the LCC that we do enough for them with our school matinées at reduced prices, and don't let them hamper us in our work. How do you suppose we can cook sausages without a gas ring? Instead of trying to make things difficult, why don't you try to get more people to come to the operas?'[6]

The office and the box were not only Lillian's headquarters: they were, in a sense, her home. Certainly she spent more time in them than she did in her Stockwell drawing-room or garden.

As a manager she demanded a great deal and often got it. People who applied for a staff job were given fair warning. To Frances Briggs, for instance, she said in 1918, 'If you come here you will have no home life of any kind. You must give up yourself entirely to the work here as I do, and you must have no private interests of any kind.' Miss Briggs worked from ten in the morning till the play or opera finished at night. 'It was very tiring, especially as she used to get busy about nine o'clock at night. On the steps of the stage door as she was going she'd suddenly start thinking she must dictate some letters.' In those days Miss Baylis was self-conscious about giving dictation. She would say, defensively, 'Of course, *I'm* not a lady. I've had no education. I don't know the right thing to do. I can only do what God tells me.' One of the things that He told her to do was to maintain an almost obsessive interest in the tiniest detail of the theatre's life. 'She pervaded everything,' said Nora Nicholson, who was there in 1914, and 'she was all ears'. When she couldn't hear for herself, she asked. She usually relied on at least one member of each company to keep her in touch with events and temperatures: if the producer was bullying people, or if any feuds had broken out, or if any backstage romances were blooming. She liked to believe that she could see and trace all the filaments in the Waterloo Road web. It was only by learning as much as she could about everyone in her empire that she could keep it responsive not only to her control but to God's will.

Early in her career at the Old Vic, Mrs Clark (who, as 'Clarkie', became one of its institutions) was at work in the box office one morning when Miss Baylis came storming in.

'They've got the wrong poster up outside,' she shouted. 'Why didn't you do something about it?'

'*Me*, Miss Baylis? It's nothing to do with *me*,' said a bewildered Mrs Clark.

'Never let me hear you say that again,' Lilian rasped. '*Everything* to do with the Vic is to do with you – and with every one of my staff. Don't forget that.'

Nobody was ever allowed to forget the audience. A prime clue to the success of the Old Vic and the curious supremacy of Lilian Baylis lies in the character of the audience and Lilian's intimate understanding of it. This became manifest in the 1920s. To quote the *Daily Telegraph* in September 1921: 'To form part of an Old Vic audience is a real tonic. These people really love the theatre for itself: they love the plays, the acting, the players. They do not come to see, and be seen by, each other . . . It is really possible to tell, at the Old Vic, what the audience think of the play, and how deeply they understand it. And they *do* understand it.' This audience, said the same critic a month later, was 'not the least important factor' in the 'traditional' teamwork acting. By 1925 the *Sunday Times* was talking of it as 'members of a great family sharing a common inheritance'; *The Times*, in 1926, said that not only Shakespeare but 'his natural audience' was 'as much alive today as when he was writing'; in the same year the *Daily News* asked, rhetorically, 'Surely the greatest happiness that can come to a player must be to act before an audience at the Old Vic?'

What was so special about this audience? It came, said Margaret Webster, 'to enjoy itself and did so vociferously. It could criticize vocally too, and laugh with a mighty derision . . . The hard core . . . didn't read the critics and didn't care about an actor's previous successes. It still liked to make its own stars, and when it made them, they stayed made.'[7] Right through the 1920s there was 'a unique flavour of intimacy, loyalty, mutual friendship and proprietary pride'. It was not (as it once may have been) proletarian, but it was democratic. 'Nobody appeared in evening dress, and, as the difference in price between the stalls and gallery was very little, and the difference in comfort still less, the whole house seemed to acquire a unity of character that was to be observed in the Old Vic and nowhere else.'[8] It was a *regular* audience, not one made up from the carriage trade and a floating population of tourists, on whom the London theatre now depends for survival. 'There will never be another audience quite like them,' said Joan Cross. 'They responded with understanding, devotion and loyalty. They partook, in the real sense of the word, and although not averse to offering criticism, they felt themselves part and parcel of the institution; it was *their* theatre as well as Miss Baylis's.'[9] But it was Miss Baylis who created this audience, not only by 'constantly presenting them with excellent things' but 'by allowing her own personality to be felt all the time as something constant and human in a world of abstract values'. Some of these words were written after the 1920s were over, but they express the especial quality of the audience and of its manager; for Lilian managed not only the players and the singers, but the people before whom they performed. If, as John Gielgud said in later years, 'the spirit of the place seemed so much stronger than any of the separate personalities who served it',[10] it was largely because of the custodian of the place, and the guardian of its spirit.

The audience changed as the years went by. In the 1930s it included – notably, in the gallery – a group of blimpish loyalists who, having discovered Shakespeare through the early Vic productions, found it hard to accept any subsequent interpretations of less roughness, less readiness and less patent 'sincerity'. This 'congregational element', as Harcourt Williams termed it, was both a tower of strength and a redoubt of resistance, and refused to welcome any newcomers until they had shown they were good enough for the Vic, to the satisfaction of the old guard. Their symbol was Miss Pilgrim, a tiny, shrill devotee who began going to opera in 1912, when she was fifty-four. She could not afford more than one visit to the gallery a week, at twopence, but she followed every season for twenty-five years. She became infected by a love of Shakespeare, and saved up so that she could go to the theatre *every* night, for opera and drama. She acquired so special a status that she never had to queue for a seat in the gallery: her accustomed place was always left for her. Every night, at the end of the performance, she sang 'God Save the King' in a cracked voice; and then she walked home to a tobacconist's shop in the Pentonville Road. That kind of devotion was part of the making of the Old Vic; and part, too, of the cross that directors and performers had to bear.

During the post-war decade the reputation of the Old Vic – both in drama and, more slowly, in opera – advanced against enormous odds, through a daunting series of financial and structural crises, with the help of some rare theatrical talents and the determined leadership of Lilian Baylis, whose confidence flowered as she and her theatre were more heavily burdened yet more widely acclaimed. But this flowering, it should be remembered, was rooted not only in religious faith but in good works: most particularly in the donations of a few charitable men and institutions, without which – in the absence of state and civic aid – the Vic would have perished. A new saviour, the Carnegie Trust, was providentially recruited in 1918. After postal approaches by the Governors had failed to secure any of the Carnegie gold, the invaluable Lady Fred was brought into play. She persuaded its chairman, Sir William McCormick, to visit the Vic and meet Lilian. Sir William fell under the spell of the theatre and the manager; and some months later the Trust made a grant of £1,000 over the next two years, to meet increases in salary and 'certain necessary alterations'. That did not go far, but all the same it was manna, and it was followed by heavier showers. These helped to pay for some of the improvements that were urgently needed, now that the war was over – and with it, Lilian's best excuse for postponing structural change and expenditure.

One of the first changes came in 1919, before the autumn season began, when – persuaded by Robert Atkins and others – Lilian set up a wardrobe in (shades of Emmie!) a disused pub in Oakley Street, three minutes walk from the stage door. Although there were other good theatrical reasons for such an addition to the Vic's resources, and Lilian had often heard them, she acted now in order to save money on the Raynes bill for hiring costumes, which was being pushed up by £100 p.a. to £600. The nucleus of the collection was the stock of the disbanded Moody-Manners opera company, which Lilian's mother bought at an auction in 1918 – Madame Konss-Baylis's last service for her daughter before she became immobilized in a wheelchair. 'By her energies in fighting the crowd of Jewish dealers at the sale', her daughter wrote in her obituary tribute, 'she had obtained over £1,000 worth of goods for the Vic with the expenditure of £400 or £500.'[11] It was a welcome reinforcement to the motley collection of tatty finery from Matheson Lang and other benefactors, with such bonuses as evening-gowns and fancy-dress clothes handed down from the Governors and their friends and relations. Major Lyttelton, for instance, generously gave 'a rich costume which he wore at the Great Shakespeare Ball before the war'. But a great deal more was needed for a company with a repertoire of over thirty plays and twenty operas. Lilian estimated the cost of an adequate wardrobe in 1919 at about £5,000; and although there seemed to be no prospect of extracting such a sum from any of the new rich, the Carnegie Trust disgorged again in 1920 to the tune of £1,500. Whether it *all* found its way into the wardrobe seems open to doubt, in view of press comments during the following decade. Many of the costumes worn in the Shakespearian repertoire had a distinctly operatic ambience – and indeed an operatic identity – for regular patrons of both companies.

The look of the stage was improved too. A new black velvet front curtain was installed, thanks to the generosity of one of the Governors, Mrs H. C. Gooch (later Lady Gooch), replacing the old tumbler curtain. The orchestra pit was sunk below the floor level. Miss Baylis at last submitted to the LCC's demand for the replacement of the old gas battens by electricity, with beneficial results for safety and visibility. The inadequacy of the stock scenery now became much more nakedly apparent; but the worst of this was jettisoned, and the old groove system was at last destroyed, by a successful conspiracy against the manager before the 1919–20 season began. Lilian's new producers, Russell Thorndike and Charles Warburton, had set their hearts on the liquidation of the grooves. But although the two young actors repeatedly begged Lilian to abandon this anachronistic technique of scene change, it seemed to her that to do so would be too sharp a break with the Cons past – and, more significantly, too expensive. She consulted God, having explained to Him the grooves' function at the Vic, but 'He withheld His opinion for a long time'. Meanwhile, Thorndike and Warburton strengthened their case by getting the local vicar, Mr Gordon, on their side – he was also on the board of Governors – and by privily killing off those 'groove-flats' that might still have seemed to Lilian to be worth patching up for a few more seasons.

At last, after they had given up hope, Miss Baylis surrendered.

'Everyone seems to agree with you boys about the grooves,' she said, with a sigh of resignation. 'I've prayed about them, and I know you have too. I suppose they must go. The workmen are in the place. They can do it. I'll be down early in the morning if you want me about anything.'[12] The two conspirators felt in their bones that she was going home to seek divine guidance once again; and in case God showed His hand and turned against them, they put their plan into action right away. They got the work started at six next morning and urged the men on to finish it before Miss Baylis might arrive. By nine o'clock all but one of the grooves had crashed to the stage, bringing down with them a century's dirt and throwing up a huge pile of rubbish. Just as the last one was ready to fall, Lilian entered, calling, 'Don't do anything yet to the grooves,' right in the path of the splintering survivor. Thorndike and Warburton pushed her to safety, as it hit the stage. 'Oh, *what* are you all doing to my theatre?' Miss Baylis cried out. 'Don't touch any more of them. And put that one back, at once.' But it was too late. 'God should have warned me to come down earlier,' she said, looking at the directors' estimate of what a new system would cost. 'He was telling me in the night not to let you remove the grooves.' But when Lilian realized that what was done couldn't be undone she did her best to get the money required for new wood, canvas and paint to make the scenery, and for braces, screws and counterweights to hold it up.

The productions, though still necessarily frugal, began to look less impoverished. Under pressure, Lilian inched up the salaries for leading players, at least, above the ten-bob-a-show dole. And with even more reluctance, because of the threat to Emmie's principles, she put up the prices to help in paying for the higher costs (largely by adding sixpence to the cost of reserved seats). A reserved orchestra stall now cost nearly twice as much as in 1914 (4s. 3d., including entertainments tax). But the gallery was still only 3d. Lilian insisted that the Vic had to be available to 'her people' at prices they could afford. That was, indeed, a condition of the grant from the City Parochial Foundation and a part of the Vic's constitution.

In opera, time – and the repertoire – seemed to stand still. 'To know the opera company of those days was to see a whole cross-section of theatrical history for the last fifty years. There were brothers of Mr Crummles and the more pertinacious students from the Royal College and Academy, who wanted to learn about opera and couldn't find anywhere else to do it in London; quiet young men who could speak authoritatively of Dresden and Salzburg; there were milkmen and miners who sang with lovely liquid vowels and lapsed cheerfully into the vernacular when they spoke.'[13] The chorus lived in a curious, classless limbo: clerks, shop assistants, students, telephone operators, singing for love – or five bob a time. Among them, in 1920, was Miss Palmer, who had been a volunteer since the early tableau recitals. 'She insisted on keeping her original stage position; and, as a production developed, was often left solitary, much to her content and the audience's amusement. She had a wealth of fair hair which (no matter what the opera was) fell below her waist. When the chorus had to draw attention to some character or object, on or off stage, Miss Palmer, by an astonishing body-movement, would fling her tresses in the appropriate direction.'[14]

'The Vic has been built upon failures,' said Lilian Baylis; and the tradition was strong in the opera. 'Failures of cast at the eleventh hour, failure of props, failures of orchestra, choir, music-stands, scores, any one of the essentials for performances of opera; yet the proud record is that never a performance has been put off.' As Kathleen Eggar wrote in 1918, 'Would you want a more breathless experience than to be faced, at the only full rehearsal before the first attempt at *Carmen*, with the failure of three of your principal characters? Most people under such circumstances would say, as the conductor did on that occasion, "Well, it's no use *rehearsing*". Few people would reply, as the Manager did, "Well, will you start rehearsing, for heaven's sake, and let me think what to do".'[15] A musical comedy company to whom the Vic stage had been lent for a rehearsal was just leaving the theatre. As Lilian, deep in thought, went to the office, one male singer asked her if she could fit him into her company for a few days.

'Do you play Zuniga?'

'Oh yes.'

'Free tonight?'

'Yes.'

'Well, come on. They're just rehearsing for tonight.'

'My wife's a very good Frasquita – I suppose you couldn't fit her in, too . . .'

Shortly afterwards the third vacancy was filled, when one of the original defaulters found he could make it after all . . .

On one celebrated occasion the tenor in *Tannhäuser* lost his voice, and every possible replacement appeared to be out of town or otherwise engaged. Then Lilian heard that a tenor travelling from the North was due at King's Cross about an hour before the curtain was due to rise at the Vic. 'We met him at King's Cross and simply listened to no excuses, kidnapped him, one could say, bundled him into a taxi, took him to the theatre where the con-ductor hummed his cues while he dressed.' There were no solu-tions for other crises in stage management, such as the 'discon-certing trick' played by one stage manager in 'pressing all the wrong buttons with a fine abandon'. Curtains went up at quite unexpected moments, in the middle of an interval or halfway through an act.[16] Again, 'it was always thrilling to watch what happened during *Faust* when Mephistopheles drew forth his sword to strike the sign outside the inn, calling, "Some wine!" Would the liqueur fall to his magic touch? Often it refused to do the devil's bidding, only to shoot forth over the chorus during a later phase . . .'[17] And the settings, like the effects, were generally primitive in execution. Rostrums were pushed together and 'bolstered up by ginger-beer boxes which never quite fitted' – so that a singer might take one step of six inches, and follow it with one of twenty-four inches: a somewhat disconcerting experience for any performer.

At this time, however, a new era seemed to open – as so often at the Vic – by accident. To Miss Baylis, of course, nothing concerning its welfare could be accidental. For her it was God's will that her theatre (and His) should discover, at precisely the right time, a director and a scholar of undoubted brilliance. It happened, obliquely, through Lilian's own initiative. She wanted to revive *The Marriage of Figaro*, and asked Muriel Gough, a light soprano who had just joined the company and who had worked in German opera houses for six years before the war, to mount a production (and sing Susanna). In declining the job of directing (though not of singing) Miss Gough recommended Clive Carey – actor, opera singer, composer and Mozart enthusiast; and Carey agreed to direct (and sing Figaro) on condition that he was allowed to use a new translation made during the war by Edward J. Dent.

At first Miss Baylis resisted, on the grounds that it would mean a lot of extra work and expense in copying new words; and that to learn them would be much disliked by the chorus and the principals, who were accustomed to the old text and could not afford (on what Lilian paid them) to rehearse a completely different one. But a new cast was assembled, who had not sung in *Figaro* before, and who made no objections to the Dent libretto; and Carey compromised with Lilian's demand that the opera must be cut to three hours, the most that her people (so she declared) would take from any composer. Carey challenged Vic tradition and the Baylis budget by insisting on far longer and more detailed rehearsals than had ever been known at this theatre, but Lilian's fears were calmed by the readiness of the singers to rehearse for nothing (without the orchestra). The production (in January 1920) was a critical and a popular success. One surprise was that the words could be clearly heard, so that the singers got laughs even in mid-ensemble. 'Superior members of the audience were gravely shocked at this; on the rare occasions when *Figaro* had been performed in Italian at Covent Garden it would never have occurred to anyone to laugh.'[18]

Lilian could see that God had again sent her the right man, even if he was inclined to ask for the impossible; and so she agreed that he should stage *The Magic Flute* – again, in Dent's translation. This opera had been largely excluded from the English stage until 1911, when Carey demonstrated at Cambridge that the legendary obstacles of its production – the demands of the spectacle, absurdities of the plot, and 'impossibilities' of casting adequately the leading roles of high soprano and low bass – could all be dissolved by a resourceful and imaginative director, using simplified scenery and a first-class translation. Carey now borrowed from Cambridge the orchestral parts and most of the costumes of that production nine years earlier so that it could be staged inside the Baylis budget; the 1911 Tamino, Stewart Wilson, repeated his performance: and *The Magic Flute* was installed in the Vic repertory after its successful introduction in December 1920.

Carey and Dent now decided, with Miss Baylis's support, to try *Don Giovanni* on the Vic audience. This was staged in November 1921 in a new translation by Dent and a new production by Carey: indeed, Dent said, 'we ... did our best to make *Don Giovanni* a new opera,' by bringing out its comedy rather than presenting it as a romantic tragedy. They restored the comic finale in Act 2, hitherto always omitted in conventional productions; and they dressed it, as best they could, in the Goya period. Lilian allowed no squandering, of course, on such perfectionism: 'practically everything had to be done out of stock'. But expert aid was given by well-wishers such as the specialist in Spanish literature, J. B. Trend, who supplied authentic combs and mantillas, plus instructions on how to wear them, and a quantity of picture-postcard reproductions of Goyas in Madrid – one of which served the ingenious wardrobe mistress, Mrs Newman, to model a dress for Zerlina.

Lilian herself came to the rescue at the first dress rehearsal. Dent asked Corri for a real mandolin for the serenade: 'I can't bear that violin playing it pizzicato, even if it is the tradition of all the great opera houses of Europe.' To Dent's astonishment, Corri replied, 'Well, ask Miss Baylis. She's the only person here who can play the mandolin.' Miss Baylis was clearly enthralled to be asked.

'Still more to my surprise', Dent recalled, 'a mandolin was suddenly produced from somewhere; she hurriedly tuned it, and, what is more, played the obbligato to the serenade from memory without a mistake, standing in the wings with the rapt expression of a seraph.' Alas, she was not to remain a feature of the production after the first performance. As she was 'a little nervous and timid' – she explained to Dent that she hadn't touched the instrument for years, which was not strictly true – the premier lady mandolinist of South Africa was barely audible in the stalls. So, after that, they went back to the violin pizzicato, at least when Dent and Carey were around. On later occasions Miss Baylis could not resist having a strum on her favourite instrument on her own stage in one of her own operas.

The Vic also acquired, at this time, two new recruits who were to be pillars of the opera seasons for years to come: Sumner Austin and Lawrance Collingwood. Their stories of their first brief encounters with Miss Baylis give vivid glimpses of the way she worked as a manager. Austin went for an audition in December 1918, having spent four years in a German prison camp. After he sang her a Mozart aria in Italian, Lilian said, 'Go and feed up till you get your strength back. Work up a repertoire in English and then come and sing to me again, and I'll see what I can do for you.' He took her advice. After touring for six months as a principal with the Carl Rosa company, he went to the Vic for a second audition and Lilian engaged him for the 1919–20 season at a pound a performance. This was among the happier instances of her flair for finding the right man for her purposes; for this gentle, intelligent artist with a passion for the theatre, a readiness for hard labour and (less common among the company) a university background proved to be a valuable servant of the Vic for years to come.

During that season Lawrance Collingwood came to see Lilian, armed with an introduction from one of the Carnegie Trustees, who had recognized him as a promising composer (his musical experience included a formative spell in pre-revolutionary Russia). A rehearsal was in progress, and as there was no room for an interview inside the theatre Lilian took him outside. She 'walked me up and down the pavement, and in a great hurry explained that she wanted a pianist to help Mr Corri, but could not afford to pay for one'.[19] As the Carnegie Trustees found that it *could* afford Mr Collingwood's salary, he came to the Vic. He hated the work at first. It was hard for a young artist – sensitive, reticent and musicianly – to labour on an ancient piano through crude versions of standard works with a motley chorus of amateurs who never got enough rehearsals; and Corri did not make it easier. But at the end of the first year he agreed to stay on at five shillings a week less (Lilian was now paying his salary), and he remained even though she increased his work 'tenfold'. According to Collingwood, 'I was so infected by her enthusiasm and so interested in the whole establishment that I did not mind';[20] and, indeed, he was partly responsible for his own extra burdens. He was, in Joan Cross's words, a 'fabulously patient' coach, 'a marvellous singers' conductor'.

Behind it all there was still the staunch, rough-and-ready musicianship of Charles Corri, who achieved one of his ambitions in 1920 by introducing *Tristan and Isolde* in a brilliantly contrived adaptation for his economy-size band (gradually extended during the 1920s from eighteen to twenty-eight). He resented Lilian's refusal to increase his salary; and he found it hard at first to stomach the newcomers to the company, especially the more educated singers (he would, for instance, deliberately slow down *tempi* in some of Sumner Austin's arias). On their side, they at first found him boorish and crude, musically and socially. But somehow they developed a working tolerance, respect, even (here and there) affection. The mixture held together largely because of Lilian, although she stirred it continually. Musicians and singers responded to her devotion to the theatre with a zeal that helped to make up for the tattiness and incongruity of many productions; for the desperately inadequate rehearsals of principals and players; for the absurd undermanning of the orchestra; for the cheese-paring economy that Lilian felt obliged to practise.

With the advent of Carey and Dent, the behaviour and appreciation of the audience began to change. It had long been the custom to applaud every separate number – scarcely surprising, when the tradition of 'recitals' was so entrenched; but Carey speeded up the scene-change and attempted to eliminate waits and interruptions. In other operas, however, the old habits persisted, along with the old-style productions, and the audience continued to give a hand to their favourites *en route*. It was not until 1926 that, according to the annual report for that year, 'the thunder of clapping for which the Old Vic audience is famous is now almost entirely confined to the fall of the curtain'. This was a response to a gruff appeal by Lilian at the beginning of the season not to applaud until the end of a scene or an act.

158

Miss Baylis herself did not always relish the processes of change in the 1920s, however slow and piecemeal they might seem to the outside observer; nor were her new brooms, like Clive Carey, always patient with her delays, her tempers, her economies, her eccentricities. They frequently and fiercely argued about salaries, rehearsal time, production costs and repertoire. She vetoed what seemed to them to be manifestly essential. She could – and did – slow down the rate of growth. She firmly refused, for instance, to allow *Fidelio* to be staged. 'I'm an ignorant woman. I don't know anything about *Fidelio*. I've never seen it. I only know it's always been a failure at Covent Garden.' That, said Professor Dent on many occasions (as a Governor), was just the reason why they ought to make a success of it at the Vic. But it took him 'ten years of persistent nagging', he claimed, before she surrendered. In the early phase of Dent's connection with the Vic he decided that 'the only hope for a rational development of opera there lay in the removal of Miss Baylis'; yet, after he had come to know the theatre and its manager better, 'I gradually became converted to the view that . . . she was the one person whose presence was indispensable'.[21] Similarly, Carey felt that the Vic was 'falling between two stools. It was attempting to be an artistic venture and at the same time a philanthropic institution.' Miss Baylis, he said, 'did not know exactly what she wanted, nor even always distinguished the best from the second best'. But – and it is a big 'but' – 'one thing she knew with all her heart and soul, and that was that her theatre should give the best of which it was capable, and that it should be ever more and more capable of the best. To this end we had too to give of our best, and we gave it, not because we were asked to, but because the fire of her enthusiasm just made us give it without the asking.'[22]

So much for opera in the early post-war years. In the Shakespeare company, too, there were new faces and new approaches: notably those of Ernest Milton, the romantic American born actor who made his Old Vic debut in the autumn of 1918 aged twenty-eight, and was later widely acclaimed as the greatest Hamlet of his time; and of Robert Atkins, who returned to the Vic in 1920. Atkins, then thirty-four, was a seasoned actor with a broad, virile power and panache, who had worked with Tree, Martin-Harvey, Forbes-Robertson and Benson before his wartime season with the Vic in London and Stratford. During 1915–16 he played Macbeth, Cassius, Richard III, Iago, Jaques, Sir Toby Belch and Prospero, until he went into the army; and on his return to the Vic, after touring with Ben Greet, he was seen in other major roles, notably Caliban and Lear. But his importance in the history of the Vic, and the English theatre in general, is not as an actor but as a director.

Miss Baylis had picked Atkins as the right man on the strength of his wartime form, when he deputized for Ben Greet – especially at Stratford in 1916, when (Atkins claimed) he 'practically ran the season' because B.G. and Lilian were not on speaking terms. He did not see a great deal of her at that time, but when he was called up, she asked him what he was going to do when he came back.

'I may not come back,' said Atkins.

'I think you *will*,' Lilian answered, with a 'most beautiful' smile. 'Would you like to come back to me? If you would, I'd like to have you here.'

Atkins said he wouldn't forget – and he didn't. One night in the trenches he scribbled a letter to her, and in what he later described as 'a very comical fashion' told her the six plays that he would like to stage at the Vic, if he got back safely. Those were the six plays with which he started his regime as its director.[23] Lilian frequently said, towards the end of the war, that she was 'waiting for Robert'. She used to preface declarations about future plans and possibilities with, 'When Robert comes back . . .' By the one-season appointments of George Foss and the Thorndike–Warburton duo she was keeping the job open for him. Lilian resisted pressure to engage Edith Craig, in spite of the reputation that this sister of Gordon Craig and daughter of Ellen Terry had made as founder of the Pioneer Players, and in spite of her admiration for Edith's mother and her sympathy with the feminist cause. 'We don't want another woman here. And anyhow we don't want Edy. She would upset the staff.' As Edy's lifelong friend Christopher St John said, 'That apprehension may have been well founded for Edy was no appeaser . . . She would certainly have upset the complacency of the Old Vic. Her appointment might have been a turning-point in its history as well as hers.'[24] Five years later Ellen Terry tried directly to get Edy the succession, but was repulsed by Lilian. The turning-point, for the Vic, came with Atkins, whose appointment was certainly one of her most successful exercises in intuitive casting. Atkins set standards in Shakespeare, as Carey did in opera, in spite of the crippling poverty of time, space and money; but his achievement was far greater. Unlike Carey he reshaped the entire Vic repertoire, for during his five years at the theatre he directed all but one of the Shakespearian canon. He revived such rarities as *Henry VI*, *Titus Andronicus* and *Troilus and Cressida*, not seen for generations in a professional production; he staged contemporary poetic drama (Laurence Binyon's *King Arthur* and Gordon Bottomley's *Britain's Daughter*); he ventured the first production in England of Goethe's *Faust* (as distinct from the W. G. Wills version used by Irving, and the Stephen Phillips variation staged by Tree); and he was responsible for the first public performance in Britain of *Peer Gynt*, an ambitious achievement miraculously presented on a budget of £100. Lilian put up a stiff resistance to this Ibsenite innovation. Atkins overcame it, he said, only by 'dangling the bait of the attraction to her opera audience of the Grieg music.' Russell Thorndike gave 'the performance of his life' as Peer. It drew many playgoers to the New Cut for the first time and marked a sudden increase in the fame and glamour of the Old Vic, which caused Lilian no little perturbation. She was inclined to stand outside the theatre and, in a loud voice, say things like 'all the people who come to the Vic in motor cars ought to pay three times as much for their seats', or, more succinctly, 'beasts and bounders', and 'thieves and rogues'.

Atkins also helped to stage several operas, including *Tristan* and *Don Giovanni*. He was, said Professor Dent, 'wonderfully ingenious at obtaining quite new effects by the rearrangement of old oddments of scenery and the clever disposition of curtains.'[25] Curtains were indispensable to Atkins in producing Shakespeare: not because they were cheap (which endeared him, professionally, to Miss Baylis), but because they helped to simplify the background to the text and speed up its delivery, as he had learned from William Poel. Atkins, like Poel, turned his back on many traditional methods – including most of the traditional cuts used by B.G.; put his faith in the text; and gave far more of it than had been heard on the stage for many years, except in the handful of pre-war productions by Poel and Granville-Barker. In the cause of scenic simplicity and verbal rapidity he persuaded Miss Baylis to let him install a permanent false proscenium of black velvet with two doors in each pediment, build a movable platform over the orchestra, eliminate the footlights and put in 'spots'. These changes were the cause of frequent feuds with the opera company, and presented many problems to Atkins's successors; but they helped him to achieve some approximation to Elizabethan staging, to minimize cuts and waits, and to keep each production as closely and fully to Shakespeare's words as he could contrive, by a mixture of charm, bullying, improvisation and flair. He had a talent for lighting, and he was a good mentor of young actors (those, at least, that he didn't take against) especially in teaching them how to speak. Apart from Ernest Milton his companies included such talents as Ion Swinley, Hay Petrie, John Laurie, Wilfrid Walter and Florence Saunders. Dozens of aspirants to Shakespearian stardom crossed Waterloo Bridge to try their luck. It became known as *the* place to get experience – even if this was, sometimes, at the audience's expense. Among those who walked on during the Atkins regime was John Gielgud. Among those who, in Atkins's first year, couldn't get in, was a girl straight from RADA, Flora Robson.

Armed with a letter of recommendation from Sybil Thorndike, I did an audition for Atkins and he was very keen to take me on. He explained that he couldn't actually do so until Miss Baylis came back from her summer holidays, and could give her approval. So I took a job and came back and did a further audition later. Miss Baylis's comment was, 'You're far too young to come to the Vic and you haven't got nearly enough experience. Go away, young lady, and get some before you come here.'[26]

Atkins built on a foundation of audience support which – although the Shakespeare experiment was only six years old – showed uncommon enthusiasm and discrimination. In a sense, his work may be seen as a natural development from the Greet era. But whereas B.G. was already a veteran when he came to the Vic, Atkins was twenty years younger when he took over, a passionate man with a burning concern to let Shakespeare speak for himself to the audience, with as little clutter and censorship as possible. The new quality which he brought to the New Cut was soon recognized; and the press notices reflect this growing awareness. In December 1920, the *Daily Telegraph* was already declaring that, 'There is no doubt that the "Old Vic" is doing great work, and work for which future generations of playgoers will owe them more thanks than they are likely to repay.' This review began:

The Royal Victoria Hall – to give it the name by which it is never known – is actually accomplishing all the time what no other repertory theatre is able to do more than dream about. It is creating, or has created, a real taste for the comprehension of good drama among the class which forms the real backbone of the playgoing public . . . The Old Vic management has realized long since that some people will not listen to what they do not understand; they know that if you are to educate public taste you must give your public plays which do not soar over their head. And, fortunately, they realize that very few of the best plays ever do soar above the heads of simple-minded people.

Unexpected recognition of the Old Vic's new status came in that season – from abroad. In June Lilian was invited by the Belgian Minister of Fine Arts to take her company to Brussels, as representatives of the British theatre. They were the first actors to play Shakespeare in English in Brussels, and were said to be the first company from a British theatre to visit a foreign capital at its government's request. Within seven years, four of them overshadowed by a world war, the Vic had become recognized as the equivalent of a national theatre – with no state subsidy, no spectacle, no stars (except those it had helped to make) and, above all, none of the space, the resources or the equipment that a normal, let alone a national, theatre needed. This Belgian honour was a milestone in the battling life of Miss Baylis, as well as in the progress of her theatre; and it was 'mucky old Shakespeare', not her beloved opera, which brought it. She appeared to take it all in her stride, although she enjoyed both the tribute and the treat with unaffected excitement. Beatrice Wilson, who acted with the company on that visit, described how Lilian made her entrance at an 'extremely swagger' official reception to welcome the Vic to Brussels. All the guests were dressed in their formal, fashionable best, but the manager of the Old Vic entered 'hot and dishevelled in a white shirt-blouse and a check skirt' – and very late, explaining breathlessly that she had just climbed to the top of the Waterloo Memorial, and needed a good wash and brush up. 'She returned with a face shining and ruddy from soap and water, and not a vestige of powder. She was quite unaware of anything unusual in her appearance . . . Suddenly she seemed to me to be the only real person there.'[27]

Such acclamation, together with the rise in box-office takings, helped to console Lilian for one disappointment which might, some years earlier, have amounted to a disaster: the temporary end of the school matinées in the early 1920s. Their undoubted wartime success had led to LCC backing for Shakespearian performances for children by Ben Greet elsewhere in London, but the legality of charging children for admission was challenged in 1919. Although the LCC then met the bill at the Old Vic and for Greet's performances, the legality of *this* payment was challenged in 1921 – and, for some years, the matinées had to be dropped. This cost the theatre a big slice of guaranteed revenue (which could have amounted to upwards of £1,500 p.a.); so it was just as well for the Vic that its new brooms, both in Shakespeare and opera, swept in a new prosperity. Between May 1921 and May 1922 the credit balance increased by over £2,800. The Governors voted an additional £200 p.a. to Atkins, in recognition of his work and his claim for a rise. This made his salary £700, and, as it seemed unsuitable that he should earn more than the manager, Lilian's pay was brought up to the same level. Frederick Hudson, who was confirmed as the opera producer and stage manager, was paid only £400.

That autumn at a symposium of drama critics all of them endorsed Herbert Farjeon's verdict that the most important theatre in London was the Old Vic. In Farjeon's view, this was largely because Robert Atkins's productions showed 'a sympathy, an insight and a fundamental appreciation of the essentially practical beauty of the poet's creations such as no other manager of the century has displayed'. In the old days, said Farjeon, the performances 'again and again reduced us to a state of such blank dismay that to have commended them would have been to betray the first principles of aesthetic criticism'. But with Atkins the Vic 'emerged for the first time out of the rut of the commonplace'.[28]

Robert Atkins's role in winning prestige for the Vic was certainly appreciated by Miss Baylis, although it seems doubtful that at the time he gave *her* much credit. After a brief honeymoon period of mutual amity their relationship became stormy and violent, even by Baylisian standards, without the gruff affection and respect that underlay her shouting-matches with, say, Ben Greet. Like B.G., Atkins often bellowed at his company – particularly at young actresses and at actors who seemed at all 'pansy' (in the current comminatory idiom). Unlike B.G., he not only barked but bit, sometimes with lacerating effect (often driven by his own physical pain: he suffered intensely in one season from mastoid trouble). His manager showed something of the same streak of cruelty (though hers was not usually deliberate) and her will – like his – was dominating, even domineering. As their immediate objectives did not always coincide, frequent clashes were inevitable; and although Atkins never pulled Miss Baylis's nose, he inflicted many verbal bruises. He detested the atmosphere of good works, the dowdiness and stinginess; he resented her 'meddling' in his productions, when she knew next to nothing about Shakespeare; and he was furious that she was honoured, as he saw it, for *his* achievements.

By Lilian's standards, Robert was a pagan – heavy-drinking, hard-swearing and womanizing. As Robert Speaight puts it, he was an Elizabethan, whereas Lilian was a Victorian. Sometimes she enjoyed his un-Victorian jokes. She asked him on one occasion whom he was casting as the Virgin Mary in Father Andrew's *The Hope of the World*.

'I haven't decided yet,' Atkins said.

'Well,' said Lilian, 'This time I *will* have a virgin.'

'When shall we hold the auditions?' asked Atkins. For a second or two he thought, 'this is the end of my contract', but she merely roared with laughter.[29] She was shrewd enough to give him plenty of rein: to turn a deaf ear, for instance, when he hurled four-letter words at the company as she was walking through the theatre. When a friend with her remonstrated, Lilian said calmly, 'Oh, he always loses his temper like that at dress rehearsals'. Robert often tended to redouble the effing when Lilian was in the offing. At one rehearsal, when a microphone had been installed on stage for one of the first BBC relays, he walked across to it, after directing a particularly lurid stream of language at his company's shortcomings, and boomed, 'And that goes for you too, Miss Baylis, if you're listening in'. When rehearsals moved slowly because of his concern with the details of production – something to which Lilian was not accustomed – she would shout from her box, 'Oh, get *on* with it, Robert'; and Robert would answer, not quite under his breath, 'Shut up, you old cow' (or something less pastoral). The slightest interference from her in rehearsals set off rumblings of protest from him. 'Krakatoa wasn't in it,' says John Laurie. But although his language was stronger than hers, his will was not. Robert was, indeed, a little afraid of Lilian, like many of the people who worked for her, and this kept in check his tendency to bully and to break actors' confidence. When she sacked Ion Swinley because his drinking was damaging his work, Atkins threatened to resign unless Swinley was reinstated. But that was not enough to influence Lilian: he had to recruit Ben Greet, who begged her to take back the offender on the promise of good behaviour. (For the time being it was kept: Swinley played Hamlet in its entirety without, said Atkins, 'missing a single comma'. And although more than commas were missed in later performances, Swinley's golden voice continued to be heard at the Vic until his death. Lilian recognized quality when she heard it.)

Somehow the Baylis–Atkins partnership survived for five years. However much she infuriated him, she gave him the chance to show how Shakespeare ought to be acted and staged – or, at least, to do the plays 'in a way that Shakespeare wouldn't have been ashamed of', (as John Laurie put it) and to attempt work that would have been impossible, at that time, in any other theatre.

By 1923, the 300th anniversary of the publication of the First Folio, all the plays in it had been staged at the Vic within ten years – a much more remarkable achievement than may appear to contemporary theatregoers, accustomed to revivals of plays that were then ignored and classified as unactable. Lilian, who had a ruling passion for anniversaries, seized the opportunity to mark her theatre's feat. A special performance of *Troilus and Cressida* – the last of the works to be presented – was given in November, and many notabilities attended, including Matheson Lang, William Poel, Stewart Headlam and other eminent allies of the Vic. When it was proposed to ask the Princess Royal and her husband, the house was already sold out, and Lilian indignantly protested that she was not going to turn any of her people out of their seats just for royalty – until the Governors finally persuaded her to let the Princess occupy their box. When the curtain fell, the stage filled up with members of past companies and other actors and actresses. All gathered in homage to Lilian Baylis and Robert Atkins; and the manager was presented with a silver rose bowl, inscribed with the congratulations of the company.

Among the further signs of change that year was the final disappearance of the lectures on Tuesdays, because the stage was needed for opera rehearsals – it was a 'temporary measure', but they never returned. Also Lilian reluctantly agreed to insert a daily advertisement in *The Times* as 'an experiment'. Moreover, the local council woke up to the Vic's importance. The Mayor suggested that, as it was a Lambeth institution, he and his councillors should attend a performance 'in state'; and the Governors agreed to invite him, although on Lilian's recommendation they accepted his offer to pay for the seats. A new patron emerged in the shape of the British Broadcasting Company, which agreed to pay fifteen guineas for the transmission of an opera and ten guineas for a play (plus five guineas if relayed to stations outside London). Official recognition – without, of course, a penny of official aid – was sealed on a more august level by the agreement of the King and Queen to become patrons of the theatre. (Lady Frederick Cavendish must have taken especial pleasure in this honour, which she helped to negotiate. It was among the last of her services to the Vic, for she died in 1925.)

Even more rewarding for the manager was the University of Oxford's decision to confer on her the degree of Master of Arts, *honoris causa*. Only one other woman to date had received this honour: Queen Mary. What is more, this was the first time that the university, which had been notoriously slow in sanctioning let alone honouring professional theatricals, had accorded recognition in such a way to the business of the stage. But then there was no business like Baylis business; and Oxford was signalling its approval of good works rather than good shows, of educational effort rather than managerial flair. On 6 May 1924 Lilian organized a characteristically eclectic expedition to Oxford from the Old Vic to witness the ceremony, including the chairman of the Governors, her father, her secretary, the box-office manager and other friends such as Mrs Edward Compton and old Bob, the stage-doorkeeper. Walking in formal procession to the Sheldonian, with four mace-bearers, Lilian looked, for once in her life, overawed – this was a production about which she had no chance to speak her mind. But everything went well on what was one of the greatest days of her life, when the Public Orator said of her (in Latin), 'it is very meet and right that we who are wont to enrol among ourselves the promoters of learning, whether male or female, should bestow a title, well deserved, upon this lady who has used the art wherein she herself is most highly skilled, to raise and foster the minds of the people'. Her escorting party were very proud, too. As one of them said, 'It was *lovely*, Miss. When I saw you come through those great big doors, it fair put me in mind of the execution of the Duke of Buckingham.' After the ceremony, the new MA entertained them all to tea at the Mitre, where she listened delightedly to a set of celebratory verses by the chairman (who was paying for the tea). She insisted that it was the theatre, not her, that was being honoured. 'This is nothing to do with me, or for anything that I have done, but it is an honour I am receiving on behalf of all the dear people who have so faithfully stood by the Vic in its hard fight for existence.' Yet her Oxford degree was, not surprisingly, a source of intense and abiding gratification. From then on she proudly wore her cap and gown at the Vic on all possible occasions – first nights, last nights, festivals, special appeals, Christmas, royal visits. She kept them at the back of her box, so that she could pop into them quickly, if the chance arose. '*Somebody* has to wear the things,' she protested when quizzed about them. 'You can't leave them hanging in the foyer or the hall. So I might as well wear them here.'

In the same year the Old Vic was honoured at Cambridge, in a way that gave Lilian almost as much pleasure – so that, in making her 1936 record about the theatre, she chose to mention it as one of the peaks of her achievement. This was a performance of *Everyman* on the chancel steps of King's College Chapel, the first to be given there, she proudly claimed, since the days of Queen Elizabeth.

While all this and more – bewilderingly more – was happening during the five years after the war, the future of both Shakespeare and opera was seriously threatened. Apart from all the multifarious worries of a management starved of money, space and time but morally committed to do the impossible, Lilian had to struggle with one Himalayan problem: the closure of the Old Vic unless reconstruction was undertaken.

Among the more surprising aspects of the theatre's history to date had been the ability of Miss Cons and her niece to keep the theatre open in conditions that would, in another kind of building less conspicuously devoted to philanthropic ends, have brought swift action by the licensing authority. Lilian continued her aunt's tactics, in defence of a weaker case (by LCC standards) and greater need (by Lilian's standards). But the greatly extended use of the building, with opera and drama companies squeezed into it for nearly forty weeks in the year, inevitably prompted the LCC to make more radical demands for reconstruction; for its inspectors knew that the old building in the Waterloo Road was quite inadequately equipped to serve one art, let alone two, while also accommodating a college on the premises. Though nobody said as much in public, the Old Vic was felt to be operating under false pretences, albeit for the very best of reasons. Lilian and the Governors had managed to defer action, on the grounds that there was a war on, but they knew that they would have to meet the LCC demands when peace came; and they also knew it would mean raising a sum of money greater than Emma had paid for the lease – estimated at some £7,000. It was, in fact, to cost far more than *that*; and to get this cash for the Vic (while saving as much as she could on its current operation) became Lilian's main and at times obsessive preoccupation. By the time the inevitable public appeal was launched in 1921, the target was set at £30,000 – of which the Vic had £10,000 in hand or promised.

It was high time for Morley College to go – that was the prime objective. What seemed so admirable in 1894 had become intolerable twenty-five years later. More space was needed imperatively for the economic and efficient running of the theatre (and the College, too). This meant, of course, a break with the Cons tradition; but it had to be made, and in March 1921 the Governors formally asked the College Council – with which, for so many years, they had been so closely linked – to quit. The Council agreed, if the Vic would provide alternative accommodation. This was found within two months, but at the cost of £20,000. Hence the appeal: there was no other way. It was launched in November with distinguished signatories, including not only the indispensable Lady Frederick Cavendish, Dame Ethel Smyth and the Bishops of Southwark and Manchester, but also three political leaders, Asquith, Bonar Law and J. H. Thomas. The audience gave generously, egged on by the exhortations of Miss Baylis: boxes were passed around at the intervals, and some £2,500 was raised. Collections were made in Morley College, too. The *Observer* took a keen interest in the campaign, and nearly £600 was raised by readers. (The editor, J. L. Garvin, said that 'although the *Observer* staff always worked together he had never known them so united in anything as in their determination that the Old Vic should be saved'.) A few individual donors gave as much as £100, including the King of Siam, 'whose interest touched all connected with the theatre very deeply'. But the money came in slowly; only £5,000 in six months, and the chance of the new site for the College began to evaporate. It was a bad time for Lilian, who was less ready than usual to cope with the crisis. Early in the season she had a nasty accident on her bicycle, and hurried back to work before she had fully recovered, so that she was obliged – with great reluctance – to take a convalescent holiday in the spring. It was the first time that she had left the Vic during the season in her twenty-four years there.

While she was away, however, her prayers were suddenly and dramatically answered. The *Observer* announced on the day after the season ended that a cheque for the whole of £30,000 had been offered by an anonymous benefactor, who was later revealed to be the theatrical manager, George Dance. Dance – who began his stage career as a writer of songs, sketches and libretti – had made a fortune from the production of musical comedies and other entertainments in a world apart from the Vic. According to W. MacQueen-Pope, who wrote of him in generally admiring terms,

Dance 'had the poorest opinion of actors and of theatrical art. His object was to make money, and he did.'[30] After his identity had been disclosed, which happened without excessive delay, he explained that he was in the theatre's debt before Miss Cons took it over, when he watched the plays from the gallery. 'The dingy old playhouse taught me what I wanted to know; there I learnt the rudiments of dramatic construction in a series of Shakespearian and standard British drama, which afterwards I was able to turn to useful account.'[31] People have given away thousands for less substantial reasons; but in this case one may perhaps look not only to Mr Dance's sudden gratitude for boyhood lessons in Lambeth, and to the power of prayer as practised by Lilian, but also to the fact that the philanthropic millionaire-author of *The Chinese Honeymoon* and other musical hits was knighted in the next honours list. The story goes that the news of his gift was not entirely unexpected by Lilian, for Lady Cunard – the celebrated political manipulator and hostess, who was by then a frequent visitor to the Vic – had volunteered to secure the theatre's future by getting Dance the promise of a knighthood if he would come to the rescue with his cheque book. When he did, Lady Cunard approached Lilian to claim her ten per cent: it was, she said, the customary arrangement. The air was sulphurous at the Vic. 'She'll never get any ten per cent out of *me*,' raged Lilian. She never did.

Whatever the cause of the Dance donation, it rapidly proved, in spite of its munificence, to be no more than a temporary solution to the problems of the Old Vic and Morley College. After a long search, new premises for the College were found that autumn in the Westminster Bridge Road; but the total bill for the building, its renovation and extension came to £27,000, and that obviously left the Vic with not enough cash for its own structural alterations. The Governors attempted to pay the College compensation based on no more than the value of its share of the old Hall; and although they had to abandon this position, they absolutely refused, after a prolonged wrangle, to pay more than £21,000.

For Lilian, brought up in the tradition of dual allegiance to College and Hall, it was a difficult time. Yet for all her loyalties she had – according to the College's historian, Denis Richards – 'nothing like Emma Cons's "parent's fondness" for the place; and her more brusque manner alienated more than one old student who had been devoted to her aunt'.[32] After the final separation was painfully accomplished she remained 'a good friend of the College'. She sometimes gave talks there; and College students continued to visit the Vic, though no longer privileged to pay half-price. But though rooms were named after Emma, the Martineau sisters and Ethel Everest, none was given the name of Auntie's niece; and the only formal link after 1924 between the College and its parent institution was the Old Vic Governors' right to nominate two members of the College Council.

This separation of college and theatre was an inevitable stage in healthy growth, the necessary rescue of both institutions from an impossible housing situation. Just as inevitable was Lilian's realization that, whatever private regrets she might secrete, there was no real doubt in her mind about her commitment to the Vic, which gave her more than enough cause for worry. And the death of Ellen Cons in 1920, at the age of eighty-one, had perhaps made it easier for her to snap one more link with the past.

Even so, there was still a long way to go before she could finally meet the LCC's demands and ensure the safety of the Old Vic. At first the LCC insisted that unless the programme was completed by March 1924 the Vic would be closed; but somehow Lilian's forces persuaded the Council to agree that the work on the auditorium should be postponed for a year or two, and that only the backstage alterations should be carried out right away. They were not, in fact, completed until two years later. Alarms and emergencies intervened. There was more need than ever for prayer – and economy.

Apart from the problems of paying for the reconstruction of the building, Lilian was tormented by the big rise in its running costs, an inevitable by-product not only of economic changes outside the Vic but of its own changes in standards. However hard she might skimp, save and haggle, she could not stop the bills from mounting. She was encouraged by one godsend, achieved after patient lobbying in that hard-pressed year of 1922: the Shakespeare Memorial Committee made a grant of £1,000 p.a. for at least three years, as long as the Vic 'pursues its present policy of making the production of Shakespeare's plays in a practically complete form the characteristic feature of their activity'. Mucky old Shakespeare was paying off, after all; and the audience for him was steadily increasing. Ten years after the introduction of drama in 1914 it overtook opera at the box office for a time. But the revenue didn't, and couldn't, meet the theatre's bills. The SMC's grant still left the Vic accounts in the red and Miss Baylis more determined than ever to get everything and everyone for the smallest pittance she could contrive to pay.

Just as the builders were about to begin on the new Morley College in March 1923, she had to meet another threat. The Vic suddenly discovered that the London Electric Railway was promoting a Parliamentary Bill empowering it to drive two new Tube lines under the College building; and was proposing to sink extraction shafts on the site. Far from being sympathetic to the desperate predicament of both Morley College and the Vic, the Railway announced that it was acquiring compulsory purchase powers, and offered miserably inadequate compensation. The LCC advised swift acceptance of the terms, but the Vic Governors and the College Council, sinking their differences, petitioned against the Bill. It all seemed in vain. The Bill started on its way through the Lords. And then, once again, salvation came out of the blue, at nearly the last moment, when the Bill was unexpectedly defeated in the committee stage. Lilian gave thanks to the proper quarter in the appropriate position: He had shown, once again, whose side He was on. And He moved the Carnegie Trust to send another cheque in 1924 towards the reconstruction: £5,000 down, with the promise of five further payments of £1,000 for each £4,000 raised from other sources.

Lilian had worked long hours under persistent strain since 1914; and, while the builders were on the job at the theatre, she took a long-promised holiday to South Africa – partly to revisit the scenes of her girlhood adventures and the landscape she loved, and partly to explore the possibilities of taking her opera company out there (a dream-project that she nursed until her death). She was so overtired that, when she received two cables inviting her to make speeches, she thought of cancelling the trip. But when she prayed for guidance on Corpus Christi Day, 'a strong voice spoke from the Reserved Sacrament, "My Grace is sufficient for thee," and she felt calm and fearless once again'.

While she was away, another storm blew up. The builders were called out on strike while the theatre roof was off, and the stage was left open to the sky. The Vic could clearly afford neither the delay nor the extensive damage that would have been caused by a prolonged stoppage. But one of the Governors, Reginald Rowe – who had organized resistance to the Railway Bill – conducted urgent, informal negotiations with the builders' union, and persuaded its leaders to classify the Vic with hospitals as an essential service in an emergency situation. Saved again, in the nick of time! Evidently Miss Baylis did not have to be on the spot for the miracles to work. (Rowe, an Under-Treasurer of Lincoln's Inn, achieved further quiet miracles on behalf of the Vic – and later for Sadler's Wells. Although his contributions in money, energy and time were inevitably overshadowed by Lilian's, he was knighted in 1934 – for his services to housing.)

Nonetheless, there were further delays in finishing the first stage of the theatre's reconstruction. The 1924–5 season – Robert Atkins's last – opened much later than usual (on 25 October); and, as Lilian Baylis (in new cap and gown) explained on the first night, the new lighting system had been handed over officially only at four o'clock that day, as work on the switchboard had been completed the night before; the company had not been able to use the stage for rehearsals until a few days before; and Atkins and his staff had not, she claimed, been to bed for three days and two nights. She herself had been in the thick of it, among all the new wonders. There was a safety curtain, which went right up into the space where Morley College Library had been, and counter-weighted scenery; there were dressing-rooms with running water, and even a bath; there was a wardrobe and workrooms on the spot; there was an orchestra room, and an outlet behind the stage for the players (who used to pass through the stalls exit); there was a lift, and a stage door with a doorkeeper; and instead of the old cubicles, there were offices for Lilian and her staff on the other side of the building. But her box remained; and so did the gas ring.

The auditorium was scarcely touched, apart from a dab of paint here and there, some rearrangement of seats in the balcony and gallery, and a new balcony exit door. It was another three years before Lilian could get the money to pay for the second round of reconstruction. But meanwhile the important thing was that while backstage efficiency was immeasurably improved – the Vic was at last operating in conditions similar to those of other London theatres – there was no deterioration in the quality of the audience. 'There is no other house like the Old Vic,' as one critic said that season. 'Everybody in it "belongs".' In spite of her new academic gear, and some new posh friends, the woman in charge 'belonged' as much as she had always done – and was seen to belong. Players and producers came and went, but Miss Lilian Baylis, MA Oxon. (Hon.) seemed to go on for ever.

Why did Robert Atkins leave that year? He was convinced, to the end of his life, that Lilian sacked him out of jealousy because he was drawing too much of the limelight. It was 'the green-eyed monster', he said in his autobiographical notes, that made her prevent him from directing *Cymbeline* in 1925, which meant he would personally have staged all thirty-six plays at the Vic in five years. She insisted instead on *Trelawny of the Wells*. Could Lilian have been so petty? Perhaps. Such observers as Sir Lewis Casson believed it; so did Atkins's successor, Andrew Leigh; so did John Laurie. Atkins said so himself, frequently and intensely, all round the theatre in that last season. He would plunge into the dressing-rooms, night after night, bitterly complaining that Lilian didn't appreciate him. He had some justification. It seems clear that Atkins was inclined to forget too often and too conspicuously that the Old Vic was Lilian's theatre, and the Old Vic's glory was Lilian's glory, under God's mercy of course, but not under Robert's. Yet there was one overriding reason for Lilian's preference of *Trelawny of the Wells* to *Cymbeline*: it was a very special gala production in aid of the new theatre-to-be. And, even if jealousy did enter into her break with Robert Atkins, there were other familiar factors in the difficulties created by his temperament and his intemperance. According to one friend, 'Robert had begun to hit the bottle too hard for Lilian to take it'. He was too much of an individualist and an egotist to fit into a team. And, in any case, he had been there five years – a long time to carry so big a workload in such bad conditions.

Ten years later Lilian said to a young actor (Marius Goring), 'Robert was impossible. He *had* to go. But there's never been anybody to touch him here. He was the best man we ever had in this place.' When other reputations have faded, it seems likely that the verdict of J. C. Trewin will be endorsed by future historians, that Robert Atkins 'did more for Shakespeare in the theatre . . . than anybody of his generation had done'.[33] And more, perhaps, for the Old Vic, than anybody except Lilian Baylis.

Lilian had dreamed, years earlier, of 'one great building which could house all the greatest achievements in art: of drama, of music, of dancing and of painting'. Although she had 'given up' that dream, she saw in the 1920s a way of accomplishing 'something a little nearer' to it – by taking over a second theatre . . .

The Way to the Wells

The Old Vic is like a child almost grown up and
by several sizes grown out of its clothes.
The way the child has grown up has been a joy to me,
and, though I can only claim it as a foster-child,
I may be forgiven for regarding it with motherly love.

Lilian Baylis (1925)

To act you must assume; and that assumption is faith.

Cardinal Newman

Right from the start of her experiment in combining opera and
Shakespeare under one roof, Lilian Baylis could perceive that one
theatre was not going to be enough. As early as 1915, even though
the Vic was sometimes almost empty and she had only a few
pounds in the bank, she was circularizing people with the news
that 'We are hoping to cooperate with some Theatre or Hall similar
to the old "Vic", where we can exchange our Companies upon our
"off" nights; and so help to establish in some other part of London,
needing such a centre, what is so much appreciated by the thousands of South Londoners in the Waterloo Road'. Visionary prospects, these, in wartime; especially when, as Lilian discovered,
there *was* no theatre or hall similar to the Old Vic, with a company
to exchange. Within ten years, however, in the era of *Peer Gynt*
and *The Magic Flute*, when the demands of the opera and drama
companies – if not, as yet, the demand *for* them – were splitting
the Old Vic at its seams, the need for another theatre seemed
inescapable. No less inescapable was the fact that, wherever it was,
Miss Baylis would have to run it.

One of the first candidates proposed in the early 1920s was the declining Surrey, but Lilian turned that idea down without hesitation. The Surrey was clearly far too near. The Canterbury, another South Bank showplace, was also ruled out. When Sadler's Wells was first suggested by Estelle Stead back in 1914 or 1915, Lilian had rejected the idea as 'a madman's dream', according to Russell Thorndike. 'It was ridiculous, she said, to think of adopting another child when one could not adequately provide for one's own.'[1] But once the decision to dislodge Morley College had been made, the notion began to take root in her imagination. 'The more she thought of it, the more she saw the vast possibilities,' especially after they had been pointed out by Reginald Rowe, who seized on the idea around 1924 (after the Wells had been rejected as a site for a pickle factory) and took her to see the building.

Sadler's Wells seemed suitable for colonization or partnership on several grounds. First, its history. It was one of the oldest theatre buildings in Europe, for its main structure dated back to 1765, although the interior had been remodelled in 1879. It had presented every kind of popular entertainment, a prime People's Theatre at its best, with Grimaldi as its greatest star; and in the 1850s it was the scene of a remarkable experiment in management by Samuel Phelps, who in his eighteen years at the Wells staged nearly all Shakespeare's plays and works by other Elizabethan dramatists, establishing a claim to be ranked – by his insistence on simple productions and relative fidelity to the text – as a forerunner of Poel and Atkins.

Second, its social geography. Like the Vic, it was in a working-class district with something of a theatregoing tradition; and it was far enough from the Waterloo Road to draw (in theory, at least) an entirely distinct audience.

And finally, its availability. As a theatre it had been closed since April 1914. Reopened as a cinema that September, the Wells shut down the following year, apparently for good. Since then it had been partly destroyed by local vandals. It needed reconstruction, but the external structure and the interior stone staircases were 'sound', or so the first appeal for funds pointed out. And it was going cheap.

When the eviction of Morley College was completed, the need to acquire a second theatre seemed urgent – despite the LCC demand for further reconstruction of the Vic, and the fact that Miss Baylis and her colleagues had no money for it, let alone for buying another building and reconstructing that. In spite of the

backstage improvements in 1924, the Vic could not cope indefinitely with the growing pressures from both opera and drama.
It could not, for instance, hope to make the best of its successes,
when no play, however well received at the box office, was given
more than a dozen performances, and when opera was presented
only ten times a month. Lilian was especially anxious that the
opera, which had for so long subsidized the drama, should be
given room to grow. To crusade for the redemption of the Wells,
moreover, offered an irresistible opportunity to follow Emma's
example; and it *was* followed in some respects – most conspicuously by getting a Duke to head a public appeal for funds. In spite
of all the social changes in the half-century that separated them,
there were some marked resemblances between the Cons and
Baylis campaigns, apart from the support of the Cavendishes.
Both had a strong vein of missionary fervour, begging for money
to acquire a theatre because it would be morally good for the
working class; and both still had to rely, in the main, on the consciences of the rich. But with ten years theatrical experience, the
King and Queen as Patrons and growing prestige on her side,
Lilian was able to recruit a starrier cast than Emma could do and
to raise far more money, without appealing to devout teetotallers
or anti-Socialists. Officially it was not Lilian's business. 'I had little
or nothing to do with the actual start of the scheme,' she said in a
letter to *The Times* in 1925. As the Old Vic was heavily in debt, the
Governors felt that they could not directly conduct a campaign to
acquire another theatre. But Lilian's achievements and prestige
were, in effect, used as the carrot for prospective donors, for it was
agreed that, when the Wells was available, the Vic would take it
over; and an Old Vic Governor, Reginald Rowe, was the honorary
treasurer (and tireless dynamo) of the separate Fund that was
established. Like Greet, Carey, Atkins and others he proved to be
the right man in the right place at the right time. One can see why
Lilian continued to believe that God took a special interest in her
work.

With Rowe and other kindred fund-raising spirits, she was
lobbying and pleading for some months before the Duke of
Devonshire launched the appeal in March 1925. (At that time the
Vic had £612 in its reserves.) The appeal committee glittered with
names from politics, literature and the arts: Churchill, Baldwin,
Balfour, Asquith, J. R. Clynes, Galsworthy, Chesterton, Gosse,
George Moore, Beecham, Ethel Smyth, Forbes-Robertson, Cyril
Maude and the Mayors of Islington and Finsbury. (Finsbury

subscribed £2,000. Islington voted against a gift of 100 guineas because, the Council majority agreed, children already learned enough about Shakespeare at school, and they could not afford such extravagances for minority amusements. Hospitals were just as deserving and the Council did not help *them*.) Money was sought, first, to buy the freehold, reconstruct the interior and save it for the nation; then, to make sure that it was properly used, the theatre would be established as a non-profit-making foundation under the Charity Commissioners and would be made available to the Vic's opera and Shakespeare companies, thus creating an Old Vic for North London.

By December the freehold and building were acquired, thanks to a gift of £14,000 from the Carnegie United Kingdom Trust (after Lord Hambleden had personally guaranteed the bank overdraft). But that was only the beginning. With some £6,000 in hand, about £40,000 was required. Six months earlier Lilian had believed that the Wells would reopen in the autumn of 1926. But she soon discovered that this was a dream. The existing fabric was much less of an asset than had originally been supposed – two of the main walls had to go, for a start, if the new theatre was to be big enough – and the money came in more slowly than the costs rose, in a way that has become depressingly familiar to all theatre builders in recent years. Nevertheless, Reginald Rowe and his colleagues – backed by Lilian – resolved to begin the reconstruction, even though they had less than half the necessary cash in sight, let alone in hand. This could not have been achieved without what Rowe described as 'a building contract of a very exceptional kind', which allowed the committee to stop the work as soon as its funds ran out; and for that (and much else) the credit must go to F. G. Minter (later Sir Frederick) who was a builder 'of a very exceptional kind', not least in his enthusiasm for the Wells, rooted – like much of its support – in moral and educational concern.

Lilian Baylis and Reginald Rowe had believed that the spectacle of the building operations would serve as an incentive to the private donors whose money they desperately needed. It did not. They were advancing into the unknown, at huge financial risk. As the Wells was a charity, no legal security could be given for bank advances to pay the mounting bills. The building had to proceed very slowly. It would have been lethally expensive to stop it completely, take down the scaffolding and, perhaps, never start again. So on it went, in fits and starts, in faith, hope and charity. It took five years to complete, at over twice the original estimated cost. For those five years Lilian's life was overshadowed, if not obsessed, by the financing and timing of the new Sadler's Wells. Emma had reached *her* objective so much more quickly. Sometimes God did move in a tiresomely mysterious way.

From the summer of 1925 onwards, while Rowe and Lilian begged and cajoled and bullied behind the scenes, the traditional propitiatory gestures of middle-class mendicants were continued in public – fêtes, garden parties, concerts, special matinées and many, many speeches on every possible occasion. Among the most august and glamorous contributors to the funds was Dame Nellie Melba, the Australian-born soprano who was for many years Britain's leading prima donna. As we have seen, she had once visited the Vic, in March 1914, to see *Rigoletto*; and, although she left before the end of the performance, she not only said kind words about it (duly passed on to the press), but also gave Lilian a cheque for £50. Thereafter she took a distant interest in the Vic, and in 1926 – at the very end of her career – fulfilled a long-standing if vague promise to sing there by agreeing to give a special concert in aid of Sadler's Wells. (She was brought into Lilian's net at last through the good offices of one of Emma's old friends, Lord Frederick Hamilton, a director of the South London Dwellings Company, as well as a backer of Covent Garden.) The concert sold out within two days of the announcement, and the long queue for tickets outside the theatre included, for once, many New Cut costers, few of whom (for all Lilian's notions) ever set foot inside the doors for Shakespeare. But nonetheless Lilian may have regretted the occasion. Not many people routed her; but Dame Nellie was one of them. She demanded her own conductor. She prescribed the billing (and exploded in fury when her instructions were not carried out). She requested a massive managerial order of violets, because she *always* had violets handed up to her from the audience. She had the front row of the stalls reserved for her friends. She even had the structure of the theatre altered, by insisting on an enlargement of the orchestra pit (to the advantage, thenceforth, of opera productions). It is not clear whether she met the cost of that operation, but she paid for the additional players, *and* for principals to sing with her in two acts of *La Bohème*. At one moment it all seemed in jeopardy. When Percy Pitt, the conductor of Melba's choice, discovered that no seats were available for his family or friends, Lilian received an ultimatum. Either she found seats for Percy Pitt, or Melba would not sing. So Lilian made a public appeal from the stage: if a kind friend of the Vic didn't make the supreme sacrifice of missing the concert, there wouldn't be a concert to miss.

At Lilian's invitation Father Hutchinson, of St John's, Waterloo Road, went along to see Melba rehearsing and found her 'working like a black, making everyone work as they'd never worked before. She was behaving as if it was *her* theatre. That, for Lilian, was unforgivable. Lilian said to me, as I came in, "That woman and I are going to have a row presently".' They did, indeed, have a row; and Dame Nellie seems to have won it. Lilian was found, in a collapsed state, sipping brandy. But she recovered after the performance. She called Father Hutchinson into her room, where Melba was standing, with masses of flowers (including the violets) piled around. 'Now, you've got a lovely lot of flowers,' said Lilian. 'But you won't want them *all*, I'm sure. There's a lot of hospitals round here. Father Hutchinson here has got a car at the door. He'll take them to the hospitals for you *now*.' Lilian felt, perhaps, that she had won that round. And she made over £300 for the Wells. It was Dame Nellie's last public concert in England. Lilian built up one of her stories about it (recorded by Winifred Holtby as 'brimming over with humour, vitality and the love of life'): how she was instructed by Melba to manufacture 'spontaneous and overwhelming' calls for 'Home Sweet Home'; and how Melba then insisted on singing it by herself, although the chorus were all *longing* to join in; but how, after all, she was 'a grand woman, a great woman'.[2]

Meanwhile, apart from the Wells, there was a sufficiency of problems for Lilian Baylis at the Vic in the twenties, with plenty of scope for prayer. In one respect at least Lilian had little to worry about (though, no doubt, she did worry): her governing board. According to Sir Adrian Boult, who was on it for a time, 'Lilian did more or less what she wanted, so there was not much left for the Governors to do beyond signing on the dotted line'.[3] There was no room reserved for their meetings: a trestle table was put up wherever they could be fitted in – often at the back of the dress circle. They included, at various times, such artists and writers as Edward Dent, Geoffrey Toye, Allardyce Nicoll, Barry Jackson, Herbert Read, Hutin Britton and Muriel Gough. As on all boards, only a few at a time were activists, among whom Reginald Rowe was perhaps the best known and certainly the most productive. However, the passive majority appear to have given Lilian steady support and a minimum of trouble, a feat seldom achieved by theatre boards today; but with Lilian in charge the Governors felt they had no cause to fear either financial extravagance or moral controversy, the most common causes in boardrooms of alarm, despondency and intervention. She was particularly fortunate in her chairmen, Everard Morrish, Sir Wilmot Herringham and Lord Lytton, who were not only distinguished figure-heads but hardworking, loyal allies. There were rows, of course, in private encounters and official meetings of the Executive Committee, to which she reported every month or so. Lilian always spoke her mind, brusquely and frankly if not always clearly, wherever she might be; and she sometimes found it no easier to keep her temper with a Governor than with a stage-doorkeeper or fire inspector. Her last chairman, Lord Lytton, said, 'She would get very excited and explosive, giving expression to vehement opinions delivered at the top of her voice. At such times I had to intervene to keep the peace. But there was never any malice in Miss Baylis's outbursts – they were always in defence of some principle which she held sacred, and the storms would subside as quickly as they arose.'[4] She was far too important to the theatre for such tempests to matter: the Governors knew her value. Even those who may have been critical of her methods and sceptical of the legend already forming around her were infected by her faith in the Vic.

In the decade since she started Shakespeare, Lilian had lost some of her gaucherie and frumpishness. When Andrew Leigh returned to work at the Vic, ten years after the first Greet season, he noticed the changes in the manager. Her manner was less abrasive. She had become 'more of a woman of the world, more sophisticated. Her hair was done in a different way. Some of her feminist friends had taken her in hand and dressed her up a bit.' But although she looked rather less like a social worker, she still – said Leigh – behaved like one; she still 'ran everything like a parish hall'. The simplicity, the dedication and the will-power were still the same, too. Whatever the adjustments in appearance, the essential Lilian remained.

As for the staff, by 1925 Miss Baylis had formed around her a tiny, dedicated team who were nearly all still in harness when she died twelve years later, and whose survivors still tended to talk of her, long afterwards, in the present tense.

The veteran of the group was Muriel Ellis, who had joined

Lilian twenty years before and, until 1914, constituted the entire office staff, acting as a general aide in secretarial, fiscal and managerial chores, although – like most of Lilian's team – she had no previous theatrical experience (or, indeed, any office experience). Like many of them she came to the Vic through her church connections: she was a clergyman's daughter. With the expansion of the theatre's work in 1914 she became treasurer and second-in-command. A genteel, plain, dowdy and rather schoolmarmy figure, her most noticeable assets were her devotion to Lilian (with whom, in their first decade together, she sometimes went on holidays) and her readiness to sacrifice herself to the Vic. Although her professional utility seems to have been questioned among the staff, Miss Ellis remained as treasurer until 1928, when Lilian suddenly fired her. The reason for her departure was never made public; but as she remained in touch with Lilian afterwards, clearly no treason to the Vic had been committed. The immediate cause is said to have been her dereliction of duty in carrying away the ledger of the Vic takings to the Lyric, Hammersmith, where the company played a short season in 1927-8. 'The ledger is the Book of Life for the Vic, and it must always stay at the Vic,' Lilian shouted at her; and after a row she told Muriel to leave. But it seems probable that her old friend was looking for an excuse to make the break at last, because Miss Ellis had not only become inefficient but an increasingly tiresome victim of sexual frustration, with a tendency to gush about the better-looking actors; to have presents left for them anonymously at the stage door; and, more perilously, to allow the kinder or more *rusé* ones to buy her drinks and pump her about the politics of the office. Not everybody mourned poor Miss Ellis's departure. One posthumous verdict was, 'she's the sort of woman who always kept her hat on in the theatre'. But others remembered her with affection and gratitude.

Muriel Ellis was succeeded as treasurer by the only man in Lilian's office team, Bruce ('Dig') Worsley. When he joined in 1923 as front-of-house manager (a job he continued until Lilian's death) his theatrical experience was limited – he had briefly managed the Croydon Grand and acted in a touring company – but, more significantly, he had a notable war record. Having got himself into the army at fifteen, he ended with a commission in the RAF, a variety of wounds that kept him going in and out of hospitals for five years after his demobilization and a silver plate in his skull. Lilian admired courage just as much as, if not more than, piety; and she admired masculine good looks, too. She could see that Mr Worsley would be a decorative figure in the foyer; she could sense he was the kind of man that the theatre needed, at this point in its growth, and she also took to him straight away. 'You poor dear, we must mother you,' was her greeting; and then she offered him £2 a week, on trial. A friendly, gentle but somewhat remote and reticent man, 'Dig' did not belong to the circle of Lilian's intimates, 'the Inner Circle', as Ethel Smyth called it, but he remained an indispensable member of the team until her death, and was named as one of her trustees.

A key figure in the Baylis regime was Evelyn Mary Williams – 'Williams', as she was always known – who joined the theatre in 1921. Like Bruce Worsley she had been in uniform (the WRAF), and her social background, like his – and unlike her employer's – was that of the middle-class gentry, with a Cheltenham and Oxford education and a sizeable private income. Nominally, Williams – a small, sparrow-like figure with 'goggle' glasses – was Miss Baylis's secretary; but in such a small organization, with so unorthodox a boss, her responsibilities soon expanded far beyond the customary secretarial limits. Although 'her typing was execrable and her shorthand non-existent,' according to Tyrone Guthrie (a lifelong friend) she was in her own style an unflappably efficient organizer and office diplomat. She underpinned Lilian's emotional guess-work with careful staffwork and cool, sometimes icy authority; helped to pour oil on troubled waters and temperaments; and attempted to translate the sometimes mysterious workings of the manager's intuition into practice, while protecting her from the possible consequences of her more dangerous blunders and indiscretions. She stood up against her employer's dominating will, matching it with her own (though she lacked Lilian's charisma). She refused, for instance, to work late, night after night, as Lilian expected her staff to do. 'I hate clockwatchers,' she would say ominously. Williams declared firmly, soon after her arrival, 'I am coming in early, and I am going early,' and she succeeded in doing that, emergencies apart, during her long reign at the Vic. Sometimes Lilian was convinced that Williams despised her, because of her lack of education; but in fact Williams seems to have regarded her as a genius, if a tiresome one, and gave Lilian her complete loyalty. It was she who started to call Lilian 'The Lady', the name by which she became widely known inside the Vic among the staff. Williams did so partly to discourage the back-stage tendency to call the manager 'Mother' (or, rather, 'Muvver'), prompted not only by protective loyalty but also, perhaps, by ironic Irish humour; for 'the Lady' was (luckily for the Vic and the theatre in general) far from being ladylike (as the term was conventionally understood) although she was, in her own domain, a great lady. Williams did a good deal, I believe, to elaborate and propagate the anecdotes about Lilian, and to help the Lady to articulate her public role and support its performance. As time went by, she took over more and more responsibilities and was indispensable to the successful operation of the theatre. She also tended (especially after the Lady's death) to adopt some of her eccentricities, together with her causes.

Williams became one of Miss Baylis's intimates at the theatre, invited to share a gas-ring snack in the office and, on occasions, a fuller and more formal meal at her home in Stockwell. Among the select few who also shared these odd collations and the confidences that went with them was Mrs Kathleen Clark, a stocky, auburn-haired Cockney, who joined the Vic in 1916 to work in the box office, at fifteen shillings a week, and was still there in 1937 when Miss Baylis died. By then she had reached the pinnacle of £7 a week, but she had never asked for a rise. 'Somehow I wouldn't have dared. She'd have made me feel I was robbing the Vic.' Clarkie never forgot her first wartime night there, when she set out for home absent-mindedly taking five shillings change. After she had gone some distance from the theatre she realized that she still had the money in her bag, rushed back to the Vic and, meeting Miss Baylis at the stage door, thrust it into her hand. Instead of thanking her, Lilian said to her sternly, '*Never* take any of the theatre's money away with you – you might get blown up on the way home, and to the Vic every shilling is precious'. Clarkie – still in 1974 an unquenchably sunny personality and vivid talker, in spite of her age and angina – came from a lower-middle-class Cockney background, closer to the manager's own milieu than that of Williams and Worsley. ('We don't believe in Mr and Miss down here,' Lilian used to declare.) She spoke her mind shrewdly and wittily, with the frankness that Miss Baylis (for whom the 'Miss' was rarely dropped down there) exercised on everyone else. She made Lilian laugh. She was, like Williams, a fighter with a strongly individual personality; and she kept Lilian in touch with audience reactions to the programmes. Those were good reasons why they got on so well together; and there was another: 'You and I have never been educated, Clarkie, have we?' Lilian used to say to her. 'We've never been trained to our jobs.' There was more pride than shame in that avowal. Clarkie was 'another Lilian Baylis, really,' said Dame Sybil.

Williams, Clarkie and Worsley were all, as we have seen, part of the permanent crew till the captain suddenly left the bridge, for ever, in 1937. Other stalwarts till the end were the two popular wizards of the wardrobe, Mrs Newman and Orlando Whitehead, who joined the Vic in 1921 and 1923 respectively, and whose ability to conjure wonders out of notoriously meagre resources has been recorded affectionately in several memoirs of the time. And down in the hold were Cockney institutions whose links with the Vic went back to the days of Miss Cons, and who enjoyed a special status as 'characters', genuine proles and friends of 'Mother'. Roland Robinson ('Old Bob') had tried many jobs at the Vic since he was engaged by Emma Cons, three months after she took it over. He started as a check-taker, became head scene-shifter, progressed to stage carpenter (in which his no less *rusé* son Rowley succeeded him) and, finally, stage-doorkeeper. By 1920 he was already relished as something of a period piece, with his battered hat tilted slightly over one ear, his yellowing Old Bill moustache, his pipe (from which he was inseparable) and his air of raffish authority. Sometimes he was urged out on the stage on the last night of the season, 'thrust unwilling forward, rose in hand, to make his bow before the curtain which has often been his business to manipulate'.[5] As Harcourt Williams said, 'He belonged to the Victorian "working classes" that *Punch* used to patronize in the eighties and which the socialism (with a dash of William Morris in it) of Emma Cons had striven to uplift. It was for Bob and his kind that the Old Vic had been invented.'[6] Certainly he did sometimes appear to regard it as his own demesne (and the Mother's), treating everyone as at best his equal with a Cockney aplomb that could never be disturbed by new arrivals from the West End accustomed to a greater show of backstage deference. 'He was a tyrant,' says Joan Cross, 'and he kept me in my place.' He would bring the Mother down to earth too at times – as on the occasion of Queen Mary's first visit to the Vic, when Miss Baylis had worked herself into a state of high excitement over such details as the width and condition of the bread-and-butter for tea. 'Don't *worry* so much,' said Old Bob, 'the Queen knows she aint acomin' to Buckingham Palace.'

A younger figure from the same Lambeth background was William Townsend ('Townie') who first worked for the Vic at the age of twelve when he left school in 1907. He was introduced to the theatre – with several other members of the family – by his uncle, a local builder, who had been 'saved' by Miss Cons and cherished a deep admiration for her. Townie started his career by selling programmes, and had stayed at the Vic ever since in many different capacities ('I've done everything in that theatre except sing *Pagliacci*'), becoming a valuable aide to Bruce Worsley. Among his main responsibilities was washing the entire auditorium, to save Miss Baylis from decorators' bills; and he also saved her from paying them at home, where he did many of her domestic odd jobs and acted as a handyman in times of need. She was, in some ways, a strict employer: Townie dared not be seen to drink while on duty, at Stockwell or at the theatre. Yet she was also a companionable one, and their relationship was flavoured with a friendly, often gruffly bantering intimacy of manner, illustrated in one of his stories about her:

She used to ride a bicycle, see, and she got dumped off this bicycle. So she was laid up in bed. When I called at her place in the morning, her housekeeper said to go up. There she was in bed. So I said, 'How d'you feel, then?' 'How do you think I feel?' she said. She pulled her clothes up and showed me her leg, all black and blue. Yes, *she* didn't care.

'There's a parcel over there,' she said. 'Open it up.' There were six photographs of her inside it. 'I want you to get them framed,' she said, and she told me where she wanted it done. And then she said, 'You'd like one of those, wouldn't you, Townie?'

For a joke, I said, 'Now, what's the good of that to me?' 'What do you mean?' she said.

'I've got no rats or mice in my cellar to put it in front of.'

She sort of laughed, and then she said, 'Give me my pen over.' And she signed one of them, and gave it to me. She'd written, 'To Townie, for his years of faithful service at the Old Vic, from his friend and manager Lilian Baylis'.

Townie, who remained on the Vic–Wells payroll for twenty years after Lilian's death, cherishes that photograph today as one of his proudest possessions. 'She was like a mother to me.'

Among the less dependable though almost as long-established Cockney retainers in Miss Baylis's entourage was Nightingale, a gloomy factotum with 'heavy feet and weeping whiskers'. He lived like an old mole in the cellarage, and his den smelt of old fish, cabbage and paraffin. His precise theatrical function puzzled members of the company, but his multifarious jobs included, at various times, those of fireman, boilerman, storekeeper, sweeper, cooking odd meals for the staff and shopping in the New Cut for Lilian. He would appear despondently at the office door, carrying his string bag, and ask her abruptly, 'Do you want 'addock, 'alibut or 'ake today?' In the 1930s Lilian entrusted him with more responsible errands, like taking money to the bank. He took some of it for himself, having borrowed heavily from his slate club to meet losses in gambling, and when his embezzlement was discovered he committed suicide. To her grief, it happened before Lilian could come to the rescue, as she had done on many other occasions. As we shall see in the following chapter, pilfering was by no means unknown at the Old Vic, but most of the offenders escaped punishment – except from Lilian's tongue.

Minor peculation, a problem in all theatres, was scarcely surprising when the level of pay was so low, the volume of work so high and the organization so essentially amateurish and dependent on part-time, untrained help – like that of the wrestler who worked as a stage-hand, a linkman and a chucker-out. What *was* surprising was the relative efficiency with which the amateurs and professionals combined under the Lady's leadership; and the zeal which informed some, if not all, of the casual labourers – like the woman from Surrey Lodge who was paid a few shillings a week for front-of-house jobs (including responsibility for the Ladies), and yet insisted on handing Lilian any tips she received. The staff was far too small; members of the inner circle, says Bruce Worsley, each played about five different roles. Yet, in their various and sometimes eccentric ways, they made an indispensable collective contribution to the achievements of the theatre, for very little money and not a sniff of glory. 'By some miracle,' Evelyn Williams wrote, Lilian 'made all of us anxious to overwork, and unwilling to go home'.[7] This devotion was far from being uncritical: Lilian's faults were blindingly and often obvious. She exploded into volcanic rages, with little or no provocation; she would pick on people, unfairly and persistently; she would sometimes fret furiously about trivia, concentrating on whether the gallery had been cleaned with the thoroughness she expected instead of on the immediate crisis of engaging a new soprano or rearranging the Shakespeare dates. She became oddly indecisive, about matters large and small (usually, no doubt, because she was waiting for instructions from God). When she went off on a retreat, she would sometimes go all round the departments and 'blow them up' – 'to keep us quiet till she came back,' said Orlando Whitehead.[8] And as soon as she was back, spiritually recharged, she was likely to start blowing them up all over again. Retreats often seemed to have an unfortunate effect on backstage relationships. Such explosions, however, usually left no lingering damage, and they came to be expected by the people who got to know her, laugh at her, respect her and like her, even sometimes love her. She hated sycophants, smugs and show-offs, milk-and-water meekness, self-pity and laziness. However maddening she often was, those were not her weaknesses. Part of the reason for her staff's dedication was that, in Williams's words, 'she never expected half as much from those she employed as she gave herself'.

After the Wells was opened Lilian was criticized because she refused, at first, to expand the staff to meet the new demands (and to jettison some of the deadwood). Yet, despite the drawbacks of understaffing – not least for the private lives of these overworked and undervalued loyalists – and of pushing untrained volunteers into situations where they were at sea, Lilian was struggling not only to maintain control over her expanding empire (or, later, to keep the illusion of such control), but also to preserve the manifest sense of personal identity in management which was among the Vic's special assets. And this is still one of its lessons for theatre managers today, with a hundred times as much to spend and no individual ambience, no tangible continuity of development, no creative authority to show for it.

Elsewhere, in the drama and opera departments, the same continuity was evident; and the company renewed its strength, trained new talent and discovered fresh slaves and 'helpers' in the same haphazard ways, directed by Lilian's hit and miss intuition. Consider the case of Joan Cross, who went for an audition one summer day in 1923. She had no stage experience and, indeed, she had no real ambition to sing in opera.

There was a ghastly upright and very tinny piano, some light on the stage, the auditorium in total darkness it seemed; I was too frightened to look. I still have that impression of nothing but old scenery, old props, all round the stage, and a strange and forbidding atmosphere which struck terror into my heart.

After she did her piece – the 'Ballatella' from *Pagliacci* – there was silence. Miss Cross walked off the stage.

It was, as I had thought, a waste of time. I tried to find the way I had come in ... when suddenly a voice unlike any I had ever heard before or since (except from those stalls outside in the market) bellowed, 'Where's that girl gone? Fetch her back!'

188

It was, of course, Lilian Baylis, who made a characteristic opening gambit.

'Any stage experience?' she rapped out. 'None? Well, I'm not going to pay you to get it in my theatre. You can come into the chorus if you want to.' She was so intimidating, so like a battleship cleared for action – and I felt so like a small dinghy trying to steer clear – that I could only stammer. I was making a lamentable impression, I felt; indeed she made it seem as though it was my obligation to pay *her* for the privilege of stepping inside her theatre.

There was no pay, and no contract, for the first season. But Miss Cross stayed on to become one of Britain's leading singers, a top opera director and a pillar of the Vic–Wells empire. She stayed in spite of such remarks from Lilian as this one after her appearance in *Lily of Killarney* in 1924: 'You sing nicely, dear. Pity you can't act.'[9] She put up with it – like Sumner Austin, to whom Lilian would suddenly say things like: 'You look like nothing on earth.' There were rows, of course. On one occasion Austin, exasperated beyond endurance, rushed into her office and said, 'If you were a man, I'd knock you down.' Lilian eyed him coldly from the desk, and said, 'Well, I'm *not* a man. So get *out.*'

Although the Vic employed new singers – like Joan Cross, Edith Coates, Henry Wendon, Heddle Nash – it staged few new works. In 1922 Lilian asked the opera audience, through a note in the programme, to tell her what kind of music they wanted. A third, she later reported, said they wanted more Verdi; a third wanted more Mozart; and the rest said they wanted nothing but Wagner – so she decided that no radical changes should be made. Three minor British works – Nicholas Gatty's *The Tempest* and *Prince Ferelon* and Ethel Smyth's *The Bosun's Mate* – were adopted as house favourites. But it was not until 1926 (after Geoffrey Toye joined the Governors) that the repertoire was extended to include *Madame Butterfly*; *La Bohème* did not arrive until 1928, and *Tosca* till 1929. Meanwhile, the standard works continued to be staged more or less as they had always been staged, less shabbily and skimpily than in the era of Recitals, but with a minimum of expenditure on costume, scenery and production. From 1922 this was in the hands of Frederick Hudson, a popular member of the company for the past decade. But he was no more than a stage manager, whose stage management was of the simplest traditional kind. As Sumner Austin said, 'you were told to come on *here* and go off *there*. The rest you filled in for yourself. There was no production whatsoever.' The same familiar bits of scenery – church, trees, cottage – were trotted out again and again. The same mossy bank served on all manner of occasions (Shakespearian as well as operatic). But although Lilian allowed a little experiment in the drama, it was forbidden in opera, which she guarded against 'arty' innovations. On one aspect of production she was insistent: no scene of what she called Lust (on the Venusberg, for instance) was complete without *pink*. 'Pink for passion was one of her main ideas. Though, of course, everybody had to behave in an exemplary fashion,' said Sumner Austin. Apart from the visual curiosities, there were frequent musical surprises – like the use of a concertina to fill in the missing woodwinds in *Don Giovanni*, or the sudden arrival in the pit of Dennis Brain. As Joan Cross says, 'We never knew what kind of brass or wind section we were going to get till we were on stage for the performance'. The singers continued to work in isolation from the actors, although Miss Cross, for one, gained valuable experience of a kind that she could never have gained in German opera houses – by watching some of the prime Shakespearian talents (notably, Gielgud) rehearsing; and the gap between the two groups was bridged by the versatile Harry Powell Lloyd, actor, singer and designer, who married one of Lilian's major artists, Edith Coates. The music was still the responsibility of Charles Corri and (until 1926) Lawrance Collingwood, who was succeeded as chorus master by Walter Wiltshire. The survivors of the ageing chorus continued to turn up ten times a month, rewarded by cake and lemonade. And the press notices continued to make allowances for the traditional difficulties, and even on occasion to give high praise, with the traditional qualifications about 'roughnesses and shortcomings'.

By the mid-1920s critics showed a tendency, however, to become somewhat less patient about these blemishes. This was reflected, for instance, in *The Times* review of *Lohengrin*, which opened the 1926 season. The critic suggested that Corri 'ought to get better playing from the strings: they might, at least, be up to the standard of the wind. The chorus master might overhaul the vowel sounds of the chorus . . . Every member of the company except Mr Sumner Austin might rethink out his part to the extent of inventing entirely new gestures. Mr S. Harrison might be told that there is no need, even for a herald, to bite off every phrase of his proclamation with a snap of the teeth. These and similar small revisions would break the deadening effect of routine, which is detracting from the value of performances which are, in the most essential respect, admirable.' But Lilian had no time for critics. And, in any case, everything would be all right once she had the Wells.

In the Shakespeare department, continuity of managerial control and resistance to higher spending were harder to maintain; but the two men who succeeded Robert Atkins – Andrew Leigh (1925–9) and Harcourt Williams (1929–33) – fitted admirably into the world of Miss Baylis at the Vic. Both had a solid Shakespearian grounding as graduates of the Benson company (in which, at different periods, each spent five years); both were influenced by Poel in their attitude to Shakespearian production (although Williams's more immediate inspiration was Harley Granville-Barker); and both had 'family' links with the Vic. Andrew Leigh had worked as stage manager, actor and director in the first war-time season; and had returned to act (primarily as a Shakespearian comic) in the 1920–22 and 1924 seasons. Harcourt Williams – who had a wider West End experience of acting, but had done little directing – was engaged by Miss Baylis, he was told, because of the way in which he produced some children's plays at a Christmas matinée. He had also been recommended by Ellen Terry; but the clinching argument in his favour was that he was married to the actress presenting that matinée, Jean Sterling Mackinlay. She had been giving recitals at the Vic since 1920, was a personal friend of the manager *and* – even more decisively – was the daughter of Antoinette Sterling, who had given Emmie such valuable and voluntary support in the pioneering days. ('She was the first great artiste to reach the hearts of the Lambeth people, and they gave her what they have never since given to anybody,' declared Lilian in the Magazine in 1923.) Compared with Atkins, both Leigh and Williams were gentle persuaders, who coaxed and manoeuvred instead of bullying and blasting. They lacked his touch of genius, but shared his belief in simplicity, speed and respect for the text (though the Atkins pace seemed slow to Leigh, and Williams found Leigh's work too sluggish and stagey). They seldom quarrelled with the Lady, although both found her, on occasion, suspicious, stubborn, unfair and irrational. They believed in compromise rather than confrontation. Leigh, in particular, managed to maintain a remarkable degree of backstage harmony. When he left, the annual report paid the tribute that 'he never lost the friendship and goodwill of a single one of those who have worked with him'. And Williams, though not so widely popular among the staff, became Lilian's favourite among her directors.

In spite of the increasing fame of the Vic in the 1920s, there were still – to Miss Baylis's continuing grief and indignation – many empty seats at many performances. But box-office business slowly and patchily improved, particularly for Shakespeare, who overtook opera around the middle of the decade. The 1925–6 season broke all records to date: on most Shakespeare nights the Vic was unprecedentedly full. The main draw – and the prime glory – was Edith Evans, the first West End star to join a company at the Vic. After appearing at Drury Lane in *A Midsummer Night's Dream*, in which she played Helena 'to the satisfaction of very few people and certainly not my own', Miss Evans decided that she must 'find out how to play Shakespeare',[10] although she had made her debut twelve years earlier as Cressida under William Poel's direction and had appeared meanwhile in several of the Works (or fragments of them) with Ellen Terry. The Old Vic was the obvious place to learn in 1924. It had seemed so, indeed, six years earlier, when Edith Evans had hoped to work there; but Lilian had turned down approaches on her behalf. 'I was a fool,' she told Sybil Thorndike years later. 'I ought to have engaged her but she didn't look the leading type.' Now Lilian saw what she had missed, although she was still slow in grasping the opportunity. The Lady and Edith Evans had mutual friends (including Ellen Terry) who told Edith to write to Lilian and ask if she could work for her. As no word came from the Vic, Edith did so. Lilian struck a bargain (as Andrew Leigh was enthusiastic), and Miss Evans was given thirteen roles, including Portia, Rosalind, Cleopatra, Beatrice, Kate the Shrew, and Juliet's Nurse. She led the company with Baliol Holloway, a fine artist and a seasoned Shakespearian who had toured the country for years with such managers as Frank Benson, and had also worked in the West End for Granville-Barker and others.

In the opening play, *The Merchant of Venice*, Edith Evans found it impossible to get into contact with the audience. It was not until the third production, *The Taming of the Shrew*, that she came to terms with it; was accepted; and was, by many, adored. During the next eight months of her education in Shakespeare her talent soared and stretched. Not only *she* changed, but so did the audience; for her name – and the news about her acting, combined with Holloway's – led an increasing number of West End playgoers to discover the virtues of the Vic. Takings dropped in the season after Miss Evans's departure (seventeen pounds lighter in weight and immeasurably richer in experience), but the Vic was never quite the same again. It had been put vividly on the theatrical map in a way that an anniversary treat (like a Birthday Festival) or an intellectual rarity (like *Faust*) could not hope to achieve. Edith Evans had been put on the road to greatness. She was also established as a friend of the Vic, where she returned during the next decade to help the theatre as well as herself. Like other leading artists who followed her to the Waterloo Road, Dame Edith was sometimes unduly credited with philanthropy in performing there. But to act at the Vic, at the right time in one's career, was – as she magnificently showed – to serve one's self-interest and one's art, as well as Lilian Baylis.

The danger of being taken up by West End actors – and West End audiences – began about this time to emerge among those problems of success that caused the Lady mounting concern in the last decade of her life. Of course, she wanted her theatre (especially her opera) to succeed: why else did she burn herself out in its service, working fourteen hours a day and more? But she wanted it to be filled with the right kind of people: poor, deserving and preferably local; and the right kind of artists, putting Service, Beauty and the People (plus, if possible, God) before their own salaries and careers. Just as it was obviously inevitable that casting could not be maintained on moral and character judgements, so it was inevitable that the composition of the audience should change. There was not enough support in the immediate neighbourhood to keep the Vic open: the growth in the public for Shakespeare since the first desperately ill-attended seasons was due to an influx of schoolteachers, students and other enthusiasts from all over London. By 1925 few Lambeth costers, the original target of Emma Cons, could be found in the gallery. It was not class solidarity or territorial loyalty that created the community of interest, freshness of response and warm family feeling in the unique audience of the 1920s. But Lilian was bound to worry. She liked to mother the audience. She knew a great many members of it personally. And she didn't fancy trying to mother a lot of uppity strangers. Being uppity was something of which Miss Baylis deeply disapproved; and one of her managerial burdens was to chasten people who were (or might well be) inclined towards uppityness. She tried to make sure that newcomers knew their place, and *her* place; not that she expected deference, but she wanted people to put personal vanity aside in the service of the Vic (as she believed *she* did) and to show them that she was not going to stand for swank and side. That, surely, lies behind some of her notoriously crushing remarks to young actors and actresses who had just joined the Vic – and who, not surprisingly, remembered those bruises long after they had forgotten later bouquets. Like her encouraging, 'Oh don't be nervous! They'll like you here whether you're good or bad'; or her remark to Nora Nicholson, after she had played Celia in *As You Like It*, 'The audience thought you were *awful*'. When John Laurie first joined the Vic, she said his legs were too thin – and made him so self-conscious that he padded them for the rest of the season. After Marie Ney's first appearance she said, 'Very good, dear, but there's something wrong with your hands'. Miss Ney, by no means a novice, knew there wasn't. 'She thought the good notices might have gone to my head.' In a different category, perhaps, was Lilian's reassurance of a young singer, leading in *La Traviata* for the first time, who said to Miss Baylis, 'I hope you don't think I overdid my make-up'. 'Oh *no*,' said Lilian, 'I always think Violetta ought to look a bit tarty.'

Among other worries in the 1920s were the stars who could not be put down by such brusquery, and the demands they made on the budget. There was, for instance, the matter of Edith Evans's wardrobe, which was newer and dressier than had been seen before at the Vic. The rule of poverty had, apparently, been bent, or at least circumvented. How? Dame Edith explained later that she had been 'rather artful'.

I wanted new clothes; but I didn't want Lilian to think that this tiresome woman from the West End, whose value as a Shakespearian actress still had to be proved, was insisting on unusual expenditure. So when any question of clothes was mooted I used to ask very politely if they would telephone down to Miss Baylis to come to the Wardrobe and discuss the matter; and before the session was finished she was wanting new clothes as much as I was, and how often and how rightly did she boast of the beautiful dresses made for the season of 1925–6.[11]

It sounds painless. It was not. But it was not allowed to set a precedent.

There were troubles outside the theatre: Lilian got very cross with the Salvation Army band which used to blast off within earshot on opera nights. Then there were the public meetings on the corner of Webber Street, right outside the theatre. Lilian tried for years to get them suppressed, at first with no success. She also protested at regular intervals to the LCC and the police about the conduct of the nearest pub and its patrons, in the hope of blocking a renewal of the licence. And she fought furiously for the destruction of the neighbouring public urinal, on whose continued immunity she angrily reported to the Governors year by year. It was not Puritanism alone which prompted these small but fierce crusades, but her protective and proprietorial concern for the welfare of her theatre and all the people who worked in it or visited it. She had eventually to acquiesce in coexistence with the pub, and the urinal was only eliminated, long after her death, because it became a popular homosexual 'cottage'; but she finally had her way about the public meetings.

There were battles, too, over the theatre's catering. Pearce & Plenty was one link with the past that Lilian longed to snap. For years there were arguments over the quality of the refreshments they served, but the firm (or so she claimed) treated her complaints with studied unconcern or rude letters. Not until 1927, when the lease ran out, could she do anything about it.

But the biggest problem of all for the Lady in the twenties, once the divorce from Morley College had been completed, was reconstructing the Vic's auditorium. At first, in July 1926, it was thought that this could be done for £15,000 without closing the theatre in the autumn. But during the preliminary work the architects discovered that parts of the main walls – now over a century old – were dangerously unstable; and Lilian was told that the entire auditorium might have to be pulled down and rebuilt. Such an operation might well have daunted and even defeated the lion-hearted manager; for, apart from the massive capital investment required – on top of the thousands she was struggling to get for Sadler's Wells through prayer, supplication and manipulation – it would have entailed prolonged closure, with disastrous consequences in loss of audiences and revenue. Happily, this complete renewal did not prove necessary; but, nevertheless, the reconstruction was so radical that the bill came to around twice the original estimate and the work lasted for nine months. Another George Dance was needed, but God omitted to find one. Generous help came from Harry Lloyd, a philanthropic local landowner, who gave £1,000; and the Carnegie UK Trust came to the rescue again with £10,000. The City Parochial Foundation lent £7,000. But nearly £4,000 had still to be found somehow – enough to pay for at least a hundred productions, or to meet Lilian's salary for the next five years.

While reconstruction was going on in the Waterloo Road, Miss Baylis had to secure a temporary home for her Shakespeare company. To find one for the opera company as well was clearly an impossibility – only the Vic could hold both (or rather, could disregard the impossibility). So the opera company did a short tour of London music halls that autumn, playing cut versions twice nightly of *Faust*, *Trovatore*, *Traviata* and *Daughter of the Regiment* at Stoke Newington, Ilford, Kilburn and other suburban dates – the Chelsea Palace was their closest point to the West End. After she had failed to find a central theatre of the right size for the right period at the right rent – the Princes, which seemed the likeliest, asked for a basic £400 a week, which appalled the penny-wise matriarch of the Vic – she accepted Nigel Playfair's offer of the Lyric Hammersmith at £90 less. In fact, the Hammersmith rent probably cost more, as Playfair took 25 per cent of the gross over £600 a week; and it also cost the possible recruitment of Edith Evans, who felt that her next stage appearance should be in the West End. But Lilian ensured that the Vic would not be overlooked when it moved from South to West London by persuading her old friend Sybil Thorndike to head the company in exile with Lewis Casson. It was a short season – only four plays were given – but a successful one; and the company returned to the refurbished Vic (without the Cassons) on 7 February 1928, having added to its kudos if not its cash reserve.

During the rebuilding, Joan Cross went down to the Waterloo Road to see what was happening to the theatre, where she suddenly came face to face with Miss Baylis.

She was, but tried not to show it, delighted to find me there, and led the way from floor to ceiling. We scrambled over bricks and mortar, and tight-rope walked along planks. In the basement she suddenly stopped and, clasping her hands, announced dramatically, 'Look dear, there! I never thought the time would come when I should jump for joy at the sight of a urinal.'[12]

Romeo and Juliet reopened the rebuilt theatre, and five more productions (including *Everyman*) were staged before the summer closure. It was a notably smaller programme than that of the previous season, when sixteen plays were presented; but this contraction was not only due to the Hammersmith migration. Andrew Leigh had already reduced the Atkins scale of twenty productions every season, and Atkins would not attempt the twenty-six that Greet somehow managed to stage. From 1928 onwards the seasonal total was never more than twelve; and in the next decade it dropped still further. This was another indication of how the Vic was changing. Its directors and playgoers demanded more; and, in this respect, more meant less. Not every member of the audience was convinced of this, as many dissidents told Miss Baylis; and she herself sometimes wondered – audibly and even angrily – if it was *worth* it. After making her beg all that money for the building, and spend all that money on salaries, sets and costumes – compared with the days of dear old B.G. – shouldn't they be giving her people *more* of everything? Because she worried about waste she insisted, into the 1930s, on passing and signing all sketches for costume and scenery. But, said Harcourt Williams, although 'she would growl at them and dismiss them as too expensive . . . they generally went through, even though they were never finally signed'. Why? His explanation was that 'when she had once tested people she knew that the work would be done up to the top of their ability'.[13] Perhaps, too, she was beginning to lose her zest for the exercise of authority. In any event, however she may have grizzled at them, she generally supported her directors. She had to accept their axiom that higher quality could only be achieved with a lower quantity of plays, and it was to achieve such quality that they were there, overworked and underpaid like her. She wanted the *best*, didn't she, rather than the *most*? Well, then . . .

The 1924 reconstruction had made it easier to improve standards of production, as well as backstage comfort and working conditions. Now, in 1928, the transformation of the old Hall was completed. Pearce & Plenty had at last been removed from the front; and an entrance from the New Cut led to a foyer with a box office, just as in other theatres. There were 'refreshment rooms' for stalls, pit, balcony and gallery. (None of them served alcoholic refreshment – the Vic hadn't changed *that* much.) Six boxes were removed. There was one new staircase to the upper house, and another from the foyer leading under the pit and into the auditorium. Among other changes, the first five rows of the pit were reupholstered and repriced at 3s. 6d. (some Governors wanted to raise the stalls above the five shilling mark, but that was going too far and too fast for Miss Baylis); both stalls and pit were raked upwards from the stage; and the apron stage was trimmed, to improve the orchestra pit.

The Vic was still far from being luxurious, but the comfort and safety of the audience was considerably increased. Their numbers went up a bit, too; but costs rose more noticeably. Better buildings always mean bigger budgets, as many repertory managers and their local-authority patrons have discovered in the last decade. What with that, *and* the bill for rebuilding, *and* the cost of Sadler's Wells, Lilian requested the Governors in 1929 to reduce her salary. And, although they assured her that 'there was not the smallest need' to accept her offer, she had her way. At her insistence it was cut by £100 p.a., to £700, and she asked for the money saved in this way to be used as the nucleus of a pension fund for the staff. Whatever her critics said, there was one charge they could not make against the Lady: that she was in it for the money.

By then she had received another kind of reward. In the New Year's honours list of 1929 (postponed till March, because of the King's illness) Lilian Baylis was granted admission to the Order of the Companions of Honour. None of the thirty-seven members were theatrical managers; only five others were women. She told friends that she had been sounded out to see if she would accept a DBE, but had turned it down: 'None of your Dames for me! I don't want to go about the country labelled, and be charged double for everything!' There was an even better reason for refusal: the CH was something that was awarded to men, not an honour reserved for women; and although she may not have consciously relished that competitive distinction, it was one that Emma would have approved. Lilian greatly enjoyed the investiture, for which she borrowed a suitably feathered hat from a friend, to 'dress up' to the occasion. The Prince of Wales performed the ceremony. The room at the Palace, she told Frederick Hudson, was 'just what we need for *Tannhäuser*, dear', and she talked ardently about the 'lovely legs' of the soldiers on duty there. 'Oh, how I'd like to have them in my chorus.' Although it may never have quite eclipsed in her affections her honorary MA (Oxon), she was deeply proud of her little blue-and-white enamel medallion with its inscription, 'In action faithful and in honour clear'.

Six months later Lilian made sure that Emma was given *her* recognition, and royalty was recruited to do the honours. One October afternoon, the Duchess of York unveiled the long-delayed memorial to Emma Cons, seventeen years after her death. It consisted of a portrait in bronze in bas-relief by Sir William Goscombe John; an inscription on a stone tablet; and, characteristically, shelters at the entrances to pit and gallery. The gesture seemed oddly belated; but Lilian was sure that Emmie would understand. The welfare of the Vic came first. Now that the building crisis was over, the dead might have their due.

It was nearly all in vain. That July a new threat to the building itself came from a new quarter: a scheme was launched to build a new bridge at Charing Cross, and to move Charing Cross station across the river close to the Vic, on which the news burst like a bombshell. Lilian and the Governors had to pull all the stops out once again. After a good deal of lobbying, negotiation and, no doubt, emotional blackmail, the LCC agreed to provide a new site for the Vic *and* to pay for the cost of building and equipping a new theatre. That was, in the context of 1929, a remarkably generous and far-sighted decision, for which both the Council and the Vic deserve full credit. But to the immense relief of both the scheme was shelved, and the theatre escaped once more.

The twenties ended at the Vic with a number of innovations and auguries of change, while the new theatre in Islington was build-ing. The opera season of 1928–9 introduced *Hansel and Gretel*, *La Bohème* and *Othello*, and all were box-office successes. The annual report gave pious thanks that 'the conservatism of the opera audience has at last been overcome'. To an observer in the 1970s, the arrival of the most popular works of Humperdinck and Puccini, and of Verdi's Shakespearian masterpiece, over thirty years after their first production in Britain, may seem something less than sensational progress. But for a theatre with such slender resources, mounting fourteen stock operas in a season, it was a feat to add three new productions; and *Othello* proved to be 'the most difficult work', apart from *Tristan and Isolde*, that the Vic had tackled. Yet, as Lilian reminded everyone, this was no time for resting on laurels – certainly not on hers.

In the next season there were more operatic innovations, but less euphoria. *Tosca* and *The Force of Destiny* were staged for the first time. The Verdi, not seen in London since 1867, was generally acclaimed, but *The Times* complained of *Tosca* (yet another straw in the wind) that 'Mr Corri must do something drastic if it is to be worth while for an enterprising company of singers to undertake new productions . . . The score was so shaken as to be constantly on the verge of trembling to pieces altogether.' The *Daily Tele-graph* praised the *Aïda*, *Tannhäuser* and *Figaro* of that season. The Mozart, said its critic, 'comes to life in the Waterloo Road in a way that it never does at Covent Garden'. But whatever the critics said, not enough people came. There was still a lot of conservatism about. Opera, once the financial backbone of Lilian's great enterprise, was in the red; and in the summer of 1930 it was decided that the orchestra must be cut for certain performances, although it was still far below strength compared with a normal opera house. More significantly, Lawrance Collingwood, back in the fold, was appointed to take complete control of three operas in the first half of the next season, which would be the first at Sadler's Wells. 'It was agreed', said the minutes of the Governors' meeting, 'that Mr Corri's age and failing grip brought the question of a pension fund to the fore.'

There were novelties, too, in the dramatic repertoire; and not all of these were supported by the public either. Lilian complained (prematurely perhaps) in the 1929 report, 'Unfortunately the Shakespearian audience seem now to have developed a conservative tendency that was once the prerogative of the opera audience'. Andrew Leigh's adventurous choice of *The Vikings*, to mark Ibsen's centenary year, proved a box-office disaster (as Lilian had warned him, and kept on *reminding* him). Clemence Dane's *Adam's Opera* and the revival of Tom Robertson's *Caste* were not much better as money-makers; though the fourth departure from tradition in the 1928-9 season – the replacement of Lilian's favourite play, *Everyman*, by Maeterlinck's *Mary Magdalene* – proved, to the manager's surprise, something of a hit. When Harcourt Williams took over in the autumn of 1929, he dropped for good not only *Everyman* but the thirteen-year ritual of religious drama in Lent. He was going to stage a morality by a Dutch author, but something went wrong and the programme 'as announced' in the Green Leaflet had to be changed – a transgression which was considered by the Lady in those days to verge on a sin against the Holy Ghost. Who else could have got away with all that, but a man related to Antoinette Sterling? What's more, he staged *A Midsummer Night's Dream* without Mendelssohn and the gauzy fairies (to the horror of the old guard) and *The Tempest* with an Ariel who seemed daringly near-nude (Leslie French's performance inspired Eric Gill's Ariel above Broadcasting House). He introduced Molière (*The Imaginary Invalid*) and Shaw (*The Dark Lady of the Sonnets* and *Androcles and the Lion*, followed by *Arms and the Man*). Billie Williams, as he was usually known, made changes not only in the programmes but also in the stage area (he added a flight of steps) and in the style of acting and verse speaking. He resolved to eliminate the surviving remnants of the old, resilient conventions of meaningless gesture, traditional 'business' and the ponderous 'Shakespeare voice' (with the 'me' instead of 'my', for instance, that Robert Atkins preserved so resonantly in his own diction). By cutting down the number of productions he secured more time for rehearsal, which meant more subtlety, more attention to psychology and poetry, more opportunity for carrying into practice some of the ideas of his guru, Granville-Barker. He wanted, and got, more money to spend on costumes and scenery: he persuaded Lilian to increase the budget from £15 to £20 per play. Even more astonishingly, he persuaded her to pay £20 a week to the young West End actor whom he wanted to lead the company. Lilian at first resented 'giving' this extortionate sum, even though she seems to have shared Williams's instinct that John Gielgud was the right kind of actor for the Vic and although he had the right 'family' connections, as the great-nephew of her beloved Ellen Terry. As soon as Williams accepted Lilian's offer to be her director of plays he decided that Gielgud must lead the company, with Martita Hunt, and he talked him into agreeing to see the Lady 'about money'. This, as Williams later discovered, was always 'a critical event' in planning.

Often I have lured some star into the Waterloo Road, having come to a perfect understanding that, money being 'all right', it would consent to shed its light there, but after the 'talk' it would become a shooting-star and disappear from my horizon for ever.[14]

Gielgud, then twenty-five, was at a turning-point in his career when he felt ready to shed *his* light there. Dissatisfied with the West End, he was looking for a place in which to develop his ideas and exercise his talents under guidance, and Williams's approach came at precisely the right time – for both Gielgud and the Vic. But Gielgud knew that it meant, with a much lower salary, giving up 'a comfortable dressing-room for myself, new suits, late rising and suppers at the Savoy', and he approached his Baylis interview with caution, trying to look 'rather arrogant, as I always do when money is discussed'. She put him in his place at once, greeting him with 'How nice to see you, dear. Of course, we'd love to have you here, but of course we can't afford stars.' By the end of the interview, Gielgud wrote, 'I was begging her to let me join the company. We both evaded the question of salary as long as possible, and a little matter of fifty shillings, over which we both obstinately failed to agree, was settled by letter some days afterwards.'[15] The settlement was nearly wrecked when Lilian had her 'talk' with Martita Hunt, whose engagement Gielgud had made a condition of his own. The Lady offered Miss Hunt ten shillings a week less than Williams had proposed in his approaches to the actress, and Miss Hunt refused. Williams was in despair, and told Lilian that she was breaking his spirit. She told him he was talking nonsense, but acquiesced in the extravagance; 'the two fish were finally landed', and in due course Williams opened his first season, which was to make theatrical history.

It appeared at first to be heading for disaster. In his determination to reform the bad habits of the tradition, Harcourt Williams speeded up his company's speech with, perhaps, excessive acceleration in his opening production, *Romeo and Juliet*. 'We gabbled in order to try and get pace, and we were not yet used to working together,' wrote Gielgud. He himself was not seen at his best in the leading role, which helped to confirm the suspicions of the thicker-headed members of the old guard in the audience about these innovations. They began to attack Harcourt Williams verbally outside the theatre, or, even less acceptably, in anonymous letters. The press complained too in a more rational and articulate but no less depressing way. When bad notices were heaped upon *The Merchant of Venice*, the season's second production (in which Gielgud played Antonio) and more anonymous letters arrived, Williams went to the office and told Miss Baylis he had decided to resign. Lilian shut the door 'rather firmly' and went for him 'hot and strong'. He was brave enough to be a CO in the war; was he going to funk it now, because of a few critics (who cares about *them*?) and some good-hearted but old-fashioned people in the gallery. 'Are you *really* a coward?' *Of course*, she said, he couldn't resign. He didn't; and he discovered that 'under the rather callous manner I had a real friend who had made up her mind to accept me for good and ill and stand by me'.[16] She did so because she liked him, and because, having engaged him as a temporary warrior in her crusade, it was her duty to give him her loyal support. There was a more practical reason: it would have been very difficult to find another director of the right kind at a moment's notice. But although she was doubtful about the detail of his ideas, she followed her instinct that he was the right man for her theatre – and kept him working for it.

With *Richard II*, Gielgud found his feet 'at last' and the audience, though not the critics, gave a warmer reception to the production. With *A Midsummer Night's Dream*, in spite of all its innovations, Williams scored a popular and a critical success. Gielgud went on to tackle two major parts, Macbeth and Hamlet, and by the end of the 1929–30 season Williams was vindicated in his 'West End' casting and his 'revolutionary' methods. Box-office business boomed. As the annual report said in 1930, 'Nothing justifies a producer's method so much as a steady increase in the size of the audience'. At the five performances of *Hamlet* in its entirety every seat was sold, many people stood throughout, and many more were turned away. Gielgud began to be acclaimed as the First Player of the English stage. The success of the Edith Evans season five years earlier was almost repeated. Lilian Baylis felt justified too and was eager to champion her director in the annual report. Harcourt Williams, it said, 'has drilled the company to use an almost incredible speed – an experiment which at first came in for as marked an unpopularity as it afterwards became markedly unnoticeable; except that on the night of Shakespeare's Birthday, when members of previous Shakespearian companies took the stage, a great difference in the tempo, if such an expression may be used, was perceptible – the Old Vic is pre-eminently the place for artistic experiment, even if some eggshells of prejudice have to be smashed in the process.' Williams returned for three further seasons of eggshell-smashing. Gielgud came back for another year of Shakespearian mountaineering to play Prospero, Antony, Hotspur, Benedick, Malvolio and Lear. Lilian was delighted: she is even said to have agreed to a rise in his salary 'without a murmur'. That, perhaps, is a little hard to swallow; but she knew – nobody can deny that – when she was getting value for money.

Apart from the new excitements in opera and Shakespeare at the close of the 1920s and the state's recognition of Lilian Baylis's services to the theatre, there was one major innovation at the Vic: the recognition by Miss Baylis of a third performing art – the art of ballet.

In the 1890s Emma Cons had recruited unpaid dancers from her source of choristers, the Church of the Sacred Heart in Camberwell, and this arrangement continued well into the present century: they were part of the first production at the Vic of *Tannhäuser* in 1904, under the direction of Madame Martha Mayall. Madame Mayall was, in fact, Mrs Charles Corri. She had been a ballerina with the Carl Rosa, and had helped to arrange dances in their operas – so Lilian got her to do the same for the Vic. It always gave her particular pleasure to recruit husbands, wives and children of the staff, if they could be used somewhere in or out of the theatre, and especially, of course, if they could be used without payment. Even if they did want money, she would attempt to get from a married couple two jobs for the price of one, or at least one and a half. (As the time drew near for Andrew Leigh to leave the Vic in the 1920s, he joked – though not in Miss Baylis's hearing – that he was going to marry the charwoman, or some other indispensable on the payroll, as the sure way to Lilian's heart.)

When the Shakespearian experiment began, Lilian enlisted the help of Mrs Henry Wordsworth, a matriarchal and imposing teacher (with one eye) whose dancing classes had long been an institution of middle-class life in London. Both Lilian and Ninette de Valois had been instructed in childhood by Wordsworthian teachers. Mrs Wordsworth specialized in 'Fancy Dancing' – 'a quaint compromise of rudimentary steps such as the *chassé* and the *glissade* combined with other steps fancy beyond belief'. She had no theatrical expertise; indeed, says Ninette de Valois, she had 'a puritanical loathing of dancing as a profession. She regarded it as the duty of anyone under her tuition to eschew the theatrical profession at all costs.'[17] (Perhaps Miss Baylis talked her into the Vic on the grounds of patriotic duty in wartime?) After Mrs Wordsworth departed, arrangements for rehearsing dances in both Shakespeare and opera were generally haphazard and minimal, even by Waterloo Road standards, in spite of Mrs Corri's help. In the early 1920s, for instance, Flora M. Fairbairn, who ran the Mayfair School of Dancing, was obliged to rehearse in 'the gap at the back of the circle, while somebody hummed the dance tunes'. Miss Baylis liked dancing herself, though she hadn't done much since the Gipsy Revellers, and teaching the wives of the Rand millionaires. (She was surprisingly light on her feet for a woman of her bulk, and usually managed at special theatre parties to do her favourite – Sir Roger de Coverley.) And she realized all too well the ludicrous inadequacy of conditions and standards in this department, insofar as there was one at all. But with so many gaps to fill, and so many ends that wouldn't meet, she could do little about it. She needed money, of course. She needed space – and she found a bit more after the 1924 reconstruction, when she established a 'permanent' dancing class under Miss Fairbairn's auspices, and allotted separate responsibility for the arrangement of dances in the plays and operas. This was, said the annual report, one of the manager's 'long-cherished ideas'. But, apart from money and space, she still needed the right person. With her usual luck, flair and judgment, she found that person two years later. Or rather, let us say, they discovered each other.

During the early 1920s there was increasing discontent in the dancing profession about the lack of employment for British dancers. A few were engaged by Pavlova or Diaghilev, but opportunities elsewhere in opera or ballet were scarce, and most dancers had to work in revue, music hall and pantomime. Inspired by the Russian example, and encouraged by Russian teachers who had settled in London, there was a good deal of talk about establishing a British ballet company. Miss Fairbairn put the case for it in the Old Vic Magazine in 1924, and later tried to put it into practice (with Cyril Beaumont), but the venture soon collapsed. When Anton Dolin opened his school of dancing in 1925, he announced his hope that it would be the nucleus of a British company; but things did not turn out in quite that way. Lilian Baylis was aware that something was brewing. Sometimes she used to 'buttonhole' Philip Richardson, editor of the *Dancing Times* – who played a significant role in the development of professional dance – and demand, 'When are we going to have a British Ballet?' But she did nothing, at that time, to help its arrival; and it seems unlikely that she had much time or inclination to think about it (as distinct from opera–ballet at the Vic).

Among those who did think about it – steadily, clearly and persistently – was Ninette de Valois (born Edris Stannus) who in 1926 opened a dancing school in South Kensington, the Academy of Choreographic Art, with the ultimate aim of training a company of her own. She was twenty-seven, and had been twelve years on the stage: principal dancer of the Lyceum panto throughout the war; in Covent Garden opera and revue; and, for the past two years, with Diaghilev. Having opened the Academy, a title chosen to distinguish it from the Wordsworthian dancing schools, Miss de Valois set out to find a repertory theatre in which to work out her ideas and give her dancers stage experience until they might be formed into a resident ballet company. First of all she tried Barry Jackson at the Birmingham Repertory Theatre, the leading regional company; and when he turned her down flat she wrote to Lilian Baylis, knowing that Sadler's Wells was 'in the air'. Having secured an appointment, she put on her summer best and a large floppy hat and set off for the Waterloo Road one sunny Saturday in May, resolved to achieve 'the formation of a British Ballet through the good offices of the Old Vic'.[18]

When Evelyn Williams saw her letter, she thought, knowing Miss Baylis's prejudices, 'with writing like that and a name like that she shouldn't waste much of our time'. But the two women hit it off right away. After Miss de Valois had outlined her dreams, her plans and her qualifications, Miss Baylis said, 'I like your face, dear. I think you're practical. And you seem to have had a great deal of experience.' She explained that she could offer very little money and that, in spite of the recent backstage improvements, there was little room or opportunity to develop a ballet group. But she did have a number of jobs that needed to be done: to arrange any dance required in a Shakespeare production; to give some basic training to those unpaid secretaries and clerks who used to 'help out' in the opera ballets (like their forerunners from the Sacred Heart), and who attended dancing classes for about eighteen pence a lesson; to organize a short ballet performance by a ballet school as part of the Christmas festivities; and to teach the drama students how to move and use their hands. Most actors and actresses had dreadful hands, which looked all the more dreadful because they didn't know what to do with them. She preferred, she said, beautiful hands to beautiful faces. The pay was a pound a week for teaching the students, and two pounds for arranging a 'little dance' in Shakespeare. Would Miss de Valois consider it? Miss de Valois jumped at it. Unlike Marie Rambert, with whom the Lady had already discussed the needs of the Vic, she was not put off by the request to 'look after my office girls'. It was quite a short interview. When Ninette de Valois left the office after half an hour, Lilian came out and said to Williams, 'with conviction', something very remarkable: 'Ninette de Valois is going to form a ballet company for us. When we open at the Wells, it will be on a whole-time basis.' As Harcourt Williams said, 'could one have a better example of Lilian Baylis's uncanny insight into character than the decision she took in those thirty minutes?' (Although, of course, that decision was not based on instinct alone. Before Ninette de Valois arrived, Lilian had asked about her among the people who *knew*.)

Once Lilian had visited the Academy with Leigh, to satisfy herself that everything looked as practical as it sounded, the deal was agreed – and a remarkable partnership began. The Lady had found the necessary person, cheap, to settle her dance problems. The necessary person had found the necessary house-room for her dreams. Above them hung the vision of the rebuilt Sadler's Wells, which Miss Baylis kept 'ever dangling in front of my eyes'. But Lilian entered the dream, too. This was not merely another instance of her ability to recruit an idealist at cut-price. She knew very little about the history or art of ballet, but that was immaterial. She recognized in Ninette de Valois a kindred spirit, both practical and visionary, a single-minded fighter with an indomitable will. (Both had worked hard from childhood, both blazed into rages, both preferred to ignore the word 'impossible'.) She not only supported the long-term plans for a ballet company, but, Dame Ninette has testified, 'never wavered or went back' on them. 'She ruthlessly championed my cause throughout those trying four and a half years of waiting for better opportunities' – until Sadler's Wells opened at last.

Lilian found little support for the ballet project among her staff. Understandably, there was alarm and resentment at the prospect of squeezing a third company into an already overcrowded theatre, where opera and drama competed for time, money and rehearsal space, for scenery, costumes and the attention of the Lady and her team. Lilian rose above such mundane anxieties. She knew in her bones that everything would be all right when she got the Wells. But many of her staff, including the ever-loyal Clarkie, did not believe in the Wells, either. They felt by 1929 that it was never going to be opened, and that if it *was* opened, it would be a big mistake. 'Bloody Wells', they used to grumble. 'All the departments were against it at heart,' said Harcourt Williams, 'and the difficulties really seemed insurmountable.'[19] He secretly hoped that they would never be overcome while he was working for Lilian, and although she frequently asked him to go and look at the building, he excused himself until it was ready to open by pleading pressure of work or some other reason. Lilian's faith was unshaken; or, if it was shaken, she quickly brought it back into its normal steadfast state without letting go. Ninette de Valois had no doubts, either. 'I knew I had a long wait, but I knew it would come in the end.'

During those years of waiting Ninette de Valois 'served her practical apprenticeship as producer, choreographer, teacher and administrator' in meeting Lilian's requirements. She was paid, on average, no more than some £40 a year, so she had to subsidize her work there – and, indeed, subsidized the Vic – by her Academy; by teaching outside it (at Heathfield School); by working at the Abbey Theatre (where she established a ballet school) and at the Cambridge Festival Theatre, run by her cousin Terence Gray; by dancing now and then – with the Diaghilev Ballet, with Dolin at the Coliseum, at Covent Garden. She became responsible for the opera ballets as well as the dances in Shakespeare; she set Rosalind Iden – later Lady Wolfit – to take charge of classes; and her own

Academy dancers appeared in productions. Two years after her agreement with Lilian – in December 1928 – her first ballet was staged at the Vic: *Les Petits Riens*, a curtain-raiser danced to Mozart, with the choreographer as a pastoral coquette. Five months later came another curtain-raiser, *The Picnic*, with music by Vaughan Williams. Both went down well with the audience, and were described in the annual report as the Old Vic's 'first tentative efforts at founding a school of English Ballet. Such a development of the operatic side of the work has always been an ideal that the Manager has set in front of her', a somewhat doubtful Managerial gloss on past history, 'and in the indomitable hands of Ninette de Valois this ideal has been translated into an achievement.' The Governors promised 'a considerable development of the scheme' in the coming seasons, but only two more short ballets were staged within the next two years. Lilian moved cautiously and slowly, too slowly sometimes for Ninette. Their tempers blazed at each other, over Lilian's stinginess and Ninette's impatience. But in 1930, with the Wells reconstruction almost complete, the dream began to materialize. Lilian and the Governors agreed to accept Ninette de Valois's proposal that they should establish the Vic–Sadler's Wells Opera Ballet, run in conjunction with a training school on the spot, in return for Ninette's gift of her Academy of Choreographic Art. The profits of the Academy would pay for the salaries of the six salaried dancers (all girls): it would cost the Vic nothing. On the horizon was the plan to add male dancers to the company and to give the company one evening a week. But not yet.

It was not until 5 May 1931 that Lilian risked the first full evening of ballet – at the Vic; but the risk was triumphantly justified, to her own astonishment. The performance was sold out; its success was repeated on two later evenings at Sadler's Wells; it was agreed to stage a ballet once every fortnight in the 1931–2 season (what hard-labouring far-sighted preparation by Ninette de Valois lay behind that decision); and the Vic–Wells Ballet was launched, on the wave of a large and enthusiastic public which had suddenly swept into both theatres. Lilian Baylis, delighted as she was with this sudden demand, could not help contrasting it with those cold, empty evenings in 1914 at the debut of her earlier experiment. Sometimes she could not help hankering for those days, grim as they were, when she felt in charge of everything and everybody, days of poverty but days of power, and a kind of camaraderie in work which was now increasingly difficult for her to enjoy in her expanding empire. She was, perhaps, a glutton for punishment. She need not have worried: there was plenty more of it to come. Yet however much she might ask for punishment, she could no longer take it in quite the same resilient, prayerful way.

Private Worlds

O Holy Spirit of God, come into my heart and fill me:
I open the windows of my soul to let Thee in
I surrender my whole life to Thee.
Come and possess me, fill me with light and truth.
I offer to Thee the one thing I really possess,
My capacity for being filled with Thee.
Of myself I am an unprofitable servant, an empty vessel.
Fill me so I may live the life of the Spirit,
The life of Truth and Goodness,
The life of Beauty and Love,
The life of Wisdom and Strength.
Guide me today in all things,
Guide me to the people I should meet and help.
Whether by my actions or sufferings, above all make Christ be
    formed in me,
That I may dethrone myself in my heart and make Him King.
Bind and cement me to Christ in all ways known and unknown.
By Holy Thoughts, unseen graces and sacramental ties.
So that He is in me and I in Him, today and for ever.

> Prayer of the Mainstream, *by Bishop Carey,*
> *found among Lilian Baylis's papers in her handwriting,*
> *together with a list of those for whom she prayed each day.*

So far in this narrative (which now moves out of chronological
sequence) we have seldom seen Lilian Baylis outside the Old Vic,
in her home at 27 Stockwell Park Road. That is partly because she
was seldom there, except to sleep. If we have appeared to over-
look her life away from the theatre, it is largely because she left
little evidence of it. Intimate recollections by friends outside the

Vic are scarce and shadowy, relating largely to her last six years. So it is hard for a biographer to describe her private life, especially as there was so little of it. She didn't give herself much time for privacy, except in her relationship with God. She spent more of her days and evenings at the theatre than is usual for a manager, even in the overworked world of repertory, and when the theatre was closed she could not insulate herself for long from its people and its problems. To a remarkable degree, her private and public lives were interfused.

Many of the hours that were left to her, after God and various good causes were served, were claimed by her family. She enjoyed no really close link with any of her relations after Emma died, except (for a time) with her young sister Ethel Dunning and Ethel's son Bobby. Emotionally, she found richer rewards in her substitute children at the Vic and her substitute Fathers. But she felt a strong sense of duty to her family, as its most conspicuously successful member, and as a woman driven by the urge to serve *and* the urge to dominate. Apart from her staff – she employed a housekeeper-cook and, in her last decade, a chauffeur–companion–secretary – there was usually a relation in residence at Stockwell, or a lame duck with a hard-luck story, or an old friend from South Africa. She mothered them all, bossily but generously. That seems to have been a necessity of her private life: she enjoyed being kind as well as powerful.

Lilian kept in touch with the family outposts in Africa and Australia, sending Old Vic programmes and cuttings; sending advice; even sending money, on occasion. She saved for them, bossed them, sheltered them. During the war she shared her home with Ethel, who arrived from Africa in 1916 after her husband joined up, bringing the four-year-old Bobby. This was Bobby's home for the best part of his next four years. Lilian, who doted on the boy, took him often to the theatre, where he fell in love with Florence Saunders and was befriended by Old Bob. He hero-worshipped his uncle Ray from Australia, who served with the Anzacs in Gallipoli and France and spent his leaves with Lilian; and he watched with awe his great-aunt Ellen Cons, a grim, 'horse-faced' old Victorian, all in black, sitting bolt upright in a straight-backed chair in the living-room, for ever thumping her stick imperiously on the floor to summon the servant from the kitchen below. Sadly, though not surprisingly, Bobby found Lilian nearly as formidable: her love for him was not reciprocated, for he never felt – then or later – really at home in Stockwell or really close to his aunt. Although he remembered his early years in London as a time of happiness, his nickname for Lilian was 'Auntie Tiger'. But Auntie Tiger continued through the years to send him postcards, presents and endearments, although she never saw him again after 1927 – when Ethel and Frank Dunning stayed for several months at Stockwell, with Bobby and his sister Gladys.

Lilian's enthusiasm for his mother (for long her favourite sister) was not sustained. The 'spoiled little darling' of the 1890s seems to have become a penitential bore in middle age, alienating her sister's affections by her flightiness and self-absorption. Lilian began to dread her letters, let alone her visits; and she was generally disliked at the theatre, and by friends of Lilian on whom, without the slightest justification or apology, she thrust her company. The memory of Ethel Dunning prompted even the all-forgiving Sybil Thorndike, years later, to pejoratives unqualified by praise: a phenomenon rare enough to indicate the size of Lilian's sisterly cross. But she continued to bear it: that was her duty.

Lilian expected her family, for their part, to recognize that they had a duty too – not so much to her as to the Old Vic. She tried to get work for the theatre out of any members of the family who might be available – partly in return for services rendered, partly because the Vic needed any help it could get, especially if the help was free; and also because it was a *family* theatre, in which they *ought* to be involved. Aunt Ellen was a Governor till her death in 1920; Ethel was recruited to dance in operas and plays, her war-work permitting; her mother was consulted on costumes and sent to sales; her nephew and nieces were roped in to do odd jobs (just as Emma had enlisted her in childhood) – she had thoughts, at one time, of training a South African niece as her assistant, with an eye to the succession, and years later (according to Bobby) she urged him to take over the management. Her father – a trim, jaunty figure with a small white imperial beard and RR (for Rand Rifles) on his lapels – was the most conspicuously helpful Baylis at the Vic. He showed people to their seats, did some bill-posting, gave Lilian advice about singing, told rambling stories about the old days in South Africa and cycled to the bank every morning with the takings. On one trip he was knocked off his bicycle, but escaped with no more than a graze. An actor found Lilian in her office looking white and shaken, and reassured her that Mr Baylis was all right. 'I *know*. It's not *that*,' Lilian snapped. 'But when I heard about my poor old father, may God forgive me, my first thought was for the money he was taking to the bank.'

Lilian had never, at heart, forgiven her mother for her childhood – and, in particular, for her face. Rightly or wrongly, she blamed Mrs Baylis for her palsy. But she discharged her daughterly responsibilities as best she could, especially when – in the early 1920s – her mother was confined to an invalid chair. Both parents were 'quite under Lilian's thumb', although Newton Baylis sometimes tried unsuccessfully to stand up to her. Yet she saw that they were given their due (as well as their keep). They were invited to first nights at the Vic in Lilian's box; and when they were staying at number 27, early callers were likely to be told, 'Go upstairs and say good morning to Mummy and Daddy'. Lilian was then in her forties.

Newton Baylis died in February 1925 at the age of seventy-nine. Libby followed him in November, at seventy-seven. Although they had long ceased to exert any authority over Lilian, their death seemed to coincide with new freedoms in her style of life. The freedom, for instance, of a car. For thirty years Lilian had been an adventurous cyclist, ever since her 'Devil on Wheels' days in Joburg, and she often cycled to and from work, undeterred by increasing traffic and even by wartime raids. She was not only ardent but accident-prone, and after a series of falls and crashes – in one of which she seriously injured her knee – she had to depend on trams, begging lifts, and even taxis (for which she was granted a quarterly allowance of £5 by the Governors). At last, in 1926, she was persuaded to buy a car. She put up a stiff moral resistance to the notion. 'How can I *afford* a car? And what will my people think? They won't give me their pennies if they see me driving around in one.' Moreover, as she explained in the Magazine, 'I have always avoided machinery'. But the cost was subsidized by the Governors; and, having been persuaded to acquire a Trojan (a solid-axle, two-stroke car), she talked her front-of-house manager, her carpenter and others into teaching her how to drive it.

Whether she ever learned to do so was warmly questioned by many of her passengers; for in the Trojan, as in other situations, Lilian displayed a style all her own – autocratic, single-minded and ruthlessly indifferent to everyday practicalities. This was indeed so unworldly, to the point of extreme peril – 'God *must* have been on the Lady's side, or she'd never have come out of that car alive' – that she was finally persuaded to employ a driver, who would also serve as a kind of companion–secretary, on the understanding that while she paid the girl's keep (it would have to be a girl) the Governors would pay her wages.

Lilian found it hard to fill this job. The demands were exacting, the hours were virtually unlimited, the pay was low. She expected the same dedication shown by her trusted servants at the Vic, the same dedication that she herself gave to her work. Not surprisingly, her expectations were frequently disappointed. There was a rapid turnover of women who seemed to her quite impossible, or who found her quite intolerable, and who included at least one recruit of quite advanced criminal tendencies. With the arrival of Annette Prevost in 1932, however, Lilian had the singular luck and judgement to discover and to keep a loyal, shrewd and highly intelligent girl who became a devoted friend and a valuable servant of the theatre. She came to occupy, in effect, the role of a younger sister – that was how Lilian cast her; and as such she inevitably aroused initial jealousies among people at the Vic, perturbed by what amounted to a shift in the balance of power. But the new private secretary was also a 'peacemaker' (as Lilian called her), who did her best to avoid civil strife, and maintained a solitary, solacing role in the hierarchy. As she played an important off-stage part in Lilian's last five years, which she helped to make happier than they might otherwise have been, and as her story of their relationship illuminates some of the complexities of the Lady's personality, it is worth looking briefly here at how she came to work at Stockwell Park Road – and to stay there.

Characteristically, Prevost – as she was always called, and as she is still remembered long after her marriage to George Chamberlain, the former general manager of the Vic – was recruited through Lilian's network of church connections. A South African bishop had given Lilian an introduction to his niece in England, a Sister of the Holy Name, who was Prevost's aunt; Lilian got to know the Sister's family; and Prevost happened to be looking for a job when Lilian came for a weekend. When Prevost (then twenty-one) went to the Vic for an interview, it was her first visit. The omens were not encouraging. She asked at the box office for Miss Baylis, and was told briskly to go to the stage door.

'I don't know where the stage door is,' said Prevost.

'If you don't know where the stage door of the Old Vic is, *go away*,' said the voice in the box office, which belonged to Clarkie.

Having found it, Prevost asked Miss Williams, while she was waiting, whether Miss Baylis was easy to get on with. Williams fixed her with a disquieting stare, and said, 'My dear girl, is anybody really *great* easy to get on with?' When Lilian saw her, she told Prevost that the pay was a pound a week. 'I can't promise you any time off. But I will *try* to let you see your friends when they are in London.' In spite of that, Prevost decided to have a go; but when she arrived at 27 Stockwell Park Road for the first time the smell of what seemed to be putrid meat on the boil (it was the dogs' dinner) drove her back from the front door, and nearly into retreat. But the friend who had driven her there persuaded Prevost first of all to look at her room; and when she did so she was won over by the sight of a bowl of flowers by the bedside. If the great Miss Baylis could find time to think of doing that for a stranger and a servant, then, Prevost decided, she was worth working for.

As Prevost soon discovered, she was not easy to work *with*. After minor skirmishes in the first three weeks, they had a major battle. It happened because Lilian insisted that Prevost should continue to practise the piano every morning (just as Lilian herself had been obliged, as a girl, to practise on the violin), between washing down the car (which had to be done every day) and driving Lilian to work. Prevost, who found this impossible to fit into a crowded sixteen-hour working day, refused. Lilian was furious, but Prevost was adamant. After some rumination, she went into Lilian's bedroom where, as usual, her employer was dispatching her morning quiverful of letters.

'When do you want me to leave, Miss Baylis?' she asked.

'What on earth are you talking about?' barked Lilian from her pillows.

'Well, you've ordered me to do something, and I've refused to carry out your orders, several times. So clearly you won't want me to stay here any longer,' said Prevost.

Lilian did not answer. Instead she groped wildly for the nearest thing to hand and threw it at Prevost. It happened to be a bottle of ink, without a top, and after hitting the mirror it splashed all over one of her dogs. 'We both laughed so much,' says Prevost, 'that the conversation was never completed.' She stayed till Lilian's death – and worked for her theatres for many years after that.

Prevost had been warned that Miss Baylis never kept anybody longer than three months. 'She only wants doormats. And when she's wiped her feet on you, you're out.' This did not turn out to be true, as far as Prevost was concerned. 'If you behaved as a doormat, she treated you as a doormat. But if, as I did, you stood up to her, it was something she liked. She respected people who weren't afraid to say "No" to her.' That was one reason for the success of their relationship. Another reason, Prevost suggests, was that 'I was prepared to make my own bed. She thought I was going to be grand. I can't think why.' Prevost was, in fact, a cut above nearly all the girls who had worked for Lilian, in background and education. The Lady – as Prevost soon learned to call her, like the rest of the office – enjoyed the knowledge that she had a *real* lady working for her, and, what's more, one who liked it. Most important of all, the Lady discovered that 'my Prevost', as she used to call her brusquely and possessively, served her with completely disinterested affection. That, in Lilian's private life, was something to treasure.

Although Lilian devoted so much of her time to good works (of which her theatres were the best) she was far from being a Puritan in many aspects of her life: in her appetite for food and drink, for example. She was, indeed, something of a glutton ('I *love* my grub,' she used to say), if not much of a gourmet; although her eating habits were influenced by her dislike of formality, her ill health and her aversion to spending money unnecessarily. She seldom went out to restaurants, except when somebody else was paying the bill. During her last decade this happened more frequently, as she had to attend a growing number of banquets, receptions and official junketings, at which she was often called upon to make a speech. But the kind of eating out that Lilian preferred was alfresco, on picnics. Even at the Vic she seldom went to the local restaurant (Wagner's was the favourite of the company). She liked to go home for lunch; but if, as often happened in the early days, she felt that she could not leave the theatre, she took a quick snack in her office. The legendary gas ring disappeared in the second reconstruction of the 1920s, but a quick fry-up could still be served on demand from a mini-kitchen nearby. The discovery that she had diabetes, as well as high blood pressure, put an end, in theory at least, to such meals. She had to observe a strict diet, and if she was held up at the Wells, her housekeeper would sometimes arrive by bus with a special thermos containing Lilian's special lunch. But she found this restriction too severe, and would frequently break its taboos by sampling somebody else's food. 'Yes, I know,' she would reply to remonstrances. 'But just this once,' sniffing decisively. Every evening she expected a large, 'slap-up' meal, often with guests, before the theatre; and she frequently entertained two or three people to lunch on Sunday. 'We kept a good table. We had to,' says Prevost.

There was always wine, in her last decade at least – both at home in Stockwell and at the between-shows meals that she shared at the Vic with Williams, Clarkie and Prevost. As Lilian raised her glass to them she would usually say briskly, 'Emmie' – a kind of ritual toast which licensed the consumption of intoxicating liquor on the premises. She enjoyed a drink in moderation, although she was no connoisseur of vintages. In the 1930s a friend sent her a barrel of wine which she kept in the office and tapped for treats and emergencies. Lilian believed in its healing powers and rare bouquet, all the richer because she hadn't paid for it; but her friends dreaded its sharp, musty taste. She also kept brandy in the office instantly available for medical emergencies, and the usual tipples at home, for social purposes. But she rarely drank spirits herself. Bruce Worsley said that when she was taken ill one evening at the Vic, he gave her a tiny noggin of brandy from his small stock of press refreshments and told her it was medicine. It did her good, she said, without evincing any sign of recognition; and quite often after that, when she was feeling well below par, she would say, 'Dig, have you got any more of that medicine, dear?' Mr Worsley was convinced that she didn't know. Certainly, Lilian was no teetotaller. In the 1930s she belatedly discovered the simple pleasures of the country pub (notably, Ploughman's Lunch), and became an enthusiastic patron. But she maintained the *theatre* as a temperance institution, carrying out her aunt's wishes, until she died; indeed, it was not until 1950 that the Old Vic acquired a spirits licence (and then it was achieved with considerable difficulty). At Sadler's Wells it was different. Within five years of its opening, prohibition was ended, after a stubborn resistance by Lilian, who suddenly changed sides. According to Ninette de Valois, 'once Miss Baylis had recovered from the disloyalty to Aunt Emma, to the coffee-house tradition and to the triumphant overthrow of gin-palaces in the past, she decided on a large-scale campaign to reinstate gin as a financial aid to culture'.[1] It was at her insistence that the Wells became the first theatre to run a bar on both sides of the stage. But then Emma had never set foot in the Wells; so Lilian's conscience could, after some prolonged scrutiny, be cleared.

Lilian was a generous host, who enjoyed entertaining, even when she was paying herself. Most of all, perhaps, she liked *organizing* simple entertainments on a large scale at the theatre, like the Christmas party for the poor children of the Waterloo Road area; the Twelfth Night ritual with home-made lemonade served from a large tin bath; the meat tea for the company between shows on Boxing Day with crackers and paper hats; and other treats at which she could mother one and all to her heart's content. She staged one of these every year in the garden at Stockwell, when she asked members of the opera company and the Shakespeare company to meet each other on the Sunday before the season opened, and egged them on not only to fraternize but to *do* things together, over the buns and lemonade. While somebody played the piano inside, part of the opera chorus was talked into delivering a bit of Gounod or Balfe under Lilian's watchful eye; or two actors (actresses, on one occasion) were cheerfully dragooned into performing one of the well-known bits, like the balcony scene from *Romeo and Juliet*, with the help of the summer house, which had a small verandah. This annual party, which led to agonies of embarrassment unsuspected by the hostess, was intended for the mutual benefit of the two companies. In addition she gave a party twice a year for the old folks of St Agnes, Kennington, her favourite church.

In private, among friends at home after tea on Sunday, for instance, she would sometimes bring out her mandolin and play some of her Gipsy Revellers' repertoire. The guests would join in the songs, and if Dr Hussey was among them, he would sometimes do his bit on the banjo. Dr Hussey, a friend and neighbour as well as Lilian's GP, was something of a hero, though he tried to keep it quiet: he had been a member of the Shackleton expeditions to the Antarctic in 1914 and 1920.

Among friends, Lilian showed an infectious sense of humour, as well as a dry, rough wit, when she could unbutton herself psychologically and relax. She had, in fact, few close friends, and scarcely any of those came from the theatre. The closest, for nearly forty years, was Louie Davey, who accompanied Lilian on her world cruise in 1910 and on most of her later, less spectacular holidays, but who took no part in the Old Vic world. Louie Davey came to Lilian through the Cons connection: her father had a philanthropic interest in the Walmer Street property that Octavia Hill had passed to Emma. The other members of Lilian's tiny, private circle included Jack Webster's sister, Harriet, and Katie Moss, composer of 'The Floral Dance' and an opera which was never staged at the Vic. Outside that circle there were several somewhat dim 'holy ladies' (as one of her staff sardonically described them), pious Anglo-Catholics who shared Lilian's intense preoccupation with the religious life; and a larger and more brilliant group of people (mostly women) whom Lilian had met through the theatre. They included such warm friends as Sybil Thorndike and Ernest Milton; Dame Ethel Smyth, with whom she had a series of stormy quarrels that left their friendship unimpaired; and a number of writers associated with *Time and Tide*, under the editorship of Lady Rhondda. Chief among these was Cicely Hamilton, actress, dramatist, critic, feminist, who published a history of the Old Vic in 1926, to which Lilian contributed background information and added a chapter of Emma Cons (the main source of information about her aunt).

Cicely Hamilton introduced Lilian to the Soroptimists, who played a significant supporting role in her offstage life. This international federation of women's clubs – a kind of feminine Rotary network – was established in California in 1921, on a basis of vocational representation and liberal idealism. The Federation – which by 1974 numbered over 55,000 members in 1,700 clubs in fifty countries – states its aims as including the maintenance of 'high ethical standards' in business and professional life; striving 'for human rights for all people and, in particular, to advance the status of women'; the promotion of international understanding, universal friendship and other 'blue horizon' objectives. The name is defined as meaning, 'Best of women, best for women'. Each club consists of women executives, invited as representatives of a business or profession. Lilian was invited to join the London club as representative of the theatre. They met formally only once a month – for luncheon at the Florence in Rupert Street (where her paternal grandfather had run his jewellery business) – but the new acquaintances and friends that she made there had an influence on the pattern of her last decade.

Lilian's friends were usually known – like the women who worked with her – by their surnames; and she herself was (and still is) often referred to as 'Baylis' by both performers and staff. This seems to have been prompted by considerations of managerial convenience and defensive habit, rather than by feminist principles of egalitarian nomenclature. Lilian was not herself a professional advocate of feminism, although she knew many of them; and she took no interest in party politics, not even, it appears, in the politics of women's emancipation. She was a regular reader of the *Daily Telegraph*, the *Church Times* and the *South London Press* (plus the notices of Old Vic productions in other papers); and she read, and skipped through, an eclectic range of library books (Prevost kept a list). She did not buy books; she seldom went to concerts, art galleries or cinemas; she did not often go to other people's theatres. She was too busy going to her own, six days in the week, every night of the season.

There was one drawback to the appointment of a chauffeur: Lilian missed the excitement of driving, and found it hard to acquiesce in being a passenger. As long as she retained the Trojan, there was still an opportunity to take over the wheel; but to keep it on the road meant hard labour of a kind which Prevost finally found beyond her physical resources. She issued a regretful ulti-matum – 'either the Trojan goes, or I must' – and the Trojan went. After a brief period with a Citroen, they acquired an Austin 14 'like a shire horse'; but Lilian never attempted to drive it. As she found it impossible to master the gears, her own motoring days were over – though not before her exploits had added a few stories to the Baylis legend.

Among the most popular of these motoring anecdotes, handed down by victims of the Trojan, is the true story of the occasion when, driving over Blackfriars Bridge to the Wells, she was amazed to see a tram coming straight at her. This was not, actually, so amazing, as the tram lines then followed the west side of the bridge, and Lilian was driving right along them. The tram driver was understandably cross, especially as Lilian kept barking at him to get out of the way; and as he failed to do so, she left the car, hurried off in search of a policeman and said, ablaze with fury, 'Officer, that tram is on the wrong side of the road. *Tell it to move.*'

Lilian was always confident that, whatever other people were doing with *their* vehicles, *she* was in the right. She left it to them to brake or take evasive action, as the Trojan bore down on them. For one thing, she was not very good at using her own brakes. 'Out of the way, out of the way,' she would shout. 'You *bounders,*' she would rage at them. And, if there was time to shout any more, she would lean out and explain. 'I'm the manager of the Old Vic, and I've got Sybil Thorndike's mother inside. She plays the organ in *St Joan*' – or whoever it was that was suffering the privilege of Trojan transport.

She found it hard to understand that anything was wrong with her driving. On one occasion, as an enraged pedestrian shook his fist at her in protest, she said delightedly, 'Oh, look! Somebody recognizes me. He's waving. Isn't that *nice*, dear!' Cutting in alarmingly on a taxi driver, with nuns in the Trojan, she yelled,

'I can't help it'; and, as he caught up with her, she shouted, 'I've got to get to Liverpool Street with these holy sisters of the Church. *You* can dawdle as much as you like. I can't.' Confronted by a policeman at Hyde Park Corner, who put up his hand to stop her, she failed to brake – she'd forgotten how – but yelled, 'Can't stop to argue with you *here*, my man. Come into the park.' Miraculously, she escaped prosecution and injury on a score of occasions; but clearly Lilian would not have stayed alive for long in post-war traffic. How could any driver hope to survive, whose highway code started with the feeling that, as she explained to Sybil Thorndike, 'once I've got the car going, I don't like to stop in case anything happens'.

Going for a drive with Lilian was one of the occupational perils of working for her or accepting her hospitality. A guest was likely to be involved in good works as well. When Winifred Oughton went to lunch one Sunday, Lilian suddenly said, 'Come on, let's go for a drive'. It was not long since she had been given driving lessons, and Miss Oughton was pretty sure that she had never been in the car on her own before. She was terrified. But Lilian had set her heart on a good deed. She had decided to drive up to Notting Hill Gate to see an old actress who was very poor and lived on her own. 'It would be such a treat for her', Lilian said, 'to go for a drive with us.' *That* old actress wasn't in; so Lilian thought of another one, a few miles further north. She found her asleep in bed, with her lunch tray beside her, untouched. Lilian made her dress and come downstairs; and then drove her all the way to Stockwell Park Road for tea. 'She had to be given this wonderful treat, you see. It was a treat for Lilian, so it *must* be a treat for her.'

Among her good causes in the 1930s was Ben Greet. If she knew that he was going to a theatre, for instance, Lilian would save his money and his legs by arranging to pick him up in the Trojan at the stage door and take him home to Lambeth – he lived not far from Stockwell. This would infuriate Lilian's dogs, if they were with her, because the old actor-manager used to delight in circling the car making faces at them, shaking his pink cheeks and leonine white mop, and jeering, 'Yah, yah, yah'. They would yap themselves into paroxysms of hysterical anger, slobbering all over the windows. It was a kind of revenge for all those who had suffered from their nips and noise; for B.G. never started his taunting until he was safely out of the car.

Apart from performing such errands, the Trojan proved to be

useful in other ways. Saving money, for instance. Lilian persuaded both Bruce Worsley and Townie, on different occasions, to come with her at night from the Vic, when the curtain was up, to a cache of road blocks in Hampstead, which were apparently there for the taking, and fill the car with fuel for her Stockwell fire. The Trojan also opened a new era for Lilian and her staff, by enabling her to bring her beloved dogs to the theatre every day. Her passion for dogs flowered late in life – prompted, perhaps, by Father Andrew in the First World War – but it was nonetheless fervent for that. Once she had the Trojan they became her inseparable companions, bridging her private and public worlds. The two terriers she took to the office (leaving one or more at home) were deeply hated by most of the staff and by all visitors to Lilian's office, where they had their headquarters behind a dirty curtain, surrounded by dishes of water, dog food and dog smells, yapping continually and hysterically through all conversations, which they regarded with feverish jealousy as competitions for their mistress's affection. Their invisibility contributed to their initial impact: newcomers were unnerved by the sudden outbreak of growling from no apparent source. Part of the Baylis legend was, as Laurence Olivier recalls, that if you asked for a rise they went straight for your ankles. Dame Ninette de Valois has described the impact of the last couple, Scamp and Sue: 'Always in the office and always in the way, they spent their time charging at their owner in an effort to get on to her lap . . . breaking up any sequence of conversation with yelps that made you long to throttle them . . . She would wander round the theatre carrying these shapeless O-Cedar mops, one under each arm. If she wished to point out any feature of interest, a dog was dropped; it would land, yelping, on your feet, successfully drowning the observation that led to its downfall.'[2] A similar chaos prevailed in Stockwell; for Miss Baylis did not – or could not – exercise over her animals the mastery with which she kept her people in order. Sue, in particular, liked to nip anyone in trousers; and when life was dull both dogs would chase Lilian's cat, which they detested. The dogs went everywhere, even to church. She would leave them in charge of the gardener, if he was in sight; if not, she put them in an old prayer-book cupboard near the door. They were among her favourite subjects of conversation with her intimates, who would learn from day to day a great deal about the dogs' ailments and mating habits in unremitting and unsavoury detail. It is scarcely surprising that among the post-humous panegyrics – indeed for many years – Scamp and Sue (with their precursors) provoked one of the few notes of recurrent criticism from her friends. They were, said Dame Ethel Smyth, 'her only grave weakness'.[3] This was the 'weakness', it seems clear, of a shy, lonely and childless woman, for whom the dogs were the most demonstrative, nursable and (in one sense) lovable members of her large substitute family.

The Trojan and its successors not only enabled Lilian to keep the dogs with her throughout the working day but also to take them with her in pursuit of two of her chief private pleasures, for which the car gave her – when she could seize the time, and be persuaded that she was not indispensable – a far greater range of choice. The first of these was swimming, which she kept up until the end. She never had any hesitation in recruiting friends or members of the company to escort her to the nearest navigable water. Back in 1916, on the company's visit to Stratford, a number of the young actresses *had* to bathe in the Avon every day, because Lilian did – encased in a striped Victorian bathing costume. At the Vic the attraction was Lambeth Baths. Eric Phillips, who was with the company in 1929, described in a broadcast talk how he was 'literally shanghaied' into such an expedition.

In the water she wore a somewhat old-fashioned bathing costume and a cap like an inverted sponge-bag. She said, 'When I go bathin', I'm a lazy girl. I like to be pushed along. That's where you come in, Eric.'

She lay on her back and floated on the water. Then, when I had swum over to her, she placed the tips of her toes on either side of my shoulders and told me to swim the breast stroke. For the best part of a quarter of an hour I propelled her up and down the Lambeth Baths.

But Lilian liked best to look up at the sky when she was floating; and the sudden mushrooming development of outdoor swimming pools in roadhouses and elsewhere during the late 1920s and early 1930s led to many erratic expeditions in the Trojan around the countryside. 'We used to go to Birmingham by way of Beachy Head so that she could get into as many pools as was possible. And she loved sea-bathing. I couldn't keep her out of the water,' says Prevost. 'Why? I think it was something to do with her size and weight. She loved the buoyancy of being afloat, of feeling *light*.' It made her forget her appearance, too.

Opportunities for swimming apart, Lilian developed an enthusiasm for exploring the countryside. She had the Trojan converted, so that she could sleep in it; and if she saw a field that she fancied at the end of the day, she would get her driver to ask the local farmer if they could camp there for the night. 'You can tell them who I am,' she would say. It did not occur to her that in that part of the country they might not have *heard* of Miss Baylis or the Vic. But if the natives proved to be friendly, she might bring out her mandolin and play for them at night after dinner (she loved to cook meals in the open). As Clarkie said, 'she was a born gipsy, at heart'; she certainly liked to think of herself as one. Perhaps, too, this was an attempt to recapture something of the South African experience. 'She never really lost her ox-waggon attitude to life,' says Prevost. With her arrival, Lilian's weekend transport improved, because they would often use Prevost's own Austin 7, which did forty m.p.h., compared with the Trojan's maximum of sixteen m.p.h. 'Can't we go faster, can't we go faster,' she would ask eagerly, relishing the excitement.

Lilian also practised a more sedentary form of weekending. During Ethel Everest's lifetime she sometimes enjoyed the hospitality of Chippens Bank, and she visited retreat-houses and the homes of religious friends throughout the country; but around 1928 she acquired a second home of her own. Lilian's country residence was not much like Chippens Bank. The Hut, as it was generally known, was a one-room shanty on Betchworth Hill in Surrey, in a clearing about 700 feet above sea level where a few like-minded spirits pursued the simple life at weekends. Lilian was introduced to it by Cicely Hamilton, who had somehow established herself there in a converted single-decker tram. The Hut had a bunk, a camp-bed, a canvas chair, a small primus cooker and a tiny veranda with splendid views into the Weald of Kent and over to Chanctonbury Ring. Lilian loved it. She brought very few friends there, but preferred to be on her own or with one of her trusted intimates such as Clarkie or Prevost, strolling in the woods with her dogs, cooking sausages on the Primus, washing in the open air, picking mushrooms or blackberries, and thinking about God, the Vic and her own successes and failures. Sometimes she would wake Prevost up in Stockwell at two or three in the morning and say, 'Come on. Let's go to the Hut,' and they would drive through a sleeping London to this pastoral retreat for an early breakfast, watching the sun come up over the hill.

In the last year of her life Lilian bought a third home, with retirement in mind. It was better equipped and bigger than the Hut, but scarcely more pretentious: a poky, rather dilapidated Victorian cottage in a working-class terrace on a cliff in Hastings, which she acquired for a couple of hundred pounds. (After her death Ethel, who inherited it, dubbed it 'Liliancot'.) Lilian chose it not only because it was cheap, but because it had a clear view of the sea, with only greenery between the house and the beach, and it gave her unrestricted opportunities of floating in the sea water whenever she could escape from London. Late at night on Saturday, after she had made her usual round of both performances at both theatres, she would be driven down to Hastings, arriving asleep at about two in the morning. But a few hours later she would be up for church – and a dip. She seemed to need both of them with increasing urgency in the last few years of her life.

Lilian seldom stayed in hotels and seldom went abroad: no more, perhaps, than half a dozen times in forty years, and then usually under persuasion – almost duress – from her friends and colleagues, because of her health, though she generally seems to have enjoyed herself a good deal more than she anticipated. Emma took her (and Ethel) on a weekend trip to Amiens in 1898; the Governors sent her on a round-the-world cruise in 1910, to recover from a breakdown; she went on a trip to Portugal in 1921, to convalesce after her cycling accident; she returned to South Africa in 1924; she went on a cruise to the Canaries, and spent two days in Paris when she attended a conference there; and she travelled with the company to Belgium in 1921 and Denmark in 1937. She had no gift for languages and little interest in foreign food. But she delighted in sending picture postcards to her family, especially her nephew Bobby, and, later, in taking her own snaps. Converted to photography, she wielded her camera with the same zeal and ineptitude that she showed at the wheel of the Trojan. And she always returned from holiday armed with little trinkets and mementoes. Most were destined for her friends and family, but she kept a few for herself, adding to the odd collection of personal junk in her office at the Vic or her home in Stockwell. One of her favourites (bought in Paris) may be seen in a portrait: a tiny clown balancing a bottle on his nose. Her affection for that grinning toy reflects one side of Lilian's nature that is often overlooked: her childlike appetite for *fun*, of the simplest possible kind – the kind she had been starved of in her own childhood.

The pivot of Lilian Baylis's private life, however, was her religious life. It centred on God, to whom – she believed – she had direct access. But the main intermediary and interpreter was, for over thirty years, Father Andrew. This Anglo-Catholic monk, whose real name was Ernest Hardy, was unquestionably the most important man in Lilian's life and her closest male friend – as close as any man could be to such a shy, celibate, self-protective loner. Only a priest vowed to poverty, chastity and obedience could, perhaps, have achieved such intimacy; but Father Andrew was no ordinary priest. A man of strong will, dominating charm and versatile talents, he became recognized – years after he first met Lilian – as one of the outstanding devotional writers of the day.

As an undergraduate at Oxford in 1890, Hardy was drawn – in the wake of Emma Cons's old hero, F. D. Maurice, and her friend Samuel Barnett – to serve God and the poor in the East End. Attracted by the personality of the Rev. A. F. Winnington Ingram, Head of Oxford House (and later Bishop of London) he worked in this Bethnal Green 'settlement' for eighteen months after leaving Keble. During the following year, at theological college, he planned with two friends to establish a new Anglo-Catholic order, in which they could combine their intense sense of religious vocation with work in the East End. The Society of the Divine Compassion, founded in 1894, was one of the small neo-monastic groups of enthusiasts to emerge in the Church of England at the turn of the century. It remained active for some fifty years, with the help of lay associates (like Lilian) who were given a bronze medal with the words, 'Put on a heart of compassion', inscribed on both sides. It took over a church and parish in Plaistow, a London working-class suburb where Father Andrew remained for most of the following fifty-two years. He is said to have been the first man ordained in a religious habit since the Reformation. In 1912, at the age of forty-three, he was elected Superior of his Order; two years later he helped to establish a home for lepers at East Hanningfield in Essex; and it was shortly after this that he met Lilian Baylis. She had been on a retreat taken by a priest of the SDC, who introduced her to his Superior. 'They were soon firm friends, and she became an associate of the SDC and one of Father Andrew's spiritual children,' according to Kathleen Burn, his biographer.[4] The leper colony (the Home of St Giles) became her main private cause, outside the Vic.

Their long friendship was clearly rooted in an intensity of religious feeling that could not be satisfied by the traditional rituals and reticences of the Church of England below the Highest level. But Lilian and Father Andrew had other enthusiasms in common – dogs, swimming and the theatre. From the beginning of his life in the SDC Father Andrew showed a crusading concern for using theatrical techniques in the service of God, reflecting the turn-of-the-century trend towards the reinstatement of religious drama, and the recognition by the churches of an art long denounced as sinfully profane and still, even at that time, dismissed by some clerics as morally dangerous.

Father Andrew was a prolific writer: although he did not begin to publish until he was fifty, he produced nine volumes of poems and eighteen volumes of prose, as well as six plays. He was also a keen painter and sketcher; had originally planned to make a career in art; and always carried a sketch-book in the pocket of his robe. At the first Christmas of his Plaistow ministry he presented in church a dramatized illustration of the Nativity story, known as the Bethlehem Tableaux, the precursor of a genre that was to become familiar to many Anglican congregations in the next century. The Tableaux – for which he painted the scenery and directed the performers – were so immediately popular that they achieved a transfer to a secular stage, in Canning Town Hall, and were revived spasmodically for many years (their final run was from 1931 to 1940). Father Andrew's introduction to the Old Vic, of which he rapidly became a *habitué* both backstage and in the box, stimulated his interest in religious drama, and through Lilian he was commissioned to write a Nativity play for the theatre. She liked to have one every Christmas: for three years she had insisted on *The Star of Bethlehem*. In 1918 George Foss persuaded her to allow a version of the Coventry Nativity Play; but in 1919 the Old Vic presented Father Andrew's first play, *The Hope of the World*. On its publication, the author dedicated it 'very affectionately to Miss Lilian Baylis and all at the dear Old Vic'. It was revived there for two further Christmases, and would perhaps have been staged *every* Christmas – until there was no room for special seasonal plays in the programme – had Lilian been able to overcome the resistance of successive directors to this devotional but undramatic exercise. None of Father Andrew's later works reached the Vic stage (although he corresponded voluminously with Lilian about his dramatization of *John Inglesant*); but his Passion Play, *The Garden*, was staged every Lent for seventeen years at Plaistow, where his plays became a parish tradition. According to his biographer, 'many of those who took part in them have testified to the influence for good which they exercised on their lives'. Lilian lent costumes, gave advice, brought guests and in other ways took a keen personal interest in the productions. She also gave practical aid to the theatricals of other religious orders – for example, to the

Shakespearian productions of the Order of the Sacred Mission at Kelham. And Father Andrew gave spiritual aid elsewhere in the theatre, as chaplain to the Theatre Girls' Club and to the Artists' Guild.

At the Old Vic the influence of Father Andrew was widely regarded – among all but the very devout – as something less than beneficent. This was partly, no doubt, because so few people knew anything about him. Even Dame Sybil, who knew and admired him, admits that he was not popular backstage, because of his 'rather smarmy' manner. Some actresses found him not only unctuous but embarrassingly friendly, with a disposition to put an arm around them in a way that seemed decidedly un-monkish. The company also tended to suspect his influence on the management, and in particular the censorship of 'ruderies' (Miss Baylis was said to have insisted on the occasional bowdlerizing of a word because 'Father Andrew wouldn't like it'). Professor Dent (who never met him) wrote: 'He haunted the theatre, and haunted is here indeed the right word, for his tall and sinister-looking figure would sometimes glide silently into the shadows of the Governors' box during a performance . . . suggesting a Grand Inquisitor escaped from the score of some forgotten opera by Mercadante or Donizetti.'[5] Others found him not so much sinister as grotesque and even comic. From season to season there were institutional jokes among the impious about the way in which Lilian shut herself up in her office with Father Andrew, and ribald speculations about the nature of her orisons. Both the resentment and the mockery were, perhaps, understandable reactions to the manifest piety that many people on the Vic payroll found incompatible with Lilian's apparent bossiness, ruthlessness and stinginess. They failed to comprehend the passionate intensity of religious feeling and self-questioning behind the brusque, confident façade, and what seems to have been the essential innocence of her relationship with her father-confessor, no matter how it may have been energized by sexual sublimation. Although Father Andrew sometimes signed himself 'Yours lovingly', it was the protective love of the shepherd for his flock, one of the traditional roles naturally (if somewhat hammily) assumed by this dominating and not a little self-dramatizing priest. Lilian was, it is true, one of his most influential sheep; yet she was not only his 'dear child in our Lord' but also his 'dearest Pal', long after she could offer him a stage for his plays.

Like all those who knew her well, Father Andrew came under

the spell of her personality; and he knew the depths and complexities of her character perhaps better than anyone. As his *Life and Letters* illustrate, he was a man of tolerant views. Writing to unnamed correspondents on sexual topics, he said, for instance, 'The old idea that human love could never be quite pure and that the flesh is bad and sex nasty is a heresy to be fought to the death'; and 'God made your sex, and there is nothing to be ashamed of in the hunger of it any more than in the appetites of hunger and thirst'. Writing about Christ, he said, 'His Hands are the Hands of an artist and a lover'. That was an image to which Lilian would have been especially responsive.

Father Andrew was, moreover, a man of genuine talent, with a passion for the theatre which may well have helped to infect Lilian and cool her impatience with 'mucky old Shakespeare' in the early years. (Robert Atkins believed that it was on the Father's advice that Miss Baylis chose him as producer.) It was not until 1933, when he was sixty-four, that he stopped going to the Vic, and then it was as a religious penance, self-imposed. He explained this to Lilian in a letter which reflects something of his enthusiasm for the drama, as well as the tone of their relationship.

I am sure you know that there is hardly a bigger sacrifice that I offer to God in my life than the sacrifice of coming to the Vic as I used to. I believe there is no one who loves the theatre more than I do, or who is more completely happy in its atmosphere and in the appreciation of dramatic art; but that good thing God, I believe, asked me to offer up as a sacrifice and I have done it. If you want me for your own or another's soul on any occasion, you know I would wish to come from one end of England to the other at once, but I must not seek anything for myself.[6]

This was not a permanent sacrifice: Father Andrew later resumed his visits, to the irritation of many on the Vic staff, who had felt reprieved.

It seems unfair that he should survive in most recollections of the Baylis era as no more than a joke or a nuisance, for he undoubtedly contributed, in his own way, towards its achievements. In Dame Sybil's words, 'he was a great help to Lilian because of his deep appreciation and his wide knowledge of art'. But even more significant was his deep appreciation and wide knowledge of Lilian Baylis. He gave this lonely woman the only kind of consolation and satisfaction that she could take from a man. He gave her, as one of her early secretaries said, 'the serenity that she needed so badly', even if she could not keep it for long.

There is little doubt about the intensity of her feeling for him. Some four years after they met, she wrote to Ivy Smithson, a young Anglo-Catholic girl who later became an actress.

I believe I never realized God's love so much as when I make my confession to Father Andrew. Though I love him I'm afraid of his tenderness, I never knew loving words could hurt so much. I feel often I'd whip myself for my rotten failings, but one feels aching from head to foot and just as if one had really been scourged all over after his words of loving encouragement. I have practised confession steadily for nineteen years now and have had many dear helpful priests but never one who makes me feel my sins as Father Andrew does, just because of his great loving heart.

This was the world of feeling which, though hidden from her people at the theatre, supplied the extraordinary energy and drive of her work there; and her confessor was her route to the main source of power. Although she believed that she could achieve direct contact with God in prayer, communications sometimes broke down – Father Andrew helped to repair them. Lilian prided herself on being able to recruit, in every department, the man who really *knew* – Father Andrew was the expert in the department of the divine.

Lilian Baylis's faith in divine immanence and in the power of prayer is the subject of many anecdotes still current in the theatre world. She sometimes asked actors and actresses at auditions if they believed in God; and if they did, it was clearly a major point in their favour. To Beatrice Wilson, for instance, she said, concluding the interview, 'Do you believe in God? All right, you'll do.' To Marie Ney, ten years later, she put the same final question. 'And you do believe in a God, dear, don't you – you do believe you're doing God's noblest work?' Some of the company were infected by her own faith. Winifred Oughton said: 'If she hadn't got the money, she went down on her knees in that poky little office of hers with anybody handy who would do the same thing, and bullied God till God sent her the money, and He *did*. There's no denying it. The money came.' Others were embarrassed by being involved in these supplications. Before *The Hope of the World* was first performed, Lilian sent for Florence Saunders and Molly Veness, who were in the cast, and both had to kneel down and pray in the office with Father Andrew and her. Both actresses 'got the giggles', and Lilian exploded into one of her unChristian rages – but later forgave them for their levity.

To some people Miss Baylis's concern with their religious views and practices seemed intrusive. During the company's visit to Stratford in 1916, she sent one Monday for Madge Whiteman – who was assistant stage manager, in addition to playing small parts – and told Miss Whiteman how glad she had been to see her in church the previous morning. 'If you had been there *every* Sunday you would have been blessed, and we should have seen God shining through your work. Don't you think so, dear?'

'No,' said Miss Whiteman. 'I don't, Miss Baylis. I was there every Sunday, but you didn't see me. So you haven't seen God shining through my work.' They did not get on well after that exchange; and Madge Whiteman believed that her employer never forgave her.

In later years Miss Baylis was less inclined to question new arrivals about their religious beliefs, or to ask visitors to pray for instant aid from the Almighty. She did such things a good deal less frequently than the stories suggest; and, true as many of these are, they overshadow other aspects of the truth about Lilian. She was, for instance, too shrewd to cross-examine a John Gielgud or an Edith Evans about *their* faith, or to thrust her own upon them. She didn't, indeed, talk about religion to a great many people, let alone ask everyone to pray with her; and although she often engaged people on the strength of their church connections she did not hesitate to get rid of them if they failed to put the Vic first. Having hired a box-office clerk because she was the sister of the housekeeper of a priest whom she knew, Lilian fired her shortly afterwards because the girl refused to work on a Good Friday. Manifest piety was not always a sufficient qualification for employment – or for personal friendship. Mrs Clark was an agnostic, as Lilian discovered soon after Clarkie started work there. Some weeks later Clarkie lost her watch, and reported it to the manager, who was closeted with two priests.

'Have you prayed to St Anthony to get it back for you?' asked Miss Baylis.

'No,' Clarkie answered hesitantly, afraid that she was going to get the sack for the revelation. 'I'm an agnostic.'

'Take no notice of her,' said Lilian to the priests. 'I've never known a better Christian. But she will insist that she isn't one.'

Lilian's own Christianity, while shot through with contradictions, was free of religiosity. 'The great thing', she told Hugh Walpole, was 'to be quite natural yourself with God as you would with anybody else'.

232

'That's very difficult. To be natural, I mean,' Walpole said. 'You feel he sees through you.'

'So long as He helps the Old Vic, dear, He can see through me as much as He likes.'[7]

Some of her friends wondered what would happen if He abandoned the Vic – would Lilian obediently turn her back on the mission of Emma and herself? 'The Vic and God were her two loves,' said one admirer. 'But if He'd interfered with the Vic, I think He'd have been *out*.' There were occasions, of course, when He disappointed her: on one of them she said to Ninette de Valois, 'God's let me down. I never thought He'd do this to me.' And she told Him so, when they were alone together. There were even moments when she felt crises of deep inner doubt and anguish; and although it is the moments of confidence and triumphant assurance that have been recorded – like her exit from a Governors' meeting, smiling broadly and declaring, 'I've got the Almighty in my pocket' – she was not only shrewd enough but humble enough to know that her prayers would be answered only, as Russell Thorndike said, if she 'did her share of helping to bring them about. "God helps those who help themselves", was a true maxim, and she followed it bravely, never sparing herself in the effort. After each prayer she would drive herself to a further effort, and then with success give no credit to herself, but all to God . . . she knew that they were answered, not for her, but for the Vic.'[8] That was on the threshold of the 1920s; in later years she was perhaps readier to keep a little of the credit for herself. But she saw herself only as the instrument of God, who had given her the Vic to work for; and that is why she saw other people as agents of His will, which coincided with hers.

She worshipped, in her time, in many churches; but it is not quite true that, as Father Andrew suggested, any church would do, and that it did not matter as long as God was there. It did matter a good deal. The church had to be sufficiently High; and, if she was travelling outside London, she always took care to get a recommendation first from Father Andrew or another of her clerical friends. For most of her life she went on about ten retreats every year. Before she died, she had stayed at most of the convents in the country, and numbered many mothers superior among her acquaintances. At home she had her favourite churches. She often visited St John's, Waterloo Road, and two of its ministers – Mr Gordon and Canon Hutchinson (generally known as 'Father Hutch') – were familiar figures at the Vic. Mr Gordon was one of the Governors, and his successor, Hutch, became Chaplain to the theatre and a close friend. Sometimes she visited St Stephen's, Gloucester Road, and sometimes she went back to the church where she was christened, All Saints, Margaret Street. But for over forty years her main church was St Agnes's in Kennington, about twenty minutes walk from her house in Stockwell, midway to the Vic. She was drawn to it by the personality of Canon Alfred Holland, who was minister from 1895 to 1925. Her parents and Aunt Ellen worshipped there, too, and as a memorial to them in 1933 Lilian commissioned two of the Kilburn sisters to make plaques of the Stations of the Cross. The church was bombed in 1941; but some of the plaques survived and, together with replicas of the others, were installed in the rebuilt St Agnes in 1958 as a memorial to Lilian, with the help of contributions from many friends and former members of the companies.

Hers was no mere Sunday observance. For years she went to Mass every morning, although towards the end of her life she went only about twice a week. 'She put all her problems before the Lord. And *whatever* came to her at the moment of communion, she would follow it out,' said Dame Sybil. 'Sometimes it seemed to be against all common sense, but it always turned out to be right.' Always? Well, often enough to make people talk, however hyperbolically, of 'miracles'. This kind of religion did not depend upon churches: it was *lived*, throughout the day. 'I've never known anyone whose religion was so much a part of every moment in her life,' to quote Dame Sybil again. God was there behind the bargaining, the bullying, the rows – in fact, some of the biggest (if least publicized) rows were with Him. If she was a 'saint in the making', as Father Andrew said, she was a noticeably bad-tempered one – 'a very *rough* saint', to use Dame Sybil's distinction. But she certainly fitted Father Andrew's definition that 'a saint is a person with a one-track mind. The life is dominated by one passionate force, and that is faith in God, and obedience to all that is believed to be His will.'[9]

Not only did Lilian think frequently and fervently about Christ: on occasions she saw Him – or so she believed. One spring Sunday in 1931, praying for help in the church on the Isle of Sheppey, she 'looked up and saw our Lord kneeling against the little table facing her. They seemed to say the Our Father together,' but when she opened her eyes again, He was not there. 'The wonder of it grew and grew. On her way to London next day passing the church she longed to get out and see if He would

234

come again but felt she could not bear any disappointment.' As a practical believer, she returned to the church a year later, and, after praying in the same chapel, checked to see if there was a large figure of Christ in the window that might have accounted for her experience; but there was not. He did not appear again then, but on another occasion she woke up one morning after sleeping in the summer house at Stockwell, and saw between the curtains in the bedroom of her neighbour, Dr Mary Smith, a 'very wonderful and glorious golden picture of our Lord'. When she asked Dr Smith about this picture, her friend replied that she had none; and when Lilian asked to be allowed to inspect the bedroom to see what might have caused it, she saw nothing. 'The Face was so lovely that she said her prayers to it and thought of it constantly for some time.'

Miss Baylis believed in works as well as faith, and she showed an especial compassion for the lepers in the Home of St Giles at Hanningfield, near Chelmsford, run by Anglican sisters under the auspices of the SDC (until the mid-1930s, when the Community of the Sacred Passion took over responsibility). When the Home was first established in 1914, patients were transported there in secret: 'It was difficult even to buy provisions and equipment locally because of the hostile attitude of people in the area'. The traditional and irrational fear of the disease was still so strong that for many years its victims had been excluded from hospitals, workhouses and nursing homes; but Lilian was not afraid. On the contrary, she spent some of the happiest days of her life among the lepers. She wrote in 1917 – characteristically dating the letter, 'St Thomas's Day', and with characteristic punctuation:

Tomorrow I hope to take my banjo and sing to each leper who is too ill to get to the common room, and then in the evening we are having a sing-song in the common room ... One boy played the violin by ear, though almost blind, a sister tells me usually, directly the eyes go the hands start.

And again, in the following year, Lilian wrote:

In this dear community Jack is as good as his master. I much prefer it. As Father Andrew says, if Our Lady came to some of our big convents she certainly would not be found with the choir sisters in the chapel or doing the more dainty jobs, but in the kitchen with the lay sisters. Here they are all the same and it's lovely.

There were few cases in Britain – no more than a hundred in the

1920s – yet even so the cluster of bungalows at Hanningfield could hold no more than a score of them. But for those who were there, no effort could be too great for Lilian; and she made sure that the effort was shared by as many of her friends and her company as she could marshal into an expedition. They would set off four or five times a season, on a Sunday morning, wet or fine, after Lilian had been to Mass. Whatever the weather, they would almost always have a picnic lunch *en route*: Lilian mobilized her friends to supply chicken legs, sandwiches, etc. They would usually stop in Epping Forest so that, as she put it euphemistically, 'the boys and girls can circle round a bit'. And when they got to the Home, they were expected to entertain the patients with songs and recitations, sometimes giving whole excerpts from an opera or a play on a tiny makeshift stage. According to Father Hutch, Lilian knew each leper personally and 'made a point of maintaining contact with every one of them. Especially those in an advanced state of the disease. It was a very important part of her life.' One of the patients in the last stages said to Sybil Thorndike, 'I want to see that nice big lass who laughs and talks so bright – she's a caution, she is'; another said, 'she makes me feel I'm going to get well'; and a woman whose husband had died of the disease, and was then nursing her son in the home, said, 'Miss Baylis is one of those who take away fear. I feel I don't mind if I get the disease or not.'[10] The Mother Superior in charge, Mother Clare, became one of Lilian's friends, and sometimes visited the Vic, concealing herself behind the curtains in Lilian's box. Father Hutch found her there once in hiding with an admiral, who turned out to be her brother. She was, said Father Hutch, 'a very unconventional kind of Mother Superior'.

Today, as the official brochure of the Home of St Giles says, 'fear of the disease has disappeared not only in the locality but to a large extent in the rest of the UK'; and Lilian Baylis played a part in dispelling that fear. The link of the Hanningfield home with the SDC has long since disappeared, too, but St Giles is still the only hospital in Britain specifically for the care and treatment of sufferers from leprosy. Lilian's work for it is remembered in the Recreation Room, where the stage is called the New Vic.

Although Lilian's sympathy with the lepers may well (as we have suggested) have been influenced by self-identification and perhaps masochism, it illustrates one important fact about the Lady that does not fit into the funny stories: in spite of her reputation for pennypinching as a manager, she was, in private, generous and kind, especially towards the very young and the very old. Apart from posting remittances to her more importunate relations abroad, Lilian contributed to the upkeep of a number of old people in the parish and helped to pay for the education of several children (in at least one case, right through university). One of these young dependants was staying at number 27 when Lilian died. She was preparing for her matriculation exams; and Lilian wanted to give her the good food and privacy that were not available at home. This girl's father was chronically unemployed, but Lilian paid all the grocery bills and bought clothes for the children. Like Octavia Hill and Emma, she preferred to give in kind, not in cash. Among her minor good deeds was meeting the cost of elocution lessons for a young curate who was suffering socially and professionally from his near-Cockney vowel sounds. The lessons were not immediately successful. After morning service Lilian cornered him. 'I don't know *what*'s the matter with you, dear. You're still saying, "Let us *pry*, let us *pry*". It's about time you started *praying*.'

It was the Old Vic's money that she hoarded so covetously and guarded so vigilantly: she gave much of her own money away on the quiet, to deserving (and not so deserving) causes. The way in which she maintained this demarcation line was illustrated by her behaviour when Annette Prevost, after nearly four years of devoted service, asked Lilian for a ten-shilling rise in her wages (which the theatre paid) – to thirty shillings a week. Miss Baylis refused, point-blank, and continued to refuse, until she realized that 'my Prevost' could no longer live on a pound a week and would have to look for another, part-time job. With great reluctance, and some resentment, the rise was approved; and Lilian showed her displeasure, even anger, for some time. Shortly afterwards they went to her dressmaker for a fitting. Before they left Lilian said she had to buy a dress for a girl about Annette's age, and asked her driver to suggest a pattern and act as model for it, as she was also about the same shape and height. Some days later she suddenly came into Annette's room, threw a parcel at her, barked, 'There you are. Drat you. You've won,' and made an equally sudden exit. Inside was the dress. It was, Prevost explains, 'her way of saying, "Sorry I was mean, but I didn't think the theatre could afford it".'

Even when the theatre's money was involved, Lilian could show a generosity that makes nonsense of the legend. When a Cockney girl (with a problem-family background) was found to be stealing from the box-office till at the Old Vic, Lilian not only forgave her but virtually adopted her, had her taught to drive, and employed her for a time as her part-time chauffeur. Some years later the Sadler's Wells box office suffered from pilfering, when a girl (call her B.) who worked in it helped herself to the takings and shared them with another of Lilian's erstwhile drivers. B. panicked, threw the keys of the safe into the Thames over Blackfriars Bridge and disappeared. The insurance company paid up. But months later Lilian learned that the runaway was working as a nursemaid in a seaside town, was miserable and repentant, but didn't dare to make the first move. At once Lilian rang up Father Hutchinson (who had recommended B. to her) and told him, 'You've got to go and find her'. Which he obediently did, somehow, without knowing any address, and B. was brought back to London for rehabilitation, but not for punishment. Lilian would not consider the possibility of prosecution. She sent the insurance company a cheque from her own account for the money; and her gesture was matched by theirs – for they returned her cheque in two pieces. On yet another occasion, pilfering from the dressing-rooms, coats and handbags at the Vic was so persistent that dyed coins were planted to trap the thief. They were found in the purse of a girl-student, who was bundled into Lilian's office with purple-stained hands and her Pekinese dog, to await the arrival of the police. Lilian was horrified at the idea. Turning to Annette Prevost she snapped out orders for instant evasive action. '*Quick*. Out of that door. Take that child. *And* her dog. Take them to Stockwell. And hide them.' And they stayed there in sanctuary until the affair blew over – to the fury of Sue and Scamp, who detested the Pekinese intruder.

Lilian's personal attitude to money was conditioned by the recollection of her childhood and adolescence. Her private fear of debt, like Emma's terror of drink, was partly influenced by the fact that she had seen too much of it in the family. Moreover, the money was not hers to spend. She was officially required to account to the Governors for the smallest item of expenditure. She took little enough for herself – indeed, she demanded to be given less, on several occasions. She had a peasant-like attitude to money, as Ninette de Valois suggests, with a deep-rooted suspicion of banks and their ways. But she demanded – and quite often got – discounts for immediate payment of bills – if they were not given as a matter of course, the fur flew. Every night one of Prevost's tasks was to separate the florins from the change in her purse, in case they should be confused with half-crowns. Although she was generous in her entertainment, she delighted in getting other people to pay for it too – whether it was a matter of making the food for a picnic, or giving a garden party to raise funds. Yet she made loans *sub rosa* to colleagues and friends (at her death Prevost had instructions to destroy several IOUs). And although she saved hard, it was not only for her own old age – she was determined not to take a penny from the Vic and the Wells when she retired, because she believed they could not and should not afford to pay her a pension and, remembering her parents' last decade, she was resolved to keep her independence – but also for all those relations, lame-duck friends and elderly pensioners who had for so long relied on her financial aid.

Although Lilian was widely believed to be a miser, especially by those who did not know her life out of the theatre (and they were the majority), the news that her estate was valued at some £10,000 was received with astonishment and, in some quarters, derision. To many people it appeared a fortune of unseemly, improbable size for a woman who had for so many years been the incarnation of managerial poverty, haggling over pennies with artists and begging for pennies from the audience. Clearly, even the most skilful miser could not have saved so much (allowing for the value of her two houses, jewellery and other personal effects) from a salary that, even at the end of her life, was no more than £1,000 a year, with a private income of some £300. (By comparison, Sir Reginald Rowe left some £6,000 when he died in 1945; Evelyn Williams left over £22,000 when she died in 1959.)

The clue to Lilian's relative prosperity at the end of her life seems to lie in her membership of the Soroptimists. Among the friends she made through this all-woman club was Miss Gordon Holmes, a brilliant financial brain in the City, where women were still not allowed to be stockbrokers and had to show exceptional talent and determination to succeed. As a partner in a bond house (or 'bucket shop', as they were familiarly dubbed) and also, more exotically, as the director of a savings bank in Budapest, she invested Lilian's savings to dazzling effect. Miss Gordon Holmes was also among the leading figures in the British Federation of Business and Professional Women, and a powerful advocate of the need for such women to organize themselves for mutual protection and progress in a man's world.

Another friend in the Soroptimists, who owned a clothes boutique in Bayswater, helped Lilian by advising on a new wardrobe, which she supplied. Although Lilian's appearance may have improved by the mid-1920s, compared with pre-war days, there was still – in the eyes of her staff – considerable room for improvement. She herself had no interest in clothes at all, but she took the advice of those she trusted, and reluctantly submitted to the persistent lobbying of her friends who felt that she had a responsibility to the Vic to put up a better show. With regret she said goodbye to her venerable bathing suit, her antique South African furs and her more governessy hats, and tried to live up to the new image with the aid of Madame Felicia. She didn't *enjoy* it; but she was, by now, inured to suffering for the Old Vic.

And what about the sexual life of Lilian Baylis? To this question, often considered to be by far the most important in any contemporary biography, the only satisfactory answer can be: she didn't have one, in the commonly accepted sense of the term. As Virgin Queen of the Vic, her sexual energies were sublimated in her religion and her work, and inextricably interfused with them; and they were also sublimated, perhaps, in her power-relationships with people, her hates (for she was, like many devout Christians, a good hater) and her crushes. 'Lil was always in love with someone,' says Dame Sybil. 'When I say "love", I mean "pash" – the innocent, childlike kind. She had pashes for a lot of men.' They were chaste, brief and unrequited; for, other considerations apart, the objects of Miss Baylis's affections were often somewhat remote – like King George of Greece; or, nearer home, Lord Lloyd. ('Fetch Lord Lloyd! Fetch Lord Lloyd!' she murmured, in her 1931 car crash. Lord Lloyd – a Conservative politician who was first Chairman of the British Council – was related to Lady Frederick Cavendish. He lived near the scene of the crash.) She was the object of many pashes – but from women, not men. She attracted lesbians, although there seems to be no question of her having had any overt homosexual inclinations herself, and indeed she was slow to recognize them in others. When Williams and Clarkie tried to discourage her from engaging an actress with notoriously proselytizing lesbian tastes she was, at first, horrified by their talebearing – 'I've never heard such a thing. I'm sure she's a dear, good woman. You've both got nasty minds – what a couple of peculiar women you are.' However, on reflection (and further consultation elsewhere) she took their advice. In her lifetime there were persistent rumours that the Old Vic was a lesbian stronghold; partly because a number of well-known lesbian actresses had, not surprisingly, played there over the years; because Miss Baylis was a dominating unmarried woman whose closest friends and colleagues (monks and clergymen aside) were mostly women (most of them unmarried); and because those who did not know her believed her, quite wrongly, to be mannish and butch. Lilian was, in fact, for all her brusqueness and bossiness, a very feminine woman. She sympathized, to some extent, with feminism in her own non-political way, and was proud of her MA and her CH because they honoured not only her theatres but also her sex. But as for love, that was a matter between her and God; and God, to Lilian, was always Him – never Her.

Once men were officially de-sexed, as it were, in cassocks, robes and clerical collars, she found no difficulty in making warm friend-ships. This is how she first introduced herself to Canon Hutchin-son, who became one of her closest friends and (unlike Father Andrew) widely popular at the Vic.

I'd just settled down at Waterloo, and I was in my shirtsleeves, trying to arrange my books. A black man who looked after me then came upstairs and said, 'There's a lady downstairs to see you'.
'What's she like?' I asked him.
'She's fat and she's got furs on,' he said.
I said, 'Show her up' – but she was already up. She came in and said, 'I'm Lilian Baylis. And I'm very glad to see you. I knew your sister, and I was very glad to hear you were coming to the Waterloo Road. I'm sure we're going to be very great friends. Anything I can do for you at any time just let me know. I'd like you to regard your church as our church, and remember that whenever you want a seat in the theatre there's always one for you.'

At the theatre she worked easily with many men, and made many professional friendships. If her intimates were women, that was not only because she was shy and a spinster, but because she was pain-fully conscious, all her life, of her size, her twisted mouth, her lack of education. 'She felt that she was a plain woman, and would never be anything else,' said Hutch.' That undoubtedly explains a lot of things about Lilian's character.'

Her attitude towards the sexual experience of other people was a mixture of prudery, ignorance and tolerance. According to Hutch, she was 'broad-minded and at the same time extraordinarily small-town'. When Bruce Worsley missed his last train to Tun-bridge Wells, because of pressure of work at the Vic, Lilian some-times put him up in Stockwell; but, in deference to convention, he slept in the summer house at the bottom of the garden. In her own bizarre way she was inclined to ask members of the company dumbfounding, personal questions, as in this story told by Laurence Olivier.

'Are you pure, dear boy?' she said to Eric Portman one day. He went red and white by turns, and stammered, 'Yes, well, I – oh, er – well, *yes*'.

'Mind you, I'm not the curious type,' said Lilian. 'I'm nobody's nosey-parker. But I won't have anything going on in the wings.'

As she grew older, her Puritanism seemed to thaw. Ernest Milton said of her, after her death, 'I cannot think of any celibate woman of her years less spinsterish in outlook'. According to Annette Prevost, she made no fuss about people 'living in sin' if it was a stable relationship. She would say, 'Well, they're married in the sight of God, *aren't* they, dear?' She steadfastly preferred to believe in the sexual innocence of the company in any year – 'All my boys and girls are good boys and girls.' But in the mid-1930s she used to go round the dressing-rooms between performances, to make sure that nothing was going on. According to Sir Frederick Ashton, 'Her anger knew no bounds when she caught the opera chorus red-handed gambling in the lavatories' (though she can't have caught many at a time). 'Even more outraged was she when she discovered that my dresser and his girl friend were having an affair. She absolutely insisted that they got married at once.'[11] In the higher echelons such insistence would not have got very far; so Lilian behaved there with more conspicuous tolerance. She remained, to the end, a practical moralist.

In the company of her intimates, however, she had a liking for broad stories which by their contemporary standards (if not by those of the 1970s) seemed 'Rabelaisian'. Some of them were about her own adventures; and she liked to suggest, frequently and vividly, that she too had been fancied and had flirted and had taken chances, long ago in the dear dead days beyond recall in South Africa. In this, as in her sense of humour, there was little of the Puritan about Lilian Baylis in maturity, though to compare her with the Wife of Bath (as Williams did) seems as far-fetched as to invoke St Joan (as Sybil Thorndike did). She had an uninhibited admiration too for the Body Beautiful, especially for male legs. Her support for the ballet was kindled by her pleasure at looking at men in tights. Standing at the back of the Vic circle one evening during a ballet performance, she loudly told Ninette de Valois – and all the nearby audience – that one of the male dancers had a most *beautiful* behind.

Did she ever regret that she had never married? Perhaps – especially in her thirties and forties. Certainly she said occasionally that she should have had a family: 'Of course I'm the sort of woman who should have married and had half a dozen children.' But did she really mean it? Perhaps. She found a substitute for them in the scores of 'boys and girls' whom she mothered at the Vic, and in her nephew, nieces, great-nieces and other children whom she helped and befriended.

Towards the end of the 1920s, she was thrown into an unusual excitement by the news that a man from South Africa who had once proposed to her was coming to visit her at the Old Vic. 'I'm having all this trouble with chauffeurs and help at home,' she said to her friends. 'It would be so nice to have someone belonging to you to drive you. So I think I might ask him to marry me. He always wanted to marry me then. Maybe it's time I got married now. But he shan't live in my house. I'll have a room built for him over the garage. And I won't take his name, either. I shan't stop being Miss Baylis.' That it came to nothing was scarcely surprising. After thirty years, the idea of marrying Lilian, under any conditions, had not occurred to her 'boy friend'. But, in any case, Lilian realized that she had been on her own too long, and was too set in her ways, to consider the give-and-take of a marital relationship, even if the marital relations were restricted to driving.

The relationship that mattered most to her was, one must repeat, with God. Christianity, for Lilian, was a deeply personal experience: only the tip of it showed to the majority of people who worked with her. Many of those who did not share her faith respected its burning simplicity and sincerity; but few could guess at the private visions, vigils and intensities of self-scrutiny reflected, for instance, in the following much-used little list in her handwriting found tucked into her Bible.

Do I pray to forgive what I cannot forget
Do I practise self-control when I feel hurt
Do I accept bitterness of speech with sweetness
Do I make allowance for mistakes and try to work with those uncongenial to me
Do I as quickly make excuses for them as for myself
Am I really merciful towards those I dislike or who dislike me
Do I check in myself the spirit of criticism?

She prayed persistently to be a better woman; to be healthy enough to complete her mission; to be worthy of the Vic – and

Sadler's Wells. Father Holland wrote in her parish magazine after her death that she was 'above all else a woman of prayer. She had a profound belief in the power of prayer – whatever she attempted she entered upon with prayer – whatever she accomplished she gratefully acknowledged that it was prayer that had done it. To her prayer was not an occasional act but a habitual gesture, it was the atmosphere in which she lived . . .' She believed, unshakably, that 'working as she did for God and His poor, she was on God's side, and He on her side; but not only ON but AT her side, a present Friend, and unfailing Helper, in all that she undertook for Him, His Church and His people'. That was the heart of her private world.

One may catch a glimpse of it in this extract from a letter to a friend who was on the point of having an operation:

I've never felt much difficulty in waiting for an op. There is the possibility of passing on, and when you have done your duty (as you have always done) and really tried to be helpful and thoughtful in everything, you can have no fears. My only fear has been in case I fail to face life bravely, and when one has to work again, that wants all one's courage. It really is an adventure, and directly the first day or two of discomfort is over, just to be obedient, no other duty, is very wonderful, and one has so much to thank God for. I've always grabbed my hanky and prayed I may breathe steadily and quietly as I lay down on the operating table. Just the thought, 'To God I commend my spirit', and I close my eyes, feeling *certain* God is close to me, really more at peace than at any other time in my life.

The Triple Crown

The master of a theatre
is a kind of general trustee for the nation.

Aaron Hill (1735)

The box office never lies.

Lee Shubert (c. 1925)

Hers was and is a theatre for the people, in the narrow sense,
and the impulse to make it so
undoubtedly sprang from the fact that she was of the people.
It was and is the theatre of a people
in the larger sense of the whole nation.

James Agate (1937)

Nearly six years after the first public appeal was launched, the new
Sadler's Wells finally opened on 6 January 1931. It was a bad night
for theatregoing – foggy and frosty – and it was a bad time for
theatre-opening, on the verge of a national crisis. But it was a
night of triumph for Lilian Baylis, and for all those whose anxious
hopes were invested in her long-dreamed-of, scraped for, prayed-
for second theatre. This was the building that was going to solve
the problems of the impossibly overcrowded Vic; to give opera,
at last, the chance to expand, and ballet the opportunity to grow;
to bring sweetness and light to the working class of North London. Lilian had hoped to open it in the previous summer, then the
autumn, but the money came in slowly. The delays, after so prolonged a campaign, were hard to bear. To add to her furies and
frustrations, she had to go into hospital some weeks before the

great event, for an operation that, unlike the opening, could not be postponed. She had to stay there longer than she wanted, but insisted on trying to run everything from her hospital bed, where staff came to bring news of the battle and carry away her orders. She was back in action, hurrying from one theatre to the other, before she had really recovered. But she willed herself to be well enough to take part in the ceremonial opening.

Although the building was soon to be reserved for opera and ballet it opened with Shakespeare; and Shakespeare inspired the permanent decoration of the proscenium – a scene from *A Midsummer Night's Dream*, crowned by the arms of the borough of Finsbury. The inaugural production was *Twelfth Night*, to fit the date. John Gielgud and Ralph Richardson were in it, and an equally distinguished cast took part (in person, or by proxy) in the surrounding solemnities. Before the play began, speeches were made by Sir Johnston Forbes-Robertson and Dame Madge Kendal, who were not only doyens of the stage but had also been pupils of the Wells's greatest manager to date, Samuel Phelps. The Mayor of Finsbury also made a speech, watched by the mayors of six other boroughs which had helped (minimally, if at all) to pay for the new building. Reginald Rowe read out telegrams from the Prince of Wales, Ben Greet, Pinero and many more. All this took about an hour; but there was more to come. When *Twelfth Night* was over, and the company had taken their calls, the curtain rose again to reveal all the eminent visitors lined up on the stage with the actors, for the culmination of the evening. From their midst stepped Miss Baylis. It was *her* turn to make a speech. It was a moment of glory. The Lady was dressed, as usual, in her cap and gown, with her CH on her chest; but instead of the flowers that she often clasped on special occasions at the Vic she held in her right hand, surprisingly and unwisely, a large basket of fruit. Although this had a somewhat inhibiting effect on her gestures, which were vigorous when she was excited, 'she ploughed bravely on until, enthralled by the force of her own argument, she swept her right arm out impulsively. An enormous apple fell from the basket with a thud. There was a slight titter from the audience. Lilian looked at the basket, and then, edging towards the truant apple, tried to hide it with her robes. She went on with her speech, but soon sincerity overcame technique, and the basket shot out to the right to accentuate another point. This time a pear fell on the stage.' John Gielgud, describing the scene, confessed that he burst out laughing – and so did the audience. 'The solemnity of the occasion was irrevocably shattered'; but not its significance, *nor* Miss Baylis's speech.[1]

It seems characteristic of this extraordinary woman that one of the biggest moments of her life should be punctured by a comic gaucherie; and that she should mind (or *seem* to mind) so little if people were laughing at her, so long as they were not laughing at her theatre – either of her theatres. Personal dignity didn't bother her much; she had more important things to worry about. She knew that *she* – the real Lilian – was more important than her physical appearance and what she described as her 'rotten body'. She was used to being laughed at. What she could not get over was the fact that the Wells was really open, at last. Nothing could spoil the pleasure of seeing the new theatre packed with people for the first time, of hearing those tributes to the realization of a great dream that had seemed, to so many people, a grand illusion. It must have been, in Sir Hugh Walpole's words, 'the gratification of her very soul'.[2]

The prospect was rosy. A permanent opera company could now be established, nearly forty years after those early Costume Recitals at the Vic. The singers would have more space and time at last for more adequate rehearsal. For the first time, the chorus could rehearse with the orchestra. And for the first time in the history of London, opera could be on view nearly every night of the week for eight months in the year. With luck and judgement, the first British ballet company would be born before very long. And the drama company might not only restore the lustre of Phelps to the Wells but also find a new strength with its new *Lebensraum* at the Vic. Most of this happened, during the next six years; although by the time it did happen Lilian was near to death.

The opening of the Wells was a great personal victory for Lilian Baylis. Yet, as she soon discovered, this victory was only the beginning of another campaign. *Building* a theatre was difficult enough, especially when the architectural, technical and organizational problems were so unfamiliar: there was no modern British model which combined drama, ballet and opera under one roof, no foreign model whose financing depended so erratically upon the begging-bowl. Keeping the theatre *open* was even harder to achieve. Apart from the handicap that the times were more than usually out of joint, Sadler's Wells started in the red – to the tune of £15,000; so the fund-raising, lobbying, wheedling had to go on unabated. There was to be no end to the begging in Lilian's life.

The theatre was not only more expensive to build than experts had calculated (theatres always are), it was also much more expensive to run than the Lady had ever imagined. In the single-minded intensity of her drive to get it built, she seems to have insulated herself from the realities of how it was to be used, and of its implications for the old system at the Vic and her own mode of government. That insulation was, no doubt, a necessity if she was to succeed, though it is hard to believe Professor Dent that she was 'utterly unprepared for the new developments'. According to him, when she announced to the Governors that the two theatres would stage alternate weeks of drama and opera, Dent said, 'Then I suppose that means that we shall now have opera every night of the week for eight months'. Lilian seemed 'completely taken by surprise. "Yes, I suppose there will," she replied with a rather dazed look, as if it had never occurred to her that the whole work of the opera department would from now onwards be doubled if not more.'[3] The new theatre plan meant more singers, producers and conductors; it meant a bigger bill for scenery, props and costumes; it meant a larger orchestra; and, above all, it meant the instant mobilization of an *audience* for opera for five nights a week, after no more than two nights for the past twenty years. Although the increase in the drama company's work was not quite so marked, a big strain would be put on the director and his team by the obligation to play five nights a week, two matinées and (frequently) a school matinée, in addition to the time and energy consumed in travelling backwards and forwards between the two theatres. Some of this *must* have occurred to Lilian, during the months of preparation and scheming, but she no doubt soon dismissed such thoughts as distractions from the main task. There would be time to consider the details later, when the theatre was built. First things first.

Before she had to shoulder the full burden of these details, Lilian went back to hospital. While still not fully recovered from the aftermath of her operation, she was injured in a car crash, two months after the Wells opened. It was this accident, which could scarcely have come at a worse time, which produced one of the most popular (and most verifiable) anecdotes in the Baylis legend. It happened on the way back from a dinner given by the Gallery First Nighters to celebrate the opening of the Wells. At the corner of Portman Square her car hit the back of a coach, and Miss Baylis, who was sitting in front next to her driver, slumped forward, apparently unconscious. Clarkie was in the back, surrounded by Lilian's flowers, and when the ambulance men came along they went straight to her aid, as she seemed to be the VIP in the car. 'Oh no,' Clarkie protested. 'It's Miss Baylis, in front, you ought to look after first. She's the manager of the Old Vic.' Lilian raised her head, said emphatically, '*And* Sadler's Wells', and slumped down again.

Lilian had struck her chest against something and, characteristically, she used to expose it to friends to show them how black and blue she was. The injury was not serious: but she came out of hospital to work, once again, too soon. How could she stay in bed, when so much was happening at her lovely new theatre? Now fifty-six, she was visibly and persistently taxing her strength beyond its limits. The anxieties and disappointments of the Wells took their toll. The Governors were so concerned that they voted £100 to her, on condition that she spent it on a sea trip or some other 'really adequate holiday'. Lilian was so tired that she accepted the gift, with much less than her usual resistance, although she did not go to sea but stayed in England and Wales.

When she returned to work she went at it, seemingly, with all her old gusto; though not quite in the old way. 'It was difficult to talk to her; to follow the trend of her thoughts,' wrote one of her most loyal and trusted colleagues, Lawrance Collingwood. 'She jumped to conclusions in a flash but not always the right ones, and she dismissed you before you had time to speak your mind.' There was so much, so very much, to do. 'She seemed to be at both theatres at once, ever active in getting things moving, spying pitfalls or inefficiencies in every department and continually striving to put them and fifty other things right at the same time.'[4]

What was wrong? First of all, there was a good deal wrong with the building itself – though it took Lilian some time to admit that the objections to it were much more than fussy perfectionism. From the start most of the actors and many of the singers hated the new Wells. They disliked its deliberate austerity and neutrality of colour scheme – 'like a denuded wedding-cake', said Gielgud; its failure to create an equivalent of the theatricality that the Vic, for all its seediness, retained; the gap in communication with the audience caused by the absence of boxes; and the poor acoustics – especially for speech. There were only two really good spots on the stage from which to sing, said Sumner Austin, and there was a good deal of competition for them. There were other things wrong as well. Most of the dressing-rooms were too small (the occupants of some had to put their costumes on in the corridor). The scene-dock was too small. The stage itself was too small.

There was inadequate storage space, inadequate rehearsal space, inadequate wardrobe facilities. There was no paint-frame: everything had to be done at the Vic and ferried over. And the gallery seemed too far from the stage.

To some critics of the Baylis regime this seemed to illustrate, monumentally, the expensive perils of doing things on the cheap, regardless; for as these inadequacies and misjudgements became apparent, an Extension Fund had to be set up, with a view to enlargement and rebuilding. In defence of Miss Baylis, Reginald Rowe and the architects, it should be recalled that underestimation of demand and cheeseparing on essential services have featured in the design of most post-war British theatres (up till 1973), none of which has had to carry the performance-load of Sadler's Wells in the early 1930s. Some demands on the Wells were unprecedented and seemed unpredictable – notably, the rapidity with which ballet expanded and acquired an audience. Moreover, one should not – with the wisdom of hindsight – make too much of the architectural defects of the building; for ballet and opera grew there in strength, quality and popularity. Compared with the Vic in comfort and resources it was a palace of delights. There were tip-up seats in the gallery, basins in the dressing-rooms, modern electrical equipment. Yet there was something missing: the warm personality and intimate atmosphere of the old theatre in the Waterloo Road. It takes time, of course, for a brand-new building – whatever the pedigree of its site – to acquire a personal patina and assert an individual identity; and some of the chill wore off as the house warmed up and structural improvements were made; but Lilian did not have quite *enough* time to put her stamp on the Wells and develop an audience there, as she had done at the Vic. She was handicapped by the absence of the box, from which she could keep an eye on both sides of the footlights. (She had a kind of peep-hole made in a wall, but it was not the same.) And to keep both theatres imbued with her personality was a gruelling exercise for a woman approaching her sixties. She had to accept Geoffrey Toye as co-director of the Wells in 1932, and by 1933 she had surrendered her autocratic control of opera planning. She was obliged to recognize that it was no longer possible to keep her finger on everything and everybody; but initially both the Lady and the Governors failed to realize that the special conditions of the Vic were rooted in a world that had almost disappeared, and that they could not be instantly transplanted from Lambeth and reproduced in Islington. Instead of thinking out the needs of the new building, they thought first and foremost of establishing a second Old Vic: an extension, not a place in its own right with its own personality. Just as the scenery and costumes of the Vic appeared much tattier in the new building, so some of the old methods seemed out of place and some of the old staff seemed out of touch. So, even, did Lilian at times. Not only a new building but a new era had opened with the Wells. It seemed to be symbolized by the sudden death of Old Bob Robinson, a week afterwards, at the age of sixty-eight.

The original plan was that each theatre should stage a fortnight, alternately, of opera and drama; but it soon became clear in the first joint season that the Wells audience preferred opera, and stayed away from plays, while drama, not surprisingly, did better at the Vic, where it had taken the lion's share for seventeen years. So Lilian agreed to alter the plan. The Vic was given two weeks of drama to one of opera, and vice versa at the Wells. When this left the revenue problem unsolved, while increasing the strain on the companies, the cake was cut in another way: six weeks to three. By 1934-5 the Wells showed only four weeks of drama; in the 1935-6 season the interchange was stopped: drama stayed at the Vic all the time, opera and ballet at Sadler's Wells. During these four years the chopping and changing confused, irritated and exhausted not only the companies but many of the customers. Operagoers and playgoers frequently turned up at the wrong box office, arriving just in time for *Hamlet* at the Vic on the *Carmen* night, or finding too late that *Rigoletto* was at the Wells instead of the *Lear* they had journeyed into Islington to see.

All this not only ran up an unexpectedly large transport bill (about £2,000 p.a.) but also had a damaging effect on both box offices, which needed every paying customer they could get. It was hard enough to make revenue meet costs. Prices at the Wells, as at the Vic, were pegged at artificially low levels, because of the basic philanthropic aims of the enterprise and its charitable constitution. Under the terms of the Sadler's Wells Foundation, with the Duke of Devonshire as President, performances had to be 'suited for the recreation and instruction of the poorer classes', at prices which 'artisans and labourers' could afford. This was, however morally and socially commendable, an anachronistic aim, inherited from Emma Cons. It was not the artisans and labourers of North London who filled the gallery at Sadler's Wells, on those nights when the gallery did fill; any more than it was the South London costers who filled the gallery of the Vic. It was not really a local audience at all: that was a chimera that led Lilian and her colleagues astray. And that was one reason why it took four years to stop the interchange between the two theatres after it was seen to be impractical and uneconomic. The official reason was that both theatres were committed by the terms of their trusts to show both opera and drama, and the Charity Commissioners had to sanction a change in those terms. But Lilian could not bear the thought that there would be no opera at all at the Vic, where it had always been closest to her heart. The delay in reorganizing the programmes was probably due less to legal than to emotional obstacles.

It was a costly delay. At the end of the first, short season the Wells had lost over £3,200. It looked as if the new theatre might have to close down within two years after its opening. Business was generally poor, especially in the stalls, although it is hard to credit Hugh Walpole's story that on one occasion he was the *only* person there at *Il Trovatore*, when the gallery was packed. (Suddenly he heard Lilian's familiar husky voice: 'Tisn't very good, dear, is it?' No, said Walpole. If the stalls were full, it would be better. If it were better, the stalls would be full. 'Yes,' said the manager. 'It's a nasty roundabout, dear.')[5] 'It would be sheer madness to go on as at present,' Reginald Rowe said in a memorandum to the Governors. In the first six weeks of the autumn season the Vic lost £400, the Wells over £1,000; but Lilian firmly opposed Rowe's proposal to shut the Wells for half the week, and other suggestions for surrender. She was less successful in her resistance to the minor proposal, supported by the Governors, for starting performances at eight o'clock instead of seven thirty. Her people wouldn't stand for it, she said. But they did. The annual report for 1932–3 said that there had been 'surprisingly little opposition' to the change; but that an effort had been made to speed up productions so as to get the curtain down by eleven, 'our people having a distinct aversion from remaining in the theatre after that hour'. The imperial capitulation was made with dignity.

To get money and to save money in the next six years Lilian prayed, harangued, wheedled and begged, pulling strings and prodding people. Artists like Maggie Teyte, Anton Dolin and Lydia Lopokova gave their services. Musicians such as Vaughan Williams cut their fees. Gustav Holst paid for an additional orchestral rehearsal of *Job*. Oliver Messel designed *A Midsummer Night's Dream* for nothing, and the cost of executing the costumes and settings was met by Lord Hambleden and his brother, the Hon. James Smith. Theatre stars with a special affection for the

Vic – notably, Sybil Thorndike and Edith Evans – returned for short seasons at cut-price salaries. Production costs were helped by friendly 'loans': Covent Garden lent costumes for a new *Figaro*; Alexander Korda lent costumes from his *Henry VIII* film; and, most significantly, the Camargo Society 'lent' the production of *Job* and other ballets which it had commissioned. Lilian was very proud of some gifts and bargains. The British National Opera Company's scenery for *Tosca* was bought cheap at an auction; cut down, it 'came in very useful for our production', said Lilian's annual report. Edith Evans sold her the sets, for a 'nominal' sum, of her unsuccessful production, *Delilah* – Samson's pillars came in very useful for *Lear* and *Antony and Cleopatra*. Madame Kirkby Lunn, the famous singer, bequeathed her theatrical effects. Madame Agnes Nicholls (Sir Hamilton Harty's wife) gave Lilian a pile of costumes from her wardrobe, including the armour worn by Florence Austral as Brunnhilde at Covent Garden. John B. Gordon, producer of *Traviata*, paid for new costumes in his production, and gave generously in other ways. John Gielgud directed *The Merchant of Venice* for nothing. The audience, too, was asked to give and to go on giving. Weekly collections were made, notably in the gallery, to pay the Wells's building debts. The gallery pennies did not go very far towards the £15,000; but for Lilian this was a kind of psychological warfare – an attempt to generate at the Wells the sense of community, of 'audience participation', that she had nurtured at the Vic. Somewhat less explicable was her insistence on sending weekly collection-boxes around the opera company, whose members were already subsidizing the Wells by their underpayment and overwork. But, then, what union organizer could explain why an orchestra should rehearse for nothing – as the Wells orchestra did for *Samson and Delilah*? J. M. Keynes, one of the theatre's most influential new supporters, booked seats for 800 economists visiting London for an international conference. Lord Hambleden, helped by Lady Ottoline and Philip Morrell, organized the Sadler's Wells Society, with the main initial aim of getting well-to-do people to buy books of vouchers for the stalls. Contributions were made in many different ways by the Vic–Wells Association, the Old Vic Circle and the Sadler's Wells Circle, whose devoted loyalists played a notable part in the struggle. Less familiar methods of raising money were summer rambles in the country, and W. R. Sickert's promise to sell his picture 'The Raising of Lazarus' for the cause. He had 'deliberately made it provocative in order to create discussion and give publicity to the theatre's needs,' Lilian explained in her annual report, to calm the prejudices of her narrower-minded Governors. (Sickert, who had once acted at Sadler's Wells, took a close interest in the Vic at this time: he painted pictures of the interior and Peggy Ashcroft as Rosalind). Not the least of all these gestures, though never publicized, was Lilian's in risking her own money. Towards the end of 1931, appalled by Reginald Rowe's warnings of possible closure, she offered at a Governors' meeting to pay £100 into the Vic funds if nine others would do the same. That offer was gratefully accepted. It may be noted that – whether Lilian meant it or not – she was returning the money they had voted her for a holiday. According to her friend Cecil Leslie, when in 1934 she was given another honorary degree – as a doctor of law at Birmingham – she went off for a swim after the ceremony, and prayed in the water, 'Oh God, no more honours. It's *money* I need'.

All this begging, borrowing, blackmail and sacrifice was not enough in itself to stave off financial collapse. Whatever its tactical value and its psychological rewards, it did not pay the running costs or the building debt. In spite of a 'deficit grant' in 1932 of £5,280 by the CPF, which also gave £3,000 for the Old Vic, the outlook seemed black. In April 1933 Reginald Rowe told the Governors that it would probably be impossible to open the Wells for another season without 'some form of endowment'. Part of this was precariously achieved, later in the year, by persuading the BBC to grant £6,000 for the coming season, in return for broadcasting rights. The Wells building debt of £20,000 was reduced to £14,000, partly by an anonymous 'loan' from the Duke of Devonshire in memory of his aunt, Lady Fred, the staunch ally first of Emma and then of Lilian. Most of this was owed to the builder, Frederick Minter (shortly to be knighted), who generously agreed to go on waiting and forgo interest charges.

A very different kind of patron was then persuaded, in the autumn of 1934, to help both theatres to stay alive. After long manoeuvring and soliciting, with two flat refusals by the Chancellor of the Exchequer to consider the case, the Old Vic and Sadler's Wells were granted exemption from the payment of entertainments tax. This tax, introduced as a wartime expedient, was retained as a peacetime convenience by the Treasury. It was levied on gross box-office receipts, not on profits, so that theatre managers frequently had to pay out large amounts in tax on productions that had lost many hundreds of pounds. Lillian had attempted to get exemption as soon as the tax was imposed in 1916, instancing the beneficial effects of her programmes upon blinded soldiers and other casualties of the war. Moreover, she had claimed, 'members of the audience have written to say they were practically saved from insanity by the healing power of our plays'. The bid for exemption was renewed, somewhat less dramatically, in 1925 by Reginald Rowe, after the Finance Act allowed exemption to entertainments 'promoted by a society or institution of a permanent character established or conducted solely or partly for philanthropic or charitable purposes'; but these purposes were interpreted narrowly as giving donations to charities. Although exemption was later permitted to entertainments 'provided for partly educational or partly scientific purposes by a society or institution not conducted for profit', the Vic was declared to be ineligible, because 'educational' was defined as 'tuitional'. So it had to go on paying tax. In 1931–2, for example, the two theatres paid nearly £3,400, which swallowed up most of the hard-won revenue from the LCC matinées (£250), the Vic students (£550), subscriptions and donations (£409), ballet classes (£470) as well as the City Parochial Foundation's grant of £2,500. (Other revenue that year: £250 from the Vic–Wells Association, £300 from the Old Vic Dance and over £900 from catering.) In the following year Lilian had to pay nearly twice as much tax – £7,640 on box-office takings of £45,777.

Although Lord Lytton has sometimes been given the credit for securing exemption in 1934, Lilian took a different view. She told Sir Oswald Stoll, among other people, that she had dealt with the Chancellor herself. She said to him, 'Look here. If you don't take it off me within a fortnight, I'll have to close both my theatres. Then I shall spend the rest of my life on a lecture tour of the United States, telling them what a philistine you are to kill Shakespeare and opera in your own country.'[6] Perhaps she did give him that ultimatum (it sounds in character), and perhaps it tipped the scales. In any event, this long-overdue decision meant that the Old Vic and Sadler's Wells could now keep some eight per cent of their box-office revenue which would otherwise have gone to the taxman. This achieved, in effect, a kind of tacit differential bonus from the authorities, discriminating between the Vic–Wells and the rest, which amounted to a negative subsidy from the state. And the Vic's belatedly successful backstairs campaign was a landmark in the development of contemporary British theatre; it pointed the way for a growing number of repertory companies and, later, for Hugh Beaumont of H. M. Tennents, who used tax exemption to consolidate his power as Britain's leading manager.

The most expensive – and therefore the most worrying – of the arts under the suzerainty of Lilian Baylis was opera. But she had few fears about the men at the helm, who were nearly all old associates, while the new one, Warwick Braithwaite, rapidly proved to be in the great tradition. Charles Corri was still there when the Wells opened. Indeed, the Lady did not finally part company with that stoic veteran for several years, after much heart-searching. But Lawrance Collingwood was in effective control of the orchestra from 1931, and in 1933 Corri's salary was halved, as his work had decreased. Submissively, he wrote then to Lilian, 'I have always been in your hands and hope to remain so until I tap for coda'. He did so for the last time on 9 May 1935, conducting '*Cav*' and '*Pag*'. The orchestra gave him a gold watch; and Lilian presented him, on behalf of the company, with a farewell cheque for £95. (How typical of her not to round it up to £100. Corri's reaction to the watch, too, was typical: looking at it impassively, he grunted and said, 'Hrrumpph! I've got one of these already'.) He also received, however, a pension of £300, the first in the theatres' history. Strenuous backstage efforts were made to get him some kind of official honour, which he richly deserved, but the Governors were informed that as he had published no original compositions he was not considered eligible for a decoration. Sadly, there is nothing to mark his work at the Vic or the Wells, though he did more for the opera than better musicians who have been commemorated there.

From 1932 productions were handled by Sumner Austin, Clive Carey and John B. Gordon (opera coach at the Royal Academy of Music). This triumvirate (known jocularly at the Wells as 'the Soviet') was left largely in peace by Lilian, although she would occasionally erupt into their meetings to insist that a favourite singer must be in the following season ('You must have Tudor Davies on the first night. I don't care what else you do'), or to protest against what she saw as the latest piece of wilful extravagance, waste or uppity behaviour. She allowed Geoffrey Toye to deal with specialized matters of musical policy. She even acquiesced (though with some difficulty) in the possibility of a scheme proposed in 1932 by Sir Thomas Beecham for cooperation between Covent Garden, the Imperial League of Opera, the Carl Rosa and Sadler's Wells, with Sir Thomas himself in command. This came to nothing; so did the proposal that Sir Thomas should act as artistic adviser to Sadler's Wells for five years. (Surprisingly, Lilian 'kowtowed' to Beecham, says Joan Cross. 'If she'd blistered him, he'd have adored it.') But Beecham's plans had one decisive effect on the Wells organization: he recruited Geoffrey Toye to run Covent Garden in 1935. The Beecham plans had been supported by some people who wanted to see Lilian pushed aside. These plotters regarded her as an ignorant, interfering vulgarian whose removal was necessary to the development of opera. But Sir Thomas's projects were somewhat too airy as the basis for a putsch, and the Lady, while prepared to do a bit more delegating, had no intention of being deposed. The 'odd little Empressario', as Ivor Brown called her, stayed put – though she stayed worried.

What worried her was the introduction of new works and new methods, and their possible effects upon the audience. She was afraid, at first, that the loyalists would resent the disappearance of many of the old conventions in productions of the standard works; but, as she admitted in the 1932–3 annual report, her warnings to the producers proved unfounded (as on the issue of later opening). 'It now appears that the one thing the majority of opera audiences had been hankering after for years was just this new viewpoint.' She realized, moreover, after some persuasion, that the Wells not only had to refurbish many of the old favourites, and even drop one or two – though she put up a fight against *that*, as they were *her* favourites – but had also to extend its repertoire. Between 1931 and her death in 1937 it staged over fifty operas, compared with little more than thirty works presented at the Vic in the preceding thirty years. Among the fifty were *Fledermaus*, *The Mastersingers*, *Falstaff* and *Fidelio*; rarities such as Rimsky-Korsakov's *The Snow Maiden* and *Tsar Saltan* (both produced in Britain for the first time) and *Boris Godunov*; and even a few works by British composers, including Stanford's *The Travelling Companion*, Holst's *Savitri*, and Collingwood's own *Macbeth*, seven years after its first concert performance. The theatre owed a debt to Collingwood for his dedicated and expert production of the Russian operas, whose presentation at the Wells realized an ambition fired years before by his experiences in Moscow and St Petersburg.

The more adventurous choice and the higher standard of production attracted a new audience. But for Lilian they didn't arrive quickly enough or in sufficiently large numbers. In the words of the 1935–6 report, 'full houses can be expected for *Faust*, *Lohengrin*, *Carmen* and so forth; anything less familiar, even Mozart, is less attractive'. If additions to the repertoire played to half-empty houses, she did her best to see that they were not revived. She knew that novelties were needed, but full houses were needed even more urgently. The Wells could not afford many empty seats at any performance. The enlargement of the orchestra to forty-eight, more than twice the size of Corri's original group at the Vic, was partly to blame for a budget whose size and growth terrified her. She had nightmares about it, she said, and used to wake up shouting, 'The orchestra! The orchestra!' Lilian felt ill at ease, too, among the exotic works, and sometimes hankered after *The Bohemian Girl*, *Maritana* and *The Lily of Killarney*, dropped for ever from the repertoire. Looking at Beecham and Barbirolli guest-conducting, did she perhaps pine for old Corri – and the simpler operatic life they had shared? But kudos and publicity there was in abundance – even a bit of glory. That she could not deny, and would not reject the burden of it (for, of course, the greater glory of God). And she was never loth to stimulate it, in her own unconventional way. When she went to a garden party at Buckingham Palace in the 1930s, and the Lord Chamberlain asked her how she wanted to be announced, she said, 'Miss Baylis of the Old Vic and Sadler's Wells – and say Sadler's Wells loud enough to advertise it.'

When the new Wells was launched, Lilian said: 'We are taking a tremendous risk, but miracles have happened before at the Old Vic, and I hope will happen at Sadler's Wells, too.' There are grounds for arguing that, in Hugh Walpole's words, her 'supreme gift was getting other people to perform miracles for her'. Certainly this is what Ninette de Valois did; she performed miracles, if not primarily for Lilian, based on meticulous and cautious planning, ruthless personal authority, visionary courage, indomitable will-power, and helped by wealth and talent of a kind not hitherto drawn to the world of the Lady. An indispensable ally in recruiting it was the Camargo Society, founded in 1930 with the aim of producing ballets four times a year at a West End theatre (on Sundays and Monday matinées) before a subscription audience. Lilian Baylis had good reason to be grateful to this Society and the leading musicians, artists and dancers who supported it. During its six seminal years it subsidized the creation of ballets at a cost that she could never – or would never – have contemplated, and then gave the productions to the theatre.

With remarkable speed the British ballet company of Ninette de

Valois's dreams emerged, first in bud, and very soon in full flower. In the second season the original group of six girls was joined by five men, including Fred Ashton (as that great choreographer was then billed). Ballet was presented once a week. In 1932–3 it took two evenings a week, plus weekday matinées. Anton Dolin and Alicia Markova, who were already established stars, helped to build up public support by their early guest appearances; and by leading the company as prima ballerina from 1933 to 1935 Markova won recognition as a channel of the classic tradition as well as contemporary choreography. Dazzling new dancing talents – Stanley Judson, Robert Helpmann, Harold Turner, Margot Fontes (as she was then) – emerged. At Ninette de Valois's instigation Lilian invited the brilliant composer and conductor, Constant Lambert, to become musical director. Artists such as Edward Burra, John Armstrong, Rex Whistler, Cecil Beaton, Duncan Grant and (most important of all, perhaps) Sophie Fedorovich were recruited as designers. The company gave the first performances in Britain of *Giselle*, *Nutcracker* and the complete *Swan Lake*. And the school, indispensable as the basis of the grand design, flourished. By 1937 the company numbered twenty women and ten men, with two resident choreographers, a resident conductor, and forty students in the school with a full-time staff. It was an artistic success, and a financial success too: for the school paid for the ballet, and the ballet helped to pay for the opera.

Here was richness for Lilian. It was, indeed, a little indigestible, for she found that many of the new works – and Ninette aimed at introducing five a season, at least, to keep the interest of the new audience – were, like some of the operas, hard to swallow, let alone relish. But she was rightly proud of the progress of Ninette and the company, and of the part that she herself had played in it. Her roles were those of banker, umpire, superviser, scapegoat, and friend. 'She recognized good dancing up to a point', said Ninette. 'That was the point at which it was recognized by the audience.' Although there were, inevitably, arguments about money, she seldom attempted to interfere in matters of aesthetics. She knew better: that is to say, she knew how little she knew – most of the time, at least. There *were* occasions when she felt herself obliged to defend her standards. She objected, for instance, to the backcloth of *Rio Grande*, because of the way in which Edward Burra had painted the statue of a naked woman. Not, Lilian said firmly, because the woman was naked, but because the painting distorted the Body Beautiful. So, while Ninette and the rest were out at lunch, she told one of her staff to paint it out. She tried, too, to make them economize. Before work started on a new ballet, she would attempt 'to palm off on one old costumes, ancient clothes, second-hand evening dresses, peers' robes and other oddments that people had given her . . . one had to go through the ritual of taking an interest in these garments – no matter how unsuitable they were,' said Sir Frederick Ashton. 'But in the back of her mind I think that she knew it was all part of a game.'[7] Sometimes the Lady was 'very noisy (even in public) in her disapproval of things she did not like', but 'the important thing was that in the final analysis she trusted us to get on with our work. And if this work resulted in something bigger than she herself had ever envisaged, then perhaps that goes to show that one of her great attributes was an instinctive knowledge about where to place her trust.' She placed it, first and foremost, in Ninette de Valois.

Yet the remarkably swift growth of the ballet was achieved in spite of unusually large handicaps (and Lilian's belief that unusually large handicaps were jolly good for people). At the beginning the Wells stage was available for rehearsals for no more than two or three hours a week; and, as the one suitable (if inadequate) rehearsal room was used extensively not only by the school, but also for the office workers' classes, it was available for not much more than two-and-a-half hours daily. For the exacting, masochistic discipline of a dance ensemble that was 'pretty damned little'. There was no chance of using the room in the evenings, because it served as a coffee room for the audience before and during the performance. And, in any case, it gave the dancers 'perpetual sore toes', because the floor was concrete. It is hard to comprehend why Lilian did not get them a wooden floor. This would have cost money, of course – possibly £100. But they earned much more than that, every week, for the Wells. The concrete would have stayed had not Ninette got somebody else to pay for a new floor. Probably that was what Lilian was relying on.

She showed more sympathy with another persistent problem, the solution of which was outside her control: the shortage of male dancers. There were so few in those early days that Job had to keep changing his Sons from one performance to another, as dancers from West End shows volunteered to taxi up to Islington and step in when the opportunity arose. Watching a rehearsal of *Job* one day, Lilian turned to one of the original six girls and said, 'Now, dear, I want all you girls to marry all those nice boys and breed me a nice strong race of male dancers'.[8] (The dancers' marital prospects were among her minor worries. She was deeply disappointed when she watched the first BBC TV transmission of her ballet company at Broadcasting House. 'That's no good,' she snorted. 'Much too small. Those girls will never get married like that.')[9] Unlike most people in the theatre at that time, however, Lilian appeared to see the potentialities of the fledgling medium – rather in the way that, thirty years before, she had seized on the Matagraph. The Sadler's Wells dancers paid eight visits to the TV studios in the year following that December transmission. *Ghosts*, *Measure for Measure* and *Macbeth* were glimpsed on the screen in 1937. Apart from bringing in revenue, these productions brought publicity. The Lady insisted on proper credits: 'by permission of Lilian Baylis' was billed in the *Radio Times* and on the screen.

There were many things that Lilian enjoyed about her new enterprise. She enjoyed looking at the men's legs and 'forms'. She relished opportunities for getting personally involved in a production, as on the occasion when John Armstrong was asked to design both costumes and scenery for the de Valois choral ballet *The Birthday of Oberon*, and Lilian went happily off with him on a shopping expedition round the bargain basements to buy materials for forty-eight chorus dresses. And she appreciated the romantic classics of the dance, which appealed to her more intimately than the classics of the drama – or new work in any of the arts. She took great pleasure in the dancing of Markova, a pleasure reflected in the unusual warmth of her letters, although these were (as usual) also concerned with trying to pay as little as could possibly be achieved. A typical Baylis approach to artists was her plea in offering Markova five guineas a performance in 1932: 'I want you to do lots of well-paid work, but hope you'll manage to come to us in between the good engagements.' In the following June she offered Markova ten pounds a week for the season, to cover her appearances and her 'help as choreographer when necessary'. When Markova accepted, Lilian – after expressing her delight – ended her letter, 'I hope you enjoyed dancing last night. You were in perfect form, and I enjoyed every minute of it.' And in January 1934, after Markova's celebrated performance of Giselle on New Year's Day, Lilian wrote, 'I *loved* your work on Monday. It made me very proud and happy.' Not so happy that she felt able to offer more than £12 a week for the following season, but she acceded to the figure of £15 ('we just feel that we would hate to lose you').[10]

Lilian was more ruthless about money with Anton Dolin. When she asked him to lighten a ballet evening at the Wells, if he had 'something up his sleeve', she offered him £10 and his fare. What he pulled out of his sleeve was the *Bolero* speciality, danced to Ravel, which Ninette de Valois thought too music hall but Lilian (and the audience) adored. She urged him to do two more, for £25 in all. At the end of the third performance she gave him the money with one hand, and took it back with the other – 'For the Endowment Fund, Anton.' According to Mr Dolin, he 'never really minded', because of his admiration for the Lady. They maintained a friendly relationship, and she persuaded him to talk to the audience about his work at performances. 'Anton, it's so nice to hear you speak,' she used to say. 'All this ballet, it's so highbrow. And, you know, I'm sure they don't understand it. Now, when you get up and say all those nice things to them, it makes it all so much more human. I love to hear a good sermon.'[11]

Lilian loved royal visits too, not so much for her own glory but because they helped the box office; and the ballet attracted royalty from the start. In the first 1932 season the Duchess of York came to see Ninette de Valois's *Nursery Suite*, because the score had originally been composed by Sir Edward Elgar for her two daughters (later Queen Elizabeth and Princess Margaret). Sir Edward was also at the Wells on the first night, and his presence, together with his tributes to the ballet and to Dolin's performance in it, added to the publicity. But Lilian took a special pleasure in the fact that the decor and costumes were designed by Nancy Allen, a girl from the Old Vic staff, who was a great-granddaughter of Mrs Stirling. (The Duchess promised Lilian on this or a later occasion that the first Shakespeare play that the Princesses would see would be at the Old Vic; and she kept her promise, five weeks after Lilian's death, when, as Queen, she took her daughters to a matinée of *A Midsummer Night's Dream*.)

In spite of Lilian's liking for traditional dance, romantic plots and the personalities of some leading figures in the ballet world, it was not *her* world. She had a Salvation Army-lass attitude towards it, said Ninette de Valois. The intellectual experiment, aesthetic sensibility and connoisseurship of the arts associated with the work of Dame Ninette, Constant Lambert and their choreographers and designers drew on a range of music and design outside the Lady's own homely tastes and the traditional diet of a People's Theatre. She felt that there was a movement away from the popular to the elitist (though she would never use such terms), and a similar trend ('They're all getting so *artistic*') seemed to be perceptible in opera and drama as well. It was in drama, indeed, that the most direct challenge was made to the old order, and to Lilian's faith in it.

By 1933 Harcourt Williams knew that he had been in Lilian's harness long enough. Although they remained on good terms and she did not press him to go, they both realized that the work-load was too exhaustingly heavy for a man of his temperament, and his productions were beginning to show it. His successor was a man in a very different mould, different not only from Williams but from any of Miss Baylis's aides in the past forty years. He was to play a major role in the last phase of her life at the Vic, and in the later history of both theatres. Tyrone Guthrie (to be known throughout the theatre world as Tony) was a six-foot-five, heron-like intellectual showman with a public-school and university background, an Ulster Scot who combined an Establishment manner and authority with a restless radicalism of mind, a sharp ambition with a visionary idealism. Like Lilian, he was full of contradictions and something of a fantasist about himself.

In the nine years since Guthrie left Oxford (he was thirty-three when he joined the Vic) he had attempted, briefly and unsuccessfully, to act; worked for radio in Belfast, London and Montreal; directed plays for the Scottish National Players and the Cambridge Festival Theatre. He had attracted attention in the West End by his productions of James Bridie's *The Anatomist* and J. B. Priestley's first play *Dangerous Corner*. Harcourt Williams was impressed by his *Love's Labour's Lost* (mounted as an emergency replacement for a new play), and on his recommendation Lilian had seen it and had asked Guthrie to meet her. They did not take to each other at that first interview; and although, in the absence of other suitable candidates, she engaged him at £700 p.a. she did so, Guthrie was sure, with 'no feeling of pleasure or confidence'. Lilian mistrusted him because of his education and his manner, which seemed uppity. He had, she was sure, expensive tastes. He would have to be watched. Still, the Langs recommended him, as well as Billie Williams, so she would have to wait and see.

Guthrie had no cut-and-dried revolutionary plan up his sleeve. Indeed, he was at first not quite sure what he wanted to do. He knew what he *didn't* want – the tatty sets and costumes, the 'Bensonian' acting and production, the general 'air of making do' that, in his view, marked the productions he had seen at the Vic.

263

'The senior actors spoke good and loud and gave vigorous stereo-
types. The junior actors were clearly beginners,' he wrote in 1960[12]
– an absurdly dismissive view of the Williams seasons that had
included, among others, Gielgud, Richardson and Ashcroft.
Guthrie decided that he would go for more glamour, more showmanship, more stars, more visual appeal, all of which meant spending more money. He had no particular plays or players in mind at
the start, except his friend Flora Robson, whom he had first met
at Oxford and had since directed in Cambridge and the West End.
It was Flora Robson to whom he made the first approach after
accepting the Lady's offer, and it was through her, apparently by
accident, that the season began to take shape. Shortly after she had
been engaged, Charles Laughton, a friend of Miss Robson's, called
on her one day, and said in the course of conversation how much
he wanted to work at the Old Vic, if he could do so with a group
of actors and actresses of some calibre. He ended up by saying,
'if *you* go, *I* will go too'. Dame Flora is not sure whether, in fact,
Laughton knew she had already decided to go. It seems more than
likely. At thirty-four Laughton was a star who had just scored a
sensational cinematic success with *The Private Life of Henry VIII*
but, although he had been an actor for seven years, he had never
played in Shakespeare. Like other stars before and after him he
saw the opportunity that the Old Vic offered for the exercise and
development of his craft and, perhaps, his reputation and market-
value. There was nowhere else in London where an actor might
play so many leading classic roles in the space of one theatrical
season. On his side, Guthrie was anxious to secure for his first Vic
season 'the most talked-of actor in London' (as he described
Laughton in his autobiography). They met over dinner at Flora
Robson's home, and agreed on all points but one: Lilian Baylis,
whom Laughton was 'inclined to underestimate'. So, at that stage,
was Guthrie, though he did not admit it; but Laughton allowed
her even less credit for her achievements, and believed that the
general dowdiness of the Vic productions was due not to poverty
but perversity, Lilian's 'wilful determination' to run the theatre
like a parochial charity.

Guthrie had to prepare a programme for submission to Lilian,
who would pass it on to the Governors for their approval. He
rapidly roughed one out with Laughton as its centre, and broke
the news to his manager next day. She showed no more enthusiasm about Laughton than Laughton had revealed for her. 'Very
clever, dear. But I don't think my people would like him at the

Vic.' Why not? Because he was too West-Endy; he would want to spend a lot of money; and, most important of all, he had never played in Shakespeare, had he? 'Why should I pay twenty pounds a week to a man who has never acted in Shakespeare?' When Guthrie reminded her that Laughton was paid twenty times as much in films, she snapped back that, in that case, he ought to 'help the Vic' by acting for nothing. She would have to consult the Governors, she said; and, no doubt, her conscience as well. 'He ought to pay *me* twenty pounds a week,' she grumbled to her staff. When, some days later, Laughton's engagement was approved, Guthrie assumed that the Governors must have overridden her scruples; but Lilian was shrewd enough to suppress her own doubts, for she knew all too well that the Vic needed money, and that Laughton's name ought to bring it in. Indeed, he brought it in even before the season began; for he somehow persuaded the Pilgrim Trust to make a grant of £1,750 to the theatre – not to the general Vic–Wells funds, but towards the cost of the Shakespearian productions, as long as he and Flora Robson appeared in them. This was Laughton's personal insurance against what he regarded as the obsessive stinginess of Lilian's management. For her it was a smack in the face, especially as she had for months been unsuccessfully wooing this new trust, set up in 1930 to administer a £2 million gift by the American millionaire Edward S. Harkness. According to Guthrie (whose account of the episode is characteristically overdramatized) 'many of her counsellors . . . pandered to her vanity, applied the salve of flattery to her wounded pride, fed with gossip her incensement against Laughton and urged her to throw at the feet of the Pilgrim Trust its thirty pieces of silver'.[13] Lilian did no such thing, of course; but there seems little doubt that this deepened her distrust of her new leading actor, who was, she believed, only using the Vic to promote his own career. Of course he was; but so were many of the people who worked at the Vic during Lilian's lifetime, as the Lady knew very well. She also saw that he didn't like her or understand her, and the frosty dignity with which she treated him made him like her even less. For Laughton, Lilian was 'a scheming, small-minded, mean-spirited old shrew, whose one idea was to keep the reins of theatrical power in her incompetent hands'.[14] That, at least, is how Guthrie put it many years later. Did it not perchance reflect something of Guthrie's own feelings?

Laughton was not the only star in Guthrie's programme: he had succeeded in getting a strong cast, as well as the costumes and sets he felt to be essential. Flora Robson, Athene Seyler, Ursula Jeans and Leon Quartermaine were all West End names, all new to the Vic. Ursula Jeans was new to Shakespeare; so, conspicuously, was the ballet dancer Lydia Lopokova, whose odd casting as Olivia in *Twelfth Night*, the opening production, was one of Guthrie's errors. This was, in fact, her only role in the season, and Quartermaine appeared in no more than two plays. The repertoire was smaller than ever before: eight plays (seven of them at the Vic) compared with Williams's twelve, Atkins's twenty and Greet's twenty-six. Three of the eight were non-Shakespearian: Guthrie introduced Chekhov (*The Cherry Orchard*), Wilde (*The Importance of Being Earnest*) and Congreve (*Love for Love*, which was staged only at the Wells). Armed with the support of the Pilgrim Trust, Guthrie persuaded Lilian to let him commission a semi-permanent set, roughly approximating to the supposed structure of the Elizabethan stage (Robert Atkins's own attempt at a near-Elizabethan framework was at last demolished). Guthrie gave the job to a leading contemporary architect, Wells Coates. The result was an imposing structure with two curving staircases, a balcony, and a recess-entrance beneath it, between two 'formidable' pillars. This set was meant to save time in scene-changes, to avoid 'any precise suggestion of period', and to eliminate irrelevant decoration. But as Guthrie freely admitted, it was a failure: Wells Coates had no theatrical experience, and Guthrie didn't have enough. The set was obtrusively contemporary, clumsy and competed with the play instead of serving it. Far from being 'permanent', it was used for only three productions. Athene Seyler recalled Lilian giving it 'a savage kick' as she walked across the stage, and barking, '*Damn the thing*'.

Six designers were used that season, instead of one, although much of Charles Ricketts's scenery and stained glass for *Henry VIII* was that of the 1928 Casson–Thorndike production. More money was spent than ever before. More West-Endy people were in the stalls than ever before. Lilian prepared herself to put down the uppity. On the first night of the season (heralded by more advance publicity than ever before) Flora Robson – who was not in *Twelfth Night*, the opening production – was greeted with a burst of cheering from the gallery when she entered the auditorium. The modest Miss Robson was 'filled with confusion. She smiled, waved, took far too long to find her seat, and subsided thankfully into it at last. After the curtain had fallen she went backstage to congratulate her colleagues, and almost walked into Lilian Baylis.

"Lovely reception, dear, before you deserved it," said that lady, deflating an actress who might be tempted to think that successes in other theatres counted here.'[15]

By the time Charles Laughton arrived for rehearsals (he was in Hollywood when the season opened) Lilian was fully armed. When he was interviewed by the press on his return, and questioned about his lack of Shakespearian experience, Laughton had said (no doubt with self-defensive irony) that he slept with Shakespeare under his pillow. At his first Vic rehearsal the Lady greeted him before the whole company with, 'Now Mr Laughton, we've all heard that you keep Shakespeare under your pillow. What we want to know is, can you speak his beautiful words?' The omens were not encouraging, and the relationship between manager and star remained on ice thereafter for most of the season. Although both made occasional approaches towards a thaw, both usually said or did the wrong thing. Mr Laughton and Miss Baylis seemed to be incompatible.

When a royal visit was in prospect, Laughton asked Lilian deferentially at a rehearsal for advice on how he should behave to Her Royal Highness. 'Well, I can tell you one thing, Mr Laughton,' the Lady barked. 'You'd better not slap her on the BTM.' She disliked his language and his manners. On perhaps his first visit to her office, when both were apprehensive and not at their best, he was severely snubbed, as she told Marie Ney. 'There he was, smoking away and flicking his ash into my dogs' water, and I said, "Excuse me, Mr Laughton, but that's my dogs' water you're flicking your ash into". And then he kept saying "My God this" and "My God that", and I said, "Now look here, Mr Laughton, are you blaspheming or are you saying your prayers? Because we don't like blasphemers here at the Old Vic." ' It is not difficult to see why he found her impossible. She was open-minded enough to recognize that Laughton was good for the box office but she couldn't help feeling that it was the wrong kind of customer that he was attracting. When she found that, because of the demand for tickets, messenger-boys, valets and maids were being sent by West-Endy people to keep places for them in the pit and gallery queues, she exploded with anger and righteous indignation. The rich were stealing her people's seats!

She was generous enough to admit at times that here, for all his Shakespearian inexperience and his incapacity for teamwork, was a fine actor of rare quality. Laughton was at his best as Angelo in *Measure for Measure*, and Lilian used to slip into her box for nearly every performance during one scene in which he excelled. 'There are many things I don't like about that man,' she said to Marius Goring. 'But I don't want to miss a minute of this.' By the time the next production opened there was even a chance, said Guthrie, that Mr Laughton and Miss Baylis might have become 'quite friendly'. But the next production was *Macbeth*. After a brilliant dress rehearsal, Laughton's first-night performance was a disappointment (not least to him); and as he sat in his dressing-room, overwhelmed by a sense of defeat, Lilian called on him, in full academic fig, to cheer him up. She slapped him on the back, with an embarrassed laugh that sounded to Laughton like 'a hyena's yell of triumph', and said, 'Never mind, dear, I'm sure you did your best. And I'm sure that one day you may be quite a good Macbeth.'[16] Laughton never forgave her. He believed that those bruising words of consolation were calculated sadism, her revenge for the Pilgrim Trust grant. He was almost certainly wrong: Lilian was a monumentally tactless woman, whose olive branches frequently appeared like knobkerries. When she wanted her words to wound, she tried no camouflage. But it is scarcely surprising that Laughton took clumsy goodwill for deliberate malice. He was among the many actors who never understood her; and he was one of the few whom she found it impossible to mother.

According to Dame Flora, there were other reasons for their differences. The 'real trouble' arose when Lilian asked Laughton, halfway through the season, if he could raise more money to finance the remaining productions. 'With Sold Out notices every night, he hadn't been able to get any more and found it hard to believe Miss Baylis's assurance that she wasn't making a penny out of the successes because our "star" salaries were costing her so much. He demanded to see the books and discovered in fact Miss Baylis had redressed the whole of the opera and the whole of the ballet out of the money she had made from us. She did what all good managers do – make one thing pay for another. You cannot blame them.'[17] Charles Laughton obviously *did* blame Miss Baylis; although, in spreading that story, he somewhat exaggerated her powers – and the profitability of his season. To supply new costumes for the dozens of the ballets and operas in the repertoire in 1934 would have demanded a somewhat larger capital investment; although, as Guthrie knew, she did her best to divert some of the Pilgrim money to her other companies. And did she *really* let her leading man 'see the books' as he claimed? She would never allow her favourite director, Harcourt Williams, to know the state of the box office or the theatre accounts during four years in her service.

Whatever Lilian's doubts about the season, she gave Guthrie her support in public and at Governors' meetings. The Carnegie Trust 'questioned the wisdom' of including *Measure for Measure* in the repertoire, but the Lady quietened their moral anxiety. 'No unfavourable comment had ever attended former productions of the play here,' she said; and, what was more, 'it was felt that the play was peculiarly suited to the cast' (Laughton might have suspected another thrust there). On the last occasion it had been staged, it had in fact taken Andrew Leigh some effort to overcome her scruples. 'If we were doing it to help a *clinic*, that would be all right. But I don't think . . .' Some of the Governors were disturbed by the dangers of exposing the Old Vic audience to the salacity of *Love for Love*, but Lilian stood up for Congreve as one of the classic dramatists; and, in the event, it was only the Wells audience that was put at risk. Among them on the first night was the Governor who had made most fuss against the play. 'Get her to sign the visitors' book', growled Lilian, when she spotted her. She found it more difficult to placate the militant opposition to Guthrie among the loyalists in the audience. This vociferous minority was led, as usual, by Miss Pilgrim, who spoke her mind about 'that man' on every possible occasion and some impossible ones. When Lilian made her customary visitations to the gallery, she had to listen to protests from some of the old guard; and some of them wrote anguished letters. One letter, from two retired schoolmistresses, implored her to get rid of Guthrie before he laid her life's work in ruins. Naturally, Lilian passed on to Guthrie some of this criticism, including the schoolmistresses' letter; and, while assuring him of her continuing public loyalty, she told him that she shared some of the uneasiness of the objectors among her audience. Less naturally, Guthrie took it personally and pointedly. He was hurt that she did not completely trust him or realize how deeply he admired her achievement and was (so he claimed years later) 'desperately anxious' that she should not damage it.[18] Yet Guthrie was, after all, deliberately challenging some of the rules on which her achievement was founded, in an attempt to jerk the Vic and its traditional audience out of the rut of her penny-wise parochialism (as he saw it). He wanted her 'to risk spectacular insolvency against a no less spectacular improvement of standard', ignoring his own spectacular errors of judgement and the abiding problem of money: who would pay the bills for such 'insolvency' and guarantee the survival of both the Vic and the Wells? He disapproved of Lilian's susceptibility to flattery, resenting the 'cloud of incense' that surrounded her. He was convinced that many of the men on the staff were incompetent and that several were rogues, making up for their low pay by a network of 'fiddles'. (He was quite right.) He believed that the Lady saved money in the wrong ways – on wages, for instance, which could attract the efficient team she needed to run both theatres in a way that would meet the demands of the time, even if it meant purging some of her old retainers and alienating the affections of Miss Pilgrim. With all this on her mind, and some of it on record, it is really not surprising if Lilian felt that he was 'an irresponsible iconoclast' (as he suspected). Yet *Guthrie* was surprised. The truth seems to be that, allowing for the retrospective gloss in his autobiography, his attitude to her in 1934 was confused and contradictory, a mixture of affection and irritation, respect and mistrust, admiration and derision; and, although his feelings changed towards both Lilian and her theatres, they remained ambivalent. That was also true of the Lady's attitude to the man who was to become her successor on the throne.

They parted on friendly terms; and his regime was warmly defended in the annual report. 'Some of his innovations have been hardly to the taste of the more conservative members of our audience, but they have, on the other hand, been instrumental in bringing into the theatre a great many of the young generation, particularly the definitely artistic section, who might otherwise never have entered it. This increased breadth of appeal has been exactly what the Old Vic and Sadler's Wells have needed in the present stage of their development.' For some of the 'definitely artistic section' of the young company the season was among the most memorable experiences of their acting lives, because of the stimulating effect of working with Guthrie and Laughton, who continually reached heights in rehearsal that he could not recapture in performance. Among these enthusiasts was John Allen, the actor–author–director (and Mrs Stirling's great-grandson) who recalls it as 'far and away the most exciting time of my life. Every night we used to walk out of the theatre, and over the bridge, in a state of intense exhilaration. We felt we were making history.' And so, in a sense, they were. But for the time being one Guthrie season was clearly enough. Lilian was not ready for any more iconoclasm.

As Guthrie's successor she appointed a cheaper, less controversial and less remarkable actor–director, Henry Cass, who had spent the past two years running a repertory theatre in Croydon and had succeeded in transferring several productions to the West End. During the next two years at the Vic he presented twenty plays, and directed seventeen of them himself. Twelve were by Shakespeare; but the seasons also included *St Joan, Major Barbara, Peer Gynt, Three Sisters, School for Scandal* and (a rarity indeed in the New Cut) a new English play, *St Helena*, by R. C. Sherriff and Jeanne de Casalis, about the last days of Napoleon.

The latter play occupies a special place in the Old Vic's history, and the episode reveals something of Lilian Baylis's special qualities as a manager. She backed Cass's choice of the play, after it had been turned down without explanation by every West End management; she resolved to spend far more money on it than was usual, even in 1936, by engaging additional players and investing in new decor; and she prepared to run it for a month at least. It is not clear why a woman who was lukewarm about most contemporary drama should be so passionately partisan about this piece, but she was. When it was generally savaged by the first-night critics, as a bore, her enthusiasm did not falter. On the morning after, although she looked as if she had been crying, she assured the authors that she had not lost 'an atom of her faith' in *St Helena*.[19] 'Even if she had known what was going to happen she would still have done it, without a moment's hesitation, and been proud to do it. As for the critics, they were a lot of hopeless dunderheads. "If I could get the editors of their papers to come and see the play tonight," she declared, "I guarantee they'd sack those idiotic critics first thing tomorrow morning, and serve them damn well right!" ' But business was really bad. It was like the old days of 1914, with less than a hundred paying customers a night, but the difference was that at over £400 a week the cost was vast (by Vic standards), not a matter of a fiver, with ten bob a head for the leads. Yet Lilian thrived on adversity. 'She was there in the theatre all day and every night, with a smile and a joke and a word of encouragement for everybody from the leading actor to the call boy.'[20] Then, suddenly and unexpectedly, in the second week, as the debts were piling up, Winston Churchill wrote to *The Times* about it. Edward Marsh (a staunch supporter of the Vic) had prompted him to see this play, Churchill said, in spite of the notices; and he discovered that it was 'a work of art of a very high order', a riveting entertainment, a dramatization of 'the end of the most astonishing journey ever made by mortal man'. Within a couple of nights the theatre was packed. Every seat was sold. Queues formed outside the Vic; and, though there was still room in the gallery every night, Lilian rearranged the programme to make the most of this unprecedented success which, two days earlier, had been an unprecedented failure. *The Devil's Disciple*, which was due to succeed it, was dropped, and *St Helena* was seen for six weeks in all before it was transferred to the West End. (This transfer was, according to Mr Sherriff, 'a complete, unadulterated flop'; according to the Vic annual report it was a 'considerable' success; in box-office terms the author was right.)

The Cass regime also saw the emergence of a new Shakespearian star, Maurice Evans, who scored a personal triumph in the 1934–5 season as Richard II. With other performances, this brought him an invitation from Katharine Cornell to work with her in the USA, and, after only a year at the Vic, Evans was translated to New York, never to return to the London stage. *St Helena* and Maurice Evans aside, there were no great successes and no great disasters either in Henry Cass's two years at the Vic. The company included such talents as Vivienne Bennett, Mary Newcomb, Cecil Trouncer, Leo Genn and William Devlin. A new director surfaced: Michael MacOwan, who had also worked at Croydon. The critics were generally approving for many productions, and the old guard in the audience seemed reasonably content. Lilian seldom interfered. According to Henry Cass, 'she left nearly everything to Evelyn Williams. It was Williams who did the fighting. *She* was the toughest woman I ever met in my life.' But the Lady still made herself felt when it seemed necessary, in matters large and small, usually on financial or moral grounds. She was delighted with Cass's production of *Hippolytus* in 1935, and told him that the Euripides meant more to her than the rest of the season's plays because it brought letters and visits from a number of top people, including academics. But the kudos was not matched by the cash; it put the Vic about £400 in the red; and so she told Cass that he had to stage his next play on a budget of no more than £10. Morally, she exercised her censorship in *Much Ado About Nothing*. The backcloth depicted a line of washing which included a pair of red drawers – after complaints from friends, Lilian had the offending garment painted out. During rehearsals of *Peer Gynt* she took a different attitude. Cass was struggling to instruct three teenage students, playing the trolls, to attack Peer with the proper degree of sexual abandon. After watching for some time in silence from the box, Lilian said brusquely, 'Cass, let me handle this'. She took the girls into her office and said, 'You don't understand what you're supposed to be doing, my dears. It's *evil*, you see. The only thing we can do is to kneel down now and pray to God – for lust.'

She was always an empiricist: 'The Vic came first,' as Mr Cass says admiringly. She demonstrated her practicality one night in *Othello*, when a cat 'decided to take part in the jealousy scene. Two seconds later Lilian's voice was heard from the wings. "Pussy, pussy, pretty pussy," said she in wheedling tones, and made alluring, smacking noises with her lips. When this failed she tried poking at the cat with a broom. When that, too, proved useless, she reached firmly on to the stage, perfectly visible to the audience, seized the animal by the tail and yanked it off.' This was, said Margaret Webster, 'typical Baylis technique, as applied to all problems'.[21]

Henry Cass was heavily overworked. 'It was either make or break at the Vic. It broke me, professionally. I feel that I've never really recovered,' he said forty years later. But, like others before him, he was sustained through the hard labour and the long hours by the personality of the Lady, about whom he talked in 1974 with admiration scarcely tinged with criticism. 'She made you give of your best, whether you liked it or not. I felt that I was in the presence of a great woman. I think so still.' There were frustrations and irritations, of course: and on one occasion – the only one, Mr Cass says – she made him really angry when she cut a key speech in *Peer Gynt* because it was 'too long, Cass, too long'. And on her side there was something less than enthusiasm. There were too many empty seats at too many performances. Although Henry Cass was a reliable and conscientious servant of the Vic, she decided after two years that it was time for a change again.

After drawing a blank with several possible candidates, and a good deal of consultation with God and the Governors, Lilian wrote to Guthrie and asked him to return. She guessed what that might entail, but she seemed ready to compromise – partly because she knew that some of his criticisms were justified; partly because she had come to recognize in that first season together some of the humility, vulnerability and humanity behind the heron-like hauteur; and, most of all, because she was very tired and ill, and longed with half her heart to hand over the reins to the right man (though with the other half she clung to the job that had given meaning to her life for nearly forty years). As the annual report for 1935–6 explained, in preparation for the change, Shakespeare and the older classics were now not so good for the box office as

Shaw, Ibsen and Chekhov. Moreover, it was no longer 'enough' to do a play *occasionally* as well as anything in the West End: 'the aim must be to make *every* production quite as good as that'.

Guthrie was eager to come back to the Vic. His motives mixed, as he said later, 'artistic ambition and integrity with an element of worldly calculations'.[22] He wanted to promote his career by establishing his name in a series of 'respectable classical productions'; and yet at the same time he wanted to 'attach himself' to something 'more significant' than that career. Having tasted the transient casino pleasures of the commercial theatre in London and New York in the intervening years, he saw more clearly the assets of the Vic and the size of Lilian's achievement, while he viewed her vagaries and the theatres' imperfections with greater tolerance and understanding. Nonetheless, he was resolved to continue the shaking-up process that he had begun in 1933–4, and he agreed to return only on the understanding that he would have greater authority than before, making a number of other conditions to which Lilian and the Governors agreed. He insisted on separate accounts and staffs for both theatres, and brought in his own nominee as stage manager, George Chamberlain, one of Guthrie's most successful exercises in casting. (Mr Chamberlain became licensee and general manager of both theatres, and served them devotedly for thirty years.) Guthrie asked for more money, to spend on stars, on costumes and scenery and on publicity. He ended the domination of the Green Leaflet: from now on only the next production was announced, and others on the horizon were mentioned with no commitment to dates, so that Guthrie might extend the run of a successful production, cut short a box-office flop or insert a play at short notice. He reduced the size of the company from a score to half a dozen, so that he could cast from a far wider range of players from one production to the next. In other words, he set out to bring some of the commercial flexibility of the West End into the rigid structure of the Old Vic repertoire; although, as he later admitted, he brought less welcome and less necessary innovations, for along with the rigidity and the 'permanent' company went some of the theatre's distinctive idealism, coherence and continuity. The old régime was over: the Vic would never be quite the same again, for better or worse.

The first season of the new deal, which was also the last complete season under Lilian Baylis's management, was resplendent with talents – notably, those of Edith Evans, Michael Redgrave, Alec Guinness and Laurence Olivier. Olivier, then twenty-nine, was at a turning-point of his career after making a name as a romantic lead in both films and plays. Guthrie chose him as the big name at the centre of the season, as he had chosen Laughton in 1933, and persuaded him to play the full-length *Hamlet* in a Freudian interpretation, with virtually any other roles he fancied: these they would work out as they went along. The season included a magical *As You Like It* (with Redgrave playing Orlando to Dame Edith's Rosalind), which transferred to the West End; and a box-office hit which broke all records at the Vic, and later transferred to New York: *The Country Wife*. The background to this production illustrates the way in which Miss Baylis and the Vic had changed. The American manager Gilbert Miller had seen Ruth Gordon play Margery Pinchwife in Wycherley's comedy in summer stock in Westport, and he was so impressed by her performance that he planned to present her in the play on Broadway, with decor by Oliver Messel. Messel convinced him of the advantages of allowing it to be staged first at the Old Vic; and Guthrie achieved the far greater feat of persuading Lilian to acquiesce, in spite of the bawdiness of the play and the fact that the Vic was, in effect, being used as a try-out theatre for a commercial production. Some admirers of the Lady found it astonishing that a woman who, not many years before, had refused to allow a Carmen to bare one shoulder should countenance the prolonged doubles entendres of Wycherley's play. The fact that she was getting decor and costumes by a top designer for nothing scarcely seemed to warrant such a capitulation. What would Miss Cons have thought of Mr Horner, a stallion freely admitted by credulous husbands to their wives' bedrooms because he shammed impotence through the pox? Certainly, some Governors thought he had no place on the Vic stage, and argued fiercely against the play. The grant from the City Parochial Foundation was threatened. But the majority, led by the chairman, supported Lilian and Guthrie. 'For my part,' said Lord Lytton to the Governors, 'I abominate censorship as much as I enjoy the vigorous performance of a masterpiece, even a masterpiece of smut.' And when the production was attacked in the *Daily Telegraph* as a 'complete abandonment' of the Vic's standards, Lord Lytton leaped to its public defence, though on somewhat different grounds. 'The coarseness of the play can only be redeemed by the rendering of the name part and the part of Mr Horner. The fact that these two parts are performed at the Old Vic by two artists whose inherent niceness is so transparent . . . makes the whole play a clean and not a dirty entertainment.'

Guthrie had, indeed, deliberately sweetened Wycherley's harshness and cynicism, going some way to quieten Lilian's fears, notably by his casting of Redgrave as Horner ('neither old enough, nor experienced enough, nor sardonic enough', said James Agate). But the dazzling performances of Ruth Gordon and Edith Evans brought critical bouquets, and the public controversy brought thousands to the Old Vic who had never been before. Many were encouraged to discover that the classics could be fun. The theatre was full every night of the run, and people were turned away.

If the criterion of success was the box-office gross, then the Guthrie shake-up was succeeding. Not, of course, every time. *Twelfth Night* – 'a baddish, immature production of mine', said Guthrie later – was not in the same league, though it included Olivier's Sir Toby and Alec Guinness's Sir Andrew. Dekker's *The Witch of Edmonton*, directed by Michel St Denis, was a box-office and critical disaster, though Edith Evans led the cast. Even for Olivier's *Hamlet*, he recalls, there were always many empty seats, especially in the front stalls. There was opposition to the new film star among the old guard, still resentfully opposed to the pernicious ways of Guthrie. Miss Pilgrim went so far as to draw up a round-robin to Lilian, requesting his dismissal; and, under pretence of asking for an autograph, secured the signature of at least one unwitting member of the company – Lawrence Payne (though, in some absurdly inflated versions, Miss Pilgrim trapped almost the entire company into signing it).

Lilian, however, was learning to live with the Guthrie approach, and she took to her new leading man. 'I remember her sitting up until about five in the morning in her box at the dress rehearsal of *Hamlet*,' says Olivier. 'She was faithfully watching and applauding all by herself at the end of a scene.' Olivier had to repeat several passages for music cues. At about the eighteenth retake of 'My thoughts be bloody or be nothing worth', he heard a chuckle from the box, and Lilian rasped, 'I bet they couldn't be bloodier than they are, dear boy'. When there were two 'entireties' in one day, she would come to his dressing-room and wrap him up in a coat belonging to Mrs Stirling. Or was it a counterpane belonging to Antoinette Sterling? Both came in useful for such mothering occasions.

The critical reception was mixed. A few talent-spotters already saw in Olivier, playing his second major Shakespearian role, a threat to Gielgud's supremacy. Nobody (not even Lilian) was prescient enough to perceive the first director of the National

Theatre Company, the future heir of the Baylis vineyard. But she recognized something of Olivier's unique quality, and he responded. Although their relationship was no closer than that between Lilian and most of her leading players, they rapidly discovered a mutual respect and affection.

The last production of the season, *Henry V* – chosen by Guthrie to chime in with the coronation of George VI – was the occasion of the director's first major row with Lilian. It was not over aesthetics, but economics: the dress rehearsal went on so long into the early hours of the morning that he sent the entire team (amazingly for the Vic, around a hundred) home by taxi, without consulting Lilian. She was furious; and she gave him a sibilant dressing-down in her box in 'devastating asides', while she greeted members of the audience on the first night. That summer, however, they drew close to each other, in the unlikely setting of Elsinore.

At the invitation of the Danish Tourist Board the Old Vic took *Hamlet* to Kronborg Castle, on the Sound between Denmark and Sweden, to inaugurate an annual festival. The company, shepherded by Lilian, arrived a week ahead of the first performance, and found itself in difficulties. The authorities refused to close the castle to visitors during the day, so they had to rehearse from midnight until 6 a.m., and every night it rained, torrentially. This is how Guthrie described Lilian's role, over twenty years later:

Miss Baylis was in her element. She was naïvely enthusiastic about Abroad, loved the hotel, was childishly greedy about the interesting foreign food, solicitous and motherly to us, her company, her children, determined that we too should enjoy the trip, and no less determined that we should be 'good' and give foreigners a nice impression of the Old Vic. Like a good commander she shared the hardships of her troops. Night after night she sat through the rehearsals, dispensing from a window sandwiches and lemonade ... One night the rain was more persistent and violent than ever before. Miss Baylis was not at her usual window, but in a sort of porter's lodge, and word got round that she had laid in a keg of rum.[23]

There was a break at 3 a.m. and everyone rushed towards the lodge. The crowd included the military cadets and the military band, in sky-blue uniform, and it was led by the colonel in charge.

'Not you!' screamed Miss Baylis in the raucous tones which Englishwomen reserve for foreigners who, naturally, are stone deaf. 'Not you!' and we heard a resounding whack on a sky-blue behind. 'You're just band. This stuff's for *my* people.'[24]

On the first night it rained as it had never rained before. A full gale was blowing across the Sound. An open-air performance was clearly impossible, and yet it was a gala occasion, with royalty and the diplomatic corps. J. C. Trewin recalls that he found himself standing at the door of the hotel with Lilian.

She was huddled into a thick black coat and looking angrily at the sky; so angrily that I felt she might be shaking her fist at it. Then she realized somebody was standing by her, turned autocratically, pointed to the streaming rain, and said: 'Look here, this must stop!' I felt for an awful moment that I was responsible for the whole affair and was just contemplating an apology when Tyrone Guthrie came out into the hall, rubbing his hands and looking surprisingly pleased. 'I'm going to do the play here,' he said to her. 'HERE!' she said, in the kind of voice Edith Evans used for 'A HANDBAG!' 'Yes,' said Guthrie very simply, 'here'. He turned away and she shrugged her shoulders and looked after him with utter astonishment.

Guthrie had decided to stage *Hamlet* in the middle of the hotel ballroom, with the audience on three sides. While he conducted the company in a lightning rehearsal, Lilian – helped by Trewin and other critics – organized the seating, and then prepared to entertain the visiting notabilities until her company was ready. As the rain hammered against the windows the play began, and Lilian stood at the back in cap and gown, 'looking as if she dissociated herself from the whole business, yet with an oddly benevolent gleam in the eye,' says Mr Trewin. But she did not dissociate herself for long, and was soon there in the front row of gilt chairs, coming to grips with Guthrie's latest innovation.

This performance, as Guthrie said in his autobiography, was theatre in the round, although the term had not yet been invented; and it strengthened his conviction that proscenium staging was unsatisfactory for Shakespeare. It also made Lilian feel (he believed) that he was a leader, ready for emergencies, something more than an ambitious intellectual. She described him to one friend (Cecil Leslie) as having 'the heart of a child and a mind like crystal'. She talked of him to Sybil Thorndike as 'one of the elect'. As Guthrie said, 'I think from this time she consciously began to regard me as one of the possible Elishas upon whom her mantle should fall'.[25]

Lilian had begun to look urgently for such Elishas, for she privately believed she could not carry on much longer. She had apparently looked first in the family – to 'little Lilian' or to Bobby Dunning. When these blood relations had to be discounted,

Evelyn Williams seemed to many people a prime candidate – and she is said to have thought so herself. But Lilian kept looking. To trusted colleagues (Williams among them) she would say, 'I'd like to die now, but there's nobody who could take it all over,' or 'I am so weary of fighting finance, and I long to give up the ghost'. It was not only weariness that was the trouble, nor the vastly heavier burden imposed by Sadler's Wells. For the last few years of her life, just as the Wells was beginning to find its feet, Lilian Baylis was a sick woman. There were times, said Lewis Casson, when he had seen her continue working in her office although she could hardly stand up for physical pain. Earlier that year she said to Father Andrew, 'I know that if I go on as I am going, my work will kill me, but I don't see why it should be otherwise'. She felt very, very tired. She talked increasingly of retirement. Perhaps she really meant to withdraw to that little cottage in Hastings over-looking the sea. Perhaps, as Lewis Casson said, she knew that was impossible, and she really *wanted* to die, because only then could she be free of the great mission that was also an overwhelming burden.

Lilian no longer flared into great rages: she knew she could not afford them. Although she could still put her foot down hard when she disapproved – as when, at Buxton that year, she stopped Guthrie from presenting nuns in a manner something less than reverential in *Measure for Measure* – she became much gentler and mellower. She no longer spent fourteen hours a day in the theatre. She left Stockwell later in the morning and often came back in the afternoon for a rest. Yet almost every evening she went to both theatres, and she often had to attend banquets, receptions and other official ceremonies. For Lilian Baylis was now at the peak of her fame, as people throughout the country began to appreciate the magnitude of her achievement. In spite of her illness, loneli-ness and fatigue; in spite of her feelings that the organization was getting out of her control; in spite of the miscalculations over Sadler's Wells, the continuing financial problems and the national crisis outside her theatres, these were years of power and pride. She was a national figure, and she enjoyed it.

On the opening night of every season it had been Lilian's custom, for nearly twenty years, to distribute sprigs of white heather, not only to the company but to the stage hands too. On the opening night of the 1937 season it was different. She handed out sprigs of rosemary . . .

Enigma Variations

When I think of all the work that has been done
by our three companies – drama, opera and ballet –
I know *we* are the National Theatre!

Lilian Baylis (1937)

She must have touched the superconscious mind.
I see no other way
of accounting for the steady direction of what she did.
It *couldn't* have been her ordinary conscious mind.

Sir Lewis Casson (1962)

In the last week of November 1937 Lilian Baylis suffered a sharp professional disappointment: for the first time in her reign at the Old Vic – through wartime raids, epidemics, financial crises, strikes – the opening performance of a production was postponed at a few hours' notice. *Macbeth* was, as so often, the cause of the trouble. Olivier caught a chill; Michel St Denis, who had been asked to direct it at Olivier's express request, was involved in a taxi accident; and these were advanced to the press as reasons for postponement. But by far the most substantial, though unpublicized, cause of the delay was that St Denis was so unaccustomed to Old Vic conditions and appeared so much of a perfectionist at rehearsals that Guthrie had had to step in to make sure that *Macbeth* would, in fact, reach the stage. In spite of the state of her health, Lilian sat up until 3 a.m. on the morning of 23 November to watch what should have been the last dress rehearsal. She was deeply distressed when Guthrie insisted that the first night must be delayed.

Lilian spent the rest of that day quite normally. She enjoyed a brief visit to the Hut, clearing things up for the winter; and, on her return to Stockwell, settled down for a rest. While Prevost was putting the car away, Ethel Dunning – who had been staying with Lilian since February – decided to go out for some wine, and to take the dog Susan with her (Scamp had died a few months earlier). Suddenly Ethel came back again with the dog in her arms. She rushed upstairs into the bedroom where Lilian was lying down, shouting hysterically, 'Susan's killed! Susan's killed!' and dropped the little corpse on top of her sister.

Susan's death – she had been run over – was, in itself, a grievous personal loss for Lilian. The way it happened, and the way she learned of it, made everything worse. For years her intimates had tried to protect her from sudden shocks: the news of Nightingale's suicide, for instance, was broken to her by Prevost in gradual stages. That evening, as a direct result of Ethel's action (rather than of the *Macbeth* postponement) Lilian had a slight heart attack. She had intended to spend the following day, 24 November, in retreat, making her confession, but she telephoned Father Andrew to cancel this arrangement. When he offered to come and see her, she said, 'I should hate you to come and see me. I am not fit to be seen.' 'There was nothing to say to this', Father Andrew recorded, 'but "God bless you, my dear". "I was just waiting for you to say that" were the last words that came back over the wire.'[1] Towards the end she complained of feeling too bad-tempered to be in the right mood for prayer, so – said Annette Prevost – 'we spent her last hours mumbling bad-tempered psalms together'.

At 5.15 a.m. on Thursday, 25 November, Lilian had a second and massive heart attack, from which she did not recover. Her last act had been to sign the treasury cheques which Prevost had farsightedly collected on Wednesday night, so that there need be no delay in paying her 'boys and girls' their wages. She was sixty-three. The cause of her death was certified by her old friend Dr Hussey as angina. A contributory cause might have been diagnosed as theatrical management. Her death came less than a week after the news that the Governors had 'a respectable balance of working capital in hand ... At last we can look into the future with confidence that we can pay our way.'

When *Macbeth* opened on Friday at the Vic, Reginald Rowe made a short speech and the audience stood in silent tribute. Most of the men had black ties, and most of the women wore 'some sign of mourning', said the *Daily Telegraph*. In Lilian's box Evelyn

Williams sat beside an empty chair. At Sadler's Wells, where *Job* was being performed, a similar tribute was paid by the audience, and Ninette de Valois said a few words before the curtain rose. Clive Carey followed suit before the opera next day. Several newspapers treated Lilian's death as a national loss. It was, said Bernard Shaw, 'an event of the greatest magnitude'. 'The English ballet has lost its greatest friend and guardian,' said Ninette de Valois. 'We have lost a pioneer, a great artist and a great person,' said Dame Marie Tempest. Tyrone Guthrie declared that she had done more for the theatre, opera and ballet than any other person of her generation. The *Church Times*, in its main editorial, described her life as 'a call and an encouragement to all Christian people. Lilian Baylis demonstrated her faith by good works, and her good works were the running of two theatres with unconquerable courage and therefore unqualified success.' (How treasurable is that 'therefore'!) Over lunch at the Garrick Club two leading critics, James Agate and Horace Horsnell, agreed that she was 'of more importance to the culture of our time and the drama of the country as a whole than the entire crop of London managers since the war'. Even her old adversary Charles Laughton responded to questioning by saying that her death was 'the greatest loss the English theatre has suffered for many years'. To the editor of the *Vic–Wells Magazine* he wrote, in apologizing for being unable to contribute to its obituary paeons, 'Lilian will always remain in all our hearts . . . She was a great woman.'

On Monday evening Lilian Baylis's body was brought to St Agnes's, where her friends kept a watch through the night. The coffin was draped in the gold and silver colours of the Actors' Church Union. A Low Mass of Requiem was said at seven thirty a.m. At eleven there was a High Mass, when the church was crowded to the doors. Father Hutch officiated, Sadler's Wells supplied the singers. In his address the Bishop of Southwark declared that he was prouder of the Old Vic than of almost any other institution within his diocese. After the service the coffin was taken first past the Vic and then past the Wells – at both theatres waiting crowds paid homage in silence. The cortège went on to Golders Green crematorium, where Father Andrew conducted the last rites. When Lilian's body had been cremated, Annette Prevost took the ashes to St Agnes's, where they remained during the night. Next day a memorial service was held at St Martins in the Fields, at which Father Andrew and Father Hutch officiated, while John Gielgud read one of the lessons and the choir from

Sadler's Wells led the singing. The service began with the prelude from *Lohengrin* and ended with the 'Awake!' chorus from *The Mastersingers*. So many people came to pay their last respects that some of them, including Laurence Olivier and the Vanbrugh sisters, had to stand in the gallery. Strangely enough, the church was arranged for a Nativity play: the altar was set on a large stage, with a curtain lent by the Coliseum – an aptly theatrical decor for this last Baylis production. After the service Father Andrew and Annette Prevost drove in Lilian's car to St Agnes's; they laid the ashes before the Sacrament; and, after her two friends had knelt in prayer for a while before the casket, they took it to the East London Cemetery. Lilian had expressly asked that there should be no grave or memorial: she wanted her ashes to be sprinkled on the ground belonging to Father Andrew's church, and on the grave of a friend, Louisa Bentley, who had worked for the Society of the Divine Compassion. There were flowers, although Lilian had requested that money should be spent, instead, on donations to the Vic–Wells Completion Fund, or to the Home of St Giles.

Miss Baylis's estate was valued at some £10,000. She left £25 to her executor, Bruce Worsley; £20 to Townie; three months' wages and a pound for every year of service to 'any servant, housekeeper or chauffeur living with me at the time of my death'; £100 to the Society of the Divine Compassion and also to the Community of the Holy Name of Jesus. She carefully divided up the main items of her jewellery among her nieces. To Bobby Dunning she left a silver tray, silver bowl and silver spoons, a pewter and turquoise enamel presentation bowl, and the family papers of Elias Konss. To the Society of the Divine Compassion she also left an antique silver and amethyst chain which Mrs Bentley had bequeathed to her. Among other trinkets which later passed to Prevost was a small brooch that Jack Webster had given her, forty years earlier – the claw of the first lion he killed, mounted on gold from a mine he had prospected. Apart from one or two other small legacies, the rest went to Ethel. At Ethel's death the income from 'trusts, investments, etc.' was to be held in trust for Lilian's nieces.

About the greater legacy of the two theatres she left no precise instructions. Legally, of course, they were not hers to bequeath. But the ideas she had planted continued to grow; the 'work' continued to develop; and many of the people she had chosen continued to meet her demands, long after her death.

Among the glowing tributes paid to Lilian Baylis during the week after her death, some of the most perceptive were written by St John Ervine in the *Observer*.

The most obvious fact about this singular woman was her utter selflessness and her unbounded devotion to her job. The Old Vic was the beginning and the end of her life . . . She had a single-track mind, the awful concentration of the saint . . . She had conceived a holy passion for the Vic, and she would not allow anything to reduce it or to distract her from it.

She ought to have been disliked, but she wasn't; and the reason why nobody had the heart to dislike her was that her devotion to the theatre was unquestionable. If she was hard on others, she was hard on herself. She did not expect any more from other people than she expected from Miss Baylis. Her selfless nature made it impossible for even the most resentful and bitter-minded man or woman to continue an enmity with her . . . In her most aggravating moments she could still command obedience, and even affection, from those she ruled by her fearless character. She had not one manner for the eminent and influential and another manner for the lowly and unimportant. She would tick off a king as severely as she would tick off the humblest of his subjects. Your value, in her estimation, depended upon your value to the Old Vic.

Among these warm and accurate words, however, were colder phrases that shocked many of Lilian's friends and admirers. 'She was as hard as nails and utterly tactless,' said St John Ervine. 'She would screw a penny off a player's salary without compunction. She was not a grateful woman, and she could be unimaginably cruel in her criticism.' He also said that her conversation gave no sign that she was a woman of the theatre, even when she was talking about it; and that, in fact, 'she generally did not know what she was talking about, as far as acting and the drama were concerned,' although this didn't appear to matter. Even though she had a 'miraculous' ability for getting money, the presentation of drama, far from being damaged by her death, 'may be affected for the better'. Many of the Old Vic's productions, St John Ervine declared, would have been booed off the stage of any other theatre, and the critics would have 'flayed alive' any other managers who had offered such 'botched' work to the public.

In spite of such asperities, the general tone of his article was not unfairly hostile; yet, in the grief and turmoil that Lilian's death caused in her little empire, he was cast by some who mourned her as not only a boor but an enemy. He seemed to confirm this six months later, after the news that Lilian's estate had been valued at around £10,000, and after the publication of two books devoted to her memory – a biographical portrait by Sybil and Russell Thorndike, and *Vic–Wells*, a symposium edited by Harcourt Williams. Provoked by some of the more fulsome homage, the irascible Ulsterman dashed off a virulent indictment. Spurning suggestions that she was a martyr to her theatres, he wrote:

> Running the Old Vic was immense fun for Lilian Baylis. She was a born boss, and nothing gave her greater pleasure than to domineer over other people . . . That they were theatres meant little to her. What meant everything was the opportunity to boss something and to indulge her illimitable love of cutting down expenses.

Far from being a good manager, he argued, she was a poor one. Indeed, he said, Lilian was 'a very bad business woman – a great deal of the financial trouble of the Old Vic was entirely due to her and her aunt's incompetence'. Nor was she the simple, natural eccentric, incapable of egotism or sham, that some idolators imagined. Gone was the selfless servant of the theatre that he himself had exalted in his earlier piece. Instead he set up the picture of a self-romanticizing, self-publicizing woman with 'a small shopkeeper's mind' who spent a 'vast amount' of her time and energy in acting out a spurious public role, as 'a mixture of Joan of Arc, Saint Teresa and Florence Nightingale'.

That was clearly going too far; and the sustained note of personal resentment and near-venom which runs through this piece may well have come from the author's bitterness about Lilian's refusal to stage one of his plays. Yet some of St John Ervine's criticisms were taken up by later iconoclasts, reacting against the more sentimental and hagiographical aspects of the Baylis legend, and his splenetic attempt at character-assassination is a useful starting-point for a look at the realities behind that legend.

Nobody knows, and nobody can know, the complete picture of Lilian as she saw herself in the mirror; or as her nearest and dearest contemporaries saw her; or as she essentially *was*. Nevertheless, there were visible elements in her complex character that have been often ignored by later commentators. So let us briefly examine the debits and credits of Lilian Baylis's life and career, as far as they may be weighed and balanced.

First of all, among the debits, Lilian Baylis did nothing to encourage new English drama. In twenty-three years she staged only five premieres (religious work aside): *Wat Tyler*, *King Arthur*, *Britain's Daughter*, *Adam's Opera*, *St Helena*. It was not until 1929 that Shaw was admitted to the Vic stage – he was then seventy-three. She resisted Ibsen, Strindberg and Chekhov (though she had to let them in) and pressed the claims of Father Andrew, John Drinkwater and R. C. Sherriff. She did little to encourage new English opera. In thirty-nine years she staged only one operatic premiere, Lawrance Collingwood's *Macbeth*, and that was seven years after its first concert production. It was only with great reluctance that she would agree to include a new work in the repertoire, and if it failed on the first night, she was inclined to assume it had failed for ever. She refused, for instance, to stage *The Wreckers* by her friend Ethel Smyth. Beecham gave the first performance of this opera in 1909. It was not until thirty years later that it was staged at Sadler's Wells. The composer was then too deaf to hear a word of it, and Miss Baylis was dead.

Lilian also fought with general success, during most of her managerial career, against new ideas in design and lighting – mainly because they were (like living authors and composers) expensive, but also because she had an old-fashioned and uncertain visual taste, as anyone might see by looking at her clothes. She judged a production largely by its appearance – 'her interest was always *pictorial*', as John Laurie says; but the criteria she applied were no more than the commonsense tests of neatness, brightness and, above all, cheapness.

Her flair for talent-spotting (emphasized by some of her colleagues as her outstanding quality) has perhaps been overpraised. Certainly she showed at auditions that she had an ear for a good voice, an eye for an arresting face and handsome legs, an alertness to charisma, a recognition of box-office appeal, within the context of the Old Vic audience. But she relied heavily in casting upon her director of productions, and it was in selecting *them* (and other team members) that she showed her skill. Many good players and singers emerged from the Vic as better artists, but Lilian Baylis did not discover them, nor did she train them; although, having agreed to engage them, she gave some of them her maternal support and a few her friendship.

Sometimes, however, she damaged an artist's confidence, for she was devoid of tact. Although many have praised this deficiency as a virtue, especially if they had not themselves been exposed to her devastating candour, and many who *were* exposed to it accepted the barks and bites without resentment once they knew her, it was not always helpful in achieving one of the main objectives of theatrical management: getting the best possible performances out of the talent available. In her determination to punish the uppity and demonstrate who was top dog at the Vic, Lilian inflicted lacerating wounds on the egos of some singers and actors, especially the younger and more vulnerable ones, by brutal criticism of their appearance or performance. 'You sing well, but your face is against you,' was her brusque epitaph (with variants) on the hopes of some operatic applicants. To those whom she did engage she was likely to offer such words of encouragement as, 'You look a perfect fright,' or 'You're the worst in that part I've ever seen, dear,' or 'Pity your voice isn't right for it, dear'. She was capable of gruff, spontaneous and heartfelt praise – but not often, not even to her friends and favourites. And she had no aptitude or inclination for those off-white lies with which most managers ensure that the show will go on and stay on until the truths of the box office break through. She *used* everybody, ruthlessly, for the good of the theatre – or any other cause dear to her heart – but without sweet talk. Many artists, moreover, resented the abruptness with which, having used them, she pushed them aside. Often they did not know until the very last night of the season that she was not going to ask them back again. Lilian's annual speech usually contained bad news for some members of the company, as they heard her announce that X or Y would be moving on to express their talent (she expected) in some other place.

Miss Baylis did her best to make it clear that nobody but Miss Baylis was indispensable; and she disliked seeing the spotlight of publicity kept for long on others. Every season she encouraged her staff, in dealing with the press, to hand out photographs of herself, rather than those of more ephemeral (if prettier) faces. She bridled even if anybody on stage in the last-night-of-the-season ritual seemed to be getting too many bouquets in relation to her own sheaves. On a larger scale of envy, she was said to be recurrently jealous of her Shakespeare directors. When the press began to praise them rather than Lilian Baylis and the Vic it was time for them to express *their* talents elsewhere.

Whatever her mothering talents, Lilian had little or no ability to help most actors or singers in interpreting roles and solving artistic and technical problems. Sybil Thorndike is not only the most eminent, but almost the only, witness to give her credit for practical aid. When Dame Sybil said that she dreaded the prospect of playing Lady Macbeth because she felt that she couldn't comprehend the evil of the character, Lilian snapped: 'You love your husband, don't you? You'd do anything for Lewis, wouldn't you?' – and that put Dame Sybil on 'the right track. She had a perfectly down-to-earth vision which could give you clues. She saw right through the outward thing, to the kernel of the parts.' Lilian would say, 'I don't know why you all make such a fuss about these great parts. I think they're all just human beings – ask Father Andrew, he knows them all in Confession – poor things – and the lovely ones too.' According to Dame Sybil, she could 'by some homely phrase . . . sweep away the difficulties that generations of great playing of great parts had invented'.[2] But the difficulties remained for the great players who emerged from the Vic, without any such aid from the manager. Ernest Milton, one of Lilian's most constant admirers, could ascribe to her no more specific help than a 'spiritual' stimulation. Others – Olivier, Richardson, Gielgud – have praised her shrewdness, loyalty, dedication, motherliness and other virtues. But very few have testified that she showed an especial insight – or, indeed, any insight at all – into the actor's aesthetic difficulties, as distinct from his moral, emotional, family or religious problems. The kind of help she could give at her best, when she warmed to an actor – especially a young actor – and was not afraid of appearing ignorant or ridiculous, is illustrated by her behaviour to Marius Goring, when he stood in heroically as Macbeth at a moment's notice (and at the age of twenty). On his first night Lilian said to him, 'Very nice, dear. You know the words, that's the main thing.' On the second night she said, 'Just knowing the words isn't good enough any longer. You drone like an old clergyman. Act, dear, *act*.' And on the third night she said, '*That's* better, dear. We all have to learn, you know.' After a week she (and, no doubt, Harcourt Williams) decided that in spite of his early brilliance Mr Goring had not yet learned enough to carry so great a burden, so she asked John Laurie to take over – and she also asked him to break the news to Goring, as she could not, for all her fabled toughness, face the job herself.

In her last years Miss Baylis had little directly to do with the majority of the company. She had less time to talk to them; there were far more of them; and she was more wary about what she did say, than during the pioneering days. Actors' stories about her from the thirties tend to be second hand or restricted to the audition, the first interview about money, or, perhaps, an encounter at one of the annual beanos. Sir Alec Guinness, for instance, remembers Lilian speaking to him only twice. On the first occasion, at his audition, she said, 'Let's have a look at your legs, dear,' and, having looked, she said, 'You'll do'. On the second occasion he dropped three pennies in a corridor, just as she came round the corner. She eyed the coins, remarked, 'Father, Son and Holy Ghost', and swept on.

As a manager she was far from being the paragon of efficiency who appears in the legend. Even an admirer like Beatrice Wilson had to admit that Lilian was not really very good at business. She was 'the last word in untidiness', as one secretary said. She kept losing things, and St Anthony – who was responsible for finding them – kept letting her down. She was vague about dates and names, and her staff had to be adept in construing her own free versions, translating 'that nice woman whose husband had a job in Jamaica' into 'a chorister whose sister had gone to Canada' (to take a somewhat wild illustration by Evelyn Williams). Lilian sometimes dithered for days, even weeks, before making up her mind, changed it, then dithered again. She sometimes behaved in her later years, says Anthony Quayle, 'like a spitting Catherine wheel whirling round' and 'running about distraught' (though behind it all was a visionary gleam). She would delay signing letters, and then add a postscript in her own handwriting that contradicted the typescript above. She admitted frequently that she was ignorant, but usually added that she knew the people who did know. Yet, while consulting Lady Fred on matters of royal protocol or Matheson Lang on the choice of a new producer, she was inclined to take as an oracle anybody she met – a postman, a bishop, a fireman, a charwoman – and to believe that God had answered her questions through them: as long, that is, as what they said did not conflict too sharply with what she wanted to hear.

In matters of organization, as in everything else, Lilian Baylis worked by intuition. She was swayed by affection, pity and generosity as well as by anger, suspicion and resentment, in ways that were notably unbusiness-like (though endearingly human). To help a friend, or the friend of a relation, or the relation of a priest, she would sometimes tolerate stupidity, inefficiency and even the loss of money. Lilian was also occasionally guilty of favouritism in casting, with no apparent regard to suitability, although her favourites were usually lame ducks, shooed away if they missed their chance. In one season, when she pressed the claims of an operatic protégée to a part for which she was unqualified, she was steadfastly opposed by the director and conductor. 'Rather than give in,' said Sumner Austin, 'we dropped the work for a whole season. When it came up for casting the following year we met the same insistent advocacy. We agreed finally to hear the lady in question sing and act a small scene from the part. This ordeal ended, Lilian Baylis turned to Warwick Braithwaite – "Quite impossible," was his verdict. She turned to me – "Out of the question," was mine. She made no reply, but walked up to the orchestra rails and called to the singer on the stage – "Very nice, my dear. When can you start rehearsing?" There was something so Napoleonic about it, that neither of us found a word to say.'[3]

Lilian was preoccupied by economy, at times to the point of obsession. In striving to save pennies she sometimes threw away pounds. This may be seen, absurdly, in her endearing passion for shopping at the sales. She would go off joyously in search of bargains for the Vic wardrobe, and come back triumphantly with piles of 'reductions' that she couldn't resist but that were of very little theatrical use. On a larger scale, Lilian's misreading of financial priorities was illustrated by her refusal for years to 'waste' money on advertising the theatre's programmes and times of performance in the daily press, or, indeed, to invest in any publicity at all, even by giving tickets to critics. 'Although in her later days the Vic did achieve very wide publicity, it was in spite of Lilian Baylis rather than because of her,' said Norman Marshall.[4] Moreover, because of her insistence on offering wages well below the levels acceptable to trained and experienced staff, a number of Cockney underlings and others on the payroll did their best to supplement their earnings by 'fiddling' and 'pinching' – pilfering materials, dipping their fingers in the till, taking bribes, cheating on bills. Lilian was not unaware of what was going on: it was one of the unpublicized traditions of the Old Vic. But she estimated that she gained more on the swings than she lost on the roundabouts. What they stole amounted to less in value than the work she got out of them *and* their relations for miserably low wages. Her practicality, on this point, is open to question: it was partly a rationalization of her reluctance to sack old retainers who, though rogues, were warm-hearted ones who knew their place and liked it.

Did she deliberately live up to her reputation for being a 'character' by exaggerating her philistinism and by eccentric role-playing? Probably she did, if it helped the two theatres – so far, at least, as her public appearances in later life were concerned. Harcourt Williams observed that when she talked to the Vic audience from the stage she seemed to assume another personality.

'There was something of the music hall artist's approach . . . something of the dancing mistress and her concert work in South Africa.'[5] Playing to the gallery – which she still saw, Williams believed, as the 'rough crowd' of Emma's day – she exaggerated her oddness, homeliness and no-nonsense materialism. Her voice was more raspingly 'common' than it was in private. Perhaps she dressed up (or, rather, down) to the role – at least in the thirties. And some of the later gaffes were not always entirely unpremeditated. Norman Marshall went so far as to say that Lilian 'invented what was really an elaborate disguise. She became a "character", half comic, half frightening.'[6]

For some years Lilian Baylis continued to attract sycophants, like all celebrities with a good deal of power and personality. 'We used to watch people kowtowing to her like mad,' said an actress who worked at the Vic in the 1920s. 'She'd watch them and listen to them, but not for long. We used to say among ourselves, "*That* one won't stay the course" – though one or two of them did, for a while.' Most of the flatterers were women, although young actors sometimes joined the tiny court. But, whereas in those days Lilian had demonstrated that flattery was all right as long as you didn't inhale, it sometimes seemed in later years to friendly critics like Guthrie that she found it hard to *stop* inhaling. Towards the end of her life she appeared to lose not a little of her distinctive humility. Dame Sybil, her most consistent and devoted champion, said, 'She did tend to think that she was – well, not Lord God Almighty in the theatre, but pretty near to that. After all, everything the Lord had told her to do had turned out right.' Is it surprising if she sometimes felt, at least, pleased with herself, and felt that He was pleased too?

And now the case for the defence, and the credit side of the Baylis ledger.

Mean? Although generous to friends in private need, Lilian Baylis was indeed Scrooge-like with the money belonging to the Vic and the Wells. But that was because there was always so very little of it in hand, with overshadowing debts and so much more to be spent, although she never knew where the cash would come from. The Lady may have believed that the Lord would provide; but not if she squandered His gifts in advance. Lilian relied on subsidy from the actors and singers (through underpayment) to keep the theatres open. Her managerial poverty was not some spinsterish delusion, but a fact of her life until the end of it. Critics who admonished her for failing to spend more lavishly on costumes, scenery and stars, for refusing to sponsor new plays and operas, underrated her practical difficulties. How could she raise capital for productions when, if they made profits, she could not distribute them; in a theatre, moreover, where the prices were constitutionally pegged at uneconomic levels; in a country with no tradition of state aid, civic subsidy or private funding in the performing arts? Moreover, the poverty of the theatre and the miserliness of the manager may be seen as blessings in disguise for the Vic, considered as a home of Shakespeare and a training-ground of talent and audiences, for it made simplicity imperative and spectacle impossible. Attention was concentrated on the text and the acting. The play was the thing, not the production – the author, not the director, was the man who mattered most.

Rude? Sometimes Miss Baylis meant to be offensive, and then she signally succeeded; but more often those who found her manner 'rude' were unaccustomed to her congenital candour, combined with a defensive gruffness and abruptness. 'Forthrightness, thy name is Baylis,' would have been a good motto for her, said James Agate. In Marie Ney's words, 'She didn't mind what she said or where she said it. She just said exactly what she felt and what she thought,' without caring what kind of impression it made. Canon Hutchinson was talking to Lilian one evening at the Vic at the back of her box, while at the front, watching a performance, was Harriet Webster, who was staying at Stockwell on her annual holiday. Suddenly Lilian pointed to her house-guest and said to Hutch, calmly and non-committally, 'I wish I didn't hate her so,' and then continued their conversation. Those who knew her well accepted her uncommon frankness and brusqueness as an inextricable part of her eccentric power; and her directors had the satisfaction (if a somewhat uneasy one) of knowing that any criticisms of their work would be made face to face, not behind their backs. At board meetings and elsewhere she would publicly defend them to the hilt, as long as they were in her employment and her confidence (which is by no means standard managerial practice today).

Domineering? Yes. But however hard she drove her staff, she drove herself harder; and, although she demanded a great deal of service from them, it did not include subservience – she liked people to stand up for themselves. Nor did she demand this service for herself, but for the theatre; and she made them feel that it was not her theatre but theirs, that the theatre was their life, and that it was all immensely worth while. Graduates of the Vic put it in different ways: 'She could twist anyone round her little finger, could Miss Baylis'; 'You couldn't help feeling that you'd do anything for her'; 'She *made* you do things you'd never have done for anyone else. It was a kind of hypnosis'; 'We laughed at her, but we were rather frightened of her, too'. The faith that drove her infected others who did not share its 'divine ground'. They believed in the Vic because she so manifestly did, burning with a single-minded intensity of purpose and self-dedication. She was a born leader.

Arrogant? Behind that gruff and sometimes grim exterior was concealed a vulnerable, self-critical woman. Professor Dent wrote that her 'repellent crust of hardness was a protective armour . . . against all sorts of spiritual enemies'.[7] Far from being smug, Lilian experienced many moments of despair and disappointment with her private self. She knew that she lacked a natural humility, and she prayed for it. In her daily devotions and on her frequent retreats she often struggled with self-interrogation. In such moods, according to Canon Hutchinson, she 'felt that her own failures had led to failures in her work, and that made the cross harder to bear'. Or, in the more melodramatic prose of Father Andrew, 'her soul was often in the wilderness, bowed down in agony, and sometimes, so to speak, with her back to the rock fighting the fiend . . . Her own self-chastisement made her sometimes seemingly rough in her dealings with others.'[8] That inner questioning, secret though it was, helped – by the way it shaped her character – to win for her not only the respect but the affection of many people who knew little or nothing of the private Lilian Baylis. A smug woman could not have done what the Lady did. Her animating faith was not a belief in herself alone.

Conceited? Yes, but . . . Lilian's pride in her honorary degrees and her CH was manifest and justified. Although she was ridiculed for wearing her cap and gown so often on the stage, she did so not only because she wanted to show them off but because they were the honours of the Vic and the Wells, and she wanted to share them in the theatre, on public exhibition. They were a reassurance to herself and, perhaps, to her audience that an uneducated, untrained woman had earned the right to stand there in command.

She was immensely proud of her job in life, but tended to assume that everyone knew what it was. It was one thing to tell shopkeepers and stallholders in the New Cut, as she did in hunting for bargains, 'I'm Lilian Baylis of the Old Vic', yet she would make the same proclamation with the same expectations to a farmer on whose field she wanted to camp or a roadhouse manager in whose pool she longed to swim. Annette Prevost recalls that after voting in a general election, Lilian went up to the candidate of her choice and announced, encouragingly, 'I've just cast my vote in your favour. I'm Lilian Baylis of the Old Vic.' He clearly did not know who or what that was, and an expression of 'total defeat' spread over Lilian's face. 'It was the only time,' Prevost says, 'that I ever saw her look really hurt.' To be of the Old Vic and Sadler's Wells was what gave her meaning, definition and identity. Without it, she felt lost in public, perhaps even in the sight of God. It was this kind of 'conceit' that made her envious and alarmed if she felt that people were moving out of her control, and if her central role seemed to be threatened even by tiny symptoms of competition. But this conceit also helped to keep the Vic and the Wells open. They would have been abandoned years earlier by a manager who needed them less, a woman with more roles to choose from.

Unbusinesslike? Some critics said that Lilian Baylis was essentially an amateur. They were quite right; and it was another contributory cause of her success. No professional manager would have accepted such a set-up, with all its absurdities and austerities for so many years, or could have persuaded so many remarkable people to tolerate them and even to share them with so little reward. Only an amateur in business could have plunged, time after time, into such desperately uneconomic enterprises and have come through with credit unimpaired. If she dithered and changed her mind, it was because she worked entirely by intuition. The 'inexplicable delays' of her management often turned out to be justified, apparently by some sixth or seventh sense, which secured her inexplicable survival. Because of her reliance on intuition she quite often found it difficult to explain *why* she was doing *what* she was doing, and this not only gave an impression of vagueness but also sometimes accentuated the customary brusqueness of her manner.

If the Lady tolerated inefficiency and even minor dishonesty on the staff, it was partly because she instinctively recognized that rigid rules were irrelevant to the growth of an organism like the Vic. Moreover, it was not merely a pious memorial cliché that Lilian's natural gifts included an unusually keen appreciation of the personal factor (though this was not always matched by an insight into individual character). As a good leader she sensed the importance of keeping the right mixture of personalities within her team, but this worked only so long as the theatre was small enough for her to know quite intimately everyone who worked for her; and only so long as it was treated as a special case by other organizations, not least by the trade unions. Once the Vic grew beyond her direct, mothering grasp, her intuition and her method faltered.

After this negative praise in defence of Lilian Baylis, how can her positive qualities be summarized? For a start, she had exceptional courage. She was brave in tackling official opposition, public apathy, private despair and in continuing a fight against apparently overwhelming odds. The dice were heavily loaded not only against her theatre but against herself: both were conspicuously handicapped. 'Guts' was the quality that, perhaps, she most admired in others – it was one of the things she liked about Lilian Baylis. She worked exceptionally hard and long hours, for exceptionally little financial reward. She was an *animateur* with exceptional drive and ultra-English empiricism. She had exceptional faith in what she was doing – a total belief in her mission, and a single-minded devotion to its accomplishment. She had an astonishing gift for making other people believe in it and slave for it. At the same time she had enough self-knowledge to realize her own limitations.

Her character combined rare, almost bleak simplicity with canniness, an almost childlike naïvety with a peasant's earthy wisdom, self-defensive wariness and belligerence with vulnerably affectionate kindness. Although she was, perhaps, most at ease among working-class people, she did not believe – as a practical woman – in dealing with 'underlings'. Her motto (as she told Arnold Haskell) was 'Always go to the big people, the people at the top'. That is why she went, directly and habitually, to God.

What did Lilian achieve? First and foremost, she kept her theatres open. This was, as we have seen, considerably easier said than done. Even supernatural help seemed, at times, of no avail. She ensured, as best she could, that they were open to ordinary people who wanted to see Shakespeare and opera in English, at a price they could afford, staged in a way they could understand: simply, directly, with humour and humanity. Ordinary people were *poor* people: unsophisticated people, badly educated, like herself rather than like the West Endy people. Within those limits, and the limits of her budget, directors and artists were free to get

296

on with their jobs. That is why so many brilliant people worked for the Old Vic, in spite of the miserable pay, the backstage discomfort and inefficiency, the pauperized atmosphere – in spite, indeed, of Lilian Baylis, as some of them saw it. This was a free theatre with no counterpart anywhere else in Britain. It was free from the censorship of intellectual fashion and (at least till the mid-1930s) from many of the commercial pressures familiar in the West End. It was a place to learn, where an artist might stretch himself in miscast and underrehearsed performances without being caught in the glare of the critical spotlights. It was also a theatre that offered an unusually alert, cohesive, informed audience, for whose tastes, at least until her last few years, Lilian showed a rare responsiveness. Indeed her creation and understanding of her audience are among the prime reasons for ranking Lilian Baylis as a great manager.

What was Lilian Baylis's aim in life? To a friend like Father Hutchinson it seemed clear. First of all, it was to 'bring the best to the poorest'.

She felt that Shakespeare represented the absolutes of truth, goodness and beauty, and that the poor people should have all the truth, beauty and goodness they could get, presented at prices which they could afford. Shakespeare was a Bible to her, in a way, though she didn't know it very well, mind you . . .

But it went further than that. Lilian wanted not only to serve other people (the poor, preferably) but also to purify herself, as an instrument of God.

She had a sort of hunger and thirst after righteousness. She had to give the best of herself not only in her work, which she regarded as her vocation, but also, at the same time, she had to give the best for herself. She believed that she was the channel for doing this job, and that she had to be as good, herself, as she possibly could be.

She was indeed, as Professor Dent wrote, 'undoubtedly a woman of deep fundamental goodness . . . and it was this . . . which made her a peculiarly lovable woman, and the only woman who could hold these two entire theatres . . . firmly together, united if for no other cause in personal loyalty to herself.'[9]

The reputation of Lilian Baylis rests in part upon the work of Robert Atkins, Charles Corri, Reginald Rowe, Harcourt Williams, Ninette de Valois and other rare talents whom she enlisted to serve her theatres and her people; but whatever the brilliance of such contributors to the achievement of the Old Vic and Sadler's Wells before 1937, it was their manager who must be given the ultimate, overall credit. In the twenty-five years between Emma's death and her own, Lilian Baylis encouraged, promoted, defended and accelerated the growth of the performing arts and their relevance to the life of ordinary people. She made a home and an audience for them; she was a great host and housekeeper of the arts; and she established an irresistible case for subsidizing them – on *moral* grounds (as was imperative in England). As S. R. Littlewood said of her work, 'She created bridges between theatre and schoolroom, theatre and church, theatre and home . . . Shakespeare, opera and ballet can be produced at popular prices by others. But it was Lilian Baylis who broke down the barriers of 300 years by her own glowing sympathy and triumphant commonsense.'

Great abysses gaped in British cultural life at the turn of the century. Lilian Baylis had no intention of trying to bridge them when she started work at the Old Vic in 1898, or even when she succeeded her aunt in its control in 1912. But she did begin to bridge them, somehow, with the help of her faith in God, some very odd methods and some very remarkable people; and the work was continued after her death. The structure changed, but the foundation lasted. I can't help feeling that the most remarkable of these people – indeed, of all the talents at large in the British theatre between 1900 and 1940 – was Lilian Mary Baylis. She had so much against her; she had, it would seem, so little to give; yet she gave abundantly, invaluably and incomparably, as the mother of a national theatre, a national opera and a national ballet.

Today her name survives, outside books, archives and newspaper-files, in a street opposite the Old Vic stage door (once called Oakley Street) off which you may find a block of flats named after Ben Greet; in the rebuilt church of St Agnes, Kennington; in the Number One dressing-room at the Vic (once her office); on a blue plaque at her old Stockwell home (now inhabited by the Water Board); in an LCC school behind the Vic in Webber Street; in her portrait in the Wells Room at Sadler's Wells; and in the rag-bag of anecdotes handed down through half a century.

Is this all that endures? Certainly the theatrical map has been so radically redrafted that it may seem futile to make comparisons or draw lessons. The Lady's technique, like her personality, is unrepeatable. Her successors in the Waterloo Road, St Martin's Lane, Rosebery Avenue and the new South Bank colossus do not depend (as yet) upon faith in divine aid. In the year of Lilian's centenary a National Theatre play and a Sadler's Wells opera cost some 500 times as much as she allowed her producers in her heyday of the 1920s. The National Theatre company received from the state in that year about twice the amount that Lilian had begged in thirty years from all her institutional patrons put together. Millions are spent by the Arts Council every year on opera, ballet and the drama, in theatres run by directors who do their sums not in pennies but in thousands of pounds. Yet, in spite of the transformation in the cultural and moral climate, and in official attitudes towards the arts, the eccentric mother-figure of our national theatres is worth remembering not only because she set an example of crusading dedication, stubborn courage and hard labour, combined with peasant prudence and good housekeeping; but also because of the attitude to the performing arts that she embodied.

For Lilian Baylis the theatre was important not as a game for personal glory, but as work for enlightenment and education. Its functions stretched beyond the immediate satisfactions of the stage to a world of wider concerns and deeper knowledge. Lilian thought of this experience in terms of God, Truth and Beauty. That kind of valuation seems unlikely to be restored to critical or administrative favour in the near future; but without the attitude that it reflects – the refusal to accept the theatre as an end in itself, the faith that the arts are made for man, not vice versa, and, ultimately, for *all* men (not an obsessive three per cent of the population) – a good deal of the cultural activity now subsidized by the state would appear to be little more than expensive occupational therapy for artists and their imitators.

Some forty years ago, long before a television set was installed in nearly every British home, Miss Baylis said in a broadcast: 'The theatre is perhaps the most important and accessible and most easily understood branch of art for the man and woman in the street . . . our greatest power for good – and evil.' Important as it is, she was both too shrewd and too simple to believe in theatre for theatre's sake. She invested her life in theatre for the people, under God. Lilian's religion, like her morality and her economics, may seem oddly Victorian both to the theatrical activists of the 1970s, queueing for state aid to change society, and to the passivists who are content with the consummation of a good show.

But the kind of commitment that Lilian Baylis exemplified is an unquenchable source of social change, cultural creativity and individual energy that can never be out of date, though it may be out of fashion.

Notes

1. PRELUDE (*pages* 17–21)

1. Sybil and Russell Thorndike, *Lilian Baylis*, Chapman & Hall, 1938.
2. Edward J. Dent, *A Theatre for Everybody*, T. & V. Boardman, 1945.
3. Sir Hugh Walpole, *Vic–Wells*, ed. Harcourt Williams, Cobden Sanderson, 1938.
4. Robert Atkins, Recording in BBC Archives, made 28 February 1963.

2. EMMA (*pages* 23–41)

1. 'Notes on the Life of Emma Cons', in a programme for a special performance of *The Merchant of Venice* at the Old Vic, 20 October 1929, when the Duchess of York unveiled a memorial to Miss Cons.
2. Beatrice Webb, *My Apprenticeship*, Longmans, 1926.
3. Cicely Hamilton and Lilian Baylis, *The Old Vic*, Cape, 1926.
4. I am indebted for much of the following information to the genealogical researches of John B. McKee.
5. C. E. Maurice, ed., *The Life of Octavia Hill as Told in her Letters*, Macmillan, 1913.
6. *The Old Vic.*
7. C. E. Maurice.
8. E. Moberly Bell, *Octavia Hill*, Constable, 1944.
9. *The Old Vic.*
10. ibid.
11. ibid.
12. ibid.
13. C. E. Maurice. (This is now Garbutt Place, off Marylebone High Street.)
14. ibid.
15. *The Old Vic.*
16. Renamed St Christopher's Place, it is now a chic shopping precinct.
17. *The Old Vic.*
18. ibid.
19. ibid.
20. E. Moberly Bell.
21. ibid.

22. *The Old Vic*.
23. J. C. Winnington-Ingram, 'A Glimpse of London in the Last Century', *Quarterly Bulletin of the Society of Housing Managers*, April 1954.
24. 'Model Dwellings', *The County Council Magazine*, April 1889.
25. *The Old Vic*.
26. 'Model Dwellings'.
27. ibid.
28. ibid.
29. G. Stedman-Jones, *Outcast London*, Oxford University Press, 1971.
30. *My Apprenticeship*.
31. 'Model Dwellings'.
32. *The Old Vic*.

3. THE PURIFIED HALL (*pages 43–63*)

1. *The Old Vic*.
2. John Hollingshead, *Ragged London in 1861*, 1861.
3. ibid.
4. F. G. Tomlins, *A Brief View of the English Stage*, 1840.
5. *The Old Vic*.
6. *My Apprenticeship*.
7. William Poel, *Old Vic Magazine*, December 1930.
8. Edwin Hodder, *The Life of Samuel Morley*, 1887.
9. *A Theatre for Everybody*.
10. *The Times*, 21 February 1930.
11. *The Musical Review*, 10 March 1883, republished in *How to Become a Music Critic*, ed. Dan. H. Laurence, 1960.
12. *Morley College Magazine*, April 1902.
13. *The Old Vic*.

4. ENTER LILIAN (*pages 65–85*)

1. The magazine of All Saints Church, Margaret Street, December 1936.
2. *The Old Vic*.
3. ibid.
4. *Daily News*, 28 April 1930.
5. *Old Vic Magazine*, March 1937.
6. *Daily Sketch*, 13 July 1931.
7. Roy Campbell, *Light on a Dark Horse*, Hollis, 1951.
8. Beatrice Wilson, *Vic-Wells*.
9. *The Old Vic*.
10. ibid.

5. ACTING MANAGER (*pages 87–111*)

1. *The Life and Labour of the London Poor*, 1903.

2. Adrian Boult, *Centenary Festival Souvenir Programme*.
3. *A Theatre for Everybody*.
4. Constance Willis, *Vic–Wells*.
5. *A Theatre for Everybody*.
6. ibid.
7. *Grove's Musical Dictionary*.
8. Denis Richards, *Offspring of the Vic*, Routledge, 1958.
9. *The Times*, 24 February 1913.
10. Constance Willis, *Vic–Wells*.
11. *The Old Vic*.
12. ibid.
13. F. Charlton Fry, letter in the *Observer*, 12 December 1937.
14. *The Old Vic*.
15. Winifred Isaac, *Ben Greet and the Old Vic*, published by the author, 1964.
16. *The Times*, 23 October 1913.
17. *The Times*, 28 October 1913.
18. *Lilian Baylis*.

6. LILIAN'S WAR (*pages* 113–44)

1. *Lilian Baylis*.
2. Tudor Davies, *Vic–Wells*.
3. *All Saints' Magazine*.
4. see Winifred Isaac.
5. *Lilian Baylis*.
6. ibid.
7. Russell Thorndike, *Sybil Thorndike*, Thornton Butterworth, 1929.
8. *Lilian Baylis*.
9. *A Theatre for Everybody*.
10. *The Old Vic*.
11. *Lilian Baylis*.
12. Margaret Webster, *The Same Only Different*, Gollancz, 1969.
13. ibid.
14. Robert Atkins, 'The Lady of Waterloo Road', *The Times*, 30 March 1974.
15. *Lilian Baylis*.
16. Henry Kendall, *I Remember Romano's*, Macdonald, 1960.
17. *Lilian Baylis*.
18. ibid.
19. *The Same Only Different*.
20. ibid.
21. *Lilian Baylis*.
22. Tyrone Guthrie, *Vic–Wells*.
23. ibid.

7. THE BUILDING YEARS (*pages* 145–74)

1. Tyrone Guthrie, *Vic–Wells*.
2. ibid.
3. ibid.
4. Robert Atkins, 'The Lady of Waterloo Road'.
5. Tyrone Guthrie, *Vic–Wells*.
6. *The Same Only Different*.
7. ibid.
8. *A Theatre for Everybody*.
9. *Tribute to Benjamin Britten*, ed. Anthony Gishford, Faber, 1963.
10. John Gielgud, *Early Stages*, Falcon Press, 1948 edn.
11. *Old Vic Magazine*, 1925.
12. *Lilian Baylis*, from which the following story is taken.
13. Irene Beeston, *Vic–Wells*.
14. Robert Atkins, 'The Lady of Waterloo Road'.
15. Kathleen Eggar, 'Music at the Old Vic', *The Music Student*, August 1918.
16. Joan Cross, *Tribute to Benjamin Britten*.
17. E. L. Lovett, *Civil Service Arts Magazine*, 1931.
18. *A Theatre for Everybody*.
19. Lawrance Collingwood, *Vic–Wells*.
20. ibid.
21. *A Theatre for Everybody*.
22. Clive Carey, *Vic–Wells*.
23. Robert Atkins, BBC Archives.
24. see *Edy: Recollections of Edith Craig*, Muller, 1949.
25. *A Theatre for Everybody*.
26. Flora Robson, Centenary Programme.
27. Beatrice Wilson, *Vic–Wells*.
28. Herbert Farjeon, *The Shakespearian Scene*, Hutchinson.
29. Robert Atkins, BBC Archives.
30. *The Footlights Flickered*, 1952.
31. Foreword to H. Chance Newton, *The Old Vic*, 1923.
32. *Offspring of the Vic*.
33. J. C. Trewin, *Shakespeare on the English Stage 1902–1964*, Cresset Press, 1964.

8. THE WAY TO THE WELLS (*pages* 175–209)

1. *Lilian Baylis*.
2. Winifred Holtby, *Letters to a Friend*, Collins, 1937.
3. Adrian Boult, Centenary Programme.
4. *Vic–Wells*.
5. *Old Vic Magazine*.
6. Harcourt Williams, *Old Vic Saga*, Winchester Publications, 1949.
7. Evelyn Williams, *Vic–Wells*.

8. ibid.
9. Joan Cross, *Tribute to Benjamin Britten*.
10. Edith Evans, *Vic–Wells*.
11. ibid.
12. Joan Cross, *Tribute to Benjamin Britten*.
13. Harcourt Williams, *Four Years at the Old Vic*, Putnam, 1935.
14. ibid.
15. *Early Stages*.
16. *Four Years at the Old Vic*.
17. Ninette de Valois, *Come Dance With Me*, Hamish Hamilton, 1957.
18. ibid.
19. *Four Years at the Old Vic*.

9. PRIVATE WORLDS (*pages* 211–44)

1. *Come Dance With Me*.
2. ibid.
3. Ethel Smyth, *Vic–Wells*.
4. *Life and Letters of Father Andrew*, ed. by Kathleen E. Burn, A. R. Mowbray, 1948.
5. *A Theatre for Everybody*.
6. *Life and Letters of Father Andrew*.
7. Hugh Walpole, *Vic–Wells*.
8. *Lilian Baylis*.
9. Father Andrew, *Vic–Wells*.
10. *Lilian Baylis*.
11. Frederick Ashton, Centenary Programme.

10. THE TRIPLE CROWN (*pages* 245–79)

1. *Early Stages*.
2. Hugh Walpole, *Vic–Wells*.
3. *A Theatre for Everybody*.
4. Lawrance Collingwood, *Vic–Wells*.
5. Hugh Walpole, *Vic–Wells*.
6. Dennis Gray Stoll, letter in the *Manchester Guardian*, 3 April 1957.
7. Frederick Ashton, Centenary Programme.
8. Mary Clarke, *The Sadler's Wells Ballet*, A. & C. Black, 1955.
9. ibid.
10. Anton Dolin, *Markova*, W. H. Allen, 1953.
11. Anton Dolin, *Autobiography*, Oldbourne, 1960.
12. Tyrone Guthrie, *A Life in the Theatre*, Hamish Hamilton, 1960.
13. ibid.
14. ibid.
15. Janet Dunbar, *Flora Robson*, Harrap, 1960.
16. *A Life in the Theatre*.
17. Flora Robson, Centenary Programme.

18. *A Life in the Theatre.*
19. R. C. Sherriff, *No Leading Lady*, Gollancz, 1968.
20. ibid.
21. *The Same Only Different.*
22. *A Life in the Theatre.*
23. ibid.
24. ibid.
25. ibid.

11. ENIGMA VARIATIONS (*pages* 281–300)

1. Father Andrew, *Vic–Wells.*
2. *Lilian Baylis.*
3. Sumner Austin, *Vic–Wells.*
4. Norman Marshall, *The Other Theatre*, John Lehmann, 1947.
5. *Old Vic Saga.*
6. *The Other Theatre.*
7. *A Theatre for Everybody.*
8. Father Andrew, *Vic–Wells.*
9. *A Theatre for Everybody.*

Bibliography

ALLEN, PERCY, *The Stage Life of Mrs Stirling*, Hutchinson, 1922.

ARUNDELL, DENIS, *The Story of Sadler's Wells*, Hamish Hamilton, 1965.

BARNETT, MRS H., *Canon Barnett: his Life, Work and Friends*, 1918.

BELL, E. MOBERLY, *Octavia Hill*, Constable, 1942.

BETTANY, F. G., *Stewart Headlam*, John Murray, 1926.

BOOTH, JOHN, *The Old Vic 1816–1916*, Stead's, 1917.

BURN, KATHLEEN E., *The Life and Letters of Father Andrew*, A. R. Mowbray, 1948.

CARTWRIGHT, A. P., *The Corner House: the Early History of Johannesburg*, Cape Town, Purnell, 1965.

CAVENDISH, LADY FREDERICK, *The Diary* (2 vols.), ed. John Bailey, John Murray, 1927.

CHADWICK, OWEN, *The Victorian Church*, Part 1, A. & C. Black, 1970.

CLARKE, MARY, *The Sadler's Wells Ballet*, A. & C. Black, 1955.

DENT, EDWARD J., *A Theatre for Everybody*, T. & V. Boardman, 1945.

DE VALOIS, NINETTE, *Come Dance With Me*, Hamish Hamilton, 1957.

DOLIN, ANTON, *Autobiography*, Oldbourne, 1960.

DOLIN, ANTON, *Markova*, W. H. Allen, 1953.

DUNBAR, JANET, *Flora Robson*, Harrap, 1960.

EARLAND, ADA, *Ruskin and his Circle*, Hutchinson, 1910.

FAGG, EDWIN, *The Old 'Old Vic'*, Vic–Wells Association, 1936.

GIELGUD, JOHN, *Early Stages*, Falcon Press, 1948.

GISHFORD, ANTHONY, ed., *Tribute to Benjamin Britten*, Faber, 1963.

GUTHRIE, TYRONE, *A Life in the Theatre*, Hamish Hamilton, 1960.

GUTHRIE, TYRONE, *In Various Directions*, Michael Joseph, 1966.

HAMILTON, CICELY and BAYLIS, LILIAN, *The Old Vic*, Cape, 1926.

HAYMAN, RONALD, *John Gielgud*, Heinemann, 1972.

HARRISON, BRIAN, *Drink and the Victorians*, Faber, 1971.

HILL, W. T., *Octavia Hill*, Hutchinson, 1956.

HODDER, EDWIN, *The Life of Samuel Morley*, 1887.

ISAAC, WINIFRED, *Ben Greet and the Old Vic*, published by the author, 1964.

KENDALL, HENRY, *I Remember Romano's*, Macdonald, 1960.

KNIGHT, ESMOND, *Seeking the Bubble*, Hutchinson, 1943.

LEYDS, F. A., *A History of Johannesburg: the Early Years*, Cape Town, Nasionale bookhandel, 1964.
MARSHALL, NORMAN, *The Other Theatre*, John Lehmann, 1947.
MAURICE, C. E., ed., *Life of Octavia Hill as Told in her Letters*, Macmillan, 1913.
NEWTON, H. CHANCE, *The Old Vic and its Associations*, Fleetway Press, 1923.
OUVRY, ELINOR SOUTHWOOD, *Octavia Hill's Letters on Housing, 1864 to 1911*, 1933.
RICHARDS, DENIS, *Offspring of the Vic*, Routledge, 1958.
ROBERTS, PETER, ed., *Souvenir Programme of the Lilian Baylis Centenary Festival*, 1974.
ROVER, CONSTANCE, *Women's Suffrage and Party Politics in England 1886–1914*, Routledge, 1967.
SMITH, WARREN SYLVESTER, *The London Heretics 1870–1914*, Constable, 1967.
SHERRIFF, R. C., *No Leading Lady*, Gollancz, 1968.
SPEAIGHT, ROBERT, *Shakespeare on the Stage*, Collins, 1973.
SPEAIGHT, ROBERT, *William Poel and the Elizabethan Revival*, Heinemann, 1954.
THORNDIKE, RUSSELL, *Sybil Thorndike*, Thornton Butterworth, 1929.
THORNDIKE, SYBIL AND RUSSELL, *Lilian Baylis*, Chapman & Hall, 1938.
TOMLINS, F. G., *A Brief View of the English Stage*, 1840.
WEBSTER, MARGARET, *The Same Only Different*, Gollancz, 1969.
WESTWOOD, DORIS, *These Players*, Heath Cranton, 1926.
WHITE, ERIC WALTER, *The Rise of English Opera*, John Lehmann, 1951
WILLIAMS, HARCOURT, *Four Years at the Old Vic*, Putnam, 1935.
WILLIAMS, HARCOURT, *Old Vic Saga*, Winchester Publications, 1949.
WILLIAMS, HARCOURT, ed., *Vic-Wells*, Cobden Sanderson, 1938.

Other sources include:

The Old Vic Magazine, 1919–30.
The Old Vic and Sadler's Wells Magazine, 1931–8.
The Octavia Hill Collection in the Marylebone Library.
Minutes of the Executive Committee of the Old Vic Governors, 1907–1938.
Old Vic/Sadler's Wells cuttings and other material, including letters and postcards in the Enthoven Collection; the British Museum Library; the Mander and Mitchenson Collection; the library of the Vic–Wells Association; and private hands.
The archives of the GLC.
BBC recording of Robert Atkins (28 February 1963); and of speeches made on the last night of the Old Vic before the arrival of the National Theatre Company (15 June 1963).

BBC recording of Lilian Baylis, interviewed by Leslie Mitchell, 29
September 1937.
BBC programmes about Lilian Baylis broadcast on the Home Service,
29 July 1952, and on BBC Radio 4, 26 May 1974.

Index

Aberdeen, Lady (wife of 1st Marquess), 75

Actors' Church Union, 120, 123, 283

Agate, James, 276, 283, 293

Ainley, Henry, 124

Alberg, Albert, 52

Alexander, Sir George, 105, 145

Alexandra, Queen, 51

Allen, John, 66, 270

Allen, Nancy, 262

Andrew, Father, 13, 142, 146, 165, 223, 226–31, 235, 241, 279, 282–4, 287, 289, 294

Archer, William, 115

Armstrong, John, 259, 261

Artists' Guild, The, 229

Ashcroft, Dame Peggy, 12, 254, 264

Ashton, Sir Frederick, 242, 259–260

Ashwell, Lena, 124

Asquith, H. H. (1st Viscount), 169, 177

Atkins, Robert, 21, 129, 132, 140, 142, 151, 159–66, 173–4, 176, 177, 191, 196, 201, 230, 266, 297

Austin, Sumner, 135, 157–8, 189, 190, 249, 256, 291

Austral, Florence, 253

Baldwin, Stanley (1st Viscount), 177

Balfe, Michael, 219

Balfour, Arthur (1st Earl), 177

Barbirolli, Sir John, 258

Barnardo, Dr Thomas John, 36

Barnato, Mrs Barney, 80

Barnett, Canon Samuel, 30, 40–41, 75, 92, 227

Barth, Alice, 94

Baylis, F. W. (Newton), 37, 65, 67–85 *passim*, 109–11, 127, 213–214, 234

Baylis, Elizabeth (Liebe and Libby), 24, 33, 37, 65, 67–85 *passim*, 109–11, 127, 151, 214, 236

Baylis, Ethel: *see* Dunning, Ethel

Baylis, Lilian:
childhood and education, 65–72; early musical experience, 72–3; a Gipsy Reveller, 74–6; touring and teaching in South Africa, 75–85; deformity, 81–3; engagement, 79; return to London, 1898, 84; starts work at Old Vic, 87; introduces Shakespeare, 101–8; as manager, 19, 139–40, 148–9, 159, 187–90, 193–5, 197, 286–300; life-style, 19–20, 212–44; appearance, 18–20, 82, 87, 146, 181, 240; religion, 20, 65–6, 83, 87, 106–7, 109–10, 118–20, 141–142, 172, 226–35, 243–4; influence of Emma Cons, 24, 28, 33, 90, 92–3, 100, and *passim*; money, 85, 90–91, 164, 198,

Baylis, Lilian—*continued*
237–9, 254, 261–2, 284, 292–3,
and *passim*; speeches, 133–5,
246–7; dogs, 147, 222–4; holidays, 98, 169, 172, 226, 249;
honours, 167, 198, 199; driving, 214, 221–2, 224–5; drinking
and eating, 217–19; swimming, 224; weekending, 225–6;
concern for lepers, 83, 142, 227,
235–6, 284; sexual life, 240–42;
death and last rites, 282–4
Baylis, Lilian (the Lady's niece),
278
Baylis, Mary, 65
Baylis, Ray, 68, 73, 98, 212
Baylis, Violet, 68, 73–4, 98
Baylis, William (the Lady's
brother), 68, 71, 72, 76, 80, 85,
110
Baylis, William (the Lady's grandfather), 66, 220
Beaton, Sir Cecil, 259
Beatrice, Princess, 145
Beaumont, Cyril, 205
Beaumont, Hugh, 256
Beecham, Sir Thomas, 108, 177,
256–8, 287
Beldon, Eileen, 17–20
Bennett, Vivienne, 272
Benson, Sir Frank, 66, 118, 130,
159, 191, 192, 263
Bentley, Louisa, 284
Binyon, Laurence, 161
Booth, Charles, 92
Bottomley, Gordon, 161
Boult, Sir Adrian, 93, 180
Brain, Dennis, 190
Braithwaite, Lilian, 124, 130
Braithwaite, Warwick, 256, 291
Brassey, Lord, 55
Bridges-Adams, W., 103
Bridie, James, 263
Briggs, Frances, 139, 148
British National Opera Company,
253

British Broadcasting Corporation, 165, 166, 254, 261
Britton, Hutin, 119, 180
Broadwood's, 24–5
Brown, Ivor, 257
Brownlow, Earl (1st), 55
Burn, Kathleen, 227
Burra, Edward, 259

Cabanel Rudolf, 44
Camargo Society, 253, 258
Campbell, Roy, 81
Carey, Clive, 155–9, 160, 177, 256,
283
Carl Rosa Company, The, 59, 93,
96, 157, 203, 256
Carlyle, Thomas, 30
Carnegie UK Trust, The, 151–2,
157, 172, 178, 195, 269
Carr, Philip, 103
Carrodus, J. T., 71–3
Carter, Agnes (Natalie Kent), 134
Cass, Henry, 271–3
Casson, Ann, 123
Casson, Elizabeth, 121
Casson, Sir Lewis, 102, 119, 134,
140, 174, 196, 279, 289
Casson, Dame Sybil: *see* Thorndike, Dame Sybil
Cave, J. Arnold, 58
Cavendish, Lady Frederick, 51,
57, 75, 98, 100–101, 137, 143,
151, 166, 169, 254, 290
Chamberlain, George, 215, 274
Chandos, Viscount (1st), 51
Chaplin, Charles, 99
Charity Commissioners, The, 55,
178, 252
Charity Organisation Society, 34
Charlotte, Princess, 44
Chekhov, Anton, 266, 274, 287
Chesterton, G. K., 177
Chirgwin, George, 99
Christian, Princess, 54, 107
Church and Stage Guild, 120, 127
Churchill, Winston, 177, 271

312

City Parochial Foundation, 55–6, 101, 130–31, 153, 195, 254–5, 275
Clark, Kathleen (Clarkie), 12, 146, 149, 184–5, 207, 215, 218, 225, 232, 240, 248–9
Clynes, J. R., 177
Coates, Edith, 189–90
Coates, Wells, 266
Cobden, Miss, 62
Coffee Music Hall Company, 41, 47, 50, 54
Coffee Tavern Company, 36
College for Working Women, 29
Collier, Constance, 124
Collingwood, Lawrance, 157–8, 190, 200, 249, 256–7, 287
Community of the Holy Name of Jesus, 215, 284
Compton, Mrs Edward, 118–19, 167
Congreve, William, 266, 269
Cons, Charles, 25, 37
Cons, Ellen, 25, 30, 37, 38, 54, 67, 82, 171, 212–13, 234
Cons, Eliza, 25, 37, 38, 67, 74, 98
Cons, Elizabeth: *see* Baylis, Elizabeth
Cons, Emma, 11, 13, 21, 101–4, 107, 127, 135, 144, 147, 151, 153, 168–71, 177, 185, 193, 199, 219, 233, 251, 254, 275; family, 24–6; friendship with Octavia Hill, 26–8; as Christian Socialist, 27; teaching slum children, 27–8; artist and engraver, 28–30; begins housing work, 31–4; launches coffee tavern movement, 35; settles in Lambeth, 36; begins Old Vic experiment, 40; work with Lilian Baylis at Old Vic, 88–100; death, 100; achievements, 23, 62; memorial 198
Cons, Esther Goodair, 24
Cons, Esther: *see* Forrest, Esther

Cons, Frederick (1788–1839), 24
Cons, Frederick (1810–70), 24–5, 37
Cons, Frederick (Emma's brother), 37
Cornell, Katharine, 272
Corri, Charles, 96–7, 119–20, 123, 144, 156–8, 190, 199–200, 203, 256, 258, 297
Craig, Edith, 160
Craig, Gordon, 128, 160
Cross, Joan, 94, 97, 150, 158, 185, 188–90, 196, 257
Cunard, Lady, 170

Dance, Sir George, 169–70, 195
Dane, Clemence, 200
Davey, Louie, 98, 219
Davies, Tudor, 256
De Casalis, Jeanne, 271
Dekker, Samuel, 276
Dent, Edward J., 21, 95–7, 126, 155–9, 161, 180, 229, 248, 294, 297
De Valois, Dame Ninette, 20, 204–8, 218, 220, 223, 233, 238, 242, 258–62, 283, 297
Devlin, William, 272
Devonshire, Duke of (7th), 51
Devonshire, Duke of (8th), 51; as Hartington, Lord, 74, 77
Devonshire, Duke of (9th), 51, 98, 177, 251, 254
Diaghilev, Serge, 205
Dolin, Anton, 205, 207, 252, 259, 262
Dove, Alfred, 96
Drinkwater, John, 287
Ducie, Countess of, 75
Dunning, Ethel, 67–8, 77–8, 80, 84, 110, 212–13, 226, 282, 284
Dunning, Frank, 110, 213
Dunning, Gladys, 110, 213
Dunning, Dr Robert, 13, 110, 212–13, 226, 278, 284

Edward VII, King, 51, 68, 74
Edward VIII, King, 198 (as Prince of Wales)
Eggar, Kathleen, 154
Elen, Gus, 99
Elgar, Sir Edward, 262
Elizabeth II, Queen, 262
Elizabeth, Queen Mother, 262
Ellis, Muriel, 181–2
Elwes, Gervase, 124
Ervine, St John, 285–6
Euripides, 272
Evans, Dame Edith, 192–4, 203, 232, 253, 274–6, 278
Evans, Maurice, 272
Everest, Ethel, 38, 53–4, 56, 62, 84, 100, 171, 225, 229
Everest, Sir John, 38

Fairbairn, Flora, 214–15
Faraday, Michael, 52
Farjeon, Herbert, 164
Fedorovich, Sophie, 259
Filippi, Rosina, 104–6, 117, 135
Fonteyn, Dame Margot, 259
Forbes-Robertson, Sir Johnston, 145, 159, 177, 246
Forrest, Esther, 25, 37, 70, 73, 98
Forrest, Lord, 37
Forrest, Robert, 37, 73
Foss, George, 141, 160, 228
Frederica, Princess of Hanover, 51, 70
French, Leslie, 200
Fry, Charles, 102, 105

Galsworthy, John, 177
Garvin, J. L., 169
Gatty, Nicholas, 189
Genn, Leo, 272
George V, King, 98; (as Prince of Wales), 100, 177
German, Sir Edward, 108
Gielgud, Sir John, 150, 162, 190, 201–3, 232, 246, 249, 253, 264, 276, 283, 289

Gill, Basil, 124
Gill, Eric, 200
Gladstone, W. E., 51
Godfrey, Dan, 52
Gooch, Lady, 152
Gordon, Rev. E. G., 152, 233
Gordon, John B., 253, 256
Gordon, Ruth, 275–6
Goring, Marius, 174, 268, 289
Gosse, Sir Edmund, 177
Gough, Muriel, 155, 180
Gounod, Charles, 219
Grant, Duncan, 259
Granville Barker, Harley, 128, 161, 191–2, 201
Gray, Terence, 207
Greet, Sir Philip Ben, 19, 119–41 passim, 160, 162–5, 177, 196–7, 222, 246, 266, 298
Gregory, Sir Charles, 67
Grieg, Edvard, 161
Grimaldi, Joseph, 11–12, 44, 176
Guinness, Sir Alec, 274, 276, 289–290
Guthrie, Sir Tyrone, 75, 94, 143, 146–7, 183, 263–70, 273–83, 292

Halifax, Viscount (1st), 75
Halliday, Henry, 26
Hambledon, Viscount (2nd), 178
Hambledon, Viscount (3rd), 252–253
Hamilton, Cicely, 103, 220, 225
Hamilton, Lord Frederick, 179
Hampden, Viscount (1st), 36, 51
Harding, Lyn, 124
Hardinge, Viscount (2nd), 75
Hardy, Ernest: see Andrew, Father
Harkness, Edward S., 265
Harrison, Sam, 94, 190
Hartington, Marquess of: see Devonshire, Duke of (8th)
Harty, Sir Hamilton, 253
Haskell, Arnold, 296

314

Headlam, Rev. Stewart, 127, 129, 166
Helpmann, Sir Robert, 259
Herringham, Sir Wilmot, 181
Hill, Caroline, 26–8, 31
Hill, Miranda, 26, 40, 69
Hill, Octavia, 26–35, 38, 40, 51, 67, 69, 75, 100, 122, 219, 237
Holland, Canon Alfred, 234, 244
Holloway, Baliol, 192
Hollingshead, John, 46–7
Holmes, E., 95
Holmes, Miss Gordon, 239
Holst, Gustav, 252, 257
Holt, Clarence, 69
Holtby, Winifred, 180
Home of St Giles, 142–3, 227, 235–6, 284
Horniman, Annie, 122
Horsley, Canon J. W., 70
Horsnell, Horace, 283
Hudson, Frederick, 164, 189–90, 198
Hughes, Thomas, 27
Hunt, Martita, 201–2
Hussey, Dr, 219, 282
Hutchinson, Rev. C. W. (Father Hutch), 180, 233–4, 236, 238, 241, 283, 293–4, 297

Ibsen, Henrik, 161, 200, 274, 287
Iden, Rosalind, 207
Imperial League of Opera, 256
Ingram, Rev. A. F. Winnington, 227
Irving, H. B., 124
Irving, Sir Henry, 127–8, 161
Isaac, Winifred, 103
Isaacson, Bernard, 58

Jackson, Sir Barry, 180, 205
Jeans, Ursula, 266
Joel, Mrs Solly, 80
John, Sir William Goscombe, 198
Judson, Stanley, 259

Kean, Edmund, 45
Kendal, Dame Madge, 246
Kendall, Henry, 131–3
Keynes, Lord, 253
King, Hetty, 99
Kingsley, Charles, 27, 45
Konss, Elias, 22, 284
Korda, Sir Alexander, 253
Kyrle Society, 40, 70

Ladies' Co-operative Guild, 25–8
Lambert, Constant, 259, 262
Lang, Matheson, 118–19, 135, 151, 166, 262, 290
Laughton, Charles, 264–70, 275, 283
Laurie, John, 162, 165–6, 174, 194, 287, 289
Law, A. Bonar, 169
Le Gallienne, Eva, 124
Leigh, Andrew, 119, 132, 174, 181, 191–2, 196, 200, 204, 206, 269
Leopold of Saxe-Coburg, Prince, 44
Leslie, Cecil, 254, 278
Lidgett, Sir John Scott, 105
Littlewood, S. R., 298
Lloyd, Harry, 195
Lloyd, H. Powell, 97, 190
Lloyd, Lord (1st), 240
Lloyd, Marie, 99
London Academy of Music, 67
London County Council, 30, 56, 62, 89–90, 99–101, 115, 120, 127, 131, 148, 163, 168, 171–2, 176, 199, 255
London Shakespeare League, 124, 127
Lopokova, Lydia (Lady Keynes), 252, 266
Lothian, Lady (wife of 9th Marquess), 50
Lunn, Mme Kirkby, 253
Lyttelton, Alfred, 51

Lyttelton, Lord (5th), 51
Lytton, Earl of (2nd), 181, 275

Maeterlinck, Maurice, 200
Mackinlay, Jean Sterling, 191
MacOwan, Michael, 272
MacQueen-Pope, W., 169
Macready, W. C., 45
Mander, Reginald, 96
Manners, Charles, 123, 130
Manning, Cardinal, 55
Margaret, Princess, 262
Marie Louise, Princess, 143
Markova, Dame Alicia, 259, 261
Marsh, Sir Edward, 271
Marshall, Norman, 291–2
Martineau, Caroline, 38, 52, 54, 56–7, 61, 84, 90, 171
Martineau, Constance, 54, 57, 171
Martin Harvey, Sir John, 159
Mary, Queen, 98 (as Princess of Wales); 100, 143–4, 167, 177, 185
Maude, Cyril, 177
Maurice, Rev. F. D., 27, 28, 56, 227
Mayall, Martha, 203
Mayhew, Henry, 27, 40
McCormick, Sir W., 151
Melba, Dame Nellie, 107–9, 179–180
Mendelssohn, J. L. F., 200
Messel, Oliver, 252, 275
Miller, Gilbert, 275
Milton, Ernest, 142, 146, 159, 162, 219, 220, 242, 289
Minter, Sir Frederick, 178, 254
Moody Manners Company, The, 59, 93, 123, 151
Moore, George, 177
Morley College, 56, 62, 117, 169–173, 176
Morley, Samuel, 53–6
Morrell, Lady Ottoline, 253
Morrell, Philip, 253
Morris, William, 30, 113, 185

Morrish, Everard, 181
Moss, Katie, 219
Mount Temple, Lord, 36, 41, 50, 55, 59
Muggeridge, Malcolm, 128

Nash, Heddle, 189
Newcomb, Mary, 272
Newman, Mrs, 156, 185
Newton, Sir Isaac, 67
Ney, Marie, 194, 231, 267, 293
Nicholls, Agnes, 253
Nicholson, Nora, 148, 194
Nicoll, Allardyce, 180
Nightingale, 186–7, 282

Old Vic:
early history, 43–7; Emma Cons takes over, 47; her problems, 48–61; licensing, 57, 93–4, 99, 101, 218; opera, 52, 58–61, 93–8, 101, 106–9, 117, 123, 126, 153–9, 188–91, 199–200, 257; *for individual operas see also* opera; LCC complaints, 89–90, 131, 152, 168, 171–3; variety, 48–9, 52, 61, 95, 98–9, 101; ballad concerts, 48–9, 59, 95, 98, 101; temperance meetings, 48, 117, 129; military bands, 52–3, 96, 98; lectures, 48, 53, 56, 95, 117, 129, 166; films, 95, 101; symphony concerts, 95–6, 98, 101; Shakespeare, 52, 58, 101–8, 118 ff.; crises, 49, 53, 98, 107–8, 168–173, 195; during First World War, 17–19, 114–17, 131; audience, 44–6, 48–50, 52, 59, 88, 91–4, 105–6, 116, 125–7, 135, 136–8, 149–50, 162–3, 193, 257, 269, 296–7; ballet, 203–8; repertoire: *see* plays
Olivier, Lord, 47, 223, 242, 274–277, 281, 284, 289

Operas and Oratorios (at Old Vic and Sadler's Wells): *Aida*, 199; *Bohème, La*, 179, 189, 199; *Bohemian Girl, The*, 60, 93, 123, 258; *Boris Godunov*, 257; *Bosun's Mate, The*, 189; *Carmen*, 96, 123, 124, 143, 154, 257; *Cavalliera Rusticana*, 93, 123, 256; *Così fan Tutte*, 52; *Daughter of the Regiment*, 60, 95, 123, 196; *Don Giovanni*, 123, 156-7, 161; *Elijah*, 130; *Falstaff*, 257; *Faust*, 60-61, 96, 123-4, 143, 154, 193, 196; *Fidelio*, 159, 257; *Fledermaus*, 257; *Force of Destiny, The*, 199; *Fra Diavolo*, 96, 123; *Hansel and Gretel*, 199; *Lily of Killarney, The*, 60, 91, 93, 123, 189, 258; *Lohengrin*, 93, 123, 190, 257, 284; *Lucia di Lammermoor*, 123; *Macbeth* (Collingwood), 257, 287; *Madam Butterfly*, 189; *Magic Flute, The*, 156, 175; *Maritana*, 60, 123, 258; *Marriage of Figaro*, 154-5, 199; *Martha*, 123; *Mastersingers, The*, 257, 284; *Messiah, The*, 52; *Pagliacci*, 123, 188, 256; *Prince Ferelon*, 189; *Othello*, 199; *Rigoletto*, 109, 123, 179; *Robert Macaire*, 61; *Savitri*, 257; *Snow Maiden, The*, 257; *Sonnambula, La*, 60; *Tannhäuser*, 93, 194, 198, 199, 203; *Tosca*, 189, 199; *Travelling Companions, The*, 257; *Traviata, La*, 123, 194, 196; *Trovatore, Il*, 60, 96, 123, 196; *Tristan and Isolde*, 158, 161, 199; *Tsar Saltan*, 257; *Wreckers, The*, 287

Order of the Sacred Mission, 229

Oughton, Winifred, 132, 222, 231

Owen, George, 103

Paganini, Niccolo, 45

Palmer, Miss, 153-4

Pavlova, Anna, 205

Payne, Lawrence, 276

Parkin, Adeline, 76

Pearce, John, 57

Pearce and Plenty, 57, 91

People's Concert Society, 41

Petrie, Hay, 162

Phelps, Samuel, 45, 176, 246-7

Phillips, Stephen, 161

Phillips, Eric, 224

Pilgrim, Alice, 150, 269-70, 276

Pilgrim Trust, The, 265-6, 268

Pinero, Sir Arthur, 246

Pitt, Percy, 179

Playfair, Sir Nigel, 196

Plays (Old Vic): *Adam's Opera*, 200, 287; *Androcles and the Lion*, 200; *Antony and Cleopatra*, 203; *Arms and the Man*, 200; *As You Like It*, 107, 124, 127, 194, 275; *Britain's Daughter*, 161, 287; *Caste*, 200; *Cherry Orchard, The*, 266; *Comedy of Errors, The*, 122, 124; *Country Wife, The*, 275; *Cymbeline*, 173; *Dark Lady of the Sonnets, The*, 200; *Devil's Disciple, The*, 272; *Everyman*, 124-5, 130, 136, 168, 196, 200; *Faust*, 161, 193; *Ghosts*, 261; *Hamlet*, 19, 123-5, 130, 202-3, 275-8; *Henry IV*, 139, 203; *Henry V*, 133, 277; *Henry VI*, 161; *Henry VIII*, 266; *Hippolytus*, 272; *Hope of the World, The*, 165, 228, 231; *Imaginary Invalid, The*, 200; *Julius Caesar*, 124, 138; *King Arthur*, 161, 287; *Importance of Being Earnest, The*, 266; *King Lear*, 203; *King Rene's Daughter*, 124; *Lady Audley's Secret*, 103; *Love for Love* (at Sadler's Wells), 266, 269; *Love's Labour's Lost*, 263; *Macbeth*, 124, 137, 140, 143,

317

Plays (Old Vic)—*continued*
202, 261, 268, 281–2; *Major Barbara*, 271; *Mary Magdalene*, 200; *Measure for Measure*, 261, 267, 269, 279; *Merchant of Venice, The*, 105, 119, 123, 128, 132, 137, 192, 202; *Merry Wives of Windsor, The*, 123, 139; *Midsummer Night's Dream, A*, 124, 192, 200, 202, 246; *Much Ado About Nothing*, 107, 115, 272; *Oliver Twist*, 103; *Othello*, 124–5, 273; *Peer Gynt*, 161, 175, 271–3; *Poor Joe*, 103; *Richard II*, 202; *Richard III*, 137; *Romeo and Juliet*, 105, 131, 196, 202, 219; *St Helena*, 271–2, 287; *St Joan*, 271; *School for Scandal, The*, 105, 124, 271; *Shaughraun, The*, 103; *She Stoops to Conquer*, 124; *Streets of London, The*, 103; *Taming of the Shrew, The*, 119, 123–4, 192; *Tempest, The*, 109, 123–4, 200, 203; *Three Sisters, The*, 271; *Titus Andronicus*, 161; *Trelawny of the Wells*, 174; *Troilus and Cressida*, 161, 166; *Twelfth Night*, 107, 124, 203, 266, 276; *Vikings, The*, 200; *Wat Tyler*, 287; *Winter's Tale, A*, 124; *Witch of Edmonton, The*, 276
Poel, William, 50–51, 53–4, 58, 102, 103, 120, 124, 127, 161, 166, 176, 192
Portman, Eric, 242
Powell, Arthur, 29
Prevost, Annette, 12, 215–21, 224–5, 237–9, 242, 282–4, 295
Price, Nancy, 130
Priestley, J. B., 263
Probyn, Edith, 76

Quartermaine, Leon, 266
Quayle, Anthony, 290
Quilter, Roger, 124

Rambert, Dame Marie, 206
Read, Sir Herbert, 180
Reade, Charles, 66
Redgrave, Sir Michael, 274–5
Rhondda, Viscountess, 220
Richards, Denis, 170
Richardson, Philip, 205
Richardson, Sir Ralph, 246, 264, 289
Ricketts, Charles, 266
Robertson, Tom, 200
Robinson, Roland (Bob), 144, 167, 185, 212, 251
Robinson, Rowley, 185
Robson, Dame Flora, 162, 264–6, 268
Rowe, Sir Reginald, 172–3, 176–180, 239, 246, 250, 252, 254–5, 258, 282, 297
Royal Academy of Dramatic Art, 162
Royal Academy of Music, 56, 71, 153, 256
Royal Coburg Theatre: *see* Old Vic
Royal College of Music, 56, 153
Royal Institution, 53
Royde-Smith, Naomi, 142
Ruskin, John, 27–30, 33–4

Sadler's Wells, 20, 21, 173, 254, 270, 279; selected as satellite theatre, 176–7; fund-raising and rebuilding, 177–9, 195, 198, 205–8; reopens, 1931, 245–58; opera, 256–8; ballet, 258–62
St Denis, Michel, 276, 281
St John, Christopher, 160
Sala, G. A., 45–6
Santley, Sir Charles, 54
Sandhurst, Lady, 62
Saunders, Florence (Dickie), 141, 162, 212, 231
School of Ornamental Art for Females, 28, 67
Seyler, Athene, 266

Sennett, Charles, 52
Shaw, G. B., 60, 105, 135, 200, 271, 274, 283, 287
Sherriff, R. C., 271–2
Siam, King of, 169
Sickert, W. R., 253–4
Smith, Hon. James, 252
Smithson, Ivy, 231
Smyth, Dame Ethel, 169, 177, 183, 189, 220, 224, 287
Society of the Divine Compassion, 227, 235, 284
Soroptimists, The, 220, 239
South London Dwellings Company, 37
Speaight, Robert, 165
Stamfordham, Lord, 100
Stanford, Sir Charles, 93, 257
Stead, W. T., 118
Stead, Estelle, 118, 120, 122, 176
Stewart, Shakespeare, 103, 107–8, 118
Sterling, Antoinette, 60, 191, 200, 276
Stirling, Fanny, 66, 146, 262, 270, 276
Stoll, Sir Oswald, 255
Swinley, Ion, 162, 165

Talbot, Bishop, 51
Tempest, Dame Marie, 283
Tennents, H. M., 256
Terry, Dame Ellen, 117, 124, 160, 191–2, 201
Teyte, Maggie, 252
Theatre Royal, Covent Garden, 43, 59, 71, 179, 205, 207, 253, 255–7
Theatre Royal, Drury Lane, 17–18, 43–4, 105, 192
Theatre Girls' Club, 229
Thomas, J. H., 169
Thorndike, Russell, 20, 105, 122, 132, 135, 140–41, 152–3, 160–161, 176, 233, 286
Thorndike, Dame Sybil, 21, 83, 105, 120–38 *passim*, 162, 185, 192, 196, 220–21, 229–30, 236, 240, 242, 253, 278, 286, 288–9, 292
Tomlins, F. G., 45–6
Toye, Geoffrey, 180, 189, 250, 256–7
Townsend, W. J. (Townie), 91–2, 185–6, 223, 284
Toynbee Hall, 30
Tree, Sir Herbert Beerbohm, 105, 124, 128, 145, 159, 161
Tree, Viola, 124
Trend, J. B., 156
Trewin, J. C., 174, 278
Trouncer, Cecil, 272
Truscott, Euneta, 93
Turner, Harold, 259
Twain, Mark, 80–81
Tyndall, John, 52

Vanbrugh, Irene, 284
Vanbrugh, Violet, 284
Veness, Molly, 231
Victoria, Queen, 44, 51, 71, 100

Walpole, Sir Hugh, 21, 146, 232–233, 247, 252, 258
Walter, Wilfrid, 162
Warburton, Charles, 141, 152, 153, 160
Webb, Beatrice, 23, 34, 39, 52
Webster, Ben, 118
Webster, Harriet, 79, 219, 293
Webster, Jack, 79, 82, 219, 284
Webster, Margaret, 120, 129, 149, 273
Wendon, Henry, 189
Westminster, Duke of (1st), 36, 54–5
Westminster, Duke of (2nd), 89
Wheeler, Ben, 75–6
Wheeler, Frank, 76
Whistler, Rex, 259
White, J. Fisher, 119
Whitehead, Orlando, 185, 187

Whiteman, Madge, 139–40, 232
Wilde, Oscar, 266
Williams, Evelyn, 183–5, 187–8, 205–6, 215–16, 218, 239–40, 242, 272, 279, 283, 290
Williams, Harcourt, 150, 185, 191, 197, 200, 203, 206–7, 263–4, 266, 268, 286, 289, 291–2, 297
Williams, Ralph Vaughan, 252
Willis, Constance, 61
Wills, W. G., 161

Wilson, Beatrice, 162, 231, 290
Wilson, Sir Stewart, 156
Wiltshire, Walter, 190
Women's Liberal Federation, 62
Wood, Sir Henry, 108
Wordsworth, Mrs Henry, 124, 204
Working Men's College, 56
Worsley, Bruce, 12, 182–4, 186–7, 218, 223, 241, 284
Wycherley, William, 275–6

BLINDED BY THE LIGHT

JOHN GRIBBIN

BLINDED BY THE LIGHT

BANTAM PRESS

LONDON · NEW YORK · TORONTO · SYDNEY · AUCKLAND

TRANSWORLD PUBLISHERS LTD
61–63 Uxbridge Road, London W5 5SA

TRANSWORLD PUBLISHERS (AUSTRALIA) PTY LTD
15–23 Helles Avenue, Moorebank, NSW 2170

TRANSWORLD PUBLISHERS (NZ) LTD
Cnr Moselle and Waipareira Aves,
Henderson, Auckland

JU05

Published 1991 by Bantam Press
a division of Transworld Publishers Ltd
Copyright © John and Mary Gribbin 1991

British Library Cataloguing in Publication Data
Gribbin, John, *1946 –*
Blinded by the light.
1. Sun
I. Title
523.7

ISBN 0–593–02064–2

Typeset in 11/12 pt Bembo by
Photoprint, Torquay, Devon

Printed in Great Britain by
Mackays of Chatham, PLC, Chatham, Kent

BLINDED BY THE LIGHT
The Secret Life of the Sun

Contents

Acknowledgements   **ix**

Introduction   **1**

1 Ancient History   **3**
Vital statistics; the French connection; the geologists'
timescale; solar thermodynamics; Victorian genius;
Kelvin's timescales

2 Seats of Enormous Energies   **33**
Radiation revealed; energy from atoms; solving the energy
crisis; making a date with radioactivity; nuclear energy;
solar energy; simple stars

3 At the Heart of the Sun   **59**
A quantum of uncertainty; tunnelling inside stars; alchemy
in the lab; the solar pressure cooker; stellar alchemy;
stardust; the Sun inside out

4 Too Few Ghosts   **86**
The need for neutrinos; the Davis detector; forecasts that
failed; desperate remedies; speculative solutions; cosmic
connections; future projects

5 Another Wild Idea   **115**
The particle connection; cosmions are WIMPs; cosmic
connections; keeping the Sun cool; credit where due; other
stars; WIMPy connections

6 The Breathing Sun   **138**
A spot or two of bother; the shrinking Sun; the breathing
Sun; the record in the rocks; solar connections; a lunar
connection

7 The Shaking Sun   **162**
Ringing like a bell; fine tuning; first results; splitting the
difference; the triumph of the WIMP; the GONG test

8 The Large and the Small   **182**
The candidates; how to catch your WIMP; results so far;
into the future

Appendix. The Supernova Connection   **196**
Discovering a supernova; blasts from the past; back to the
present; death and glory; the supernova inside out

Bibliography   **215**

Index   **220**

ACKNOWLEDGEMENTS

This book has benefited from discussions with many astronomers at various scientific meetings over the past few years. In particular, it was John Faulkner's boyish enthusiasm for the WIMP theory that first made me aware that there was a story worth telling. Jack Eddy, Ron Gilliland and Douglas Gough should also be singled out for mention and thanks for their helpful responses to my requests for more information about their own work. Mick Kelly, Hubert Lamb and Stephen Schneider share most of the credit (if there is any to be shared) for educating me on the subject of climatic change, which features in Chapter Six.

Douglas Gough also followed John Faulkner, more years ago than any of us care to remember, in the unrewarding task of acting as my supervisor when I was a research student in Cambridge. I hope they feel that my efforts here live up to their exacting standards, and I am grateful to them for not writing a better book on the subject first.

John Gribbin
December 1989

Introduction

The Sun has always kept its secrets well. Less than a hundred years ago, nobody knew, even in general terms, how the Sun maintained its heat. Less than a human lifetime ago, nobody knew what the Sun was made of. And it is scarcely fifty years since details of the nuclear processes that fire the Sun began to become clear. For centuries, progress towards an astronomical understanding of the deep workings of the Sun was painfully slow – and it was slow for an ironic reason.

Our Sun is simply a star, much like many of the other stars we see in the night sky. It looks so bright to us simply because it is so close, a mere 150 million kilometres away. Because it is so close, and its surface so hot (roughly 6,000°C), it shines with dazzling brightness, and it is all too easy for astronomers to study the surface and the atmosphere of our neighbourhood star. But studying the deep interior – the work I describe here – is another matter entirely.

Not just astronomers, but their sensitive instruments as well, would be blinded by the light from the *surface* of the Sun if they stared at it for long. The very brightness of the surface helps to conceal the workings of the deep interior, telling us only that something, deep inside the Sun, is indeed generating enormous quantities of energy. Pioneers of astrophysics – the study of the workings of the stars – never dreamed that they would be able to see inside the heart of the Sun, and make direct measurements of the conditions there. But in recent years two entirely separate and independent probes of the solar interior have been developed. They involve such bizarre developments as a telescope buried deep beneath the ground in a mine, and instruments so sensitive that they can measure vibrations that move patches of the solar surface in and out by a few tens of metres. Even stranger, some of these new studies of the conditions deep in the heart of the Sun may be telling us important things about the evolution and ultimate fate of the whole Universe.

As we move into the 1990s, astronomers are no longer completely blinded by the light from the surface of the Sun, and are able to measure, directly, what goes on in its heart. This book tells the story of how the astrophysical pioneers began to unlock the secrets of the Sun – and points the way ahead to the way they will be probing the solar interior in the years and decades ahead.

1

Ancient History

No other object has so stirred the imagination of mankind as the Sun. In earliest times, it was worshipped as a god, since our ancestors could clearly see that the Sun brings life to Earth, and makes things grow. The ancients thought that the Sun was a ball of fire, which travelled across the sky of our planet Earth by day, and returned to its starting place, ready for the next dawn, through underground passages and caverns by night. The first recorded attempt to put these ideas on what we would nowadays regard as a scientific footing was made as long ago as the fifth century BC, by the Greek philosopher Anaxagoras, of Athens. His scientific reasoning was pretty good, as far as it went; but unfortunately the observational facts on which his reasoning was based were incomplete, so that his ideas about the Sun turn out, with hindsight, to be very misleading. Nevertheless, Anaxagoras deserves pride of place for at least making the effort to understand the Sun as a physical phenomenon, subject to the same laws as the rest of the Universe, and not simply treating it as a supernatural object beyond mortal comprehension.

One of the things which started Anaxagoras thinking about the nature of the Sun was a meteorite which fell one day at Aegospotami. The meteorite was hot, so the philosopher reasoned that it must have come from the Sun. It contained iron, so he deduced that the Sun must be made of iron. A ball of red-hot iron, moving high over the land, could certainly, as far as anyone knew in those days, provide the warmth of the Sun and the cycle of day and night. This description of the Sun was, by the standards of the day, what modern scientists would regard as a good working hypothesis, a basis for further investigations. But like all good scientific hypotheses, this one raised new questions for the philosophers to puzzle over. How big would the ball of red-hot iron have to be, and how far above the Earth was it moving?

In those days, philosophers didn't really do much in the way of experiment and observation themselves. They listened to reports of interesting phenomena, and they tried to fit the various pieces of hearsay evidence into a coherent picture. Anaxagoras himself, for example, had never travelled to the upper reaches of the River Nile, but he had heard reports from travellers who had. They said

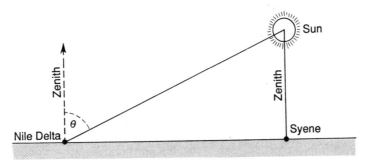

Figure 1.1   Assuming that the Earth was flat, and using the geometry of right-angled triangles, Anaxagoras calculated in the fifth century BC that the Sun must be 4,000 miles overhead.

that in the city of Syene, which was located near the present position of the Aswan dam, on the day of the summer solstice (the 'longest day') the Sun was directly overhead at noon, and cast no shadow. Now, Anaxagoras may not have been much of an experimenter or a traveller, but he knew his geometry, and he also knew that at noon on the day of the summer solstice the Sun at the Nile Delta, about 500 miles north of Syene, made an angle of about 7 degrees with the vertical. Since he 'knew' that the Earth was flat, Anaxagoras was quickly able to calculate the height of the Sun above the Earth, using the straightforward geometrical properties of right-angled triangles (Figure 1.1). He found that the Sun was just 4,000 miles above the heads of the observers at Syene. And because he also knew the apparent size of the Sun (its angular diameter, about half a degree), he was also able to calculate, from the geometry of triangles, how big the Sun must really be in order to appear the size it does to our eyes. His estimate, about 35 miles for the diameter of the Sun, suggested that it was very similar in size to the southern peninsula of Greece, the Peloponnesus.

This was a shocking and subversive suggestion to make in

Greece in the fifth century BC. Anaxagoras was first arrested for heresy, and then banished forever from his home city of Athens – treatment very similar to the fate which Galileo Galilei suffered at the hands of the religious authorities of his day when he, too, dared to suggest that the Sun was a natural phenomenon. That, however, came more than two thousand years later, in the seventeenth century. For all that time, from Anaxagoras to Galileo, nobody, as far as we know, attempted to understand the Sun in scientific terms – a dark age, indeed. But even in the twentieth century, when we like to think we are more open-minded, and understand the Universe in which we live better than any of our predecessors, the example of Anaxagoras is worth taking to heart. Even his mistakes can teach us a great deal about science, and about the hazards of complacency.

The speculation that the Sun might be a ball of red-hot iron was quite reasonable at the time, and Anaxagoras cannot be faulted for that. His geometrical calculation of the height of the Sun above a flat Earth was also impeccable. Where he made his big mistake was in taking for granted what 'everyone knew' to be true – that the Earth was flat. Only a couple of hundred years later, another Greek philosopher, Eratosthenes, used exactly the same evidence to calculate the diameter of the spherical Earth. Whereas Anaxagoras assumed the Earth was flat, and deduced that therefore the Sun was just 4,000 miles above it, Eratosthenes assumed that the Sun was so far away that rays of light from the Sun reach the Earth as parallel lines, and he used the measured angle of the Sun below the vertical at the solstice, as viewed from the Nile Delta, to calculate the diameter of the Earth (Figure 1.2). Because the angle involved in the geometrical calculation is the same, he got the same 'answer', 4,000 miles; but he interpreted this as the radius of the Earth, not the height of the Sun above the Earth. We now have an overwhelming weight of other evidence which shows that Eratosthenes was more or less correct in his reasoning.

But the moral to this tale is not that Anaxagoras was 'wrong' and Eratosthenes was 'right'. Good scientists don't regard even their best theories as being 'right' in any absolute sense. There are simply good theories and bad theories. Good theories enable you to make accurate predictions about the way things will behave in the real world; bad theories make inaccurate, or unreliable, predictions. The best theories, such as general relativity, are so very good indeed that they have never been found to make an inaccurate prediction. But even lesser theories, such as Newton's theory of gravity, may be perfectly adequate for many purposes, provided their limitations are understood.

In that sense, the two ideas about the relationship of the Sun and Earth provided by the two Greek philosophers form a good set of hypotheses. The geometrical evidence obtained by observing the height of the Sun at the Nile Delta and at Syene tells us *either* that the Earth is flat and the Sun is 4,000 miles above it *or* that the Sun is at a vast distance and the Earth is a sphere with a radius of 4,000

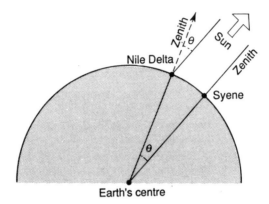

Figure 1.2　Assuming that the Earth was round, and that the Sun is at a vast distance, a later Greek philosopher, Eratosthenes, used the same geometrical calculation as Anaxagoras to infer that the radius of the Earth must be about 4,000 miles. Both calculations were correct; it was Anaxagoras's assumption that was wrong.

miles. The evidence available at the time was consistent with either possibility. Only further observations and measurements could reveal which hypothesis was correct. Together, the two interpretations of the one set of data make good science. But the lesson to be drawn from the tale is that even a radical and far-sighted thinker, who was not afraid to fall foul of the established authorities of the day in his search for the truth, could not rid himself of the dogma of the flat Earth. Anaxagoras was so certain that the Earth was flat that he never questioned the assumption – otherwise he, and not Eratosthenes, might have been credited with the first accurate measurement of its radius. The history of science is littered with such unfortunate examples of theories that are argued with complete logic and perfect accuracy, but which start out from a basis of unquestioning faith in something which later turns out to be completely untrue. The true scientific method is to take nothing for granted; but some assumptions, like the flatness of the Earth in Anaxagoras's day, are so deeply ingrained that they are hard to eradicate.

If I seem to have laboured the point, the reasons will soon become clear. The story of how astronomers developed an understanding of the way the Sun maintains its internal fires is full of similar examples of things that seem blindingly obvious to one generation being totally rejected by the next. No theory is any better than the assumptions that are built in to it, and the only real test of a theory is its predictive power. By those criteria, the story I have to tell may lead in unexpected directions, but it follows an inevitable path. It is concerned primarily with the interior of the Sun – the secret Sun – and how it has maintained a steady supply of heat for thousands of billions of years. This only became a puzzle for scientists in the nineteenth century, when the discovery of the laws of thermodynamics revealed that nothing, not even the Sun, could stay hot forever. In terms of the history of astronomy, even nineteenth-century science is ancient history; but before we move on to the main theme of our story, I should, perhaps, explain why astronomers today are so confident that, unlike Anaxagoras, they really do have a good idea of how far away the Sun is, how big it is, and how hot.

Vital statistics

Distances to astronomical objects, including the Moon and nearer planets, can indeed be measured using the same basic technique, triangulation, that Anaxagoras tried to use to determine the distance to the Sun. This is exactly the technique used by surveyors and mapmakers here on Earth. If we want to know the distance to a landmark, such as a high mountain, that it would be inconvenient to travel to, we can simply measure an accurate baseline, place surveying instruments at either end and line them up on the landmark. By measuring the angle from each end of the baseline to the landmark, we can calculate the length of the sides of an imaginary triangle stretching out from the baseline with the landmark at its tip. The further away things are, of course, the more subtle the measurements become. The Sun is too far away for the technique to work. The difference in the angles measured at either end of the baseline is too small to detect. But it is fairly simple, using this technique, to establish that the distance from the Earth to the Moon is about 60 times the radius of the Earth.

Similar geometrical techniques provided the first estimates of the distances to the nearest planets, Venus and Mars; in the second half of the twentieth century, such measurements have been improved by bouncing radar echoes off these planets and calculating the distances on the basis of the time it takes for the radio pulses, travelling at the speed of light, to travel there and back again. Either way, the key measurement is the distance to Venus, because Venus orbits the Sun within the orbit of the Earth. Since the orbits are tilted slightly, we don't actually see Venus pass across the face of the Sun in every orbit. But on the rare occasions when Venus does pass across the face of the Sun, as viewed from Earth, it can be used to provide a measurement of the distance to the Sun.

The technique depends on making simultaneous observations (or taking simultaneous photographs) from two widely separated observatories. Each observer watches the dark spot of Venus moving across the solar disk. Because the two observatories are viewing the transit of Venus across the Sun from different angles, they will see the planet's image against different parts of the solar background, as a result of the parallax effect (Figure 1.3; the effect is greatly exaggerated here, but you can see parallax for yourself by holding up a finger at arm's length in front of a distinctive background, then closing each of your eyes in turn and watching the finger 'move' across the background). In particular, the moment at which Venus crosses the edge of the Sun's disk will be different as viewed from the different observatories. Once the distance from Earth to Venus is known, together with the distance between the two observatories, it is straightforward to calculate the distance from either observatory to the Sun.

All of these, and other observations, give the same result. The average distance from the Earth to the Sun ('average' because the distance varies slightly during the year) is 149,597,893 kilometres. In round terms, amply accurate enough for our needs in this book, we can call it 150 million kilometres, or 93 million miles. Astronomers regard this as such a fundamental measure of distance that they also call it the Astronomical Unit, or AU, and measure distances to other stars in terms of the AU.

How can we put this distance into perspective? It takes light, travelling at 300,000 kilometres per second, a full 8 minutes and 20 seconds to travel from the Sun to the Earth – but the speed of light is itself too big to be familiar to us. The fastest object which any ordinary person is likely to encounter is a jet airliner, which might travel at a speed of 800 kilometres per hour. As a passenger inside such a vehicle, you could cross the Atlantic in a few hours, or travel from New York to Sydney in little more than a day. But if you could keep airborne long enough to fly the equivalent of the distance from the Earth to the Sun, you would be flying, non-stop, for 21 years.

Space really is big, and so is the Sun. If the Sun is so far away, then, obviously, it must be a lot bigger than the 35-mile diameter calculated by Anaxagoras when he thought it was just 4,000 miles above the Earth. In order to show as a disk half a degree across at a

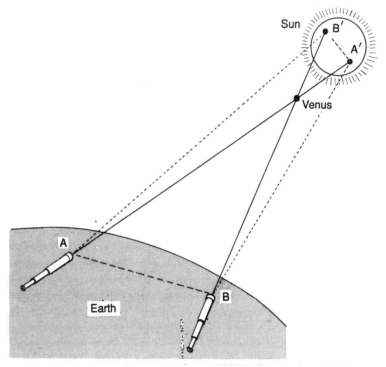

Figure 1.3 Observers in different places on Earth see Venus against different parts of the Sun's face. The difference helps them to calculate the distance to the Sun.

distance of 150 million kilometres, the Sun must, in fact, be 1,390,500 kilometres across, 109 times the diameter of the Earth. We know how far away the Sun is, and how big it is. How much matter does it contain?

One way of measuring the quantity of matter is by volume. With a diameter just over a hundred times the diameter of the Earth, the Sun is a million times bigger than the Earth, in the sense that a million globes the size of the Earth could fit within a globe the size of the Sun. This is because volume goes as diameter cubed, and 100 cubed is 1,000,000 (written in mathematical shorthand as 10^6; similarly, a billion, written in full as a 1 followed by nine zeroes, can be abbreviated as 10^9, and so on). The distance from the centre of the Sun to its surface is roughly twice the distance from the Earth to the Moon; while a hundred Earths side by side would just stretch across the Sun, a hundred Suns side by side would stretch from the Sun to the Earth. But none of this tells us how much mass the Sun contains.

It is the amount of matter in the Sun that determines the strength of its gravitational pull, holding the planets in their orbits around it. Isaac Newton discovered the law of gravity, the rule which says that the force pulling two bodies together depends on their two masses, multiplied together and divided by the square of the distance between them, all multiplied by a constant, the gravitational constant, written as G. In the eighteenth century, Henry Cavendish carried out a series of painstaking measurements, using large and small masses in the laboratory, and obtained a value for G. Once this was known, it was easy to calculate the mass of the Earth, by measuring the force with which the Earth pulls on an object – its weight. The distance that comes into the equation is simply the distance to the centre of the Earth, the Earth's radius, which Eratosthenes showed us how to measure; and the calculated mass of the planet is just under 6 × 10^{27} grams (that is, a 6 followed by 27 zeroes). So the average density of the Earth is 5.5 times the density of water.

With the mass of the Earth determined, astronomers immediately knew the mass of the Sun. The Earth orbits the Sun once every year, at a distance of 150 million km, so astronomers know how fast it must be moving in its orbit. The force required to hold a planet in this orbit is known from basic physics. It doesn't matter whether the planet is being held in place by a long piece of string fastened at the centre of the Solar System or by the gravity of the Sun; the force has to be the same. And from the known mass of the Earth and distance to the Sun, the only way to provide the right gravitational force is if the Sun itself has a mass of just under 2 × 10^{33} grams. The Sun has a mass of a third of a million Earths, occupying the volume of a million Earths. Overall, therefore, its average density is only one third that of the Earth, just about 1.5 times the density of water. That doesn't sound particularly impressive, but remember that it is an *average*. As we shall see, although the outer layers of the Sun are composed of tenuous layers of gas, deep down inside the density, pressure and temperature build up dramatically. But first, we need some idea of how much heat the Sun is radiating at its surface.

I won't go into all the historical details here, because there is a beautifully simple example of the power of solar radiation which astronomer Herbert Friedman provides in his book *Sun and Earth.** Friedman tells how C. A. Young, of Princeton University, used to put the point across to his students by starting off from the observation, made by William Herschel in the late eighteenth century, that the heat of the noonday Sun in summer would be able to melt a layer of ice one inch thick in 2 hours and 12 minutes.

This only begins to seem truly impressive when you realize that as far as we know the Sun is pouring out radiation equally energetically in all directions. So if there is enough energy to melt a piece of ice one inch thick that quickly at the point where the Earth in its orbit happens to intercept the Sunlight, there must also be the same amount of energy crossing every square centimetre of space at the same distance from the Sun. In other words, there is enough energy pouring out of the Sun to melt a whole shell of ice, one inch thick and 300 million km in diameter, in 2 hours and 12 minutes. Young used to ask his students to imagine this shell of ice shrinking in diameter, closing in on the Sun so that its area got less and less, but with its thickness increasing so that it always included the same total amount of ice. By the time the inner surface was touching the surface of the Sun, this imaginary layer of ice would be more than a mile thick, but it would still be thawed in exactly the same brief span of time.

The temperature of the surface of the Sun, sufficient to achieve this feat, is 5,770K.† We can calculate this today by measuring the amount of heat arriving at each square centimetre of the Earth's surface (or, indeed, warming the detectors on a satellite in space), and making suitable allowance for the distance to the Sun. There is also another way to measure the temperature of a hot object, from its colour. Just as a white-hot piece of iron is hotter than a red-hot piece of iron, so a blue or white star is hotter than a yellow or orange star. This colour-temperature connection follows a precise law, studied in detail in laboratory experiments, and can be quantified. The figure we end up with is still the same – the temperature of a yellowish star like our Sun is about 6,000K.

---

* Details of titles cited in the text can be found, with other books of interest, in the Bibliography.
† Measured from the thermodynamic zero point of temperature, −273°C.

This is not, in truth, a particularly remarkable figure. The glowing filament of an electric light bulb runs at about 2,000K, and although it is a little hotter than red-hot iron, the *surface* of the Sun, at least, is not at a temperature that even Anaxagoras would have had any difficulty comprehending. The trouble came in the nineteenth century, when geologists and evolutionary biologists began to appreciate the extreme age of the Earth, and pointed out that the Sun must have been shining this brightly for many hundreds, probably thousands, of millions of years.

This posed a major problem for science, because it was also at about this time that physicists began to appreciate that the laws of thermodynamics and conservation of energy set very strict limits on how long the Sun could maintain its present-day output of energy. By all the known laws of nineteenth-century physics, there was simply no way in which the Sun could have stayed hot as long as geology and biology seemed to require. Were the geologists and biologists wrong? Or was the understanding of physics deficient? One of the greatest scientists of the day was convinced that, if something had to give, it certainly was not going to be the laws of physics, and he mounted a determined attack on anyone who dared to suggest otherwise. And yet, the weight of geological evidence certainly had to be taken seriously.

The French connection

As recently as the eighteenth century, it was widely accepted that the Earth was created about 6,000 years ago. In 1654, John Lightfoot had refined a famous calculation originally made, earlier in the seventeenth century, by Archbishop Ussher. This refinement set the moment of the creation as 9 AM, Mesopotamian time, on 26 October, 4004 BC on the Julian calendar. The estimate had no basis in scientific calculation or observation, but was arrived at simply by counting back the generations referred to in the Bible, from Jesus Christ back to Adam. Today, even theologians accept that the Bible should not be taken literally at that level, and that the Earth, our Sun and the Universe at large have been around for a vastly greater span of time than even our recent ancestors could have imagined. The first attempt to extend the timescale, the first real scientific estimate of the age of the Earth, only pushed this out to 75,000 years or so, still far short of the figure calculated today. But this still increased the age tenfold, and it flew in the face of established religious doctrine, just as Anaxagoras had rejected religious doctrine in his approach to the problem of the nature of the Sun. Georges-Louis Leclerc, Comte de Buffon, who made the calculation, did not suffer the same fate as Anaxagoras, however, and it took less time for the seed he planted to bear fruit.

Buffon, as he became when he inherited the title and an estate in his mid-twenties, was born in 1707 at Montbard, in Burgundy. He was the son of a magistrate, and received a good education, studying first law and then mathematics and science. His formal education, at Angers, was cut short when he had to leave following a duel, and in the early 1730s he travelled to Italy and England. When his mother died and he came into his inheritance, Buffon returned home and settled down. He made his mark as a gentleman scientist – rich enough to investigate whatever interested him, but serious enough (and able enough) to produce valuable contributions to knowledge. After Buffon had carried out some important research on the strength of timber – a crucial military material in those days – the delighted minister of the navy used his influence to have him installed in 1739 as the keeper of the Jardin du Roi in Paris. He managed the botanical gardens, and the associated museum, for almost half a century, doubling the area under cultivation and acquiring many new specimens.

Buffon's great work, his *Histoire naturelle*, started out as a catalogue of the king's museum, but grew into an attempt to describe the whole of the natural world, in a projected fifty volumes. He only lived to complete thirty-six of them, and died in 1788. But he had done more than enough to make his mark on eighteenth-century science.

Most of Buffon's work had no direct bearing on the puzzle of the nature of the Sun, but among his many interests he worried about the age of the Earth. Buffon was not convinced that the heat of the Sun was enough to keep the Earth warm, and he assumed that heat from inside the Earth was essential to provide conditions suitable for life. Since he knew of no way in which heat could be generated inside the Earth today, he also assumed that the Earth had been formed as a molten ball of rock, and had been cooling down ever since. The molten, primeval Earth, he suggested, had been torn out of the Sun by a collision with a passing comet; but how long would it have taken to cool to its present state?

Newton had pointed out, in his *Principia*, that a globe of red-hot iron as big as the Earth would take 50,000 years to cool down. Buffon actually carried out experiments with balls of iron and other substances of different sizes, observing how long it took for them to cool down from red heat. Armed with this information, and the accurate knowledge scientists already had of the size of the Earth, he improved Newton's calculation, suggesting that if the Earth had been born in a molten state it would have taken 36,000 years to cool to the point where life could appear, and a further 39,000 years (75,000 in all) to cool to its present temperature.

Theologians of the day, naturally, attacked this extension of the timescale of Earth history. But at least Buffon wasn't sent into exile, and his ideas, breaking completely with religious dogma, had a lasting influence after his death, into the nineteenth century.*

The direct line of Buffon's influence on subsequent generations of scientists was through Jean Fourier, who is best remembered today for his development of the mathematical tool known as Fourier series, developed as Fourier (or harmonic) analysis. In fact, Fourier, who was born in 1768 in Auxerre, was primarily a physicist, and developed his mathematics as a means to an end, in order to be able to analyse accurately interesting physical problems.† In particular, he was fascinated by the problem of providing an accurate means to calculate the way in which heat is transferred through an object; the attention which Buffon's estimate of the age of the Earth gained led Fourier to his own study of heat conduction, and on to the mathematics he needed to describe the process. Buffon had simply measured the rate at which hot objects cooled, and tried to extrapolate this up to an object the size of the Earth. Fourier, on the other hand, tried to develop laws – mathematical equations – to describe the rate at which heat could escape from a body, and used them to calculate how long it would have taken the Earth to cool. On this picture, the Earth must be coolest on the outside, but still at the temperature of molten rock at its centre, even today (that means a

---

* Buffon's son, born in 1764, came to a more sticky end. Although the boy showed signs of a brilliant mind, he was not interested in academic (or any other) work and became a spendthrift and wastrel, like so many members of the French aristocracy of the time. And, like them, he went to the guillotine, in 1794. There can hardly be a better example to young people of the importance of working hard at your studies!

† He was primarily a physicist, that is, as far as his scientific interests went. He was also politically active at the time of the French Revolution, and accompanied Napoleon on his expedition to Egypt. He was in charge of the publication of the 21-volume *Description de l'Egypte* which came out of that expedition and which established 'egyptology' as a branch of study. Back in France, Fourier became an able administrator, eventually rising to become prefect of the Rhône department and being appointed first a baron and then a count by Napoleon – but that didn't stop him resigning during the last days of Napoleon's rule in protest against the excesses of the regime. Strictly speaking, much of his scientific work was carried out as a hobby, in his spare time – including what seems to have been the first scientific mention of what we now know as the greenhouse effect.

temperature above 6,000K, more than the temperature at the *surface* of the Sun today). There is a steady fall in temperature – a thermal gradient – from the inside to the outside, and a steady flow of heat outwards. Because the layers of cooler material surrounding the hot core act as an insulating blanket, holding heat in, it takes much longer for the Earth to cool, according to these estimates, than even Buffon had realized. In 1820, Fourier wrote down the formula for the age of the Earth based on these arguments; but as far as anyone has been able to find out, he never wrote down the number which comes out of this formula. Perhaps he regarded the value he had derived for the age of the Earth as too big to be taken seriously – for, instead of Buffon's 75 *thousand* years, Fourier's equations implied an age for the Earth of 100 *million* years.

The figure caused no immediate stir, simply because it wasn't publicized. Fourier himself died in 1830, and it was to be another thirty years before essentially the same calculation was taken up and promoted widely as indicating the true age of the Earth. But by then, so rapid had been the pace of change that the enthusiastic promoter of this timescale, William Thomson,* was making the case that 100 million years was such a *short* timescale that it ought to be causing embarrassment to the geologists and evolutionists.

The geologists' timescale

One of the most basic tenets of modern geological science is the idea that only the same sort of processes that we see at work on Earth today – erosion, volcanic activity, earthquakes and so on – are needed to explain how the world got into its present state, provided that there has been enough time for the forces of wind and weather, and the rest, to do their work. The notion seems as natural to us as the notion of a flat Earth did to Anaxagoras, and would pass without comment (except, perhaps, for a muttered plea to get on with it?) as part of a prefatory introduction to geophysics. But this 'obvious' idea only surfaced in the late eighteenth century, when it was put forward by the Scot James Hutton, a contemporary of Buffon; and it only became an established fact of scientific life in the nineteenth century, after a vigorous debate between the 'uniformitarians', who held that the Earth has always been much the same as we see it now, and the 'catastrophists', who argued that such dramatic features as

* Later Lord Kelvin.

mountain ranges and ocean basins could only have been created during epochs of great upheaval and turmoil, when the Earth was wracked in the grip of mysterious and perhaps supernatural forces.

Hutton, who was born in 1726 and was the son of a merchant, was intended by his family to follow a career as a lawyer, but turned instead to chemistry. With a friend, John Davie, he invented a method for production of the valuable industrial chemical ammonium chloride, and made enough money out of this, together with a modest inheritance, to set himself up as a gentleman farmer in Berwickshire. The farm, too, was successful; but while he was involved in agriculture Hutton became interested in the effect of running water on rocks and soil, and he made several trips, ostensibly to study farming techniques, to the continent, where he took advantage of every opportunity to learn more about rocks and minerals. In 1768, financially independent, he returned to Edinburgh, and he spent the rest of his life in scientific work, mainly geology.

Hutton's uniformitarian ideas appeared in print first in a scientific paper published in 1788, and later in a book, *Theory of the Earth*, in 1795, shortly before his death. Although the ideas provoked a strong response from some critics in the 1790s, Hutton's rather impenetrable writing style meant that they did not reach a wide audience until 1802, when his friend John Playfair published an edited version of the work under the title *Illustration of the Huttonian Theory*. This was the point at which the idea began to be taken seriously, and geologists began to divide into two camps, for and against.

Uniformitarianism is so well accepted now that there is no need to labour the point, but it is worth noting that Hutton was the first person to point out, for example, that the heat of the Earth could explain, without any supernatural intervention, how sedimentary rocks, laid down by water, could be fused into granites and flints. Heat from inside the Earth, he said, was also responsible for pushing up mountain chains and twisting geological strata. But, as Hutton realized, this would take a very long time indeed.

His style may have been impenetrable, but Hutton did come up with one particularly striking example. The forces of erosion work very slowly today, and this is neatly shown by the fact that Roman roads are still visible, more than two thousand years after they were laid down. Clearly the time required for such slow processes to carve the face of the Earth into its modern appearance must be vastly longer than the biblical 6,000 years. Hutton regarded the age of the Earth as beyond comprehension, writing that 'we find no vestige of a beginning – no prospect of an end.'

Hutton's pioneering idea was taken up and developed in the nineteenth century by another Scot, Charles Lyell, who was born in 1797, the year Hutton died. Like Hutton, Lyell was steered by his family towards a career in law. He was actually admitted to the bar in 1825; but, also like Hutton, his interest in science, especially geology, diverted him from a legal career. In the late 1820s, Lyell was able to travel extensively on the continent – his father was wealthy enough to support him – and everywhere he went he saw evidence of the way natural forces could mould the features of the Earth. The region around Mount Etna, in particular, provided striking reinforcement for the ideas he already held. The fruits of Lyell's travels appeared in his three-volume work *Principles of Geology*. The first volume was published in 1830, the second in 1831 and the third in 1833. The subtitle of Volume One says it all: 'Being an Attempt to Explain the Former Changes of the Earth's Surface by Reference to Causes now in Operation'.

Lyell's books caused an immediate stir, and made a particularly striking impression on a young naturalist just setting off on a voyage in HMS *Beagle*. Charles Darwin took Volume One with him; Volume Two caught up with him during the voyage, and Volume Three was waiting for him when he returned home in 1836. Darwin never failed to acknowledge his debt to Lyell, who showed him that the Earth was very old indeed, and that all that was needed to explain its present appearance was the same set of forces that we see at work today. Lyell applied that doctrine to the rocks; Darwin applied it, with equal success, to living things. Evolution by natural selection required, above all else, a long timescale in which to operate, and Lyell gave Darwin that timescale.

The two scientists became firm friends in later life, although Lyell was slow to come round to the idea of evolution. After the *Origin of Species* was published in 1859, however, Lyell gradually allowed himself to be persuaded by Darwin's evidence, and lent his support to Darwin in a major new edition of *Principles of Geology*, published in 1865. This counted for a lot; Lyell was by then a knight and a friend of both the royal family and politicians, and held many professional honours, as well as being widely known to the general public. By standing up to be counted alongside Darwin, at a time when opposition to Darwin's ideas was fierce, he persuaded many other people that there must be something in this evolution business, after all. Darwin was delighted, and commented 'considering his age, his former views, and position in society, I think his action has been heroic.'

Just at that time, however, both Darwin and Lyell were coming under attack, not from religious fundamentalists but from physicists who argued that no known natural processes could have provided conditions suitable for life on Earth for long enough for geological processes to have shaped the planet, or for evolution to have produced the diversity of life we see today. There was no obvious answer to this criticism, which had to be taken seriously. Biology and geology seemed to be telling scientists that the Earth, and the Sun, were much older than was physically possible.

Solar thermodynamics

Fourier's work on the mathematics of how heat flows from one place to another became part of one of the greatest achievements of nineteenth-century science, thermodynamics. The realization that heat energy is exactly equivalent to mechanical energy (work), that heat flows only from a hotter object to a cooler one, never the other way (the second law of thermodynamics), and that the amount of disorder (entropy) in the Universe is always increasing ('things wear out', expressed in rigorous mathematical terms) revolutionized science and made it possible for physicists to investigate and quantify many phenomena that had previously been inexplicable in strictly scientific terms. One of those phenomena – by no means regarded, at the time, as the most important piece of nature to be caught in the thermodynamic net – was the age of the Earth and Sun.★

In the decades following Fourier's death, the realization that energy and heat could be quantified, and that the energy even of sunlight might be a limited resource, began, slowly, to spread. A few scientists began to worry about the profligate way in which the Sun pours energy out into space, and to wonder where the energy came from, and how long the supply might last. In those days, anyone who puzzled about such things naturally thought in terms of the energy produced by burning coal, the basic power supply that was fuelling the Industrial Revolution. Today, we can update those calculations by thinking in terms of the modern successor to coal, gasolene. If the Sun were made entirely of

★ For more about the broad sweep of thermodynamics, see *The Omega Point* by John Gribbin and *The Second Law* by Peter Atkins.

gasolene, burning in the most efficient way possible, then it could maintain its present heat for only a few tens of thousands of years. The same is true of any form of chemical burning, in which energy is released as atoms combine together into molecular arrangements which are more efficient, in energy terms, than the arrangements they were in before combustion. No form of chemical energy can keep the Sun hot for more than a few tens of thousands of years.

It took some time for the message to sink in, and for physicists to appreciate its importance. The first two people known to have tackled the problem head on were both largely ignored at the time, and although they have received some belated credit for their work, in view of the way they were treated it seems quite possible that some completely forgotten scientific hero may have been thinking along the same lines before either of them. As far as anyone now knows, however, the first person to express the law of conservation of energy, which says that energy can be converted from one form into another, but can never be created or destroyed, was Julius Mayer, a German physician living in Heilbronn.

Mayer was born in 1814, in that same city, and studied medicine at the University of Tübingen and in Vienna and Paris. In 1840 he took a post as ship's physician on a vessel sailing to the East Indies. In those days bleeding a patient was still an accepted part of medical routine, and when Mayer bled some of the crew of the ship during their sojourn in the tropics, he was surprised at the bright red colour of the blood from their veins. Coming from Europe, Mayer was used to a different appearance of arterial and venous blood. Arterial blood is bright red, because it is carrying plenty of oxygen from the lungs to the muscles and other tissues of the body; venous blood, returning to the lungs, is a much darker, purplish-red, because it is depleted in oxygen. Or so Mayer had always thought; when he opened the vein of a sailor in Java, however, he thought at first he had cut an artery by mistake, because the blood was so red. When he found that he had not made a mistake, and that the venous blood of all the sailors was just as red, Mayer was alert enough to realize that this must mean, first that the venous blood was carrying more oxygen than it did in colder climates, and secondly that this must be because the body needed less oxygen in order to maintain body temperature in warmer climates. He knew of the idea, pioneered by Antoine Lavoisier in the eighteenth century, that warm-blooded animals keep themselves warm by a form of slow combustion in the body, in which food is combined with oxygen; and he made the great intuitive leap to the conclusion that work (such as muscular exertion), heat (including the warmth of the body), and other forms of energy (such as the chemical energy released by oxidation of food, or by burning coal), are all interchangeable, and that work or energy is never created but only transformed from one form to another.

Mayer returned to Germany in 1841, and settled down in Heilbronn as a general medical practitioner. He had a successful practice, but remained intrigued by these new ideas on the nature of heat, teaching himself physics, carrying out experiments (not very adroitly, it seems) and publishing the first scientific papers on such important topics as the way mechanical energy is converted into heat when air is compressed in a pump, and what should have been a key discussion of the energy source of the Sun. Yet his work was almost completely ignored at the time, and when the same ideas were discovered independently by other people, who began to get a great deal of publicity and credit, Mayer became so depressed that he attempted suicide in 1850, and spent several years in a mental institution. After 1858, however, his work began to be recognized, his health recovered and he received many accolades before his death in 1878.

The other pioneer of solar thermodynamics fared even worse than Mayer. John Waterston was born in 1811 in Edinburgh, and as a young man he was allowed time off from his work as a civil engineer to study at Edinburgh University. He began publishing articles – scientific papers – in the research journals in 1830, and kept up his scientific activities after he moved to London in 1833 to work on the rapidly growing railway system. In 1839 Waterston went to India, where he worked as a teacher of the East India Company's cadets; by saving hard he was able to retire in 1857 and return to Edinburgh to devote himself to research. But he had increasing difficulty in getting his papers published, and became a bitter recluse; on 18 June 1883 he walked out of his home and was never seen again.

The turning point in Waterston's life had come as early as 1845, when he sent a paper to the Royal Society in London, spelling out some important new ideas of what is now known as the kinetic theory of gases. Waterston showed how energy is distributed among the atoms or molecules of a gas, an important step forward in what became the branch of science known as statistical mechanics. The Royal Society, after consulting two experts who were unimpressed by the efforts of this largely unknown teacher writing from half a world away, decided not to publish the paper, and left it lying, forgotten, in their files. Waterston, in those days before the typewriter and the photocopier, had neglected to keep a copy of the paper himself, and he never reworked it fully for publication anywhere else. Although briefer summaries of his ideas were published and circulated, it was nearly fifteen years before his basic discoveries in kinetic theory were rediscovered, independently, by other researchers who took all the credit. It was only in 1891, too late to do Waterston any practical good, that his paper was found in the vaults of the Royal Society by Lord Rayleigh, the secretary of the society at the time, who had it published in 1892, establishing Waterston's priority to the idea and adding a warning to young scientists about the reluctance of learned societies to accept new ideas.

During his time in India, probably in the late 1840s, Waterston had also developed his ideas about the thermodynamics of the Sun, and he did receive some credit for these after they were presented to a meeting of the British Association in 1853, and published shortly after. Ironically, however, the one piece of Waterston's work which did make a minor splash in the scientific community was itself at least partly pre-dated by Mayer's work along similar lines, which had been carried out a few years before, but was then virtually unknown. What both Mayer and Waterston realized was that if chemical energy was insufficient to maintain the heat of the Sun for more than a few tens of thousands of years, then it must be powered by the only other source of energy known to nineteenth-century science which might keep the Sun hot for a longer period of time – gravity. In terms of the conservation of energy, what they needed was some reservoir of energy which could be drawn on steadily for millions of years and converted into heat. Gravity might fit the bill, if a way of converting gravitational energy into heat could be discovered.

Both Mayer and Waterston suggested that the Sun might be kept hot if it were 'fuelled' by a continuous supply of meteors falling on it from space. This is a source of energy which comes directly from the gravitational field of the Sun. When a meteor – essentially, a lump of rock – in space falls towards the Sun, it does so, as Newton realized, because of the mutual gravitational attraction – or force – between the Sun and the meteor. Gravitational energy is converted into kinetic energy, energy of motion, as the meteor falls faster and faster. When the fast-moving rock hits the surface of the Sun and stops, all that energy has to go somewhere. In exactly the same way, when a fast-moving car is brought to a halt using its brakes, all the energy of motion of the car has to go somewhere. In the case of the car, the energy is converted into heat in the brakes, and can easily be felt if you hold your hand near the brake disks or drums just after the vehicle has stopped; in the case of a meteor falling onto the Sun (or, indeed, onto the Earth) the kinetic energy is also converted into heat, raising the temperature of both the meteor and whatever it happens to hit. When a meteor strikes the Earth, the impact can melt rock explosively, blasting out a huge crater with the power of many millions of tons of TNT – far bigger than any man-made explosion, including nuclear blasts. Because the Sun contains more mass than the Earth, it has a correspondingly stronger gravitational field, meteors fall that much faster when they hit the Sun, and the energy released is even greater than it would be if the same meteor struck the Earth.

In principle, you could indeed make the Sun hot in this way, if there were enough meteors around to fall onto it. There is nothing in the laws of physics which says that it is impossible to heat a star in this way. In the real Universe, however, there are nowhere near enough meteors around to do the job. Waterston himself realized this, and later modified his argument to suggest that the Sun might maintain its internal heat by gradually contracting, shrinking down upon itself. This, too, would convert gravitational energy into heat, and this basic idea became the cornerstone of the arguments used by physicists in the second half of the nineteenth century to 'prove' that the Sun could not have existed in its present form for more than 100 million years. Having given due credit to the pioneering efforts of Mayer and Waterston, however, the best way to appreciate the full impact of the calculations which provided such a contrast with the timescales required by Darwin and the geologists is to look at the work of the man who became the supreme advocate of this gravitational timescale – William Thomson, who later became Lord Kelvin.

Victorian genius

William Thomson was born with the scientific equivalent of a silver spoon in his mouth, and had the ability to take full advantage of the unusual opportunities he was given. When he was born, in 1824, his father was the Professor of Mathematics at Belfast University, and both William and his older brother James were educated at home. They were taught as children the latest mathematical ideas, still new to university lecturers (let alone students) at the time, and both of them went on to become successful scientists, although William was by far the outstanding physicist in the family (indeed, ranking with James Clerk Maxwell as one of the two greatest physicists produced by Britain in the nineteenth century). In 1832, their father became Professor of Mathematics at Glasgow University, where William became a student at the age of ten, in 1834. In 1841, still only seventeen, he moved on to Cambridge University, graduating near the top of his year in 1845. By then, he had already begun to publish scientific papers – his first efforts, written when he was sixteen and seventeen, provided English readers with a summary and 'defence' of Fourier's work on heat flow, which Thomson had read in French but which was not very well known in Britain up to then. Thomson developed the idea that Fourier's equations could be used not just to describe the flow of heat, but to calculate the flow of energy in general, including fluids moving through a pipe and electricity flowing along a cable.

After he graduated from Cambridge, Thomson worked in Paris for a time, but in 1846 the position of Professor of Natural Philosophy became vacant at the University of Glasgow. Thanks to a careful campaign mounted by his father (and, of course, his own obvious ability), Thomson was elected to the post – at the age of twenty-two. He stayed there for the rest of his career, retiring fifty-three years later in 1899. Although the puzzle of the age of the Earth and Sun was a lifelong fascination for Thomson, this was just one of the many facets of his glittering scientific career. In 1851, he put forward the second law of thermodynamics, that heat cannot flow from a colder object to a hotter one. He developed the scale of temperatures which starts from the absolute zero of temperature, $-273°C$, the temperature at which, thermodynamics predicts, all the thermal motion of the molecules and atoms in an object, jostling against one another, is stilled. In his honour, the temperature scale is now known as the Kelvin scale, with degrees the same size as degrees Celsius, but starting from absolute zero and with 0°C, for example, given as 273K (*without* the 'degrees' symbol).

Even these achievements, however, did not provide the basis for Thomson's fame in the public eye in Victorian England. That came for his work on the design of the first successful telegraph cable laid across the Atlantic, putting Fourier's equations to good, practical use; he was knighted by Queen Victoria for this work in 1866, and became a rich man out of the royalties on his cable patents (and other inventions). The elevation to the peerage, as

Baron Kelvin of Largs, came in 1892 as a further recognition of his broad achievements in engineering and physics.

The public knew him best as a brilliant inventor, in the great Victorian tradition. But this eminently practical man of science had also been puzzling over the more esoteric theory of the age of the Earth ever since he had formulated the second law of thermodynamics in 1851. For, as Thomson immediately realized, the second law tells us that the Earth is getting colder and cannot live forever – things wear out. In 1852, he wrote:

> Within a finite period of time past the earth must have been, and within a finite period of time to come the earth must again be, unfit for the habitation of man as at present constituted, unless operations have been, or are to be performed which are impossible under the laws to which the known operations going on at the present in the material world are subject.★

But Thomson did not immediately follow up this broad conclusion with any detailed calculations of the age of the Earth – partly because, as historian Joe Burchfield disarmingly expresses it, he was 'diverted' to the problem of solar energy.† It was at the annual meeting of the British Association in 1853 that Waterston's version of the proposal that the Sun might be kept hot by meteors falling onto it was aired. Thomson was immediately taken with the idea, and set out to calculate how long the Sun could be kept hot by such means.

Thomson spent a lot of time trying to make the meteor idea work, but eventually he had to admit defeat. There is no need to go through all the painful steps, since the ultimate version of the 'meteor' idea, developed by Thomson, makes its deficiencies brutally plain. As it became clear that there were not enough small, rocky objects in the Solar System to provide the required input of energy to the Sun, Thomson toyed with the idea that the Sun might maintain its fires by consuming not mere meteors but whole planets, one by one. On this picture, Mercury, the innermost planet, might slowly spiral into the Sun, giving up its gravitational energy as heat – but this would only provide enough to keep the Sun hot for seven years. Venus would do little better, providing enough energy to heat the Sun for eighty-four years, and even Neptune, the most distant large planet in the known

★ Quoted in *Lord Kelvin and the Age of the Earth* by Joe Burchfield, p. 22.
† Ibid., p. 23.

Solar System, could contribute only enough energy, if it fell all the way into the Sun, to keep the fires hot for some 2,000 years. Even by gobbling up all of the planets in the Solar System in turn, the Sun still could not maintain its fires for more than a few thousand years – the 'meteoric' fuel supply is no better than the chemical one.

By the 1860s, Thomson was able to do better by invoking the idea of a shrinking Sun. But by then he had, in fact, been pre-empted not only by Waterston's still little-known work but by a German researcher Hermann Helmholtz, whose career had some curious parallels with that of the other unsung hero of the solar energy puzzle, Julius Mayer.

Helmholtz had been born in Potsdam in 1821. He was a delicate child, and scarcely left his home for the first seven years of his life, but was educated by his father, a teacher of philosophy and literature at the Potsdam Gymnasium (a school for pre-university students).★ Young Hermann showed great academic ability, and when he was old enough, and well enough, to attend the Gymnasium himself he was particularly interested in physics. But since his father could not afford to pay for him to go to university, he turned instead to medicine, taking advantage of an arrangement whereby his university fees were paid in return for a promise that he would serve eight years in the army after he qualified. During four years at the Friedrich Wilhelm Institute in Berlin, Helmholtz studied medicine, as required, but managed also to take courses in physics and mathematics, and to become a skilled pianist. He obtained his MD in 1842, and by 1843 he was back home in Potsdam, as surgeon to his regiment, which was stationed there. His medical duties were not too arduous, and Helmholtz was able to carry out experiments in a laboratory which he set up in the barracks.

The official biographies report that Helmholtz's skill and reputation as a scientist soon became so great that he was 'released' from his military duties in 1848; there are suggestions, however, that after an official leave of absence to carry out scientific work he simply refused to return to army life, and was actually dismissed from the service under something of a cloud. Either way, in 1849 he was appointed Assistant Professor of Physiology in Königsberg, and he went on to a series of other academic posts in a long and distinguished career. It was also in 1848 that he had

★ On his mother's side, incidentally, Helmholtz was a descendant of William Penn, the founder of Pennsylvania.

independently discovered the law of conservation of energy, from
an investigation of the heat produced by muscles in animals –
almost exactly the same course that had led Mayer to his discovery
of the law several years previously. This in turn led Helmholtz, as
it had Mayer, to further work in thermodynamics, and to his
contributions to the debate about the origin of the Sun's energy.

Helmholtz's first contribution on the subject appeared in
February 1854, a few months before Thomson presented his own
first paper on the meteor impact hypothesis to the British
Association – Thomson probably saw Helmholtz's paper after his
own paper was complete, but before it was read to that meeting.
The brilliantly simple new idea which Helmholtz contributed was
the suggestion that the whole mass of the Sun itself, not merely
the planets, might provide the gravitational energy to make it hot.
The argument is straightforward. If the whole Sun were made of
rock, and it was broken into small pieces, and all the pieces were
carried far out into space, then each piece would have a large
amount of gravitational energy, and they would all fall towards
the centre of the cloud of stones. We can measure, or calculate, the
energy involved in terms of the amount of work that would have
to be done to spread the rocks apart. In the same way, if someone
carries a heavy object up a flight of stairs, it requires a lot of effort,
because the heavy object is being raised in a gravitational field and
given energy. If the person now pushes the object out of the
window, it drops, hitting the ground; and when it hits the
ground, it stops and warms up. Gravitational energy has been
converted first into kinetic energy and then into heat.

The kinetic energy provided by the mass of all the planets
falling into the Sun could only keep it as hot as it is today for a few
thousand years. But the gravitational energy provided by the mass
of the Sun itself, initially spread out in a cloud of rocks, then
falling inward (converting gravitational energy into kinetic
energy) and bashing together in a molten ball of fire (converting
kinetic energy into heat), would release as much energy as the Sun
radiates in 20 *million* years. At the time, Helmholtz had not made
the precise calculation, simply pointing out that a great deal of
energy could be turned into heat in this way. Thomson soon put
the numbers in, but didn't think much of the proposal; he
considered the idea that the original stuff of the Universe consisted
of a spread-out cloud of irregular lumps of stone rather
implausible. Besides, what was the point of having 20 million
times as much energy as the Sun radiates in a year produced all at
once, long ago when the Sun formed? What was needed was a

way to release energy slowly, over millions of years, not a means to generate a great cosmic explosion.

Kelvin's timescales

In 1854, nobody took much notice of the contributions from either Helmholtz or Thomson, and Thomson was soon preoccupied with other matters. But in December 1860 a happy accident (for science; doubtless quite painful for Thomson) left him with a broken leg, and ample time to lie in bed thinking. This was just a year after the publication of Darwin's *Origin*, and that may well have been the reason why one of the things Thomson thought about was the origin of the Sun's energy supply, and the problem of the age of the Sun and Earth. The fruits of his thinking appeared in 1862 in *Macmillan's Magazine*,★ and this time they did make a big impact.

At this time, Thomson based his arguments very much on the image of a mass of stony meteors coming together, distasteful though that had appeared earlier. He didn't worry too much about how the vast amount of energy available was stored up and allowed to trickle out slowly over millions of years, but concentrated on the calculation of how much energy was available, and how long it could, *if* it were spread out, keep the Sun shining at its present brightness. In round terms, the theory showed that there was enough energy stored in the original cloud of rocks to provide for 10 to 20 million years of solar output at present rates. Even allowing for the possibility of errors in the calculations or the assumptions on which they were based, Thomson could see no way in which this might be increased by more than about a factor of 10, and in that article he wrote:

> It seems, therefore, on the whole most probable that the sun has not illuminated the earth for 100,000,000 years, and almost certain that he has not done so for 500,000,000 years. As for the future, we may say, with equal certainty, that inhabitants of the earth cannot continue to enjoy the light and heat essential to their life, for many million years longer, unless sources now unknown to us are prepared in the great storehouse of creation.

It isn't giving too much of my story away to say that, with hindsight, these comments are remarkably prophetic. But Thom-

★ William Thomson, 'Age of the Sun's Heat', *Macmillan's Magazine*, 5 March 1862, p. 288.

son surely did not really expect that sources of energy unknown to nineteenth-century science would, in fact, turn up, as his attack on Darwin later in the article makes clear.

Building from Lyell's version of uniformitarianism, Darwin had, among other things, calculated how long it must have taken for erosion to produce the present-day appearance of the chalk hills and valleys of the English Weald, from measurements which showed that chalk cliffs are now being eroded at a rate of one inch per century. He meant the calculation to be illustrative of the long timescale of the Earth; it wasn't a centrepiece of his story, and he carried it through rather carelessly, living to regret ever setting it down in print. But, although the number he came up with is a little on the high side, it isn't so ludicrously incompatible with the timescale envisaged for the evolution of the Earth today, which is several billion years. The figure Darwin came up with – for one relatively recent phase of geological activity – was, however, longer than the figure Thomson had now calculated for the age of the Sun. Thomson was scathing in his rebuttal of Darwin's estimate:

> What then are we to think of such geological estimates as 300,000,000 years for the 'denudation of the Weald'? Whether is it more probable that the physical conditions of the sun's matter differ 1,000 times more than dynamics compels us to suppose they differ from those of matter in our laboratories; or that a stormy sea, with possibly channel tides of extreme violence, should encroach on a chalk cliff 1,000 times more rapidly than Mr Darwin's estimate of one inch per century?

With battle joined in such strong terms, Thomson initiated a debate that continued for the rest of the nineteenth century, during which he forced the uniformitarians back on the defensive. His article on the Sun's heat in 1862 was quickly followed by new calculations of the age of the Earth, based on the application of Fourier's equations of heat flow. Thomson assumed that the Earth had been formed in a molten state as a result of heat generated by colliding meteors – very much the same picture that astronomers have today. He knew that measurements made down mine-shafts showed that the Earth's interior was still hotter than the crust, even today, and by using sound physics and known measurements of how long it takes heat to flow through an insulating blanket of rock he calculated how long it would have taken for the original molten planet to cool to the state it is in today. He came up with a figure of 98 million years for the age of the Earth, happily agreeing almost exactly with his calculation of the age of the Sun. Cautiously, allowing for a margin of error, he said that the calculations set limits on the possible age of the Earth. It might be as young as 20 million years; it might be as old as 200 million years, but there was no way (within the laws of physics known to Thomson) that it could be as old as Darwin and the geologists required. His calculations were impeccable, and his conclusions were correct. Thomson believed that the entire Universe could be described by the same set of physical laws that held in the laboratory and on Earth, and he held unshakably to that belief. The fact that his two age calculations, for the Sun and the Earth, independently came up with much the same number of years strengthened his position in the debate that followed.

In some ways, indeed, Thomson held more steadfastly to his views than Darwin did to his. Later editions of the *Origin* show Darwin wriggling uncomfortably on the hook of Thomson's calculations of the age of the Sun and the Earth, and taking on board some now discredited ideas, essentially in an attempt to find a way to speed up evolution. This is why the first edition of his great work is still the best and clearest exposition of his ideas.

Although the uniformitarians were forced into some tactical withdrawals, however, the debate did continue, and Thomson continued to revise and improve his calculations. It wasn't until 1887 that he came up with the version that is enshrined in many student texts today, and which provides the complete description of how a star like the Sun does, indeed, get hot in the first place. The idea actually drew upon a suggestion made by Helmholtz in his own paper on the Sun's heat, back in 1854 – though Thomson did not give Helmholtz any credit when he presented his own calculations in a lecture at the Royal Institution in London in 1887, and may well have forgotten that Helmholtz had pointed the way.★

The important feature of this final step in Thomson's work on the heat of the Sun was the realization that as long as the same amount of matter – the same mass – is involved, it isn't important how big, or how small, the original 'rocks' from which the Sun formed might be. Just two half-Suns, falling directly onto each

★ A nice irony, indeed, that Helmholtz, who had unwittingly upstaged Mayer and contributed to his depression, should now be upstaged himself, either by accident or design, by Thomson. Today the credit is shared in the English-speaking world, with the final version of the thermodynamic age of the Sun called the 'Kelvin-Helmholtz' age, or timescale. German astronomers, unforgivingly, still often refer simply to the 'Helmholtz' timescale.

other from far away, would collide with as much kinetic energy as a cloud of meteors collapsing to its centre. And the objects involved in the collision could also be much *smaller* than the kind of meteoric rocks envisaged in the earlier version of the theory. Tiny pebbles, gravel, a cloud of dust – as long as the *total* mass is the same, the energy available is the same. There is still, indeed, as much energy available if the original cloud from which the Sun formed was made of atoms and molecules – a cloud of *gas*, spread out initially over a huge volume and collapsing under the influence of its own gravity (under its own weight). By the time such a collapsing gas cloud had shrunk to roughly the size the Sun is today, the temperature at its core would be millions of degrees, and its surface would glow with a temperature of a few thousand degrees. Astronomers today accept this as the most likely explanation of how stars do, indeed, get going.

Once such a proto-star is hot inside, there is a great deal of pressure pushing outward, because the heat makes the atomic particles very energetic. The powerful jostling of the particles against one another tends to hold the star up against further collapse; as long as the star is hot inside, it can never collapse completely, and Thomson knew that it would take a considerable amount of time for the heat liberated in the centre to work its way outwards. What would happen, however, when such a glowing ball of gas did cool a little? Thomson (and Helmholtz) had the answer. If the Sun were a glowing ball of gas, and it cooled a little inside, it would begin to shrink. But what did shrinking really involve? All the atomic particles in the Sun would be moving closer to the centre – they would be falling in a gravitational field. What happens when things fall in a gravitational field? They gain kinetic energy, which is converted into heat when they jostle against one another! All that was required to ensure that the gravitational energy stored up in the Sun was released slowly, over millions of years, was that the Sun should be shrinking slowly, at a rate of about 50 metres a year. This didn't provide any more energy – the total was still restricted to the 20 million years' supply that Thomson had estimated previously. But it did provide the means to spread the heat out over 20 million years, instead of releasing it in one huge blast. And the required shrinkage, at a rate of 50 metres a year, was certainly far too small to be measured by nineteenth-century astronomers, so the fact that nobody had noticed it was no problem at all.

As Thomson zeroed in on such a restricted timescale for the Sun, even though his physical reasoning improved at each stage, the uniformitarians became less inclined to accept it. Maybe they could have tried to live with 500 million years – but 20 million years was definitely insufficient to account for the changes wrought in the Earth and its living inhabitants since it had formed. In a sense, Thomson's timescale was a victim of its own success; the more clearly it pointed to a low age for the Sun and the Earth, the more clear it was that there was a real conflict between the physics and the geology.

In 1889, Thomson wrote 'it would, I think, be extremely rash to assume as probable anything more than twenty million years of the sun's light in the past history of the earth, or to reckon on more than five or six million years to come.'[*] In 1892, the year he received his peerage at the age of sixty-eight, he repeated almost exactly the comment he had made as a young man of twenty-eight in 1852, but now with the numbers to back it up:

> Within a finite period of time past the earth must have been, and within a finite period of time to come must again be, unfit for the habitation of man as at present constituted, *unless operations have been and are to be performed which are impossible under the laws governing the known operations going on at present in the material world.*

And by 1897 Kelvin, as he then was, had accepted the best estimate for the age of the Sun and the Earth as 24 million years.

All of Thomson's calculations, like those of Anaxagoras, were impeccable. Today, with the benefit of nearly a further century of observations of the Sun and stars, with more practice in the application of the laws of thermodynamics to the calculations, and with the aid of electronic computers to speed those calculations (though they are hardly necessary for solving so simple a problem), astronomers agree that a star like the Sun can keep itself hot by slow contraction for a few tens of millions of years, the Kelvin-Helmholtz timescale. This is all the energy that is available from the conversion of gravitational energy into heat. But it is nowhere near enough to satisfy the geologists' appetite. Well before the end of the nineteenth century, it was clear that this figure was incompatible with the requirements of geology and evolution. Something had to give, and the way ahead was pointed most clearly in 1899, neatly at the end of the nineteenth century, by Thomas Chamberlain, Professor of Geology at the University of Chicago. Thomson had always been careful to point out that

---

[*] The quotations on this page from Thomson's writings are both taken from Burchfield.

the only way to provide a longer solar timescale was by invoking unknown sources of energy and new laws of physics, but the way he had done so made it clear that he was using this as an example of something too ridiculous to take seriously. Chamberlain, however, was prepared to contemplate the unthinkable. Writing in the journal *Science*,★ he commented:

> Is present knowledge relative to the behavior of matter under such extraordinary conditions as obtained in the interior of the sun sufficiently exhaustive to warrant the assertion that no unrecognized sources of heat reside there? What the internal constitution of the atoms may be is yet open to question. It is not improbable that they are complex organizations and seats of enormous energies. Certainly no careful chemist would affirm that the atoms are really elementary or that there may not be locked up in them energies of the first order of magnitude. No cautious chemist would . . . affirm or deny that the extraordinary conditions which reside at the center of the sun may not set free a portion of this energy.

Clearly, geology was fighting back; and it was right to do so. The scientific world was ready for a completely new explanation of how the Sun maintained its fires. Although hints of this 'new' source of energy were already available when Chamberlain wrote those words, however, it was to be fully thirty years before the outline of what was going on in the Sun became clear, and more than forty years before the details were worked out.

2

Seats of Enormous Energies

How much heat does the Sun produce? What are the 'enormous energies' we need to unlock from the atom in order to prove Chamberlain right? In one sense, the energy production of the Sun is not so remarkable, compared with the rate at which energy is produced even by chemical reactions here on Earth. George Gamow, in his book *A Star Called the Sun*, came up with a striking analogy back in the early 1960s. If a coffee pot is advertised as producing heat at the same rate that heat is produced (on average) in the Sun's interior, he asked, how long will it take to start the water boiling?

The surprising answer to Gamow's question is that even if the pot were perfectly insulated, so that no heat could escape, it would take many months for the water to boil. *On average*, each gram of the Sun's mass produces very little heat, as a simple calculation shows. With a radius of 6.95×10^{10} centimetres, the surface area of the Sun is 6.07×10^{22} square cm, and 8.8×10^{25} calories of heat energy cross that surface each second. The mass of the Sun, however, is 2×10^{33} grams. So it is only necessary for each gram of material to produce, on average, 4.4×10^{-8} calories per second – less than half of one ten-millionth of a calorie per second. This is not only low by the standards of the average coffee percolator; it is much less than the rate at which heat is released in your body through the chemical processes of human metabolism.

The reason why such a modest production of energy, compared with the mass or volume of the Sun, is enough to keep it so hot is that the heat from inside the Sun can escape only through the surface, an area which depends on the square of the radius. The mass, or volume, however, is proportional to the cube of the radius, so the mass and volume get bigger much more quickly than the surface area does when we compare spheres with bigger and bigger radii. Every time the radius is doubled, the surface area increases four times, but the volume of the sphere is eight times bigger.

We can see the effect at work, very clearly, in warm-blooded animals. A mouse has a very small volume, and a small mass, with a relatively large surface area. It loses heat quickly, and has to stay active and eat almost continuously in order to keep warm. An elephant, on the other hand, has a large mass and a proportionately smaller surface area. It has trouble losing heat, which is why it has evolved large ears, which act as radiators, and why it spends a lot of time, if it can, splashing about in water. No land mammal can be significantly bigger than an elephant, or it would cook inside through the heat generated by its own metabolic processes – which is one reason why, of course, the elephant is the largest land mammal that has evolved.

So, as the nineteenth-century astronomers appreciated, it is easy to make the Sun hot enough to shine, using a modest release of gravitational energy as it shrinks. Even burning coal would keep the Sun hot, for a time. The problem is explaining how it has been able to shine for so long. Which is where the new physics of the 1890s and the early twentieth century was able to lend astronomy a hand.

Radiation revealed

On 1 March 1896 Henri Becquerel, working in Paris, discovered the phenomenon we now know as radioactivity. His discovery led to the realization that the atom is not indivisible, and to the identification of the source of energy of the Sun and stars. But it came about partly by accident, and it took many years for the implications to be followed up, and to become a cornerstone of physics and astronomy.

Becquerel was the third member of a unique lineage of eminent French physicists. He was born in Paris on 15 December 1852, and although he trained as an engineer and became chief engineer in the department of roads and highways in Paris, fate, and family tradition, ensured that his lasting achievements were in physics. The tradition had begun with Henri's grandfather, Antoine, who investigated electric and luminescent phenomena and achieved such success that in 1838 a chair (professorship) of physics was set up for him at the French Museum of Natural History. Antoine's third son, Edmond, helped his father with experiments, and was himself drawn into the study of phosphorescent solids, crystals which glow in the dark. As early as 1858, Edmond Becquerel noted in a scientific paper published in the journal *Comptes Rendus*★ that 'the bodies which produce the most brilliant effects are uranium composites.' When his father died in 1878, Edmond succeeded him as professor at the Museum.

So when Henri, in spite of his engineering training, began to help his father out in the laboratory in 1875 nobody was surprised. He soon proved his ability as a physicist. In 1889, still only thirty-six, he was elected to the Academy of Sciences, and when his father died in 1891 he became the third person, and the third Becquerel, to become Professor of Physics in the Museum of Natural History. In due course, Henri's only son, Jean, succeeded him as Professor (Henri died in 1908). It was only in 1948, when Jean, who left no heir, retired, that the professorship passed out of the Becquerel family, 110 years after the chair had been established. But out of all this remarkable dynasty, it is Henri Becquerel who is assured of scientific immortality as a result of the discovery he made that grey day in Paris in 1896.

The 1890s were exciting times for physics, with new discoveries being made about the nature of matter and radiation. These discoveries were to lead the way to the development of the two great theories of the twentieth century, quantum physics and relativity, and to a completely new understanding of the nature of the physical world. As we move into the 1990s, many physicists are confident that they will soon be able to unite these two great theories into one package, a unified description of nature, completing a revolution that effectively began almost exactly a hundred years ago, in 1895, with the discovery of X-rays. It was this discovery that led directly to Becquerel's work on radiation, and to the discovery of the energy source of the stars.

X-rays were discovered by the German Wilhelm Röntgen, who was then fifty years old and had a distinguished career to look back on. He was Professor of Physics at Wörzburg University, and had become interested in the investigation of cathode rays. These 'rays' (we now know them to be streams of electrons) are emitted from the negatively charged plate (cathode) of an electric discharge tube, a roughly cylindrical glass vacuum tube. Such a vacuum tube is the direct antecedent of the picture tube in a modern television set, and the picture on the screen of a TV is painted by flying electrons emitted from a cathode at the other end

★ Volume 46, p. 969; the quotation comes from p. 971.

of the tube. All that, however, lay far in the future when Röntgen began to study cathode rays in 1895.

It was on Friday 8 November, that Röntgen made a chance observation in his darkened laboratory. Although the tube was encased in a sleeve of thin black cardboard, Röntgen noticed that a paper screen, painted with barium platinocyanide and lying near the apparatus, glowed whenever the tube was switched on. Cathode rays, it had already been established, could only travel a few centimetres outside the tube; the screen, not being used in the experiment, was about a metre away. Something else must be making it glow – and, Röntgen soon discovered, the something else could still make it glow when the tube was switched on, even if the screen was taken into the room next door. He had discovered X-rays, a previously unknown form of penetrating radiation.

The news was announced on 1 January 1896, and already included the dramatic discovery that X-rays could be used to photograph human bones, through the living flesh. It created a sensation, both in scientific circles and in the press, where, following almost instant reports in European papers, on the other side of the Atlantic the *New York Times* carried an account of the discovery on 16 January and followed it up with later reports in February. The learned journals *Nature* and *Science* were just behind the popular press, for once, and carried translations of Röntgen's paper on 23 January and 14 February, respectively. In France, *Le Matin* had carried the story on 13 January, and X-rays were the main topic of discussion at a meeting of the French Academy of Sciences on 20 January. Becquerel was present at the meeting, and learned from his colleagues that Röntgen had identified the source of the X-rays – they came from the bright spot where the cathode rays struck the glass wall of the vacuum tube, and made it fluoresce. Continuing the family interest in phosphorescence, Becquerel immediately decided to investigate whether other phosphorescent objects could emit X-rays. Among the crystals he set out to test were some uranium salts, including potassium uranyl disulphate, that had been prepared fifteen years earlier, during his work with his father.

Becquerel soon found the effect he was looking for. The phosphorescent salts he was using became active when exposed to sunlight. After the sunlight had made the salts active, they would glow for a while, before fading and needing a further charge of sunlight. He simply wrapped a photographic plate in two sheets of thick black paper, and laid it out in the sunlight with a dish of the phosphorescent material on top of it. When the plate was developed, he found the outline of the phosphorescent material on the plate, and if he placed an object such as a coin between the dish and the plate while it was sitting out in the Sun, the developed plate showed its image. In a paper Becquerel submitted to the Academy of Sciences on 24 February 1896, he concluded; 'the phosphorescent substance in question emits radiations which traverse paper opaque to light.'*

At this stage, it seemed that the phosphorescent activity, stimulated by sunlight, was producing radiation similar to X-rays – perhaps, indeed, X-rays themselves. Just a week later, however, Becquerel was back at the Academy, reporting that the effect had nothing to do with sunlight or phosphorescence. For the last few days of February 1896, Paris was overcast. Becquerel had prepared another experiment, in which a piece of copper in the shape of a cross was interposed between a dish of uranium salts and a wrapped photographic plate. As there was no sun, he kept the experiment in a cupboard for several days. Then, perhaps tired of waiting, on Sunday, 1 March, he developed the plate anyway, and was astonished to find the image of the copper cross, clear and sharp. It seems to have been a total surprise, since Henri's son Jean, who was eighteen at the time, later recalled that Henri was 'stupefied' when 'he found that his silhouette pictures were even more intense than the ones he had obtained the week before.'

There was certainly an element of luck in the discovery, even if, as a good scientist, Becquerel planned to check out the 'null result' he expected, that the plate would be blank if the salts had not been exposed to sunlight. Becquerel himself, as Pais reports, felt that it was destiny, the culmination of sixty years of work by three generations of Becquerels working in the same laboratory on related problems in phosphorescence.

Unlike Röntgen's discovery, however, Becquerel's work made no immediate impact outside a small circle of scientists. Perhaps the discovery seemed too much like that of X-rays for the popular press to notice the difference. But its deep implications quickly became clear, at least to a few cognoscenti. Becquerel himself soon showed that the source of the radiation was uranium itself, which, as a pure metal, is not phosphorescent at all, and by the end of 1896 he was already speculating about where the energy of the radiation came from, since it did not depend on sunlight after all.

* The dates and quotations are taken from Abraham Pais' epic history of particle physics, *Inward Bound*.

This was a mystery unique to his discovery, since the energy of X-rays, of course, very clearly came from the electricity put into the cathode ray tube. The uranium radiation, however, seemed to be something for nothing. In the journal *Comptes Rendus*, Becquerel wrote, late in 1896, 'one has not yet been able to recognize wherefrom uranium derives the energy which it emits with such persistence.'* But after the end of that year, he turned his attention to other scientific matters, and published only occasional short papers on radioactivity. It was left to two younger researchers to take up his discovery and carry its implications forward into the twentieth century.

Energy from atoms

The story of Marie Curie and her work with her husband Pierre in purifying and identifying radioactive substances is very well known, and I won't go into any details here. Marie was born in Poland in 1867 and moved to Paris in 1891, marrying Pierre in 1895. In the wake of Becquerel's discovery of radioactivity, she analysed many metals, salts, oxides and minerals, and found that radioactivity (she first used the term 'radioactive substance' in a paper published in 1898), although rare, did not occur in uranium alone. She showed that the amount of radioactivity in a sample containing uranium depended on the amount of uranium in the sample, and, also in 1898, she identified two previously unknown radioactive elements, polonium and radium. All of this led to the Curies sharing with Becquerel the 1903 Nobel Prize for Physics, for their pioneering work on radioactivity.

Their work also had tragic consequences. The dangers of radioactivity were unknown at the time, and the conditions under which Marie and Pierre laboured would never be permitted in a modern laboratory. Marie's notebooks from the 1890s are so radioactive, as a result of contamination by the materials she worked with, that they are considered dangerous to handle even today; both Marie and Pierre suffered from what we now know as radiation sickness. This contributed to Marie's death in 1934; it probably also contributed, indirectly, to Pierre's death in 1906, when after a period of illness he slipped while crossing a road and fell under the wheels of a horse-drawn truck.

In 1911 Marie received a second Nobel Prize, this time in chemistry, for her work on radium. No doubt Pierre would have

---

* Volume 123, 1896, p. 855.

shared the award had he lived, since, as Marie stressed in her Nobel Lecture, although she had carried out the chemical work which led to the isolation of radium as a pure salt, this was intimately connected with their joint research on radioactivity. In terms of unlocking the secrets of the Sun, however, Marie's work was by now being overtaken. Pierre Curie, working with his assistant Albert Laborde, had measured the amount of heat generated by the activity of radium in 1903; and the young New Zealand physicist Ernest Rutherford was beginning to probe the structure of the atom, and to work out the rules of radioactive decay. He, too, was involved, as early as 1903, in measuring the heat produced by radium.

Rutherford had been born in New Zealand in 1871. In 1895, he became the first graduate of another university (Canterbury College, in New Zealand) to be admitted to Cambridge University as a research student, under a new regulation which had just come into force. There, he worked at the Cavendish Laboratory under J. J. Thomson, who was about to discover that cathode rays are actually particles (now called electrons). Thomson's discovery was announced in April 1897, and provided the first evidence that atoms could be subdivided. Electrons are much smaller than atoms, carry negative electric charge and, it became clear from Thomson's work and that of other researchers at the time, were, literally, pieces that could be knocked out of atoms. Hardly surprisingly, working in Thomson's laboratory and with news of Becquerel's work soon coming from Paris, Rutherford turned his attention to the study of atomic processes. Following his spell as a research student in Cambridge, Rutherford took up a post at McGill University, in Canada, in 1898. In 1907 he became Professor of Physics at Manchester University, in England, and in 1919 he succeeded Thomson as Director of the Cavendish Laboratory. Although he never worked directly in the field of astrophysics, his pioneering work on radioactivity was a key development in unlocking the secrets of the Sun.

The young researcher working in Cambridge from 1895 to 1898 became intrigued by the discoveries of X-rays, the electron and Becquerel radiation. In a series of investigations, Rutherford showed that the radiation Becquerel had discovered was actually a mixture of two varieties of radiation, which he called alpha rays and beta rays. By 1902 it had been established, by other researchers, that beta rays are, in fact, fast-moving electrons. Rutherford himself concentrated his efforts on the alpha rays, and after a long series of experiments, interlaced with periods of other work, he was able to show first that alpha rays are also streams of particles, and finally, in 1908, that each alpha particle has a mass roughly equivalent to the mass of four hydrogen atoms, but carries only two units of positive charge. An alpha particle, he deduced, must be the same as a helium atom which has lost two electrons. This conclusion rather neatly explained the discovery, made in 1895 and something of a puzzle at the time, that traces of helium gas are found in minerals that contain uranium. Helium had first been identified in 1868, by the British scientist Joseph Lockyer, who pioneered the study of the Sun using spectroscopy. In this technique, elements are identified by the characteristic patterns of lines they produce in the spectrum, as distinctive as fingerprints are for individual people. When Lockyer found spectral lines in sunlight that belonged to no known element, he claimed that they must be due to an element found only in the Sun, which he called helium from the name of the Greek sun–god Helios. Nobody expected to find helium on Earth; Rutherford's work showed how it could have been produced by radioactivity, with alpha particles gaining a respectable cloak of two electrons from their surroundings to become helium atoms.

Working with Frederick Soddy in Canada, Rutherford had also explained that radioactivity is associated with the disintegration of atoms, with atoms of the radioactive element being converted into atoms of another element. And he showed that half of the atoms in a radioactive sample will decay in this way in a certain time, characteristic of the radioactive element, now called the half-life. This is a very curious pattern of behaviour. In a sample of radium, for example, just half of the atoms will decay in 1,602 years, being converted into atoms of the gas radon as alpha and beta particles are emitted. In the next 1,602 years, half of the rest of the radium (one quarter of the original) will decay, and so on. How does an individual atom 'know' whether it ought to decay or not, and when? The answers to these questions came only in the 1920s, when the quantum theory of atomic behaviour was developed.

Meanwhile, Rutherford himself soon went beyond studying alpha particles to using them to study atoms. He encouraged Hans Geiger and Ernest Marsden, in Manchester, to investigate the way alpha particles were scattered by gold foil, and they discovered that although most of the alpha particles in a beam would travel straight through the foil as if it were not there, a very few particles were bounced back as if they had struck something solid. It was this work that established that atoms are made of tiny, dense nuclei, carrying positive charge, which are surrounded by tenuous clouds of electrons. A fast-moving alpha particle (now identified as a helium nucleus) can brush through the electron cloud like a rifle bullet through tissue paper, but if it happens to head directly for a nucleus, then the positive charge of the nucleus repels the positive charge on the alpha particle and bounces it back from whence it came.

It is hardly surprising, in view of all this activity, that Rutherford received a Nobel Prize in 1908. The surprise is that it was awarded for chemistry, for 'his investigations into the disintegration of the elements, and the chemistry of radioactive substances'. Why should this be a surprise? Because Rutherford had little time for chemistry, or indeed anything except physics, and had once remarked that 'all of science is either physics or stamp collecting.' He accepted the prize with good grace, however, and commented in an after-dinner speech at the Nobel banquet that he 'had dealt with many different transformations with various time-periods, but the quickest he had met was his own transformation from a physicist to a chemist.'[*] Chemist or physicist, though, Rutherford had by then also made a major contribution to astronomy, through the developing understanding of the sources of solar energy, and to the geological puzzle of the age of the Earth. No doubt he would have seen this as further proof that all of science derives from physics.

Solving the energy crisis

Rutherford's key contributions stemmed from the pioneering work on radioactivity in the 1890s, but were directly triggered by the work of Curie and Laborde. When radiation was first discovered, researchers such as Henri Becquerel and Marie Curie speculated that the energy involved might come from outside, some external energy source tapped by certain elements and converted into detectable radiation. But at the time they did not appreciate just how much energy was being released. Rutherford and R. K. McClung, at McGill, showed as early as 1900 that the different kinds of rays actually carry enormous energy – but their paper pointing this out made little impact.

The next key step was taken by two young German researchers, Julius Elster and Hans Geitel. Both schoolteachers, they showed as early as 1898 that the source of the energy in radioactivity could not come from outside. They put radioactive substances into

---

[*] A. S. Eve, *Rutherford* (Cambridge University Press, 1939), p. 183; quoted by Pais, p. 63.

vacuum jars and down deep mines to shield them from the effects of any energy flowing in from outside the Earth, and they found no diminution of their radioactivity. The energy had to come from the atoms themselves.* Nobody was greatly worried at the time, although opinions differed on where the energy was coming from. In 1899, Rutherford commented that the origin of the energy in the radiation was 'a mystery'; J. J. Thomson, on the other hand, always assumed that the energy was produced as a result of some internal rearrangement of the then unknown structure of the atom, and like most physicists was prepared to leave it to future generations to find out just how the trick was achieved.

In 1901, Elster and Geitel showed that there is natural radioactivity present even in the air and in the soil; before long, other enthusiasts had found radioactivity everywhere, in snow, rain, lakes and rocks. Here, at last, was a 'new' source of energy, one which could keep the Earth, at least, hot inside for far longer than implied by Thomson's calculations of a cooling sphere. The first suggestion that radioactivity was at least partly responsible for the heat of the Earth and Sun came in 1903, from George Darwin, in Cambridge, and John Joly, of the University of Dublin. Robert Strutt, of Imperial College in London, was quick to suggest that the presence of radium and other radioactive substances inside the Earth provided a source of heat which could extend the geological timescale indefinitely. And if the coincidence between Thomson's timescales for the age of the Earth and the Sun was broken, it was surely time to look again at how the Sun might get its energy.

The key was the realization of just how much energy is involved in radioactive processes. Rutherford's work on this topic with McClung might have been largely ignored, but once Rutherford and Soddy had established that radioactivity involves the conversion of atoms of one element into those of another, it seemed clear, as Rutherford put it in the first edition of his book *Radioactivity*,† that 'the continuous emission of energy from the

---

* For this reason, even though the existence of atoms was not fully established in 1898, Elster and Geitel are sometimes regarded as the discoverers of atomic energy. The actual term 'atomic energy' was first used by Rutherford and Soddy in 1903, to refer to the energy stored in any atom. But the expression became common currency only in the 1940s, by which time, ironically, it was appreciated that the energy actually comes from the *nuclei* of atoms, which had not been identified in 1903. It seems that this misuse of the term was a deliberate decision by advisers involved with the political side of the 'atomic bomb' project, who felt that the public would not be familiar with the term 'nuclear' (see Pais, p. 116).
† Cambridge University Press, 1904.

active bodies is derived from the internal energy inherent in the atom.' And just at that time, in 1903, the measurements made by Curie and Laborde brought the whole puzzle of the energy involved in radioactivity back to the forefront of physics, demonstrating more dramatically what Rutherford and McClung had pointed out in 1900.

Before March 1903, scientists knew that elements such as uranium and radium released energy through their radioactivity, but most of them regarded the amount of energy involved as small enough not to worry them greatly. Then, Curie and Laborde actually measured the heat released by a gram of radium, and found that the amount produced every hour was sufficient to heat 1.3 grams of water from 0°C to boiling point. Putting it another way, radium generates enough heat to melt its own weight in ice in an hour. This caused consternation. Such a productive release of energy simply could not be dismissed as a minor problem for future generations to solve, and some physicists even speculated that the law of conservation of energy, the most basic law of physics, might be violated in radioactive processes. Ignoring the work of Elster and Geitel, the former William Thomson, by now Lord Kelvin, said in 1904, the year of his eightieth birthday, 'energy must be supplied from without . . . I venture to suggest that somehow etherial waves may supply energy to radium.'*

Rutherford, meanwhile, had been working on the problem in Canada with Howard Barnes, who was to succeed him as professor at McGill when Rutherford returned to England in 1907. Six months after the work by Curie and Laborde, they were able to show that the amount of heat produced during radioactivity depends on the number of alpha particles emitted by a substance. These relatively massive particles are emitted by radioactive atoms (we now know, by radioactive *nuclei*) and collide with other atoms (nuclei) nearby, giving up their kinetic energy as heat. Rutherford himself soon turned the discovery of this new source of energy to the question of the age of the Earth. He later told of the occasion, in 1904, when he presented these ideas to an audience at the Royal Institution in London:

> I came into the room, which was half dark, and presently spotted Lord Kelvin in the audience and realized that I was in for trouble at the last part of the speech dealing with the age of the earth, where my views conflicted with his . . . a sudden

* Quoted by Pais, p. 113.

inspiration came, and I said Lord Kelvin had limited the age of the earth, *provided no new source of heat was discovered*. That prophetic utterance refers to what we are now considering tonight, radium! Behold! the old boy beamed upon me.★

What Rutherford had realized was that radioactive events inside the Earth must be supplying heat, at a then unknown rate. The planet could no longer be regarded simply as a cooling body, and Kelvin's timescale for the age of the Earth could be no more than a minimum possible age. It was to take several decades for all the doubters to be persuaded, and for the idea to be put on a firm footing following the development of quantum physics in the 1920s; but Rutherford's basic insight, that the interior of the Earth is kept hot – hot enough to be molten, even today – by radioactivity, is now established as firmly as anything in science. The *surface* of the Earth, though, is kept warm today not by the relatively tiny trickle of heat leaking out from the interior, but by the heat of the Sun in the sky. In the early 1900s it was already clear, at least to a few perceptive physicists, that radioactivity held the key to understanding the energy of the Sun, as well; but it was to take more than twenty years for that early insight itself to be put onto a proper scientific basis, since that, too, required the development of quantum physics. During those two decades, however, the age of the Earth, at least, was established on a secure basis at last.

Making a date with radioactivity

Rutherford and Soddy realized that radioactivity is a result of the transformation of atoms of one element into atoms of a different element. When alpha and beta particles are emitted by an atom (nucleus), then what is left behind is a different kind of atom (nucleus). One of the most important features of this process is that it occurs at a regular rate. As I have mentioned, in any sample of a particular radioactive element, exactly half of the atoms will 'decay' into different atoms in a characteristic time, called the half-life of that element. It doesn't matter how much, or how little, of the radioactive element you have; just half of it is transformed into something else in one half-life. Half of the rest is transformed by radioactive decay in the next half-life, and so on.

Each radioactive element produces a characteristic mixture of

---

★ *Radioactivity*, quoted in Burchfield, *Lord Kelvin and the Age of the Earth*, p. 164.

elements – decay products – when it decays. But while some radioactive elements have such short half-lives, fractions of a second, that they never occur naturally on Earth, others, such as uranium, thorium and radium, have very long half-lives, and are still found on Earth even though they have been decaying since the Solar System was born.

Atoms of one radioactive element may decay into a stable element, or into another radioactive element. If the product is itself radioactive, then the process repeats, until stable atoms are formed. By measuring the proportions of these characteristic decay products in rocks today, and comparing these with the proportions of the parent radioactive elements such as uranium, physicists armed with a knowledge of the appropriate half-lives can infer the age of the rocks. What matters is not the actual quantities of each element present, but the proportions – the ratio of the quantities of stable elements like lead to unstable ones like uranium and thorium.

The trick of dating rocks by means of radioactivity depends on a thorough knowledge of the way radioactive elements decay, and of what they decay into. This was pioneered by Rutherford and Bertram Boltwood in the first decade of the twentieth century. Boltwood, an American chemist, became interested in the problem after he heard Rutherford give a talk at Yale in 1904 describing his work with radioactivity.

At that time, Rutherford already suspected that an alpha particle is exactly equivalent to a helium atom from which the two electrons have been removed; he was able to prove this in 1908. In 1904, Rutherford's old colleague Soddy, working with Sir William Ramsay at University College, London, had established the rate at which a sample of radium produces helium – which, Rutherford realized, was simply a result of alpha particles released by the decay of radium picking up two electrons each from their surroundings and becoming atoms of helium. Using this rate as a guide, Rutherford calculated the ages of samples of rock simply by measuring the amount of helium they contained, and assuming that all of it came from radioactive decay, and (rather optimistically) that none had escaped since it was formed. This gave an age of 40 million years for a particular piece of rock Rutherford had in his possession – not yet a challenge to Thomson's timescale, even though, assuming some helium gas had escaped over the aeons, the real age of the rock was almost certainly more than this figure.

But Boltwood took the argument a stage further, looking at the overall products of radioactive decay, not just the helium. He knew in 1904 that the decay of uranium produces radium, and how quickly this happens; a year later he established that the further decay of radium ultimately produces lead. From measurements involving the uranium-radium-lead series, by the end of that year he had calculated ages ranging from 92 million years to 570 million years for different samples of rock. Unfortunately, though, these numbers were all wrong. They were based on measurements by Rutherford which turned out to have been inaccurate, and on a half-life for radium which was soon revised in the light of further studies.

By 1907, however, Boltwood and Rutherford were on the right track. Their figures were still not as accurate as modern estimates, but they were sufficient to show that something was seriously wrong with Thomson's estimate of the age of the Earth. The new estimates (which involved, among other little problems, measuring a trace of just 380 parts per billion of radium, compared with uranium, in samples of rock) gave ages for different rocks ranging from about 400 million years to more than 2 billion years. Even allowing for the remaining inaccuracies in the technique, they showed that the Earth must be about a billion years old – at least ten times older than Thomson's estimate.

Even so, the geological community was not persuaded overnight to take these age estimates seriously. The techniques involved were difficult and tedious, and nobody seems to have cared enough to try to duplicate the work immediately. Even after the new estimates for the age of the Earth appeared, many geologists continued to argue that radioactive heating could not really extend the lifetime of the Earth very much at all, and Thomson's age estimate was still widely accepted.

Boltwood went on to other work, and Rutherford maintained only a desultory interest in the age of the Earth. It was left to the next generation, in the form of Arthur Holmes, to finally carry the radioactive dating technique through to universal acceptance.

Born in 1890, Holmes studied at Imperial College, London, and returned there to carry out research after an expedition to Mozambique in 1911. In 1920, he went to Burma to work as an oil geologist, and he returned to England in 1925 to become professor of geology at Durham University, where he was an early supporter of the idea of continental drift. He moved to Edinburgh University in 1943, and wrote a standard textbook, *Principles of Physical Geology*, which is still widely used; he died in 1965.

During his time at Imperial College, Holmes dated many rock samples using the uranium-lead method, and decided that the oldest were about 1.6 billion years old. In 1913, Holmes was the first person to use radioactive dating to determine the ages of fossils, putting absolute dates into the fossil record for the first time. He refined the radioactive dating technique both before and after the First World War, taking on board the new discovery that elements could come in different varieties (isotopes) with slightly different atomic weights, and building up such an impressive body of data that even the doubters were eventually forced to admit that the radioactive dating technique was revealing something significant about the age of the Earth.

By 1921, a debate at the annual meeting of the British Association for the Advancement of Science showed that there was a new consensus: geologists, botanists, zoologists and physicists agreed that the Earth is indeed a few billion years old, and that the radioactive technique is the best guide to its age. The final seal of approval came in 1926, in the form of a report from the National Research Council of the US National Academy of Sciences endorsing the technique. Since then, further refinements have given an age of 3.8 billion years for the oldest rocks found in the Earth's crust; the oldest samples of rock from meteorites, which have fallen to Earth from interplanetary space, are 4.5 billion years old, and it is now widely accepted that the Solar System, including the Sun and Earth, was formed roughly 4.5 billion years ago.

By 1926, however, it would have taken a real stick-in-the-mud to contest the new age of the Earth. For it was in the early 1920s that real progress at last began to be made in the search for the Sun's source of energy. And the way forward had been pointed out, in no uncertain manner, in 1920, at the meeting of the British Association *before* the one at which Holmes finally persuaded his colleagues that he knew what he was talking about. To see why, we have to backtrack a little to 1903, and the sensation caused by the investigation of the heat output of radium by Curie and Laborde.

Nuclear energy

Gamow's coffee-pot analogy shows just how little heat each gram of the Sun produces, on average; the experiment carried out by Curie and Laborde showed just how much heat a gram of radium produces. In July 1903, four months after their results were announced, the journal *Nature* carried a suggestion from the English astronomer William Wilson, that radium could provide the heat of the Sun. He showed that just 3.6 grams of radium in every cubic metre of the Sun's volume would be enough to supply all of the heat now being radiated from the solar surface.

Wilson's suggestion failed to make much of a splash in scientific circles. But a few months later the theme was taken up by George Darwin (the son of Charles). Hardly surprisingly, George Darwin had long had his doubts about Kelvin's chronology of the Sun and Earth, which seemed to conflict so badly with the requirements of evolution. The younger Darwin also aired his views on radio-activity as a source of solar energy in *Nature*, but he was initially quite conservative in his claims, suggesting only that Kelvin's timescale might be multiplied by ten or twenty. The name 'Darwin' attached to this speculation, reviving echoes of the great debate between Kelvin and the evolutionists in the nineteenth century, immediately roused interest, and produced a flurry of letters to *Nature*. By the end of 1903 there was a clear body of opinion that the Sun's heat must, ultimately, derive from radioactive energy. But even those researchers who held this opinion knew that it was based entirely on speculation, and that the actual processes by which energy was released from atoms inside the Sun were unknown. In a sense, the claims were premature, and in the absence of a solid theory of solar energy production by any other means, Kelvin's contraction hypothesis, and the short timescale it implied, lingered on – just as his timescale for the age of the Earth lingered on past its sell-by date. They still had supporters ten years later.

The main objection to the idea of radioactive energy powering the Sun was that spectroscopy showed no trace of the characteris-tic 'fingerprints' of elements such as uranium and radium in the light from the Sun; but the most prescient comment at this time came from the prolific pen of Rutherford, who suggested in 1913 that 'at the enormous temperature of the sun, it appears possible that a process of transformation may take place in ordinary elements analogous to that observed in the well-known radio-elements', and went on 'the time during which the sun may continue to emit heat at the present rate may be much longer than the value computed from ordinary dynamical data.'[*]

By then Rutherford knew, as Wilson and Darwin had not ten years previously, of Albert Einstein's proposal that mass and energy are interchangeable, through the relation $E = mc^2$, where c is the speed of light. Einstein's first paper on special relativity,

---

[*] Quoted by Burchfield, p. 168, from Rutherford's *Radioactive Substances*.

establishing, among other things, the mass–energy relation, was published in 1905. In the same year, in a second paper on the subject, he specifically addressed the radioactive energy question, and said 'if a body gives off the energy L in the form of radiation, its mass diminishes by L/c^2.' He stated quite categorically that 'the mass of a body is a measure of its energy', and speculated that 'it is not impossible that with bodies whose energy is variable to a high degree (e.g. with radium salts) the theory may successfully be put to the test.'*

Einstein was too optimistic, by far, in his hope that anyone might be able to measure the reduction in mass of a radioactive substance as it released energy. In everyday terminology, we are used to measuring the flow of energy in watts, or kilowatts. A hundred-watt lightbulb radiates one hundred joules of energy every second, and Einstein's equation tells us that we can also measure this flow as a little more than 10^{-12} of a gram (that is, a decimal point followed by 12 zeroes and a 1 grams). A hundred-watt heater would raise the temperature of a gram of water from 0°C to boiling point in just four seconds, far more swiftly than the heat produced by a gram of radium; there is no hope of measuring the change in mass of the radium as it loses radioactive energy, on any sensible timescale.

Turning the argument around, the mass of the Sun, usually written as 2×10^{33} grams, can be thought of as just under 2×10^{47} joules, or, in the units used by Gamow, about 5×10^{46} calories. With 8.8×10^{25} calories of heat escaping from the Sun each second, even if only 10 per cent of its mass can be converted into heat energy it would still have a potential lifetime of almost 6×10^{20} seconds, that is 2×10^{13} years (20 trillion years). The Sun radiates energy equivalent to four million tons of matter every second – but even if it has done so for four billion years, the amount of matter 'lost' in this way represents only one five-thousandth of its original mass. 'Atomic energy' can certainly solve the solar energy puzzle, and provide the timescale required by evolution. But how does it do the trick?

The next step towards understanding the seats of enormous energies in the Sun and stars was made by Arthur Eddington, the pioneering British scientist who was the first person successfully to apply the basic laws of physics to tackle the problem of what went on *inside* stars, and thereby invented the subject of astrophysics.

* *Annalen der Physik*, Volume 18, p. 639; quoted by Pais, p. 104.

Eddington had been born in 1882, and by 1920 he was Plumian Professor of Astronomy in the University of Cambridge. He was also one of the best-known scientists of the time, since he had been responsible for organizing the expedition to measure the way light from stars was bent by the Sun, during the solar eclipse of 1919, and had confirmed the prediction made by Einstein's general theory of relativity – popular folklore of the time had it that Eddington was the only person, apart from Einstein, who really understood general relativity. But he found time for a great deal more work besides this, and during the 1920s he speculated, at various times, that the source of energy in the Sun might be the total annihilation of matter to release energy, or the breakdown of heavy elements by radioactive decay (now called fission), or the building up of heavy elements from light elements, the process we now call fusion.*

Eddington had a clear idea which of these proposals was the best bet. 'Annihilation of protons and electrons', he wrote in 1926 in his epic book *The Internal Constitution of the Stars* (p. 295), 'or the disintegration of unknown elements of intense radio-activity are speculative hypotheses; these processes may or may not be capable of occurring. But in the formation of helium we have a process which *must* have occurred at some time and place – and where more likely than in the stars?' Why did he single out the formation of helium, rather than any of the other elements? Largely because of a discovery made by Francis Aston, working at the Cavendish Laboratory in Cambridge.

Aston had developed an instrument, called a mass spectrograph, which could be used to determine the masses of atoms of a chosen element. The technique, still used today, depends on measuring the way in which positively charged ions (atoms which have had one or two, or a few, electrons knocked off) are deflected by a magnetic field. The deflection depends on the speed of the particles, their charge and their mass, and the technique is so useful, and so important, that Aston received a Nobel Prize for his

---

* Both fission and fusion can release energy, we now know, because the nuclei of atoms in the middle range of masses are the most stable forms, with the lowest energy. The reasons have to do with details of quantum physics, which I won't go into here. But the most stable nucleus of all is iron-56, and in energy terms all other nuclei would 'like' to move towards this stable state, either by fission, in the case of heavier nuclei such as uranium, or by fusion, in the case of lighter nuclei such as carbon, oxygen or hydrogen. A common analogy is to think of iron as at the bottom of an energy valley, with lighter nuclei ranged up one side of the valley and heavier ones up the other side. Given the right conditions – and the inside of a star provides the right conditions – other nuclei will move down the slopes to the low point represented by iron.

work in 1922. His first mass spectrograph was operating in 1919, and one of the first discoveries he made with it was that an atom of helium has 0.8 per cent less mass than the mass of four atoms of hydrogen. Other atomic weights were *nearly*, but not quite, multiples of hydrogen. The 'not quite' gave Eddington his clue; the 'nearly' resolved a puzzle dating back more than a century.

In 1816, the English chemist William Prout had suggested that the atomic weight of any atom is an exact multiple of the atomic weight of hydrogen, and although later research showed chemists that the rule did not hold precisely, the weights they determined for other atoms were tantalizingly close to whole multiples of the weight of a hydrogen atom.

Puzzlement over why this should be so persisted throughout the nineteenth century and into the twentieth. Chemists could only measure atomic weights by studying the behaviour of large numbers of atoms in chemical reactions, comparing, for example, the weight of oxygen involved in reactions with a certain weight of carbon, or of hydrogen. The weights they found must always be the average of the weights of all the atoms involved in the reactions. In 1913, Frederick Soddy, who had worked with Rutherford in Canada and was by now at Glasgow University, explained the discrepancies by introducing the idea of isotopes, atoms of the *same* chemical element which had slightly different masses. If a sample of an element contained a mixture of atoms with slightly different weights but identical chemical properties, then chemical tests would indicate a single 'atomic weight' which would be an average of the actual atomic weights, and therefore not necessarily a precise multiple of the atomic weight of hydrogen, even if each isotope did have a weight that was a precise multiple of the atomic weight of hydrogen. Soddy's mass spectrograph also dealt with large numbers of atoms, but atoms of each isotope, with the same charge and speed, are deflected by different amounts in a magnetic field, and show up in their own right. He could measure each isotopic atomic weight, and average out the weights of the isotopes to get exactly the 'atomic weights' measured by chemical tests.

At the time, Soddy did not have the complete picture of isotopes, and did not know how two atoms could have different weights but identical chemical properties. The key to that understanding came only in 1932, when James Chadwick discovered the neutron, a particle very similar to the proton but with no net electric charge. We now know that, for example, there are two isotopes of helium, the rare helium-3, which contains two protons and one neutron in its nucleus, and the far more common helium-4, which has a nucleus made up of two protons and two neutrons (a helium-4 nucleus is an alpha particle). Eddington, in 1920, knew nothing of neutrons, and thought of what we know as the proton simply as the nucleus of the hydrogen atom.* But, like his contemporaries, he appreciated that Soddy's work had strongly re-established the idea that all atoms could be thought of as multiples of the hydrogen atom, perhaps built up by, somehow, sticking hydrogen atoms together. And he immediately seized on Aston's discovery that the nucleus of helium-4 weighed *less* than four nuclei of hydrogen 'weighed' separately.

Solar energy

In August 1920 the British Association for the Advancement of Science held its annual meeting in Cardiff. Eddington chose to address the gathering on the subject of solar energy, and began by knocking a few nails into the lid of the coffin of the contraction hypothesis:

> Only the inertia of tradition keeps the contraction hypothesis alive – or rather, not alive, but an unburied corpse. But if we decide to inter the corpse, let us freely recognize the position in which we are left. A star is drawing on some vast reservoir of energy by means unknown to us. This reservoir can scarcely be other than the sub-atomic energy which, it is known, exists abundantly in all matter; we sometimes dream that man will one day learn to release it and use it for his service. The store is well-nigh inexhaustible, if only it could be tapped. There is sufficient in the Sun to maintain its output of heat for 15 billion years . . .
>
> Aston has further shown conclusively that the mass of the helium atom is even less than the masses of the four hydrogen atoms which enter into it – and in this, at any rate, the chemists agree with him. There is a loss of mass in the synthesis amounting to 1 part in 120, the atomic weight of hydrogen being 1.008 and that of helium just 4. I will not dwell on his beautiful proof of this, as you will no doubt be able to hear it from himself. Now mass cannot be annihilated,

---

* The proton itself was only named in 1920, by Rutherford, in a paper in *Nature* (Volume 106, p. 220). It is virtually impossible to tell the story of the development of astrophysics in the 1920s without slipping in concepts that became common currency only in later years!

and the deficit can only represent the mass of the electrical energy set free in the transmutation. We can therefore at once calculate the quantity of energy liberated when helium is made out of hydrogen. If 5 per cent of a star's mass consists initially of hydrogen atoms, which are gradually being combined to form more complex elements, the total heat liberated will more than suffice for our demands, and we need look no further for the source of a star's energy.

If, indeed, the sub-atomic energy in stars is being freely used to maintain their great furnaces, it seems to bring a little nearer to fulfilment our dream of controlling this latent power for the well-being of the human race – or for its suicide.*

Subrahmanyan Chandrasekhar, in his book *Eddington*, describes these comments as 'some of the most prescient statements in all of astronomical literature'. This comment has the benefit of hindsight but is at least partly true. Eddington himself did not stand firmly by the idea of energy being produced by the conversion of hydrogen into helium, but, following what we now know to have been a wrong turning, he also considered the possibility of the complete annihilation of protons and electrons into energy. For years, the transmutation idea was just one possibility for consideration. On the social implications, however, he was certainly prescient. Eddington, a Quaker who had run into some difficulties with the authorities in Britain because of his pacifist beliefs during the First World War, saw not only the implications of Einstein's equation for energy production in stars, but the mixed blessing it implied for the inhabitants of planet Earth.

Simple stars

Eddington's astronomical work developed into one of the landmarks in science, the book *The Internal Constitution of the Stars*, written between May 1924 and November 1925, and published in 1926. Even today, more than sixty years later, it is still essential reading for astrophysicists. Eddington set out in this book the basic rules needed in applying physics to the study of stellar structure – how the inward pull of gravity is balanced by the

* From *Observatory*, Volume 43, p. 353; quoted in Chandrasekhar, *Eddington*, p. 17. As Eddington himself acknowledged, the Frenchman Jean Baptiste Perrin also pointed out the implications of Aston's discovery in 1920 (*Revue du Mois*, Volume 21, p. 113; cited by Eddington in *The Internal Constitution of the Stars*, p. 296). But he never developed as complete an understanding of stellar structure, and the implications of this release of sub-atomic energy, as Eddington achieved.

outward pressure of the hot interior, how density and temperature vary from place to place inside a star, the relationship between the mass of a star and its brightness (luminosity), and more. He also followed up some wrong turnings, like the idea of matter annihilation in stars. I won't delve into those here, but will focus on the key developments which led, at last, to the identification of the seats of enormous energies.

One of the most important of Eddington's insights, though, was the realization that in order to describe what he called 'so simple a thing' as a star you *don't* need to know where the star gets its energy from. The laws of physics tell us that a ball of gas containing a certain amount of matter and held up by the pressure inside itself must have a certain size and radiate a certain amount of energy. It doesn't matter where that energy comes from – without an energy supply, as we have seen, the star will shrink slowly, but the way the material of the star behaves is the same whatever the source of energy in its heart. To non-physicists, it is almost equally surprising that the scientific laws that describe the nature of a star are the laws of behaviour for a so-called 'perfect gas' – even though the *average* density of the Sun is about one and a half times the density of water, and the density in its centre is many times that of lead. Not what we usually think of as a 'gas'. But the fact that this dense material behaves like a gas is directly related to the way pressure holds the star up against the inward pull of gravity.

It is easy to understand why the inside of a star is hot. As we have seen, as the star forms, gravitational energy is liberated as heat; also, anything that is squeezed gets hotter, like the air in a bicycle pump (the opposite effect, that gas which expands gets cooler, is the principle on which your domestic refrigerator is based). Part of the pressure inside a star which holds it up is simply caused by the particles in its interior bashing against one another at high speeds – gas pressure. But if the particles are bashing together hard enough (if they are hot enough), negatively charged electrons get knocked off atoms in the process, and roam freely through the star. Atoms that have had electrons knocked off are called ions, and are left with a positive electric charge; a mixture of ions and electrons is known as a plasma.

This is what makes the inside of a star behave as a perfect gas. Atoms consist of a tiny nucleus surrounded by a much bigger cloud of electrons. To put the two components in perspective, if the nucleus of an atom were the size of a pea, the electron cloud would be the size of a concert hall. In a solid, atoms (the electron clouds) are touching one another, and do not move about. In a liquid, the electron clouds of atoms are still just about touching one another, but the individual atoms have enough energy to slither past one another. The density of a solid at its melting point is scarcely any more than the density of the liquid it melts into. But in a gas, the atoms have so much energy that they fly about freely through space, occasionally bumping into another atom. So the density of a conventional gas is much less than that of the liquid it evaporates from. Atomic nuclei are so much smaller than atoms, however, that when the surrounding cloud of electrons is stripped from atomic nuclei to form a plasma, the nuclei are nowhere near touching each other, and can be squeezed closer together, even to densities many times that of lead, while still flying free and behaving like gas particles. You can put a *lot* of peas in the Carnegie Hall without them touching each other. The nuclei fly freely through the interior of a star, occasionally colliding with each other. In doing so, they follow exactly the laws of physics describing ideal gases.

In a relatively small collection of matter, like a planet, atoms stay as atoms and the pressure in the centre is enough to hold the outer layers up even without a plasma being formed; the matter behaves as a solid or, depending on what it is made of and the temperature and pressure, a liquid or a gas. But more interesting things start to happen, as Eddington realized, for larger globes of material with higher internal pressures and temperatures, where ionization becomes important. Once plasma forms, electromagnetic effects become important. Fast-moving charged particles convert some of their kinetic energy into the form of electromagnetic radiation, and this radiation in its turn interacts with charged particles, especially electrons, being absorbed and re-radiated. The effect of all this on the plasma is an additional outward pressure, radiation pressure, which helps to hold the globe of material – what we must now think of as a star – up against the pull of gravity. A glowing, stable star is held up by a combination of gas pressure and radiation pressure.

But now look at the other extreme. Imagine a huge ball of gas that tries to form into a star. The temperature in the centre will rise so high that there will be an enormous radiation pressure, which blasts the star apart.

So there are three possible fates for a ball of gas that collapses under its own gravity, depending on its mass. It can become a cool, small globe held up only by gas pressure; it can become a glowing star, held up by a mixture of gas pressure and radiation pressure; or it can become a short-lived, superhot gas globe that is quickly blown apart by radiation pressure. Stars only exist in the range of masses where gas pressure and radiation pressure contribute roughly equally to the support of the ball of gas against the tug of gravity. And this is only true for a limited range of masses.

Exactly which range of masses depends slightly on what the star is made of, because that affects the number of electrons around to interact with the radiation. As we shall see in the next chapter, Eddington made a wrong guess about the composition of the Sun in his classic book; but this is a trivial mistake compared with the power of his discovery of the importance of applying the gas laws to stars. In *The Internal Constitution of the Stars*, Eddington asked the reader to imagine a series of globes of gas of various sizes, starting with 10 grams, then 100 grams, 1,000 grams and so on. The nth globe contains 10^n grams of material. The *only* globes in which, according to the gas laws, radiation pressure and gas pressure combine to produce stable, glowing stars are numbers 32 to 35 in the series.* And this prediction from basic physics is borne out when we look at the real Universe. Globe 31 has a mass about five times that of Jupiter, the biggest planet in our Solar System. Globe 32 has a mass of 10^{32} grams, just about one tenth of the mass of the Sun; and globe 35 is about a hundred times more massive than our Sun. A star cannot begin to glow until it is bigger than Jupiter and about one tenth of the Sun's mass, but if it has more than a hundred times the Sun's mass, gravity is insufficient to hold it together against the outward blast of radiation from its hot interior. Out of the infinite range of possible globes of gas that we can imagine, only globes 32 to 35 in Eddington's list correspond to stars. Eddington told astronomers, using basic physics, how bright stars of each mass should shine. And our Sun sits nicely at the lower end of this range, obeying the basic laws of gas physics, *whatever* its source of energy might be.

Eddington's calculations also fitted in with discoveries being made from observations of other stars. The discovery of a relationship between mass and luminosity (stars with low mass are dim; more massive stars shine more brightly) was particularly significant in developing an understanding of how stars work. But Eddington also found that all stars in the same family as our Sun (so-called 'main sequence' stars), regardless of their mass and

---

* I am using here the modern version of Eddington's calculation, with numbers appropriate to the actual composition of the Sun.

luminosity, must have the same central temperature. It happens that the figure Eddington worked out for this crucial central temperature, 40 million degrees, was rather too high. Since his pioneering work, the calculations of the physics of stellar interiors have been improved in several small ways, and today the accepted figure is about 15 million degrees.★ But this relatively minor adjustment has no effect on his important discovery that all main-sequence stars 'burn' energy in their hearts at the *same* temperature.

'Taken at face value', as Eddington pointed out when considering in his book (p. 179) the energy released by two specific stars, 'it suggests that whether a supply of 680 ergs per gram is needed (V Puppis) or whether a supply of 0.08 ergs per gram (Krueger 60) the star has to rise to 40,000,000° to get it. At this temperature it taps an unlimited supply.' Later in the book (p. 299) he elaborated on the notion. A star will 'contract until its central temperature reaches 40 million degrees when the main supply of energy is suddenly released . . . A star on the main series must keep just enough of its material above the critical temperature to furnish the supply required.'

This is a beautiful example of a feedback process which maintains equilibrium in such a star. Suppose the star – any star – shrinks a little more. It would get hotter in the middle, as gravitational energy is converted into heat, and so more sub-atomic energy would be released, which would have the effect of making the star expand, restoring equilibrium. Or suppose that for some reason the star expanded slightly. That would make it cooler in the middle, slowing down the release of energy and making it shrink again. Stars have an inbuilt thermostat which keeps their centres just at the right temperature for sub–atomic energy to be released. In general terms, the physics worked out beautifully. But Eddington still had one major problem in trying to persuade his physicist friends that this was, indeed, the way stars worked. 'The difficulty is that from the physicist's point of view the temperature of the stars is absurdly low. He regards the stars as practically at absolute zero, because in regard to nuclear processes 40 million degrees is a small quantity which it is scarcely worth while to take notice of' (*Internal Constitution*, p. 300).

The problem was that in the mid-1920s physicists were able to carry out calculations which showed that the energy required to

★ These are, of course, degrees Kelvin (K), measured from the absolute zero of temperature, −273°C.

make nuclei interact with one another in the first place was much more than the energy of motion of particles inside the Sun at the temperature Eddington calculated. There was plenty of nuclear energy available in principle, but how could the stars release energy at so low a temperature? This was the main objection, in the mid-1920s, to Eddington's theories of stellar energy generation; but he stuck firmly to his guns. 'The helium which we handle must have been put together at some time and some place', he pointed out. 'We do not argue with the critic who urges that the stars are not hot enough for this process; we tell him to go and find *a hotter place*'★ (p. 301).

Even as these words were going through the printing presses, however, a new understanding of physics that would solve the problem was being developed. In his preface, dated July 1926, Eddington mentions that 'as we go to press a "new quantum theory" is arising which may have important reactions on the stellar problem when it is more fully developed'† (p. xi). He was right. The first great revolution in physics in the twentieth century, relativity theory, had provided an understanding that mass could be converted into energy, in principle, and opened up the possibility of a star like the Sun living for billions of years. The second great revolution in physics in the twentieth century, quantum physics, showed how the trick could be achieved in practice, and that the conditions of temperature and pressure at the heart of the Sun, calculated by Eddington, were, indeed, exactly right to permit a series of interactions that effectively converted hydrogen nuclei (protons), four at a time, into helium nuclei (alpha particles).

The message was one that Chamberlain would have appreciated, and one that recurs throughout science. When observations tell you that something is happening, but theory says it is impossible, it is time to change your theory, not the observations! But it took well over ten years for the hopes expressed by Eddington in July 1926 to become reality, with the development of a full understanding of the way energy is produced inside the Sun and stars.

★ Eddington, stressing his faith in the laws of physics which unambiguously revealed the temperature at the heart of the Sun, was in fact telling his critics to 'go to Hell'.
† For a discussion of the quantum revolution of the 1920s, see *In Search of Schrödinger's Cat*, by John Gribbin.

3

At the Heart of the Sun

In his address to the British Association in 1920, mentioned in Chapter Two, Eddington made a particularly prescient comment about the source of solar energy. He referred to the possibility that 'sub-atomic energy is actually being set free in the stars', and mentioned that 'Aston's experiments seem to leave little room for doubt that all the elements are constituted out of hydrogen atoms bound together with negative electrons. The nucleus of the helium atom, for example, consists of four hydrogen atoms bound with two electrons. But Aston has further shown conclusively that the mass of the helium atom is less than the sum of the masses of the four hydrogen atoms which enter into it.' Transmutation of elements could, if it occurred, set free energy, corresponding to the difference in mass, and 'if 5 per cent of a star's mass consists initially of hydrogen atoms, which are gradually being combined to form more complex elements, the total heat liberated will more than suffice for our demands, and we need look no further for the source of a star's energy.'

The only doubt, at that time, seemed to be that transmutation of the elements might not actually be possible inside stars. But Eddington had an answer to that. Rutherford, he told his audience, had recently been breaking down atoms of oxygen and nitrogen, driving out an isotope of helium from them; and 'what is possible in the Cavendish Laboratory may not be too difficult in the sun.'* Eddington was tantalizingly close to the truth, but his intuitive speculation had run ahead of scientific understanding. Before the real importance of the transmutation of hydrogen into

---

* The version of Eddington's talk published in *Nature* can also be found in *A Source Book in Astronomy and Astrophysics*, edited by Kenneth Lang and Owen Gingerich.

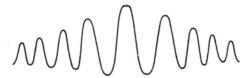

Figure 3.1   A wave packet. Fundamental 'particles', such as electrons and protons, are best thought of as tiny wave packets, not mathematical points. A wave packet is, by its nature, a spread-out object, with a finite size.

helium could be established, and astronomers could come to appreciate that hydrogen makes up far more than 5 per cent of the bulk of a star like the Sun, the quantum revolution had to provide physicists with a new set of tools to describe the way particles interact under the conditions found at the heart of the Sun. The most important of these was uncertainty.

A quantum of uncertainty

I have told the story of the quantum revolution in detail in my book *In Search of Schrödinger's Cat* – the story of the strange quantum world of particles like electrons and protons, where particles have to be regarded as being waves as well as particles, and waves, like light, must also be regarded as particles (in the case of light, photons). One of the strangest aspects of quantum reality, closely linked to this wave/particle duality, is known as uncertainty. In the quantum world, you can never be quite sure exactly where a particle is – not simply because of the difficulty of measuring the position of something as tiny as an electron, but because it *does not have* a precisely defined position. This is because the particle is also a wave – and a wave is, by its very nature, a spread-out thing (Figure 3.1). It was this feature of the quantum world that explained how alpha particles – what we would now call helium nuclei – could escape from the nuclei of radioactive atoms.

By the 1920s, it was clear that atoms consist of a cloud of negatively charged electrons surrounding a tiny kernel, the positively charged nucleus. In a normal, neutral atom, the number of electrons in the outer cloud is exactly balanced by the number of protons in the positive nucleus – but the nucleus also contains neutral particles, similar to protons but with zero charge. They are called neutrons, and they were only discovered in 1932.★ A nucleus of the most common isotope of radium contains 88 protons and 138 neutrons, and when it decays two protons and two neutrons are ejected together, as an alpha particle, leaving a less massive atomic nucleus behind.

Like charges, of course, repel each other. Because the alpha particle carries a positive charge, and so does the nucleus being left behind, it is no surprise that, once the alpha particle is outside the nucleus, it should be repelled strongly, and rush away from the nucleus. But all nuclei contain positive charge, and they don't blow apart as the like charges in each of the protons repel one another. This is because there is another force at work inside the nucleus. It is called the strong nuclear force, and over very short distances – just across the nucleus of an atom – it overwhelms the electric force repelling the protons from each other, and glues the mixture of protons and neutrons together. The strong nuclear force only has a very short range, but it completely dominates over the electric force over that short range. One of the puzzles that quantum physicists had to solve at the end of the 1920s was how the escaping alpha particle from a radioactive nucleus could overcome this attractive force long enough to make its getaway.

The answer came from uncertainty, and it was found by a young Russian, George Gamow, who was visiting the University of Göttingen in 1928 (and who later moved to the United States and became an American citizen). Gamow realized that the strict rules of quantum uncertainty allowed – indeed, *required* – the alpha particle in some nuclei to be smeared out over a short distance, extending out of the nucleus proper and beyond the range of the strong nuclear force. Together, the combined influence of the strong nuclear force and electric repulsion produced the energy equivalent of a hill surrounding the nucleus, a barrier which the alpha particle had to climb over in order to escape. Measurements of the energy of escaping alpha particles showed that they did not have quite enough energy to climb over this hill; Gamow's work showed how quantum uncertainty would allow them, in effect, to 'tunnel through' the hill. When the numbers were put into the

---

★ It was because neutrons hadn't yet been discovered that Eddington talked, in 1920, of helium atoms containing two extra electrons, bound up in the nucleus to cancel out some of the positive charge possessed by four hydrogen nuclei (four protons). In fact, a helium-4 nucleus, or alpha particle, consists of two protons and two neutrons, not four protons and two electrons. But a neutron left on its own for more than about 10 minutes will 'decay', spitting out an electron and turning into a proton, so Eddington's description wasn't really so wide of the mark after all.

equations, they matched precisely; quantum uncertainty and the tunnel effect exactly explained how alpha particles with the measured energy got out of radioactive nuclei (Figure 3.2).

But what has this to do with sticking hydrogen nuclei together to make helium nuclei? The relevance is that the tunnel effect also works the other way round. If a proton is approaching a positively charged nucleus, it 'ought' to be repelled by the positive electric charge in the nucleus, and bounced away. If it is moving fast

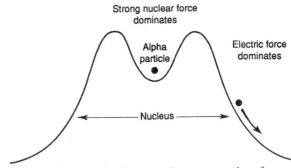

Strong nuclear force dominates

Alpha particle

Electric force dominates

Nucleus

Figure 3.2   The interplay between the strong nuclear force and the electric force makes a 'potential well' in which particles in the nucleus of an atom are trapped. An alpha particle inside the well that does not have enough energy to climb over the barrier ought to be trapped forever. But quantum uncertainty, related to the fact that the particle is really a wave packet that extends beyond the confines of the nucleus, allows some alpha particles to 'tunnel through' the barrier and escape.

In a similar way, during fusion reactions some particles from outside tunnel into the nucleus, through the barrier.

enough – with enough kinetic energy – it can get close enough to 'touch' the nucleus, and then the strong nuclear force can grab hold of it. The nucleus has gained a proton and has been transmuted. But the energy needed for the incoming proton to get close enough for this to work is very high – far higher than the energy possessed by protons at the temperatures that, simple physics told Eddington, exist inside the Sun. The tunnel effect, however, changes the picture. Because of its wave-like character, the proton only has to get near enough to the nucleus for its wave to overlap with the wave of the nucleus before it is grabbed. In effect, it tunnels through the electric barrier holding it at bay. And *that* is why there is no need of 'a hotter place' than the heart of the Sun to transmute hydrogen nuclei (protons) into helium nuclei. This was the key insight that set astrophysicists on the trail of the transmutation processes that keep the Sun, and other stars, hot. But it still took them ten more years to sort out the details.

Tunnelling inside stars

Gamow's insight, and the discovery of the tunnel effect, set physicists off along two separate, but related, trails. It gave them a chance, at last, to understand where the enormous energies that powered the stars came from; and it opened up the possibility of achieving the alchemists' dream, and changing one element into another in laboratories on Earth. The astrophysicists were quicker off the mark, but took longer to achieve their goal.

The first steps were taken astonishingly quickly after Gamow came up with the idea of tunnelling in 1928. By the next year, the physicists Robert Atkinson and Fritz Houtermans had taken up the idea and used it to demonstrate that in principle solar energy could be produced by sticking atomic nuclei together – the process now known as nuclear fusion. Their calculations showed how hydrogen nuclei (protons) could indeed get close enough to other nuclei for fusion to take place even at the kind of relatively low temperatures that straightforward physics said must exist in the heart of the Sun. Rudolf Kippenhahn, who worked with Atkinson in the 1960s, tells (in his book *100 Billion Suns*) how Atkinson remembered what had set him thinking along the right lines. He clearly recalled that Eddington's book *The Internal Constitution of the Stars* had first made him aware of the problem that the temperatures inside stars were not hot enough for fusion to take place, but that Eddington was convinced that nuclear energy *must* be the source of the light and heat radiated by stars. And the debt to Gamow was paid in the first sentence of the 1929 paper by Atkinson and Houtermans (published in the *Zeitschrift für Physik*, Volume 54, p. 656), which reads: 'Recently Gamow demonstrated that positively charged particles can penetrate the atomic nucleus even if traditional belief holds their energy to be inadequate.'

The key to an understanding of how the tunnel effect makes the energies of protons inside the Sun adequate to do the job is that a little fusion goes a long way. So much energy is released each time four protons are converted, by whatever means, into one alpha particle that the reaction can be quite a rare one, and yet (given that the Sun is made up of many billions of particles) provide enough energy to keep the Sun hot. Even at the temperatures at the heart of the Sun – about 15 million K by modern estimates – *most* protons are not moving fast enough to tunnel through the electric barrier. The temperature of anything, including the Sun, is indeed a measure of how fast the particles it is made of are moving and jostling against one another, but that doesn't mean that all the particles have exactly the same energy, or exactly the same speed. There is a particular average speed which is most common, and which is appropriate for that particular temperature. But some particles will be moving faster than average, and others more slowly, in a very well-defined way which obeys a precise statistical

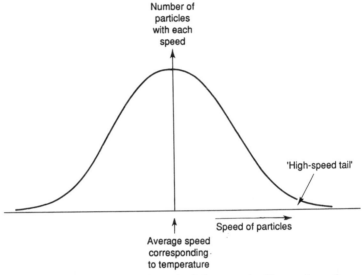

Figure 3.3   Even with the aid of the tunnel effect, only a few particles are moving fast enough for fusion to occur inside the Sun. They belong in the 'high-speed tail' of the distribution of velocities that corresponds to the temperature at the heart of the Sun.

law. At any temperature, it is possible to calculate not only the average speed but also what fraction of the particles will be moving 10 per cent faster, 50 per cent faster, twice as fast as the average, or whatever speed you are interested in (Figure 3.3). These rare fast particles are said to lie in the 'high-speed tail' of the distribution of velocities. The triumph of the application of Gamow's tunnel theory to the conditions inside the Sun was that it showed that at the right temperature just enough particles from the high-speed tail (by no means every proton) could tunnel through the electric barrier. But the 1929 paper was only a first step along the road to unlocking the secret of what keeps the Sun hot, because at that stage not only did nobody know exactly which fusion reactions were at work inside the Sun, they had completely the wrong idea about what the Sun was made of.

Anaxagoras, remember, had thought that the Sun must be a ball of red-hot iron. In 1929, astrophysicists' ideas about the composition of the Sun hadn't really moved on far from that idea. It was natural to guess that the composition of the Sun might not be so very different from that of the Earth, and the idea that the Sun's energy might come from the radioactive decay of elements such as radium, which are heavy metals, encouraged the view that most of the Sun's bulk consisted of heavy elements. So, although Atkinson and Houtermans had shown that protons could penetrate other nuclei of heavier elements and fuse with them under the conditions that existed inside the Sun, at the end of the 1920s nobody guessed that what kept the Sun hot was, in fact, the fusion of protons with other protons to make helium nuclei more or less directly – the fusion process which is, in fact, the most efficient energy source of them all.

Atkinson went on to develop these ideas in more detail in the 1930s, while Houtermans turned to other work. In 1928, Albrecht Unsöld had shown for the first time, using spectroscopic evidence, that hydrogen is not only the most abundant element in the atmosphere of the Sun, but that there are roughly a million times more hydrogen atoms there than anything else. This was confirmed, using evidence from a completely different spectroscopic technique, by William McCrea in 1929. But although Unsöld and McCrea had proved that hydrogen is by far the dominant element in the atmosphere of the Sun, it took a long time for astrophysicists to appreciate that it is comparably dominant *throughout* the Sun and stars. Even in the 1930s, less than a human lifetime ago, the Sun still kept the basic secret of what it was made of. Nonetheless, there was clearly ample hydrogen available to provide energy by fusion, and in the early 1930s Atkinson developed the idea that heavier nuclei might absorb protons one after another until they became unstable and, as a result of a kind of nuclear indigestion, spat out alpha particles instead – a way of turning hydrogen into helium through an intermediary. He was nearly right – as we shall see, some stars do get their energy in this way, but this is not the main fusion process at work inside the Sun. But Atkinson did show, by 1936, that the single most likely fusion reaction under the conditions prevailing at the heart of the Sun would be the simple fusion of two hydrogen nuclei to form a deuteron. In this process, one of the protons is converted into a neutron by spitting out a positively charged counterpart to the electron, known as a positron. The deuteron is a nucleus consisting of a single proton and a single neutron held together by the strong nuclear force, and it is also known as heavy hydrogen.

But all this talk of protons changing into neutrons and spitting out positrons shows how much the world of physics had changed by 1936, because in 1929, when Atkinson's work with Houtermans was published, nobody knew that either neutrons or positrons existed. They were part of the laboratory physics version of the story of twentieth-century alchemy.

Alchemy in the lab

In 1928, when Gamow came up with the idea of the tunnel effect, physics only knew of two 'fundamental' particles, the proton and the electron. The alpha particle seemed to be a group of four protons and two electrons bound together in one unit, and all atoms could be envisaged as built up from protons and electrons alone. But there was still a long-standing puzzle about the nature of radioactivity, involving these particles and dating back to the distinction Rutherford had found, in 1898, between alpha and beta 'rays'. Although beta rays had been firmly identified with electrons at the turn of the century, at the end of the 1920s it was still far from clear how the electrons got out of atomic nuclei. In particular, measurements made in 1914 had shown that when a radioactive atom (we would now refer to the radioactive nucleus) emitted beta rays (electrons) some energy seemed to be lost. This is related to the way mass is converted into energy, or the other way around.* In nuclei that are prone to beta decay, the mass of the nucleus before it emits the electron is not quite the same as the mass of the nucleus plus the electron after the decay. An energy equivalent to about one and half times the mass of an electron is released in the decay, and this energy ought to be taken up by the electron, giving it a very well-defined speed – the *same* speed for all beta decay electrons. But the statistics of many measurements of electrons produced by beta decay showed that they emerged from the nucleus with a whole range of energies, always less than the

---

* The discussion here, and elsewhere in this chapter, often uses ideas and names that were not common until much later; I give what is essentially the modern version of beta decay (and other processes) at work in order to avoid confusion. Some of the historical byways that led to the modern understanding – often by devious routes – are explored in my other books.

magic figure corresponding to 1.5 electron masses. Energy seemed to have vanished into thin air.

In 1930, Wolfgang Pauli explained the discrepancy by invoking the presence of another kind of particle, with no electric charge and very little mass, that had never been detected in any experiment. The sole raison d'être for this particle was to carry away the missing energy in beta decay. The hypothetical particle was later given the name 'neutrino', and later still neutrinos were actually detected. We shall hear much more about them in Chapter Four. But in 1930 it was a breathtaking act of daring to suggest that there might be another kind of fundamental particle besides the proton and the electron.

Just two years later, in 1932, the discovery of the neutron confirmed that there was more going on inside atoms than just interactions involving protons and electrons. This helped to give the neutrino idea respectability, and very soon beta decay was explained in terms of the workings of another kind of force, called the weak nuclear force, which describes how a neutron can convert itself into a proton by emitting *both* an electron *and* a neutrino. In beta decay, the radioactive nucleus loses a neutron but gains a proton, being converted into a nucleus of a different element in the process. With neutrons and neutrinos added to the list, the number of known fundamental particles had doubled in a couple of years. But where do positrons come into the story?

In 1929, at about the same time that people were beginning to think seriously about the implications of tunnel theory, the British physicist Paul Dirac came up with an idea which seemed, at first, outrageous. Working with the new equations of quantum physics (which he had developed himself), he had found that the equations that describe the behaviour of the electron (including its curious wave-particle duality) seemed to have two sets of solutions. This is rather like the way in which simple quadratic equations have two solutions. Just about the simplest quadratic equation of all, $x^2 = 4$, has two solutions, $x = 2$ and $x = -2$. Both 2×2 *and* $(-2) \times (-2)$ are equal to four. Of course, Dirac's equations were rather more complicated than that. But still, they had two solutions, and only one solution was needed to describe electrons. Dirac didn't want to waste any of the mathematics he had lovingly developed, so he suggested that the 'extra' solutions to his equations described a particle like the electron but with positive charge. Very few people (if any) took the idea seriously until 1932, when studies of cosmic rays (high-energy particles from space) revealed the existence of positive electrons – positrons. Dirac's chutzpah was vindicated, and by 1933 all the main players in the game of solar alchemy were known, even if the neutrino, in particular, was not yet taken fully seriously by all physicists.

We now know that just as there is a kind of mirror-image particle for the electron, so there are mirror-image 'antiparticles' for the neutron, proton, and neutrino. We can imagine whole planets and stars made of this mirror matter – but there is very little of it around in our part of the Universe, because any antiparticle that meets one of its particle counterparts annihilates in a blast of pure radiation, with all of the mass from both particles being converted into energy. Almost certainly, the entire Universe is, in fact, made almost entirely of matter, not antimatter. But that doesn't stop antiparticles like positrons being created in nuclear reactions, and taking part in other nuclear reactions during their brief lives. Which brings us back to the modern alchemists.

While other people were worrying about what the quantum equations meant, and 'inventing' new particles to explain where the missing energy from beta decay was going, some of the more pragmatic physicists were still indulging in the kind of experiments that had started the particle physics revolution in the first place – essentially, bashing atoms (or nuclei) as hard as possible and watching to see what happened to them. But this particular phase of atom bashing was a direct result of the development of new quantum ideas: it stemmed from Gamow's tunnel theory.

Early in the 1930s, physicists developed the first machines which could accelerate beams of protons, using electric fields, to fairly high energies. The energy of the beams produced by these particle accelerators is usually measured in terms of the energy that an electron would gain by being accelerated across an electric potential of one Volt (1 eV). The old-fashioned equations that described collisions between protons and atomic nuclei said that the protons could only approach close enough to 'stick' to the nuclei – to come within range of the strong nuclear force – if they had energies of millions of electron Volts (several MeV). Just as the heart of the Sun was too cold for such reactions to occur, according to the old theory, so, in the late 1920s, particle accelerators that might be built on Earth were, physicists knew, not energetic enough to make protons stick to nuclei in the lab. But Gamow's tunnel-effect equations apply just as much in laboratories on Earth as they do inside the Sun.

In the late 1920s, one of the junior members of Rutherford's research team at the Cavendish Laboratory was John Cockcroft, a physicist who had made rather a late start in his eventual speciality (he was born in 1897) because his education had been interrupted by army service during the First World War. He had a background in electrical engineering, related to his army work in signals, and this would stand him in good stead in the work which was to make his name famous. At that time, the only particles which physicists had available to bombard atomic nuclei with in atom bashing experiments were alpha particles produced by radioactive decay. These had produced the first successful transmutations of elements when Rutherford discovered, in 1919, that when a fast-moving alpha particle strikes a nucleus of nitrogen the nitrogen is transformed into oxygen, while a hydrogen nucleus, to which Rutherford gave the name 'proton', is ejected. Even before Rutherford identified the proton as a fundamental particle, physicists had discovered that positively charged hydrogen nuclei could be produced by stripping the electrons off the atoms electrically. Ten years after his first transmutations of nitrogen into oxygen, they knew how to produce protons in profusion. But there seemed little point in trying to develop a proton accelerator if the protons would not have enough energy to penetrate the electric barrier around nuclei. In a conversation with Gamow in 1929, however, Cockcroft learned that protons with energies of only a few hundred keV could penetrate the nuclear barrier – and he knew that a machine to accelerate protons to such energies could be constructed using the technology of the time. But it wouldn't come cheap.

Cockcroft persuaded Rutherford to use his influence to obtain what was then a very large sum of money to begin work on the particle accelerator project – one thousand pounds. In a couple of years of intensive work, with a research student from Ireland, Ernest Walton, Cockcroft developed the first particle accelerator, producing a beam of protons with energies of more than 700 keV. The rationale behind the project was, in fact, a neat reversal of one of Eddington's quips from his 1920 British Association lecture, although no latter-day Eddington seems to have pointed this out. Eddington had said that 'what is possible in the Cavendish Laboratory may not be too difficult in the sun.' Gamow had pointed out that the way in which fusion could work inside the Sun at the relatively low temperature of 15 million K meant that fusion should be possible in the laboratory using protons with energies of a few hundred keV – in effect, that 'what is possible inside the *Sun* may not be too difficult in the Cavendish Laboratory.' It is entirely fitting that the first particle accelerator was indeed built in the Cavendish Lab – and that in 1932 it produced nuclear fusion reactions (the work for which Cockcroft and Walton received the Nobel Prize in 1951).

This may be a surprise to anyone who knows that researchers today are still struggling to obtain energy commercially by reproducing on Earth the kind of fusion reactions that take place inside the stars. But their problem is rather more difficult – to produce a stable, sustainable reaction that can be used safely in power stations on a regular, day-to-day basis. All that Cockcroft and Walton had to do was bombard nuclei of a chosen substance with protons and test to see if any of those nuclei were absorbing protons and being converted into other elements in the process. That's all – but it achieved the age-old dream of the alchemists, transmutation of elements, and it took physics a crucial further step towards unlocking the secret of how the Sun stays hot.

The target that Cockcroft and Walton chose to bombard with their proton beam was a thin layer of lithium. This is the third lightest element, after hydrogen and helium, and is the lightest solid that exists under everyday conditions. Each lithium nucleus carries only three units of positive charge. Obviously, the smaller the positive charge on the chosen nuclei the easier it would be for the protons in the beam to tunnel through the electric barrier. We now know that the nucleus of a stable lithium atom consists of three protons and four neutrons held together by the strong nuclear force. Most of the protons in the beam from Cockcroft and Walton's accelerator passed through the almost empty spaces between the lithium nuclei, brushing aside electrons like armour-piercing shells bursting through wet Kleenex. But just a few protons hit their nuclear targets head on, and, in accordance with Gamow's prediction, tunnelled their way into the nuclei. In each case, the result was a nucleus containing four protons and four neutrons – an isotope of the element beryllium. But this isotope is highly unstable, and whenever it is formed it almost immediately splits into two alpha particles (helium nuclei) each containing two protons and two neutrons. Mass is converted into energy in the process, and the two alpha particles hurtle out of the lithium layer, and can easily be detected.

In the popular press of the day, and almost always since, the Cockcroft-Walton experiment was described as 'splitting' the atom, as if the flying protons simply blasted the lithium nuclei apart, like a cannon ball demolishing a brick wall. But there is much deeper significance in the fact that the atomic nucleus that splits is actually an unstable *beryllium* nucleus, created, if only fleetingly, by the *fusion* of a proton with a lithium nucleus. The tunnel effect could be seen at work in the Cavendish Laboratory, and nobody could doubt any longer that it was also at work in the heart of the Sun. But which atomic nuclei did it operate on?

The solar pressure cooker

Throughout the 1930s, astrophysicists trying to pin down the exact cycle of fusion reactions that keeps the Sun hot were hamstrung by their misconceptions about what the Sun is made of. Unsöld and McCrea had convinced them that there was a lot of hydrogen in the Sun (at least in its atmosphere), and so they knew that there were probably many protons available inside the Sun, with the right kind of energies to participate in the kind of reactions that Cockcroft and Walton had demonstrated in the Cavendish Laboratory (and which were very soon being demonstrated in other laboratories, in the United States and elsewhere). The approach pioneered by Eddington, using the standard equations of physics that describe how heat is transmitted outwards from the interior of a globe of gas like the Sun, showed how the flow of heat, and therefore the stability of the globe of gas, depended on the composition of the star. Electromagnetic radiation interacts strongly with charged particles, such as electrons and protons, and according to these calculations a star like the Sun could only be stable provided that there was the right mixture of electrons and nuclei inside it. Too many charged particles, and they would hold the radiation in, making the star swell up as it pushed them out of the way; too few, and the radiation would escape too easily, so that the star would deflate like a pricked balloon. And it makes a difference whether the protons all roam about freely, as hydrogen nuclei, or whether they are packed together, 26 at a time (plus the appropriate number of neutrons, 30 in the most stable form of iron), into nuclei of iron, as Anaxagoras supposed. For the same total mass of the Sun, the number of electrons is always the same as the number of protons. There are most electrons if all of the nuclei are simple protons, and far fewer electrons if a large fraction of the mass is locked up as neutrons (for a Sun made of pure iron, less than half the mass would be protons, and the rest neutrons, so the number of electrons would be less than half that of a Sun made of pure hydrogen).

Unfortunately, as it turned out, the calculations showed that a globe exactly the size of the Sun, with the Sun's temperature and measured rate of energy generation, could exist as a stable star provided that the proportion of hydrogen in its interior was *either* about 35 per cent *or* at least 95 per cent (at least 95 per cent made of hydrogen *and helium*, in fact, with very little scope for any heavier elements). Once again, what 'everybody knew' was to colour ideas about the Sun, and to hold back progress. Until Unsöld and McCrea showed otherwise, 'everybody knew' that the composition of the Sun was rather like that of the Earth. Once everybody knew that there was a lot of hydrogen inside the Sun, and that the laws of physics said that 'a lot' meant either 35 per cent hydrogen and 65 per cent heavy elements, or less than 5 per cent heavies, it was 'obvious' that the lower figure for hydrogen, closer to what everybody had known before, must be correct. So theorists began to look for ways in which protons could combine with heavier nuclei to produce unstable nuclei which would spit out alpha particles and liberate energy, just like the 'atom splitting' of lithium carried out in the Cavendish Laboratory by Cockcroft and Walton.

This misconception coloured the work of Robert Atkinson, when he developed the ideas he had first put forward in collaboration with Houtermans. In 1931, he suggested that the proportions of different elements inside stars and the energy generation process might both be explained if heavier nuclei absorbed successive protons and spat out helium nuclei – but he thought then that a star like the Sun contained only 35 per cent hydrogen. Even handicapped by these misconceptions, by 1936 Atkinson had established that the single most common nuclear reaction occurring in the heart of the Sun is the collision of two protons to form a deuteron (a nucleus containing one proton and one neutron) and a positron. The next step was to establish the way in which some stars, at least, really do extract nuclear energy.

Once again, George Gamow comes into the story. In April 1938, he organized a conference in Washington DC, bringing astronomers and physicists together to discuss the problem of energy generation inside stars. One of the young nuclear physicists at that meeting, Hans Bethe, had a thorough understanding of the conditions required for protons to penetrate more massive nuclei, but had not been aware of the astrophysical problems. Bethe was born in 1906 in Strasbourg (then in Germany, now part of France) and worked at several German universities before moving to Britain in 1933 (when Hitler came to power) and on to the United States in 1935, where he worked at Cornell University in New York.

By 1938, astrophysicists knew that the energy of the stars must originate from nuclear processes, but they didn't know which nuclear processes. The problem is fairly simple to sum up, using a couple of examples. A reaction like the classic interaction between hydrogen nuclei and lithium nuclei – the Cockcroft and Walton 'atom splitting' process – is far too efficient to explain how the Sun stays hot. Even at a temperature of 15 million degrees, if there were very much lithium in the Sun's core it would all be rapidly converted into helium nuclei, releasing so much energy so quickly that the Sun would blow itself apart. On the other hand, reactions between protons and (for example) oxygen nuclei are far too slow, at these temperatures, to produce the right amount of energy on their own. If the Sun depended on those reactions, it would fizzle out (in fact, it would shrink until it got hot enough in the centre to make the reactions go faster). Bethe, and the other participants in the conference, were asked which nuclear reaction, or set of reactions, would go at just the right rate at the temperature inside the Sun to produce the amount of energy the Sun actually does radiate.

In his book *The Birth and Death of the Sun*,* written just after these events, Gamow describes how Bethe decided that this shouldn't be a very difficult problem to solve, and how he set out to find the secret of stellar energy on the train back to Cornell. According to legend, Bethe promised himself he would solve the problem before the steward called the passengers to dinner – and he did so, with seconds to spare. At the same time, early in 1938, another German, Carl von Weizsäcker, had identified the same solution to the stellar energy problem, back in Berlin. But he lacked the presence of an ebullient Gamow to make the discovery memorable by spreading the news of a (possibly partly apocryphal) hasty calculation while waiting for dinner on a train.

Stellar alchemy

In its modern version, only slightly improved since 1938, this energy generation process is called the carbon cycle, or the carbon-nitrogen-oxygen (CNO) cycle. It works like this.

First, a proton tunnels into a nucleus containing six protons and six neutrons (a nucleus of carbon-12). The nucleus that is

* Viking, New York, 1940.

produced, nitrogen-13, is radioactive, and emits a positron and a neutrino, converting into carbon-13. If a second proton now tunnels into this nucleus, we get a nucleus of nitrogen-14, and if a third proton tunnels into the nitrogen-14 nucleus it is transformed into oxygen-15, which is also radioactive and spits out a positron and a neutrino, transmuting into nitrogen-15 (in every case, the *name* of an isotope depends on how many protons it contains; its *number* is the combined total of neutrons + protons). But now, if yet another proton tunnels into the nucleus of nitrogen-15, it ejects an alpha particle – two protons and two neutrons bound together to form a helium nucleus. What is left behind is a nucleus of carbon-12, just what the cycle started with; along the way, four protons have, in effect, been combined to make one helium nucleus, with a couple of positrons, two neutrinos and a lot of energy released along the way. A relatively small amount of carbon-12 in the heart of a star will act as a catalyst for many cycles of this kind (Figure 3.4), steadily converting hydrogen into helium and releasing energy to keep the star hot – even though, overall, the amount of carbon, nitrogen and oxygen in the star is unchanged (and if Bethe really did work all that out on the train before dinner, he deserves all the credit Gamow gave him).

The process explains beautifully the way in which many stars stay hot. But it turns out that it is *not* the most important process for generating energy inside the Sun. As astrophysicists improved their calculations, and their observational colleagues obtained more accurate estimates of stellar masses and luminosities, it became clear that the carbon cycle is the dominant energy source in stars with more than about one and a half times the mass of the Sun, and correspondingly higher internal temperatures, but that it can only produce a modest amount of energy at the temperatures inside the Sun itself. By the time this was realized, it was no embarrassment to the astrophysicists, because Bethe had already found the nuclear process which really does keep our Sun hot.

This time, there was no train ride involved, just steady work back at Cornell, with Bethe's colleague Charles Critchfield. Their work on what is known as the proton-proton (p-p) chain was also first published in 1938, although it was not until the 1950s that astrophysicists were able to say for certain that it is the p-p chain, not the CNO cycle, that produces most of the Sun's energy (one of the main reasons it took so long to sort this out was the confusion about the Sun's composition; everything fits together neatly once it is realized that the Sun is, indeed, more than 95-per-

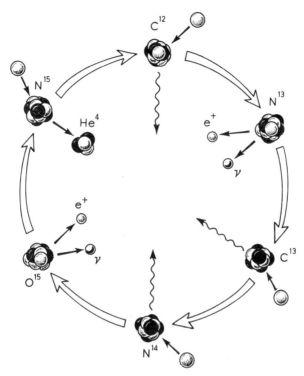

Figure 3.4 If there is just a little carbon-12 inside a star, and the temperature is just right, then hydrogen can be converted into helium and energy released by the carbon-nitrogen-oxygen cycle. Start at the top of the diagram, and follow the arrows clockwise; each incoming particle from outside the ring is a proton, and the net effect is to convert four protons (hydrogen nuclei) into one alpha particle (helium-4 nucleus), while the carbon nucleus is reformed. Wavy lines indicate gamma rays.

cent made of hydrogen and helium, and the modern estimate sees the Sun as 70 per cent hydrogen, 28 per cent helium, and just 2 per cent for everything else, the heavy elements).

The p–p chain starts with the reaction that Atkinson had pointed to as the starting point for nuclear fusion inside stars, a collision between two protons in which the tunnel effect allows them to get close enough together to fuse into a deuteron, spitting out a neutrino and a positron in the process. Another proton can then tunnel into the deuteron, producing a nucleus of helium-3, containing two protons and one neutron. Finally, when two nuclei of helium-3 collide they form a stable nucleus of helium-4,

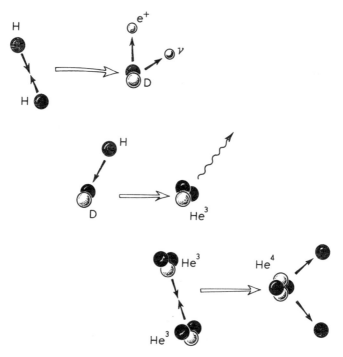

Figure 3.5   Our Sun is not hot enough to be powered by the CNO cycle, although other stars are. It gets its energy from another fusion process, the proton-proton chain. Thanks to the tunnel effect, two protons can combine inside the Sun to form deuterium, from which first helium-3 and then helium-4 is formed. But even in the heart of the Sun, only rare fast-moving particles are able to take advantage of the tunnel effect and fuse in this way.

spitting out two protons as they do so (Figure 3.5). About 95 per cent of the helium-3 nuclei do suffer this fate; the other 5 per cent have a choice of two slightly different fates, which we shall learn more about in Chapter Four. Just as in the CNO cycle, the net effect is that four protons have been converted into one nucleus of helium-4, and energy has been released. But whereas, we now know, the CNO cycle needs temperatures above about 20 million degrees to work effectively, the p-p chain is an efficient energy source even at a temperature as low as 15 million K.

It is very hard to put all of this in any kind of everyday context. Temperatures like 15 million K and densities many times that of lead are simply not part of our experience. But there are some slightly mind-boggling features of these nuclear reactions that are worth trying to take on board (and which, if nothing else, will make you appreciate what engineers are up against in trying to reproduce fusion processes as a source of energy for power stations here on Earth).

First, the tunnel-effect calculations show that even at a temperature of 15 million K the basic proton-proton interaction that starts the chain off occurs only if one of the colliding protons is travelling five times faster than average, way out in the high-speed tail of the velocity distribution. And even then, the collision has to be almost exactly head on – a fast-moving proton that strikes another proton only a glancing blow will not be able to tunnel through the electric barrier. Inside the Sun, just one proton in a hundred million is travelling fast enough even for a head-on collision to do the trick. And unless one of the two interacting protons spits out a positron during the tiny split second that they are within tunnelling range of each other, they will still not form a stable deuteron – a 'nucleus' consisting of just two protons is not stable in its own right. Each proton in the heart of the Sun is involved in a collision with other protons millions of times in every second. But even so, the quantum calculations show that on average it would take an individual proton 14 billion years to find a partner able to join it in forming a deuteron through a head-on collision. Some will take longer than average; some will find their partners more quickly. The Sun is only about 4.5 billion years old – which is why most of its protons have not yet found such partners. But there are so many protons inside the Sun that, even at this incredibly slow rate of reactions, with just one collision in every ten billion trillion (1 in 10^{22}) initiating the p-p chain, and just 0.7 per cent of the mass of each set of four protons being converted into pure energy when a helium-4 nucleus is formed, about *five million* tons of mass is converted into energy every second inside the Sun. And so far, the Sun has processed only about 4 per cent of its initial stock of hydrogen into helium, although the p-p reactions have been going on steadily for 4.5 billion years.

Strictly speaking, these mind-blowing statistics bring us to the end of the story I set out to tell at the start of this chapter, the secret of how the Sun stays hot. But it would be a pity to move on to other secrets of the Sun without mentioning, if only briefly, how more complex nuclear reactions inside other stars, long ago, explain our presence here on Earth today.

Stardust

Astronomers now have good evidence that the clouds of gas from which the first stars formed, after the Big Bang in which the Universe was born, contained only hydrogen and helium (about 25 per cent helium) with just a tiny trace of a few other light elements.* Everything else has been made inside stars.

The first stage is the processing of hydrogen into helium. This affects the nature of the star in which the hydrogen is being 'burnt', and has, astrophysicists calculate, already changed the size and appearance of our own Sun over the past 4.5 billion years. Because each single nucleus acts like an individual particle in the 'gas' at the heart of the Sun, every time four protons are combined to make one helium nucleus there are three less particles to contribute to the gas pressure holding the Sun up. As the gas pressure slowly decreases as a result, the core of the Sun shrinks slightly and gets hotter, so that extra radiation pressure exactly makes up for the deficiency. But shrinking and getting hotter in its heart means that the Sun's *outer* layers actually expand slightly, as they become hotter in response to the increased flow of energy out from the core. Over its life so far, the Sun's brightness has increased by about 40 per cent. In another 1.5 billion years, when it is 6 billion years old, it will be 15 per cent brighter still. This has interesting implications for life on Earth – the climate of Norway will then, other things being equal, be like that of northern Africa today, and there will be no polar ice caps. But at least the Sun will still be recognizable.

In 6 billion years from now, when the Sun is rather more than 10 billion years old, it will no longer be recognizable. By then, almost all of the hydrogen in its heart will have been converted into helium, and although plenty of hydrogen will remain in the outer part of the star, those regions are not hot enough for the proton–proton process to operate. Without hydrogen fusion in its heart, the Sun's core will shrink in upon itself and get hotter still. Hydrogen burning will take place in a shell around the burnt-out core, making the surface layers expand until the Sun swells to more than three times its present size. Although a lot of energy will be flowing out through this large star, it will have a vast area of surface to flow through, and so the surface itself will be cooler than today, and dark red in colour. The Sun will be a red subgiant,

* See my book *In Search of the Big Bang*.

and will continue to swell slowly for the next couple of hundred million years. It will become a true red giant, reaching a size 100 times bigger than its present diameter and engulfing Mercury, the innermost planet.

But then, according to astrophysical calculations, another dramatic change will occur. Over all this time, the temperature in the core has been rising, and when it reaches about 100 million K a new kind of nuclear fusion, helium burning, begins. Helium burning starts almost literally in a flash, releasing so much energy that the outer layers of the giant star are blown away into space, and the core settles down to a new life as a helium burning star – which takes us the next step along the road of stellar alchemy.

Helium nuclei – alpha particles – cannot combine in pairs to form another stable nucleus. The nucleus that corresponds to two helium-4 nuclei combined is beryllium-8 – and as Cockcroft and Walton noticed, beryllium-8 is *extremely* unstable. The only way helium-4 nuclei can be used to build something more complex is if a *third* alpha particle collides with the beryllium-8 nucleus during its very brief lifetime – within ten millionths of a billionth of a second after the first two alpha particles collide. Ridiculous though it may seem, this does happen, just often enough for helium burning to be a major source of energy in stars further along the evolutionary trail than our Sun. The end product is carbon-12, a respectable, well-behaved and stable nucleus.*

Other fusion processes occur at higher temperatures in correspondingly more evolved stars (more massive stars go through their life cycles, or evolve, more quickly than less massive stars, so many stars in our Galaxy have already died, even though our own Sun is barely middle-aged). Once carbon-12 has been produced inside a star, it is relatively easy for another alpha particle to tunnel into the nucleus, making oxygen-16, so the end product of helium burning is a mixture of carbon and oxygen nuclei. 'Carbon burning' occurs at a temperature of around 500 million K (after the core has shrunk appropriately), when pairs of carbon nuclei interact to produce a mixture of products including neon, sodium and magnesium nuclei. 'Oxygen burning', at around a billion K, produces silicon, sulphur, and other nuclei. The most important product of the combined transmutation of oxygen and carbon is

---

* The story is even more surprising than it seems from this simple outline. Three alpha particles can only form a stable carbon-12 nucleus because of a striking quantum coincidence involving the energy levels of the carbon-12 nucleus. This coincidence (among others) is discussed in *Cosmic Coincidences*, by John Gribbin and Martin Rees (Bantam, New York, 1989).

silicon-28, which is the key element in the last, and most complex, version of the fusion energy-generation process.

Silicon 'burning' is, in fact, rather more complex than the simple addition of two silicon-28 nuclei together to make one nucleus of iron-56. In effect, alpha particles break away from one nucleus and join the other one, one at a time. But the end result is the same – silicon is converted into iron. All the way from helium to iron, the elements that are produced in large quantities by this stellar alchemy are, in effect, combinations of alpha particles, with masses roughly a whole number of fours times that of a proton (only roughly – remember that the whole point is that at each stage some mass is converted into energy). Some of these nuclei spit out a positron as a proton is converted into a neutron to make a more stable configuration; but that doesn't change the mass number significantly, since the mass of a positron (or an electron) is only about one two-thousandth of the mass of a neutron or proton. Elements with mass numbers that are not multiples of four form when these nuclei capture stray neutrons from their surroundings; they may then spit out electrons to convert some of those extra neutrons into protons. But everything stops at iron-56. Nuclei of iron-56 have the most stable arrangement of protons and neutrons that any nucleus can have. In order to make more massive nuclei – things like lead, or uranium, or gold – energy has to be put *in* to force the extra particles into the nucleus.

Instead of each nucleus being lighter than the sum of its parts, now the addition of an extra alpha particle or neutron makes the new nucleus even heavier than the sum of its parts, as the energy needed to force the particles together is converted into mass.

The extra energy is only available in the last stages of the life of a few heavy stars. When such a star runs out of nuclear fuel, its core collapses, pulling the floor from under the outer layers, which are no longer supported either by radiation pressure or by gas pressure. As they hurtle inwards onto the burnt-out core of the star, so much gravitational energy is released that not only are nuclei of elements lighter than iron-56 forced together to make more massive nuclei, but the whole star then explodes outwards, scattering the elements it has created across the space between the stars. Such an exploding star is called a supernova; some idea of the energy involved is indicated by the fact that a supernova may shine, temporarily, as brightly as a whole galaxy of stars – and a galaxy contains tens of billions of stars like our Sun. The Sun itself is too modest a star ever to suffer this fate. When its nuclear burning options are exhausted, it will settle down quietly into a cooling lump of star stuff, basically white-hot iron, fading away into old age as a so-called white dwarf. Anaxagoras's guess about the composition of the Sun would have been right – if he'd been born a few billion years later. But even Anaxagoras never imagined that he was himself made of stardust.

All the elements except hydrogen and helium (and even some of the helium) have been manufactured inside stars. But the only stars that these elements ever escape from are supernovas.★ The mass of our Milky Way Galaxy is about 100 billion times the mass of our Sun; astronomers estimate, from studies of the spectra of stars, that just one per cent of this matter, only a billion solar masses, is in the form of heavy elements ('heavy' meaning anything except hydrogen and helium). Since the Galaxy is about 10 billion years old, this means that just one tenth of a solar mass of material is processed into heavy elements each year. Allowing for the fact that there were probably more supernova explosions when the Galaxy was younger, this requires about one supernova explosion, each releasing two solar masses of processed material into the void, roughly every thirty years today. Supernovas make stardust, and some of that stardust eventually gets into clouds of gas collapsing to form new stars and planets. That is where the heavy elements in the Sun, a relatively young star, and on Earth came from. The silicon in the computer I am using to write these words was formed inside a star at a temperature of a billion degrees, and was later shot out into space when that star exploded. Our Sun will never turn itself inside out in this way – it isn't massive enough. But by the 1960s, it seemed to astrophysicists that even without being able to see inside the Sun, they could describe its structure, from the inside outwards.

The Sun inside out

The structure of the Sun, inferred from astrophysical calculations in the 1950s and 1960s, but never probed directly at that time, is described in terms of a series of layers, or shells. The heart of the Sun – the core in which nuclear processes generate energy – extends just one quarter of the distance from the centre of the Sun

★ This has recently been confirmed by studies of a supernova that exploded relatively near to us, literally in the galaxy next door to our Milky Way, and was first visible from Earth early in 1987. Even though the Sun itself is *not* destined to become a supernova, this is such an important and exciting development in astronomers' understanding of the way stars work that I have included a detailed discussion of the event, known as SN 1987A, at the end of this book.

to the surface, and represents only 1.5 per cent of the Sun's volume. But this is the region where electrons are stripped from atoms to leave nuclei that are packed together at a density 12 times that of solid lead, even though they behave like the particles of a perfect gas. So half of the mass of the Sun is concentrated in this inner core (the total mass of the Sun is, in round terms, 330,000 times the mass of the Earth, while its radius is 109 times that of the Earth), The temperature inside the core, according to the standard astrophysical models, is 15 million K (the temperature at the outer edge of the core is about 13 million K), and the pressure is three hundred billion times the pressure of the atmosphere at the surface of the Earth. Under these extreme conditions, even a photon (a quantum of radiation, the particle component of light) only travels a fraction of a centimetre before it collides with a charged particle. The photons produced by the nuclear reactions are gamma rays – created out of the mass that is 'lost' when four protons form an alpha particle. When these photons are absorbed by charged particles, the energy is promptly re-radiated as X-rays, and it is as X-rays that the energy produced by nuclear fusion in the core begins to make its way outward through the Sun.

It does so very slowly, in one sense, even though each X-ray travels at the speed of light. When a photon is absorbed and then re-radiated by a charged particle in the hot plasma outside the core, it may be radiated in any direction, at random, including back the way it came. The result is that it moves in an erratic, zig-zag path known as a random walk, with each step in that walk just about one centimeter long, on average. Over a range of one centimetre, there is very little difference in temperature in this part of the Sun, called the radiation zone. But that tiny difference ensures that just a few more photons work their way outwards than inwards at each distance from the centre. If a photon could fly in a straight line from the core of the Sun to the surface, its journey would take just 2.5 seconds; in fact, on average it takes a photon 10 million years to get from the core to the surface. During all that time, it has been travelling at the speed of light – so its zig–zag path is actually 10 million light years long. If the zig-zag could be straightened out, it would stretch five times further than the distance to the Andromeda Galaxy, a neighbour of our own Milky Way. Looking at this another way, it means that the conditions on the surface of the Sun today are the conditions that correspond to what the core of the Sun was doing 10 million years ago. We cannot, simply by looking at the Sun's surface, be sure that nuclear reactions have not, in fact, stopped converting hydrogen into helium in the Sun's core some time during the past few million years.

The radiation zone extends out to about one million kilometres, 85 per cent of the distance from the centre of the Sun to the surface. All the way out, the plasma is getting cooler and thinner. Halfway from the centre of the Sun to the surface, the density is the same as that of water, and two thirds of the way out it has dropped to the density of the air that we breathe. At the outer edge of the radiation zone, the temperature is only about half a million K, and the density of the solar material is just 1 per cent that of water (because the dense core is so small, incidentally, the *average* density of the Sun, from the centre to the surface, is just one and a half times the density of water). Under these conditions, nuclei can cling onto a cloud of electrons, and at the same time the energy of each photon has been degraded, shifting the radiation to longer wavelengths which interact less violently with the particles. At this point, the atoms of gas are able to absorb the energy of the photons and hang on to it, without immediately re-radiating it in all directions. The energy they absorb makes the atoms hot – they seethe with energy, dumped at the bottom of the shell known as the convection zone by radiation which has, almost literally, run into a brick wall.

The material of the convection zone, heated from below in this way, responds like the water in a pan that is heated from below on a stove. The hot material rises upwards through the zone and is replaced by colder material from the surface sinking down into the depths – in other words, living up to its name, it convects (the cooler material that sinks down to complete the convective cycle and replace the rising hot gas has lost its energy by radiating away photons at the surface). This seething activity extends over the last 15 per cent or so of the Sun's radius, from a depth of 150,000 kilometres up to the visible surface of the Sun. The convection zone is a bit less than half as thick as the distance from the Earth to the Moon, and is thought to consist of three main layers of convection, one on top of the other.

The top of the convection zone corresponds to the visible bright surface of the Sun. In this very thin zone, called the photosphere, the temperature is a mere 5,800K, the pressure is down to one sixth of the atmospheric pressure on Earth, and the density is less than a millionth of the density of water. Under these conditions, atoms can no longer block the flow of radiation outwards, and photons stream freely out into space. The light we see all comes from this layer, no more than 0.1 per cent of the Sun's radius (500

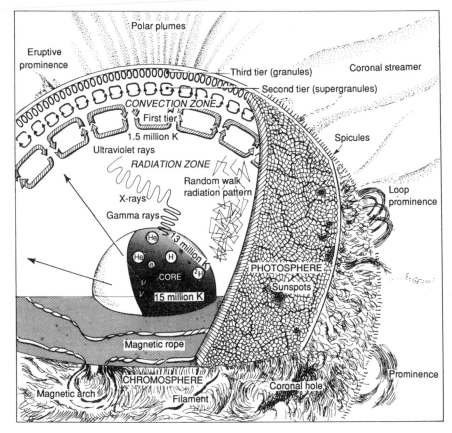

Figure 3.6 The structure of the Sun, from inside to outside. Adapted from an illustration in Sun and Earth, *by Herbert Friedman (Scientific American Library, 1986), with permission of the publishers.*

kilometres) deep. The energy in that light has travelled for millions of years at the speed of light on its zig-zag journey through the radiation zone, then been carried up through the convection zone (at a modest 75 kilometres an hour, but essentially in a straight line) in about 90 days. It then speeds across the further 150 million kilometres to the Earth in just over eight and a half minutes.

Until recently, light from the photosphere provided all the information we had about the interior of the Sun. In effect, it told us what the Sun's core was doing ten million years ago. But in the 1970s and 1980s two new techniques were developed, one probing the core itself to find out what it is doing today, and the other 'looking' down into the Sun from its surface layers. Those new techniques have shown that the astrophysicists were very nearly right in their calculations of conditions in the solar interior – but they have also revealed new secrets about the workings of the Sun and stars, and provided new mysteries for researchers to puzzle over.

4

Too Few Ghosts

The cosy picture of steady progress by astrophysicists towards a thorough understanding of the way stars work was shattered in the second half of the 1960s. It turned out that astronomers might not, after all, understand 'so simple a thing', in Eddington's words, as a star – and the embarrassment was compounded because the observations that showed their understanding to be flawed were not made on some distant, faint star that might be expected to be hard to understand, but on the Sun itself, our nearest star and the one we ought to understand best. The problem, which emerged in 1968 and has remained for twenty years, is that the Sun is producing too few of the ghostly particles called neutrinos – too few, that is, if the standard models of how stars work are correct.

The implications seemed to spread wider the more seriously physicists took the problem, and the longer the experiments continued to show this paucity of solar ghosts; today, this difficulty in understanding what goes on in our own astronomical back yard is seen as part of a major difficulty in understanding the evolution of the Universe at large. Both problems, local and cosmic, may, as we shall see, be solved in one neat package. But first we have to go back sixty years or more, to the late 1920s, when atomic physicists were grappling to understand the puzzle of the phenomenon known as beta decay, which I mentioned briefly in Chapter Three.

The need for neutrinos

In beta decay, the nucleus of an atom emits an electron, which is also known as a beta ray. We now know that in the process a neutron inside the atomic nucleus is converted into a proton – but in the 1920s nobody knew of the existence of neutrons, which are particles with roughly the same mass as the proton (2,000 times the mass of an electron) but which carry no electric charge. Part of the puzzle of beta decay was that it seemed possible for electrons to emerge from atomic nuclei in all kinds of directions, at all kinds of energies, without this being balanced by the recoil of the nucleus itself. This seemed to conflict with the law of conservation of momentum – if an electron shot out of the nucleus in one direction, something else ought to shoot out on the other side, just as a rifle 'kicks' when a bullet is fired from it. Nobody could find the missing 'other particle' that ought to be carrying momentum away from the nucleus in beta decay, and for a time physicists seriously considered the possibility that the laws of conservation of energy and momentum might not work in atomic nuclei – just as their not so distant predecessors had speculated that energy might not be conserved in radioactive processes. An alternative explanation came from an Austrian-born physicist in 1930, and gradually became accepted as the right answer to the puzzle.

Wolfgang Pauli had been born in Vienna in 1900, and already had a reputation as one of the leading theorists of his day. He had obtained his doctorate in 1922, at the University of Munich, and he had worked with both Max Born and Niels Bohr in the pioneering days of quantum physics. By 1930 he was Professor of Physics in the Federal Institute of Technology, Zurich; he later became a Swiss citizen. Pauli was known for his clear thinking – he had made his name as a nineteen-year-old student by producing what was then the clearest account of Einstein's two theories of relativity – and he saw how to cut through the Gordian knot of the beta decay problem. In a letter to Lise Meitner, one of the physicists whose work led to an understanding of nuclear fission (the process that powers the atom bomb and nuclear reactors), he made the straightforward proposal that the 'extra' energy was indeed being carried off by another particle which must be emitted from the nucleus at the same time as the electron observed in beta decay, but which was unobservable by the technology of the day, and might never be detected.

This idea was published formally in 1931, but it did not gain much immediate support, in spite of Pauli's reputation. It looked like too easy a cop-out, and in 1931, remember, only two fundamental particles, the electron and the proton, were known. 'Inventing' a new one was a much bigger step then than it became in later decades – we can imagine other physicists of the day reacting along the lines that if theorists invented a new particle every time the experimenters couldn't balance their books, where would physics end up? Besides, Pauli's hypothetical particle seemed too odd to be believed. Not only would it have to have zero charge, it would also have to have scarcely any mass, otherwise it would have been detected already. The only property it was allowed to have, said Pauli, was 'spin', a quantum property which is rather different from the concept of spin in everyday life (for example, a quantum object has to rotate completely *twice* to get back to where it started).

He called the particle the 'neutron'. But the idea had so little impact, at first, that this name was hijacked, in 1932, when the particle we now know as the neutron was discovered. A year later, however, Pauli found an ally, in the form of the Italian physicist Enrico Fermi, who suggested the name 'neutrino' ('little neutral one'), and made the particle respectable by developing a new theory of particle interactions in which the neutrino played an integral part. (It also helped, of course, that the neutron itself had been discovered. If one neutral particle was known to exist, physicists were more willing to accept the possibility that another one might exist, as well.)

Fermi's description of beta decay is essentially the same as the modern interpretation. When a neutron decays, it emits both an electron and a neutrino (strictly speaking, an antineutrino), and becomes a proton. The scientific books were kept in balance, and the new understanding of the particle world developed in the wake of Fermi's interpretation of Pauli's insight helped in the development of an understanding, in the late 1930s and beyond, of the nuclear fusion reactions that keep the Sun and stars hot. In all of this theoretical work, the neutrino played a key role, and became indispensable. But its existence was not finally proven, by experiment, until 1956.

The reasons are not hard to see – indeed, the surprise is that neutrinos were ever detected at all. Pauli himself considered it so unlikely that in 1931 he offered a case of champagne to any experimenter who successfully took up the challenge, and he seemed to be on a safe bet. According to the original concept of the neutrino, it has zero charge, zero mass and travels at the speed of light (later refinements suggest that it may have a tiny mass and travel at very nearly the speed of light). A neutrino does not interact with other particles through the electromagnetic force that holds molecules together, or through the 'strong' force that holds nuclei together. Apart from gravity, which has little effect on a particle with so little mass, neutrinos only interact with the rest of the world through what is called the 'weak' nuclear force, introduced by Fermi to explain the behaviour of nuclei during decay. This is a very weak interaction indeed – if a beam of neutrinos like those thought to be produced by nuclear reactions inside the Sun were to travel through solid lead for 3,500 light years, only half of them would be absorbed by the nuclei of the lead atoms along the way.

If the standard theory of how stars work is correct, the nuclear processes going on in the heart of the Sun produce roughly 2×10^{38} neutrinos each second. About one tenth as much energy as we observe in visible light actually emerges from the Sun in the form of neutrinos. But, unlike the visible light, the neutrinos come directly from the heart of the Sun. Only one in a thousand billion of them are absorbed on the way out through the Sun itself, and the Earth, and our own bodies, are virtually transparent to neutrinos. Billions of these ghostly particles are zipping right through you every second, as you read these words, without your body noticing them, or them noticing your body.

So, how do you catch a neutrino? You need a big detector (one with lots of atomic nuclei in it, for the neutrinos to have a chance of interacting), and you need a lot of neutrinos (so that even though the chance of any one neutrino interacting is small, just a few out of the billions passing by will be stopped by nuclei in your detector). The trick was first achieved beyond any reasonable doubt in 1956, by Frederick Reines and Clyde Cowan. They used a tank containing 1,000 pounds of water placed alongside the Savannah River nuclear reactor in the United States. According to theory, the flood of neutrinos from the nearby reactor crossing the tank of water should have been 30 times greater than the amount of solar neutrinos reaching the detector across 150 million kilometres of space, so there would be just a chance of catching one or two of them in the tank every hour. The reaction that Reines and Cowan actually looked for, during a series of tests they called 'Project Poltergeist', was the reverse of beta decay. In this reaction, an antineutrino strikes a proton and converts it into a neutron, while a positron (the antiparticle counterpart of an electron) carries away the positive charge. It was the positrons that the Savannah River experiment actually detected. Hints of the anticipated 'neutrino signal' came in 1953, and full confirmation that Pauli's idea was correct came in 1956. Reines and Cowan sent Pauli a telegram informing him of their success; Pauli, in turn, duly paid up on his twenty-five-year-old bet by giving them a case of champagne.

The successful discovery of the neutrino put nuclear physics on a firmer footing than ever before, and gave theorists renewed confidence. It also suggested a new challenge, if any experimenter were brave enough to take it up. If neutrinos – or, at least, events directly attributable to neutrinos – could be detected coming from a nuclear reactor here on Earth, maybe it might be possible, after all, to capture a few of those billions of solar neutrinos that pass by us, and through us, every second. The idea of a 'telescope' that would not look at the surface of the Sun, but would provide a direct probe of conditions in the solar interior, caught the imagination of one man, who has since devoted his working life to the hunt for solar neutrinos.

Many theorists dismissed his efforts as a waste of time. They knew how stars worked – the standard model of the Sun told them how hot it was inside, what pressures were encountered there, and what nuclear reactions were going on. It hardly seemed worth the enormous effort of catching a few neutrinos just to prove the theories right. But they were wrong.

The Davis detector

The man who took up the challenge was Raymond Davis, Jr, of the Brookhaven National Laboratory, on Long Island. But New York is no place to build a solar neutrino detector. There are many other things that can interact with atomic nuclei to make them transmute, notably the cosmic rays – protons, electrons and other particles striking the Earth from space. Davis and his colleagues had to build a detector where it would be shielded from everything except solar neutrinos. Paradoxically, because only neutrinos pass unaffected through the Earth, that meant burying the new solar telescope deep down a mine, where light from the Sun is never seen. Then, the detector had to be big, in order to have any hope of capturing even a few out of the enormous number of solar neutrinos passing through each cubic centimetre of its bulk every second.

Beginning in 1964, the experiment was installed 1,500 metres below the ground in the Homestake gold mine at Lead, South Dakota. Seven thousand tons of rock had to be removed to make room for the detector, a tank the size of an Olympic swimming pool (Figure 4.1), containing 400,000 litres of perchlorethylene (C_2Cl_4, commonly used as a cleaning fluid in so-called 'dry cleaning' processes). It was the chlorine in the cleaning fluid that Davis planned to use to detect solar neutrinos.

Figure 4.1   The neutrino detector deep underground at the Homestake gold mine. 400,000 litres of cleaning fluid fill the tank of the 'telescope'. Photograph supplied by Ray Davis.

The reasoning behind this choice of detector runs like this. About a quarter of all the chlorine atoms that occur naturally on Earth are in the form of the isotope chlorine-37, each nucleus of which contains 17 protons and 20 neutrons. With four chlorine atoms in every molecule of perchlorethylene, that means that in round terms there is one atom of chlorine-37 for every molecule of cleaning fluid in the tank – about 2×10^{30} potential 'targets' for the neutrinos to hit. On the very rare occasions that a neutrino from

Figure 4.2   When a neutrino from the Sun interacts with a nucleus of chlorine-37 in the tank at the Homestake mine, it is turned into a nucleus of argon-37. The Davis detector actually counts the number of argon nuclei produced in this way.

the Sun does interact with a nucleus of chlorine-37, one of the neutrons in that nucleus is converted into a proton, and an electron is emitted – a kind of forced beta decay. The resulting nucleus now contains 18 protons and 19 neutrons, and 'belongs' to the element argon – specifically, the isotope argon-37 (Figure 4.2). This interloper is released from its place in the former perchlorethylene molecule, and as more neutrinos strike their targets argon-37 builds up in the tank of cleaning fluid as a dissolved gas. If the Brookhaven team can count the number of argon-37 atoms in the tank, they know how many neutrinos have interacted with chlorine nuclei in the tank.

But that is easier said than done, and because argon-37 is itself unstable and decays back into chlorine-37 by capturing an electron, you can't wait forever to let the argon build up in the tank. The half-life of argon-37 is about 34 days, so the tank has to be swept clean of argon, and the atoms counted, every few weeks.

Davis's experiment, and the technique for counting the argon atoms in particular, is one of the most beautiful pieces of work in the whole of physics. People have certainly won Nobel prizes for less, and even the brief summary that we have room for here is enough to inspire awe. First, the huge tank of cleaning fluid has to be 'purged' of argon-37 by bubbling helium gas through the tank. In fact, some inert argon gas, either argon-36 or argon-38, is also added to the fluid, to help flush the argon-37 out. The argon atoms (including the argon-37 atoms) mingle with the helium, and are carried out of the tank with the gas. They then have to be separated from the helium (a fairly simple technical feat, compared with the rest of the work). Then, the Brookhaven team takes advantage of the fact that argon-37 decays back into chlorine-37. When this decay takes place, the atom involved releases a characteristic, precisely defined burst of energy. Automatic counters, shielded from cosmic rays, record every flicker of activity from the argon over a period of up to 250 days, and record each pulse that has the appropriate energy 'signature'. After all that effort, an average of 12 counts are recorded in each run of the experiment. It is an astonishing tour de force.

The first results from the experiment emerged in 1968, and seemed to disagree with the predictions of standard solar theory. At that time, nobody was very worried, since it seemed hard to believe that the difficult experiment was really being carried out with sufficient accuracy to be a reliable guide to what was going on inside the Sun. Confidently, the astrophysicists waited for the experimental figures to 'improve' and come in line with the predictions of their theories. But over the past twenty years the experiment has been repeated time and again, and every step has been repeatedly tested (for example, by adding a known quantity of argon-37 to the tank and seeing how the detectors respond). Always, the answer is the same. Davis and his colleagues detect only one third of the number of solar neutrinos that theory says they should detect. On average, only one argon-37 atom is produced in the tank every two or three days. The far-reaching implications of this can only be seen by looking at how the theorists made their confident predictions that Davis would actually detect three times as many neutrinos.

Forecasts that failed

I described in Chapter Three how energy is produced in stars in general, and in the Sun in particular. According to the standard model, less than 2 per cent of the Sun's energy is produced by the carbon–nitrogen–oxygen (CNO) cycle; the Sun simply is not hot enough for this process to dominate, even though it happens, through an accident of history, to have been the first stellar nuclear energy source to have been 'discovered' in 1938. Most of the Sun's energy, astrophysicists are convinced, comes from the fusion process known as the proton–proton (p-p) chain. It's worth recapping on just how this works, with emphasis on the ways in which this step-by-step fusion of hydrogen nuclei (protons) into helium nuclei (alpha particles) releases neutrinos along the way.

The Sun is made chiefly of hydrogen, and in the heart of the Sun the nuclei of the hydrogen atoms (the protons) are separated from their electrons and travel at high speeds, constantly colliding with and ricocheting off other protons. Occasionally, in such a collision two protons will stick together, with one proton releasing a positron and becoming a neutron. The neutron-proton pair is a deuteron, the nucleus of an atom of deuterium, an isotope of hydrogen. Along with the positron, a neutrino is released and passes virtually unhindered out of the Sun and into space. Such neutrinos are referred to as p-p neutrinos, to remind us of their origin; they are no different from other neutrinos produced when protons are converted into neutrons, but have a characteristic energy. The next step in the fusion process occurs when a proton combines with a deuteron to make a nucleus of helium-3; no neutrino is involved in this reaction.

Helium-3 nuclei cannot combine directly with protons, but when two helium-3 nuclei collide a more complex interaction can take place. *Two* protons are released in the interaction, leaving behind a nucleus of helium-4, which contains two protons and two neutrons. Overall, four protons have been converted into one helium-4 nucleus, with the release of part of the energy that keeps the Sun hot, and two positrons, each accompanied by neutrino. These are *not* the neutrinos that Davis can detect.

In all the activity at the heart of the Sun, a helium-3 nucleus and a helium-4 nucleus will occasionally collide to make a nucleus of beryllium-7. Under the conditions in the solar interior, beryllium-7 can do two things. The nucleus might capture an electron, and give off a neutrino, becoming an isotope of lithium (lithium-7), as one of its protons is converted into a neutron by inverse beta decay. Lithium-7 can then capture another proton and split into two helium-4 nuclei (the Cockcroft-Walton reaction). Alternatively, the beryllium-7 nucleus might capture a proton first, becoming a nucleus of boron-8, which then decays, in less than a second, giving off a positron and a neutrino and becoming beryllium-8 and then splitting into two helium-4 nuclei. The neutrinos produced in these reactions (mainly the boron-8 neutrinos) are the ones that Davis can detect. They are only produced rarely, compared with the p-p neutrinos, but they carry much more energy.

The p-p neutrinos do not have enough energy to trigger the

conversion of chlorine-37 into argon-37. The beryllium-7 neutrinos have enough energy so that some of them can do the trick; the boron-8 neutrinos have ample energy to make the transmutation take place.

So, how many neutrinos should be produced by each process inside the Sun, and how many should Davis detect, according to the standard model? At this stage, theory and experiment combine. Astrophysicists tell the particle physicists what the

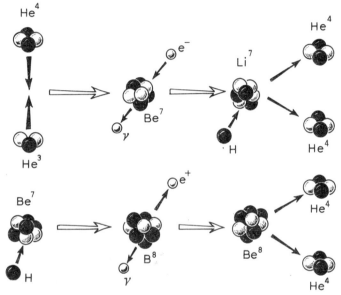

Figure 4.3   The neutrinos that Davis detects actually come from a side-reaction to the proton-proton chain. Sometimes, in the heart of the Sun a helium-4 nucleus will fuse with a nucleus of helium-4, not another helium-3. This produces beryllium-7, which can follow two different routes, shown here, to becoming two nuclei of helium-4. It is the neutrinos produced in these reactions, mainly the boron-8 neutrinos from the lower chain, that Davis can detect.

conditions at the centre of the Sun are like, according to the standard model. Experimenters – notably, in this particular story, researchers working at the Kellogg Radiation Laboratory at CalTech – accelerate beams of protons, deuterons, helium-3 and helium-4 nuclei in particle accelerators, and watch as they interact, measuring the numbers of the different kinds of nuclei produced. They are able to reproduce – one at a time – the actual reactions that go on in the heart of the Sun, and to measure the efficiency of those reactions in terms of quantities that are known, for obvious reasons, as cross-sections.

Of course, the conditions in the colliding beams are very different from those inside the Sun. Willy Fowler, of Kellogg, likes to paraphrase Eddington's famous remark by saying that 'what is possible in the Sun is very difficult in the Kellogg Radiation Laboratory'. But once the cross-sections are measured over a range of energies, it is possible to extrapolate the figures and to deduce the appropriate reaction rates under the conditions of temperature and pressure that, the theorists say, exist inside the Sun.

When Fowler and his colleagues do this, they find that the main p-p reaction should be producing a flood of 60 billion neutrinos crossing each square centimetre of the Earth every second. Unfortunately, none of these have enough energy to be detected by the Davis experiment. The predictions for beryllium-7 and boron-8 neutrinos are very sensitive to the exact temperature fed in to the calculations. The standard model of the Sun has a central temperature of 15 million K. For that temperature, there should be 4 billion beryllium-7 neutrinos crossing each square centimetre of the Earth each second, and these should produce five events per *month* in the tank at the Homestake mine. The figures for the standard model also imply a flux of just 3 million boron-8 neutrinos per square centimetre per second at the tank, but these are so energetic that they should produce 20 events per month. Overall, the Davis experiment should be producing 25 events per month; in fact, over 20 years he has found an average of about 9 events per month that can be attributed to solar neutrinos.

There is another way of expressing this result, but it boils down to the same thing. Theorist John Bahcall, now of Princeton, has been closely involved in the search for solar neutrinos, and has kept tabs on all the possible sources of error in the calculations. He was born in Shreveport, Louisiana on 30 December 1934, graduated from Berkeley in 1956, and obtained his PhD from Harvard in 1961. His early training was in theoretical physics, but in the 1960s he worked for several years at CalTech, where he became 'converted' to astrophysics. From 1963 onwards, he has carried out successively more precise and sophisticated theoretical calculations of the rate at which solar neutrinos should be expected to be observed on Earth, and his work, in 1964, provided the theoretical basis for Ray Davis's confidence that he could build a detector that would indeed 'see' solar neutrinos.

For convenience, Bahcall has invented a unit called the 'solar neutrino unit', or SNU, for measuring events like those detected by Davis. The standard model predicts that the Davis detector should be recording between about 6 and 8 SNU, allowing for uncertainties in the calculations. In these units, the observed events correspond to between 2 and 3 SNU. Whichever way you look at it, in round terms the detector sees just one third of the expected number of neutrinos. Why?

Desperate remedies

Either we don't understand how neutrinos are made in nuclear reactions, or we don't understand how stars work – at least, not as

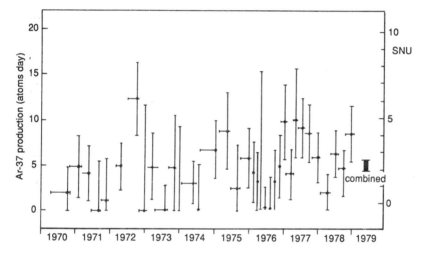

Figure 4.4   The first complete decade's worth of solar neutrino measurements, given both in numbers of argon-37 atoms produced and in solar neutrino units (SNU). The standard solar model predicts a 'flux' of 6 to 8 SNU; the measurements showed no more than a third of that. This is the 'solar neutrino problem'.

well as we thought we did. Any lingering hopes among theorists that there might, after all, be something wrong with the Davis experiment that would let them off the hook were well and truly squashed in 1988, when results from a Japanese detector (actually designed for another purpose, but capable of detecting boron-8 neutrinos from the Sun) confirmed the lack of solar neutrinos. Though nobody had really doubted Davis's results, the confirmation was reassuring to the Davis team, even if it left the theorists squirming to decide whether they had to revise their astrophysical theories or the particle physics. These two alternative explanations of the results of the Davis experiment are so alarming that they have led theorists into an almost desperate search for remedies to the solar neutrino problem. But before we look at some of those wild ideas, it is worth taking at least a crumb of comfort from the one piece of positive news to emerge from the Homestake mine. We mentioned that the standard model of the Sun predicts that less than 2 per cent of the solar energy is generated by the CNO cycle. If all of the Sun's energy were being produced by this cycle, then the predicted neutrino capture rate in the Davis detector would be 25 SNU. This is very definitely not observed, confirming that the theorists at least got that much of the energy generation process right.

How reliable are their other calculations? In the early and middle 1960s, estimates of the neutrino production rate in the Sun were amended, as the theorists thought of extra factors that they should include in their calculations. Stimulated by the knowledge that Davis and his team were working on a neutrino detector, they made an intense effort to get their forecasts as accurate as possible, to include every relevant factor, and to use the best computer models of how the Sun was thought to work. Because nobody had made this intense effort before, it took a few years to develop the best possible models. By 1969, however, they ran out of 'new' effects to include, leaving only the possibility of modest fine tuning of the standard model. The physics has stayed the same since then, and although computer power has improved enormously, the predictions are still around 6 SNU. The only way to shift the figure downwards by the required amount is to make a drastic change in the standard model of the Sun.

'Drastic' is, in this case, a relative term. Because the Davis experiment only detects the kind of solar neutrinos whose own production rate is very sensitive to the temperature at the heart of the Sun, the simplest way to bring the theories in line with observations is to set the temperature at the heart of the Sun about 10 per cent lower than in the standard models – a little below 14 million K instead of around 15 million K. Eddington would hardly have regarded that as a drastic step. When you recall that his first stab at calculating the temperature at the heart of the Sun gave a figure of 40 million K, only a human lifetime ago, and that this figure was later revised downward to 15 million K, a reduction by another million degrees or so might seem like nothing to worry about. But it is a measure of the sophistication and apparent accuracy of modern models of how stars work that an adjustment in the central temperature of the Sun of a mere 10 per cent *cannot* be incorporated within the standard model.

As this realization sank in, astrophysicists tried every imaginable way to produce the necessary change in the structure of the Sun, rejecting each piece of the standard model in turn (or sometimes all at once!). A few of these ideas were serious attempts to find out why the standard model does not work for the Sun, and to consider how this might affect our understanding of stars in general. Most were what John Bahcall calls 'cocktail party solutions', ideas dreamed up (probably over a few drinks) on a 'one-off' basis to account for the solar neutrino problem alone, without attempting to provide any serious insight into the structure of stars in general.

The more serious proposals included the idea that the Sun might be rotating much more rapidly in its deep interior than it is on the surface. This rapid rotation would help to hold the Sun up against the inward tug of its own gravity, and reduce the pressure and temperature at its centre. A similar argument proposes that there is a strong magnetic field inside the Sun, resisting compression by gravity. But either of these effects should distort the shape of the Sun, making it oblate (bigger across the equator than from pole to pole), instead of spherical; no such distortions are seen.

Wilder ideas – all of them published in the pages of serious scientific journals – include: the possibility that there is a tiny black hole at the heart of the Sun, producing more than half its energy; a suggestion that the Sun formed in two stages, and has a core rich in iron surrounded by an 'atmosphere' of hydrogen that it gathered up from space at a later date; and (essentially the opposite of that proposal) the idea that the Sun's interior is totally devoid of heavy elements, so that radiation can escape more easily from the centre than it can in the standard model.

One of the most intriguing of the desperate remedies to the solar neutrino problem is that the Sun might not be in a 'normal' state today. The standard models of the theorists only tell us, after all, about the long-term, average conditions inside the Sun. As Kelvin and Helmholtz appreciated, the Sun need not be in a steady state today. Taking their idea forward, in modern terms, if we were to turn off all the nuclear reactions going on inside the Sun, it could maintain its present brightness for millions of years by shrinking slightly and converting gravitational energy into heat. The Kelvin-Helmholtz idea won't work as an explanation of how the Sun has stayed hot while life has evolved on Earth, but it is still, potentially, a useful buffer mechanism available to smooth out any temporary hiccups in the nuclear energy supply. Alas, all the ideas put forward to 'explain' how the Sun could have gone off the boil, temporarily, are in the category of cocktail party solutions.

Perhaps helium, produced by the fusion of protons, builds up in the centre of the Sun as a kind of cosmic ash, until fusion stops for a while and then there is some great internal hiccup and the whole central region of the Sun is turned over by convection, mixing in more protons from outside to start things rolling again. Or perhaps the Solar System recently passed through a cloud of gas and dust in space, with the Sun gathering up material on its *surface*, temporarily disrupting the outward flow of heat and causing internal adjustments which have reduced the nuclear activity. Perhaps – but all such solutions seem contrived. And they raise a new question: if the Sun does indeed *usually* produce the flux of neutrinos predicted by the standard model, but has temporarily reduced its output, isn't it rather odd that we are here to witness this very rare event in solar history?

I could go on, but to continue the catalogue of desperate remedies would be pointless. When one of the suggestions put forward is that the constant of gravity itself might be varying as the Universe ages, so that the standard calculations of how the Sun evolved are all wrong, it is surely time to call a halt. Not to all the speculations – when standard ideas fail, speculation becomes an integral part of science.★ But constructive speculation has to be compared with observation and experiment to weed out the wilder flights of fancy, and none of the proposed changes in the standard solar model survives this test. In a review published in 1985,† Bahcall mentioned that between 1969 and 1977 he and Davis had kept track of all the new 'explanations' of the solar neutrino puzzle as they were published, and counted nineteen independent ideas of what might be wrong with the standard model. They then gave up keeping detailed track, but 'new ideas have been suggested at the rate of 2 or 3 per year since then.' When speculation is so unfettered, a different approach to the problem is needed. In the past few years, this has come from the particle

---

★ Of course, a theory has to be in trouble before speculation is called for – which is why, for example, no scientist takes seriously the many attempts by amateurs to find fault with relativity theory. Any competent physicist at a cocktail party can dream up alternatives to Einstein, but such efforts are as contrived and speculative as the cocktail party solutions to the solar neutrino problem. The difference is that Einstein's theory passes every test, while the standard solar model does not.

† *Solar Physics*, Volume 100, p. 53.

physicists, who have put forward several suggestions which, while still speculative, at least have the merit that they can be tested in the not too distant future.

Speculative solutions

If we understand how stars work, and *if* we have the right numbers for the cross-sections involved in the boron-8 interactions, then there remains one possibility. Perhaps, a few physicists suggested in the 1970s, we don't understand the *neutrinos* as well as we thought we did. Could something be happening to neutrinos on their way to us from the Sun, so that even though the 'right' number start out, only a third of them are left for Davis to detect by the time they reach the Earth?

The idea isn't completely crazy, because many particles are now known which do decay in this way, turning into something else after an appropriate interval of time, be it long or short. Even the neutron decays, within a few minutes (if it is not in an atomic nucleus), into a proton and an electron. But there is a slight problem in finding something else for neutrinos to turn into. According to the best modern understanding of the particle world, protons and neutrons are not truly 'fundamental' particles, but are composed of another kind of particle, the quarks, which are themselves the most basic building block of matter. Electrons, on the other hand, *are* truly fundamental, and never decay; and neutrinos are always associated with electrons, part of the same family, called leptons. There is nothing more fundamental for a neutrino to decay into; but perhaps just possibly, it might turn into another kind of neutrino.

This idea, called neutrino oscillation, was first suggested in the early 1960s by Soviet and Japanese researchers, working independently of one another. The motivation for their speculation goes back to the discovery of a particle called the muon, back in 1936. The muon is similar to the electron, but has a mass 200 times greater than the mass of an electron; it is a member of the lepton family, but its place in the particle world remained a mystery until the 1970s. Left alone, a muon will decay into an electron, a neutrino and an antineutrino, within 2.2 microseconds. The neutrinos, of course, could not be detected in the 1930s, and no significant advance in understanding the muon was made until 1959, when Bruno Pontecorvo, born in Italy but by then working at Dubna in the Soviet Union, and Melvin Schwarz, at Columbia University in the United States, suggested a technique for creating beams of muons, and their associated neutrinos, which was later carried out at CERN and Brookhaven. By 1962 Schwarz and his colleagues had proved that the neutrinos associated with muons are different from those associated with electrons. An electron neutrino, when it strikes a neutron, will always produce a proton plus an electron; a muon neutrino, when it strikes a neutron, will always produce a proton plus a muon.

This was the discovery that led to the suggestion that the electron neutrino might be able to change its spots. Perhaps, the argument ran, a beam of neutrinos that initially contained only the electron variety might somehow metamorphose into a mixture of muon and electron neutrinos. The implications for the Davis experiment, which can only detect *electron* neutrinos, is clear; and in 1975 the fact that Davis detects just one third of the expected number of electron neutrinos became striking, with the discovery of yet another member of the lepton family, the tau particle, which is just like the electron and muon except that its mass is twice as great as that of a proton. It is generally assumed that there must be a third type of neutrino associated with the tau particle, although this has not yet been confirmed by experiment.

This made for the striking coincidence. If a beam of electron neutrinos somehow became mixed into all three possible varieties, in equal numbers, then exactly one third of the original number of electron neutrinos would be left for detection. Of course, the coincidence would fail if yet more members of the lepton family were discovered; but, as it happens, there are just three principal types of pairs of quark, each associated with one of the three lepton pairs, and physicists now have sound reasons for believing that this is all the kinds of basic particle the Universe has room for.* But there is still the question of how a beam of electron neutrinos could change its spots – a process Reines has likened, graphically, to a dog trotting along the road and transforming itself into a cat as it goes along.

This kind of transformation is, in fact, well-known in the particle world, under the right circumstances. The crucial factor is that the 'right circumstances' include the particles involved having a little mass – it doesn't have to be very much mass, but it does have to be more than zero. Everyone had always *assumed* that the neutrino mass was precisely zero, but nobody had ever measured it – think a little about the difficulty of even detecting a neutrino, let alone weighing it, and you'll see why. There are ways to

* See *The Omega Point*, by John Gribbin.

estimate the masses of the neutrinos, by measuring the amount of energy they carry away during certain interactions and in recent years Soviet researchers have consistently claimed that their experiments show that neutrinos do have mass, around 30 electron Volts each, 0.006 per cent of the mass of an electron. Other researchers disagree – their experiments only set limits on the maximum possible mass a neutrino might have, and these limits are typically around 20 eV. That doesn't mean neutrinos *do* have this mass; it means that there is no way, according to these experiments, that they can have *more* mass, and they might very well have a lot less – even zero mass. Obviously, there is a conflict here, and the situation calls for more and better experiments. It is not likely to be resolved to everyone's satisfaction in the immediate future. But at least it is still on the cards the neutrinos do have a small mass, and therefore it is on the cards that they can change their spots during the 8½ minutes or so it takes for them to travel from the Sun to the Earth. On this picture, each neutrino would be repeatedly changing its 'flavour', millions of times every second, and the Davis experiment would only be picking out the ones that happened to be flavoured 'electron neutrino' at the moment they hit his tank of cleaning fluid.

Although Pontecorvo, and Masami Nakagawa in Japan, had suggested years before that electron and muon neutrinos (the only two kinds known in the 1960s) might change form in this manner, it took the impetus of the discovery of the tauon, and growing concern about the solar neutrino problem, to push experimenters into trying to measure the hypothetical effect in the early 1980s. The man who took up the challenge was an old hand at spotting neutrinos – Frederick Reines. Working now with Henry Sobel and Elaine Pasierb, he went back to the scene of his earlier triumph at the Savannah River reactor, and tried to find out if the electron neutrinos produced in the reactor were changing into other varieties as they sped along. The test they used depended on the different way different neutrinos interact with nuclei of heavy water (deuterium oxide) placed in a tank 11.2 metres from the core of the reactor.

Some nuclear reactions involving electron neutrinos produce two neutrons in these interactions, but reactions involving other flavours of neutrinos produce only a single neutron each time. Some of the electron neutrinos also give rise to single neutrons, just to confuse the picture, but Reines and his colleagues were confident that by careful analysis they could deduce what proportion of electron neutrinos (if any) had changed into other varieties on the brief flight to their detector. They claimed to have found evidence of this effect, in the spring of 1980. But these claims have not stood up to detailed scrutiny. Other experiments show no sign of the neutrino spot-changing at work, and like the Soviet claims of measurements of neutrino mass, the suggestion that Reines and his team really have observed neutrino oscillations is, at best, controversial. But, as I said, at least the idea can be tested, in principle.

So things stood until the spring of 1986. Then an old hand at the solar physics game suddenly reappeared on centre stage. Hans Bethe, back in 1938, had worked out, with Charles Critchfield, the details of the p-p chain which keeps the Sun hot. Now he took up and publicized a proposal to solve the solar neutrino problem developed by two Soviet researchers, S. P. Mikheyev and A. Yu. Smirnov, on the basis of a suggestion made by a US physicist, Lincoln Wolfenstein. The human interest of a scientist coming back, almost fifty years later, to a field of research he had pioneered, caught the imagination of scientists and popularizers alike, and ensured that this new version of the neutrino oscillation idea received a blast of publicity. The idea is worth mentioning briefly, but it has since been overtaken by events, and no longer looks the front-runner it seemed to Bethe in 1986.

The key to the Mikheyev-Smirnov-Wolfenstein (MSW) variation on the neutrino theme is that the transformation of electron neutrinos into some other variety might occur *inside* the Sun, as a result of an interaction between the neutrinos and the material of which the Sun is made. Once again, some of the neutrinos involved have to have mass. But this time, it turns out, the mass must be tiny; and the electron neutrino itself need not necessarily have mass. According to the MSW model, electron neutrinos do experience a very weak interaction with solar particles on their way out of the Sun. The effect of this is to increase the energy being carried by the neutrinos, and since mass and energy are interconvertible this is equivalent to increasing their mass – but not by much. Provided that the mass of an electron neutrino is increased above that of a muon neutrino, the electron neutrino will decay into a muon neutrino. The muon neutrino, however, once formed does not, on this picture, change back into an electron neutrino.

The amount of mass-energy that an electron neutrino can pick up in this way depends on the density of matter in the Sun, and it is very small. That limits the possible range of masses of the neutrinos, if the effect is to work. Specifically, the mass of the electron neutrino must be essentially zero, and the mass of the muon neutrino must be no more than about 0.01 electron Volts. This might seem as implausible and contrived as any of the cocktail party 'solutions' to the solar neutrino problem, except for the fact that there is a class of theories which predict that neutrinos ought to have masses in the range from about 0.00001 to 100 eV. They are called 'see-saw' models, and represent one of the many attacks by theorists on the problem of finding one mathematical framework in which to describe all of the material world – a Grand Unified Theory. But there are other versions of Grand Unified Theories, or GUTs, and the see-saw model is by no means the most favoured these days, so that doesn't really mean a lot.

What really seems to have blown the MSW interpretation of the Davis experiment, however, is something that happened long ago in a galaxy far, far away.

Cosmic connections

Early in 1987, astronomers detected an outburst of light from a star in the Large Magellanic Cloud (LMC), a small galaxy that is a neighbour of the Milky Way. A star in the LMC had exploded as a supernova, which became known as Supernova 1987A. The distance to the LMC is 160,000 light years, which means that the light of the explosion had been 160,000 years, as measured on Earth, on its journey across space to us. The supernova actually happened 160,000 years ago, before the onset of the most recent ice age on Earth. This is the closest supernova to have been observed since telescopes were invented on Earth, and it has been the subject of intense scrutiny and debate. It was also the first supernova to have been detected not only by its visible light, but by the neutrinos that were produced during the explosion.

Two experiments in different parts of the world recorded neutrino bursts now interpreted as due to the supernova. At Kamioka, in central Japan, a research team is using a tank containing 2,140 tonnes of water as part of a programme attempting to determine whether protons decay. The detector is also very sensitive to neutrinos (indeed, this is the detector that has confirmed the accuracy of the Davis experiment), provided they have certain energies; and when news of the supernova came in, the Japanese team searched back through their records and found that it had 'observed' a burst of 11 neutrino events, spread over a period of 13 seconds, with energies in the range from 7.5 to 36

Mega electron Volts (MeV). A similar detector near Cleveland, Ohio, is being operated by Irvine and Michigan Universities, and by the Brookhaven National Laboratory. It too found a pulse of neutrinos at the right time – eight events spread over six seconds, with energies in the range from 30 MeV to 100 MeV (these energies far exceed those of solar neutrinos, which cannot be detected by these experiments). The similarity of the results from the United States and Japan, plus the fact that most of the neutrinos arrived in the first second of the pulse, has convinced scientists that these really were neutrinos from Supernova 1987A. And the tightness of the burst sets definite limits on neutrino mass.

If neutrinos have zero mass, then they all travel at the speed of light, and would arrive together even after a journey as long as 160,000 years. But if neutrinos have mass – even if they all have the same mass – then the speed at which they travel will depend on their energy. Just as a baseball hit more powerfully will fly faster through the air, the neutrinos given the biggest boost in the supernova explosion will travel more quickly, and arrive first. The effect is more pronounced if the neutrinos have more mass; the fact that several neutrinos with different energies arrived within a second of each other, after a journey of 160,000 light years, shows that their mass must be less than 15 eV, the best limit yet set. This, of course, conflicts with the Soviet claims, but is consistent with the neutrinos having zero mass, or having the tiny mass needed to make the MSW trick work. But at least one researcher, Ramanathan Cowsik, from the Tata Institute in Bombay, thinks he can take things a step further.

At a meeting of astronomers in Hungary in June 1987, Cowsik suggested that instead of there being one pulse of neutrinos from the supernova, spread out over about 13 seconds, there were actually two pulses, separated by a few seconds. If that interpretation is correct, then a simple physical argument implies that one of the pulses represents the arrival of electron neutrinos, and these neutrinos have a mass of about 4 eV each; the other pulse would be either all muon or all tauon neutrinos, and each neutrino in that pulse would have a mass of 22 eV. And that would completely pull the rug from under the MSW hypothesis. According to Cowsik, there is only a one-in-five possibility that the pattern of neutrinos that was seen arose by chance, and that neutrinos do not have these masses.

What this interpretation takes away from astronomy with one hand (a 'solution' to the solar neutrino problem), it gives back with the other. If the mass of a set of the neutrinos, one of each type, adds up to more than 1.4 eV, then the total mass of all the neutrinos in the Universe would add up to more than the mass of all the bright stars in all the visible galaxies put together. Some astronomers would welcome this, since there is now an overwhelming weight of evidence that bright stars and galaxies make up less than 10 per cent of all the matter in the Universe, and that some form of 'dark matter' is needed to hold things together gravitationally.*

At present the Universe is expanding, with galaxies moving further apart as time passes. One of the big questions in cosmology today is whether this expansion will go on forever, or whether it will one day reverse and become a contraction, as the gravitational pull of all the matter in the Universe overcomes the expansion. There is nowhere near enough bright matter visible to do the job, but a combined mass of 25 eV for all three neutrino types would suffice. There are simply so many neutrinos around that even such a tiny mass for each of them would add up to 100 times the mass of all the stars and galaxies put together.

So studies of relatively local events in our own cosmic back yard – the solar neutrino problem – have a major bearing on our understanding of such deep cosmic questions as the ultimate fate of the Universe. It is more important than was ever appreciated before that the solar neutrino problem is resolved, and at last there is the prospect, as we move into the 1990s, of a new generation of detectors to investigate the many neutrinos from the Sun that cannot be studied by the Davis detector which has done such sterling work for two decades.

Future projects

Solar neutrino astronomy today needs a new experiment – preferably several new experiments. There is just one substantial set of data, from just one experiment, and this tells us only that there are neutrinos arriving at the Earth. The Kamiokande detector confirms that the Davis experiment is working properly, but adds no new information. Strictly speaking, since the Davis detector cannot tell which direction the neutrinos are coming from, we don't actually even know that it is detecting *solar* neutrinos, although this scarcely seems in doubt, since no other cosmic source is within range. There are still ways in which more information might be gleaned by this experiment. For example, it

* See *The Omega Point.*

already seems to show hints that the number of neutrinos recorded in the tank depends on the activity of the Sun, and varies over the eleven-year 'sunspot cycle'. This is a totally unpredicted result, which is very hard to explain, since neutrinos are thought to come from the secret heart of the Sun, while sunspots are a surface phenomenon.

I shall go into more detail about the nature of sunspots in Chapter Six. Getting ahead of my story a little, what matters here is that dark spots come and go over the surface of the Sun with a cycle roughly eleven years long. It is not *quite* a crazy idea that there might be more solar neutrinos detected on Earth when there are more sunspots, because the spots are associated with increased magnetic activity in the Sun, and the changing magnetic activity might influence the kind of neutrino oscillations I have already mentioned. On the other hand, if that is the case, then occasional outbursts on the Sun, called flares, which are also associated with magnetic activity, would also increase the number of detectable neutrinos. But a search made by the Kamiokande team covering the period from July 1983 to July 1988 shows no significant neutrino signals at the time of solar flares. Another possibility is that solar cosmic rays, energetic particles produced by the Sun, might be producing neutrinos by interactions that take place in the atmosphere of the Earth. John Bahcall, though, believes that the apparent correlation between sunspots and solar neutrinos (Figure 4.5) is a fluke. Statistical tests, he says, show that a correlation as strong as this can occur purely by chance in 2 per cent of the cases where random sets of data are placed alongside each other. And he points out that many important things in our lives, such as the sequence of events which leads to our first meeting with our spouse, have a probability of less than 2 per cent. Such rare events certainly do happen! Ray Davis, on the other hand, believes that the correlation is real – and, echoing Pauli's famous bet but in a more modest way, Bahcall and Davis have a bottle of champagne wagered on the outcome of further tests of this coincidence.

Those tests are now being made. The Sun's activity was rising to a peak late in 1989, as I was writing this chapter, and it will be in decline again after about 1992. Observations up to about 1995 should provide the definitive test of this strange correlation. That alone would be sufficient reason to keep the Davis detector running. But it is hard to see any dramatic new breakthrough coming from the swimming pool of cleaning fluid.

Some researchers have suggested searching the records, or

making new observations, to try to find out if more neutrinos arrive in the daytime, when the Sun is overhead, than at night. Again, there shouldn't be any effect – neutrinos are 'supposed' to pass through the solid Earth as if it were not there. But if solar neutrinos don't match up to predictions in some ways, it may be worth testing what 'everybody knows' about their ability to pass through the Earth. Some variations on the MSW idea, in fact, would suggest that oscillations occur inside the Earth, and might produce a measurable daily effect. But such tests are pushing beyond the limits of the Homestake neutrino 'telescope'.

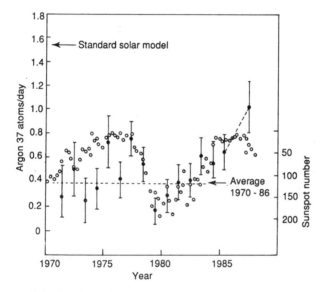

Figure 4.5   With nearly twenty years of solar neutrino data (dark spots) it looked as if there might be a correlation with sunspot number (open circles). Observations over the next few years should tell us whether this is a real effect or not.

There is, however, no shortage of proposals for new kinds of neutrino telescopes, detectors using technology that was either too expensive or too difficult to contemplate in the 1960s. If Davis had found exactly the expected number of neutrinos, then most of these ideas would still be regarded as too expensive or too difficult to bother with. It is because of the puzzles raised by his twenty years of observations that it now seems worthwhile – even urgent – to measure the energies of neutrinos, the directions they are coming from, and the flavours of the neutrinos themselves. I know of at least twelve different types of experiment now proposed to measure at least some of these properties of solar neutrinos. Each of the twelve techniques could be applied in several different ways. I will mention only the few possibilities that seem to have a realistic chance of becoming operational in the next few years.

The next logical step is to build a detector that will respond to the lower-energy neutrinos produced in vast quantities by the p-p reaction. Front runner for this is likely to be some variation on the idea of an experiment using gallium to capture the neutrinos. The experiment is simple in principle, and depends on the fact that when an electron neutrino interacts with a nucleus of gallium-71, the nucleus is transformed into one of germanium-71 and an electron is emitted. Without going into details here, chemists are happy that they can count the number of germanium atoms produced, using techniques which are conceptually similar to those used by Davis to count argon atoms. The great advantage of gallium-71 is that it interacts with p-p neutrinos. The immediate snag with a gallium detector is its cost; a secondary problem is that it might give an ambiguous answer to our questions about solar neutrinos.

Gallium itself is a metal with a very low melting temperature. If you hold a lump of it in your hand, it melts into a shiny puddle, like a little pool of mercury. It is also a very valuable metal, already used in the electronics industry to make light-emitting diodes (LEDs), the familiar little red lights on calculators and other pieces of electronic equipment. By the time this book is in print, gallium arsenide may be becoming a commonly used semiconductor, providing a generation of electronic equipment faster than the present one. All that makes gallium useful, and desirable to modern industry. But it is also rare – less than 100 tons of gallium are produced each year, and a good solar neutrino detector would need at least 30 tons, perhaps as much as 60 tons, all to itself. The cost of the gallium for the detector alone would be between five and ten *million* dollars, at present prices – but, as the scientists have been quick to point out, you could always sell it to the electronics industry after you had finished with it!

Both Soviet researchers and a collaborative European team are, nevertheless, planning such projects, and it had been hoped that by detecting p-p neutrinos a gallium experiment would solve the puzzle of why Davis detects only one third of the expected number of neutrinos. According to the standard model, such a detector should 'see' about 120 SNU of neutrinos, with about 70 per cent coming from the p-p process and most of the rest from the beryllium-7 interaction. If the new detector actually finds one third of the predicted number of neutrinos, that will certainly suggest that neutrinos are oscillating between the three flavours en route from the Sun to the Earth, since the p-p process is not very sensitive to the temperature at the heart of the Sun. But if the p-p neutrinos are present in about the predicted quantities, that could be explained in either of two ways. It might mean that there are problems with the astrophysics that influence only the Davis neutrinos (such as a central solar temperature 10 per cent below that of the standard model). That would affect boron-8 neutrinos but not p-p neutrinos. Or it could still leave room for the MSW type of mixing of neutrino flavours *inside* the Sun, since that process may itself only work for high-energy neutrinos.

Another proposal involves using the metal indium instead of gallium to detect solar neutrinos. Norman Booth, of Oxford University, has plans for an experiment using a ton of indium-115, which should catch one solar neutrino every three or four days. When that happens, a nucleus of indium-115 is converted into tin-115, and an electron is released. Because the tin is created with excess energy – in an excited state – it immediately falls back into its most stable state, by emitting two photons (gamma rays) that can be detected relatively easily. This technique has the advantage that the gamma-ray flashes signalling the arrival of neutrinos will be detected instantly, in 'real time', as the neutrinos arrive, instead of experimenters having to wait for days or weeks before doing the equivalent of flushing out the tank and counting the number of neutrinos that arrived over a long period of time. It has the disadvantage that indium-115 is naturally radioactive, and a ton of the stuff will emit 200,000 electrons every second. But Booth thinks he can get round the problem of this huge 'background' of electrons that threatens to swamp his detectors.

At the other extreme from Booth's approach, at least in terms of size, comes a series of proposals which depend on the fact that neutrinos can simply bounce off electrons – scattering, as it is called – and give up energy to the electrons. Such an event is rare, but if you have enough electrons in a detector, with enough neutrinos passing through, it is bound to happen occasionally. Build a big enough tank of almost anything, since all atoms contain electrons, and some of the solar neutrinos passing through will give energy to some of the electrons in the tank. 'All' you have to do is to capture the fast-moving electrons and work out where the scattering took place – feats which are far from easy, but are routine for physicists who work with fundamental particles.

The detectors that 'found' neutrinos from Supernova 1987A work in this way, but have not yet been capable of detecting neutrinos at the lower energies typical of those coming from the Sun. The advantages of the technique are that it works in real time, recording the neutrinos as they arrive, and that in principle it is possible to work out both the energy and the direction of the incoming neutrinos. The disadvantage is the enormous amount of material you need. One proposal, involving 6,600 tons of liquid argon placed in a tank in the Gran Sasso tunnel under the Alps, might be able to do the trick. The experiment is called ICARUS (a tortuous acronym for Imaging Cosmic and Rare Underground Signals), and it would be able to measure the energies of the electrons, and thereby infer the energies of the incoming neutrinos.

This proposal is worth picking out for special mention because one of the physicists involved is John Bahcall, the world's authority on the theory of solar neutrino interactions. According to his calculations, the detector should 'find' 4,700 solar neutrinos per year, and would be able, he claims, to confirm (or refute) the accuracy of the standard solar model in just one day of operation.

The argument is disarmingly simple. According to standard theory, the electrons monitored in the ICARUS detector should have energies (gained from solar neutrinos) distributed evenly around a peak of 5 MeV, with the same number of events at 3 MeV, for example, as at 7 MeV. But any version of neutrino oscillations will shift the distribution of energies, either up or down depending on which detailed theory you prefer. If ICARUS finds very few electrons on one side of the peak (which side doesn't matter), that will be a sure sign that oscillations are at work, and would imply that the standard model of the Sun is correct, and it is the neutrinos themselves that are playing tricks.

There are still other ways of detecting the arrival of solar neutrinos in the lab. Blas Cabrera, of Stanford University, is working on what is known as a bolometric detector. This relies on the simplest concept of all, the fact that when a neutrino interacts with the nucleus of an atom it produces an electron with a lot of energy. Instead of trying to detect the electron itself, however, Cabrera plans to measure the energy indirectly, from the rise in temperature of the detector that results. This is only possible if the detector is cold to start with, and its atoms are arranged in a solid crystal. Then, when the emitted electron flies out of one nucleus it collides with other nearby atoms, jostling them into a tiny vibration. This shaking of the atoms is equivalent to a rise in temperature – cold atoms move about only a little bit, hot atoms move about a lot. So if you start out with a very cold crystal of, say, silicon, and it is struck by a neutrino whose energy is absorbed, there ought to be a tiny rise in temperature of the silicon crystal. The trick is measuring this tiny rise in temperature – you certainly have to be operating the whole thing at temperatures close to absolute zero, a few K, where helium is a liquid.

Cabrera's step-by-step approach to the problem involves plans to build first a prototype detector using a kilogram of silicon, and study the way it responds to being bombarded with energetic particles and X-rays. Then he hopes to build a larger detector, perhaps containing 100 kilos of silicon, and to place it alongside a nuclear reactor to see how it responds to neutrinos. Only then will he be ready to proceed with a full-size solar neutrino experiment, involving 10 tons of silicon.

That timetable gives you some idea of how long it is likely to be before any definitive new data on solar neutrinos come in. A gallium detector, ICARUS, or the Cabrera bolometer could be operating in the early 1990s, if funds become available. More exotic ideas could really pin down the overall distribution of solar neutrinos at different energies (their spectrum) but are scarcely even on the drawing board yet. They are unlikely to be applied in practice until the twenty-first century. And, in spite of the optimistic claims made for ICARUS, somehow I doubt that one day of operation will suffice to solve the puzzle. In 1966, many physicists (perhaps including Bahcall) would have told you that only a month of observation with the Davis detector would suffice to confirm the accuracy of the standard solar model!

After two decades of puzzling over the results from the Homestake mine, maybe the prospect of waiting another five or ten years for the next insight into solar neutrinos ought to be bearable. When such costly, long-term projects are planned, however, it is the duty of the theorists to try as best they can to predict what the experiments will find. Just as the advent of the Davis experiment itself concentrated the minds of astrophysicists in the 1960s on refining their calculations of the standard model, so the plans for a new generation of detectors cry out for the astrophysicists to make testable predictions of what those detectors might find. There is also the challenge, for theorists, of using their ingenuity to find a satisfactory solution to the solar neutrino problem that does not require spending years of effort and millions of dollars building detectors deep down in holes in the ground, but which (unlike the cocktail party solutions) does relate what is going on inside the Sun to what is going on inside other stars and in the Universe at large.

Observational astronomy can also help. In the 1980s, while physicists have struggled with their designs for neutrino detectors, and made technological progress towards a new generation of experiments, astrophysicists and astronomers have not been idle. They, too, have improved their instruments and their techniques, gaining new insights into the nature of the Sun, and finding new ways to probe the secrets of its interior. Those new insights suggest that some of the cocktail party discussion of the solar neutrino puzzle may not have been so crazy after all. In order to see why, we must go back to 1977, when the solar neutrino problem was less than ten years old and cocktail party solutions were a dime a dozen, to pick up the threads of what seemed at the time to be just another wild idea about what might be going on in the heart of the Sun.

5

Another Wild Idea

John Faulkner is a British-born astrophysicist, now living in California, where he works at the Santa Cruz campus of the University of California and at the Lick Observatory. An acknowledged expert on the physics of stellar interiors, he made his scientific name in the 1960s for research into the way stars evolve when they contain two sources of nuclear energy, with helium burning into carbon in their cores, while a shell of hydrogen is still burning into helium outside the core. These calculations explained the appearance of what are known as 'horizontal branch' stars,* fitting into place the last main piece of the puzzle of how stars evolve. When researchers began to be interested in the possibility that there might be 'new' kinds of particle in the Universe, and that the presence of these particles might affect the way stars evolve, it was natural for Faulkner to become involved in these speculations, in the latter half of the 1970s. But at first, nobody thought that the speculations might be relevant to the story of solar neutrinos.

At that time, many astronomers were beginning to take seriously the idea that there might be a lot more matter in the Universe than we can see. Bright stars, and galaxies containing billions of bright stars, had to be the main focus of astronomical attention over the years, because only bright objects could be studied directly, by the light which reaches our telescopes. But ever since the 1930s there had been a suspicion among many astronomers, and a deeply felt belief among a few, that there is

---

* The name comes from the location of these stars in a diagram which relates the brightness of a star to its colour. It is called the Hertzsprung-Russell, or H-R, diagram, after the two astronomers who developed this method of classification. Stars like the Sun, burning hydrogen in their hearts, lie in a band on the diagram known as the main sequence. Red giants and white dwarfs occupy their own regions of the diagram.

more to the Universe than meets the eye. Studies of the way in which stars move in a galaxy like our own, and studies of the way galaxies in groups (called clusters of galaxies) are moving suggest that they are being tugged by gravitational forces that are stronger than the combined gravity of all the visible bright stars added together. There must be dark matter in the Universe, as well as the bright stuff. But what was the dark matter, and where did it congregate?

The dark matter is sometimes referred to as 'missing mass' – a name that has gone out of favour as astronomers have persuaded themselves, during the 1980s, that the matter really is there, and it is the light that is 'missing'. At first, the natural assumption was that this dark matter might be in the form of very faint stars, or clouds of gas that had not condensed to form stars, or even planet-like objects, enormous numbers of 'Jupiters' spread throughout the Galaxy. But in the 1970s new developments in particle physics led to the daring new suggestion that some, or all, of the 'missing mass' might be found in the form of particles never detected in any laboratory on Earth, left over from the Big Bang in which the Universe was born.

The particle connection

Particle physicists had no idea, at first, that their new theories might have cosmic repercussions. They were interested in developing a unified set of equations that would describe the behaviour of all of the four forces of nature (gravity, electromagnetism, and the strong and weak nuclear interactions) in one package. A first, and major, step along the road to such a 'Theory of Everything' (TOE) had been made by combining electromagnetism and the weak interaction into one package, the electroweak theory. But some versions of this theory required the existence of a new kind of particle in the Universe – a particle even more massive than the proton. The specific particle envisaged in calculations of this kind carried out in 1977 was a type of heavy neutrino. That proposal has since fallen from favour as these theories have been improved, and has been replaced by other candidates for dark-matter particles; but it provided the impetus to set some astrophysicists thinking along new lines. Such a particle could never be manufactured in accelerators on Earth, like those at CERN in Geneva or Fermilab in Chicago. The energy E required to manufacture particles with mass m several times bigger than the mass of a proton, in line with Einstein's equation $E = mc^2$, simply is not available. But astronomers have very good evidence that the Universe itself was born, about 15 billion years ago, out of a state of superdensity and superheat, the Big Bang.* The energy available in the Big Bang was ample to make vast numbers of these hypothetical particles – indeed, it is energy from the Big Bang, converted into mass in line with Einstein's equation, that is locked up in the form of protons, neutrons and electrons in all stars, planets and your own body today. If protons and neutrons could be left over from the Big Bang, then so could these other heavy particles. If there were enough of them around, their gravitational influence could add up to explain the way stars and galaxies move, and perhaps even help to explain how galaxies had formed from collapsing clouds of gas in the first place. But what effect would the presence of such particles have on the behaviour of stars themselves?

Faulkner's interest in the problem was hooked during a visit to the US National Radio Astronomy Observatory, in Green Bank, West Virginia, in 1977. There, he met up with other astronomers interested in various aspects of the cosmic implications of the presence of a previously unrecognized form of heavy particles in the Universe. Three of those researchers, Gary Steigman, Craig Sarazin and H. Quintana, plus Faulkner, joined forces in a study of the way in which the presence of such particles would affect the evolution of the Universe at large, the formation of galaxies, the behaviour of galaxies once they had formed, and the behaviour of stars. They concluded that particles with masses between twice and twenty times the mass of the proton could represent 'a dynamically significant component of the mass density of the Universe' and that they 'would have all the required properties to form the "missing mass" in clusters of galaxies, and galactic halos'.†

The effect of these heavy particles on stars, though, seemed to be small, since it turned out that very few of the particles would collapse along with the hydrogen and helium in the clouds from which stars form – the dark matter particles stay spread out over a large spherical region surrounding a Galaxy like our own (the 'halos' mentioned by the team). This is all to the good, since we know that the dark matter, whatever it is, is spread out and not concentrated inside the visible stars. But Faulkner had become intrigued by the possibility that even a few of these particles

* The evidence is summarized in my book *In Search of the Big Bang*.
† *Astronomical Journal*, Volume 83, p. 1050.

accumulating in the core of the Sun might change their structure just enough to account for the deficiency of neutrinos recorded by the Davis experiment. After all, it only needs an adjustment of 10 per cent in the temperature given by the standard solar model to resolve the neutrino problem. Back at Santa Cruz, he enlisted the help of a research student, Ron Gilliland, to carry the calculations through. Sure enough, the trick worked. Adding heavy particles to the heart of the Sun *could* cool it enough to reduce the flow of neutrinos to match the measurements made by Davis. But Faulkner's colleagues were far from enthusiastic at the idea of including yet another cocktail party solution to the solar neutrino problem in their joint paper. Grudgingly, they allowed Faulkner to include a brief summary of his work with Gilliland at the end of sub-section *c* of section five of the paper, just above the conclusions. The last sentence of the paper ended 'one could solve the solar neutrino problem without seriously affecting other aspects of stellar evolution'. But nobody, not even Faulkner, thought at the time that this was the most important aspect of the joint paper. And although during 1978 Faulkner and Gilliland got as far as writing up a detailed account of their work, ready to present to the world in the form of an article in a scientific journal, they received so much flak from their colleagues about the stupidity of the whole notion that they gave up the idea. The draft article was quickly buried under an accumulation of other paper in Faulkner's office at Santa Cruz, and soon forgotten. Steigman became convinced that new arguments ruled out the existence of heavy neutrinos (the whole basis of the original collaboration) anyway, and although Faulkner sometimes gave the idea an airing at scientific meetings the response was generally sufficiently unenthusiastic to discourage him from pressing the case – even though he now fondly recalls that one of the few people who actually liked the idea in the early 1980s was Nobel laureate Murray Gell-Mann.

But while Faulkner's enthusiasm for the idea was being squashed by his colleagues, in the world of particle physics theorists were, in the early 1980s, being forced ever more firmly to the conclusion that some form of 'extra' particles must exist in the Universe, even if these particles are not heavy neutrinos. And at the same time astronomers were finding more and more evidence of dark matter exerting its gravitational influence across the Universe. It was only a matter of time before someone else combined the two sets of ideas. That someone was William Press, of the Harvard-Smithsonian Center for Astrophysics, who, with his colleague David Spergel, followed up the implications in the mid-1980s. Neither Spergel nor Press had read the 1978 paper in which the calculations made by Faulkner and Gilliland had been briefly summarized, nor had they happened to be at any of the meetings where Faulkner had tried to rouse interest in the idea since. Quite independently, and starting from scratch, they developed their own calculations of how such massive particles, which they called cosmions, might affect the behaviour of the Universe at large, galaxies, and individual stars. And they, too, found that the presence of such particles inside the Sun might solve the solar neutrino problem.

Cosmions are WIMPs

The two pieces of work are essentially the same, and now is the time to look at them in detail. The Harvard team avoided one mistake made by Faulkner and his colleagues, however, by resisting the temptation to nail their theory to the existence of one particular kind of 'new' particle. A theory based on the existence of massive neutrinos looks very silly, as Steigman realized, if evidence comes in that massive neutrinos do not exist; but by 1985 the particle theorists were invoking a plethora of new particles to go along with various ideas about how the forces of nature might be unified into a TOE. The underlying point is that *whichever* theory turns out to be right, there will be room for *some* form of extra-massive particle. So don't specify which one you are invoking in your astronomical calculations – just give it a catch-all name, like cosmion.

Unfortunately, cosmion is not such a good catch-all name, since it doesn't make the connection with developments in particle physics theory clear. In fact, the astronomical observations *specify* what kind of particle must be out there filling the role of missing mass, and that tells the particle theorists what they should be looking for in their calculations (the solar studies, as we shall see, even pin down the mass of the particle). The term that most theorists prefer now is an acronym based on a description of the important properties that any such hypothetical cosmion must have. It must be weakly interacting, in the sense that it does not 'feel' the strong nuclear force, otherwise such particles would be destroyed by nuclear interactions; and it must have mass, in order for it to produce a gravitational force and play the role of dark matter in galaxies. So it is known as a Weakly Interacting Massive Particle, or WIMP.

Where do WIMPs come from? There are still several detailed possibilities, and they cannot all be right. But my own preference is for the idea that the existence of WIMPs in the Universe is intimately connected to the existence of everyday matter, the protons and neutrons (collectively known as baryons) of which we are made (we can leave electrons out of the discussion, for now, since they have so little mass compared with protons, neutrons or WIMPs). And this can best be understood in terms first expressed by the Soviet physicist Andrei Sakharov, in the 1960s.

The puzzle Sakharov addressed was why, if the Big Bang theory is correct, should there be any matter in the Universe at all? In the Big Bang itself, energy was in the form of radiation at very high temperatures. At such high temperatures, the energy in electromagnetic radiation (photons) can convert directly into pairs of particles – an electron and a positron, a proton and an antiproton, a neutron and an antineutron. Almost all tests that can be carried out in terrestrial laboratories show that this kind of mass-energy interchange obeys a basic law of symmetry, that particles and antiparticles are created together. Because a baryon that meets its antibaryon counterpart annihilates in a puff of energy, leaving no particle behind, the making of particle-antiparticle pairs does not, in a very real sense, add to the number of baryons in the Universe. If each baryon counts for +1 and each antibaryon counts for −1, each particle-antiparticle pair adds precisely zero to the number of baryons in the Universe.

If this law of nature operated precisely in the Big Bang itself, then at a later stage, when the Universe had cooled down from its hot beginning, every baryon would, sooner or later, meet up with its antibaryon partner and annihilate. After 15 billion years, we would be left with a Universe full of energy, but no matter at all.

Sakharov pointed out that there must have been processes at work, very early in the history of the Universe, that selectively produced a surplus of baryons over antibaryons when matter was created out of energy. Like many insights of pure genius, this seems obvious – once somebody has spelled it out for you (and, of course, I have made it look even simpler by leaving out the mathematics that surrounds this neat insight and puts it on a secure scientific footing). Astronomers actually know how much radiation there is in the Universe today. They can monitor a weak hiss of radio noise, coming from all directions in space and known as the cosmic background radiation. This radiation is what is left of the fireball of the Big Bang after it has been cooling for 15 billion years; it fills the entire Universe, and now has a temperature of just under 3K (less than $-270°C$), which corresponds to the presence of just 488 photons in every cubic centimetre of space throughout the Universe. If all the matter in all the bright stars and galaxies (all the baryonic matter) were distributed uniformly across the Universe, there would be just one particle in every ten million cubic centimetres. In other words, for every proton or neutron in the Universe there are, in round terms, a billion (10^9) photons.

That ratio, a billion to one, is a measure of the tiny size of the breakdown in the law that particles and antiparticles are always created in pairs – small wonder that it has never been measured directly under laboratory conditions! What it is telling us is that for every billion antibaryons that were produced in the Big Bang, there were a billion and one baryons. In each case, a billion pairs annihilated to produce a billion photons, and a single baryon was left over.

Physicists are still struggling to develop a version of a unified theory that will produce exactly the right balance between baryons and photons from the reactions that took place in the Big Bang. There are several contenders for such a theory, but as yet none of them gives exactly the 'right' answer. But that is not what matters here. The important point is that measurements made by astronomers *tell* us what the right answer is – that there are a billion photons for every baryon. If there is dark matter in the Universe as well – as there must be, if observations of the movements of stars and galaxies are taken at face value – then the simplest and most natural assumption to make is that the dark stuff (the WIMPs) was made in much the same way. That is, until there is a good reason to abandon simplicity and go for some more complicated theory of how things got to be the way they are, we might guess that for every billion antiWIMPs created in the Big Bang there were a billion and one WIMPs, so that the surplus left over today is one WIMP for every billion photons, or one WIMP for every baryon.* If that is indeed the case, then WIMPs with a mass of about 5 to 10 times the mass of the proton would be

---

* To make both sets of particles, of course, we need two billion left-over photons. Don't worry – the calculation is sufficiently vague that the difference between one and two billion photons (a factor of two) is not important. What matters is that in each case the ratio is a billion to one, not a thousand to one, or fifty to one, or a hundred billion to one. Factors of ten *are* important; a factor of two is neither here nor there.

exactly right to provide all of the dark matter needed in our Galaxy. One implication would be that bright stars – baryonic matter – make up just 10 per cent of the mass of the Universe, and that 90 per cent of the mass of the Universe is actually in the form of WIMPs. For people made of baryons (and electrons), living on a baryonic planet circling a baryonic star, this is hard to accept. But that doesn't make it any less true. There is a wealth of evidence that what we see really is only one tenth of the Universe, and that the rest is hidden from our gaze.

Cosmic connections

Apart from the fact that the way stars and galaxies move indicates that they are being tugged by the gravitational hand of a great deal of dark matter, cosmologists have puzzled for a generation over the problem of how galaxies ever came into existence at all. A typical galaxy has a mass equivalent to a hundred billion Suns, and galaxies like this are the basic features of our Universe on the large scale – sometimes referred to as 'islands in space'. The Universe itself is expanding. We know this from measurements of light from distant galaxies, which shows a consistent displacement towards the red end of the spectrum. This redshift is explained if all galaxies are moving apart from each other – it is an effect on light equivalent to the effect on sound that makes the note of the siren on a police car deeper if the car is racing away from you. The redshift does not, however, mean that galaxies are moving through space, in the sense that the Earth moves through space as it orbits the Sun, or the Sun moves through space as it orbits the centre of our own Milky Way Galaxy. Rather, it is interpreted as indicating that space itself is expanding – something that was actually predicted, before the redshift was observed, by Einstein's general theory of relativity.

Long ago, in the Big Bang, the Universe was a hot, dense fireball, a maelstrom of violence. As it has expanded, it has thinned and cooled – all the way down to a temperature of 3K and a baryon density of just one particle for every ten million cubic centimetres of space. But how could clouds of gas containing as much matter as a hundred billion Suns condense out of the expanding Universe, when the expansion of space was trying to spread the gas thinner, pulling clouds apart before they could collapse?

The answer, cosmologists had realized by the 1980s, is that they can't – unless they have help. The gravity of all the bright stars in a galaxy, or even a cluster of galaxies, is insufficient to explain how the original cloud of gas held itself together in the early phases of the expanding Universe. But computer simulations of the way clouds of gas collapse as the Universe expands show that the trick *can* be done, provided that there is ten times more dark matter spread out around each galaxy in an extended halo. WIMPs of the kind described in the previous section are exactly what are needed to make the equations balance and to provide the extra gravity needed to hold proto-galaxies together in the expanding Universe.*

But WIMPs don't form clouds that collapse down to form stars. Only baryonic matter does this. This is because WIMPs carry no electric charge, and so cannot radiate energy away into space. When a cloud of particles shrinks under the tug of gravity, it gets hotter because gravitational energy is released – the particles move faster, and the pressure inside the cloud increases, resisting any further collapse. The rule applies just as much to a cloud of WIMPs bigger than our Galaxy as it does to the Sun itself. If the cloud is made of baryons, the heat is converted into electromagnetic radiation by the charged particles, and escapes. So the pressure is relieved, and the cloud carries on shrinking and getting hotter inside until nuclear burning starts up and provides the extra radiation pressure needed to halt the collapse (as John Faulkner is fond of remarking, in this sense nuclear reactions keep stars *cool*, by preventing them from collapsing even further and getting still hotter inside!). But if there is no way to release the energy from inside the cloud in the form of radiation, then the cloud stabilizes at an appropriate size. For WIMPs left over from the Big Bang, the appropriate size is quite large. The WIMPs are spread out through a roughly spherical halo around our Galaxy, reluctant to interact either with baryons or each other except through gravity. But a star like our Sun, ploughing through the WIMPy sea, must inevitably accumulate a relatively modest number of these particles in its interior, captured and held there by the Sun's own gravity. Which is how the Santa Cruz team and the Harvard researchers, independently of each other and working on opposite sides of the North American continent, explained why the Sun is colder in its heart than it ought to be.

---

* Confusingly, the researchers who carry out these computer simulations of galaxy formation usually refer to the dark stuff as 'cold dark matter', or CDM. Cosmions, CDM and WIMPs are the same thing under three different names. In this book, I shall stick to the term WIMPs.

Keeping the Sun cool

It all depends on how many WIMPs the Sun has captured during its lifetime, and where exactly they lurk inside the Sun. Fortunately, these properties are very easy to calculate. A single WIMP can pass right through the Sun without bouncing off more than one proton (or other nucleus) – they are nearly as reluctant to interact with everyday matter as are neutrinos. So gravity is, indeed, the only thing that matters, as far as trapping WIMPs inside the Sun is concerned. At the surface of the Sun, a particle would have to be moving at 617 kilometres a second in order to escape from the Sun's gravity – this is the 'escape velocity'. Any particle that moves slower than this will be captured. Inside the Sun, at a distance where there is just half the solar mass between a particle and the centre, the escape velocity is 2,100 kilometres a second. But this is much more than halfway from the surface to the centre – remember that 40 per cent of the Sun's mass is contained in a core filling just 25 per cent of its radius. At the core itself, a particle would have to be moving at 3,000 kilometres a second, and be lucky enough to avoid colliding with a proton or some other nucleus on its way out, in order to escape entirely into space.

Each WIMP in the halo of particles around our Galaxy moves in its own orbit, held in place by gravity. The velocity needed to stay in that orbit is the same, whatever the mass of the particle is, for any particular orbit. At the Sun's distance from the galactic centre, the appropriate orbital speed is about 300 kilometres a second, whether the orbiting object is a star, a WIMP, or a hypothetical dark planet. So it is easy to see that most of the WIMPs swept up by the Sun during its passage through space will indeed 'stick'. If the Sun is overtaking the WIMP, there is hardly any difference in speed at all, and even if the WIMP is moving the opposite way to the Sun, in a head-on collision its relative speed is only 600 kilometres a second, scarcely enough to escape even from the surface of the star. The accurate calculations take account of the way particles are gathered in by the Sun's gravitational field, allow for the distribution of WIMPs through the halo required to provide the 'missing mass', and give a total for the present WIMP population of the Sun, allowing for the four and a half billion years it has spent ploughing through the halo to date. The concentration of WIMPs required to provide the missing mass in our Galaxy, for example, is equivalent to one solar mass of material spread through every thousand cubic light years of space.

When this and the other relevant numbers are put into the calculation, it turns out that there should be just one WIMP inside the Sun for every hundred billion protons, provided that each WIMP has a mass (the same for each WIMP) in the range from five to ten times the mass of a proton.

This is a pretty small ratio. The proportion of WIMPs to protons inside the Sun is, in fact, one hundred times *less* than the proportion of baryons to photons in the Universe at large – and that seemed like a small number when we first encountered it. Can such a minute fraction of WIMPs really affect the way the Sun works? Astonishingly, the answer is 'yes'.

WIMPs with masses in this particular range, about five to ten times the mass of a proton, will settle down into stable orbits inside the Sun that spread over no more than about 10 per cent of the solar radius. They form a tenuous WIMPy core, moving through the densest part of the Sun almost as if the baryons were not there. But that 'almost' holds the key to the way they cool the heart of the Sun. The neutrinos that Ray Davis and his colleagues can detect are produced only by the nuclear reactions that take place in the very hottest part of the Sun, the innermost 5 per cent of its radius. But some nuclear reactions are still going on just outside this inner core, where the temperature is a little lower. Although the temperature is lower in this outer part of the core, so that nuclear fusion proceeds less vigorously, the volume (which, of course, depends on the *cube* of the radius) is greater. So most of the energy being produced by nuclear reactions inside the Sun actually comes from the region outside the innermost 5 per cent, out to about 12 per cent of the radius of the Sun. This is exactly the region where WIMPs with masses in the interesting range congregate. Unlike particles in pure orbits affected only by gravity, WIMPs orbiting inside the Sun are also affected by the occasional collisions with protons and other nuclei, so the region where the WIMPs settle does depend on their mass. Lighter WIMPs would pick up energy from collisions with protons and escape from the Sun; more massive WIMPs would lose energy in collisions and sink down into the innermost core, so they could never affect what turns out to be the interesting region between 5 and 10 per cent of the way out from the centre. But if WIMPs have masses in the range required to provide the dark matter in the Universe, then their orbits take them across the inner 10 per cent of the Sun's core.

In each orbit, each WIMP suffers one collision, on average, with a proton. If that collision takes place in the innermost core (the inner 5 per cent), the WIMP will pick up energy, and move faster as a result – it has got hotter. At the same time, the proton it collided with has lost energy and moves more slowly – it has got colder. But when a fast-moving WIMP collides with a slower-moving proton slightly further out from the centre, it gives up some of its energy. The WIMP slows down and gets colder, the proton speeds up and gets hotter. Moving rapidly about the inner 10 per cent of the Sun, and occasionally colliding with protons and other nuclei, the effect of the WIMPs is to average out the temperature conditions across the innermost 10 per cent of the Sun, making the central peak of temperature less than it ought to be according to the standard model. The WIMPs make the innermost 5 per cent of the Sun a little cooler, and the next 5 per cent a little hotter, with the overall effect that exactly the same amount of nuclear energy is produced, but from a larger, more evenly hot core than in the standard model.

The WIMPs can do this, in spite of their scarcity, because of the speed with which they transport the energy. A photon, remember, colliding against billions of protons in its frantic pinball-machine random walk out of the heart of the Sun, will take hundreds of thousands of years to cross the innermost 10 per cent of the Sun's radius. But a WIMP traverses that distance in about 17 minutes. Each WIMP makes the round trip across the innermost 10 per cent of the Sun roughly twice every hour, 48 times a day, nearly 18,000 times a year, year in and year out through all the billions of years that the Sun has been shining. And each time it carries its quota of energy outward. The ratio of the time it takes for a WIMP to cross the inner 10 per cent of the Sun to the time it takes a photon to negotiate the same journey is, in fact, about 100 billion to one – the same as the ratio of the number of baryons to the number of WIMPs. The scarcity of WIMPs inside the Sun is almost exactly compensated for by their efficiency at moving energy outward over the critical region (Figure 5.1).

When the effects of WIMPs are added in to the standard computer models of the Sun, they show that the temperature of the innermost core, where the Davis neutrinos are produced, is automatically reduced by the 10 per cent required to match the neutrino measurements to date, provided that the WIMPs have masses between five and ten times the mass of the proton and that there are about three WIMPs for every hundred billion protons – the same, within the limits of accuracy of all these calculations, as the properties required for WIMPs to provide the dark matter in our Galaxy, and to help galaxies form in the first place. The effect

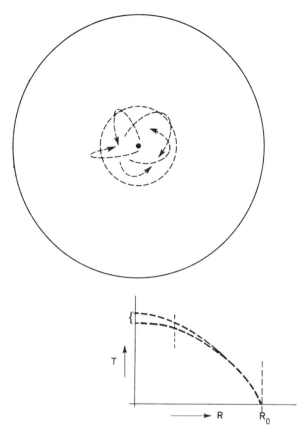

Figure 5.1   WIMPs circulating in the innermost 10 per cent of the Sun transport heat outwards and make the temperature in the centre drop by about 10 per cent, indicated by the curly bracket on the temperature plot. This simplified schematic does not show how the redistributed heat actually warms the region just outside the solar core, so that overall just as much energy is produced. With or without WIMPs, conditions at the surface of the Sun (R_0) are the same. The key point is that the decreased central temperature exactly explains the scarcity of neutrinos detected by Ray Davis and his colleagues. (Based on figures supplied by John Faulkner.)

of this cooling on nuclear reactions is to reduce the number of neutrinos that would be detectable by the Davis experiment by a factor of two or three, bringing theory and observations nicely in line with each other.

By cooling the very heart of the Sun, of course, the WIMPs also reduce the radiation pressure there, and that means that the density of matter must be a little higher than in the standard model, in order for gas pressure to take on a bigger share of holding the Sun up against gravity. But this is no problem, and may actually, as we shall see in Chapter Seven, be an advantage.

Credit where due

All of this actually emerged in a flurry of scientific papers published in 1985 and 1986, with credit eventually being shared equally between Faulkner, Gilliland, Press and Spergel – but not without a little excitement along the way. It isn't hard to imagine the consternation felt by John Faulkner, early in 1985, when an advance copy (a 'preprint') of the first paper on cosmions by Spergel and Press arrived at Santa Cruz. With a sinking feeling, he realized that the paper presented essentially the same solution to the solar neutrino problem that he and Gilliland had worked out seven years before, but had never published. And the Spergel and Press paper was already set for publication in the most prestigious journal read by astronomers, the *Astrophysical Journal*. So much time had passed that Faulkner simply couldn't remember how much detail of his work with Gilliland had actually got into print (over Steigman's proverbial dead body) in the 1978 collaboration with Steigman and the others. But he knew only too well that in science the credit for a new idea goes to the person who *publishes* the idea first, whether or not someone else thought of it first.

He searched his office for a copy of the 1978 article, only to find that he had long since given all his copies away. Then he went to the library on campus, only to find that the relevant volume of the *Astronomical Journal* was out on loan. He couldn't even find the unpublished draft of the paper he had worked on with Gilliland in 1978, and Gilliland himself, having completed his PhD studies, had long since gone off to the High Altitude Observatory in Boulder, Colorado (home of Mork and Mindy), where he was pursuing a quite different line of research into the behaviour of the Sun (more of this in Chapter Six). Gloomily, Faulkner decided to call Press and compare notes. The reaction, he later recalled,★ was understandable jubilation on the part of Press, who said 'Well, it's too bad, John' and laughingly went on 'You realize that all the credit goes to he who has the courage of his convictions and first puts [the idea] in the literature.'

★ *San Francisco Examiner*, interview by Keay Davidson, 2 October 1986, p. E-1.

This did nothing to lift Faulkner's gloom. But next day he found that the 1978 volume of the *Astronomical Journal* had been returned to the library. Hurriedly, he flipped through the pages to the relevant article, scanning down to subsection *c* of part five. To his surprise and delight, he found that not only was the basic idea mentioned in there, but that he had squeezed in four out of the five main conclusions that had emerged from his work with Gilliland. There was enough there to establish scientific priority beyond a shadow of a doubt. With the boot now firmly on the other foot, he called Press back with the news. 'He sort of cursed me out, in a genial fashion,' says Faulkner, but once the chaffing was over the two teams quickly agreed that the sensible thing to do was to join forces to produce a definitive paper describing the WIMP scenario.

First, though, Faulkner had one enjoyable task to perform. A more thorough search of his office revealed the draft of the Faulkner and Gilliland paper, seven years old and literally covered in dust. It needed only a few changes to make it ready to send off for publication in the *Astrophysical Journal* – a revised introduction, acknowledging the independent work of Spergel and Press, and a new acknowledgements section, in which the authors thanked 'many colleagues for discussions over the years, including especially Gary Steigman (without whose counsel this work would have been published prematurely)'. With that off his chest, and the paper duly published before the end of 1985, Faulkner was ready once more to start work on the implications of WIMPs for stellar evolution.

The collaboration with Press and Spergel (which was also published in the *Astrophysical Journal*, in July 1986) was a natural progression from both teams' earlier work, not just a diplomatic exercise. Faulkner and Gilliland had used approximate techniques to estimate the way WIMPs would interact with other particles in the core of the Sun, but had used detailed solar model calculations to determine the implications in terms of the output of detectable solar neutrinos. Spergel and Press, on the other hand, had worked out the WIMP properties in great detail, using the advances in particle physics theory and cosmology during the early 1980s, but had not worked out the details of the changes in solar structure, only that WIMPs could indeed lower the temperature at the heart of the Sun. Together, the two teams were able to tell the complete story, essentially as I have outlined it in the preceding section.

Nobody has yet been able to *prove* that WIMPs exist – that would require catching one in the laboratory (which may not be impossible; see Chapter Eight). But the circumstantial evidence in

their favour is compelling. John Bahcall, who is the theorist who
has made the most intense study of the solar neutrino problem,
and who has also been involved in the search for the missing mass,
has commented 'WIMPs solve two fundamental and exasperating
problems; this is such a beautiful idea that if it isn't right, God
missed a great opportunity',* while late in 1988 Roger Tayler, of
the University of Sussex, gave a keynote lecture to the Royal
Astronomical Society in London where he said that although
'there have been many attempts' to solve the solar neutrino
problem, 'the only one which is at present under active study
involves the presence of weakly interacting massive particles
(WIMPs) in the solar interior'.† In ten years, the WIMP theory had
gone from being 'just another wild idea' to being the *only*
respectable theory currently on offer to explain the solar neutrino
problem. And meanwhile Faulkner, in particular, had been
applying it to resolve some other long-standing problems in stellar
theory, as well.

Other stars

The most useful tool that astronomers have for studying the way
stars change as they age is called the Hertzsprung-Russell diagram,
after the two astronomers who pioneered its use. Stars live for so
long, and change so slowly, by and large, that there is no hope of
studying stellar evolution by watching an individual star or two
age. But the H-R diagram enables astronomers to do the
equivalent of a botanist who studies a forest of trees that includes
seedlings, saplings and mature specimens, and uses those studies
to work out the life cycle of a tree.

The H-R diagram is a kind of graph, in which the overall
brightness of a star (usually measured in units where the
brightness of the Sun is 1) is compared with its surface
temperature (which is equivalent to its colour, with blue stars
being hotter than red, and so on, in a precisely quantifiable way).
Most stars follow the fairly simple rule that brighter stars are
hotter than fainter stars, and they lie on a band in the H-R diagram
running from top left (hot and bright) to bottom right (cool and
dim). The Sun is a main sequence star (Figure 5.2). But there are
exceptions to this rule. Some stars are both bright and cool, while

---

* Quoted by Gilliland, *Griffith Observer*, January 1987, p. 9.
† The George Darwin Lecture for 1988, published in *The Quarterly Journal of the Royal
Astronomical Society*, Volume 30, p. 125, 1989.

others are both hot and faint. A star can be bright, even though it has a cool surface (and therefore looks red), if it is very big. The amount of heat crossing each square metre of the surface is small, so it is cool; but the number of square metres involved is huge, so it is releasing a lot of energy altogether, and is bright. Such stars are red giants, and lie in the upper right of the H-R diagram. Similarly, a faint star can be hot if it is very small, so that even though a great deal of energy flows through each square metre of

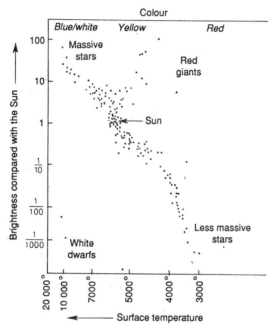

Figure 5.2 The H-R diagram relates the brightness of a star to its surface temperature, or colour. The Sun lies on the main sequence, a band running from top left to bottom right on the diagram.

the surface, making its light white, there are very few square metres for the energy to flow through. Such stars are called white dwarfs, and occupy the bottom left of the H-R diagram.

The main sequence corresponds to stars that are, like our Sun, burning hydrogen into helium in their hearts. The rate at which such a star is burning its nuclear fuel, and therefore its brightness, depends on its mass. The heavier a star is, the more energy it must produce in its heart each second in order to hold itself up against the inward pull of gravity. So the bright stars at the top of the main sequence are bright because they are more massive than stars at the bottom of the main sequence, and use up their fuel more quickly.

All this has been determined largely from studies of the H-R diagrams for different groups of stars. In particular, there are some groups, known as globular clusters, which each seem to have formed from a single collapsing cloud of gas when the Galaxy was younger. So every star in a globular cluster must have the same age. When astronomers look at the H-R diagram for such a cluster

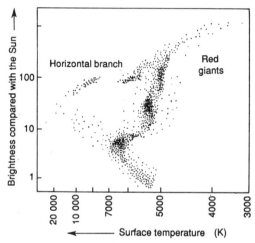

Figure 5.3   In H-R diagrams of some clusters of stars the upper part of the main sequence is missing, and has been replaced by red giant stars. The point at which the main sequence bends away to the right indicates the age of the cluster.

(Figure 5.3), they find that the stars at the bright end of the main sequence have gone, and been replaced by cooler stars, further to the right in the diagram. There is also, usually, a trail of stars between the position where the upper main sequence 'ought' to be and the new 'red giant branch'. This trail is the horizontal branch that I mentioned earlier.

Detailed studies of many stars in many globular clusters, compared with the computer models of how stars work based on standard physics, have produced a clear picture of how a star like our Sun evolves (very massive stars get involved in supernova explosions, of course, but that is a different story and I won't discuss it here). When hydrogen burning can no longer be sustained in its heart, the core of a main sequence star shrinks and gets hotter, while its outer layers expand. The star becomes a red giant, with an inert core of helium surrounded by a shell in which hydrogen is still being 'burnt'. The star moves to the right and upward, off the main sequence in the H-R diagram and along the red giant branch. At the tip of the red giant branch, the core becomes so hot that nuclear burning can begin in the helium core. This makes the core itself expand, moving the hydrogen-burning shell out to a cooler region of the star and *reducing* the intensity of hydrogen burning. The combined effect is to shift the star, abruptly, onto the horizontal branch, where it stays while helium burning continues in its core and hydrogen burning continues in a shell outside the core. When all the helium in the core has been converted into carbon (and probably some oxygen as well), the inner part of the star again contracts, while its outer layers expand. Helium burning takes place in a shell around the inert carbon core, and hydrogen burning still goes on in a shell even further out from the core. The star has once again become a red giant, at the top end of the red giant branch (the 'asymptotic giant branch'). After further evolutionary adventures, in which a great deal of its mass is lost, literally blown away into space during its life as a giant, what is left of the star shrinks in upon itself and moves down into the white dwarf part of the H-R diagram.

It took heroic efforts by generations of astronomers to work all this out. Just one key feature is particularly important to the story I have to tell here. More massive stars lie near the top of the main sequence, and more massive stars run through their life cycles faster. As a cluster of stars that were born together ages, the point at which the H-R diagram for that cluster bends away from the main sequence moves down the main sequence from top left to bottom right. So the point at which the main sequence bends away towards the red giant branch tells us how old the cluster is. The H-R diagrams of globular clusters, like Figure 5.3, provide the best measures we have of stellar ages. And, as a bonus, it turns out that globular clusters are the oldest stars in our Galaxy, formed when the Galaxy itself was just collapsing down from a huge cloud of hydrogen and helium gas, held in the gravitational grip of an even more massive cloud of WIMPs.* But there is a problem. The ages of the oldest stars in the Galaxy, inferred from

---

* Without wandering too far from the thread of my story, it is worth just mentioning that we know these are the oldest stars, formed when the Galaxy was young, because they contain almost all hydrogen and helium (revealed by spectroscopy) and very little in the way of heavier elements. Heavy elements are only made inside stars, so the *oldest* stars must contain least, as they formed from virgin clouds of hydrogen and helium before any supernovas had been at work enriching the interstellar medium.

these main-sequence turnoff points, are uncomfortably close to the age estimated by cosmologists for the whole Universe. There is scarcely any time available, after the Big Bang, for the WIMPs to do their work of pulling clouds of gas together to make proto-galaxies, and for some of the gas in at least one of those proto-galaxies, our own, to form the first stars. The effect of WIMPs *inside* those stars, however, goes some way towards alleviating the embarrassment caused to astronomers by this problem.

WIMPy connections

The ages of globular clusters, estimated from comparison of actual main-sequence turnoff points with standard computer models of how stars work, lie in the range from 13 billion to 19 billion years. This is not a spread of real ages, since all the globular clusters are thought to have formed together when the Galaxy was born. Rather, the spread is a measure of the remaining uncertainties in the technique, with 16 billion years being the best bet for the age of the oldest of our Galaxy's stars. The age of the Universe (the time that has elapsed since the Big Bang) cannot be measured directly, and the inferred age depends on detailed theories of how the Universe has evolved.★ As far as this can be pinned down, however, the best evidence is that the Universe is between 15 billion and 18 billion years old, and probably nearer to 15 than to 18. Obviously, you cannot have stars 19 billion years old in a Universe just 15 billion years old (taking the worst possible disagreement between these two estimates), and even the middle value for each range, giving stars 16 billion years old in a Universe 16.5 billion years old is embarrassing to astronomers, who cannot find any way in which galaxies could have formed just 500 million years after the Big Bang.

WIMPs change the picture, because they alter the rate at which stars like the Sun age. Interestingly, the effect is *only* important for stars with masses rather like that of our Sun. Much more massive stars capture more WIMPs each year than our Sun does, because their stronger gravity pulls in the particles from a wider range. But much more massive stars don't live long enough to gather in significant numbers of WIMPs even allowing for their wider gravitational influence. Stars that are much less massive than our Sun, by contrast, have ample time to gather in WIMPs, but their more feeble gravitational range means that they gather them in

★ See *In Search of the Big Bang.*

more slowly. The accumulation of WIMPs in the hearts of low-mass stars will eventually have an important influence on their behaviour – but the Galaxy is nowhere near old enough for them to have had a chance of accumulating sufficient WIMPs to do this yet.

The way the presence of WIMPs in its core affects the evolution of a star like the Sun is seen by adding the influence of WIMPs to those standard computer models of stellar evolution. The calculations show that the age of the star when it leaves the main sequence is *less* than the age at which an otherwise identical star with no WIMPs in its core will leave the main sequence. In other words, if the globular cluster stars contain WIMPs then all of the ages inferred from measurements of the main-sequence turnoff points in the H-R diagram should be revised downward. The effect is small, but as Roger Tayler commented in his George Darwin lecture 'problems relating to the ages of the clusters would be eased if their stars contained WIMPs'. Faulkner is cautiously (but only cautiously) pleased by his discovery of how this effect works. He told me that just about the biggest effect you can produce with realistic WIMP models is to reduce the turnoff ages by about 15 per cent, bringing the 'standard' age of 16 billion years down to about 13.6 billion years. 'WIMPs,' he says, 'can turn modest embarrassment into modest agreement. Certainly, they go in the right direction (thank goodness!).'

This, of course, is the important point. If WIMPs had made the embarrassment worse, that would have been a major blow to the theory, hinting strongly that such particles might not exist at all, and that astrophysicists might have to find some other solution to the solar neutrino problem. Just such a suggestion has, in fact, been made by some astronomers, who base their arguments on a study of horizontal branch stars. But Faulkner, who cut his teeth as a researcher by finding out how horizontal branch stars work, has responded with a counterblast that puts this criticism very much in question, at least for now.

This attempt at WIMP-bashing depends on the way in which the presence of WIMPs in the heart of a star smooths out the temperature in the core (making it isothermal). In the standard models of horizontal branch stars, pioneered by Faulkner in the sixties, the core of the star, where helium is being converted into carbon, is a convective region. The temperature at the centre of the star is a lot higher than at the edge of the helium-burning zone, and the core material is being turned over by convection as a result. One effect of this is that fresh helium is dragged down into the centre of the star from the region just outside the core proper, providing additional nuclear fuel for this phase of its life. If WIMPs are present and smooth out the temperatures to produce an isothermal core, convection will be suppressed. In that case, only the helium in the heart of the core will ever get burnt, and no additional helium will be brought down into the heart of the star by convection. As a result, this phase of the star's life will be more short-lived, and once the innermost core of helium is burnt it will quickly move off the horizontal branch and along the asymptotic giant branch. The overall effect of this process at work on the members of a globular cluster would be to reduce the number of horizontal branch stars visible at any time, compared with the number of asymptotic branch stars. We actually see a higher proportion of horizontal branch stars in globular clusters than can be explained if core convection is suppressed.

Faulkner's response to this (worked out in collaboration with David Spergel) is that although suppressing core convection would indeed shorten the time spent by globular cluster stars on the horizontal branch, convection is not, in fact, suppressed. The changes that take place inside a star during its evolution, after it leaves the main sequence and goes up the red giant branch and down onto the horizontal branch, make it very unlikely that there are any WIMPs left in the core by the time it reaches the horizontal branch. Even if any WIMPs survive the blast of energy produced when the helium core ignites (the 'helium flash') and avoid being blown away into space, under the changed conditions in the heart of the star many of them will be moving at faster than the appropriate new escape velocity. They will 'evaporate', escaping from the core and out into space – in as little as a hundred years if their mass is around five times that of the proton, and rather longer if they have a bigger mass. WIMPs with more than about 8 times the mass of a proton can survive in the heart of a horizontal branch star for a lot longer – but they are held so tightly that they occupy only the innermost part of the inner core, leaving ample scope for convection to take place in the region just outside their sphere of influence.

These arguments about the influence of WIMPs on horizontal branch stars surfaced only in 1988, and there is sure to be more toing and froing between the protagonists in the debate while this book is going through the presses, and in the years ahead. The issue is a subtle one, and may never be resolved to everybody's satisfaction. But it is worth mentioning here because of the suggestion that WIMP masses might lie at the lower end of the range suggested by the original calculations. Although cosmologists would like WIMPs to have a mass of about 10 proton masses each, in order to provide all of the dark matter in one form, there is, in fact, no reason why WIMPs could not have half this mass, leaving half of the dark matter in some other form. And the most beautiful prediction of the WIMP model, now borne out by observations of the Sun itself, also favours a mass in the lower end of the range, around 5 times the mass of the proton.

More of this in Chapter Seven. But I wouldn't want you to run away with the idea that the only studies of the Sun that revealed anything new and interesting during the 1980s revolved around the idea of WIMPs. While the WIMP theory was languishing under a pile of paper in Faulkner's office at Santa Cruz, and even after it was given the kiss of life by Spergel and Press, there was a great deal of other work going on to probe the secrets of the Sun. The most exciting of this work, as we shall see in Chapter Seven, turned out to be directly relevant to the WIMP story (although that is not why it was originally carried out), and points the way to a more detailed understanding of the deep interior of the Sun in the 1990s than ever before. Before we move on to this denouement of the story of solar studies to date, though, there is still something else to tell about the outer layers of our neighbourhood star, and the way changes in those outer layers may influence life on Earth. But there is still a connection with the WIMP saga – or, at least, with one of the participants in that saga. Just in case you were wondering what Ron Gilliland was up to in Boulder all the while the WIMP theory was languishing, here is your chance to find out.

6

The Breathing Sun

The work Gilliland went on to when he left Santa Cruz also concerned the Sun – but in the early 1980s he was more interested in what was going on in the outer layers of our nearest star, not in the secrets locked deep in the solar interior. After he completed his graduate studies in California, Gilliland went to Boulder, Colorado, where he became (and still is), a member of the High Altitude Observatory of the National Center for Atmospheric Research. This was in 1979, at a time when one of the senior scientists at the Observatory, John A. ('Jack') Eddy, was making headline news with his claim that the Sun was shrinking measurably, at a rate of 0.1 per cent per century. Such a dramatic change in the diameter of the Sun – far more rapid than anything envisaged by Kelvin or Helmholtz – could only, of course, be some sort of short-term phenomenon, a fluctuation that had been going on for, perhaps, a few hundred years. Shrinking at a rate of 2 metres *per hour*, as Eddy's claims implied, the Sun would vanish entirely in less than 100,000 years. Put it another way, and if the Sun had been shrinking at that rate for more than a few thousand years then conditions on Earth would have been drastically different a few thousand years ago. All the old, familiar geological and evolutionary evidence showed that that simply was not on the cards.

So, what *was* going on in the Sun? It was natural that Gilliland, joining the team in Boulder at this exciting time, should turn his attention to the problem. He was, indeed, to be instrumental in showing that the solar variation is not as large as Eddy thought at first, but is real, and certainly large enough to have important repercussions for life on Earth. But in order to put these discoveries in perspective, we have to go back to the puzzle that started Eddy off on the trail of the shrinking Sun – the curious case of the missing sunspots.

A spot or two of bother

Astronomers have known that the Sun is imperfect, and that dark spots sometimes pass across its face, since the time of Galileo, in the early seventeenth century. Chinese and Greek sky watchers knew about sunspots even before Galileo's time, but it was with his invention of the astronomical telescope that the era of modern observations began. By projecting an image of the Sun through a telescope and onto a white screen (never, of course, looking directly at the Sun through a telescope), Galileo and his successors were able to monitor the comings and goings of these strange, dark spots. But it was only in the nineteenth century that astronomers realized that these sunspots come and go with a more or less regular rhythm, some eleven years long. And it was only in the 1980s that the rhythms of sunspot variations were linked with rhythms of changes in the size of the Sun itself, which 'breathes' in and out on a timescale of decades and centuries.

Individual sunspots range in size from about 1,500 kilometres in diameter to irregularly sprawling dark features 150,000 kilometres across. They usually occur in groups of several spots which together spread over hundreds of millions of square kilometres on the surface of the Sun. They look dark against the bright background of the solar surface because they are relatively cool. But 'relatively' is the watchword, for with the Sun's surface at a temperature of about 6,000K, the darkest central region of a spot is still at about 4,000K, and the lighter, outer region is at a temperature of around 5,500K.

Astronomers believe that sunspots are regions where the convection currents which usually carry hot material up to the surface from deeper layers of the Sun are temporarily inhibited by strong, local magnetic fields. Certainly, the magnetic fields – measured, like the temperature of the spots, by analysis of the spectral lines in light coming from a region of sunspot activity – are always associated with sunspot groups, and the spots themselves seem to be just the most obviously visible manifestation of a whole range of solar activities. These activities include great storms, and flares which send tongues of solar material licking far out into space. All of this activity varies over the roughly eleven-year solar cycle of activity, from a quiet Sun to an active state and back again. The overall pattern of magnetic changes in the Sun takes two of these cycles to get back to where it started – in one eleven-year cycle, the north and south magnetic poles of the Sun swap places, and in the next cycle they swap back again. So many astrophysicists argue that the basic cycle of activity is the 'double sunspot' cycle, about twenty-two years long.

Each sunspot cycle follows the same overall pattern, although the details differ from cycle to cycle. Starting from the quiet point of the cycle, a few sunspots appear at latitudes about 40° north and south of the solar equator. Each spot group builds up over about ten days, then dies away slowly over a month or so. As the solar cycle develops, not only do more and more spot groups form, but they form closer and closer to the equator, so that during the time of maximum solar activity they are concentrated near latitudes 10° north and 10° south.

Although this pattern is regular and to some extent predictable, we still do not know exactly what processes inside the Sun drive the solar cycle. The most favoured explanation involves a tightening of magnetic lines of force, wound up by the rotation of the Sun and pulling the spot groups towards the equator. But the life of a theorist trying to explain the exact behaviour of sunspots and the solar cycle in general is not made any easier by the fact that individual cycles differ not only in length but in strength. Some cycles may be only nine years long, measured from minimum to minimum; others stretch to about fourteen years. Although both extremes are rare, it is only on average that we can talk of a sunspot cycle of eleven years. Sometimes there are few sunspots even in years of maximum activity; in other cycles, hundreds of sunspots are produced during the peak sunspot years.

Even without knowing details of how the cycle works, however, some researchers have drawn attention to apparent relationships between solar activity, as measured by sunspots, and the weather on Earth. Solar activity can be measured in terms of an index called sunspot number, which is related to the area of the visible solar disk that is covered by dark spots, and is usually averaged over a month or a year. A sunspot number of 100 on this scale does not mean that there are 100 individual spots on the disk, but tells us how much of the disk is covered by spots – on this scale, 100 corresponds to a good, strong maximum, while anything over 150 is a bit special, and in the quiet years of a solar cycle the sunspot number falls well into single figures, sometimes actually to zero.

One of the reasons why it took astronomers so long to notice that there was an eleven-year sunspot cycle is that in the decades following Galileo's observations of the Sun there were, indeed, very few spots at all to be seen. For the best part of a century, it was as if, in modern terminology, the Sun was experiencing an extended minimum of activity. Of course, nobody at the time had any way of knowing that this was unusual. Sunspot activity picked up in general after about 1715, and by the middle of the nineteenth century astronomers had enough observations to notice the eleven-year cycle, which was first reported (as a ten-year cycle) by Heinrich Schwabe, and then checked out in detail by Rudolf Wolff, who showed that it had persisted since the early eighteenth century. What, then, had happened in the seventeenth century? In the 1880s and 1890s both Gustav Spörer, a German researcher based in Potsdam, and Walter Maunder, who worked at the Royal Greenwich Observatory in London, published the results of their studies of old records, which showed that there had been very few sunspots at all between about 1645 and 1715. Maunder continued to try to persuade his colleagues of the importance of this discovery, right up until his death in 1928. Astronomers paid little attention, preferring to believe that it was the fault of seventeenth-century observers, failing to notice, or failing to record, sunspots, rather than the fault of the Sun, failing to produce any sunspots. It was easier to assume that astronomers of past centuries (who were safely dead and couldn't argue back) were incompetent than it was, even in the twentieth century, to believe that the Sun was imperfect and variable. But some climatologists and popularizers took up the idea of a dearth of sunspots in the seventeenth century, and it was their claims that drew Eddy into the debate in the 1970s.

Until very recently, the idea that the climate of the Earth might change on a timescale of decades and centuries seemed as ludicrous to climatologists as the notion that the Sun might vary on the same timescale seemed to astronomers. Climate was regarded simply as a kind of 'average weather', which might experience random fluctuations, so that one year or one decade might be colder or hotter than another, but which didn't really alter much from century to century. That idea began to lose its grip as the twentieth century developed, and climatologists and historians realized that the weather in the 1930s and 1940s was distinctly warmer than that of the nineteenth century. A subsequent cooling of the Northern Hemisphere, in the 1950s and 1960s, encouraged more interest in climatic change, and led to some scare stories

about a new Ice Age being just around the corner. Largely
through the pioneering efforts of Hubert Lamb, first with the
Meteorological Office in London and later at the University of
East Anglia, the study of climatic variations in historical times
became respectable.

Those studies showed, among many other interesting features,
that the seventeenth century contained the coldest decades of a
period of climate so extreme that it is now known as the Little Ice
Age.* Rivers and lakes across Europe froze on an unprecedented
scale in winter, many crops could not be grown as far north as
they are found today, and sea ice extended much further south
from the Arctic than anyone now living has seen. Some
climatologists confronted by the fact that the world was colder in
the seventeenth century than it is today, but lacking any
explanation for why this might be so, conjectured that the Sun's
output of heat was weaker then, and pointed to the evidence of the
prolonged lack of sunspots, that happened at the same time as the
Little Ice Age, and is now known as the Maunder Minimum in
recognition of the astronomer who had most vigorously tried to
draw attention to it.

But the climatologists, of course, knew nothing of the
workings of the Sun, and the astrophysicists dismissed their
claims of a link between sunspots and the weather as ludicrous.
Still the claims persisted, remaining unproven but, equally,
unrefuted, like a skeleton in the closet of solar physics. Nobody
knew for sure if the Maunder Minimum was real. In the 1970s,
this all became too much for Eddy, who later told reporter Sam
Bleecker† 'I was annoyed by occasional references to it in
connection with a coincident change in the world climate. As a
solar astronomer, I felt certain that it never could have happened,
and my interest in history made the prospect of cross-examining
Maunder's assertions an appealing one.' Eddy expected to find
that Maunder (and Spörer) had been wrong, and that a proper
cross-examination of the historical records would show, not that
there were no sunspots in the late seventeenth century, but that
nobody had kept proper records of solar activity then. He soon
found out that he was wrong.

Eddy's research took him to the pages of long-unread journals
in the dusty corners of astronomical libraries, and to Europe and
the Royal Greenwich Observatory in search of ancient manus-

---

* See Lamb's book *Climate, History and the Modern World.*
† *Star & Sky,* June 1979, p. 14.

cripts. What he found was a sobering reminder that modern scientists are no more intelligent or dedicated than their predecessors, just better equipped in terms of instruments and technology. Astronomers of the seventeenth century were certainly motivated to study the Sun – Galileo's discovery of sunspots had caused enormous scientific interest. Records of observations of the planets and the rings of Saturn made at the time also showed how skilful the observers were, and how meticulously they recorded their observations – there was no question, Eddy realized, that they might not have had the skill to study sunspots. But did they have the inclination? Here, too, his expectations were shattered. He found that several observers had made regular observations of the Sun throughout the Maunder Minimum, specifically searching for dark spots, and had kept records of their findings (or lack of findings) every bit as scrupulous as the records they kept of planetary observations. Precisely because sunspots were so rare in the seventeenth century, when one *was* discovered an observer would report it to his colleagues with a flourish, and would achieve a modest measure of fame. Sunspots were eagerly sought during the decades of the Maunder Minimum, but they just weren't there to be seen – for 32 years, not one sunspot was seen in the northern hemisphere of the Sun, and for three score years and ten, from 1645 to 1715, no more than a single small group of spots was seen at any one time.

Setting out to lay the myth that world climate was linked to sunspot activity, Eddy had, in fact, succeeded in establishing the link as much more than a myth. He went on to develop the work by looking further back in time, using other techniques, such as records of auroral activity in the sky of the Earth (known to be caused by solar activity) and the measurement of traces of radioactive carbon in old tree rings (known to be caused by cosmic ray particles from the Sun), to show that the link between climate and solar activity is not only real but extends back to well before the time of Christ. When the Sun is quiet – when there are few sunspots for decades at a time, and even the peaks of the solar cycle of activity are low – the world cools.

The evidence was summarized at a meeting of the Royal Society in London during February 1989. Records of solar activity going back much further than the beginning of modern astronomical observations of sunspots are stored in the wood of trees (living or dead), in the form of radioactive atoms of carbon-14. Carbon-14 is produced by the interaction in the atmosphere of cosmic rays and atoms of nitrogen, and some of these carbon-14 atoms are taken up by living trees and laid down in the wood of their annual growth rings. The rings can be dated, simply by counting in from the outside of the tree, and the proportion of carbon-14 in each ring can be measured. By comparing the radioactive carbon content of rings laid down over the past two centuries with astronomical records of solar activity, it has been established that the amount of carbon-14 laid down each year is directly related to the Sun's level of activity.

Charles Sonett, of the University of Arizona, told the meeting that there is a cycle about 200 years long which dominates the tree-ring record of solar activity. The same 200-year cycle shows up in the thickness of the rings themselves. Every two centuries, the rings tend to be narrower, indicating that the trees suffered some form of stress. The pattern suggests that there was not one Little Ice Age but many, with the Sun's activity declining, and the weather turning colder, every couple of centuries.

In fact, Sonett had been saying this for years, long before the February 1989 meeting of the Royal Society. It was one of the claims that Eddy set out to refute; but it was Eddy's work, in particular, that had now made such studies respectable enough to grace those hallowed halls. Why?

The shrinking Sun

As a result of his interest in old sunspot records, Eddy learned of the existence of another series of intriguing solar observations, carried out at the Royal Observatory in Greenwich. Ever since 1750, astronomers at the observatory had been taking daily measurements (weather permitting) of the size of the Sun. The observations were made with an instrument called a transit telescope, which is mounted so that it can swing 'up and down' along a north-south line, but cannot move from side to side. It happens that this particular instrument defines, by international agreement, the zero meridian. The north-south line through the telescope is the Greenwich Meridian, from which we measure longitude; and the passage of the Sun directly over this telescope defines noon, Greenwich Mean Time.* Although the records of measurements of the Sun's diameter don't start until after the

---

* It also happens that the Greenwich Meridian passes within a hundred metres of the house where I live, and these words are being written due south of Greenwich. This has no significance whatsoever for the story.

Maunder Minimum, Eddy was still curious about them. During a spell as a visitor at the Harvard-Smithsonian Center for Astrophysics, he examined the records with Aran Boornazian, and saw immediately that there was a consistent downward trend in the measurements of solar diameter – taken at face value, the records implied that the Sun was shrinking dramatically.

At first, the two astronomers didn't believe what they saw. They assumed that the astronomers of the past, working without the aid of modern clocks and measuring instruments, had simply been inaccurate in their measurements. But when Eddy and Boornazian studied copies of similar records from the US Naval Observatory in Washington, they found a similar trend. Astronomers on both sides of the Atlantic, making the same kind of observations over the nineteenth and twentieth centuries, came up with similar figures suggesting a rapid shrinking of the Sun. Clearly, something *was* going on, after all. So Eddy and Boornazian went back to the records, pulled out the information on solar shrinking, and published it – to the consternation of many of their colleagues.

It is important to appreciate exactly how the measurements were made, since this has a crucial bearing on the arguments that followed about how reliable the observations were. The early observers determined the Sun's diameter by measuring how long it took for the image of the Sun to pass the cross-hairs of the telescope, as the Sun moved from east to west across the sky because of the rotation of the Earth. They started counting when the edge of the Sun touched the cross-hair, and stopped when the other side of the Sun left the cross-hair. But, of course, the early observers had no stop watches or digital clocks to help them in this task. Instead, they had to count the number of ticks of a pendulum clock as the image passed the cross-hairs, and their measurements simply cannot have been as accurate as modern ones. So Eddy and Boornazian relied chiefly on the records since 1854, when a more accurate timing system (a chronograph) was installed at the observatory. The continuous records go up to 1954, when the observatory moved out of London to Herstmonceux, in Sussex, and the daily observations of solar diameter from Greenwich ceased, although the transit telescope defining the Greenwich Meridian is still in place at the old Observatory.

It was this series of observations, together with the data from the US Naval Observatory, that led to the claim that the Sun was shrinking at a rate of about 1,500 kilometres per century – a dramatically large fraction of its 1,392,000 kilometres diameter. In terms of the angle the Sun makes in the sky, which is just under 32 minutes of arc, the estimated shrinking amounted to 2 seconds of arc per century. It seemed astonishing, but Eddy had some other evidence to back the claim up.

When the Sun is eclipsed by the Moon, there is sometimes a complete blackout, and sometimes a ring of light is still visible around the edge of the Moon. Such an annular eclipse occurs when the Moon is slightly further away from the Earth in its orbit, so that it covers slightly less than 32 minutes of arc on the sky (it is an astonishing coincidence that the Moon and Sun both appear the same size as viewed from the Earth). In 1567, the astronomer Christopher Clavius observed an annular eclipse from Rome. But modern calculations suggest that the Moon was too close to the Earth on that occasion for this to be possible – *unless* the Sun was a little bigger in 1567 than it is today!

There is some argument about what exactly Clavius saw. Was it really an annular eclipse, or did he just see flashes of light from the Sun (known today as 'Bailey's Beads') passing through the valleys between the mountains at the edge of the Moon? Unfortunately, there are no photographs from 1567 to tell us. Even if Clavius did see an annular eclipse, that doesn't give very much guidance as to exactly how big the Sun was then, simply a hint that it was bigger than it is today. As circumstantial evidence in support of a case made by the transit telescope observations, though, it looked persuasive to Eddy and Boornazian.

Others were not convinced. In spite of this corroborative evidence, most astronomers dismissed the claims made by the Harvard-Smithsonian team. Critics pointed out that the observations from Greenwich (and, indeed, the ones made in Washington) had been made by a series of different astronomers, using different clocks and different techniques. At Greenwich, six different observers might be involved in the measurements in any one year, each one using his best judgement of exactly when the edge of the Sun touched the cross-hair of the telescope. When other researchers calculated the average diameter of the Sun determined by each of these observers, they found that even in the same year two different observers would produce figures that differed by well over a thousand kilometres.

Eddy was slightly chastened, but he still had another card to play. As well as counting the time it took for the Sun to pass across the hair line in the telescope, the old observers had also used another technique. While the noonday image of the Sun was in the field of view, an observer would quickly adjust a micrometer gauge to measure the vertical diameter of the Sun, the distance from the north pole to the south pole across the image. These measurements showed the same sort of effect as the horizontal measurements – a decline in solar diameter – but only half as much, at a rate of about one second of arc per century. At first, Eddy had assumed that this technique would be less reliable than the timing technique, because of the speed with which the observer had to work, and the wear and tear, over the years, on the micrometer screws. But when he visited the old Royal Observatory at Greenwich, and tried the technique out for himself, he found that he was wrong. In fact, the observer had *more* time to judge the position of the top and bottom on the Sun's image in the telescope's cross-hairs, and these measurements ought to be more reliable than the horizontal measurements.

Even so, there were questions about the reliability of some of the records, and the exact number that you got for the rate at which the Sun was shrinking depended on which observations you decided to trust most. Eddy and Boornazian interpreted the vertical measurements as implying a decline in solar angular diameter of 1 arc second per century; Sabatino Sofia and colleagues at the Nasa Goddard Space Flight Center interpreted the same observations as implying a shrinking of 'only' about 0.2 arc second per century.

By now, in 1979, Eddy had stirred up a hornets' nest with his claims, and many astronomers started to get in on the act, some claiming to have proof that the Sun's diameter was not changing, others equally convinced that there was a shrinkage, but much less than Eddy and Boornazian had claimed. Dusty old records of various kinds were dug out of the files and re-interpreted. Irwin Shapiro, of MIT, looked at old records of transits of the planet Mercury across the face of the Sun. This is a beautiful technique, but can only be applied about thirteen times every century, when Mercury passes across the solar disk, as viewed from Earth. Because we know the distance from Earth to the Sun, and from Mercury to the Sun, astronomers can calculate the size of the Sun by measuring how long it takes for the planet to pass across the Sun's disk. Shapiro showed, using this technique, that the Sun has not been shrinking by more than 0.3 arc second per century since 1700, and he suggested that it might not be shrinking at all.

Another gorgeous technique for measuring the diameter of the Sun involves eclipses. The exact position of the edge of the path of an eclipse (the shadow of the Moon on the Earth) depends on the positions of the Sun and Moon, and their distances from Earth, which are all known very accurately and can be calculated even for eclipses that occurred centuries ago. It also depends on the size of the Moon (which nobody suggests is changing) and the size of the Sun. It happens that in 1715 there was a total eclipse of the Sun visible from England, and Sir Edmund Halley, later Astronomer Royal, collected data on the eclipse from many observers. These data can be used to work out where the edge of the shadow was, and therefore how big the Sun was in 1715. A re-analysis of these records carried out in 1980 led to one of the most delightfully ironic scientific juxtapositions of all time.

In the issue of the scientific journal *Nature* dated 11 December 1980, one of the featured articles was headlined 'The constancy of the solar diameter over the past 250 years'. It was written by John Parkinson, Leslie Morrison, and Richard Stephenson, three British astronomers, and it drew on studies of the meridian circle evidence, the transits of Mercury, and eclipse observations (including the 1715 eclipse) to conclude 'there has been no detectable secular change in the solar diameter.'

That same week, *Nature*'s American counterpart, *Science*, in the issue dated 12 December 1980, featured another contribution on the problem. This one was headlined 'Observations of a Probable Change in the Solar Radius Between 1715 and 1979'. It came from an equally eminent team of astronomers, David Dunham, Sabatino Sofia, Alan Fiala, and David Herald in the United States, and Paul Muller in England. They used the records of the 1715 eclipse, compared with data from an eclipse seen in 1976 in Australia and one visible in 1979 in North America, to conclude that 'between 1715 and 1979, a decrease in the solar radius of 0.34 ± 0.2 arc second was observed.'

It looked as if someone had to end up with egg on their face. In fact, though, in spite of their dogmatic statements, both teams could still be right. The clue lay in the 'error bars' on the numbers they quoted, their own estimates of the reliability of the evidence they were working with. Dunham and his colleagues said that the Sun *was* shrinking, at a rate between 0.14 and 0.54 (that is, 0.34 ± 0.2) arc second per century; Parkinson's group said there was *no* evidence for shrinkage, and that their observations ruled out any change bigger than 0.15 arc second per century (the figure they quoted for the 'constancy' of the solar diameter was a 'change' of 0.08 ± 0.07 arc second per century, which they interpreted as zero within the limits of the error bars; 0.15 lies at the other limit of the error bars).

The time was clearly ripe for someone to take a long, hard and careful look at *all* the available data, and to try to find out just what the Sun was really doing. It was a measure of the concern caused by Eddy and Boornazian's original claim that astronomers did not seem hugely bothered by a suggestion that the Sun might be shrinking at 'only' a rate of 0.2 arc second per century. Such a shrinkage of the *whole* Sun would still release 20 times more energy each year than the Sun actually does put out, and would pull the rug from under all the standard models of the Sun, let alone the solar neutrino puzzle. It was Ron Gilliland who put things in a (slightly) more comfortable perspective, by showing that the changes are part of a long-term cycle of gentle solar pulsations, with the implications that they are indeed something to do with the outer layers of the Sun – its atmosphere – not its deep interior.

The breathing Sun

Gilliland took all five of the available data sets which contained long-term records of measurements of the diameter of the Sun, and subjected them to a searching statistical analysis, using techniques developed by mathematicians to find long-term trends and periodic variations in such samples. Two of the sets of data used by Gilliland are the same as those used by Eddy and Boornazian, two additional sets of data involve records of transits of Mercury across the Sun's disk, and the fifth data set is a compilation of timings of various solar eclipses. Between them, these historical records provided him with information about changes in the size of the Sun over a period of 265 years, from the eclipse of 1715 up to 1980.

The results of Gilliland's analysis were published in September 1981 in the *Astrophysical Journal*. That fact is almost as significant as the results themselves, since although the weekly journals *Nature* and *Science* are prestigious and usually reliable, they are by their nature places where scientists sometimes go for quick publication, and some of the work published quickly in their pages is later proven to be in error, or incomplete. The *Astrophysical Journal*, on the other hand, has long had a reputation for the toughness of its refereeing system, whereby submitted papers are carefully checked by other experts before being published. Meaning no disrespect to the weekly journals, where I have published papers myself, their pages are the first place you would look for slightly offbeat research on sunspots and changes in solar diameter; when this work appears in the *Astrophysical Journal*, it has (like the various publications on solar WIMPs in 1985 and 1986) an added stamp of credibility.

It is a mark of how respectable Gilliland's work was that essentially no further progress has been made since it was published. After all the flurrying of sometimes contradictory papers here, there and everywhere, he provided the definitive 'state of the art' analysis.

So, what did he find? By combining the five sets of data, the statistical analysis shows that there is a long-term decline in the size of the Sun, amounting to 0.01 per cent per century, and that this has been going on since at least the early 1700s. Of course, there are still problems with the uncertainties of many of the measurements, but, as Gilliland put it, 'one is not inexorably led to the conclusion that a negative secular solar radius trend has existed since AD 1700, but the preponderance of current evidence indicates that such is likely to be the case.'★ Even more strikingly, though, the analysis showed up two cyclic patterns of changes in the size of the Sun.

One of these is a gentle pulsation, in which the Sun breathes in and out over a cycle 76 years long. Other researchers had found hints of this before, using very limited sets of data; Gilliland showed that the effect is real, and covers a range of about 0.02 per cent of the Sun's radius, some 140 kilometres. And the picture is further complicated by a hint (no more than a hint) that there is an even smaller scale oscillation in the size of the Sun over the familiar eleven-year solar cycle. Intriguingly, both the eleven-year and 76-year oscillations follow the rule of thumb that when the Sun is bigger there are fewer sunspots.

That rule of thumb would also tie in with the decrease in solar radius, and increase in sunspot activity, since the seventeenth century. In addition, astronomers have long suspected that there might be a sunspot rhythm about 80 years long, and some climatologists have related this to an apparent 80-year cycle in average temperatures on Earth. Could they be linked with the 76-year rhythm of solar pulsations?

The long-term decline in solar radius is, perhaps, the most important piece of information to emerge from this analysis, since stellar evolution theory predicts that the Sun should actually be growing, although by an even smaller and undetectable amount. The best guess at present is that this, too, is part of a long, slow

★ *Astrophysical Journal*, Volume 248, article beginning p. 1144; quotation from p. 1150.

pulsation cycle – a guess reinforced by the evidence that there were sunspots hundreds, thousands and (as we shall soon see) millions of years before the Maunder Minimum. The discovery of the shorter cycles, though, has implications which may be of practical value over the next few decades.

The Sun was at its smallest, on the 76-year cycle, in 1911, at a time when it also showed strong activity throughout its sunspot cycle. The next minimum in radius should therefore have been in 1987. Nobody will be sure if the Sun did start expanding again in 1988, or thereabouts, until several years have passed and several series of measurements have been made. But recent events certainly fit the pattern of a smaller Sun being linked with more sunspot activity. The latest peak of the eleven-year cycle was around 1979–80, when the measured mean sunspot number rose rapidly from 28 in 1977 to 93 in 1978, 155 in 1979, and about the same in 1980. These are high peaks. At the time of writing, the Sun has passed through a quiet state, with sunspot numbers in single figures in 1986, and is rapidly building up to the next peak of the eleven-year cycle, expected early in 1990.* The observations so far show that this is going to be another high maximum, very much in line with Gilliland's calculations. But then we can expect a smaller peak of activity next time, roughly in eleven years from now, early in the twenty-first century.

Gilliland explored the practical implications of all this in a paper published in the journal *Climatic Change* in March 1982. He found that many features of the pattern of temperature changes of the Earth since 1850 can be explained in terms of a combination of the effects of dust from volcanoes (rising high in the atmosphere and blocking out heat from the sun), a build-up of carbon dioxide in the air (trapping heat by the so-called greenhouse effect) and a 76-year cycle linked with the breathing of the Sun. If he is correct, the solar influence has been acting in the opposite sense to the greenhouse effect for the past thirty years, trying to cool the Earth while the Sun expanded. But as we pass the minimum of the present 76-year cycle, the Sun will start to provide more heat, contributing an additional 0.28 per cent over the next three decades and warming the globe by a quarter of a degree, Celsius, over and above anything that happens due to the greenhouse effect.

* The peak duly arrived on schedule. As this book goes to press, the Sun's activity is once again in decline.

That effect is itself a result of human activities, including the burning of coal and oil, and destruction of the tropical forests. Climate experts predict a continuing build-up of carbon dioxide in the air, warming the globe as we move into the twenty-first century. With solar and greenhouse effects combining, the rise in temperatures could be more rapid than any of the climate experts have calculated.

One of those experts, Tom Wigley, from the University of East Anglia, discussed the implications at the Royal Society meeting in February 1989. He pointed out that because it takes the Earth a long time to respond to small changes in heat arriving from the Sun (mainly because the oceans take a long time to warm up or to cool down), climatologists would not expect tiny fluctuations over the eleven-year cycle to show up in their records – the Earth doesn't have time to respond to a dip in solar output before the output increases again. But, as Wigley pointed out, a 200-year (or 76-year) cycle would be long enough for even small changes in the output of the Sun, over a range of about 1 per cent, to account for climatic fluctuations on the scale of Little Ice Ages.

This suggestion is still controversial (especially where astrophysicists are concerned) and unproven, but it points the way for future research on links between solar activity and climate that could have great practical value. This serves to emphasize the urgency of further efforts to measure the size of the Sun.

One attempt came in 1983, when an eclipse of the Sun was visible from Java. An expedition jointly sponsored by *New Scientist* magazine and University College, London, duly set out to measure accurately the edge of the path of the eclipse, with the aid of twenty-five senior students from a local school, who formed a human chain three kilometres long at right angles to the edge of the path of totality. Their observations show that the size of the Sun today is smaller by about 0.2 arc second, about 0.01 per cent, than the standard value set by astronomical observations in the nineteenth century and used trustingly by astronomers ever since.

The ultimate test of the breathing Sun idea will only come, of course, when modern instruments far more accurate than those used in previous centuries have built up a reliable, day-to-day record of measurements of the solar diameter. Following Eddy's work, a new meridian telescope has been installed at the High Altitude Observatory in Colorado, and this is automated, to time the transits of the Sun at noon with greater accuracy than ever before. More than 500 light-sensitive diodes are used to measure both vertical and horizontal dimensions of the solar disk at noon each day – but it will take at least another five years before the measurements can reveal whether or not the size of the Sun is changing. If Gilliland is right, of course, we will not find a shrinking going on over the next decade or so, but rather an expansion of the Sun – an expansion which will, paradoxically, lend credence to the idea that the Sun has shrunk since the seventeenth century.

Even while solar astronomers wait for those genuinely new data to come in, a French team headed by Elizabeth Ribes, at the Observatoire de Paris, uncovered some 'new' old data, to add to Gilliland's five data sets. The study was actually carried out by Jean Picard, in the second half of the seventeenth century. Picard was a pioneering astronomer who designed precision instruments and, among other things, made many measurements of the size of the Sun, even before regular daily measurements with the transit telescope started in Greenwich. In a careful re-analysis of his old records, the Paris team found in the mid-1980s that the Sun was indeed about 2,000 kilometres bigger during the Maunder Minimum than it is today. And, perhaps the most compelling evidence of all, they found that there was a clear decrease of 3 arc seconds in the measured size of the Sun, as recorded by the *same* skilful observer (Picard), using the *same* instruments and techniques, between 1683, in the depths of the Maunder Minimum, and 1718, when the sunspots returned in modest force. Records of the few sunspots that appeared during the Maunder Minimum can also be used to explore the Sun's behaviour at the time.

Although the sunspots were few in number throughout the Maunder Minimum, they were slightly less rare in the years 1674, 1684, 1695, 1705 and 1716, suggesting that the familiar eleven-year cycle was still operating, in a quieter way, at the time. In all these years except 1716 spots were seen only in the southern hemisphere of the Sun, and the observers of the day kept careful drawings of what they saw. Because there were so few spots, there is no ambiguity about these drawings, and the life history of each spot can be traced as it moves across the visible disk of the Sun, carried around by the Sun's rotation. Rotation measurements based on these old drawings show that the Sun was rotating more slowly at the time it was bigger. This is exactly what we would expect if the increase in size represents a genuine swelling of the material in the outer part of the Sun. Like a spinning skater whose arms are spread outward, the Sun slows as its outer layer expands. Ribes and her colleagues pointed out, in 1987, that the observations fit the expected pattern of behaviour for a real pulsation of the outer layers of the star, rather than hinting at any changes in the deep interior (where neutrinos are produced).

The key question that arises, as far as any understanding of the deeper secrets of the Sun is concerned, is whether this kind of behaviour is 'normal' in terms of the long history of the Sun, or whether the whole pattern of solar cycles and sunspot activity is something peculiar, which has been going on only for a few hundred or a few thousand years. If we are living at a time of unusual solar activity, then perhaps those ideas which hold that there are few solar neutrinos detected today because the Sun is in an unusual state should be taken seriously, after all. But if there were some way of finding a trace of similar solar cycles of activity from a few million, or a few hundred million years ago, then we really would be forced to conclude that it is normal for the Sun to produce fewer neutrinos than the standard model predicts. Almost incredibly, just the evidence we require turned up in sediments laid down 680 million years ago, in what is now Australia, and analysed in the 1980s.

The record in the rocks

The sediments were deposited in late Precambrian times, somewhere between about 650 million and 700 million years ago. Although the exact dating depends on assumptions about the geological timescale, for convenience we can say that the ancient rocks studied by George Williams, of the Broken Hill Proprietary mining company, are roughly 680 million years old. At the time they were being laid down, the world was in the grip of a severe ice age, and part of the ground of what was to become South Australia was permanently frozen, like the permafrost regions of northern Canada today. On the edge of the permafrost region, a long, shallow lake or inland sea stretched roughly north-south, and fine sand and silt particles accumulated on the floor of this lake, gradually building up to form the rocks now known as the Elatina Formation. In summer, the temperature over the permafrost terrain to the west of the lake may have risen just above freezing; in winter, it dropped to −30°C or −40°C.

Today, the rocks laid down in that lake form part of the Flinders

Ranges, west of Adelaide. During his geological work in the region, Williams noticed an unusual section of siltstones in the Elatina Formation. This section of sedimentary rock is roughly 10 metres thick, and is formed in fine layers, or laminae, each between 0.2 millimetres and 3 millimetres thick. The pattern made by these narrow bands of clay and sand looks very much like the pattern of tree rings in a large piece of wood; in this case, the characteristic pattern of the bands in the Elatina Formation has dark red-brown layers, spaced between 2 millimetres and 16 millimetres apart, separated by several paler bands of material, the narrow laminae. The pattern persists over an area several hundred metres across.

The sediments were formed by fine particles of material settling on the bottom of an ancient lake, and the regular pattern of the stripes in the rocks shows that some more or less regular rhythm was bringing in water, laden with sediment, from outside. It might have been a monthly rhythm, associated with tides raised in the lake by the Moon; or it might have been an annual rhythm, associated with the seasonal melting of the nearby glaciers. Simply by counting the layers, Williams found that the pattern of thick and thin sediments repeated roughly every eleven layers with a 'double cycle' of alternate thick and thin eleven-layer cycles common in the sediments. The implication seemed obvious, and the discovery was reported in 1981, as evidence of a solar influence on climate in late Precambrian times. The laminae were identified as annual layers of sediment, which are produced in some lakes today, and are known as varves.

Astronomers in general did not exactly fall upon this discovery of the same solar rhythms operating 680 million years ago as operate today with cries of delight. Many were suspicious about how any solar 'signal' in the weather could appear so strongly, when there is only a very weak influence of the solar cycle on weather today; some wondered whether the claimed eleven-layer cycle might really be linked with the lunar tides, and not the Sun. Were they 'really' twelve-layer, monthly cycles, which Williams had miscounted? But one senior Australian solar astronomer, Ronald Giovanelli, enthusiastically supported Williams's work, and helped him to obtain funding for a drilling programme to obtain a complete core through the ten-metre-thick varve layer. Armed with this core, Williams went to the Laboratory of Tree-Ring Research in the University of Arizona, and analysed the patterns in the layers exactly as if they were tree rings, using a battery of powerful statistical techniques developed by the tree-ring researchers.★

First he analysed 1,337 consecutive laminae (varves) from one continuous section of the core; then he analysed 1,580 consecutive 'sunspot cycles', flagged by the darker bands in the core. In 1985, he reported that as well as the basic cycle, which varies from eight to sixteen years in length, there are several other rhythms present. For example, the length of each basic cycle, in terms of the number of layers in a cycle, varies over a longer cycle thirteen basic cycles long. And there is a sharp, distinctive pattern that recurs every twenty-six cycles in the Elatina record.

By now, there was enough evidence to make more astronomers sit up and take notice. One who did so was Robert Bracewell, of Stanford University, who has made a lifetime study of sunspot variations. The reliable record of sunspot variations goes back less than 200 years, but what Williams seemed to have found was a record of sunspot variations spanning 1,337 years. Never mind how the solar activity was influencing the weather, 680 million years ago; Bracewell dived in to analyse the record on the assumption that it was indeed a pattern of sunspot activity, and compared it with the modest historical record with which he was already familiar.

He found that he could explain the pattern of the varves in terms of basic eleven-year and 22-year rhythms, modulated by two longer cycles, spanning 314 years and 350 years. The length of the 'eleven-year' cycle varies regularly over the 350-year modulation, while the size of the 'sunspot peak' reached in any eleven-year cycle seems to depend on the position of the cycle within the 314-year modulation. Of course, there is no hope of finding cycles more than 300 years long in the historical record of sunspots, less than 200 years long. But Bracewell found a neat way to test his discoveries.

Using all the rhythms found in the Elatina varves, Bracewell set his computer running at the sunspot minimum that actually occurred in the summer of 1986, and ran it *backwards* in time to 'predict' the pattern of sunspot activity back to 1800. He got an almost perfect match with the actual record of solar activity, with

---

★ Some trees respond quite sensitively to changes in the weather, laying down thick or thin rings each year as a result of favourable or unfavourable fluctuations. Cores drilled from the trunks of still-living trees, and samples of older, dead wood, can be used to reconstruct patterns of climatic variations in some parts of the world going back a couple of thousand years. Which is why just the techniques Williams needed to analyse his varve layers were ready and waiting for him in Arizona.

all the high and low peaks in the right years, and the variation in length of the cycles themselves correctly calculated. Using *only* the record in the rocks from 680 million years ago, Bracewell had obtained the best agreement ever between any theory of solar variations and the actual sunspot records from historical times. There seemed little room to doubt that the clock inside the Sun keeps a steady time, and that the Sun today is in the same basic state that it was in 680 million years ago.* We are *not* living at a time of unusual solar activity.

Solar connections

Why, then, is the solar signal so strong in the Elatina varves? This may have nothing to do with our present story, but perhaps it is worth a slight detour to look at the explanations on offer. One possibly important point was noted by Williams in his original report on the discovery. In the late Precambrian, geological records show, the Earth's magnetic field was only 10 per cent as strong as it is today. This was not particularly unusual; the Earth's magnetic field does vary over the eons, though nobody quite knows why. Whatever the reason, when the field was weak, charged particles from the Sun (protons and electrons of the solar wind) could then have penetrated deeper into the atmosphere of the Earth than they do today, thereby influencing the weather.

Another possible explanation for the link gives us a good feel for just how long ago the late Precambrian really was. At that time, life on Earth (we should say, life in the *sea*, since even plants did not begin to colonize the land until about 420 million years ago) had not yet released much oxygen into the atmosphere. Today, oxygen in the atmosphere absorbs ultraviolet radiation from the Sun. This happens chiefly in the stratosphere, about 20 to 30 kilometres above our heads. The stratosphere gains energy as a result, and is warmer than the upper layers of the troposphere, the layer of the atmosphere from the ground up to the stratosphere. Because the stratosphere is warmer than the troposphere, convection stops at the top of the troposphere,† and weather (which is driven by convection) is confined to the troposphere. In Precambrian times, there was little or no stratosphere, because there was little or no oxygen to absorb incoming ultraviolet radiation.

---

* Such room to doubt as there is may be removed in 1990/91, when, according to Bracewell's calculations, the Sun should reach a peak level of activity, with sunspot numbers above 125.
† Hot air rises, but only if the air above it is colder than the rising air.

This would have had at least two potentially important effects. First, weather would not be confined so close to the ground, and convection columns could rise higher into the atmosphere than they do today. Secondly, the ultraviolet radiation from the Sun could penetrate virtually to the ground, so any changes in solar ultraviolet associated with the sunspot cycle could have a big effect on temperature at the surface of the Earth. And anything that affects temperature and convection, of course, is also going to affect rainfall patterns.

Perhaps *that* explains why the Sun had a bigger influence on climate 680 million years ago than it does today. Even so, the effect would only have shown up in regions very sensitive to seasonal changes in rainfall, and we are extraordinarily lucky that the preserved remains of just such a sensitive set of sediments are exposed to view today. The important point to grasp, however, is not which possible explanation might be right, but the fact that conditions were so very different on Earth in the Precambrian that we cannot really make comparisons with the climatic patterns of the present day. Or can we? Just as this chapter was being prepared, another variation on the theme was produced by Kevin Zahnle, of NASA's Ames Research Center, and James Walker, of the University of Michigan. I can't resist including it here, even though it adds very little to our attempts to unravel the secrets of the Sun.

A lunar connection

Zahnle and Walker have linked the Elatina cycles with the cycles of lunar tides raised in the Earth's atmosphere 680 million years ago. The record in the rocks shows, they say, a strong 'beat' effect between two cycles, one 10.8 years long and the other 20.3 years long. These precisely fit the lengths of cycles associated with the Sun and Moon in the Precambrian.

One of the jumping-off points for their analysis is work by Bob Currie, of the State University of New York, which has shown that there is a lunar influence on rainfall patterns around the world today. This is due to the so-called lunar nodal tide in the atmosphere of the Earth. It arises from the precession of the Moon's orbital plane about the ecliptic (the plane of the ecliptic is defined by the apparent motion of the Sun across the stars).

The Moon's orbit is inclined at 5° to the ecliptic, and the ecliptic is inclined at 23.5° to the equator. So the inclination of the lunar orbit, viewed from Earth, varies between 18.5° and 28.5°, producing a regular variation in the tides raised in the atmosphere (and in the sea, but that isn't relevant to our story), following a period 18.6 years long.

This period was, however, different in the past, when the Moon was closer to the Earth. Astronomers calculate that at the time the Elatina varves were laid down, the cycle was 20.3 years long, so any lunar influence on the ancient varves should show up at around this period.

The Sun itself should also have been behaving slightly differently long ago. Today, the principal cycle of activity exhibited by the Sun is the sunspot cycle, some eleven years long. Robert Noyes and colleagues at Harvard University have studied the evidence for starspot cycles in stars like our Sun, and concluded that the length of the cycle is proportional to the rotation period of the star. Standard stellar theory suggests that the Sun was rotating faster when it was younger, so that 680 million years ago the length of the sunspot cycle of activity would have been about 10.6 years.

When Zahnle and Walker examined the varve record, they decided that the best interpretation of the variations implies a basic periodicity of 10.8 years, closely agreeing with the astronomical calculations of solar activity at the time. But they do not agree with Williams's suggestion that the second feature in the varve pattern is best explained as a 'double sunspot' cycle.

The basic cycle is strongly modulated by an almost perfect sine wave 28.4 sunspot cycles long, and this can be explained if there is a beat effect operating between the basic cycle and a cycle *almost*, but not quite, twice as long.* The lunar nodal tide of the period exactly fits the bill.

This still leaves the big puzzle: if the lunar and solar influences on climate were so strong 680 million years ago, why are they so weak today? Zahnle and Walker think they have the answer.

Six hundred million years ago, the Earth itself rotated significantly faster than it does today, and the day was only 21 hours long. Even today, the Sun produces a daily tide in the

---

* This is exactly the sort of beat effect that is familiar to musicians. If two pure tones that are very nearly, but not quite, the same are sounded together, they produce a third, deeper note as the two notes interact. You get the same effect if one note is at almost, but not quite, twice or three times the frequency of the other – if the second note is near to a harmonic of the first note. The pitch of the beat note depends on the difference between the two original notes that are beating together; in the same way, according to Zahnle and Walker, the length of the long-term modulation of the Elatina varves depends on the difference between the lengths of the two basic cycles. Such beat effects occur naturally in many circumstances, and it would not be at all surprising if they operate in the atmosphere of the Earth.

atmosphere caused not by gravity but by heating, as water vapour and ozone absorb incoming solar radiation. In the Precambrian, there must have been a similar effect as the atmosphere warmed by day and cooled by night, even though the structure of the atmosphere, with less oxygen around, was different. This raises the possibility of another phenomenon, called resonance.

All systems have a natural period of vibration, and if they are shaken at that natural period they will respond with larger vibrations than if they are shaken at any other period. A trained opera singer who can strike a note so pure that it shatters a glass is making use of resonance, hitting the note that corresponds to the natural period of vibration of the glass (which is also the note that you hear if you wet a finger and rub it gently round the rim of the glass; the trick works best with expensive crystal goblets). A plucked guitar string, or the air inside a flute (or a bottle) when you blow across the opening, will vibrate at its natural frequency.

When the day was 21 hours long, the frequency of the daily tide in the atmosphere was the same as the natural vibration period of the atmosphere, so there should have been a resonance producing a much larger tidal effect than today. Because the *daily* influence of the Sun on the atmosphere (and therefore on the weather) was bigger then, any changes in the Sun's output from year to year (for example, if the amount of ultraviolet energy put out by the Sun varied over the sunspot cycle) would have had a disproportionate influence on the atmospheric tides at that time. It should come as no surprise to learn that the amount of ultraviolet energy put out by the Sun does indeed vary over the sunspot cycle. At the time the Elatina varves were laid down, the length of the day on Earth was just under 21 hours, and slowly getting longer.

It seems that a *nearly* resonant atmospheric tide 680 million years ago could very well explain why the Elatina formation shows such a strong 'signal' of effects that are much weaker today. Indeed, the influence may have been even more dramatic 600 million years ago, when the resonance was perfect, but we haven't been lucky enough to find any varves from that period to analyse.

What is particularly nice about the work by Zahnle and Walker is that it shows how changes in the Earth, rather than changes in the Sun, can explain the record in the rocks of climatic events 680 million years ago. The Sun seems, on this picture, to have been behaving very steadily over the past 700 million years or so, and the very small adjustments in the length of the sunspot cycle that are needed to fit the varve record are themselves exactly in line with the standard model of a Sun rotating a little more rapidly then, and exactly in line with observations of other stars. The Sun is not in an unusual state today. It is a normal star, doing normal things. So we can confidently expect that any tricks astronomers can use to probe the secrets of the solar interior will be telling us things that are relevant to the whole life history of the Sun, not just to some special conditions that happen to be operating just at the time intelligent life has arisen on Earth to look into those mysteries. This is good news indeed – for astronomers *do* now have a means to probe the solar interior, using techniques reminiscent of the way seismologists study the interior of our planet by monitoring earthquakes. Vibrations in the atmosphere of the Earth may explain links between Sun and weather 680 million years (Myr) ago. But now, it seems, vibrations in the outer part of the Sun reveal what is going on in its deep interior today. The new technique is called 'helioseismology' – and it has a direct bearing on the solar neutrino problem.

7

The Shaking Sun

T he shivering Sun opened its heart to astronomers, revealing its innermost secrets for the first time, only in the 1980s. But the discovery which made it possible to probe the solar interior had actually been made in 1960, years before the first solar neutrino was halted in Ray Davis's underground tank. For ten years nobody realized just what those observations were telling us, and then it took a further ten years (and more) to design and bring into operation equipment to monitor the Sun's shivers with sufficient precision to probe the interior. The 1990s will probably prove to be the great decade of helioseismology; but already the first detailed observations are telling us more than we ever knew about the structure of the Sun and its internal temperature variations. Those revelations do not match up perfectly to the theorists' standard model of the Sun; but they do match up, very well indeed, to the modifications to the standard model calculated to be caused by the presence of WIMPs.

The story began with the discovery, by researchers from the California Institute of Technology, that all over the surface of the Sun there are little patches which move in and out with periods around five minutes long. The discovery was made by accident, using instruments designed to study what the observers expected to see – random, or chaotic, movements of gas at the Sun's surface, being turned over by convection. In order to measure such motions, Robert Leighton and his colleagues used a sensitive refinement of the doppler technique, measuring the varying positions of spectral lines in the light from the Sun with great precision.

All hot gases produce characteristic patterns of lines, as uniquely identifiable as a fingerprint, in the spectrum of light – this was the way the various elements were identified in the atmosphere of the

Sun, and their proportions calculated back in the 1920s. If the gas is moving bodily towards you or away, those lines are shifted to slightly different wavelengths from the ones associated with the same elements when they are at rest. When these lines are shifted towards the red end of the spectrum (stretched to longer wavelengths), it means that the gas emitting the light is moving away; when they are shifted towards the blue end of the spectrum (squeezed to shorter wavelengths), it means that the gas is coming towards us. You can get some idea of the precision of the instruments used by the CalTech team from the nature of their discovery – they found that patches of the Sun oscillate intermittently, bouncing in and out five or six times in the space of roughly half an hour, with velocities of about 500 metres a second and an overall displacement of about 50 kilometres. The oscillations move a patch of the Sun's surface roughly in step over a distance equivalent to no more than 2 per cent of the Sun's diameter, and at first they seemed to be some sort of localized phenomenon, nothing to do with the behaviour of the Sun as a whole. But this was wrong.

Ringing like a bell

It wasn't until the beginning of the 1970s that several astronomers independently came up with the insight that enabled these solar oscillations first to be understood, and then to be used to probe into the heart of the Sun. The key realization was that each of these short-lived bouncing movements of a patch of the solar surface was not due to some purely local effect. They could be better explained as an effect caused by literally millions of much smaller vibrations, sound waves trapped inside the Sun and making the surface ring like a bell. What seemed to be a series of five-minute oscillations was actually the superposition of hundreds of different frequencies of oscillation, with periods ranging from about three minutes to about an hour. Whereas a gong might be struck once with a hammer to produce a pure tone, the Sun was behaving like a gong in a sandstorm, being repeatedly struck by tiny particles of sand, with new vibrations starting up and old vibrations dying away all the time. The trigger for all this activity might very well be the random 'blows' struck by the chaotic motions that Leighton and his colleagues set out to investigate in the first place – but the Sun was responding to those blows like a many-stringed instrument. Mixing the metaphor slightly, the mixture of tones is the sort of thing you might expect if the lid of a grand piano is being repeatedly thumped at random. Along with the random banging there would be the sound of all the strings vibrating gently, each with its own pure note.

There are no strings inside the Sun, but there are many pure notes that can resonate between the surface of the Sun and the bottom of the convective region. These are sound waves, akin to the waves that sound in an organ pipe when it is blown (I mean the pipe of a traditional church organ, of course, not an electronic version!). And they combine to shake the surface of the Sun in a regular way because of the way the speed of sound varies at different depths inside the Sun.*

It works like this. From the surface of the Sun down to the bottom of the convective layer, the speed of sound increases as you go deeper. There is no mystery about this – deeper layers are hotter, and the speed of sound is greater in hotter gas. So however and wherever it starts in the convective zone, as a sound wave angles down below the surface of the Sun, the bottom of the wave moves faster than the top. This bends the moving sound wave away from the bottom of the convective zone, and back up to the surface of the Sun.† At the surface, however, the wave cannot escape – there is only empty space outside the Sun, and sound cannot travel through a vacuum. So it bounces from the surface, reflecting back into the depths like light reflecting from a mirror. The whole process repeats, and the sound wave loops its way around the Sun, diving repeatedly into the convective zone and repeatedly being bent back and reflecting off the surface (Figure 7.1).

The depth a wave penetrates to, and how far it travels around the Sun in each hop between reflections off the surface, depend on the wavelength. Many waves bounce around inside the Sun and eventually fade away without contributing much, if anything, to

---

* Because it is so hot, the speed of sound in the interesting region of the Sun is about 150 times the speed of sound in the Earth's atmosphere. But the distance from the centre of the Sun to the surface is about five million times greater than the length of a wind instrument such as a clarinet. The solar equivalent of the vibration of air inside a clarinet would be a wave oscillating with a period roughly thirty minutes long, five million times the vibration period of sound in a clarinet. Douglas Gough, who made this neat analogy, stresses that although such a low 'note' is far outside the range of sound to which our ears are sensitive, it is still correct to call these solar vibrations sound waves, because they are sustained by exactly the same physical processes that sustain sound waves inside a clarinet on Earth.

† The same sort of thing happens to sound waves in the atmosphere of the Earth. On a hot, still day, the air just above the surface of a lake may be significantly cooler than the air a little higher up. Sound waves that start moving up from one shore of the lake are bent back down towards the surface, and may carry the sound of voices, for example, clearly for a great distance across the surface of the water – a kind of acoustical mirage.

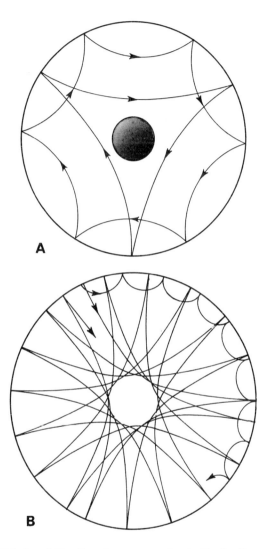

Figure 7.1 A and B   Sound waves moving inside the Sun are bent as they pass through the hot interior, and reflect when they strike the surface from below. So patterns of standing waves can build up inside the Sun, as indicated in these two diagrams. Where such standing waves touch the surface of the Sun, they cause a regular oscillation which can be measured from Earth.

the regular oscillations discovered in the early 1960s. But for some waves the length between bounces is just right to make an exact

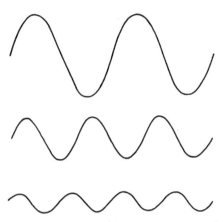

Figure 7.2   A standing wave is like the waves on a plucked guitar string or in air vibrating in an open-ended organ pipe, shown schematically here. These three waves are part of the same family of overtones, and each fits the same space – one with two peaks and two troughs, one with three peaks and three troughs, one with four peaks and four troughs. A physicist could tell how big the organ pipe that made these notes was by analysing the notes. The same technique tells astrophysicists about conditions inside the Sun.

number of hops fit into a complete circuit around the Sun. The wave may bounce three, or six, or some other number of times on its travels, but as it goes round and round the Sun it always touches the surface in exactly the same three, or six, or whatever number it is, places. So those particular patches of the Sun's surface are pushed in and out by the wave not once but every time it passes right around the Sun. The pattern it makes is called a standing wave (Figure 7.2), and it is exactly equivalent to the standing waves that make a plucked guitar string, or a blown organ pipe, vibrate to produce a pure note. By analysing the notes produced by an organ pipe, a physicist could tell you what the dimensions of the pipe were without ever seeing it.★ Similarly, by analysing the 'notes' produced by sound waves travelling around the Sun, an astrophysicist can tell you about conditions inside the

★ Indeed, the eminent geophysicist Sir Edward Bullard once told me that trying to work out the detailed structure of the Earth by analysing earthquakes (geoseismology) was like trying to work out the detailed structure of a grand piano by analysing the noise it made when pushed down a steep flight of stairs. Happily for astrophysicists, the structure of the Sun is simpler than either a grand piano or the interior of the planet we live on. Once solar sound waves were identified, helioseismology became practicable.

Sun, without ever seeing below the surface. The situation is more complicated, because the 'cavity' inside the Sun is three-dimensional, not a straight, one-dimensional tube. But the principles are exactly the same.

Fine tuning

During the 1970s, improved observations confirmed that the Sun really was 'ringing' in this way. First, astronomers found that the five-minute vibrations can even be seen in the overall brightness of the Sun, as a tiny variation in what they call the 'integrated' light. This, in effect, treats the Sun as if it were a distant star, looking at its total brightness, not at the variations from place to place over the surface. Then, by refining their spectroscopic studies, they were able to show that each patch of the Sun that we see moving in and out with a five-minute period is actually being pushed by an enormous number of much smaller standing waves.

Measuring the way such a small region of the solar surface moves up and down over a distance of a few tens of kilometres five or six times in half an hour is impressive enough. But by using a technique known as Fourier analysis this movement can be broken down into its constituent parts. Once again, there are appropriate musical analogies. The deepest note that can be produced by an organ pipe, for example, corresponds to sound with a wavelength just the right size for one wave to fit into the length of the pipe. This is the fundamental note of that particular pipe, and organs are made with pipes of various lengths in order to be able to play different notes. But there is another way to get different notes out of the same length of pipe.

The fundamental note has a wavelength that fits once inside the pipe. This is the 'natural' note produced by the pipe, the one you get just by blowing across the end and making the air inside resonate (blowing across the top of an empty bottle does the same trick). But you can also fit a wave with half that length into the pipe twice; a wave with one quarter that wavelength will fit in four times, and so on. These shorter waves that also fit the pipe are known as harmonics, or overtones, and correspond to appropriately higher notes, related to the fundamental. Even if the organist is trying to play a pure note – the fundamental – some of the vibration of the air in the pipe will be producing the overtones, and this helps to give different kinds of wind instrument different sound textures, even when they are playing the same note.

Using Fourier analysis, a physicist could unravel this complexity of overlapping notes, and tell you exactly which pure notes, harmonic and overtones, have been combined in the pipe to produce the rich sound that we hear. Exactly the same technique makes it possible to break down the pattern of vibrations actually observed at the solar surface into the individual standing waves that have combined to produce the observed variation. Although the number of individual standing waves cannot be counted precisely, the statistical evidence shows that there are actually tens of millions of separate vibrations – separate 'notes' – interfering with each other (adding in some places and cancelling in others) to produce the observed effects. Each individual vibration moves the surface of the Sun in and out by only a few tens of metres (compare this with the diameter of the Sun, which is about a *million* kilometres) at speeds of only a few tens of centimetres a second. But any one standing wave may persist for several days, always moving the same patches of the Sun's surface in and out, and this longevity helps the observers to gather enough information for the Fourier analysis to be effective. It is the combined effect of millions of these tiny vibrations that produces the larger, short-lived pulses of vibration that were first noticed in the early 1960s.

There is another way in which you can get a grasp of just how subtle this fine tuning of the spectroscopic technique really is. It all depends, remember, on the way in which lines in the spectrum of light from the Sun are shifted to and fro, over a small range of wavelengths, as the region of gas that is being observed moves towards or away from the spectroscopic instrument. This is equivalent to a change in the colour of the light. A particular wavelength (colour) of light that is emitted from the surface of the Sun becomes shorter (bluer) when the patch of the solar surface we are studying is moving towards us, and longer (redder) when that patch of the surface is moving away. As the Earth rotates, the observing instrument itself is carried, during the course of the day, first towards the Sun and then away from it, with velocities that cover a range of about 800 metres a second, comparing dawn with dusk – far bigger than the effect being studied on the Sun, but a regular, well-known cycle which can easily be allowed for in the calculations.

But even this effect on the measured wavelengths – colours – of the light is small. The speed of light itself is 300 *million* metres a second. In principle, if you drove fast enough down the road towards a red stop light you could change the colour you would see at the light to green, by the blueshifting of the light (green is a bit more than halfway through the visible part of the spectrum from red to blue). But in order to do the trick, you would have to move at about one third of the speed of light, some 100 million metres every second. The effects being measured on the surface of the Sun correspond to motions with speeds of around 10 *centimetres* every second, about a gentle walking pace, an effect one billion times more subtle. Perhaps it is not so surprising, after all, that even though the solar oscillations were first observed in the early 1960s, it was not until the 1970s that they began to be understood and analysed in detail, and only in the 1980s that the subtleties of the information they contained began to provide new insights into the inner workings of the Sun. But those insights were worth waiting for.

First results

The depth where a travelling sound wave is turned around and bent back towards the surface of the Sun depends on how quickly the speed of sound increases as the wave goes deeper into the Sun. That, in turn, depends on the way the temperature increases. So by analysing different standing waves (different vibration modes) which probe the Sun to different depths (Figure 7.1), helioseismologists can construct a temperature profile for the outer layers of the Sun – a picture of exactly how temperature increases as you move deeper below the surface. The speed of sound also depends on the exact composition of the Sun – whether it contains 25 per cent helium, or, for example, 30 per cent, or even 20 per cent.

Before helioseismology was developed, there was no way to measure temperatures inside the Sun directly. They were inferred from computer models using standard physics. Now those models could be tested. The standard model of the Sun that astrophysicists had developed before the advent of helioseismology could be used to make predictions about the frequencies of the acoustic vibrations that have now been discovered and analysed (indeed, this could have been done *before* the vibrations were discovered, but nobody imagined that such subtleties would actually become part of observational studies of the Sun). The frequencies predicted by the standard model were a little higher than the ones that are actually observed. But the predictions of the model can be made to fit the observed pattern if the convective zone in the outer part of the Sun extends a little deeper than the astrophysicists had thought, down to about 200,000 kilometres, roughly 30 per cent of the way from the surface of the Sun to the centre. Once that adjustment is made, the standard model and the observations are in broad agreement, provided that the outer convective region of the Sun does indeed contain about 25 per cent helium, exactly the proportion required by another standard model of astrophysics, the one that describes the Big Bang in which the Universe was born.

Solar seismology immediately made it possible for astrophysicists to fine-tune their standard model of the Sun. But these subtle adjustments do not change the way the solar standard model calculates the temperature at the heart of the Sun, so the solar neutrino problem was still present in full force.

Indeed, in a way the study of solar vibrations initially made the solar neutrino problem look worse. It did so because the insight into solar structure the vibrations provide pulls the rug from under some of the ideas put forward over the years to 'explain' the scarcity of solar neutrinos. It is easy to dream up cocktail party solutions to the neutrino problem, unhindered by actual observations of the solar interior, as long as the inside of the Sun is uncharted territory (like the regions labelled 'Here be Dragons' on old maps); but it is much harder for those wild ideas to survive once we begin to find out how the inside of the Sun actually does work. I'll give just one example.

This particular 'explanation' of the solar neutrino problem depended on the possibility that some of the material in the heart of the Sun, processed by nuclear fusion reactions, could have got mixed outwards, contaminating the outer layers with processed material (a kind of nuclear ash) and changing the composition of the core by dragging in unprocessed material (extra fuel) from above. Such mixing can be arranged to produce a computer model which forecasts a lower output of solar neutrinos – but it also affects the way in which the speed of sound changes with depth inside the Sun. And the kind of change that this mixing would produce can now be ruled out from helioseismology; astrophysicists have looked for it, but it is not there.

The first results from helioseismology rule out not only this particular astrophysical 'solution' to the neutrino problem, but also virtually all the other attempts to get round the problem by interfering solely with the astrophysics of the standard model. The way the Sun shakes shows that the solution to the problem must not lie simply in adjusting the astrophysics, but must involve 'new' particle physics as well. It is, indeed, almost time to bring WIMPs back into the story. First, though, the power of the new discipline of helioseismology can be emphasized by the way in which it has settled a dispute that has run for decades, concerning the way in which the Sun rotates.

Galileo knew that the Sun rotates, because he discovered the dark spots on its surface and watched some of them move as they were carried round by rotation of the Sun. Modern astronomers study solar rotation in the same way. Because the Sun is not a solid object like the Earth, but is a fluid body, it doesn't all rotate at the same speed – the gas at the equator takes about twenty-five days to spin once, while the polar regions rotate once in thirty days. Obviously, in each case this is only the speed of rotation at the surface – the Sun might rotate faster (or slower) inside. This possibility has especially intrigued astronomers who have studied the way in which the planet Mercury (the closest planet to the Sun) moves in its orbit.

The orbits that planets follow around the Sun are not circles, but ellipses, with the Sun at one focus of the ellipse. This has been known since the pioneering work of Johannes Kepler, early in the seventeenth century. But in the nineteenth century astronomers realized that even after taking into account all known factors, such as the gravitational tug of each of the other planets, the orbit of Mercury was a little more complicated still. Instead of the planet always tracing out the same ellipse, the orbit shifts sideways slightly, pivoting around the focus that is locked to the Sun, each time the planet goes round the Sun. If you could trace out the looping complexity of the orbit on paper, it would form a series of overlapping ellipses like a child's drawing of the petals of a daisy. The effect is tiny – it amounts to a shift of only 43 seconds of arc per century. But it is real, and nobody could explain it until the second decade of the twentieth century, when Albert Einstein came up with the general theory of relativity. Among its many other triumphs, general relativity (which is a theory of gravity subtly different from Newton's gravitational theory, on which all previous orbital calculations had been based) *exactly* explained the change in the orbit of Mercury over the centuries.

More recently, partly out of bloody-mindedness and partly through a laudable wish to test general relativity to the limits, some astrophysicists have pointed out that there is another way to make the orbit of Mercury shift in the observed way (indeed, the nineteenth-century astronomers *could* have thought of the trick, but didn't). If the inner core of the Sun is rotating very fast, and bulging outward as a result, the gravitational influence of the bulge will also make the orbit of Mercury shift around the Sun.

And if that really is happening, then general relativity is not needed to explain the phenomenon!

The debate didn't exactly rage through the halls of science – there is plenty of other evidence that general relativity works OK. But the idea of a rapidly rotating solar core remained as an irritating possibility until the end of the 1970s. Then, astrophysicists realized that the fast-spinning, bulging core of such a solar model would also affect the pattern of vibrations in the Sun. When the observations were compared with appropriate model calculations they showed no sign of the effect. If anything, they suggest that the Sun may actually be rotating slightly slower in its interior than outside (which nobody seems to have predicted). General relativity *is* needed to explain what is happening to the orbit of Mercury, as well as all the other things it explains so well. And since, of course, general relativity is actually rather well established as a 'good' theory, the argument can be turned around – the accuracy of using the solar vibrations as a probe of the Sun's interior is confirmed by the fact that the internal structure the vibrations describe matches the internal structure we expect if the shift in the orbit of Mercury is indeed produced by relativistic effects. So, what *can* this new technique of helioseismology tell us about surviving attempts to solve the neutrino problem?

Splitting the difference

The answer emerged as a result of a visit by John Faulkner to the Tata Institute in Bombay in November and December 1985. There he met an Indian graduate student, Mayank Vahia, who was interested in the solar neutrino problem, and asked Faulkner how the presence of WIMPs in the models would affect the expected vibrations of the Sun. Faulkner did not, at that stage, know; but both he and Vahia were already planning to attend a meeting of the International Astronomical Union, in New Delhi at the end of November. There, Faulkner knew, Douglas Gough, from Cambridge, would be giving a talk on solar variations. It would be the perfect opportunity to find out.★

★ These General Assemblies, as they are properly called, are the biggest international gatherings of astronomers, and are held only once every three years; it is even more rare for such a meeting to take place outside the main astronomical research centres of Europe and North America. Faulkner's visit to Bombay had been partly planned to fit in with the IAU meeting, so the coincidence was not entirely serendipitous; the fact that he and Gough were old friends who had been students together in Cambridge was, however, entirely down to good luck.

Gough's talk opened the eyes of Faulkner and Vahia to the fact that as well as there being a solar neutrino problem, there was also a solar pulsation problem. It concerns measurements one stage more subtle than the ones I have discussed so far, dealing not with the periods of vibration of the acoustic waves inside the Sun that cause the five-minute oscillations, but with the *difference between* the vibration periods of closely related acoustic waves. The waves I have described so far are technically known as p-modes, or pressure waves. They are exactly equivalent to the pulse of sound waves that would ripple through the bulk of the water in your bathtub if you slapped the palm of your hand down on the surface of the water. Some of the pressure waves that disturb the surface of the Sun pass right through the solar core, so you might guess that they would be useful for studying conditions in the heart of the Sun. But because the temperature of the core is so high, the speed of sound there is very high, and the pressure waves pass through the core very quickly, so they only have time to be affected in subtle ways. One of those subtleties involves the difference in vibration frequency between sound waves that have very nearly the same period – in the jargon, 'the frequency separation of adjacent p-modes'. This was the feature of Gough's talk that caught Faulkner's attention.

Gough mentioned that the standard solar model (even after the fine tuning mentioned above) not only 'predicts' too many solar neutrinos – it also predicts a separation of these p-modes that is about 10 per cent bigger than the value revealed by helioseismology. That doesn't seem too bad on its own. But, as Gough also pointed out to his audience in New Delhi, all the existing solar models which 'solved' the neutrino problem by making the centre of the Sun 10 per cent cooler (the models with internal mixing, which I have already mentioned) made the situation worse – for those models, the frequency separation is too big by as much as 50 per cent.

Faulkner immediately asked what happened with the WIMP models. Gough replied that he had not carried out the calculation for those models, and didn't know; but since WIMPs also made the centre of the Sun cooler he guessed that they would also make the vibration problem worse. But Faulkner chewed the problem over in his mind, and became convinced that the WIMP model differed from all other models with a cooler core in one critical respect, so that whether or not the shift in frequency separation was the right *size*, it would certainly go in the right *direction*, reducing the discrepancy that Gough had highlighted. After all, the mixed models have a *higher* sound speed in their centres, in spite of the lower temperature, because of the difference in composition compared with the standard models; but the WIMP model has a *lower* sound speed, because the temperature is lower and the composition is basically the same as the standard model. But would the effect be big enough to do the job?

When Faulkner tracked Gough down, during the evening following his talk, his colleague was intrigued by the idea, and agreed that it was worth looking into properly. But when? And where? It turned out that Gough was, in fact, heading for the Tata Institute for a couple of weeks – quite unaware that Faulkner would also be there. It was too good an opportunity to miss.

Working intensively for five days at the Tata Institute, the two friends from Cambridge and their new colleague Vahia were able to show that the change in the internal structure of the Sun caused by the presence of just enough WIMPs to solve the solar neutrino problem shifts the vibration periods so that the p-mode separation predicted by the model exactly matches the separation measured by helioseismologists. Figure 7.3 shows just how beautifully the WIMP model fits the observational constraints – and how all other astrophysical 'solutions' to the neutrino problem make the vibration problem worse. In these days of electronic computers, Faulkner takes great delight in telling how the calculations were carried through in the old-fashioned way, using pencil and paper – and how, because all his data had been left back in Santa Cruz, they had to read off the numbers they needed for their calculations from the graphs published in the printed version of the earlier WIMP papers he had co-authored (the Tata Institute library, of course, stocks the *Astrophysical Journal*). The collaboration between Faulkner, Gough and Vahia was completed early in December 1985, and reached the offices of the journal *Nature*, in London, on the last day of the month. Faulkner also sent a copy to his former student, Gilliland, in Boulder – and then learned, on his return to California, that Gilliland had already been thinking (and working) along the same lines.

For once, pencil and paper had beaten the computerized approach. Gilliland and his colleagues in Boulder had been 'number crunching' in the now standard way, using a large computer to work out many different vibration modes and the physical conditions needed to make the modelled oscillations match the observations of the Sun. They came up with the same answer – that the presence of the right amount of WIMPs brings theory and observation in line with each other. But it turned out

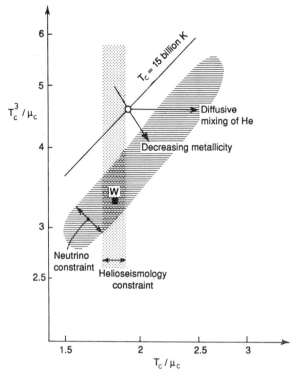

Figure 7.3   John Faulkner's pièce de résistance. *He invented this plot to show just how good the WIMP theory is. In this diagram, the standard model of the Sun is represented by an open circle, on the diagonal line corresponding to a central temperature of 15 billion K. This is barely within the region allowed by helioseismology studies, and well outside the region allowed by solar neutrino studies.*

Standard tricks to 'solve' the solar neutrino problem, by changing the assumed composition of the Sun ('decreasing metallicity') or mixing helium more thoroughly take the models away from *the region allowed by helioseismology. Only the WIMP model (W) sits smack in the heart of the region allowed by* both *helioseismology* and *neutrino studies.*

(Don't worry too much about the strange coordinates, which Faulkner chose to make everything interesting in the diagram happen along straight lines. T_c is the calculated temperature at the centre of the Sun, and μ_c is the molecular weight there. The abscissa ('X coordinate', along the bottom) is proportional to the square of the speed of sound in the Sun's heart, and the ordinate ('Y coordinate', up the page) is proportional to the square of the sound speed multiplied by the square of the temperature.)

that the two approaches were complementary. One group (Boulder) had started with oscillations, picking the ones that match observations and working back to find out what that told them about conditions in the heart of the Sun. The other group (Tata) started out with the temperature profile that matched the WIMP model, calculated what kind of vibration modes that ought to produce, and found that these match the observations. The key, in each case, is that the presence of WIMPs in the model lowers the temperature at the heart of the Sun without mixing the interior, and therefore without changing its structure, so the sound speed is also lowered. And because the two approaches were different, the Boulder team hurriedly prepared their version of the story for publication in *Nature* as well, while Faulkner and his colleagues agreed to wait, so that the two papers appeared alongside each other in the issue dated 15 May 1986. But this was far from being the end of this particular burst of excitement about WIMPs.

The triumph of the WIMP

Using a new theory to explain a puzzle you already knew about – the shortage of solar neutrinos, the splitting of p-mode frequencies, or whatever it might be – is all very well, but never entirely satisfactory. The best test of a scientific theory is when it predicts something that has never been measured before, but can be. Then, if the new measurement is carried out and matches the prediction, the theory gains hugely in credibility. This was the moment, in the late spring of 1986, when the WIMP theory was to take that giant step towards full respectability. It all came out of the collaboration in Bombay, and it involves another kind of solar vibrations.

Waves on the surface of the sea, or the waves you can make in your bathtub by sloshing the water from one end to the other, are not p-modes. They are known, instead, as gravity waves (or g-modes), because it is the force of gravity that determines how quickly they rise and fall.* Gravity waves occur where there is a difference in density between two layers of fluid, such as the difference between air and water, or the difference between layers inside the Sun. Such waves should be produced deep inside the Sun, and should be very sensitive to conditions in the core. But there is a big snag for helioseismologists who want to use g-modes

---

* Not to be confused with gravitational radiation, ripples in the fabric of spacetime that are predicted by general relativity, and which are also sometimes referred to as gravity waves.

to probe the heart of the Sun. Gravity waves have periods of hours or days, quite different from the five-minute oscillations of p-modes, so, as yet, they can only be studied from space, since instruments on the ground cannot view the Sun at night. And even from space it is no easy job to pick them out; their influence is strong in the core, but extends only weakly out to the surface, where any effect they produce on the motion of patches of the solar surface is very small indeed.

In spite of the difficulty of identifying such vibrations – much smaller than the famous five-minute oscillations – several groups of researchers had been looking for them before the Tata team's paper was published. After all, the observers knew that *if* they could find traces of gravity waves they would have a direct clue to the structure of the deep interior of the Sun. Standard models predicted that there should be an identifiable g-mode feature in the spectrum of solar vibrations with a ‹period› of about 36 minutes.* Solar models with mixing, designed to resolve the neutrino problem, shift this ‹period› by 40 per cent or more, out to about 56 minutes. Trustingly, the observers who had been looking for such a feature in the spectrum of solar vibrations had searched for anything from a little below the value appropriate for the standard model, around 32 minutes, up to the values appropriate for the mixed models, 56 minutes and even longer. In their *Nature* paper, however, Faulkner, Gough and Vahia pointed out that, just as in the case of the p-modes, the WIMP model produces the opposite effect. For the WIMP model, the g-mode feature should appear at around 29 minutes – where, as far as they knew, nobody had looked, or even gathered data.

Within three weeks of the *Nature* paper appearing, Faulkner heard that a researcher based in Switzerland, Claus Fröhlich, had found a trace of just the effect they had predicted. The evidence actually came from old data, observations of the Sun carried out from space by the Solar Maximum Mission satellite, and dating back to 1980. Nobody had found the 29-minute feature before because the researchers (with the aid of their computers) had only looked for longer ‹periods›, having put too much faith in the theory that the neutrino problem could be solved by mixing! Fröhlich had read the *Nature* paper and immediately ran the data through the computer to search for shorter ‹periods›; the only one

---

* The feature is actually not a true 'period' but, as in the case of the p-modes, a difference between periods: technically, 'the asymptotic normalized period spacing of high-order g-modes of low-degree'. With apologies to my astrophysical friends, I will use the (strictly speaking, incorrect) term ‹period›, with angle brackets, as shorthand for this mouthful.

he found was the one that had been predicted by Faulkner and his colleagues, on the basis of the WIMP model.

There is, in all honesty, no more than a hint that the ⟨period⟩ can be picked out from the data – but there isn't even a hint of any other ⟨period⟩, and the feature is exactly where it was predicted to be. Assuming the feature is real, more detailed analysis shows that the g-modes are being affected by rotation deep in the heart of the Sun in exactly the same way as the p-modes (that is, the two sets of observations both tell us that the Sun's core is rotating at the same rate). The two sets of data are completely independent – they are obtained from different instruments (one set on the ground, one in space) using different techniques to study two different kinds of oscillations (p-modes and g-modes) which have completely different period ranges (about five minutes as against many hours). And yet the 'answers' they give are the same! The WIMP model is the *only* model of the Sun which simultaneously explains these details of the spectrum of solar vibrations *and* resolves the neutrino problem.

There are astronomers – many astronomers – who are still not persuaded by the WIMP model, and prefer at least to stay sitting on the fence until the next phase of solar observations has been completed. But the weight of evidence that the heart of the Sun is kept cool by the presence of previously unknown particles, one for every hundred billion protons inside the Sun, and each with a mass somewhere around four to six times the mass of the proton, has, surely, now become something more than merely circumstantial. This is no longer 'just another wild idea'. Those who still want to 'wait and see', however, will not have to wait long, since the next generation of instruments, designed to monitor solar vibrations for twenty-four hours a day over a time span of several years is even now coming into operation.

The GONG test

The major problem for astronomers attempting to improve their observations of solar oscillations is the rotation of the Earth. Observations made from a single site on Earth are affected by the cycle of day and night. Because solar oscillations are so small, long runs of observational data must be added together and analysed to reveal the tiny periodic fluctuations. The only way to do this, if you are restricted to observing the Sun from a single site on the ground at one of the great observatories, is to add the data from different days together, taking care to join the records up so that the oscillations you are studying stay in step, and do not cancel each other out. But such 'artificial' long runs of data, from different days added together, contain spurious 'signals' caused by the night-time gaps – signals not only with a rhythm twenty-four hours long but at many harmonic frequencies associated with this fundamental. These signals show up in the Fourier analysis, and confuse the picture, making it hard for the researchers to be sure which periods are real solar variations and which ones are artefacts.

There are three ways to get round this problem, all of which are being tackled by different research groups as we move into the 1990s. A joint team from France and the United States has tried making observations from the South Pole in summer, when the Sun never sets. It worked – they obtained a stretch of observations spanning five days back in 1980. But working conditions at the Pole are hardly ideal, even in summer – and the weather conditions are so poor that five days without cloud is about the best continuous observing run you can hope for.

The second approach is to make the observations from space, from a satellite placed in an orbit where it can monitor the Sun continuously. Just such an approach was used for the Solar Maximum Mission, whose data seem to bear out the Tata team's prediction. A joint mission of the European Space Agency and NASA, called the Solar Heliospheric Observatory (or SOHO), is scheduled to fly in 1995, and will carry an instrument to monitor solar oscillations. It should send back data for several years.

But even before SOHO is launched, the third technique for eliminating the night should be coming into its own. This involves making observations of the Sun from different sites around the world, and combining the measurements to provide a continuous record spanning many years. There are three such projects now underway, and I'll mention just one of them in a little more detail. This is known as the Global Oscillation Network Group, or GONG. In principle, you need a minimum of three observing sites, evenly spaced around the world 120 degrees of longitude apart, cloudless skies, and instruments that never break down. In practice, GONG is going for six sites, spaced as evenly as possible around the globe.

Ten sites are being tested, as I write in 1989: at Mauna Kea and Haleakala in Hawaii; Mount Wilson and Big Bear in California; Yuma in Arizona; Cerro Tololo and Las Campanas in Chile; Izana in the Canary Islands; Udaipur in India; and Learmouth, in Western Australia. In addition, there is a 'reference instrument' at the US National Solar Observatory in Tucson, Arizona – the parent institute for the project. During site testing, there have already been several runs of a few days when the Sun never set on the functioning prototype GONG network, and the longest such run spanned more than a fortnight.

At each site, an automated instrument with a 50 millimetre aperture (the size is so modest that astronomers are reluctant to call them 'telescopes' – they are more like camera lenses) will take a snapshot of the Sun every minute. The design philosophy of the package resembles that of a space mission – the team chose a low-technological-risk, rugged instrument that works without any help from a human operator. Two instruments should be looking at the Sun at any one time, to cover the inevitable occurrence of cloud or breakdowns. And each measures velocities as patches of the Sun move in and out, using an instrument known as a Fourier tachometer, which can measure redshifts and blueshifts as small as one part in a billion.

The GONG instruments make these measurements at 65,000 points across the surface of the Sun simultaneously, generating an enormous amount of data to be stored (initially on tape, later on optical disks) and processed. I won't go into details of the computer power required for all this – but there certainly wouldn't have been much point in making observations of this kind in the 1970s, since the computers of that time would not have been up to the job of analysing it (one reason for saving the data on optical disks is the hope that twenty-first-century scientists may have even better techniques for analysing it than we have today). The whole network should become fully operational during 1991, and is funded to run initially for three years, generating a gigabyte of data every day. The project involves more than 150 individual scientists from sixty-one different research centres in fifteen different countries.

That should be enough to settle the question of whether the vibrations really do match the predictions of the WIMP theory. But that will surely not be the only important result to come out of the GONG project – most astronomers will be highly surprised if the new observations do not throw up new and unexpected surprises to puzzle over in the 1990s, just as every new observing technique, from Galileo's telescope to radio astronomy and X-ray satellites has thrown up new and unexpected surprises about the Universe. Most astronomers will also be disappointed if the funds are not found to keep the GONG project running for at least the length of a full solar cycle, eleven years, so that we can see how the solar vibrations change, if at all, as the Sun runs through its overall cycle of activity.

And *I* will be disappointed if half this book isn't completely out of date by the year 2000. The chances are that over the next ten years GONG, SOHO and other observations will provide us with a completely new picture of the workings of our neighbourhood star, a picture painted with unprecedented attention to detail. What matters is not so much whose pet theory is correct, but that we are about to find out more of the inner secrets of the Sun than have been revealed throughout all of history to date. The most exciting thing about the WIMP theory, and the evidence so far that it is on the right lines, is that it links these anticipated new discoveries both to the Universe at large and to the sub-microscopic world of elementary particles – while raising the possibility of building new kinds of detectors, much cheaper than GONG or SOHO, which can be constructed in individual laboratories here on Earth and which may reveal not only the innermost secrets of the Sun but also the ultimate fate of the Universe itself.

8

The Large and the Small

The most dramatic development in theoretical physics in the 1980s has been the way in which particle physicists and cosmologists have been forced to combine their talents in order to improve their descriptions of the world around us. Particle theorists, trying to develop the elusive unified theory that will explain the behaviour of all the particles and forces of nature in one mathematical package, have been forced to contemplate the implications of processes that go on at energies far greater than anything which can be achieved artificially, in their accelerators here on Earth, or even in the heart of a star like the Sun. The only place where the interactions that the theorists describe actually took place was in the big bang in which the Universe was born, some fifteen billion years ago. So the latest theories of particle physics are 'tested' by finding out whether the kind of reactions they describe could have produced the kind of Universe we live in. Improved particle physics helps the cosmologists to develop a better understanding of how the Universe began; improved cosmological observations of the Universe at large help to set limits on what could possibly have happened in the Big Bang, and thereby constrain some of the wilder speculations of the particle theorists.

At the same time, cosmologists themselves have found a need, as I have mentioned, for more matter than meets the eye in the Universe. From studies of the way galaxies and clusters of galaxies move, and measurements of the rate at which the Universe itself is expanding, it is clear that as well as all the bright stars and galaxies there is at least ten times and possibly one hundred times more 'dark matter' in the Universe, exerting its gravitational influence on the bright stuff.

The calculations of conditions in the Big Bang, in which particle physics and cosmology combine so fruitfully, establish beyond reasonable doubt that this dark matter cannot all be in the form of atoms like those of which the Sun, stars and planets are made. The bright stuff of the Universe is predominantly composed of protons and neutrons (which make up most of the mass of atoms), and the laws of physics tell us how much (or rather, how little) of this kind of stuff (known as baryonic matter) can have been made in the Big Bang. The limit roughly matches the amount of matter in all the bright stars and galaxies – a coincidence which fooled astronomers for decades into thinking that stars and galaxies were, indeed, the only stuff in the Universe. Now that there is compelling evidence for the influence of additional dark matter, the inescapable conclusion is that most of this dark matter – the *bulk* of the stuff of the Universe – is not in the form of homely baryons, but must consist of particles never yet detected here on Earth.

This, of course, was the rationale behind the first attempts to resolve the solar neutrino problem by considering the effects of WIMPs on the structure of the Sun. There is little point in inventing a 'new' particle just to explain the paucity of solar neutrinos. But if cosmology *requires* the existence of extra particles anyway, it is natural to consider how they might affect the behaviour of stars. In fact, the unified theories being developed by particle theorists all require the existence of extra kinds of particle in the Universe. These requirements are a result of theories developed independently of cosmological studies of how galaxies move. Cosmology needs extra matter, not in the form of baryons, to explain how things move in the Universe; particle physics needs extra particles, not in the form of baryons, to make the unified theories work. Theorists studying the largest observable objects (galaxies) and theorists studying the smallest known entities (sub-atomic particles) independently find that they need the same sort of new stuff to make everything fit together. This is a powerful indication that both groups of theorists are working along the right lines. And it is an impressive coincidence, if that is all it is, that one type of particle which meets the needs of theorists working with the very large *and* the very small also solves the major outstanding puzzle concerning a middle-sized object, our Sun.

But not all of the particles postulated to make the unified theories work would affect the solar interior in the right way to resolve the neutrino puzzle; nor, indeed, do the particles required by cosmologists to hold the Universe together have to fit the description of WIMPs outlined in this book. Instead of particles which each have a mass of around five times the proton mass, there could be a correspondingly larger number of correspondingly lighter particles, or even a relatively small number of *very* massive particles. I have described in detail the evidence that the Universe must indeed contain dark matter in my book *The Omega Point*; with Martin Rees, I have described in *Cosmic Coincidences* the enormous variety of possible candidates for the dark matter now being actively considered.

But these candidates cannot all be present in the actual Universe, and here I want to focus only on the small proportion of them that also solve the solar neutrino problem. After all, that problem has to be resolved somehow. If particle physics tells us that there must be 'extra' varieties of particle in the Universe, cosmology tells us the same thing, and solar studies show that some of the candidates to meet *both* the cosmological needs and the particle physics needs can also solve the neutrino puzzle, the simplest and most parsimonious assumption is that this kind of WIMP really might be the most important constituent of the dark matter. There may be other dark-matter particles as well – one very light particle, the axion, almost certainly exists, if unified theories are on the right track, and some of the dark matter (equal to the amount we see in bright stars and galaxies, at a pinch) could even be in the form of baryons. But 80 per cent of the mass of the Universe (at least) is definitely not in the form of baryons, and a sizeable fraction of that may well be in the form of WIMPs with masses around five times the mass of the proton. How could we ever hope to detect them, except by their influence on the Sun, and by the invisible tug of their gravitational fingers?

The candidates

Neutrinos themselves were once considered to be candidates for the dark matter, and in their early work on the effects of massive particles inside the Sun on the solar neutrino flux Faulkner and Gilliland, back in the 1970s, were thinking in terms of a heavy variety of neutrino. But this was mainly because, in the 1970s, scientists had not yet got used to the idea that there might be completely different varieties of particle around – they knew neutrinos existed, though, so it was natural to try to make neutrinos fit the astrophysical requirements. But it was a frame-up, and it didn't stand up to further investigation.

In 1987 astrophysicists received the gift of a pulse of neutrinos from a supernova in a nearby galaxy, the Large Magellanic Cloud. According to astrophysical theory, the supernova produced 10^{58} electron neutrinos, ten times more than the total number of electrons, protons and neutrons inside the Sun. About three thousand trillion (3×10^{15}) of these are calculated to have passed through a detector on Earth which has a volume of 7,000 cubic metres, and is run by a joint team from Irvine, Michigan and Brookhaven, and therefore known as IMB. Out of this flood, the IMB detector actually recorded just eight neutrinos, arriving over a six-second interval. If neutrinos had mass, then, as explained in Chapter Four, the ones with more energy would travel faster and arrive at the detector sooner. If they have no mass, then like photons, they travel at precisely the speed of light, always, and would arrive together (assuming they set off together). Other researchers, as I described earlier, have tried to estimate neutrino masses by considering the implications of the arrival times of neutrinos from the supernova in various different detectors on Earth. But what happens if you look at the IMB data alone, assume that all of the events it detected were caused by the arrival of electron neutrinos, and ignore the rest? Measurements of the spread in arrival times of this pulse of neutrinos from the supernova show that they cannot possibly have a mass bigger than 10 eV, and probably have masses close to 3 eV, while they may not have any mass at all. These units (electron Volts) are tiny, and so the estimated masses are very small – it would take the combined mass of 150,000 such neutrinos to equal the mass of one electron. And the estimates have a direct bearing on the solar neutrino problem, in two ways.

First, if the 3 eV estimate (or even the 10 eV limit) is correct, then, as with the calculations by Ramanathan Cowsik described in Chapter Four, the masses are *too big* to permit the kind of neutrino oscillations that some theorists have proposed to resolve the puzzle (the MSW effect). Secondly, neutrinos with so little mass could not provide anywhere near all of the dark matter required by cosmologists, leaving ample scope for unknown particles to fill the gap. On both counts, the supernova neutrino studies make the case for WIMPs more compelling.

That doesn't *quite* rule out the possibility that another kind of neutrino might masquerade as such a WIMP. There are, remember, three kinds of neutrino already known to exist, associated with, respectively, the electron, the tau particle and the muon. None of them has enough mass to be the WIMP we are looking for. This tripling is, however, a very tidy arrangement which fits neatly within the framework of the most highly regarded of the present crop of unified theories,* and seems to relate the three neutrino 'families' to the varieties of fundamental particles known as quarks. It also happens that the combination of particle physics and cosmology to describe what happened in the big bang suggests that there should be just three such families. But there is just enough leeway in these calculations to allow for the possibility of a fourth type of neutrino – and ample uncertainty in any predictions about the nature of such a particle to allow for the possibility that it might have a mass of about five times the proton mass. Suggesting such fourth-generation neutrinos as WIMP candidates is stretching credulity, but not absolutely forbidden by the current crop of particle theories or our understanding of the big bang.† More plausible candidates, though, are not hard to find.

I mentioned one way to make WIMPs – my favourite – in Chapter Five. We know that an asymmetry in the laws of physics allowed the production of just one baryon (proton or neutron) for every billion photons ('particles' of light) that emerged from the big bang. If there happens to be another kind of particle which has a mass in the range from five to ten times the mass of a proton and which is also produced in the same way, obeying the same asymmetry with the same billion-to-one ratio, then there would be one WIMP in the Universe for every baryon, and in a galaxy like our own the mass of all the WIMPs put together would be just right to account for the way stars move, perhaps leaving some leeway for more dark matter in the Universe in the form of light neutrinos or the axions that particle physicists are so fond of.

The second plausible way to make WIMPs concerns not *asymmetry* but *symmetry*. In a manner reminiscent of the way the laws of physics indicate a symmetry between matter (electrons, protons and the like) and antimatter (positrons, antiprotons and so on), modern ideas about the relationship between particles and forces suggest that there should be another counterpart for every type of particle that we know. Some particles, like photons, are actually the carriers of forces in our world. Photons carry electromagnetic forces, gravitons carry gravity, and so on. Other particles, like neutrons and protons, are lumps of matter that are

---

* I explain why in *In Search of the Big Bang*.
† Just after I had written these words, late in 1989, physicists at CERN reported new measurements which definitely restrict the number of possible neutrino types to three. If these new results stand up to closer scrutiny, as seems likely, that will close this particular loophole for good.

affected by forces, but which do not in themselves carry a force. As part of their search for a unified theory to explain forces and particles in one package, physicists see a need for symmetry between the two, and this can best be achieved by allowing every type of particle to be accompanied by a 'new' force-carrier, and every type of force-carrier to be accompanied by a 'new' particle.*

This is not as bad as it sounds, since out of all this menagerie of new particles only one variety should be stable. All the new heavy particles, in this scheme of things, decay into successively lighter particles, except for the lightest one of all, which has nothing to turn into. For obvious reasons, this kind of theory is known as supersymmetry. It predicts that there should be just one previously unknown variety of particle at large in our Universe, the 'lightest supersymmetric partner', or LSP. And the most likely candidate for the LSP is the counterpart to the photon, which is dubbed the photino. *Completely independently* of any of the cosmological considerations about dark matter, or the speculation that WIMPs in the heart of the Sun may resolve the solar neutrino problem, supersymmetry theory predicts that the photino will have a mass a few times bigger than the mass of the proton, and that it will interact only weakly with everyday matter. The photino, if it exists, is *exactly* the kind of WIMP I have been talking about.

Even if cosmologists were not eager to find dark matter to explain how stars and galaxies move, and even if there were no solar neutrino problem to be resolved, particle physicists would be eager to carry out experiments aimed at detecting WIMPs in the laboratory. With three compelling reasons to search for WIMPs (and bearing in mind the Bellman's comment, in *The Hunting of the Snark*, that 'what I tell you three times is true'), it is hardly surprising that such experiments are now moving out of the planning stage.

How to catch your WIMP

If WIMPs do provide the solution to these separate problems of cosmology, astronomy and physics, there ought to be plenty of them about to find. The averaged-out density of such dark matter required in our part of the Galaxy must be equivalent to about one proton mass in every three cubic centimetres of space. If WIMPs

---

* This is explained in more detail in *Cosmic Coincidences*, where Martin Rees and I also explain why the axion is so highly favoured by particle theorists.

each have a mass of about five times the mass of a proton, there should be one WIMP in every fifteen cubic centimetres – and that doesn't just mean in 'empty space' out above the Earth's atmosphere, but passing through the room I am sitting in as I write, your body as you read these words, and every physics laboratory on Earth. Each litre of air around you actually contains between sixty and seventy WIMPs, on this picture.

Each WIMP is moving with its own independent velocity through the Galaxy – but it is only independent up to a point. Like the planets orbiting around the Sun, the stars orbiting around the Galaxy, or, indeed, the molecules of air in the atmosphere of the Earth, the motion of a WIMP is constrained by gravity. The appropriate average velocity for objects held by the gravity of the whole Milky Way system and orbiting at about the distance of our Solar System from the centre of the Milky Way is the same whatever the mass of the object is, for a proton or a star – no more than roughly one thousandth of the speed of light, which works out at just 300 kilometres a second. The speed of the Sun and Solar System in orbit around the Galaxy is about 220 kilometres a second, for a circular orbit; this is roughly the same as the speed of a WIMP in our neighbourhood, because the Solar System has to obey the same law of gravity – but the WIMPs may be moving in any direction, not in circular orbits, so the range of speeds relative to the Earth covers the span from zero (for WIMPs moving the same way round the Galaxy as we are) up to about 500 kilometres a second (for WIMPs moving the opposite way, colliding with us head on).

Although this sounds like a lot of WIMPs moving with impressively high speeds, we get a different perspective if we compare the numbers with those appropriate for molecules of air itself. The all-important (for us) oxygen, for example, is in the form of molecules made of two atoms of oxygen, so that each molecule has a mass roughly 32 times the mass of a proton – several times more massive than a WIMP. And a mass of 32 grams of oxygen would contain rather more than 600,000 billion billion molecules (6×10^{23}, the Avogadro number). There are *many* billions of everyday atoms and molecules, each of them more massive than an individual WIMP, in the same volume of air in which we might find a hundred or so WIMPs. And those molecules are themselves moving pretty fast – about 500 metres a second for the oxygen in the air that you breathe – though not as fast as many of the WIMPs. But unlike those molecules of air, the WIMPs do not take part in everyday interactions involving electromagnetism – they interact only weakly with everyday matter, which is almost as transparent to WIMPs as it is to neutrinos.

Among other things, electromagnetic forces are what makes a solid object solid. Tiny atomic nuclei are surrounded by much bigger clouds of electrons, and it is the electrons that interact with the electrons from other atoms in a solid to lock the atoms in place in a rigid lattice. Rigid, that is, as far as other atoms and molecules are concerned. When I hit the keys on my Zenith computer with my fingers as I type these words, my fingers don't go through the keyboard because the electrons surrounding the atoms in my fingertips meet resistance from the electrons surrounding the atoms in the keys. The nuclei buried deep within those atoms take no direct part in this process at all – compared with the electron cloud, the size of the nucleus is roughly equivalent to a pea in the centre of a concert hall. A molecule of oxygen will bounce off a lump of lead, say, because its own electron cloud interacts with the electrons in the atoms at the surface of the lead. But a WIMP doesn't notice the existence of electrons. Any WIMP that arrives at the surface of a lump of lead will plough on happily through the clouds of electrons, brushing them aside like a cannonball moving through fog. It will only 'notice' the lead if it runs head on into a *nucleus* – a rare, but not impossible, occurrence. The WIMP detectors being designed and built today are intended to take advantage of such rare events, by measuring changes in a solid crystal caused by the impacts of WIMPs with nuclei.

The task is just feasible, but requires some sophisticated measuring techniques. What makes it feasible is that atomic nuclei happen to have masses in the range of possible masses for WIMPs. The lightest element, hydrogen, has a nucleus (a single proton) with just one proton mass; carbon nuclei have twelve times the proton mass; and so on. Energy is transferred from one particle to another most efficiently in a collision when the two particles have roughly the same mass – so ordinary materials are just right to 'notice' the impact of WIMPs.

There should be somewhere between 1 and 100 WIMP collisions to be noticed in each kilogram of a lump of matter per day* – the exact numbers depend on details of the properties of

---

* For anyone unfamiliar with these units, a kilo is a bit more than two pounds. A two-pound bag of sugar should experience several WIMP interactions (maybe fifty) per day; a 12½-stone (175-pound) person will stop several thousand WIMPs in the nuclei of the atoms in his or her body each day.

WIMPs, details which we can only find out about by detecting some and measuring their influence on lumps of matter. So you don't need an impossibly large lump of, say, germanium to act as a WIMP detector (you certainly don't need as much mass as the mass of cleaning fluid in Ray Davis's neutrino detector, for example). But you do need sensitive means to detect the changes in your lump of germanium (or whatever) caused by the arrival of WIMPs.

Researchers are now pursuing several different lines of attack on this problem. Some of them are rather subtle, and concern changes in the properties of the 'target' that can only be properly understood if you have a thorough grounding in quantum physics. But others are easier to understand in principle, and more straightforward to interpret in practice. I'll stick to just three of the less esoteric examples.

One possibility is that the impact of WIMPs with the nuclei of a semiconductor, such as germanium, will alter the electrical properties of the material in a measurable way. Semiconductors are rather curious materials in which some of the electrons that are attached to the nuclei in a crystal lattice are only loosely held in place. Under the right conditions, an electron can be encouraged to jump out of its place in the crystal, leaving a hole behind. Because electrons carry negative charge, the hole, in a sea of electrons, behaves exactly like a positively charged electron. And the impact of a few WIMPs on the nuclei in such a crystal ought to shake things up sufficiently to produce a few electron-hole pairs, which could be detected.

Another possibility is to listen, literally for the sound made by a WIMP striking a nucleus in a crystal. As the nucleus recoils from the blow, it will jostle its neighbours slightly, sending a ripple of disturbance – a sound wave – through the crystal. Blas Cabrera and his colleagues at Stanford University propose mounting an array of small sensors on each surface of a suitable crystal, sensitive enough to measure the tiny vibration, like miniature earthquakes, produced when the shock wave from the impact of a WIMP sends ripples out to the surface. This is my favourite technique, since it raises the possibility of using 'crystal seismology' to detect WIMPs in the lab, tying in nicely with the use of helioseismology to measure the effects of WIMPs on the Sun. If they can do this, it will be a very neat trick, indeed.

But perhaps the simplest approach to the problem of monitoring WIMP impacts with everyday matter (and the one most likely to succeed first if WIMPs do have the properties suggested by solar studies) is simply to measure the heat released by the impact. Heat is simply a measure of the amount of movement of the molecules and atoms that make up a solid, liquid or gas – a hotter object is one in which the atoms and molecules are moving faster (vibrating to and fro in a solid, wandering about more freely in a liquid or gas) and jostling each other more vigorously. When a WIMP slams into a nucleus and sets it jostling its neighbours, the temperature of the crystal has increased as the kinetic energy of the incoming WIMP has been converted into heat. Unfortunately, the amount of heat released is tiny – for a detector made of pure silicon, weighing one kilogram, under ideal conditions, the impact of a single WIMP will raise the temperature by less than five thousandths of a degree (less than 5 millikelvin). Nevertheless, if the crystal is very cold to start with (cooled by liquid helium down to a temperature of only a few K, around *minus* 270°C), there is a real possibility of measuring such modest temperature changes.

The effort involved certainly seems worthwhile, given that it may reveal the whereabouts of the 'missing' nine tenths of the Universe. Nobody has yet done the trick – indeed, nobody has yet measured any of these effects that could be unambiguously attributed to WIMPs. But all of these possibilities, and more, will be tested by operational experiments during the 1990s. So far, like experiments to measure the masses of neutrinos, the results only set limits on the range of possibilities for WIMP masses. The limits will get tighter as new experiments come into operation over the next few years – unless, or until, an actual WIMP detection is made. But as of now, the limits are far from being embarrassing to those theorists who so eagerly anticipate the eventual detection of WIMPs.

Results so far

The best limits on WIMP masses so far come from experiments that were designed and built to study other particle interactions, but which happen to be sensitive to certain kinds of WIMPs as well. No dedicated WIMP detector searching in the 'right' mass range is actually running yet. But one of the existing experiments gives you a good feel for the kind of effort involved.

This particular experiment was actually built to investigate another phenomenon, known as double beta decay, which, like

'new' particles, is required by the best unified theories of physics. ★
It works by monitoring the behaviour of electron-hole pairs in a
germanium crystal – in fact, it detects the pulse of energy released
by an electron when it falls back into the hole, shortly after the
original impact from an outside particle disturbs the semiconductor and creates a hole. Such equipment is now fairly standard, and
in the case of the detector developed by Ronald Brodzinski, of
Battelle Pacific Northwest Laboratories, and Frank Avignone, of
the University of South Carolina, consists of a germanium crystal
weighing 0.72 kilos, and associated paraphernalia. The problem is
that almost anything that collides with the nuclei in the crystal
lattice will trigger the electron-hole response. So it has to be
shielded from cosmic rays, and from any background radioactivity. Where better to site the apparatus than alongside the
Davis neutrino detector, 1,600 metres underground in the
Homestake gold mine?

Even there, the team ran into problems. The surrounding rocks
are themselves radioactive enough to trigger the detector, which
has to be shielded by some inert material that contains no
radioactive nuclei at all. Such material is, in fact, very hard to find
on the surface of the Earth today. As well as short-lived
radioactivity induced by the impacts of cosmic rays themselves,
most modern materials are contaminated by traces of radioactivity
from all the nuclear bombs that have been exploded in the
atmosphere since the Second World War. One source of non-
radioactive steel, still being 'mined' for use in some scientific
work, lies in the remaining hulks of German battleships of First
World War vintage, scuttled in Scapa Flow on the north of
Scotland after the German fleet surrendered at the end of that war.
But lead provides an even better shield against radiation, and the
apparatus in the Homestake mine is actually shielded by lead
obtained from the ballast in the wreck of a Spanish galleon that
sank early in the sixteenth century.

After all this, and other efforts to reduce background 'noise'
affecting the apparatus, the team could still 'only' set an upper
limit on WIMP masses. They found no evidence of any particles
with masses more than twenty times the mass of a proton, and
they are confident that such particles would have been found, if
they were present. As far as it goes, this is good news; the
discovery of WIMPs with such high masses would have been a

★ In case you are wondering, double beta decay *has* now been observed, confirming that
those unified theories are on the right lines – circumstantial evidence that WIMPs also exist.

severe embarrassment for astrophysicists trying to resolve the solar neutrino problem.

Yet another detector in the Homestake mine, actually intended to search for neutrinos, sets a limit at the low-mass end of the range. Edward Fireman, from the Smithsonian Astrophysical Observatory in Cambridge, Massachusetts, headed a team which reported this new limit in 1988. Their apparatus consists of six tons of potassium hydroxide, in which argon-37 might be produced by the interaction of either neutrinos or (as it happens) certain kinds of WIMP with nuclei of potassium-39. After three years of operation, the experiment produced no evidence for either neutrino or WIMP interactions. The way this detector works actually makes it more sensitive to *lighter* particles (it was, after all, designed to detect neutrinos) – so the absence of any observed interactions tells us that if there are any WIMPs around, they must have masses *above* one proton mass, and probably greater than three proton masses.

This is beginning to get interesting, since the solar physicists need WIMPs with masses in the range from about five to ten proton masses, with a preference for the low end of that range. It is even more interesting since another germanium detector, run by a team from three research centres (the University of California, Santa Barbara; the Lawrence Berkeley Laboratory in California; and the University of California, Berkeley), came up with a tighter *upper* limit, also in 1988. That experiment says that the mass of the WIMP must be *less* than nine times the mass of a proton. Tantalizingly, the range of possibilities still allowed by the observations is *exactly* the range required by the astrophysics; but until that crucial experiment that actually measures the mass of a WIMP, we won't know for sure that the astrophysicists were right. The answer should, though, be in before the year 2000.

Into the future

It is a sign of how astronomy has changed in recent years that the detectors involved in this search are not telescopes mounted in observatories high on mountain tops on the surface of the Earth, but contain tons of potassium hydroxide (or whatever) buried deep below ground at the bottom of mine shafts. By any standards, the Homestake mine, where several astronomical particle detectors may be found running simultaneously, surely now deserves the description 'Homestake Observatory'. But still, conventional optical telescopes are pretty impressive structures in their own right, tons of steel instead of potassium hydroxide, mounted in purpose-built domes and surrounded by computers and electronic detectors. Is there really such a big difference? The answer must be 'yes', not least because in a particle detector 'telescope' the tons of material form the *detector*, not part of the infrastructure.

Once this is appreciated, the contrast between the old and the new ways of astronomy is even more marked than it appears at first sight. John Faulkner makes the point with striking force when he talks about the solar neutrino problem. The important piece of a telescope like the 120–inch reflector at the Lick Observatory, where Faulkner works, is *not*, he stresses, the 50 tons or so of girders in the supports and the mirror (120 inches across) itself. The important part of the telescope, the bit that actually interacts with photons of light and focuses them onto the detectors, is a thin film of aluminium spread over the surface of the mirror. That film amounts to just one cubic centimetre of aluminium – which is all you need if you want to study photons.

But while the mirror surface of the 120-inch telescope is coated with just one cubic centimetre of aluminium, the interior 'surface' of the rectangular steel box that holds the Davis detector is 'coated' with a hundred thousand gallons of perchloroethylene. And you need all that 'working surface' if you want to study neutrinos. This contrast in volume provides a genuine measure of the intrinsic differences between photon and neutrino telescopes – and WIMP detectors closely resemble neutrino detectors, to such an extent that, as we have seen, some detectors can double up in both roles.

New kinds of detectors always open up new horizons in astronomy. Telescopes like the 120-inch at Lick were themselves instrumental in transforming our understanding of the Universe, and we are on the threshold of a new revolution, which will once more transform our understanding of the Universe, when positive results begin to emerge from the new generation of detectors. In the light of all the circumstantial evidence, the indications are strong that we stand at the threshold of a wonderful new discovery, the identification of the kind of particles that make up more than 90 per cent of the mass of the Universe. *Everything* studied by previous generations of astronomers represents only the tip of the cosmic iceberg. Alternatively, all of the assumptions and observations on which those experiments are based may be wrong. Disconcerting though that would be, especially to astrophysicists seduced (like myself) by the beauty of the WIMP solution to the solar neutrino puzzle, in some ways it would be an even more exciting discovery, forcing theorists to start afresh in trying to work out how stars operate, what holds galaxies together, and how it might be possible to unify the description of particles and forces in one mathematical package.

We, or rather our recent ancestors, have, in fact, been in this situation before – not once, but twice, in little more than a hundred years. And then, as now, it was studies of the Sun that held the key to developments with implications that would reverberate through the world of science. William Thomson (later Lord Kelvin), convinced that the power of the Sun must come from gravitational collapse, was as sure of his assumptions in the 1860s as any proponent of WIMP theory was sure of his* own assumptions in the 1980s – but Thomson lived to hear Rutherford describe the discovery of a new source of energy, from the breakdown of radium. And almost exactly halfway in time between Thomson's definitive expression of the gravitational contraction theory and the work by Faulkner and others which makes the case for WIMPs with equal eloquence, just over sixty years ago the puzzle of how nuclei could be stuck together in stars when standard physics said that the temperatures there were too low was a factor in the development and establishment of a new quantum physics describing nuclear fusion and the tunnel effect.

Are we, like Thomson in the 1860s, deluding ourselves in thinking that the laws of physics as we understand them today are adequate to solve the mystery of how the Sun works? Or should we, like Arthur Eddington in the 1920s, be right to be looking for a revolution in physics to enable us to explain the observed fact that the solar furnace does, indeed, operate at a temperature which is not the one that standard theory tells us it 'ought' to be operating at? Either way, solar astronomy seems certain to be one of the most exciting areas of science in the 1990s, after decades in which more remote and superficially more exotic objects, such as pulsars, quasars and black holes, have held the centre of the astronomical stage. My story ends here; the revelation of the innermost secrets of the Sun, though, is just beginning.

---

* This is not a sexist remark; none of the WIMP theorists happens to have been a woman.

Appendix

The Supernova Connection

Our Sun is not fated to become a supernova. But it was born out of the debris of supernova explosions of the distant past, when our Milky Way Galaxy was young. Apart from hydrogen, every atom in your body, and every atom on Earth except for hydrogen and helium,★ was manufactured inside stars and then expelled into space by supernova explosions to lace the clouds of hydrogen and helium from which the Sun and its family of planets formed. Without an understanding of supernovas, we would have no understanding of the origin of the Sun (let alone of our own origins), and the story I have told in this book would be incomplete.

Over the previous three decades, theorists had developed what seemed to be a satisfactory understanding of supernova explosions, based on their understanding of the laws of physics, on observations of such explosions in distant galaxies and of the debris from old supernova explosions in our own Galaxy, and on computer models of how stars work, like those I have described earlier. But until 1987 they had no means of checking this understanding directly. The explosion of a star known as Sanduleak −69° 202 to become a supernova first visible from Earth on the night of 23/24 February 1987 was, therefore, possibly the single most important event in astronomy since the invention of the telescope. The event, dubbed SN 1987A (denoting the first supernova observed in 1987), took place in the Large Magellanic Cloud, a galaxy so close to our own Milky Way that it is part of the same system of galaxies, held together by gravity and known as the Local Group. At a distance of 160,000 light years (just next door, by cosmological standards), SN 1987A was by far the

★ There is no helium in your body.

closest supernova to have occurred since 1604, when the last known supernova exploded in our own Galaxy, just before the development of the astronomical telescope. It was close enough to be studied in detail by a battery of instruments – including conventional telescopes on mountain tops, X-ray detectors on board satellites in space, and, as we have seen, neutrino detectors buried deep beneath the ground. Both in broad outline and most of the details, those observations showed, over the two years following the outburst, that the astronomers did have a good understanding of how supernovas work. Although some details did not match up to expectations, there were no major surprises. It seems that we do, indeed, understand where the material that made the Sun and ourselves came from, and it also seems appropriate to celebrate this landmark in astronomy by looking at SN 1987A in a little more detail before I finally bring this book to a close.

Discovering a supernova

In one sense, the story of Supernova 1987A begins about 160,000 years ago, when Planet Earth was experiencing the ice age before last. Since the star which exploded is about 160,000 light years away, it took that long for the light to reach Earth. But as far as residents of this planet are concerned, the story begins on the night of 23/24 February 1987, when a young Canadian astronomer, Ian Shelton, was making observations from the Las Campanas Observatory, high on a mountain top in northern Chile. Shelton was using a modest telescope, by professional standards – one with an aperture of only ten inches. He had just got permission to use this instrument in a survey of the Large Magellanic Cloud, a search aimed at finding variable stars, ones that change in brightness from one day to the next, one week to the next, one month to the next, or on longer timescales. Professional astronomers scarcely ever 'look through' their telescopes these days; apart from the battery of electronic technology that can be hung in the business end to obtain information from starlight, even the humble photograph reveals more than the human eye can see, because it can be exposed for a long time (hours, in many cases) building up an image all the time. The human eye will see no more after staring at a star for hours than it will at first glimpse.

Shelton took his first photographic plate of the Large Magellanic Cloud (LMC) on the night of 21/22 February – and because he hadn't yet got used to the system, it was a pretty poor snapshot. On the night of 22/23 February, he did rather better, obtaining a reasonable plate of the LMC using a one-hour exposure. This photograph was to assume great importance as the last one of the region taken by that instrument before the supernova became visible.

On the night of 23/24 February, Shelton had everything working properly, and obtained a good, long exposure, three hours ending at 2.40 a.m. Satisfied with a job well done, he was ready for bed – but decided to develop the photographic plate first. As soon as he did so, he noticed a bright spot, looking like a star, which hadn't been there when he photographed the same region the night before. At first, he thought it might be a flaw on the plate. Any star that bright, he realized, would be easily visible to the naked eye. Just in case, he stepped outside the telescope building to take a look. The new star really was there.

Earlier that same night, around midnight, one of the people working on the nearby 40-inch telescope had gone out to take a look around. Oscar Duhalde, the night assistant on the 40-inch, knew the southern skies, where the Large Magellanic Cloud is a prominent feature, well. He noticed that there was a new star in the LMC, but didn't draw the attention of the two observers using the telescope to the phenomenon. One of them later commented wryly, 'We must have been working Oscar too hard.'[*] Shelton, though, was quick to share his discovery with his colleagues. He went over to the control room of the 40-inch, and asked them how bright a nova would look at the distance of the LMC. A nova (from the Latin for 'new' star), though by no means common, is a fairly routine astronomical event, when a star passes through an unstable phase and flares up brightly for a short time. It isn't really a new star, but an old star which has suddenly brightened enough to be noticed. The more experienced astronomers working with the 40-inch told Shelton that such a nova would reach a magnitude of about 8, on the standard astronomical brightness scale (on which a *lower* number indicates a *brighter* object). That was interesting, commented Shelton, because he'd just photographed a star in the LMC that had a magnitude of 5. Barry Madore immediately said that it must be a supernova[†] – at which point

[*] Ronald Schorn, *Sky & Telescope*, May 1987, p. 470.
[†] The origin of the term is obvious, but a supernova, in fact, has nothing in common with a nova except that it is a star which suddenly increases in brightness.

Oscar Duhalde mentioned that he, too, had seen a bright new star in the LMC earlier that night. Everybody went outside to take a look – but, ironically, they could do nothing to study the phenomenon immediately. The supernova lay too low in the sky to be investigated by the 100-inch telescope at the site, while the 40-inch was rigged up for that night's observing with an instrument called a charge-coupled-device, used for studying faint objects and so sensitive that pointing it at the supernova would have burnt it out in less than a second.

All they could do was alert the rest of the astronomical community – which is easier said than done from the top of a mountain in Chile. After fruitless attempts to telephone the clearing house for astronomical discoveries (the International Astronomical Union's Central Bureau in Cambridge, Massachusetts) a messenger was sent down the mountain to telex the news from the nearest town. The report eventually arrived in Cambridge just half an hour ahead of the second report of the discovery. By that margin, Shelton and Duhalde were officially recognized as the discoverers of the supernova.

The discovery caused huge excitement among astronomers, spilling over into the general press and making the cover of *Time* magazine on 23 March. The reason for all the excitement was partly the importance of supernovas themselves – the biggest explosions that have taken place since the Big Bang in which the Universe was born, and the source of all the heavy elements – and partly their rarity. Only four definite supernova explosions have been observed in our Galaxy over the past thousand years, and the last one visible to the naked eye (and that only just) blew up in the Andromeda galaxy, two million light years away (ten times further than SN 1987A) and was visible as long ago as 1885.

Blasts from the past

The study of supernovas begins, after a fashion, in the mists of antiquity, with records of what Chinese astronomers called 'guest stars', in the centuries before Christ. Of course, those astronomers (or astrologers, as they really were) did not know what it was they were seeing. But they regarded the appearance of 'new' stars in the sky as highly significant, and kept records of their occurrence. Unfortunately, those records are not always simple to decipher. Some of the objects recorded as guest stars may have been the less spectacular novas, not supernovas; some may even have been a different kind of phenomenon altogether (perhaps comets). But what might be the earliest known mention of a supernova is an inscription on a bit of bone that dates from 1300 BC, and records a bright star appearing out of nowhere near the star we call Antares.

The first unambiguous identification of a supernova dates from AD 185, and describes the brightness of the star and its slow fade back into obscurity in terms that leave no doubt about the identification. Over the next thousand years, Chinese sky watchers recorded five more supernovas in our Milky Way Galaxy, some of which were also noted by observers in other parts of the world, including Japan, Egypt, and, possibly, the Americas. The last of these was the one that has made the biggest impact on modern astronomy – a bigger impact, indeed, than any other object outside our own Solar System.

That supernova blazed in the sky above Earth on 4 July 1054. It shone in the constellation Taurus, and marked the death throes of a star just 6,000 light years away from us. Although Chinese and Japanese observers recorded the event, no records of the supernova of 1054 have come down to us from their European contemporaries, although the star must have been visible from Europe. Curiously, though, this is the supernova that may be recorded in images left by native Americans on rock walls in Arizona – though they could have had no knowledge of the significance the fourth of July would have in that part of the world a few centuries later.

Because this supernova was so close, astronomically speaking, and so recent, it has left behind a glowing mass of gas that can be studied in great detail by modern telescopes, and a rapidly spinning, dense neutron star in its heart, detectable as a pulsar at radio frequencies, in optical light, and even using X-ray equipment. This Crab Nebula (so called because its outline in some astronomical photographs resembles a crab – if you have a vivid imagination) is virtually an astrophysics laboratory, a site where many phenomena can be observed and many theories tested, almost on our astronomical doorstep. The study of this object is so important that astronomers have been known to quip that the observational side of their craft can be divided neatly into two roughly equal portions – the study of the Crab Nebula, and the study of everything else.

Since 1054, less than a handful of other supernovas have been observed, and Europeans only got in on the act in 1572. The last supernova seen in the Milky Way occurred as long ago as 1604.★ Although this was studied in detail by Johannes Kepler, frustratingly for astronomers today his records were entirely based on observations with the naked eye. The supernova was visible from Earth just five years before Galileo first applied the telescope to the study of the heavens. Before the astronomical telescope was invented, supernovas visible from Earth had been popping off in our Galaxy at a rate of about four every thousand years. By blind chance, *two* had been visible in the span of a single human lifetime, in 1572 and 1604. But in all the time from 1604 to 1987, as telescopes lay waiting for their prey, the only supernova that could (just) have been seen by the unaided eye was the one which occurred in the Andromeda galaxy, just over two million light years away, visible from Earth at the end of the nineteenth century. Which explains why SN 1987A caused so much excitement among astronomers. It wasn't quite in the Milky Way, but in the galaxy next door; it was, though, certainly visible to the naked eye, and it could be studied in unprecedented detail by all of the instruments that now exist to supplement Galileo's simple telescope.

Back to the present

The news that came into the International Astronomical Union's Bureau in Cambridge just half an hour after the telex from Chile was from an astronomer in New Zealand, Albert Jones, who spotted SN 1987A that same night. But what turned out to be key observations had been made even before the supernova was noticed, by astronomers taking routine photographs of the Large Magellanic Cloud. Robert McNaught, in Australia, photographed the brightening star about sixteen hours before it was identified as a supernova, using a large astronomical camera known as a Schmidt telescope – but the photographs were only developed and studied after the news from Chile reached Australia. And about three and a half hours later, two astronomers testing a new piece of guiding equipment on a telescope in New Zealand just happened to pick the LMC as the target for their test photographs. Together with the observations from Chile the night before the supernova burst into view, these photographs help to establish the

---

★ Curiously, though, modern astronomers have found the remains of a supernova that ought to have been visible from Earth in the middle of the seventeenth century, but which nobody seems to have noticed at the time. It is called Cassiopeia A.

timing of the event, and the speed with which the progenitor star, Sanduleak −69° 202, flared up. Even better for astronomers, this is the first time that the star which became a supernova has been identified on old photographic plates, so that we know in some detail what it was and what it was doing, before it flared.★

All of this helped astronomers to test their theories of how supernovas work. The key theoretical insight actually dates back more than half a century, to 1934. At that time, less than two years after the discovery of the neutron, Walter Baade and Fritz Zwicky made the dramatic suggestion that 'a supernova represents the transition of an ordinary star into a neutron star.' But although half a century of observations of distant supernovas and theorizing had filled in the details of how that might happen, the theories could only be tested fully by studying a nearby supernova at work.

By the late 1980s, astronomers were satisfied, from their studies of supernovas in other galaxies, that there are two basic, different types of supernova. In each case, an ordinary star is indeed converted into a neutron star, releasing gravitational energy along the way just as William Thomson would have appreciated, from its store of gravitational energy. Nineteenth-century physics is enough to explain the energy released in a supernova – once you know that neutron stars exist. The difference between a supernova and the mechanism Thomson proposed to keep the Sun hot is primarily one of scale – the formation of a neutron star from an ordinary star involves a collapse so dramatic that the energy released makes the biggest bang since *the* big one – the one in which the Universe was born. A neutron star contains roughly the mass of our Sun packed into a volume comparable to that of a mountain on Earth. Such a star will form from any lump of matter that is no longer kept hot by nuclear fusion in its heart (a dead star) provided that its mass is a little more than a critical amount (actually slightly bigger than the mass of our Sun), when the inward tug of gravity overwhelms the forces that give atoms their structure. If the mass is *much* bigger than this, even neutrons are crushed out of existence by gravity, turning the dead star into a black hole. The range of masses for stable neutron stars is, therefore, only from a little over the mass of our Sun to about twice the solar mass.

★ Strictly speaking, this is the *second* known progenitor. Supernova 1961V, in a disk (spiral) galaxy known as NGC 1058, was probably the explosion of a star that had been recorded in a photograph taken thirty-seven years previously. But in that case there was not enough information to study the progenitor star in detail.

The first way to make a supernova (Type I) is if a cold, dead star which has *less* than the critical amount of mass gains matter from a companion. Such a star starts out as a white dwarf, a dead star with about the mass of our Sun, maybe a little less, contained in a volume the size of the Earth. It is the fate of our own Sun to end its life as a white dwarf, because it does not have enough mass to become a neutron star and it has no companion to steal mass from. But a star like our Sun which has become a white dwarf and orbits around another star can gain mass, tugging streamers of gas off its companion through tidal forces and swallowing them. When its mass reaches the critical value, the atoms of which the star is made will collapse, with electrons being forced to merge with protons to become neutrons. The star, more massive than our Sun, will shrink from the size of the Earth to the size of a mountain, releasing the appropriate amount of gravitational energy in the process.

But that is not what happened in SN 1987A. There is another way to make a supernova, known as Type II. This happens, according to theory, when a very massive star, near the end of its life, runs out of nuclear fuel to keep its heart hot. The inner part of such a star, already with more than the critical mass needed to make a neutron star, collapses all the way to the neutron star state, without stopping off as a white dwarf. Comparably huger amounts of energy are liberated – at least a hundred times as much energy, in a few seconds, as our Sun has radiated in its entire lifetime – blasting the outer layers of the star outwards at speeds of around 20,000 kilometres a second (actually 17,000 kilometres a second in the case of SN 1987A) and triggering a wave of nuclear reactions that manufacture heavy elements that can be formed naturally in no other way.

This broad description of supernovas as Type I and Type II can, like most simple definitions, be refined and subdivided. The experts split each main category into at least two sub-categories. But that is not important for now. What matters is that SN 1987A was a Type II supernova, a representative of the most energetic kind of stellar event that can ever take place. And, because the progenitor star has been identified, astronomers can reconstruct the history of the supernova, from the time the star was born right up to the dramatic events observed in 1987.

That story is reconstructed, of course, with the aid of the computer models of how stars work that I mentioned earlier. Different researchers have developed slightly different models which tell a slightly different set of stories, although the broad outlines are always the same; the outline I give here is based on the models used by Stan Woosley and his colleagues. Woosley, a supernova expert, works at the University of California, Santa Cruz (the same campus where John Faulkner is based), and he has told his version of the supernova story in some detail in an article with Tom Weaver in the August 1989 issue of *Scientific American*. According to this model, the star we are interested in was born only about 11 million years ago, in a region of the LMC particularly rich in gas and dust. Because the star contained about 18 times as much matter as our Sun, it had to burn its nuclear fuel more quickly in order to provide enough heat to hold itself up against the inward tug of gravity. So its fuel was exhausted more quickly than the fuel of a star with the mass of our Sun, and it shone about 40,000 times brighter than the Sun. In just ten million years, it had burned all the hydrogen in its core into helium. As a result, the core slowly shrank and got hotter until helium burning could begin.

It is during this phase of its life that such a massive star becomes a supergiant, with the outer layers swelling up to stretch across a distance roughly the same size as the diameter of the Earth's orbit around the Sun (that is, from here to the same distance the *other side* of our Sun). One of the surprises that astronomers found when they examined old photographs of SN 1987A's progenitor, Sanduleak −69° 202, was that the star was actually not a red supergiant but a blue supergiant, a smaller and hotter type of star. The outer parts of the star had contracted again slightly, perhaps as recently as 40,000 years before the explosion. This does not affect the basic understanding of Type II supernovas, but gives the theorists plenty of interesting detail to get their teeth into. A favoured explanation at present is that this late shrinking of the outer part of the star has to do with the fact that the Large Magellanic Cloud, unlike our own Milky Way Galaxy, contains only relatively modest amounts of heavier elements than helium. One of those elements deficient in stars of the LMC, oxygen, helps to make a red supergiant swell up, because a little oxygen in the outer part of the star absorbs radiation that is trying to escape, holding it in and making the star swell like an inflating balloon. With less oxygen present, once such a star reaches the stage of its evolution where the outward flow of radiation drops slightly, the 'balloon' might deflate again. While helium burning was going on, the star probably was a red supergiant; but helium burning could only sustain the star for about a further million years after hydrogen burning in the core ended.

In the last few thousand years of its life, Sanduleak −69° 202 must have gone through its remaining possibilities for energy production with increasing speed. Carbon, itself a product of helium burning, was converted into a mixture of neon, magnesium and sodium; neon and oxygen (another product of helium burning) 'burned' in their turn; and at the end nuclear fusion reactions were consuming silicon and sulphur in the heart of the star, while all the other nuclear fuels were being burned in

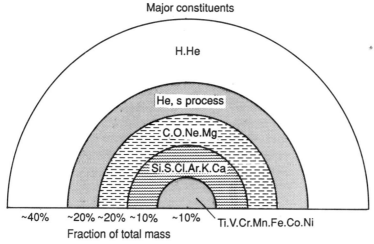

Major constituents

H.He

He, s process

C.O.Ne.Mg

Si.S.Cl.Ar.K.Ca

~40%   ~20% ~20% ~10%   ~10%   Ti.V.Cr.Mn.Fe.Co.Ni
Fraction of total mass

Figure A.1   The structure of a heavy star like the precursor to SN 1987A, just before it explodes. The iron-rich core is ready to collapse; the various fusion processes described in the text are all taking place in different layers out through the star, at lower temperatures in each successive shell.

successively cooler layers working outwards from the centre (Figure A.1). All the while, the pace of change quickened. According to the calculations made by Woosley and his colleagues, helium burning lasted nearly a million years, carbon burning only 12,000 years; neon kept the star hot for twelve years, oxygen provided the necessary energy for a mere four years; and silicon was burnt out in a week. And then, things began to get really interesting.

Death and glory

Silicon burning is the end of the line even for a massive star, because it produces a mixture of nuclei, including cobalt, iron and nickel, that is among the most stable arrangements it is possible for protons and neutrons to form. Sticking lighter nuclei together to make iron nuclei releases energy (once you overcome the electric barrier between the lighter nuclei). But sticking iron nuclei and other nuclei together to make heavier elements uses up energy, *over and above* the energy needed to overcome the electric barrier. Indeed, heavier elements may fission, splitting to form nuclei more like those of iron and giving up energy in the process. There is a kind of natural energy valley for nuclei, with iron at the bottom and light elements up one side of the valley while heavier elements lie up the other slope of the valley. All nuclei would 'like' to roll down the valley and become iron, light ones through the fusion route and heavy ones through the fission route. In this sense, iron and nickel are the most stable nuclei. So, where do elements heavier than iron (lead, uranium, and all the rest) come from? From supernovas, like SN 1987A. And although that statement was well founded in scientific calculation before February 1987, it has only been proved correct by studies of SN 1987A.

In fact, there are two kinds of elements that cannot be produced inside stable stars. The lightest elements (deuterium, helium-3, lithium, beryllium and boron) must have come from somewhere else, before the first stars formed. That 'somewhere else' can only have been the Big Bang, in which the Universe was born. The standard model of the early Universe is derived by winding back (in our imagination, and with the aid of computer models) the observed expansion of the Universe today. If we do this, like Gamow did, we arrive at a 'moment of creation', some fifteen billion years ago, when density was infinite. Leaving aside exactly what this infinity means,★ cosmologists can use information from their understanding of particle physics, and the description of the Universe provided by general relativity, to describe how the Universe evolved from a few seconds after this moment of creation.

At an 'age' of about twenty-five seconds, the temperature is about four billion degrees and the energy density is roughly two tonnes per litre. The fireball that is the Universe consists essentially of neutrinos and photons, with just a trace of protons, neutrons and electron-positron pairs. The density of *matter* is only 10 grams per litre – ten times the density of the air we breathe. At

---

★ I discuss it in some detail in my book *In Search of the Big Bang*.

this stage, protons cannot link up electromagnetically with electrons to form stable atoms of hydrogen, because atoms would be broken apart by the intensely energetic radiation. For the same reason, protons and neutrons cannot yet combine to form deuterium nuclei.

But when the Universe is about a minute old, it has expanded and cooled sufficiently for deuterium nuclei to hold together. This triggers a chain of nuclear reactions, lasting a couple of minutes, that converts almost all of the deuterium into helium, and produces very small quantities of a few other very light elements. But with all the deuterium used up, as the Universe cools further, fusion reactions stop. After a further hundred thousand years or so the Universe is so cold (about the temperature of the surface of our Sun) that naked protons and helium nuclei link up with electrons to form atoms.

The proportion of primordial material that is converted into helium depends on how rapidly the Universe expands in its early stages. This in turn depends on the number of varieties of elementary particle present, and the way they interact. Taking all of these factors into account (including the latest evidence that there are just three types of neutrino) the standard model tells us that about 23 per cent of the matter in the early Universe was processed into helium. The fact that we see 25 per cent helium, by mass, in old stars today is a striking vindication of the standard model of the Big Bang – a model which also accounts for the existence of small amounts of lithium and the other light elements in our Universe.

So the lightest elements come from the Big Bang, and everything else up to iron can be made inside massive stars. Particle theorists, drawing on the studies of their experimental colleagues, can also explain how elements heavier than iron can be produced, provided that nuclei are bathed in a sea of neutrons. And neutrons are one thing that a supernova produces in abundance – although there are, in fact, more gentle processes also at work transforming lighter elements into heavier elements in the Universe.

Most of the elements more massive than iron, as well as some of the isotopes of less massive elements, are produced when nuclei built up by nuclear fusion processes capture neutrons from their surroundings inside a star. Any free neutron is itself unstable, and emits an electron by beta decay, turning into a proton, if left to its own devices for a few minutes. So the neutrons involved in these capture processes have to be freshly released, by other nuclear interactions. This is no problem inside a star where nuclear burning is going on. For example, every time one nucleus of deuterium and one of tritium fuse to produce helium-4, one neutron is released; this and similar reactions inside stars provide a profusion of neutrons – as many as a hundred million in every cubic centimetre of the interesting region of a star – which may interact with other nuclei.

Adding a single neutron to a nucleus increases its mass by one unit, but does not change its electric charge or its chemical properties – it becomes a different isotope of the same element. In many cases, however, the newly formed isotope is unstable, and given time (in some cases, a few seconds; in others, a few years) it will eject an electron by beta decay, converting one of its neutrons into a proton and becoming a different element. Then, the whole process may repeat, when the same nucleus captures another neutron. This step-by-step build up of heavy elements, in which a nucleus has time to convert into a stable form in between interactions with neutrons, is known as the slow, or **s**, process of neutron capture.

But when large numbers of neutrons are available, which certainly happens as a result of explosive interactions occurring during the early stages of a supernova, there may be so many neutrons around that a nucleus can capture several of them before it has time to spit out an electron, or decay in some other way. A density of a mere hundred million neutrons per cubic centimetre is nowhere near enough to make this happen; it requires a density of about three hundred billion billion (3×10^{20}) neutrons in every cubic centimetre of star stuff. The result, when these enormous neutron densities are briefly achieved as a supernova explodes, is a rapid build up of elements and isotopes which have a surplus of neutrons, and which are almost all unstable. This is the rapid, or **r**, process of neutron capture. Once the wave of neutrons has been absorbed, the unstable, neutron-rich nuclei that are left behind will decay into stable nuclei, losing neutrons (converting them into protons) and becoming more like the isotopes produced by the **s** process. Many isotopes are produced by both processes. A handful of stable, slightly neutron-rich nuclei are produced only by the **r** process and subsequent beta decays. And just twenty-eight isotopes, astrophysicists calculate, can be produced only by the **s** process.

In a diagram of the elements which plots the number of neutrons in a nucleus against the number of protons, stable isotopes lie on a roughly diagonal band along which the number

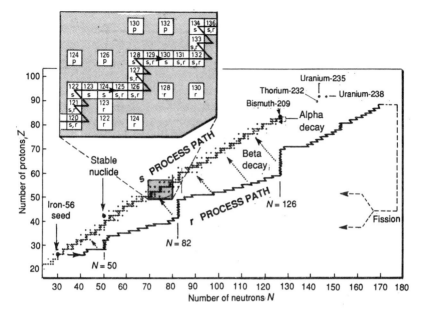

*Figure A.2   The **r** and **s** processes at work. Stable heavy elements are built up from iron-56 by the **s**-process, described in the text. They lie on a diagonal line (the valley of stability) in this plot. The inset shows in detail the **s** process at work, building up new nuclei by absorbing a neutron (moving one space to the right) and emitting an electron (moving up and to the left) as required. The number in each box indicates the total number of particles (protons plus neutrons) in a particular nucleus. 's' indicates that particular element can be made by the **s** process, 'r' by the **r** process. 'p' indicates elements formed by the still poorly understood **p** process.*

*When many neutrons are available, in a supernova explosion, neutron-rich nuclei build up rapidly through the **r** process (lower line). These then decay by emitting electrons (beta decay), raining down into the valley of stability. Very heavy nuclei split apart by fission or alpha decay.*

of neutrons is slightly greater than the number of protons. Elements formed by the **s** process (and by the ultimate beta decay of **r** process elements) lie on a zig-zag track through this 'valley of stability'; unstable isotopes produced by the **r** process lie far off to the right, in the neutron-rich half of the diagram, and as they decay they shift towards the bottom of the valley of stability, 'raining down' on the **s** process elements (Figure A.2). Both processes end for very massive elements where nuclei are split apart either by alpha decay (emitting a helium nucleus) or by fission (producing two roughly equal nuclei each with about half the mass of the one that splits).

Both these processes are very well understood. Studies of the way nuclei and neutrons interact in experiments here on Earth, combined with computer models of conditions inside stars, satisfactorily explain how almost all of the known elements are built up. The main exceptions are some isotopes rich in protons, which are thought to be formed by a proton capture process, but this is not fully understood; there are also some rare isotopes which are produced in space by interactions involving cosmic rays. But these are minor effects. The studies of SN 1987A showed just how well astrophysicists really do understand the way elements are built up in supernovas. But I don't intend to get bogged down in the details. The key thing to remember is that making elements heavier than iron requires an *input* of energy, which comes from the gravitational collapse of the supernova's core to become a neutron star.

The supernova inside out

Except in the case of our Sun, where neutrino studies may be providing a direct clue to conditions in the deep interior, we cannot study any of the nuclear processes at work inside stars directly. The observations that provide both the input to theories of stellar astrophysics and the tests of those theories are indirect studies of material expelled from inside stars. First, the material has to be processed inside a star, carried to the surface and ejected into space; then it can be studied from Earth by the way in which the elements produced either radiate or absorb light. Everything has to fit together – and it does.

One simple example shows what is involed. The carbon-nitrogen (C-N) cycle should, according to particle physics theory, convert carbon into the most common isotope of nitrogen, nitrogen-14. At the same time, the set of interactions reduces the amount of the isotope carbon-13 relative to carbon-12. All of the products of these interactions should, according to astrophysics theory, get mixed up to the surface of red giant stars. And when stellar spectroscopists analyse the light from red giants, they find just the mix of nitrogen and carbon isotopes predicted by theory.

Clouds of gas ('planetary nebulas') produced by relatively small stellar explosions (mere novas) also show the 'right' mix of elements and isotopes in line with the kind of stellar cooking of the elements described earlier in this book. But as well as providing the biggest input of energy to make heavy elements, supernovas also provide the biggest blast to blow material out into space, giving astronomers their best opportunities to study star stuff. Many old supernova remnants have, indeed, been identified and studied by spectroscopy. But there's a snag. A cloud of gas blown out into space by a supernova explosion sweeps up gas and dust from between the stars as it moves through space. So when astronomers study the glowing cloud of material today, hundreds or thousands of years after the supernova explosion lit up the night sky for our ancestors, they cannot untangle the information they want about the elements produced in the supernova itself. SN 1987A, caught on photographic plates before, during and after its explosion, was different.

According to astrophysical theory, just before the supernova exploded, all of the standard nuclear reactions leading up to the production of iron-group elements were going on in shells around the core, and in addition the s process should, theorists were confident, have been at work in the region of the star rich in carbon and oxygen (Figure A.1). Silicon burning, remember, had held the star up against the inward tug of gravity for just about one week (as it happens, barely long enough for Ian Shelton to get his photographic survey of the Large Magellanic Cloud under-way), and had left a core composed of the most stable nuclei – iron, nickel and the rest – incapable of releasing energy *either* by fusion *or* by fission (although, as we shall see, some of those iron group nuclei can decay to iron itself). After eleven million years, the heart of the star was left with no means of support, and it collapsed, in a few tenths of a second, into a lump no more than a hundred kilometres across. During this initial collapse, very energetic photons ripped iron nuclei apart, undoing the work of eleven million years of nuclear fusion processes, and electrons were squeezed into nuclei by such enormous pressures that beta decay went into reverse, converting protons into neutrons. Gravity provided the energy for all this. All that was left was a ball of neutron material, essentially a giant 'atomic nucleus', two hundred kilometres across and containing nearly one and a half times the mass of our Sun.

The squeeze of the infalling material was so great that at this point the centre of the neutron ball was compressed to densities even greater than those of the nucleus of an atom. Then, like a golf ball being squeezed in an iron grip and then released, it rebounded, sending a shock wave out through the ball of neutron stuff, and into the star beyond. Material from further out in the core of the star, plunging inwards at a speed roughly one quarter the speed of light, met the rebounding shock from the core of neutron stuff and was literally turned inside out, becoming a shock wave racing *outwards* through the star. It was this shock wave that blew the star apart – but not before a flood of neutrons emitted by all this activity had caused a sizeable production of heavy elements through the r process.*

The neutrinos easily outpace the shock. They travel at nearly the speed of light (exactly the speed of light if they have zero mass), but the shock moves at about 2 per cent of the speed of light, even after getting a boost from the neutrinos, taking a couple of hours to push the outer layers of the star into space and light up the star visibly – which is why the neutrinos were captured by detectors on Earth shortly before the star brightened visibly.

While all this was going on, even though the iron core of the star had been converted into a ball of neutrons, according to theory there should have been a massive burst of nuclear reactions further out in the star, in the hot, high-pressure shock wave, producing iron group elements. Most of the elements produced inside the star by such fusion reactions are made, in effect, from successive additions of alpha particles (helium-4 nuclei, each made of two protons and two neutrons combined together), and have equal numbers of protons and neutrons in their nuclei. Carbon-12 (six protons, six neutrons) and oxygen-16 (eight protons, eight neutrons) are typical examples. When these nuclei are processed by explosive interactions, then according to theory most of the material is converted into nickel-56, which has 28 neutrons and 28 protons in each nucleus. But nickel-56 is unstable; it decays, emitting positrons to convert protons into neutrons (inverse beta decay). The first step in this decay has a half-life of just over six days, and produces cobalt-56; the cobalt-56 then decays into iron-56 (26 protons, 30 neutrons) with a half-life of 77 days.

---

* The shock wave is actually helped on its way by a blast of neutrinos from the core as it collapses all the way down to become a neutron star just twenty kilometres across – a relatively leisurely process that takes several tens of seconds (not tenths of a second) to complete. And by the time it is completed, the neutrinos are long gone. The outgoing shock wave, trying to push more than fifteen solar masses of material along in front of itself, becomes so dense that it can absorb a significant fraction (a few per cent) of this neutrino outburst (as I describe in more detail in my book with Martin Rees, *Cosmic Coincidences*), gaining enough energy to finish the job of blowing the star apart. The rest of the neutrinos – carrying a couple of hundred times as much energy as the supernova radiated in visible light – went on through the star and out into the Universe at large, where just a few ended up in detectors on Earth.

The unstable nickel-56 has been built up by the input of gravitational energy from the collapse of the core of the supernova. When it decays, it gives up some of that borrowed energy. The standard theory of supernovas, developed before SN 1987A was seen to explode, predicted that almost all of the energy radiated by the star during the first hundred days of its life as a supernova would come from the decay from cobalt-56 to iron-56. This decay follows a characteristic pattern, a decreasing exponential curve; and the fading of the supernova itself followed exactly the predicted curve. During that first hundred days, this evidence showed, 93 per cent of the output of the supernova was indeed provided by the decay of cobalt-56; indeed, the slow fade of the supernova was still following the appropriate curve at the end of 1989, when I was finishing this book, almost three years after Shelton first noticed the brightening of the supernova. Astrophysicist Roger Tayler, of the University of Sussex, says these observations of cobalt decay 'are probably the most important and exciting ones concerned with the origin of the elements, confirming that the theoretical model is broadly correct.'

It wasn't just the 'light curve', as it is called, that he was referring to. As the material expelled by the supernova moves out into space, successive layers of its interior are revealed to the telescopes of the patiently watching observers, in a kind of cosmic striptease. Eventually, they could see material coming out from the regions where the explosive nuclear interactions should have taken place – and what their spectroscopic studies revealed was characteristic lines associated with nickel-56, just as expected, indicating (after allowing for the decay that had already taken place by the time this part of the star could be observed) that as much nickel-56 as the equivalent of 8 per cent of the mass of our Sun had been manufactured in the supernova – closely in line with theoretical calculations. The spectroscopic studies also reveal the presence of barium, strontium and scandium – all **s** process elements produced before the star became a supernova. And studies of helium and nitrogen in the outermost layers of the expanding cloud of material around the supernova are helping astrophysicists to improve their understanding of how material produced by the C-N cycle gets mixed up to the surface of a star.

Of course, there were also surprises. Details of the behaviour of SN 1987A do not in every case match precisely with the details of the theories, and there is ample scope yet for astronomers to refine their understanding of how stars like this explode. But the mention of new insights into the way carbon and associated elements are produced and mixed into the Universe provides a cue to bring my present discussion to an end. These, after all, are the elements of which we are, in large part, made – carbon, oxygen and nitrogen have a key importance for life as we know it. And observations of the spectra of these elements in the expanding cloud of material around SN 1987A provide a reminder that while such an explosion marks the death of a star, it is quite literally the beginning of the story of life forms like ourselves. We would not be here, wondering about such puzzles as the solar neutrino problem, how the Sun stays hot for so long, and why it rings like a bell, if it were not for those previous generations of supernova explosions that scattered their share of carbon, nitrogen, oxygen and other elements through interstellar space billions of years ago. As far as life forms like us are concerned, in fact, my story ends – in the beginning.

Further reading

For anyone with a serious interest in stellar astrophysics and not afraid of a few equations, the place to find out more about how stars live and die is *Cauldrons in the Cosmos*, by Claus Rolfs and William Rodney, University of Chicago Press, 1988.

Bibliography

If you want to know more about the secrets of the Sun, the following books will provide more detailed information on some of the topics I have discussed.

Peter Atkins, *The Second Law*, Scientific American/W. H. Freeman, New York, 1984.
An accessible, non-mathematical account of the importance of thermodynamics to our understanding of the world.

Peter Brent, *Charles Darwin*, Heinemann, London, 1981.
A good 'popular' biography which makes clear the debt Darwin owed to Lyell.

Joe Burchfield, *Lord Kelvin and the Age of the Earth*, Macmillan, London and New York, 1975.
The definitive history of Kelvin's contribution to the debate about the ages of both the Earth *and* the Sun. Mainly for the specialists, or anyone with a passion for the story of how science developed in the nineteenth century.

Subrahmanyan Chandrasekhar, *Eddington*, Cambridge University Press, 1983.
A tiny little monograph, based on lectures given by Chandrasekhar in Cambridge to mark the centenary of Eddington's birth. The best instant insight into the man described as 'the most distinguished astrophysicist of his time'.

Frank Close, *The Cosmic Onion*, Heinemann Educational Books, London, 1983.
Don't be put off by the 'Educational' in the publisher's name. This

is one of the best and most accessible quick guides to the particle world, and will in particular put the neutrino in its place for you.

Frank Close, Michael Marten and Christine Sutton, *The Particle Explosion*, Oxford University Press, 1987.
A wonderful illustrated history of all the known particles, from the electron to the W and Z. Particle physicist Close, picture researcher Marten, and science writer Sutton combined their talents to produce a book that is both informative and an attractive addition to any coffee table. Unfortunately, they stop short of any serious discussion of particles that haven't yet been detected, but might be soon – such as axions and WIMPs. Very good on neutrinos, though they don't really give Ray Davis his due.

Charles Darwin, *The Origin of Species by Means of Natural Selection*, Pelican, London, 1968.
An accessible version of the great work, in a reprint which includes some later material as well, but is essentially the first edition of 1859. Darwin showed from the outset that the time required for evolution to do its work was far more than a few thousand years, and he also appreciated how long it must have taken for natural forces to have moulded the landscape.

Arthur Eddington, *The Internal Constitution of the Stars*, Dover, New York, 1959.
This is the edition you are most likely to find around today; the original was published in 1926 by Cambridge University Press, and the Dover text is virtually the same. A textbook for astrophysicists, not something to dip into for light reading, but a classic well worth seeking out if you have the necessary scientific background.

Kendrick Frazier, *Our Turbulent Sun*, Prentice-Hall, New Jersey, 1982.
A journalist's view of puzzles such as the dearth of solar neutrinos, the sunspot cycle, and links between solar activity and terrestrial climate. Fun, but slightly breathless; a good light read.

Herbert Friedman, *Sun and Earth*, Scientific American/W. H. Freeman, New York, 1986.
A well-illustrated layman's guide to established current knowledge of the Sun and its influence on the Earth, with more emphasis on the traditional observational side of astronomy than I give here.

George Gamow, *A Star Called the Sun*, Viking Press, New York, 1964.
Now out of print, but worth seeking in second-hand shops or libraries. Like all Gamow's popularizations it is easy to read, full of anecdotal examples, and scientifically accurate. This one is particularly interesting because it was Gamow's work on alpha decay which led to an understanding of how nuclear fusion can occur inside the Sun at a temperature of 'only' 15 million degrees. Slightly outdated but still worth reading.

John Gribbin, *In Search of Schrödinger's Cat*, Corgi, London, and Bantam, New York, 1984.
The story of the quantum revolution which transformed physics in the first third of the twentieth century.

John Gribbin, *In Search of the Big Bang*, Heinemann, London, and Bantam, New York, 1986.
More about the relationship between particle physics and cosmology.

John Gribbin, *The Omega Point*, Heinemann, London, and Bantam, New York, 1987.
A book about the ultimate fate of the Universe, which includes a discussion of thermodynamics and the nature of time.

John Gribbin and Martin Rees, *Cosmic Coincidences*, Bantam, New York, 1989 (published in the UK by Heinemann under the title *The Stuff of the Universe*).
More about the variety of candidates for the dark matter in the Universe.

Fred Hoyle, *The Nature of the Universe*, Blackwell, Oxford, 1950.
A short book, based on a series of talks on BBC radio, which includes a chapter on the Sun. Historically interesting – Hoyle went on, among other things, to make the key contribution which unlocked the secret of how elements are made inside stars – and full of powerful analogies and examples. But long out of print, and not really worth spending much effort to track down if you cannot find it easily.

Mick Kelly and John Gribbin, *Winds of Change*, Headway, London, 1989.
More about the greenhouse effect, which I have mentioned here

briefly in Chapter Six, and which may be the most pressing problem facing humankind in the twenty-first century.

Clive Kilmister, *Sir Arthur Eddington*, Pergamon, Oxford and New York, 1966.
A book about Eddington's work and his place in science, which includes extensive quotations from his key publications, including *The Internal Constitution of the Stars*. Mainly for students of the history of science.

Rudolf Kippenhahn, *100 Billion Suns*, Weidenfeld and Nicolson, London, 1983.
A highly readable account of how stars work, from a leading German astrophysicist.

Hubert Lamb, *Climate, History and the Modern World*, Methuen, London and New York, 1982.
The best single-volume guide to the changing climate of historical times, and the impact of climatic change on human affairs. Includes a brief mention of sunspots, and a great deal on the Little Ice Age.

Kenneth Lang and Owen Gingerich, *A Source Book in Astronomy and Astrophysics, 1900–1975*, Harvard University Press, 1979.
A wonderful treasure trove of historic scientific papers, far too big and expensive to buy for yourself but well worth seeking out in a library.

Robert Noyes, *The Sun, Our Star*, Harvard University Press, 1982.
The best non-specialist description of the Sun and its workings at the time it was written, but now being overtaken somewhat by new events. Noyes, Professor of Astronomy at Harvard University, includes only a brief mention of the neutrino problem and solar oscillations, and nothing at all, of course, on WIMPs, but is authoritative on topics such as solar spots and flares, the changing face of the Sun and energy production in stars.

Abraham Pais, *Inward Bound*, Oxford University Press, 1986.
An astonishing book, a genuine tour de force, which covers the history of particle physics from the discovery of X-rays in 1895 to atomic fission in the late 1930s in great detail but also with great clarity. This part of the book comes to 444 pages; in a mere 182

further pages Pais skips lightly over the post-war years to end with the discovery of the W and Z particles, seen by many as indicating that physicists are on the right track to a 'grand unified theory' of all the particles and all the forces of nature.

Although full of scrupulously accurate science, the book essentially tells a story about physics and the people involved in these great years of discovery. The price, rather than any impenetrability of the contents, might put you off buying it, but it is well worth digging out of any library that has it, or can be persuaded to put it, on its shelves. If you *are* intimidated, either by the price or the size of the volume, try Frank Close's books, mentioned above.

Index

Academy of Sciences, French, 35–6, 37
Alpha particles, 43–4, 60–2, 69, 80, 82; and helium, 40, 45, 60–2, 65, 66; and tunnel effect, 61–2, 63
Alpha rays, 39–40, 66
Ames Research Center, 158
Anaxagorus, 3–7, 9, 12–13, 15, 31; on iron in Sun, 3–4, 12, 65, 71, 81
Andromeda Galaxy, 82, 199, 201
Antimatter, 88, 89, 101, 120–1, 186; see also positrons
Aston, Francis, 50–1, 52, 59
Atkinson, Robert, 63, 65–6, 72, 75
Atom, structure of, passim; 54–5, 60–1, 86–7, 101, 120; mass and weight, 50–2
Avignone, Frank, 192
Axions, 184, 187

Baade, Walter, 202
Bahcall, John, 96, 99, 100, 108, 112
Bailey's Beads, 146
Barnes, Howard, 43
Baryons, 120, 122–3, 126, 183–4, 186
Becquerel, Henri, 34–5, 36–8,

39, 41; Antoine, Edmond and Jean, 34–5, 37
Beryllium, 70–1, 79, 94–6, 111, 206
Beta decay, 66–7, 86–9, 191–2, 207–8, 209, 211; rays, 39, 66, 86
Bethe, Hans, 72–3, 74, 104
Big Bang, 122, 134, 170, 186, 199; mass and energy from, 116–17, 120–1, 182–3, 206, 207
Black hole, 99, 202
Bohr, Niels, 87
Bolometric detector, 112–13
Boltwood, Bertram, 45–6
Boornazian, Aran, 145–7, 149
Booth, Norman, 111
Born, Max, 87
Boron, 94, 96, 101, 111, 206
Bracewell, Robert, 156–7
Brightness (solar), 54, 56–7, 115, 130–1
British Association for the Advancement of Science, 21, 24, 26, 47, 52, 59
Brodzinski, Ronald, 192
Brookhaven National Laboratory, 90–3, 102, 185
Buffon, George-Louis Leclerc, Comte de, 13–15
Bullard, Sir Edward, 166

Burchfield, Joe, 24, 31

Cabrera, Blas, 112–13, 190
California Institute of
　Technology, 95, 162–3
Cambridge, University of, 23,
　39, 42, 50, 172–4
Carbon, 51, 189, 205, 214;
　carbon-12, 79, 210, 212;
　carbon-14, 143–4
Carbon cycle (CNO), 73–5, 76,
　93, 98
Carbon dating technique, 143–4
Carbon-nitrogen cycle (CN),
　210–11, 213
Catastrophists, 15
Cathode rays, 35–6, 38, 39
Cavendish, Henry, 10
Cavendish Laboratory, 39, 50,
　59, 69–71, 72
CERN, 102, 116
Chadwick, Sir James, 51
Chamberlain, Thomas, 31–2,
　33, 58
Chandrasekhar, Subrahmanyan,
　53
Chlorine, 90–1, 95, 190, 194
Clavius, Christopher, 146
Clerk-Maxwell, James, 23
Cockcroft, Sir John, 69–71, 72,
　73, 79, 94
Cockcroft-Walton reaction, 70–
　1, 72, 73, 79, 94
Coffee-pot analogy, 33, 47
Colour, 11, 115, 130–1, 168–9
Columbia, University of, 101
Comptes Rendus, 38
Conservation laws: energy, 12,
　19–22, 26–7, 43, 87;
　momentum, 87
Contraction hypothesis, 48, 52
Cornell University, 72, 73
Cosmions *see* WIMPS
Cowan, Clyde, 89
Cowsik, Ramanathan, 106, 185
Crab Nebula, 200
Critchfield, Charles, 74, 104

Curie, Marie and Pierre, 38–9,
　43, 47
Currie, Bob, 158

Dark matter, 107, 116–20, 121–
　3, 137, 182–7; *see also* WIMPS
Darwin, Charles, 17–18, 22, 27,
　28–9
Darwin, Sir George, 42, 48, 135
Davie, John, 16
Davis detector, 90–3, 107, 109,
　113 190, 192
Davis Jn, Raymond, 90–2, 100,
　108, 109, 110; Davis
　experiment, 90–3, 102–3, 109,
　110–11, 126; neutrino
　shortage, 94–8, 101, 110, 118,
　127
Deuterium, 94, 206, 207, 208
Deuteron, 65–6, 72, 75, 77, 94
Dirac, Paul, 67–8
Doppler technique, 162–3, 168
Dublin, University of, 42
Duhalde, Oscar, 198–9
Dunham, David, 148

Earth, 5–7, 10, 13–15, 65, 157;
　age of 12–18, 23–4, 28–31,
　42, 43–7; flat, 4–7; climate,
　78, 140–4, 150, 151–3, 155–60
East Anglia, University of, 142,
　152
Eclipse, solar, 50, 146, 147–8,
　152
Eddington, Sir Arthur, 49–51,
　52–6, 59, 61–3, 195; heat of
　Sun, 57–8, 69, 71, 98
Eddy, John A (Jack), ix, 138–9,
　142–7, 149, 152
Edinburgh, University of, 20,
　46
Einstein, Albert, 48–9, 50, 87,
　122, 171; *see also* mass-energy
　equation; relativity
Elatina Formation, 154–7,
　158–60

Electromagnetic radiation, 55, 71, 120, 123
Electromagnetism, 55, 88, 116, 189, 206–7
Eleven-year cycle, 139–41, 150–1, 153, 156, 181; solar neutrinos, 108
Elster, Julius, 41–2, 43
Energy, conservation of, 12, 19–22, 26–7, 43, 87
Energy, solar, 20–1, 24–5, 27, 29–33, 42; CNO cycle, 73–4, 98; contraction hypothesis, 52; fusion, 63–5, 72; p-p chain, 74–7; radiation, 34, 42, 48–9; Sun's zones, 82–4; and temperature, 58
Eratosthenes, 5–6
Evolution (Earth), 12, 17–18, 28–9, 48–9, 138; see also Darwin, Charles

Faulkner, John, 115, 117–19, 135–7, 194, 204; Press and Spergel, 118–19, 128–30, 137; Santa Cruz team, 118–19, 123, 128–30, 137; Vahai and Gough 172–6, 177
Federal Institute of Technology, 87
Fermi, Enrico, 88–9
Fermilab, Chicago, 116
Fiala, Alan, 148
Fireman, Edward, 193
Fission, 50, 65, 87; and supernovas, 206, 209–10, 211
Flares, 108, 139
Fourier, Jean, 14–15, 18, 23, 28, 180; analysis, 167–8, 179
Fowler, Willy, 96
Friedman, Herbert, 11
Fröhlich, Claus, 177–8
Fusion, nuclear, passim; 50, 63, 77, 88, 195; in burning stars, 79–80, 205–6, 208, 211; chain, 75, 77, 93–4; in Sun, 65–6, 69–71, 79, 82, 125

Galileo Galilei, 5, 141, 201; sunspots, 139, 143, 171
Gamma rays, 82, 111
Gamow, George, 33, 47, 49, 72–4, 206; tunnel theory, 61–5, 66, 68, 69–70
Gas, passim; 10, 54–6, 162–3; pressure, 54–6, 78, 80, 128
Gases, kinetic theory of, 20–1
Geiger, Hans, 40
Geitel, Hans, 41–2, 43
Gell-Mann, Murray, 118
Geology, 12, 15–18, 28, 31–2, 42; Elatina, 154–7; radioactive dating, 45–7
Germanium, 110, 190, 192–3
Gilliland, Ron, ix; neutrino problem, 118–19, 128–9, 184; solar variation, 137–8, 149–51, 153; WIMPs, 174–6
Giovanelli, Ronald, 155
Glasgow, University of, 23, 51
Global Oscillation Network Group (GONG), 178–181
Globular clusters, 132–6
Gough, Douglas, ix, 164, 172–4, 176, 177
Gravitational collapse, 55–6, 195, 210, 212–3
Gravitational energy, 21, 123, 195; into heat, 26, 34, 54, 99, 157; supernovas, 80, 202, 210, 212–13
Gravity, 5–6, 10, 100, 116, 196; black holes, 202; dark matter, 107, 122–3; neutrinos, 88; and stellar structure, 53–4, 55–6; and Sun, 21–2, 30, 99, 124, 160, 171; supernovas, 204, 211; and WIMPS, 117–20, 122–3, 124, 184, 188
Gravity waves (g-modes), 176–8
Greenhouse effect, 151
Greenwich Meridian, 144, 145

Halley, Sir Edmund, 148

Harvard, University of, 96, 123, 159
Harvard-Smithsonian Center for Astrophysics, 119, 145–6
Helioseismology, 161, 162, 169–71, 190
Helium: passim; 50–3, 70, 81, 92–3, 113, 131; alpha particles, 40, 45; burning, 79, 115, 204–5; dark matter, 117; and hydrogen, 50–3, 117, 131, 133; from hydrogen, 58, 59–60, 62, 65, 77–8, 82–3, 94; in Sun, 65, 72–3, 78–9, 94, 100, 135–6; in supernovas, 196, 204, 205, 208–9
Helmholtz, Hermann, 25–7, 29–30, 31, 99, 138; timescale, 26–31, 42, 45, 48
Herald, David, 148
Herschel, William, 11
Hertzsprung-Russell diagram, 115, 130–4, 135
High Altitude Observatory of the National Center for Atmospheric Research, 128, 137, 138, 152, 174–6
Holmes, Arthur, 46–7
Homestake gold mine, 90–2, 96, 98, 109, 192–3
Horizontal branch stars, 115, 132, 135–7
Houtermans, Fritz, 63, 65–6, 72
Hutton, James, 15–17
Hydrogen, 51–3, 65, 71, 73, 81, 189; burning, 115, 132–3, 204; and helium, 58, 59–60, 62, 65, 77–8, 82–3, 94; in Universe, 196, 207

Ice Ages, 105, 142, 152 154, 197
ICARUS, 112–13
Imperial College, London, 42, 46
International Astronomical Union, 172–3, 199, 201
Irvine University, 106, 185

IMB detector, 106, 185

Japanese research, 97, 101, 103; Kamiokande, 105, 107, 108
Joly, John, 42
Jones, Albert, 201

Kamiokande detector, 97, 105, 107, 108
Kellogg Radiation Laboratory, 95–6
Kelly, Mick, ix
Kelvin, William Thomson, 1st Baron, 22–5, 43–4, 52, 99–100, 138; and timescale, 15, 26–32, 42, 45–6, 48
Kelvin-Helmholtz timescale, 15, 26–32, 42, 45–6, 48
Kepler, Johannes, 171, 201
Kinetic energy, 29–30, 43, 55, 62, 192; from gravitational energy, 21, 26–7
Kippenhahn, Rudolf, 63

Laborde, Albert, 39, 43, 47
Lamb, Hubert, ix, 142
Large Magellanic Cloud, 105, 185, 196–9, 201, 204, 211
Lavoisier, Antoine, 19–20
Lawrence Berkeley Laboratory, 193
Leclerc, Georges-Louis, 13–15
Leighton, Robert, 162, 163
Lick Observatory, 115, 194
Lightfoot, John, 12
Lithium, 70–1, 72, 73, 94, 206
Lockyer, Sir Joseph, 40
Luminosity, 54, 56–7, 115, 130–1
Lunar tides, 155, 158, 159
Lyell, Sir Charles, 17–18, 28; *see also* uniformitarianism

McClung, R.K., 41, 42–3
McCrea, Willam, 65, 71–2
McGill University, 39, 41, 43
Macmillan's Magazine, 27

McNaught, Robert, 201
Madore, Barry, 198
Marsden, Ernest, 40
Mass-energy relation, 48–9, 59,
    66, 70, 120; and Sun, 49, 58,
    77, 104
Mass spectograph, 50–1
MIT, 147
Maunder, Walter, 141–2
Maunder Minimum, 142–4,
    145, 151, 153
Mayer, Julius, 19–20, 21–2, 25,
    27, 29
Meitner, Lise, 87
Meteor impact hypothesis, 21–
    2, 26–7, 28–30
Meteorological Office, 142
Mercury, 24, 79, 147–8, 149,
    171–2
Michigan, University of, 106,
    158, 185
Mikheyev, S.P., 104
Mikheyev-Smirnov-Wolfenstein
    theory, 104–5, 106, 109, 111,
    185
Milky Way, passim; 81, 122,
    123, 188; and supernovas,
    196, 199, 201
Momentum, conservation of, 87
Morrison, Leslie, 148
Muller Paul, 148

Nakagawa, Masami, 103
Nasa Goddard Space Flight
    Center, 147
National Research Council (US
    National Academy of
    Sciences), 47
Nature, 36, 52, 148, 149, 176–7;
    on solar energy, 47–8, 59
Neutrinos, 67–8, 75, 86, 88–93,
    214; oscillation, 101–5, 108–9,
    111, 112, 185; p-p chain, 94–
    5, 96–114; and supernovas,
    212; and WIMPS, 118–19,
    124, 183; see also Davis; Davis
    detector; solar neutrinos

Neutron, 51–2, 60–1, 65–6, 88,
    101; capture, 208; star, 202
New York, State University of,
    158
Newton, Isaac, 5, 10, 13–14,
    21, 171
Nitrogen, 59, 69, 214; CN
    cycle, 210–11, 213; CNO
    cycle, 73–5, 76, 93, 98
Noyes, Robert, 159
Nuclear fusion see fusion

Observatoire de Paris, 153
Oxford University, 111
Oxygen, 59, 69, 79, 188, 214;
    CNO cycle, 73–5, 76, 93, 98;
    Sun's radiation, 157;
    supernovas, 204, 205, 212

Parkinson, John, 148
Particle accelerators, 68, 69–70
Pasierb, Elaine, 103
Pauli, Wolfgang, 67, 87–9, 108
Perchloroethylene, 90–1, 190,
    194
Photon, 82–3, 120, 126, 186–7,
    194; photino, 187; see also
    electromagnetic radiation
Picard, Jean, 153
Plasma, 54, 83
Playfair, John, 16
Pontecorvo, Bruno, 101–2, 103
Positrons, 66–8, 72, 75, 89, 94
Press, William, 118–19, 123,
    128–9, 136–7
p-modes (pressure waves), 163–
    8, 173–4, 176–7, 178
Project Poltergeist, 89
Proton-proton (p-p) chain, 74–
    77, 78, 94–6, 104, 110–11
Prout, William, 51

Quintana, H., 117, 123

Radiation: electromagnetic 71;
    pressure, 55–6, 80, 128; zone
    of Sun, 83; in supernova, 204

Radioactive dating, 44–7, 143–4
Radioactivity, passim; 34–8, 38–
47, 48–50, 66
Radium, 38–9, 43, 44, 45–6, 47;
decay of, 46, 61, 65; Sun's
energy, 44, 47–9, 195
Ramsay, Sir William, 45
r process, 208–210, 212
Rayleigh, John, 3rd Baron, 21
Red giant, 78–9, 131, 133, 210
Rees, Martin, 184, 187, 212
Reines, Frederick, 89, 102,
103–4
Relativity, theories of, 87, 100;
general, 5, 50, 122, 171–2,
206; special, 48–9, 58; see also
mass-energy relation
Resonance, 160
Ribes, Elizabeth, 153
Röntgen, Wilhelm, 35–6, 37
Royal Astronomical Society,
130
Royal Institution, 29, 43–4
Royal Greenwich Observatory,
141–3, 144–7
Royal Society, 20–21, 143–4
Rutherford, Ernest, 1st Baron,
39–41, 42–4, 44–6, 51, 66;
protons, 52, 59, 69; solar
energy, 195

s process, 208–210, 211, 213
SN 1987A, 196–99, 201–2, 203–
6, 210, 213–4
Sakharov, Andrei, 120–1
Sanduleak-69°, 202, 204, 205
Sarazin, Craig, 117, 123
Savannah River reactor, 89, 103
Schneider, Stephen, ix
Schwabe, Heinrich, 141
Schwarz, Melvin, 101–2
Science, 32, 36, 148, 149
Scientific American, 204
Seventy-six year cycle, 150–2
Shapiro, Irwin, 147
Shelton, Ian, 197–9, 211, 213

Scientific method, 4–7, 58, 100,
176
Silicon, 80, 205–6, 211
Smirnov, A. Yu, 104
Smithsonian Astrophysical
Observatory, 193
Sobel, Henry, 103
Soddy, Frederick, 40, 42, 44,
45, 51–2
Sofia, Sabatino, 147, 148
Solar Heliospheric Observatory,
179
Solar Maximum Mission, 177,
179
Solar neutrinos, 89–93, 98–100,
101–5, 115, 125, 214;
detectors, 90–3, 97, 105, 106,
109–14, 154; helioseismology,
161, 162; p-p neutrinos, 94–5,
96–7; solar vibration, 170,
172–8; and WIMPS, 118–19,
128–30, 135, 172–8, 183–7,
190–5
Solar pulsation problem, 173–4
Solar thermodynamics, passim;
20–22, 24–5, 26–7, 29–32
Solar vibrations, 163–9, 170,
172–8
Sonett, Charles, 144
Sound waves, solar, 163–8
Soviet research, 101, 103
Spectral lines, 40, 162–3, 168
Spectroscopy, 40, 48, 65, 167–8;
and supernovas, 211, 213
Spergel, David, 119, 123, 128–
9, 136–7
Spörer, Gustav, 141–2
Stanford University, 112, 156,
190
Steigman, Gary, 117–19, 123,
128–9
Stephenson, Richard, 148
Strutt, Robert, 42
Sun, passim; age of, 7, 12, 18;
magnetic field, 99, 108, 139–
40; rotation, 99, 140, 153,

171–2, 178; size, 4, 9, 34,
144–9, 149–51, 152–3;
structure, 81–5, 98–9, 129,
164, 176–7, 183; temperature,
27–8, 47–9, 64–5, 82–4; *see
also* energy, solar
Sunspots, 108, 139–41, 143,
144, 159–61; cycle, 139–41,
150–1, 153, 156, 181; and
Elatina, 155–7, 158–9; and
Maunder Minimum, 143,
149–51, 153–4; solar
neutrinos, 108
Supernovas, 80, 132, 185, 196–
214; SN 1987A, 105–6, 112,
196–9, 201–6, 210–14
Sussex University, 130, 213

Tata Institute, 106, 172–4, 176–7
Tayler, Roger, 130, 135, 213
Telescopes, 139, 193–4, 197–9,
201; meridian, 152; transit
144–5
Thermodynamics, 12, 14–15,
18–19, 20–5, 26–32; laws of,
7, 18, 23–4, 31
Thomson, Sir Joseph (J.J.), 39,
42
Thomson, William see Kelvin
Transmutation, passim; 69–70,
79–80; hydrogen and helium,
53, 59–60, 94–5
Tree-ring dating, 143, 155–6
Tunnel effect, 61–4, 67, 68, 71,
195; and p-p chain, 75, 76, 77

Ultraviolet radiation, 157–8, 160
Uncertainty, 62
Uniformitarianism, 15, 17, 28–
9, 30–1
US National Radio Astronomy
Observatory, 117
US National Solar Observatory,
180
US Naval Observatory, 145

University College London, 45,
152
University of California:
Berkeley, 96, 193; Santa
Barbara, 193; Santa Cruz,
115, 123, 138, 204
University of South Carolina,
192
Unsold, Albrecht, 65, 71–2
Uranium, 35, 37–8, 45–6, 48,
80
Ussher, Archbishop, 12

Vahai, Mayank, 172–3, 174–6,
177
Varves, 155–6, 159, 160

Walker, James, 158–61
Walton, Ernest, 69–71, 72, 73,
79
Waterston, John, 20–22, 25
Wave/particle duality, 60, 67
WIMPs, 120–2, 123–8, 133–7,
162, 172–8; neutrino problem,
129–30, 183–4
Weaver, Tom, 204
von Weizsäcker, Carl, 73
White dwarfs, 81, 131, 133
Wigley, Tom, 152
Williams, George, 154–6, 157
Wilson, William, 47–8
Wolfenstein, Lincoln, 104
Wolff, Rudolf, 141
Woosley, Stan, 204, 205

X-rays, 35–8, 113, 180, 197,
200; in sun, 82

Yale University, 45
Young, C.A., 11

Zahnle, Kevin, 158–61
Zwicky, Fritz, 202